Windows® XP
Professional

The Ultimate User's Guide

Joli Ballew

President and CEO
Roland Elgey

Publisher
Al Valvano

Associate Publisher
Katherine R. Hartlove

Acquisitions Editor
Charlotte Carpentier

Product Marketing Manager
Tracy Rooney

Project Editor
Mark Janousek

Technical Reviewer
Felicia Buckingham

Production Coordinator
Peggy Cantrell

Cover Designer
Laura Wellander

The Coriolis Group, LLC
14455 North Hayden Road
Suite 220
Scottsdale, Arizona 85260

(480) 483-0192
FAX (480) 483-0193
www.coriolis.com

Library of Congress Cataloging-in-Publication Data
Ballew, Joli
    Windows XP Professional : the ultimate user's guide / by Joli Ballew.
      p.   cm.
    Includes index.
    ISBN 1-58880-228-0
    1. Microsoft Windows XP   2. Operating systems (Computers)   I. Title.

QA76.76.O63 B3598 2001
005.4'4769--dc21

2001047656

Printed in the United States of America
10 9 8 7 6 5 4 3 2 1

The Coriolis Group, LLC • 14455 North Hayden Road, Suite 220 • Scottsdale, Arizona 85260

A Note from Coriolis

Coriolis Technology Press was founded to create a very elite group of books: the ones you keep closest to your machine. In the real world, you have to choose the books you rely on every day very carefully, and we understand that.

To win a place for our books on that coveted shelf beside your PC, we guarantee several important qualities in every book we publish. These qualities are:

- *Technical accuracy*—It's no good if it doesn't work. Every Coriolis Technology Press book is reviewed by technical experts in the topic field, and is sent through several editing and proofreading passes in order to create the piece of work you now hold in your hands.

- *Innovative editorial design*—We've put years of research and refinement into the ways we present information in our books. Our books' editorial approach is uniquely designed to reflect the way people learn new technologies and search for solutions to technology problems.

- *Practical focus*—We put only pertinent information into our books and avoid any fluff. Every fact included between these two covers must serve the mission of the book as a whole.

- *Accessibility*—The information in a book is worthless unless you can find it quickly when you need it. We put a lot of effort into our indexes, and heavily cross-reference our chapters, to make it easy for you to move right to the information you need.

Here at The Coriolis Group we have been publishing and packaging books, technical journals, and training materials since 1989. We have put a lot of thought into our books; please write to us at **ctp@coriolis.com** and let us know what you think. We hope that you're happy with the book in your hands, and that in the future, when you reach for software development and networking information, you'll turn to one of our books first.

Coriolis Technology Press
The Coriolis Group
14455 N. Hayden Road, Suite 220
Scottsdale, Arizona
85260

Email: ctp@coriolis.com
Phone: (480) 483-0192
Toll free: 800)410-0192

Look for these related books from The Coriolis Group:

Windows XP Professional Little Black Book
by Brian Proffitt

MCSE Windows XP Professional Exam Prep
by Michael D. Stewart and Neall Alcott

MCSE Windows XP Professional Exam Cram
by Dan Balter and Derek Melber

Also recently published by Coriolis Technology Press:

Windows 2000 System Administrator's Black Book, 2nd Edition
by Deborah Haralson, Stu Sjouwerman, Barry Shilmover, and James Michael Stewart

Windows 2000 Security Little Black Book
by Ian McLean

Windows Admin Scripting Little Black Book
by Jesse M. Torres

Exchange 2000 .NET Server Black Book
by Philip Schein, Evan Benjamin, and Cherry Beado

C# Black Book
by Matt Telles

PC Technician Black Book
by Ron Gilster

To Mom and Dad. Thank you for always being so encouraging and supportive, from my early years as a would-be rock star, to college, to teaching, to school again, and finally to writing. I'm not sure how you do it, but you always make me feel like I could be or do anything I want.
Thank you.

About the Author

Joli Ballew (MCSE, MCT, A+) is a technology trainer, writer, and network consultant in the Dallas area. Some of her previous employment positions have included technical writing, educational content consulting, and working as a PC technician, a network administrator, a high school algebra teacher, and college instructor. She is currently working on several projects with The Coriolis Group.

Joli attended high school at the Performing Arts Magnet in Dallas where she studied music and the arts and was a member of the National Honor Society. She attended college at the University of Texas at Arlington, and graduated with a B.A. in Mathematics and a minor in English. Currently Joli has three books available: *Windows 2000 Professional Test Yourself* from Syngress Media, and *Windows 2000 Server On Site* and *Windows XP Professional - The Ultimate User's Guide* both published by The Coriolis Group. Joli has also been published in MCP *Magazine* and maintains a Web site at **www.swynk.com/friends/ballew**.

Acknowledgments

Quite a few people made this project a success. First, special thanks to Charlotte Carpentier, the acquisitions editor at Coriolis, for giving me another project and assigning to me the most wonderful people to work with. The team members include Mark Janousek, my project editor, who made this project not only enjoyable, but successful as well. Thanks once again to Catherine Oliver who stood by me for a second book, and who always makes me laugh; Catherine, you have a wonderful sense of humor. Special thanks to Felicia Buckingham my technical editor, who kept my words on the straight and narrow, and a group thank you to everyone at Coriolis who had faith in my abilities and let me do things as I saw fit. I am always amazed at the creative freedom I have when writing for all of you, and I do appreciate it greatly.

Finally, I'd like to thank my family for all of their support and encouragement. First, my parents, who are the most wonderful and supportive people in the world; without you I wouldn't be who I am today. Also my daughter Jennifer, who is so beautiful, patient, and smart; how I wish I could be half as good a person as you. Finally, Cosmo, who is always there with words of encouragement, a laugh and smile, and who drags me out to the golf course when I get too stressed. I could not be surrounded by more beautiful and wonderful people.

Contents at a Glance

Chapter 1   Getting Started   1

Chapter 2   Personalizing Your Computer   63

Chapter 3   Users and Groups   111

Chapter 4   Printing and Faxing   149

Chapter 5   Scheduled Tasks and Windows Update   187

Chapter 6   Using System Restore   201

Chapter 7   Device Driver Rollback   223

Chapter 8   Installing and Removing Software and Hardware   247

Chapter 9   Internet and Email   285

Chapter 10   Small-Office Networks   331

Chapter 11   Corporate Networks   403

Chapter 12   Disk and Computer Management   463

Chapter 13   Security   531

Chapter 14   Backup, Restore, and Recovery   595

Chapter 15   Mobile Computing   645

Appendix   Troubleshooting   699

Table of Contents

Introduction xv

Chapter 1   Getting Started 1
Basic Tasks   2
Files and Folders   40
Burning CDs   47
Microsoft Management Consoles   48

Chapter 2   Personalizing Your Computer 63
The Desktop   64
Sounds and Audio   79
Using Multimedia Utilities   90
Accessibility Options   101

Chapter 3   Users and Groups 111
Overview of User Accounts   112
Creating and Configuring User Accounts   117
User Rights, Privileges, and Permissions   122
Adding New Users to a Group   125
Group, Local, and Account Policies   139

Chapter 4   Printing and Faxing 149
Installing Printers   149
Configuring and Using the Printer   164
Faxing   178

Chapter 5   Scheduled Tasks and Windows Update 187
Introduction to Scheduling Tasks   187
Basic Tasks   189
Managing Scheduled Tasks   192
Windows Update   196

Chapter 6   Using System Restore 201
   Understanding System Restore   202
   Basic Tasks   206
   Restoring System State Data   213
   When System Restore Doesn't Work   217

Chapter 7   Device Driver Rollback 223
   Introduction to Device Drivers   224
   Plug-and-Play Driver Support   226
   Driver Signing   228
   Installing Device Drivers (New Hardware)   231
   Upgrading Device Drivers (Existing Hardware)   235
   Device Driver Problems   237
   Device Driver Rollback   238
   Removing a Driver Completely   240
   Device Manager   242
   Obtaining Drivers from the Internet   242
   Drivers and Safe Mode   245

Chapter 8   Installing and Removing
            Software and Hardware 247
   Installing Hardware   247
   Troubleshooting Hardware Installations   262
   Installing Software   267
   Adding New Windows Components   275
   Removing Software   278
   Removing Hardware   283

Chapter 9   Internet and Email 285
   Connecting to the Internet   285
   Outlook Express   291
   Instant Messaging   307
   Internet Explorer Version 6   313
   MSN Explorer   321
   NetMeeting   324
   Phone Dialer   326
   HyperTerminal   327
   Games on the Internet   327

Chapter 10   Small-Office Networks 331

Workgroups   331
Setting Up a Small-Office Network   335
Troubleshooting the Small Network   354
ICS Discovery and Control   362
Users and Computers   365
Sharing Resources   375
Using the Shared Documents Folder   393
Advanced Access Control for Administrators   396
A Little About Protocols   399

Chapter 11   Corporate Networks 403

More About Domains   404
Group Policies in a Domain   411
Windows XP and the Domain   411
Sharing Documents and Resources   422
Remote Assistance   430
Remote Desktop   438
Remote Access   448
Wireless Networking   452
License and Registration, Please!   457
Temporary and Seasonal Domain Users   459

Chapter 12   Disk and Computer Management 463

Disk Management   464
Types of Disks (Drives)   475
Adding a New Disk   486
Disk Status Descriptions   490
Disk Quotas   493
The Computer Management Console   498
Enhancing Performance   526

Chapter 13   Security 531

Security for Users   532
Security for Administrators   563
Additional Security Features   574

Chapter 14 Backup, Restore, and Recovery 595
   Types of Backups   596
   Types of Data   598
   Types of Backup Media   599
   Precautionary Measures   600
   Configuring the Backup Utility   602
   Performing a Backup   604
   Simple Backups and Backup Media   611
   Using the Restore Utility   615
   How System Restore Fits In   618
   Using Automated System Recovery   618
   The Files And Settings Transfer Wizard   620
   Windows Media Services   626
   Other Restore Options   629
   Preparing for and Recovering from a Virus Attack   630
   Using the Recovery Console   633

Chapter 15 Mobile Computing 645
   Power Management   646
   Best Performance   654
   Offline Files   662
   The Briefcase Tool   673
   Remote Desktop for the Laptop User   677
   Message Queuing   680
   Online Conferencing   683
   Mobile Dialing Options   688

Appendix Troubleshooting 699

   Glossary 765

   Index 791

Introduction

Thanks for buying *Windows XP Professional-The Ultimate User's Guide*.

In this book, I've covered all aspects of Windows XP Professional, from Windows basics such as finding and organizing files, to using multimedia utilities, to setting up a network or connecting to one. I have also included information for business users of XP, from securing their desktops to incorporating their laptops. This book is an "Ultimate User's Guide," a book that can be read from cover to cover by novices, or used as a desktop reference for users familiar with other operating systems.

Windows XP has many new features that previous Windows OS users will want to use. For example, System Restore is a new feature that takes a snapshot of the system state at various times so users can easily repair problems. Another feature, Device Driver Rollback, allows driver problems to be solved effortlessly. In addition, Windows XP offers wizards for setting up a network, and offers utilities such as Remote Assistance, Remote Desktop, disk quotas, automatic backup utilities, and more.

For business users of XP, there is information on Smart Card support, IPSec, Internet Explorer version 6, Group Policy, and support for remote and mobile users. Mobile users can enjoy offline files and folders, enhanced online conferencing, and improved power management. For all users, there is a complete troubleshooting guide in the Appendix that can be used to help you solve multiple types of problems.

Is This Book for You?

Windows XP Professional-The Ultimate User's Guide was written with the beginner, intermediate, and the advanced user in mind. Among the topics that are covered are:

♦ Personalizing the computer including the Start menu, files and folders, the desktop, multiple user accounts, and passwords.

♦ Using Remote Assistance and Remote Desktop in a corporate environment.

♦ Setting up and maintaining an office network using Internet Connection Sharing, Group Polices, security utilities, and sharing files and folders.

♦ Using System Restore and Device Driver Rollback to keep the computer working efficiently and effectively.

♦ Using mobile computing applications such as NetMeeting, configuring hardware profiles and power options, and security the laptop.

How to Use This Book

This book has been written for any level of user, in any environment, and can be used as a desktop reference or as an informational text to be read from beginning to end. If you are a novice user, consider starting at the beginning and working your way through. If you have used Windows operating systems before, but are uncomfortable with the new graphical user interface, work through the first two chapters, and then skip around as necessary. For more experienced users, or users with specific tasks in mind, use the book as a desktop reference.

Chapter 1
Getting Started

This chapter is for those of you who are fairly new to computing in general or those who have never used Windows XP Professional before. Even experienced users will find this chapter useful because the Start menu, My Computer, the Control Panel, and other areas of the graphical user interface (GUI) look quite a bit different than they did in Microsoft's previous operating systems.

In this chapter, I'll cover only the basics of using the operating system, including how to use the Start menu and the taskbar, what is available on the desktop, what My Computer and the Control Panel have to offer, and how to use Windows Explorer to find files, folders, and programs. Finally, I'll discuss how to get help and support when you need it, including using Windows Help and the Microsoft Web site.

After introducing those basic tasks, I'll introduce files and folders, and explain how to create, save, and delete them, as well as how to use the Search utility to find them. You'll learn how to switch between applications, how to minimize, maximize, and restore application windows, and how to use Cut, Copy, and Paste when working with files.

Another basic task is learning how to burn CDs. Burning CDs is the process of transferring information from the hard drive to the CD by either copying it or moving it for archiving. Because Windows XP Professional comes with its own software for this, it will be detailed in this chapter as a way to preserve and back up data.

Finally, the Microsoft Management Console (MMC) will be introduced. The MMC allows you to create custom workspaces, called *consoles*, for performing such tasks as using Device Manager, managing disks, using Event Viewer, and configuring local users and groups. You can create many kinds of consoles and use them to personalize your computer and work environment. You'll learn how to use the most common console snap-ins and how to create and use taskpad views.

Basic Tasks

Windows XP Professional, when first installed, looks quite a bit different from Windows 2000 Professional, Windows NT 4 Workstation, or Windows 98. Windows XP has a new background, new and more vivid colors, and a different-looking Start menu. The taskbar can be configured to hide inactive items, and it has several new offerings for configuration. The desktop has the same features as always, with a few new backgrounds and themes to choose from. What makes the GUI look so different at first is that when Windows XP is installed, the Windows XP theme is enabled. Other areas of difference include My Computer, the Control Panel, Windows Explorer, and Microsoft Help. Each of these items will be discussed in this section.

The Start Menu

The first thing you'll need to get familiar with is the Start menu in the bottom-left corner of the screen. The Start menu identifies who is logged on, lists commonly used programs in the left pane, and has icons for My Documents, My Pictures, My Music, My Computer, Control Panel, Network Connections, Help And Support, Search, and Run in the right pane. The bottom of the menu also has two options to allow you to either log off or turn off the computer. Each of these items will be discussed at length in later sections of this chapter, but for now, I'll focus solely on using the Start menu and personalizing it to meet your needs.

Click the Start button. You'll see something similar to what is shown in Figure 1.1.

To see what other programs are installed on your computer, click All Programs. You'll see something similar to what is shown in Figure 1.2. Notice in Figure 1.2 that I have Microsoft Access, Excel, FrontPage, Outlook, PowerPoint, and Word (all Microsoft Office applications), along with other programs that you may or may not have installed on your computer. You might have these applications or another brand of office suite software on your computer.

Adding or Removing Programs in the Start Menu

You can add or remove programs from the Start menu to customize how it looks and to make it work more efficiently for you. For instance, you might not have any music on your computer, so you wouldn't need the My Music folder on the Start menu. You can remove folders from the Start menu as described in the next exercise. (Doing so removes them only from the Start menu, not from your computer.) You can also add folders or program icons to the Start menu. For instance, I might want to add a Printers folder or My Favorites because I access these programs often.

Figure 1.1
The Start menu.

To add or remove a program or folder icon from the Start menu:

1. Either choose Start and then right-click a white area of the Start menu, or right-click an empty area of the taskbar and choose Properties.

2. In the Taskbar And Start Menu Properties dialog box, select the Start Menu tab if it isn't already active, and notice the Start menu options.

3. Choose the Customize button to open the Customize Start Menu dialog box.

4. Select the Advanced tab.

5. In the middle of this dialog box, notice the area that is labeled "Start Menu Items." Use the up and down arrow keys to see what the Start menu contains.

6. To add an item to the Start menu, check the checkbox beside the item. To remove an item from the Start menu, uncheck the checkboxes.

7. Select the General tab.

8. To clear all of the most recently used programs from the left pane of the Start menu, choose Clear List in the Programs area. You can also change the number of programs

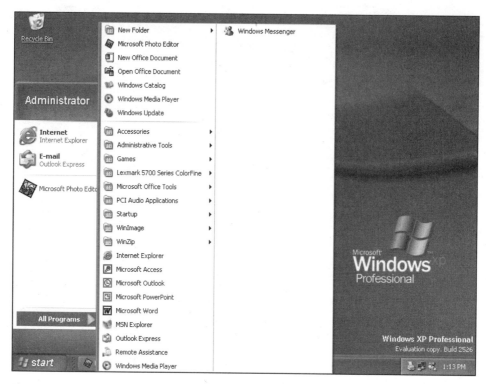

Figure 1.2
All Programs.

shown on the Start menu from the default of six to any number between zero and thirty. If you have web-browsing and email applications, you can show or hide these from the Start menu as well. Choose OK twice to close the two dialog boxes.

Changing the Start Menu's Style

Throughout the first couple of chapters, I'll be using the Windows XP theme with the Start menu because that's what you'll see by default when Microsoft Windows XP Professional is installed. However, there are certainly other styles or looks to choose from, and one of them is the Windows Classic look. The classic look is shown in Figure 1.3. This look can differ depending on the programs installed on your computer.

If you are used to the look of a Windows 2000 Professional or Windows NT 4 Workstation desktop, you might prefer the classic theme to the default theme. When you choose the classic theme, the icons My Computer, My Network Places, My Documents, and Internet Explorer are added to the desktop.

To change the Start menu and desktop to the Windows Classic look:

1. Either choose Start and right-click a white area of the Start menu, or right-click an empty area of the taskbar and choose Properties.

Figure 1.3
The Windows Classic look.

2. In the Taskbar And Start Menu Properties dialog box, select the Start Menu tab if it isn't already active, and notice the Start menu options.

3. Select the Classic Start Menu option. Choose OK.

Adding a Submenu

You can add a submenu to the Start menu to personalize your computer, or you can add submenus for groups of users who access your computer. You can also add shortcuts to the Start menu for any application or program.

To add a submenu to the Start menu for personal use:

1. Open the Taskbar And Start Menu Properties dialog box:

   ♦ If you're using the Windows Classic theme, choose Start | Settings | Taskbar And Start Menu.

   ♦ If you're using the Windows XP theme, right-click an empty area of the taskbar, and choose Properties Windows XP.

2. Click the Start Menu tab, and select Classic Start Menu if it isn't already selected.

3. Select the Customize tab.

4. Choose Advanced to open the Customize dialog box.

5. Choose File | New | Folder.

6. Type in the name of the new submenu. Then close the window by clicking on the X in the top-right corner.

7. Choose OK in the Customize dialog box.

8. If you want to use the Windows XP theme, select the Windows XP option before choosing OK for the last time.

If you are using the Windows Classic theme, the new submenu will appear at the top of the Start menu. If you are using the Windows XP theme, the new submenu will appear under All Programs in the Start menu. Figure 1.4 shows two new submenus named Test Submenu 1 and Test Submenu 2.

Moving a Folder to Another Area of the Start Menu

If you are using the Windows XP theme, you might need or want to move a program from the All Programs area of the Start menu (which would take three clicks of the mouse to access) to the top level of the Start menu (which only takes one click to access). You can achieve this simply by performing the following steps. Notice the difference by comparing Figure 1.4, shown earlier, to Figure 1.5, shown next.

1. Choose Start | All Programs and then the name of the newly created submenu.

2. Click the new submenu, and then drag it to the Start Menu.

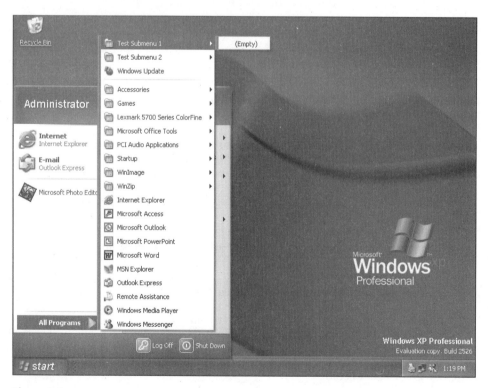

Figure 1.4
New submenus.

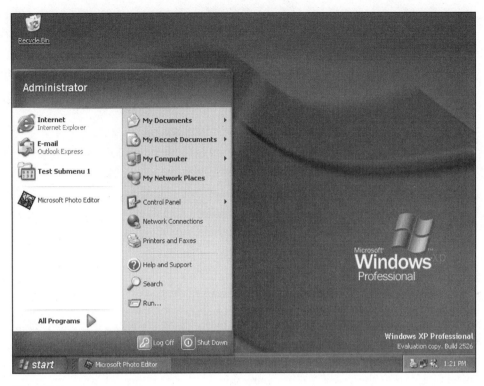

Figure 1.5
Start menu with new submenus.

Notice that the submenus are now on the top level of the Start menu (see Figure 1.5). They are also still on the All Programs menu (but not shown in Figure 1.5).

Making Other Changes in the Start Menu

Microsoft Windows XP Professional allows you to manipulate the Start menu in many ways. You can add or remove items, and even rename items. You can also see the properties of the folders and applications. Listed next are a few extra Start-menu configuration changes you can make easily and quickly:

Note

Throughout the first few chapters, I'll be staying with the default Windows XP theme. If you make many changes in the Start menu, the taskbar, or other desktop options described in this chapter, the screenshots provided here might not look exactly like what you'll see on your computer at work or at home.

♦ You can remove an item from the Start menu by right-clicking that item and choosing Remove From This List.

♦ You can rename an item in the Start menu by right-clicking the item and choosing Rename.

♦ You can manage your computer by right-clicking My Computer and choosing Manage. This opens the Computer Management window, where you can use System Tools (including Event Viewer, Device Manager, and Local Users and Groups), storage utilities (such as Disk Defragmenter and Disk Management), and Services And Applications (such as the Indexing Service or WMI Control). These utilities and how to use them will be detailed in Chapter 12.

♦ You can right-click My Network Places and choose Search For Computers to open the Search Results–Computers screen and the Search Companion. My Network Places and other networking options will be detailed in Chapter 10.

♦ You can right-click various icons on the Start menu and compress, email, copy, or send them, or perform many other tasks. The best way to see what you can do is simply to explore the Start menu and choose some of the options.

The Taskbar

The taskbar is the blue bar at the bottom of the screen; the taskbar contains the Start menu, icons for Internet Explorer, MSN, and Outlook Express, and the time. The programs listed on your computer can vary from these, but generally, this is what you'll see by default with Windows XP. The taskbar identifies which programs are running and active on the computer. To see an example of this, turn back to Figure 1.3 and notice that Microsoft Photo Editor is shown in the taskbar. This means that Microsoft Photo Editor is running and is being used, but it has been temporarily minimized. It is running in the background, ready for use when I need it again.

You can move the taskbar around on the screen, and you can hide it. You can also use the Auto-Hide option to configure the taskbar so that it comes and goes each time the cursor is moved in that area. By showing the taskbar only when it's needed, you can increase the workspace on your screen.

Before starting the following exercises, unlock the taskbar and turn on the Quick Launch Toolbar:

1. Right-click on the taskbar and choose Properties.

2. Choose the Taskbar tab.

3. Uncheck the checkbox Lock The Taskbar.

4. Check the checkbox Show Quick Launch.

5. Click OK to close.

Moving the Taskbar

As you know, the taskbar is shown at the bottom of the screen by default. I kind of like my taskbar on the top of the screen and occasionally on the right side. You can move the

Figure 1.6
The taskbar moved to the right side of the screen.

taskbar by dragging it to the area of the screen where you'd like the taskbar to be. Figure 1.6 shows the taskbar on the right side of the screen.

Locking the Taskbar

If you don't want the taskbar to be moved to any other area of the screen, and you don't want it to be hidden or resized, then right-click the taskbar and choose Lock The Taskbar. Doing so will prevent changes in the taskbar's appearance and behavior.

Displaying, Resizing, and Hiding the Taskbar

If the taskbar isn't locked, you can display it, hide it, auto-hide it, or resize it. By default, the taskbar is shown.

To auto-hide the taskbar:

1. Right-click the taskbar, and choose Properties.

2. If it isn't already active, select the Taskbar tab in the Taskbar And Start Menu Properties dialog box.

3. Check the checkbox Auto-hide The Taskbar. To keep the taskbar underneath and out of sight when other applications are running, uncheck the checkbox Keep The Taskbar On Top Of Other Windows. Choose OK.

To permanently hide the task bar until you want to display it again:

1. Right-click the taskbar, and choose Properties.

2. If it isn't already active, select the Taskbar tab in the Taskbar And Start Menu Properties dialog box.

3. Move the mouse pointer over the top edge of the taskbar until the arrow changes from a one-arrow pointer to a pointer with an arrow on each end. Hold down the left mouse button and drag down. The taskbar will disappear.

4. To restore a hidden taskbar, follow the directions for resizing the taskbar, given next.

To resize the taskbar (or show it after it's been hidden):

1. Move the mouse over the top edge of the taskbar until the mouse pointer changes from a one-arrow pointer to a pointer with an arrow on each end. For a hidden taskbar, this will be the extremely small blue line at the bottom of the screen.

2. Hold down the left mouse button, and drag the taskbar to the size you want it to be.

You can make the taskbar as large as half of the total screen area of your display. Of course, this isn't usually efficient, but occasionally you might need to increase the size of your taskbar to show multiple programs that are running.

Taskbar Grouping

If you have multiple programs running at once and multiple documents open, the taskbar can become quite crowded. Windows XP offers a new feature called *taskbar grouping*, which can help you manage these open programs and documents more efficiently and make them easier to find. When multiple documents are open, Windows XP groups them by type; for instance, all Word documents are grouped together, or all Excel documents are grouped together. They are then labeled as a group with the name of the program and a triangle on the right side of the button. The triangle signifies multiple documents in the group.

By default, the grouping of similar taskbar buttons is enabled. To disable this feature:

1. Right-click a blank area of the taskbar, and choose Properties.

2. Make sure the Taskbar tab is active in the Taskbar And Start Menu Properties dialog box.

3. Uncheck the checkbox Group Similar Taskbar Buttons.

4. Choose OK.

Starting a Program with a Taskbar Button

The taskbar contains several icons, some at the bottom-left corner by the Start menu button and possibly some on the right by the left arrow button, depending on what programs are installed on your computer. The icons shown in Figure 1.7 are common ones, and they include icons for showing the desktop, launching the Internet Explorer browser, launching Outlook Express, and launching MSN Explorer, and in this example, even a printer. You can see if you have any of these icons by clicking on the left arrow on the taskbar.

To start any of these programs by using the taskbar, simply double-click their icons. The programs will open up and run. Often, when a program such as Internet Explorer is run from the taskbar, the program runs in Normal mode. This means that the window containing the program can be stretched and resized to accommodate the user's preferences. If your preferences are like mine, however, you'll want the programs to open in a maximized window, meaning that when they open, they take up the entire screen and are shown as large as possible.

To change the programs on the taskbar so that they open in Maximized mode, Minimized mode (listed only on the taskbar), or Normal mode:

1. Right-click an icon in the taskbar, and choose Properties.

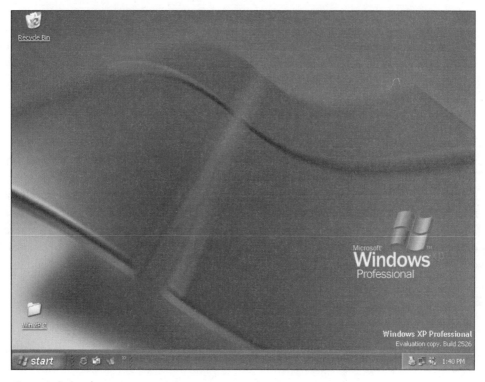

Figure 1.7
Taskbar icons.

Figure 1.8
Taskbar icons and maximizing windows.

2. On the Shortcut tab, notice the arrow next to the Run drop-down list box. See Figure 1.8. You can click on that arrow to change the program to run in Maximized, Normal, or Minimized modes. Make your choice.

3. Choose OK.

Adding Toolbars

When you look at the taskbar, you see the time, icons for programs, and icons for whatever is currently running, such as any programs or documents. You can add toolbars, shown in Figure 1.9, to personalize your computer. In this figure, notice that the taskbar contains several new toolbars, including Desktop, Links, Address, and Games. These toolbars are not shown by default, but you can add them by right-clicking the taskbar and choosing Toolbars. After you add the toolbars, you can click on these icons, as shown in the figure, to quickly access the programs in these folders. By clicking on the arrow next to Games, for example, you can choose from Freecell, Minesweeper, Pinball, and Solitaire.

To add toolbars for Address, Links, Desktop, or Quick Launch:

1. Right-click an empty area of the taskbar, and choose Toolbars.

2. In the resulting menu, place a check by the toolbar you want to add. Repeat these steps to add additional toolbars.

To add a toolbar for any other program or folder:

1. Right-click an empty area of the taskbar, and choose Toolbars.

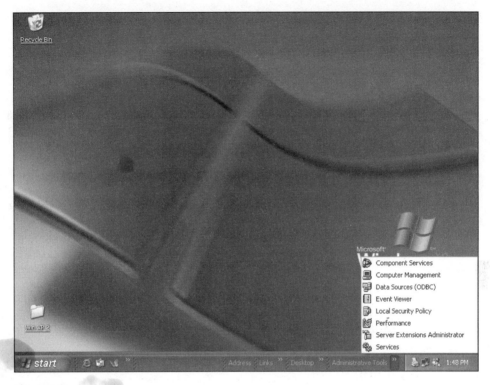

Figure 1.9
Toolbars added to the taskbar.

2. From the resulting menu, choose New Toolbar.

3. In the New Toolbar dialog box, locate the program or folder to add, and choose OK. You can also choose to create a new folder.

Note

This is one of my favorite configuration options in Microsoft Windows XP. Because I use the same programs most of the time, I simply add them to the taskbar, and they're always available quickly. Throughout this book, the screen captures will show different items in the taskbar, depending on what task is being performed.

Moving All Open Programs to the Taskbar (Minimizing)

To minimize all open programs or documents to the taskbar, you'll need to have the Quick Launch toolbar checked. You will then see the Show Desktop icon on the taskbar. To minimize all windows at the same time, all you have to do is click this icon.

To enable Quick Launch and minimize all open windows at once:

1. Right-click the taskbar, and choose Toolbars.

2. Select Quick Launch.

3. Find the taskbar icon called Show Desktop, and click it. All open windows will be minimized. Click it again to return all of the windows to their previous sizes.

The Desktop (An Overview)

In the previous example, if you were confused about the desktop and what exactly it is, I will explain it here. The desktop is simply what you see on the computer screen when you first turn on your computer. If you are still not sure, take a look back at Figures 1.6 and 1.9. Both show the desktop and the icons on it.

What's on the Desktop?

The desktop will look different on your system depending on what is installed on your computer and how you have the settings configured. In Figures 1.6 and 1.9, the items on the desktop are few and far between. However, if you use the Classic theme, your desktop will look more like Windows 9x, Windows NT 4, or Windows 2000 and will have more icons. Either way, the items on the desktop allow you to access programs and files more quickly than you can by using Windows Explorer or Search functions.

When you're using the Windows XP theme, the desktop has very few icons. This is great for people who don't like a lot of clutter in their workspace. There's the Recycle Bin, but really not much else. If you are using the Classic look, though, you'll see many more icons.

A desktop with the Classic look usually contains these icons:

♦ My Documents

♦ My Computer

♦ My Network Places

♦ Internet Explorer

♦ Recycle Bin

♦ Programs such as Outlook or similar applications that automatically place icons on the desktop

These icons that are on the desktop are also available in other areas of Windows XP, and they are accessed a little differently when you're using the Windows XP theme. I'll discuss these icons later in this chapter.

Adding a Shortcut

You can add your own icons to the desktop for any application, file, folder, Web site, or any number of other items very easily.

To add a shortcut to the desktop:

1. Right-click an empty space on the desktop, and choose New | Shortcut.

2. In the Create Shortcut dialog box, choose Browse.

3. Locate the program, file, folder, or other item by expanding the trees in this box.

4. Select the item, and choose Next.

5. In the Select A Title For The Program screen, type a name for the new shortcut. Choose Finish. Notice the new icon on the desktop.

Adding a Folder

You can also add folders to the desktop. I typically have several folders that I've labeled so that documents can be grouped together and accessed efficiently. You might have folders that are named Inbox, In Progress, and Outbox or, at home, perhaps Letters, Personal, and To Do. Whatever the case, adding and naming your own desktop folders certainly makes working with documents easier and faster.

To add a new folder to the desktop:

1. Right-click an empty space on the desktop, and choose New | Folder.

2. Find the folder on the desktop, type a name for the folder, and press Enter. To save items in this folder, browse to this folder when saving.

Arranging Icons on the Desktop

After you add icons or folders to your desktop, they will probably not be lined up just the way you'd like them. You can change how the icons are arranged on your desktop by right-clicking an empty area, choosing Arrange Icons By, and then choosing one of the following: Name, Size, Type, Modified, Auto Arrange, or Align To Grid. You can also uncheck Show Desktop Icons to remove the items from the desktop.

Adding My Network Places and Other Icons to the Desktop

Whatever theme you've chosen to use, whether it is the Windows XP theme or the Classic theme, you can add or remove items from the desktop to suit your individual needs. For instance, if you are using the Windows XP theme, but you would like to see the icon for My Network Places or My Documents, you can add those through Display Properties.

To add or remove desktop icons for the standard folders (My Documents, My Network Places, My Computer, or the Recycle Bin):

1. Right-click an empty area of the desktop, and choose Properties.

2. In the Display Properties dialog box, select the Desktop tab.

3. Choose Customize Desktop.

4. Under Desktop Icons, place or remove checkmarks for the icons you'd like to add or remove.

5. Choose OK twice.

Changing the Look of the Icons on the Desktop

You can also change what the icons look like for My Documents, My Network Places, My Computer, and the Recycle Bin by performing similar steps. I'd be careful about this if you're a beginner, though, because your new icons won't look like the ones in this book.

To change an icon:

1. Right-click an empty area of the desktop, and choose Properties.

2. In the Display Properties dialog box, select the Desktop tab.

3. Choose Customize Desktop.

4. Under Desktop Icons, make sure the item you want to change has a checkmark by it. Place a check beside the choice if necessary.

5. Highlight the icon you'd like to change next, and choose Change Icon.

6. Each icon has different choices, and some have a lot of choices. Choose the icon you want to select, and choose OK.

7. Choose OK twice to close the dialog boxes.

My Computer

Use the My Computer icon—on the Start menu or on the desktop—when you need to manage your computer and see the different drives on it. From here, you can see the contents of all of the drives on your computer, including the hard disk drive (usually C:), the floppy disk drive (usually A:), the CD-ROM, DVD-ROM, or CD-RW drives (usually D:), and any network drives that you have configured. Take a look at Figure 1.10.

My Computer Icons

In Figure 1.10, you can see that this computer has two hard disk drives: one that is called Windows 2000 (C:) and another that is called Local Disk (D:). Both are hard disk drives and are internal (inside the computer). If the computer has other drives configured such as logical drives or partitions, those will be shown here as well. Most computers are not generally configured this way; your computer most likely has only one hard disk drive.

Notice also that there is an area called Devices With Removable Storage. In that section are icons for the 3½ inch floppy drive (A:), the Audio CD drive (E:), and another CD drive, for a CD-RW (F:). The icons on your computer will differ depending on the types of drives you have installed.

You can see what's on any of these drives or run a program simply by clicking on the corresponding icon. If you choose your local disk, most likely C:, you'll be asked to check the Start menu, or you'll have to configure the software to let you look at the programs here by choosing Show The Contents Of This Drive. You can also add or remove programs that are installed on your computer, search for files or folders, or access other places on your computer.

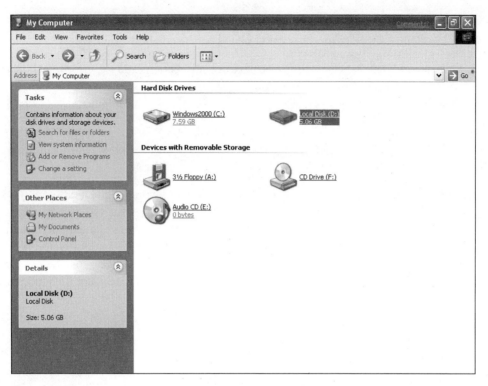

Figure 1.10
My Computer.

Back at the My Computer window, though, are other areas to note besides the list of drives available and their contents. These other areas are called Tasks, and Other Places, and Details.

Tasks

From the Tasks section of the My Computer window, you can do three tasks. They are:

♦ *View System Information*—Select this to see the System Properties screen, which shows the computer name, computer type, workgroup or domain information, hardware settings, and more.

♦ *Add Or Remove Programs*—Select this to add or remove applications on your computer.

♦ *Change A Setting*—Select this to change settings related to desktop appearance and themes, network and Internet connections, sounds, speech, audio, performance, maintenance, printers and other hardware, user accounts, date, time, language, regional options, and accessibility options.

Throughout this book, I'll return to this window as necessary, and I'll eventually cover all aspects of these options.

Other Places

From My Computer, you can access other places on the computer, including the following:

♦ *My Network Places*—Select this to see network connections and to perform such tasks as creating network shortcuts, setting up a home network, or searching for computers on the network.

♦ *My Documents*—Select this to see the files and folders stored in the My Documents folder, including two folders automatically created when Windows XP is installed: My Music and My Pictures. From here, you can make a new folder or publish a folder to the Web.

♦ *Control Panel*—Select this to open the Control Panel (detailed in the next section). The Control Panel is used for changing the appearance of the desktop and for changing settings related to network and Internet connections, sounds, speech, audio, performance, maintenance, printers and other hardware, user accounts, date, time, language, regional options, and accessibility options. Note that this is similar to the System Tasks Change A Setting described earlier. There are several ways to customize features in Windows XP. Here, you also have the option of switching to Classic view.

Details

The Details area of the My Computer window simply states what the active window is and what its contents are used for. Shown in Figure 1.10, the Details area states that My Computer is a system folder and is used to display the contents of your computer.

Note

You can press the up and down arrows shown in the top-right corner of these sections to hide the contents of the section. Pressing the up arrow in the Details area leaves the Details section there, but the information included in Details is hidden.

Introduction to the Control Panel

The Control Panel is available from the Start menu and is the most convenient way to customize your computer. From the Control Panel, you can install new programs and install printers, scanners, or other hardware. You can also set the date and time, set the appearance and theme, and more. The Control Panel also offers a place to type in a word or a question to search for just about anything you need. In this section, I'll discuss the Control Panel, including the two views, Category and Classic, as well as each of the available icons.

Category View

Figure 1.11 shows the Control Panel using Category view. To access this screen, choose Start | Control Panel if you are using the Windows XP theme, or choose Start | Settings | Control Panel if you're using the Classic theme.

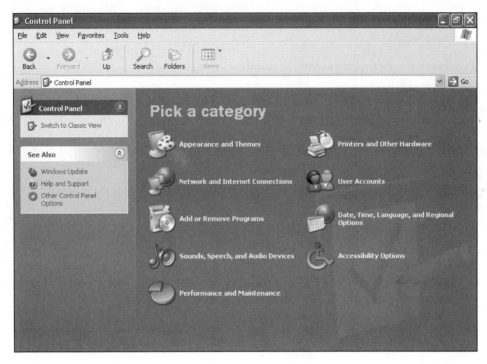

Figure 1.11
The Control Panel in Category view.

To change configurations for your computer, simply choose the appropriate icon in the Control Panel. After making your choice, you'll see a second screen that offers one of three things, depending on the icon chosen:

◆ You can choose a task, such as changing the computer's theme or creating a new user account.

◆ You can pick a Control Panel icon, such as Network Connections, Internet Options, or Sounds And Audio Devices.

◆ You can use a utility, such as Add Or Remove Programs, for performing a task.

There are so many options that it would be nearly impossible to introduce every scenario here. However, the section "Control Panel Icons and What They Do" explains the icons shown in the Control Panel through the Classic view. Even if you use the Category view, you will eventually see the windows described in this upcoming section.

Classic View vs. Category View

For anyone who's used a computer before, either a Windows 98 machine at home or a Windows NT or 2000 workstation at work, the Classic view in the Control Panel will look more familiar. The difference between the two views lies mainly in how tasks get done. For instance, changing the background used on the desktop in Category view goes something like this:

1. Choose Start | Control Panel or Start | Settings | Control Panel, depending on the theme used.

2. Choose the Appearance And Themes icon.

3. Choose Change The Desktop Background.

4. Select a new background from the Display Properties dialog box. (Notice that the Desktop tab is already active.)

5. Choose OK.

Changing the appearance of the desktop in Classic view is done this way:

1. Choose Start | Control Panel or Start | Settings | Control Panel, depending on the theme used.

2. Choose the Display icon.

3. In the Display Properties dialog box, select the Desktop tab. (This tab is not already active as it is in Category view.)

4. Select a new background.

5. Choose OK.

The important point here is that eventually, the same utility or program will be accessed for performing tasks. Notice that in both views, the Display Properties dialog box is shown, and the background is changed on the Desktop tab.

The Control Panel provides an option you can click to change views anytime you want. (See again Figure 1.11.)

Control Panel Icons and What They Do

Because all tasks performed through the Control Panel are eventually completed through the same utilities, I'll introduce the utilities in the Control Panel as shown through the Classic view. I'm doing this because Classic view is a bit more straightforward than working through the questions and options in Category view. However, you can use either, and you can simply access the programs and utilities shown here by choosing the appropriate icon or choosing to perform a specific task while in Category view. In the following descriptions, I'll note at the end of each one how the options can be accessed through Category view.

Accessibility Options

You can configure your computer with accessibility options so that any user with special needs (users who are hearing impaired, vision impaired, or physically disabled in a way that makes using the keyboard difficult) can use the computer more easily. Accessibility options including the following:

- On the Keyboard tab:

  - *Sticky Keys*—You can use the Shift, Ctrl, Alt, or Windows logo keys by pressing only one key at a time instead of two.

  - *Filter Keys*—The computer ignores repeated keystrokes or can be set to slow down the repeat rate. Settings made for the repeat rate here override the settings made in the Keyboard Properties dialog box.

  - *Toggle Keys*—The computer will sound a tone when any of the following keys are pressed: Caps Lock, Num Lock, or Scroll Lock.

- On the Sound tab:

  - *Sound Sentry*—For hearing-impaired users, the computer will generate a visual warning when the computer makes a sound. This can be configured as a flash of the active caption bar, the active window, or the desktop.

  - *Show Sounds*—Windows will instruct all programs to display captions for any speech or sounds that those programs make.

- On the Display tab:

  - *High Contrast*—For vision-impaired users, this option allows you to use colors and fonts that make reading the screen easier. There are multiple options for high-contrast schemes, including ones that use large letters or white letters on a black background.

  - *Cursor Options*—You can change the blink rate and the width of the cursor.

- On the Mouse tab:

  - *Mouse Keys*—You can use the numeric keypad to move the mouse pointer.

- On the General tab:

  - *Automatic Reset*—Use this to turn off the accessibility features if the computer has been idle for a period of time. This can be set from 5 minutes to 30 minutes.

  - *Notification*—Use this to give a warning message when turning a feature on, or to make a sound when turning a feature on or off.

  - *SerialKey Devices*—This option allows you to install other hardware, besides the mouse and keyboard, for inputting data. The devices can be installed on available COM ports.

  - *Administrative Options*—This option is used by administrators to apply settings to the logon desktop or as defaults for all new users.

Note

You can access accessibility options from Category view by clicking the Accessibility Options icon and choosing either a task or the appropriate Control Panel icon.

Add Hardware

After you've physically installed a new device—such as a video card, mouse, keyboard, CD-ROM drive, mass storage device, or modem (among others)—you can use the Add Hardware icon in the Control Panel to help you install the device's software. You can also use this icon to troubleshoot problems with existing hardware. Clicking the Add Hardware icon in the Control Panel starts the Add Hardware Wizard. (Wizards are short programs that assist you in performing certain tasks.)

When the wizard starts, it first searches for the new device. If you have installed a plug-and-play (PnP) device, Windows XP will probably find it and assist you in installing the software for it. In some cases, Windows XP has the software necessary for the device and installs it without any additional user interaction. The software that is installed with most devices is called a *driver*, and it is this driver that allows the operating system to communicate properly with the device. Other software that may be installed includes applications that work with the device, such as scanner applications or digital-camera programs.

Note

You can access the Add Hardware Wizard from Category view by clicking the Printers And Other Hardware icon and then choosing Add Hardware from the See Also section.

Add Or Remove Programs

The Add Or Remove Programs icon is used to install new applications on your system or to remove programs that are no longer needed or do not work properly. From the Add Or Remove Programs window, you can do three things:

- *Change Or Remove Programs*—Use this option to remove programs from the computer or change the components that are installed.

- *Add New Programs*—Use this option to install new programs on the computer.

- *Add/Remove Windows Components*—Use this option to add or remove components native to Windows XP, such as the Fax Service, Management and Monitoring Tools, and Networking Services.

Note

You can access Add Or Remove Programs from Category view by clicking the Add Or Remove Programs icon.

Administrative Tools

Choosing the Administrative Tools icon in the Control Panel gives you access to seven additional components of Windows XP. The administrator of the computer uses these components to protect it from other users, set policies for all users who access the computer, view event logs that tell how the computer is performing, and more. Each of these eight components is described briefly next, and each will be further explained in later chapters of this book.

The Administrative Tools are:

♦ *Component Services*—This component is used by administrators, software developers, and programmers to deploy and administrate COM + applications and to automate administrative tasks through scripts and programs. COM + is an extension of the Component Object Model and is used to simplify the creation of these types of applications.

♦ *Computer Management*—Used by administrators, this service helps you manage the local computer or a remote one by using a graphical interface. The Computer Management window combines several of the most-used administrative tools, such as Event Viewer, Local Users And Groups, and Disk Defragmenter.

♦ *Data Sources (ODBC)*—ODBC stands for Open Database Connectivity, which is an open (standard) application programming interface used for accessing databases on the local machine. The ODBC Data Source Administrator stores information about how to connect to specific databases—such as dBASE files, Excel files, and Access files—on the local computer. Also available from this component are the ODBC drivers that are installed on the system, their version numbers, the manufacturer names, and the dates.

♦ *Event Viewer*—Event Viewer stores logs that are created either automatically or manually to record the performance and integrity of programs, security, and system events on the local computer. Event Viewer can be used to troubleshoot problems related to these items.

♦ *Local Security Policy*—Used by administrators, the Local Security Policy icon opens the Local Security Settings console. From this console, an administrator can configure account policies, local policies, public key policies, software restriction policies, and IP security policies for the local machine. Setting these policies keeps the computer free from both accidental and malicious tampering or harm.

♦ *Performance*—The Performance icon opens the Performance console, which includes both System Monitor and Performance Logs And Alerts. System Monitor logs information about the system's performance and health, and it can be configured to log information about all kinds of events, such as %Processor Time and Memory Pages Per Second. Performance Logs And Alerts can be used to configure three types of data: counter logs, trace logs, and alerts.

♦ *Services*—Used by administrators, the Services icon opens the Services console, which can be used to view all of the services installed on the computer. From this console, you can also stop, start, pause, or resume a service, see a description of a service, configure what will happen if the service fails, and more.

Note

You can access Administrative Tools from Category view by clicking the Performance And Tools icon and choosing either a task or the appropriate Control Panel icon.

Date and Time

This icon opens the Date And Time Properties dialog box, which is used to change the date and time on the computer, change the time zone, or automatically synchronize your computer's time with an Internet time server. By default, that time server is **time.windows.com**.

Note

You can access date and time options from Category view by clicking Date, Time, Language, And Regional Options and choosing either a task or the appropriate Control Panel icon.

Display

The Display icon opens the Display Properties dialog box, where several choices can be made regarding the appearance of the computer. I'll briefly discuss them here, but they will be detailed further in Chapter 2.

The Display Properties dialog box has five tabs:

♦ *Themes*—For changing the theme of the operating system to Classic, Windows XP, My Current Theme, or others.

♦ *Desktop*—For changing the background of the desktop or otherwise customizing the desktop.

♦ *Screen Saver*—For choosing a screensaver and configuring the settings for it so that your computer screen is protected from having a single image "burned" on it when something is left up for a long period of time.

♦ *Appearance*—For changing the colors of the windows and buttons, the color scheme, and the font size. You can also change various effects, including using the fade effect, smoothing the edges of screen fonts, and using large icons.

♦ *Settings*—For changing the screen resolution from the default of 800×600 pixels to 1,024×768, 1,152×864, and others. This tab is also used for changing the color quality and troubleshooting video problems.

Note

You can access display options from Category view by clicking the Appearance And Themes icon and choosing either a task or the Control Panel icon.

Folder Options

Personalizing your computer goes even further than changing the background or screensaver. In Folder Options, you can configure such things as opening each new folder in its own window and single-clicking instead of double-clicking. The Folder Options dialog box has four tabs:

◆ *General*—Used to configure the Web view, how folders will be browsed to, and whether icons will open with a single click or a double-click of the mouse.

◆ *View*—Used to configure folder views and advanced settings, including showing hidden files, hiding file extensions, and showing My Network Places on the desktop.

◆ *File Types*—Shows file types and their extensions on the local computer. File types include audio files, recovered file fragments, clipboard items, security certificates, and bitmap images. You can also add new files and file types from here.

◆ *Offline Files*—Used to work with files and programs that are stored on network servers. When this option is enabled, you can work on the files even when your computer is not connected to the network server. Other options include synchronizing files when logging off and creating a shortcut to offline files on the desktop.

Note

You can access folder options from Category view by clicking the Appearance And Themes icon and choosing the Folder Options icon.

Fonts

The Fonts icon in the Control Panel opens up a window that lists all of the installed fonts on your system. By default, there are approximately 80 fonts.

Note

You can access the Fonts window from Category view by typing "fonts" in the address bar at the top of the page.

Gaming Options

The Gaming Options dialog box is used to view installed game controllers and add new ones. You can also view the status of the controllers and configure advanced options or troubleshoot problems.

Note

You can access gaming options from Category view by clicking the Printers And Other Hardware icon and then choosing the Gaming Options icon.

Internet Options

This dialog box can also be opened by choosing Internet Explorer | Tools | Internet Options, and it is often the most used utility after an Internet connection has been established. From this dialog box, you can configure just about anything that has to do with how you will access and use the Internet, including what your home page will be and what connections you'll use.

The Internet Options dialog box has seven tabs:

♦ *General*—There are several things you can change here, and the first one is your home page. A home page is the page your browser automatically opens to when you connect to the Internet; you specify this page with a Web address such as **www.microsoft.com** or **www.yahoo.com**. You can also configure what you want the computer to do with temporary Internet files. Temporary files can be cookies, stored pages, and so on; you can delete them from here or set preferences for them. Also, the History folder contains links to pages you've visited lately; this can be set to keep pages in the History folder for a certain number of days, or you can manually clear the History folder.

Finally, you can change the colors, fonts, languages, and accessibility options for your Internet browser.

♦ *Security*—This tab has four zones available for configuration: Internet, Local Intranet, Trusted Sites, and Restricted Sites. For each zone, you can set the security level to balance functionality with security needs. Multiple configurations can be made here; to see them, simply choose a zone and select Custom Level. Some options include how to handle downloads, whether installations to the desktop are enabled, and how users will be authenticated in each zone.

♦ *Privacy*—Web sites often use the information they get from users and computers to guess what you might like to see next, to help you when you're purchasing items on a site, to remember what you preferred from your last visit to the site, or to display targeted ads based on these remembered preferences. If you are concerned about privacy issues on the Web, you might want to change some of the settings here. By default, privacy settings are set to Medium, meaning that Internet sites will be checked for privacy policies, and those policies will be compared to your settings. The Web sites can use cookies to remember your preferences, and the Medium setting is compatible with most Web sites. Changing any of these policies simply requires moving a slider to a higher privacy level.

♦ *Content*—The Content tab has three areas for configuration. The first area, called Content Advisor, is used to filter out unwanted content from Internet sites that contain graphic language, nudity, sex, or violence. The Content Advisor is a great tool for administrators (and parents) who want to prevent users from accessing such sites. The Certificates section is used by administrators and other support personnel to issue and check certificates of Web sites to verify that the entities on the Internet are indeed who they claim to be. Certificates can be used to secure the computer against harm from hackers and other evils. Finally, you can store your personal information by selecting My Profile and filling out the information or by using AutoComplete to automatically fill in information such as Web addresses, forms, or usernames and passwords.

♦ *Connections*—This tab lists the dial-up and local-area-network connections on your computer. The Internet connections can be added, deleted, or configured. You can also start the Internet Connection Wizard from here and set up a new connection to the Internet.

♦ *Programs*—This tab lists which programs run by default and acts as the HTML editor, email program, newsgroup program, Internet call program, calendar, and contact list. Web settings can be set to their defaults here also.

♦ *Advanced*—This tab offers a place to change the default behavior of the Internet browser, including such items as printing default colors and images when printing Web page information, displaying notifications when script errors occur, and enabling a personalized Favorites menu.

Note
You can access Internet options from Category view by clicking the Network And Internet Connections icon and choosing Internet Options.

Keyboard

The Keyboard icon opens the Keyboard Properties dialog box, which contains two tabs: Speed and Hardware. If you have a special keyboard installed, such as a wireless keyboard, there might be other tabs as well.

♦ *Speed*—Allows you to set the repeat delay of the keyboard from long to short, set the repeat rate from slow to fast, and set the cursor blink rate from none to fast. You can also test the repeat rate after setting it.

♦ *Hardware*—Specifies the keyboard device that is installed on your computer and lists its properties, including how it is attached to the system and whether it is working properly.

Note
You can access keyboard options from Category view by clicking the Printers And Other Hardware icon and choosing Keyboard.

Mail

The Mail icon opens the Internet Accounts dialog box, which displays information about the Internet mail accounts on the local computer. This icon can also be used to add or remove Internet mail accounts or to set or change properties for these accounts.

Note
You can access mail options from Category view by clicking the Other Control Panel Options icon and choosing Mail.

Mouse

The Mouse Properties dialog box has more tabs and configuration choices than you'd probably think. Four tabs can be used to perform tasks ranging from switching the functions of the left and right mouse buttons to changing the speed of the double click. (If you have a special mouse installed, such as a wireless mouse or one with a wheel, there might be other tabs as well.) The four tabs are:

♦ *Buttons*—Used to switch the functions of the primary and secondary buttons on the mouse, change the double-click speed, and turn on ClickLock. ClickLock enables you to highlight or drag without holding down the mouse button.

♦ *Pointers*—Used to change the mouse pointer icon from the default arrow to other icons, including a hand, an extra large arrow, or a gold 3D arrow. You can customize any of the mouse pointers, including those for normal selection, help selection, working in the background, the busy state, precision selection, and moving.

♦ *Pointer Options*—Used to adjust how fast the pointer moves, to have the pointer "snap to" the default button in a dialog box, to display pointer trails, to hide the pointer while typing, and to show the location of the pointer when you press the Ctrl key.

♦ *Hardware*—Shows the type of mouse installed on the system, the mouse's manufacturer, the method by which the mouse is attached to the computer, and the status of the device.

Note
You can access mouse options from Category view by clicking the Printers And Other Hardware icon and choosing Mouse.

Network and Internet Connections

The Network Connections window offers a place to view LAN connections and Internet connections, connect to them, or make a new connection. From the configured connections on the computer, you can install protocols such as TCP/IP or Client for Microsoft Networks, configure the network adapters, or limit access to the Internet. Just about anything that needs to be configured for your network connections can be done here.

In addition, choosing the Create A New Connection under Network Tasks opens the Network Connection Wizard. This wizard helps you create a connection to the Internet, to a workplace network, or directly to another computer through a parallel or serial port or through infrared technology.

Note
You can access Network Connections from Category view by clicking the Network And Internet Connections icon and choosing either a task or the Network Connections icon.

Phone And Modem Options

Using the Phone And Modem Options dialog box, you can set options for a modem that is already on your system. (If you're adding a new modem, see the "Add New Hardware" section.) This dialog box has three tabs:

♦ *Dialing Rules*—Use this tab to add, delete, or edit dialing locations (the locations from which you will be dialing). You can have multiple dialing locations configured, and each will have its own name and dialing rules, area code rules, and calling card numbers. You can also configure these locations to dial a number, such as 9, before connecting, or to disable call waiting.

♦ *Modems*—Use this tab to see the modem installed on the system, the port it's attached to, and the name of the modem. You can also view the modem's properties, including its manufacturer and driver, or set options such as the maximum port speed or the speaker volume.

♦ *Advanced*—To connect to the Internet, send email, or talk on the phone through your computer, you probably access the Internet through a phone line or cable of some sort. For your computer to connect and to send data, it must have some service providers to assist in this transmission. The Advanced tab lists the telephony providers installed on your system. TAPI (Telephone Application Program Interface) and telephony providers allow communications such as faxing, conference calling, adding a voice to an email, and using video communications over the Internet.

Note

You can access phone and modem options from Category view by clicking the Network And Internet Connections icon and choosing the Phone and Modem Options choice in the left pane.

Power Options

Power Options in the Control Panel offers a number of ways to configure your Windows XP Professional computer to save energy and lengthen the life of your computer and monitor. These options are not just for laptop users but are for all users in any workplace environment. The Power Options Properties dialog box has four tabs:

♦ *Power Schemes*—Power scheme options include Home/Office Desk, Portable/Laptop, Presentation, Always On, Minimal Power Management, and Max Battery. For maximum efficiency, you should choose the one that best describes how you use your computer. Here, you can also set when the monitor should turn off, when the hard disks should shut down, and when the system should go on System Standby.

♦ *Advanced*—Use this tab to specify whether the power icon will be shown on the taskbar, whether the computer will require a password when it resumes from sleep, and what will happen when the computer's power button is pressed. The choices for the power button include shutting down, doing nothing, asking what to do, or going to sleep.

- *Hibernate*—When the computer hibernates, it stores any unsaved information to the hard disk and then shuts down. When the computer comes out of hibernation, the information is restored to its original place. You can enable hibernate support from this tab and view the amount of disk space available for hibernation.

- *UPS*—Use this tab only if there is an uninterruptible power supply (UPS) installed on the computer and if it is in use. On this tab, you can configure and manage such devices.

Note

You can access power options from Category view by clicking the Performance And Maintenance icon and choosing either a task or the Power Options icon.

Printers And Faxes

The Printers And Faxes window shows which printers and faxes are installed on the local computer and on any network computers that this computer can access. From here, you can set printing preferences, paper quality, paper size, and more, as long as you have the appropriate permissions to do so. You can also add a printer by using the Add Printer Wizard.

Note

You can access Printers And Faxes from Category view by clicking the Printers And Other Hardware icon and choosing either a task or the Printers And Faxes icon.

Regional And Language Options

Because there are so many people all over the world using Microsoft operating systems, and because there are corporations with offices spread all across the globe, it is necessary for Windows XP to offer options that support all of these areas. For instance, if Company A has its headquarters in Argentina, with branches in Chili, Colombia, and Mexico, and they mainly do business in these countries, then a branch office in the U.S. would probably need to use numbers, currency, times, and dates configured with those countries in mind. You can change the regional options and languages from this dialog box.

The Regional And Language Options dialog box has three tabs:

- *Regional Options*—Used to set standards and formats for decimal symbols, currency, time, and date configured by country or by component. For instance, English (United States) could be chosen from Standards and Formats, but the currency and dates could be changed to match the needs of a particular organization (in the previous example, Spanish).

- *Languages*—Used to change the input language of the computer. You must add language services through this tab before changing the input language, and there are multiple languages to choose from. Once the services are added, preferences can be set accordingly.

- *Advanced*—Used to enable non-Unicode programs to display menus and dialog boxes in their native language. This option applies to all users on the computer.

You can access regional and language options from Category view by clicking the Date, Time, Language, And Regional Options icon and choosing either a task or the appropriate Control Panel icon.

Scanners And Cameras

Similar to the Printers And Faxes window, the Scanners And Cameras window shows which scanners and cameras are installed on the local computer and on any network computers that this computer can access. From here, you can set preferences for these devices as long as you have the appropriate permissions to do so. You can also add a scanner or camera by using the Scanner Or Camera Installation Wizard.

You can access Scanners And Cameras from Category view by clicking the Printers And Other Hardware icon and choosing either a task or the appropriate Control Panel icon.

Scheduled Tasks

Although I'll talk more about each of these items in various upcoming chapters, this item has its very own chapter because Scheduled Tasks is a very powerful tool. From here, you can add tasks—such as Disk Cleanup and the Files And Settings Transfer Wizard—and programs—such as Microsoft Excel or Outlook—to be run on your computer. You might find out that your computer came preconfigured to run specific tasks that you didn't even know about. When you click Add Scheduled Task, the Scheduled Task Wizard opens to assist you with the process.

You can access Scheduled Tasks from Category view by clicking the Performance And Maintenance icon and choosing Scheduled Tasks.

Sounds And Audio Devices

Computers almost always have sound and audio devices installed by default these days, and you can see what is installed and configure it in this dialog box. The Sounds And Audio Devices dialog box has five tabs:

♦ *Volume*—Used to change the volume on the default sound device on your system. Depending on the system, you might have advanced controls for different options such as Line In, MIDI, and CD Audio.

♦ *Sounds*—Used to change the sound scheme on your computer. Two are available: the Windows Default and the Utopia sound schemes.

♦ *Audio*—Used to configure the computer's default audio devices that are used for recording and playing back music files.

◆ *Voice*—Used to configure advanced audio properties such as the performance of speakers or voice recording devices.

◆ *Hardware*—Lists the hardware on your system that might be able to play music or record sound. These devices can include CD-RW drives, CD-ROM drives, Zip drives, audio drivers, or unknown devices.

Note

You can access Sounds And Audio Devices from Category view by clicking the Sounds, Speech, And Audio Devices icon and selecting Sounds And Audio Devices.

Speech

Microsoft Windows XP operating systems include text-to-speech conversion software. You can control the voice properties, speed, and other options for this text-to-speech translation from the Speech dialog box. On the Text To Speech tab, you can also preview the voice and make other voice selection changes.

Note

You can access Speech from Category view by clicking the Sounds, Speech, And Audio Devices icon and choosing Speech.

System

There are times when you'll need to look at the properties of the system as a whole. To do that, you can use the System icon in the Control Panel to obtain information and change basic configurations of the system.

The System Properties dialog box has seven tabs:

◆ *General*—Here you can see which operating system (OS) is installed on the computer, what version the OS is, who the computer is registered to, and the type of processor, speed of the bus, and amount of memory (RAM) installed on the computer.

◆ *Computer Name*—Here you can view the computer's description and name and see what domain or workgroup (if any) the computer belongs to. You can use the Network Identification Wizard to join a domain and create a local user account, or you can rename this computer or join a domain.

◆ *Hardware*—This tab contains three sections:

    ◆ *Add New Hardware Wizard*—Starts the wizard responsible for adding new hardware to the system.

    ◆ *Device Manager*—Lists all of the hardware devices installed on the computer and can be used to change the properties or the drivers of any device.

♦ *Hardware Profiles*—Provides a way to set up and store different hardware configurations for different users or different locations.

♦ *Advanced*—Used mainly by administrators, this tab offers a place to change the performance of the computer by configuring visual effects, processor scheduling, memory usage, and virtual memory. This tab also allows administrators to set user profiles and startup and recovery options. These options will be covered later in the book.

♦ *System Restore*—This tab is used to track the changes made to your computer. If any of those changes cause the system to fail or become unstable, System Restore can be used to reverse those changes. System Restore is enabled by default.

♦ *Automatic Updates*—Microsoft offers automatic updates about service packs, hot fixes, and bug fixes, which can be downloaded from the Internet for free. You can configure how you want to be notified of these updates.

♦ *Remote*—Here you can configure how you want this computer to be used from another location. The choices are Remote Assistance and Remote Desktop. Remote Assistance means that you will allow Help Desk personnel to access your computer from the Internet to provide assistance. They will be able to view and control your computer. Remote Desktop means that you can have access from your computer from another location, such as at home. Using Remote Desktop, you can access all programs, files, and applications at home just as you can access them while physically sitting at your desk at work.

Note

You can access System Properties from Category view by clicking the Performance And Maintenance icon and choosing either a task or the Control Panel icon.

Taskbar And Start Menu

The Taskbar And Start Menu icon opens the Properties dialog box as detailed in the "Basic Tasks" section earlier in this chapter. This dialog box allows you to change the look of both of these components, including locking the taskbar or changing the Start menu from the Classic theme to the Windows XP theme.

Note

You can access the Taskbar and Start Menu options from Category view by clicking the Appearance And Themes icon and choosing either a task or the Taskbar And Start Menu icon.

User Accounts

After clicking the User Accounts icon, you have many choices. There is no User Account Wizard that appears, nor is there a User Accounts Properties dialog box. Instead, you see a User Accounts window and you have some choices to make depending on what you'd like to do. For instance, you can choose to learn more about user accounts, account types, or switching between users, or you can choose a task, such as changing an account, creating an account, or changing the way users log on or off. You can also pick an account to change (by default, Administrator or Guest).

Once you've made a choice, a wizard may or may not appear, depending on the choice. However, Microsoft Windows XP is quite user-friendly, and creating accounts is quite intuitive. Creating and managing user accounts will be detailed in later chapters of this book.

Note

You can access User Accounts from Category view by clicking the User Accounts icon and choosing either a task or a Control Panel icon.

Windows Explorer

The files and folders on your computer are stored in a hierarchical manner, with some folders inside other folders and with those folders named and organized appropriately. To see how those folders are organized, you can "explore" what's on your computer by using Windows Explorer. Explorer not only displays the structure but also allows you to move these folders or the files in them to other areas. You can also see who's on your LAN (local area network), view any mapped network drives, and rename, copy, and search for files or folders that you need. In this section, I'll introduce Explorer and how you can use it to your advantage.

Note

If you find you're not comfortable with Windows Explorer, you can access all of your computer files and folders by using other methods.

The Windows Explorer Window

To see Windows Explorer, right-click the Start button and choose Explore All Users from the context menu. You'll see something similar to what's shown in Figure 1.12.

Notice that the Start Menu folder is highlighted by default. This folder lists the programs that are installed on your computer, Windows Update, and any other items that automatically place themselves there when programs are installed, such as Microsoft Office utilities.

Also notice the other drives on the computer. These drives will vary from system to system, but in this example, there are drives called CD Drive (F:) and a Audio CD (E:), both located at the bottom-left corner of the screen. At the top of the screen is another drive, called Windows 2000 (C:), which is a separate physical hard drive on this computer. Your system may or may not have these drives, but there might be others.

Windows Explorer displays either a plus sign or a minus sign beside each folder. A plus sign indicates that a folder contains other files or folders and can be expanded. A minus sign indicates that the folder is already expanded. You can view the contents of your computer by clicking on these signs.

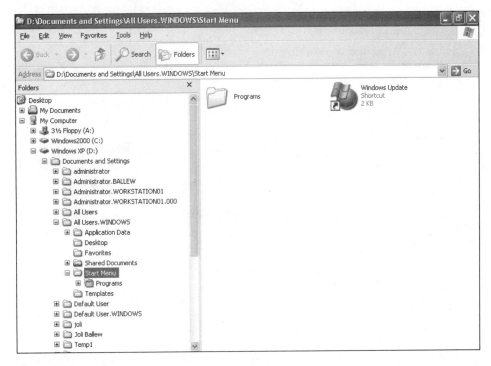

Figure 1.12
Windows Explorer.

There are other sections as well. The middle section contains tasks that can be done and other places you can go.

The File Menu

You can do several tasks in Explorer, and the tasks you'll see listed under the File menu will differ depending on which folder is highlighted in Explorer. If you choose New | Folder, a new folder will be created in the Start menu.

If a different folder is highlighted—for instance, the My Network Places folder—different tasks are available. Figure 1.13 shows these options.

Warning

Be careful when moving, deleting, or renaming folders that the operating system uses. You shouldn't perform functions like these on folders such as Programs, Winnt, Shared Documents, or My Network Places. Doing so might cause the operating system to be unable to find the files and folders it needs to run properly.

Changing Folder Options

You can change how Windows Explorer looks and many options related to the computer as a whole by using the Tools menu (at the top of the Explorer window). Choosing Tools | Folder Options opens the Folder Options dialog box, which has four tabs:

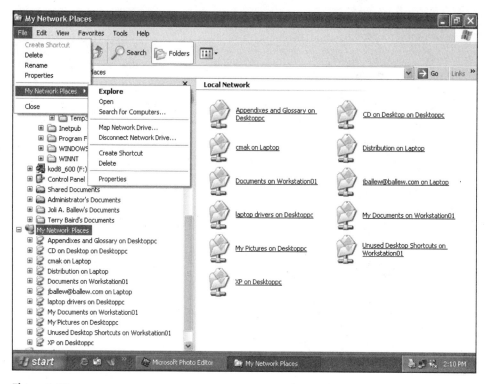

Figure 1.13
My Network Places.

♦ *General*—Here, you can choose to enable Web content in folders, use Windows classic folders, open each folder in the same or a different window, single-click (or double-click) to open a folder, and configure settings for single-clicking.

♦ *View*—Tasks available here include automatically searching for network folders and printers, displaying all Control Panel options and all folder contents, showing or hiding hidden files and folders, hiding protected operating system files, showing encrypted files and folders in a different color, showing pop-up descriptions for folder and desktop items, and restoring previous folder windows at logon.

♦ *File Types*—Here, you can view all of the different file types that can be used or accessed on your computer. If you need to add different file types for specific programs, you can do so here.

♦ *Offline Files*—Offline files allow you to store network information on your computer so that you can work with it even when your computer is not physically connected to the network. You can enable offline files here and configure how you want to use them. You can synchronize the offline files, encrypt offline files, and set the amount of disk space that can be used by offline files.

To change the folder options for your computer:

1. Right-click the Start menu, and choose Explore or Explore All Users.

2. Choose Tools | Folder Options.

3. Select the General and View tabs, and make your changes by selecting the appropriate options. When finished, choose OK.

Help And Support

No matter how hard you try or how many books you read, there will come a time when you need a little extra help, and luckily, there are several ways to get help for Windows XP Professional. You can use the XP help files, get help from dialog boxes, call or otherwise contact Microsoft, visit newsgroups, and subscribe to email communities. Your best bet however, is to contact the technical support line for the company from which you purchased the PC. The technical support is usually free and accurate.

Using Windows XP Professional Help

The first stop for getting help with a problem is the help system included with Windows XP. You can access this by choosing Start | Help And Support. You'll see the Help And Support Center window shown in Figure 1.14.

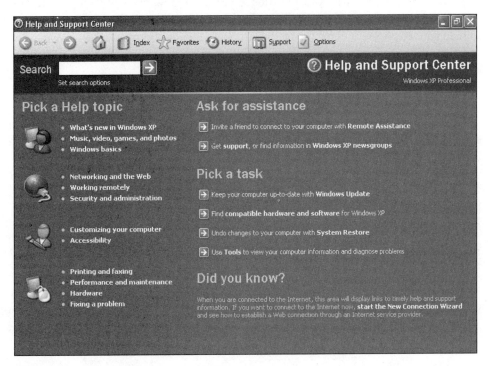

Figure 1.14
Help And Support Center.

The left side of the screen has several options offering help for many of the tasks you'll need to do. If you are having trouble with the performance of your computer, you can select the Performance And Maintenance section; for setting up a computer so that you can work remotely with another, choose Working Remotely.

The right side contains several other options for getting help, including using Windows Update, finding compatible hardware and software, and using tools such as System Restore. These options require an Internet connection and take you to the most up-to-date resources available from Microsoft's Web site.

You can also simply type a word in the Search box and obtain help about anything from using the taskbar to configuring access for other users. When you use the Search utility, the results are shown in the left pane, and the information related to each result is shown in the right pane. The screen looks like a Web site and is created this way on purpose. Microsoft Windows XP not only imitates the look of the Web but also integrates the Internet with Windows Explorer and Help. For instance, searching Help for "updates" produces three types of results: Suggested Topics, Full-Text Search Matches, and Microsoft Knowledge Base. Some of these topics are stored locally on the computer, while some are stored on a Web site belonging to Microsoft. Additionally, the Support button at the top of the Help Window allows you to decide what type of support you need: asking a friend, getting help from Microsoft, or going to a Web site forum. You can highlight search words in topics by choosing Options from the toolbar at the top of the window, choosing Set Search Options in the left pane, and then choosing Turn On Search Highlight. Other options are available to help you set preferences for navigating the help menus and topics. You can also choose Index (at the top of the screen) to search through the help system's index to find the information you need.

Getting Help from a Dialog Box

Besides the Help And Support Services utility, you can get quick answers while in a utility by clicking on the question mark in the top-right corner of the dialog box and then selecting what you'd like information about. Figure 1.15 shows an example of this.

The question-mark icon does not appear in all programs and utilities, but you will see it in Windows XP utilities such as System Properties, Local Area Connection Properties, My Documents Properties, and the like. This information can be just what you need in many instances and can provide a quick explanation of the options available.

Newsgroups and Email Communities

If you want to talk with others about Windows XP, you can do so by joining newsgroups and email communities on the Internet. To see what the Internet has to offer, simply log on to the Internet using a Web browser and type in "Windows XP Newsgroups" or "Windows XP email communities" in the browser's search window. From there, you can explore the possibilities.

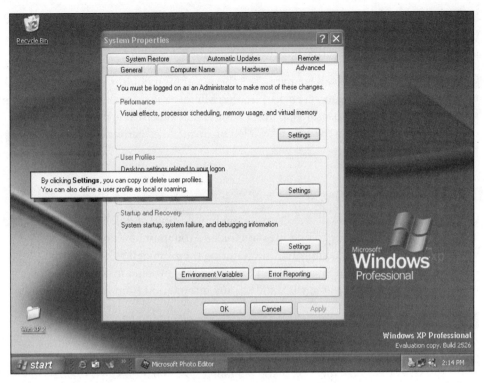

Figure 1.15
An example of What Is? help.

Microsoft offers several newsgroups at **http://communities.Microsoft.com/newsgroups/ default.asp**. From here, you can search down the list of choices to locate **whistler.professional. general**. In this group, users of all levels share problems and solutions, and write posts searching for answers or sharing ideas. Thousands of other newsgroups are available as well, and these can be found by simply surfing the net.

Email communities are a little different. Sometimes called "email groups," an email community is made up of a group of subscribers who exchange email about a certain subject. When one member of the group sends an email, all members of the group receive it. Then all members can respond to find a solution to the proposed problem or expand on ideas that are introduced. Email communities are a good way to meet people of different abilities and interests, and offer lots of great information.

Microsoft Assisted Support

Finally, you can obtain support from Microsoft by using its Web site options. To see the support options, point your Web browser to **http://support.microsoft.com/directory/**, select Support Options Overview, and scroll down to see all of the options. One of these options is Custom Support, which includes specific levels of support for specific users: Alliance, Premier, Authorized Premier, Professional, and Personal.

Several support options are free, including the Microsoft Knowledge Base, Frequently Asked Questions And Tasks, and Downloads, Updates, and Drivers (for downloading the latest updates). You can also subscribe to newsgroups.

Other support options typically require a fee; these options include logging into online Web broadcasts, asking a question via email, phoning Microsoft and speaking directly to a representative, and obtaining custom support for business customers. The rates for these vary, but to see the latest rates, go to the Microsoft Web site mentioned earlier and choose the appropriate link.

Files and Folders

Other basic, yet needed, skills are creating, saving, finding, and deleting files and folders and using the Search utility to find files and folders. You must also know how to work with windows by minimizing, maximizing, and restoring them, as well as how to switch between open windows (which can also be called "applications" in some instances). Finally, you'll need to be adept at cutting, copying, and pasting information from one file to another.

Note

If you are familiar with these tasks already, you might want to skip around in this section, or skip over it completely. For these basic tasks, not much has changed in Windows XP, even though the look of the operating system has changed dramatically.

Create, Save, Find, and Delete

Files are generally created automatically by an application when you begin working on a particular task. For instance, a Microsoft Word document will be created when you open the program and begin typing. Saving a file, finding it again, and deleting it when necessary require a little more knowledge. Folders, on the other hand, are not generally created automatically when programs are used. Folders contain files that are created by the user. If you've noticed previously, the Start menu contains some folders created by Microsoft. Those folders are My Documents, My Pictures, and My Music.

When you open a word processing program such as WordPad (choose Start | All Programs | Accessories | WordPad) and begin typing, the document you are creating is a file. By default, this file will be saved in the My Documents folder. If you open Windows Media Player and save a music file, that file is saved in the My Music folder by default. When you're saving photos from a scanner or a digital camera, those files are saved in the My Pictures folder by default. These folders can make it easier for you to find your files when you want to access them again, or, if you prefer, you can create your own folders and use them.

Creating Files and Folders

Once you have begun your work on a document, you can save the file to the hard drive. Depending on the type of file it is, it will be saved in one of the default folders unless you specify a different one.

Note

There are, of course, exceptions to this general rule. If you have a digital camera, a scanner, or a program that was added after Windows XP was installed, those programs might have created their own folders for saving files. My digital camera saves files in a folder called "My Digital Pictures," created when the camera's software was installed.

For the purpose of instruction, let's create a WordPad file:

1. Open WordPad (choose Start | All Programs | Accessories | WordPad).

2. Type this sentence: "This is a test."

3. Choose File | Save As.

4. Notice that the file has the default name, Document, highlighted in the File Name text box, and that the file will be stored in the My Documents folder, listed in the Save In box. See Figure 1.16. Choose Cancel.

Warning

Although the file has technically been created, it isn't saved to the hard drive until you choose the Save button shown in this figure. If you choose Cancel, the file will not be saved.

Creating a folder is a bit different. To create a folder on the desktop:

1. Find an open place on the desktop by closing out any open programs. Right-click any empty space.

Figure 1.16
Creating a file.

2. Choose New | Folder.

3. When the new folder appears on the desktop, type the name "Test Folder". Press the Enter key.

Saving Files

Creating a file and saving a file are similar. A file is created when an application is launched and data is added. However, the file isn't saved until you finish the task started in the previous section. This time through, save the file:

1. Open WordPad (choose Start | All Programs | Accessories | WordPad).

2. Type this sentence: "This is a test."

3. Choose File | Save As.

4. In the File Name box, type "Test File"; then choose Save.

This file has been saved in the My Documents folder. You can also save files to other folders. In the previous example, you created a Test Folder on the desktop. In this example, you'll create another file and save it to that folder:

1. Open WordPad (choose Start | All Programs | Accessories | WordPad).

2. Type this sentence: "This is a test -- 2."

3. Choose File | Save As.

4. In the File Name box, type "Test File 2".

5. Click the down arrow by the Save In box and choose Desktop, or click the Desktop icon on the left side of the Save As dialog box.

6. Notice that the items on the desktop appear in the list box. Select Test Folder. (This is the folder you created previously.)

7. Choose Save.

You have now successfully created two files and saved them in two different places.

Finding and Opening Files

There are several ways you can find and open files that you have created and saved to the hard drive. Because this is an introduction to the basics, I'll just stick to one method for now. The easiest way to open a saved file is to open the folder containing it.

In the previous exercises, you saved two files, Test File and Test File 2, in two folders: My Documents and Test Folder.

To open the file Test File, saved in My Documents:

1. Choose Start | My Documents.

2. Click Test File.

To open the file Test File 2 from the Test Folder on the desktop:

1. Open the Test Folder on the desktop by double-clicking the folder.

2. Open Test File 2 by double-clicking it.

Deleting Files

Files can be deleted the same way; just open the folder they are stored in, and delete them.

To delete the file Test File 2:

1. Open the Test Folder on the desktop by double-clicking the folder.

2. Right-click Test File 2, and choose Delete.

3. When prompted "Are you sure you want to send 'Test File 2' to the Recycle Bin?", choose Yes.

To delete the folder Test Folder:

1. Locate the folder on the desktop.

2. Right-click the folder Test Folder, and choose Delete.

3. When prompted, choose Yes to verify that you want to delete this folder.

Warning

Don't delete any of the folders that were included with Windows XP, such as My Documents, My Music, or My Pictures. For now, don't delete any folders that you did not create yourself.

The Search Companion

If you've searched for files or folders in any other operating system, this utility will look familiar to you. The Search command on the Start menu gives you yet another way to locate files or folders that you need to access. Even if you know only part of the name, you can type in wildcards to locate the files or folders with similar names. For instance, you can type in "Te*" to locate files starting with "te."

To search for the file created earlier called Test File:

1. Choose Start | Search

2. Choose Documents from the What Do You Want To Search For? choices.

3. Type in the document's name.

4. Specify advanced options if desired.

5. Choose Search.

You can also change how the Search Companion looks for files. You can choose Change Preferences from the What Do You Want To Search For? choices. These choices include choosing an animated screen character, using the Indexing Service, how files and folders will be found, and if balloon tips and AutoComplete should be enabled.

Minimizing, Maximizing, and Restoring Windows

When you open an application, it opens a window containing the application and places information on the taskbar. When several programs are running at the same time, multiple programs are listed on the taskbar. As you work, you'll probably move between programs to do various tasks. For instance, you might have an Excel spreadsheet open with database information, a word processing program for a letter you're writing, an email program, and a graphics program. When all of these programs are running, you need to know how to minimize, maximize, and restore their windows.

Figure 1.17 shows multiple programs running on a computer. This window is maximized, or as large as it can be. To minimize it, you can click on the dash (the Minimize button) in the top-right corner of the window. When the application window is minimized, the program is still running and available, but it's not shown on the desktop. Instead, it's shown on the taskbar.

The Restore button is available so that you can size the window as you'd like. Clicking the Restore button restores the application window to the size it was in before it was maximized. Restore makes the window smaller so that you can grab the edge of the window and resize it or move it around. Although this is an extreme example, Figure 1.18 shows the uses of the Restore button.

Switching Between Applications

When multiple programs are running, as shown in Figures 1.17 and 1.18, you can switch between them in many ways. A common way is to simply maximize all of the windows and then click the taskbar to work with the program you'd like. For instance, if you are using Outlook Express and want to switch to WordPad, you can simply click WordPad on the taskbar. The WordPad program will be brought "in front of" or "on top of" the other programs and will be available to work with.

A second way to switch between programs is to minimize the program that is "on top." This is the last one maximized. You can bring that program back up by clicking its name on the taskbar.

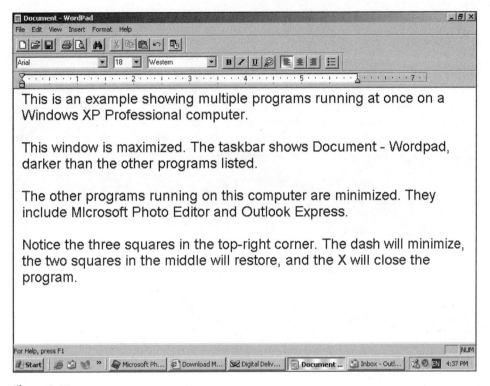

Figure 1.17
Multiple programs open (using the Windows Classic theme).

You can also press Alt+Tab to switch between programs. This is my favorite way because usually my hands are on the keyboard and not on the mouse. It's all a matter of preference.

Cut, Copy, Paste, and the Clipboard

Some of the more useful basic skills to have are cutting, copying, and pasting. You can perform these tasks in just about any program, but the easiest place to learn them is in a word processing program.

These terms are important to understand:

◆ *Cut*—When you highlight a word, sentence, graphic, or other piece of data and cut that material, the material is saved to the clipboard and deleted from the document.

◆ *Copy*—When you highlight a word, sentence, graphic, or other piece of data and copy that material, the material is saved to the clipboard while also remaining in the document.

◆ *Paste*—When you have placed something on the clipboard by either cutting or copying data, you can place that data into a document by using the Paste command.

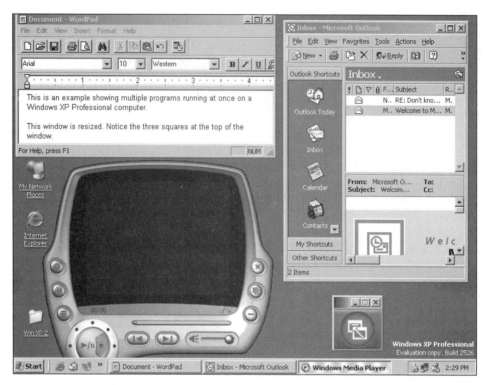

Figure 1.18
Application windows resized and arranged.

♦ *Clipboard*—The clipboard, included in Windows XP, is a utility that holds information that has been cut or copied. It can hold up to 12 items.

To use Cut, Copy, or Paste:

1. Open a word processing program such as WordPad or Microsoft Word from the Start menu.

2. Type the words, "Today I will learn to cut, copy, and paste."

3. Highlight the sentence, and then right-click it.

4. Choose Cut.

5. Right-click the blank page, and choose Paste.

6. Repeat Steps 4 and 5, using the Copy command in Step 4.

Of course, you can use Cut, Copy, Paste, and the clipboard in a multitude of other ways. These commands can be used with graphics, Internet addresses, and more.

Burning CDs

Many of the newer computers come with CD-RW (compact disc-rewritable) drives. These drives hold CDs that you cannot only read from, but also write to. If your computer came with one of these drives, you can use some Windows XP utilities to write, erase, and archive your data on CDs.

Writable CDs hold lots of data. Whereas a floppy disk can hold only 1.44MB, a CD can hold 650MB or more. This is a great way to save data and to back up crucial information stored on your computer.

Note
If the CD-RW drive did not come with your computer but was added on after-wards, you might need to use the program that came with the CD-RW drive instead of this utility.

Copying Files and Folders to the CD-RW

To copy information from your computer's hard drive to the CD-RW, you first use My Computer to select the files and folders you want to copy. Then you'll use the CD Writing Wizard to do the copying.

To select files and folders for copying and to use the CD Writing Wizard:

1. Insert a blank, writable CD into the CD drive's bay.

2. In My Computer, highlight the folders you want to copy to the writable CD. (You might have to select Show The Contents Of This Drive to see them all.) To select more than one, hold down the Ctrl key while selecting.

3. Right-click the selected items and choose Copy This File, Copy This Folder, or Copy Selected Items. If necessary, you can perform these steps again to obtain all of the files for the writable CD.

4. In the Copy Items dialog box, select the CD drive's letter, usually D: or E:, and then choose Paste.

5. In My Computer, click the CD-RW drive. Make sure all of the files you intend to place on the writable CD are listed in the temporary holding area named Files Ready To Be Written To The CD. If they aren't, perform Steps 2 through 4 again.

6. In the Tasks section in the left pane of My Computer, choose Write To CD. Follow the instructions provided by the CD Writing Wizard.

After the files have been copied, you'll see a notification message in the bottom-right corner of your screen.

Erasing

Depending on the CD used and the type of CD-RW drive you have installed, you may be able to erase data on your rewritable CDs. If this is the case, read the manufacturer's instructions for erasing data on CDs, and follow the directions carefully.

Third-Party Software

Most CD-RW drives come with their own software, which might be more useful than what comes with Windows XP Professional. I have an external Adaptec DirectCD drive installed on my computer, and it comes with lots of software, including Help files, CD-RW Eraser, DirectCD Wizard, Reference Guide, and ScanDisk. These utilities have more options than the Windows XP software does, and I like them much better.

To use third-party software for a CD-RW drive, you can usually perform steps similar to the ones listed here:

1. Place a new CD-RW in the drive bay.

2. Open the software from Start | All Programs | *<name of program>*.

3. Generally, a wizard of some sort starts and guides you through the process of creating the CD. This usually involves formatting and naming the CD first. Follow the instructions as given by the program. Once the CD is ready, you'll be asked to continue.

Microsoft Management Consoles

The Microsoft Management Console (MMC) is used to group administrative tools, folders, Web pages, and other administrative items so that working with these objects is more efficient. A console is made up of panes. The left pane holds the console tree, sort of like Windows Explorer trees, and other panes are configured to provide different views of the available consoles. These panes separate and organize the information in the consoles. Consoles are a very useful addition to the operating system; they were introduced in Windows 2000 and have been carried over into Windows XP.

Before getting too far into consoles, you need understand some of the basic terms associated with them:

♦ *Console*—A console is a place to group programs, tools, or folders so that you or other users can access them more easily and from one location.

♦ *Console tree*—Located in the left pane, this tree can be hidden if necessary. The tree lists the contents of the console. Clicking an area of the tree displays the corresponding console item in the right pane.

♦ *Container object*—Containers are used to group similar objects, such as printers, computers, or data. For example, a folder is a container object because it holds files.

♦ *Details pane*—This console pane displays the details for the item that is selected in the console tree. These details might be a list, properties of the item, or services or events that work with the utility chosen.

♦ *User mode*—When a console is saved in user mode, the users who access it cannot add or remove snap-ins or save it. This is the best setting if a console has been created for users in a department or company.

♦ *Author mode*—When a console is saved in author mode, users can add or remove snap-ins, view all portions of the console tree, and save consoles.

♦ *Snap-ins*—These are tools that can be added to MMC consoles. There are two types: standalone snap-ins and extensions. Standalone snap-ins can be added independently; extension snap-ins can be added only to extend the functionality of another installed snap-in. Examples of snap-ins include Event Viewer, Folder, Group Policy, Performance Logs And Alerts, Remote Desktops, and Security Templates.

Both preconfigured and blank consoles are available. There are many preconfigured consoles that you can use and literally thousands of personalized consoles that you can configure. In the last two sections, I'll introduce a few of the preconfigured consoles and then explain how you can create your own consoles.

Preconfigured Consoles

There would not be any reason to go into depth here about any particular console, but understanding what they look like and what they have to offer will certainly be useful. Many companies configure MMC consoles for their employees, and all administrators must use MMC consoles for completing administrative tasks. The following consoles are widely used.

Computer Management

Take a look at Figure 1.19, which shows the Computer Management console. It is a preconfigured console, which you open by choosing Start | Control Panel | Administrative Tools | Computer Management. Administrators often use this console to perform tasks related to managing users and groups, reviewing the performance of the computer, reinstalling drivers, and more.

Notice the console tree in the left pane. It contains three main categories, which are also listed in the details pane on the right side. Those categories are System Tools, Storage, and Services And Applications. Listed next are some of the tasks that can be performed with each section of this console:

♦ *System Tools*—Used for viewing application, security, and system logs (Event Viewer); viewing and managing shares, sessions, and open files (Shared Folders); viewing and managing users and groups (Local Users And Groups); viewing and managing counter logs, trace logs, and alerts (Performance Logs And Alerts); and viewing, configuring, and troubleshooting hardware (Device Manager).

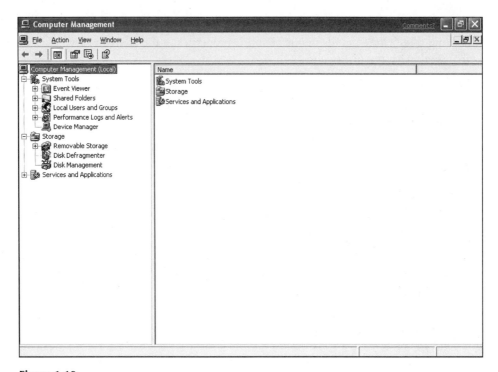

Figure 1.19
The Computer Management console.

- ◆ *Storage*—Used for viewing and managing removable storage devices (Removable Storage) such as backup devices, Zip drives, or tape devices, and for using Disk Defragmenter and Disk Management. Disk Defragmenter is a utility that can clean up files on a computer's hard disk. The Disk Management utility allows an administrator to view and manage all of the disks on the computer.

- ◆ *Services And Applications*—Used for starting, stopping, restarting, and pausing services that the computer and network use, including the Alerter Service, Indexing Service, Plug and Play, Task Scheduler, and the Workstation Service for using Windows Management Instrumentation (WMI), and for accessing the Indexing Service. Usually only experienced administrators use the latter two services.

Local Security Policy

If you are the administrator of your computer, or if you have administrator's rights or are a member of the Administrators group, you can set the local security policy on your computer from the Local Security Policy console. You can access this console from Administrative Tools in the Control Panel. Local policies affect every user who accesses the local computer, and they apply to the specific computer. Account policies apply only to user accounts and affect those users no matter what computer they've logged on to. If there are other policies in effect, the local security policy is overridden by both the domain policy and the organizational unit policy.

The local security policy is used to secure the computer from both intentional and unintentional acts of harm. Harm can be done to a computer in many ways, including a user giving out a password, a hacker trying multiple passwords to break into a computer, or someone changing the policies on the computer without proper credentials or with fake ones. These are only a few of the dangers that can be prevented through this console.

Listed next are some of the policies that can be set in the Local Security Settings console. This is not a complete list, but it introduces you to at least a few policies. You can see the Local Security Settings console in Figure 1.20. The Maximum Password Age Properties dialog box is also shown. You can change any policy by double-clicking it and making the appropriate changes.

♦ *Account Policies*—There are two choices: Password Policy and Account Lockout Policy.

    ♦ Password policies include enforcing password history, setting a minimum and a maximum password age, setting a minimum password length, and setting a password complexity requirement. You can also store the passwords using reversible encryption. These policies can be set for domain and local user accounts.

    ♦ Account lockout policies include restrictions on how many times a user can try unsuccessfully to log in before that user's account is locked out. This prevents a

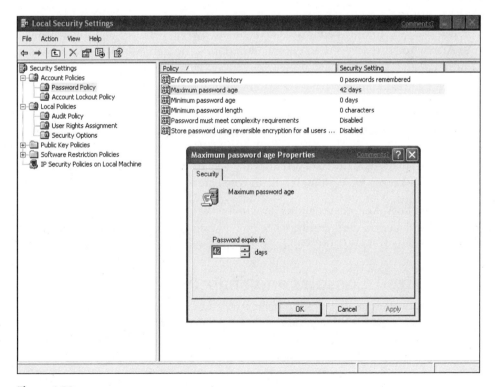

Figure 1.20
The Local Security Settings console.

hacker from gaining access to the network or the computer by using a password-breaking program.

♦ *Local Policies*—There are three choices: Audit Policy, User Rights Assignment, and Security Options.

    ♦ Audit policies allow an administrator to track such things as account logon events, directory service access, object access, and policy change.

    ♦ User Rights Assignment allows an administrator to view and change default settings for users on policies such as adding workstations, changing the system time, and shutting down the system.

    ♦ Security Options allows an administrator to enable or disable settings regarding guest account status, interactive logons, and other advanced options.

Although there are other options in both of the previously mentioned consoles, the purpose of this section is just to introduce you to some of the available consoles. Keep in mind that these consoles will be used throughout the book to perform tasks as necessary, and they are an integral part of Windows XP Professional. I'd like to introduce one more preconfigured console, the Performance console.

Performance

The Performance console comprises two utilities: System Monitor and Performance Logs And Alerts. You can access the Performance console through Administrative Tools in the Control Panel.

Figure 1.21 shows the Performance console with System Monitor running. System Monitor allows you to collect real-time information about any component in your computer, including RAM, the CPU, hard disk performance, network activity, paging files, and processes. This information can be vital when you're troubleshooting system problems such as slow access to information on the hard drive or excessive paging. (If all of this sounds a little over your head right now, don't panic. It will all come clear to you soon enough.)

Performance Logs And Alerts allows an administrator to view or configure counter logs, trace logs, and alerts. Alerts can be set to go off when certain thresholds are met such as a full hard drive or 100 percent CPU usage for a period of time.

Personalized Consoles and Snap-Ins

Administrators often group certain programs together in a console so that users can access them more easily. As you've seen previously, preconfigured MMC consoles contain utilities that are used to perform administrative tasks, and those utilities are grouped together for ease of use. Now you, too, can create a console of your own.

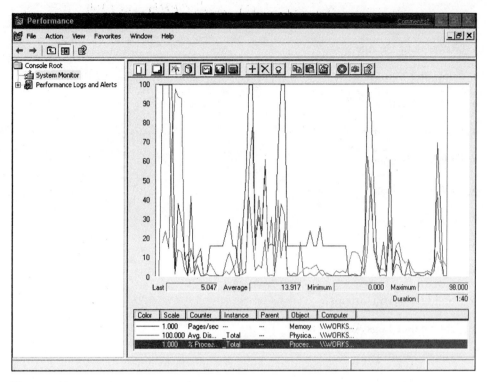

Figure 1.21
System Monitor and the Performance console.

To open a blank console ready for your personalized configuration:

1. Choose Start | Run to open the Run dialog box.

2. In the Open box, type "mmc".

3. Choose OK.

4. Maximize both the console, named Console 1, and the Console Root screens.

The console is now ready to be configured.

What Snap-ins Can Be Added?

You are aware of the preconfigured consoles, but you may not know that the utilities in those consoles are available as snap-ins. With this as an option, you can add only the utilities you need, and not the ones you don't. For instance, you might add Device Manager, Disk Defragmenter, and Disk Management to a console that you'll name Manage Disks, and you might not add Component Services or Services.

Many snap-ins can be added; the following is a partial list. Some of these utilities have been discussed previously, while others will be discussed later in this book. Here are just some of the snap-ins available:

- Certificates
- Component Service
- Computer Management
- Device Manager
- Disk Defragmenter
- Disk Management
- Event Viewer
- Folder
- Group Policy
- Indexing Service
- Local Users And Groups
- Performance Logs And Alerts
- Remote Desktops
- Removable Storage Management
- Security Templates
- Services
- Shared Folders
- System Information

Adding Snap-ins to an MMC Console

To use Windows XP Professional efficiently, you'll need to know how to create MMC consoles and how to add and remove snap-ins. Throughout this book, we'll be using these consoles to perform tasks of all types, thus making the creation of custom consoles a basic skill.

To create a custom console:

1. Choose Start | Run to open the Run dialog box.

2. In the Open box, type "mmc".

3. Choose OK.

4. Maximize both the console, named Console 1, and the Console Root screens.

5. Choose File | Add/Remove Snap-in.

6. In the Add/Remove Snap-In dialog box, choose Add.

7. In the Add Standalone Snap-In dialog box shown in Figure 1.22, select Computer Management and choose Add.

8. In the Computer Management dialog box, choose Local Computer and choose Finish. (Not all snap-ins have a second configuration box; only a few do.)

9. In the Add Standalone Snap-In dialog box, select Folder and choose Add.

10. In the Add Standalone Snap-in dialog box, select System Information and choose Add.

11. In the Select Computer dialog box, select Local Computer, and then choose Finish.

12. Choose Close in the Add Standalone Snap-In dialog box.

13. Choose OK in the Add/Remove Snap-In dialog box.

14. Choose File | Save As in Console 1.

15. Name the file "Management".

You can now use Windows Explorer to locate the new console, and if you'd like, you can create a shortcut to it on the desktop.

Adding Extensions

Extensions to snap-ins provide added functionality to those snap-ins. You can add extensions for only those snap-ins already installed in the custom MMC console. You cannot add snap-ins or extensions to preconfigured consoles.

Figure 1.22
The Add Standalone Snap-in dialog box.

To see which extensions are installed for the snap-ins added to the Management console, which you created in the previous exercise:

1. Open the Management console created earlier.

2. Choose File | Add/Remove Snap-In.

3. In the Add/Remove Snap-In dialog box, select the Extensions tab.

4. In the Snap-Ins That Can Be Extended window, click the arrow to see the three snap-ins created earlier. Choose Computer Management.

5. Uncheck the Add All Extensions checkbox.

6. To remove any of the Available Extensions, uncheck their checkboxes. Choose OK.

Removing Snap-Ins

You can remove a snap-in from a preconfigured console by taking steps similar to the previous procedure. To remove a snap-in:

1. Open the Management console created earlier.

2. Choose File | Add/Remove Snap-In.

3. In the Add/Remove Snap-In dialog box, select the Standalone tab.

4. Select the snap-in to be removed.

5. Choose Remove.

6. Choose OK to accept the changes, or choose Cancel if you do not want to remove the snap-in.

Tip

The Management console will be used for the rest of this chapter. If you have removed a snap-in from this console, you should add it back in now.

Changing the Icon, Mode, and Name of the Console

You can change the name of the console, the console mode, and the icon from a single options page in the custom console. (These changes cannot be made for preconfigured consoles.) To change these options:

1. Open a custom console such as the Management console created earlier.

2. Make sure that the Console Root entry is highlighted and not one of the snap-ins.

3. Choose File | Options.

4. Make sure the Console tab is active.

If there is not a Console tab, then you have opened a preconfigured console. Return to Step 1 and open a custom console instead.

5. To change the name of the console, highlight the current name and type a new one.

6. To change the icon for the console, click the Change Icon button and select a different icon from the icon window, or browse to an icon of your choice.

Remember, if you change the icon, the screenshots in this book will look different from what you'll see on your computer.

7. To change the console mode, click the arrow in the Console Mode window and select the option you want. (To see more information about console mode types, see the sidebar.)

8. If you've changed the console mode to a type of user mode, make any necessary changes to the additional options: Do Not Save Changes To This Console and Allow The User To Customize Views.

Adding, Removing, and Moving Columns

You can add, remove, or move columns (if you have the proper access) from both preconfigured and custom MMC consoles. Removing columns can be useful when the information given in those columns isn't necessary, and moving columns can be useful when a user wants to personalize his or her workspace.

Figure 1.23 shows a preconfigured console, Component Services. The Add/Remove Columns dialog box is also shown. In this instance, an administrator might want to remove the

---

Console Mode Options

There are four options for the console mode. One is author mode, and the other three are different type of user modes. Author mode grants users full access to all MMC functionality, allowing them to add and remove snap-ins, create new windows, create taskpad views and tasks, and view all parts of the console tree. This mode is generally reserved for the person creating the console. Once the console is created, it can be saved in one of three user modes:

- *Full access*—Grants users full access to all windows management commands and the console tree. This type of user mode prevents users from adding or removing snap-ins or changing the properties of the console.

- *Limited access, multiple windows*—Grants users access to only limited areas of the console tree. The administrator configures the console tree before it is saved. Users can create new windows but cannot close existing ones or add or remove snap-ins.

- *Limited access, single window*—Is the same as the previous choice except that users cannot open new windows.

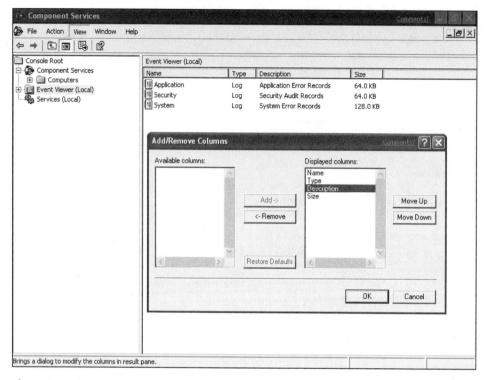

Figure 1.23
Configuring console columns.

Description column because he understands the description already. He might also choose to switch the order of the Size and Type columns.

To change the columns in a console:

1. Open the Management console created earlier. (You could choose a preconfigured console, but I'd suggest not changing those just yet.)

2. In the console tree, expand Computer Management (Local).

3. In the Computer Management (Local) tree, expand Services And Applications.

4. In the Services And Applications tree, select Indexing Service.

5. Choose View | Add/Remove Columns.

6. Remove four columns from the Add/Remove Columns dialog box by highlighting them and choosing Remove.

7. Click a remaining column and click Move Up or Move Down.

8. Choose OK.

Note

Each part of the console tree has different columns.

Customizing the View

You can further customize the view of the MMC console by choosing View | Customize. This action open the Customize View dialog box, which has several choices. By default, all choices are checked except the Description Bar. The choices are:

♦ Console Tree

♦ Standard Menus (Action and View)

♦ Standard Toolbar

♦ Status Bar

♦ Description Bar

♦ Taskpad Navigation Tabs

♦ Menus

♦ Toolbars

You can understand the importance of these options by thinking about creating an MMC console for a group of coworkers to use. To prevent those workers from causing problems because of having access to the Action and View menus, you could remove them. Additionally, you might choose to remove a console tree to further limit the view. You can then save the console in a user mode that suits your needs.

Creating a Taskpad View

Taskpad views appear in the details pane of a console and display shortcuts to different commands that are chosen when the taskpad view is created. These shortcuts are referred to as *tasks* and are shown as large icons in the details pane. Creating taskpad views makes the console more efficient for users by displaying the tools they'll need as large and familiar icons.

To create a taskpad view and explore what these views have to offer, perform or read through the following steps:

1. Open the Management console created earlier, and make sure that the Console Root entry is highlighted.

2. Choose Action | New Taskpad View. When the New Taskpad View Wizard appears, choose Next.

3. On the TaskPad Display page, you can choose a style for the details pane of the console: Vertical List (default), Horizontal List, No List, or Hide Standard Tab. You can also

select a style for the task description (Text or InfoTip). The List Size options are Small, Medium, and Large. Select the following options, and choose Next:

- ◆ Vertical List

- ◆ Text

- ◆ Medium

4. On the Taskpad Target page, accept the defaults for applying this taskpad view to more than one tree item. Choose Next.

5. On the Name And Description page, type a name and description for this taskpad. I'll use "TaskpadTest" for both. Choose Next.

6. The wizard has obtained the necessary information. Make sure there is a checkmark in the Start New Task Wizard checkbox, and choose Finish. As the New Task Wizard begins, choose Next to continue.

7. On the Command Type page, read through the command options, and choose Menu Command. Choose Next.

8. On the Shortcut Menu Command page, shown in Figure 1.24, accept the default Command Source option: List In Details Pane. From the snap-in choices, choose System Information, and from Available Commands, choose Properties. Choose Next.

9. On the Name And Description page, accept the defaults and choose Next.

10. On the Task Icon page, select an icon that somewhat conveys the properties of a system. I will choose the green wire notebook. Choose Next.

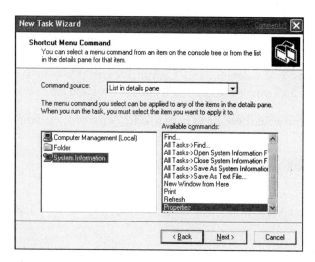

Figure 1.24
The Shortcut Menu Command page of the New Task Wizard.

11. On the Completing The New Task Wizard page, select Run This Wizard Again and two other tasks. When finished, uncheck the box and choose Finish.

Exploring Taskpad View

After you have created a few taskpad views, return to the Management console and perform the following steps:

1. In the Management console, highlight Console Root.

2. Select the TaskpadTest tab at the bottom of the screen.

3. Click System Information. Figure 1.25 shows this screen. Click the green notebook to the left to open the property sheet for this item.

4. Work through the other tasks you added in the same manner. Close the Management console when finished, saving your changes when prompted.

Wrapping Up

This chapter introduced the basic skills necessary to work with Microsoft Windows XP Professional and to use this book successfully. Windows XP users, even those fairly new to

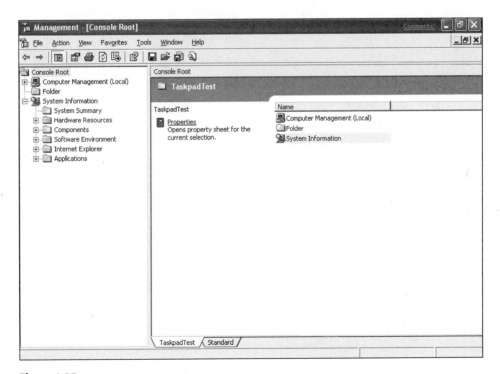

Figure 1.25
The TaskpadTest taskpad view.

computing in general, should be familiar with how to use the Start menu and the taskbar, what is available on the desktop, what My Computer and the Control Panel have to offer, and how to use Windows Explorer to find files, folders, and programs.

Also introduced was information about files and folders, including how to create, save, and delete them, as well as how to use the Search utility to find them. Before continuing with this book, you should know how to switch between applications, how to minimize, maximize, and restore application windows, and how to use Cut, Copy, and Paste when working with files.

This chapter also explained how to burn CDs. Archiving data on CDs is a good way to keep your hard drive clean and up-to-date.

Finally, the Microsoft Management Console (MMC) was introduced. MMC consoles allow you perform many of the tasks necessary to use Windows XP successfully, and customizing these consoles can make your work even more efficient.

Chapter 2
Personalizing Your Computer

There are so many ways to personalize your computer with Windows XP that it's usually the first thing a user does when getting a new computer. Personalizing your computer is important; not only does it make you feel like the computer is yours, but also it helps you work more efficiently. Often, the first step people take is to change the background and select a screensaver. Some people will take it a step further, selecting a theme or creating their own, changing the fonts and colors used in windows, installing special keyboards or wireless mice, or changing the screen resolution.

Even more options are available for personalizing Windows XP. In this chapter, you'll learn how to make the changes just mentioned, and many more. You'll learn how to customize sounds for specific events, use volume controls, use the sound recorder and multimedia utilities, and configure multiple monitors. You'll also learn how to use speech and handwriting recognition utilities, Magnifier, Narrator, and the On-Screen Keyboard utilities. Several additional components can be configured for users with special needs, and these accessibility options will also be discussed.

At the end of this chapter, what you see on your computer screen might look quite a bit different from the screenshots you'll see in the book. However, changes made here will not impair your ability to follow along and understand the latter chapters. Have fun.

The Desktop

You know what the default desktop looks like, and chances are you've either already changed some things on it or are itching to. In this section, I'll detail how to make all the changes you'd ever want to the desktop. Let's start with a new background and screensaver.

Changing the Background and Screensaver

Windows XP provides several backgrounds and screensavers to choose from, and you can download plenty more from the Internet.

To change backgrounds and screensavers:

1. Right-click an empty place on the desktop, and choose Properties.

2. *To change the background*—Select the Desktop tab, and select a new background from the list of available backgrounds.

   From the Position drop-down list, select Stretch, Center, or Tile. (You can see the effects of these changes in the window.) Choose Apply.

3. *To change the screensaver*—Select the Screen Saver tab. Select a screensaver from the Screen Saver list.

4. Select the Settings button located in the middle of the Screen Saver window.

5. Make any necessary changes in the Settings box that appears for the selected Screen Saver. If no settings exist, an information box will appear.

6. Choose OK twice.

Icons

The longer you use your computer, the more cluttered with icons your desktop is likely to get. You might have a few new icons already, especially if you've installed any programs or configured an Internet connection. To keep your desktop clean and up-to-date, you'll need to be able to delete unnecessary icons as they appear. You may also need to add icons.

Arranging Icons

Arranging icons is easy; simply right-click the desktop and choose Arrange Icons By from the context menu. Icons can be arranged in these ways:

♦ *Name*—Arranges the icons alphabetically.

♦ *Size*—Arranges the icons from the smallest size (in MB) to the largest of each application or folder.

♦ *Type*—Groups the icons according to their type.

♦ *Modified*—Groups the icons according to when they were last modified. They are listed from the earliest date to the latest date modified.

♦ *Auto Arrange*—Arranges the icons as Windows XP sees fit. When Auto Arrange is chosen, icons that are moved are still arranged in the grid and remain neatly organized.

Deleting Icons

To delete an icon from the desktop, just right-click the icon and choose Delete. (Of course, if you are part of a network, or you share your computer, these changes might not be permitted.)

Adding Icons

You can add to the desktop a number of new items by right-clicking in a blank area of the desktop and choosing New from the context menu. Once the icon is created, you can open it and add information to it. For instance, you could create several folders—named Inbox, In Progress, and Outbox—and use them to organize your desktop instead of just placing everything in the My Documents folder.

Here are some of the items that you can add to the desktop:

♦ Folder

♦ Shortcut

♦ Briefcase

♦ Bitmap image

♦ Text document

♦ Wave sound file

Adding Shortcuts to the Desktop from the Start Menu

You can also add a shortcut to the desktop by left-clicking on the program name and dragging it from the Start menu to an empty place on the desktop. This does not move the program but only creates a shortcut. Right-clicking and dragging gives the option to either move the application or folder or copy it to the desktop.

Desktop Cleanup

Even the most organized person can eventually have a cluttered desktop. This usually happens because icons are added as they are used, but they are not generally deleted when the utility, file, or folder is no longer used much. Many people are afraid to delete things from their desktops for fear that they'll never be able to find them again or that those items will be forgotten and never used. What this all leads to is a messy desktop with lots of icons that are rarely, if ever, used.

To solve this problem, the Desktop Cleanup utility is available. Desktop Cleanup moves unused shortcuts to a desktop folder called Unused Desktop Shortcuts. This utility does not move, change, or delete any files or programs; it moves only the shortcuts.

To use Desktop Cleanup:

1. Right-click an empty area of the desktop, and choose Properties.

2. Select the Desktop tab.

3. Choose the Customize Desktop button.

4. Choose the Clean Desktop Now button. (To run this utility automatically every 60 days, make sure that the Run Desktop Cleanup Wizard Every 60 Days checkbox is checked.) Choose Next when the Desktop Cleanup Wizard appears.

5. The first page is Shortcuts. To leave a shortcut on your desktop, clear the shortcut's checkbox; to remove the shortcut from your desktop, check its checkbox. Choose Next, then Finish, and then OK twice.

6. On the desktop, notice the new folder called Unused Desktop Shortcuts. Double-click it to see its contents.

Themes and Appearance

Several themes are available for you to use to personalize your computer. You can find them by right-clicking the desktop and choosing Properties, as in previous examples. From the Themes tab, you can choose from Windows XP, My Current Theme, or Windows Classic, or you can choose More Themes to download the latest ones from Microsoft.

You can further alter the theme you've chosen by using the Appearance tab in the Display Properties dialog box. The following example will walk you through making these changes:

1. Right-click an empty area of the desktop, and choose Properties.

2. Select the Themes tab.

3. Under Theme, select Windows Classic.

4. Choose Apply.

5. Select the Appearance tab.

6. Under Windows And Buttons, select either Windows XP Style or Windows Classic.

7. Under Color Scheme, select a scheme that meets your needs.

8. Under Font Size, select Normal, Large, or Extra Large.

9. Choose the Effects button. Make whatever changes you want in the transition effect, smoothing edges of screen fonts, using large icons, showing shadows under menus, showing window contents while dragging, and more. Choose OK.

10. Choose the Advanced button. To change the color of any item, select that item from the Item list, and then alter the colors from the color palette offered by Color 1 and Color 2 for the item. When you're finished with all of the items you'd like to change, choose OK.

Personalized Menus

Personalized menus, sometimes called smart menus, can be very helpful to many different types of users. The purpose of these personalized menus is to offer only those menu choices that you use most often. For instance, when you're using the Start menu to access Programs, notice that not all of the programs that are available are shown. The information bubble states that these programs are not shown because they haven't been used recently. You can turn this feature off by using the taskbar and Start menu settings.

If you leave the personalized menus enabled, you can access the remaining menu choices in one of two ways. If nothing is chosen from the menu after a few seconds, the other menu options are shown automatically. You can also select the arrow to show the other programs immediately.

Note

From here on, you'll notice that I've changed the look of my desktop, as you probably have also. I have chosen Windows Classic because I suspect a lot of readers will choose this look out of familiarity. If it makes following along easier, you can change the look of your desktop temporarily to look like the one shown here.

Turning Off Personalized Menus

To turn off personalized menus:

1. Right-click the taskbar, and choose Properties.

2. Select the Start Menu tab.

3. Select the Classic Start Menu option, and choose Customize.

4. Scroll down to the last option, Use Personalized Menus, and uncheck its checkbox. Choose OK twice.

Advanced Start Menu Options

Several other advanced Start menu options are available from Taskbar And Start Menu Properties when you're using Windows Classic, and several advanced options are available when you're using the Windows XP theme. In this section, I'll go over both, although I'll be sticking with the Windows Classic theme from here on out.

Options for Windows Classic Theme

To access the advanced options for the Windows Classic theme:

1. Right-click the taskbar, and choose Properties.

2. Select the Start Menu tab.

3. Select the Classic Start Menu option, and choose Customize.

4. Once you've made the choices that suit your needs, choose OK twice.

Using these options does not remove programs or folders from the computer; they only change the Start menu. The advanced options are shown in Figure 2.1 and are:

♦ *Display Administrative Tools*—This is great for administrators to have but is possibly not so useful for the general user.

♦ *Display Favorites*—This is useful if you access your objects or places through Favorites.

♦ *Display Logoff*—The Logoff command is useful if several users use the same computer and log on and off frequently.

Figure 2.1
Advanced Options.

♦ *Display Run*—The **Run** command, which opens a dialog box for entering commands, might not be necessary for general users.

♦ *Enable Dragging And Dropping*—Checked by default, this option allows you to drag and drop items from the Start menu to the desktop.

♦ *Expand Control Panel*—This option lists all items available when you're using the Control Panel from the Start menu. This is useful for those who work in the Control Panel frequently.

♦ *Expand My Documents*—This option adds to the Start menu the files shown in the My Documents folder. This is useful for those users who work mostly with documents in this folder.

♦ *Expand My Pictures*—This option adds to the Start menu the pictures shown in the My Pictures folder. This is useful for those users who work mostly with pictures in this folder.

♦ *Expand Network Connections*—This option shows the network connections on the Start menu.

♦ *Expand Printers*—This option shows the available printers on the Start menu.

♦ *Scroll Programs*—If more menu items are available than the screen space can accommodate, the list can be continued in a second horizontal page or be configured as one long scrolling menu. If you enable this, you'll need to click an arrow at the bottom of the menu to access the programs or files not shown.

♦ *Show Small Icons In Start Menu*—This option is used to reduce the size of the icons on the Start menu.

♦ *Use Personalized Menus*—This option sets menus so that the only choices offered from menus are the ones that you use most often. Waiting a few seconds will bring up the other choices, or you can click an arrow to show them.

Options for Windows XP Theme

To access the advanced options for the Windows XP theme:

1. Right-click the taskbar, and choose Properties.

2. Select the Start Menu tab.

3. Select the Start Menu option, and choose Customize.

4. There are two tabs: General and Advanced. The choices for these are listed next. After making the appropriate choices, choose OK twice.

The General options are:

♦ *Large Icons Or Small Icons*—Use this option to change the size of program icons on the Start menu.

♦ *Number Of Programs On Start Menu*—By default, five shortcuts are listed on the Start menu, and they are chosen by the system based on what is used most recently and most often. You can change this number from 0 to 9 and/or clear the list. Clearing the list does not remove any programs; it removes only the shortcuts from the Start menu.

♦ *Show On Start Menu*—There are two choices here: Internet and Email. You should consider removing these from any computer that doesn't use the Internet or email.

The Advanced options are:

♦ *Open Submenus When I Pause On Them With My Mouse*—Opens submenus when you hover over them with the mouse.

♦ *Highlight Newly Installed Programs*—Shows newly installed programs in boldface type on the Start menu.

♦ *Show These Items On The Start Menu:*

  ♦ *Control Panel*—Can be shown as a link or a menu.

  ♦ *Favorites Menu*

  ♦ *Help And Support*

  ♦ *My Computer*—Can be shown as a link or a menu.

  ♦ *My Documents*—Can be shown as a link or a menu.

  ♦ *My Music*—Can be shown as a link or a menu.

  ♦ *My Network Places*

  ♦ *My Pictures*—Can be shown as a link or a menu.

  ♦ *Network Connections*

  ♦ *Printers*

  ♦ *Run Command*

♦ *Recent Documents*—Can be used to provide quick access to the documents you have used most recently. You can show the most recently used documents or clear the current document list. Clearing the list does not delete the documents from the hard drive.

Figure 2.2 shows a modified Start menu with Control Panel highlighted. In this example, Control Panel was switched to a menu, My Computer was switched to a menu, My Documents

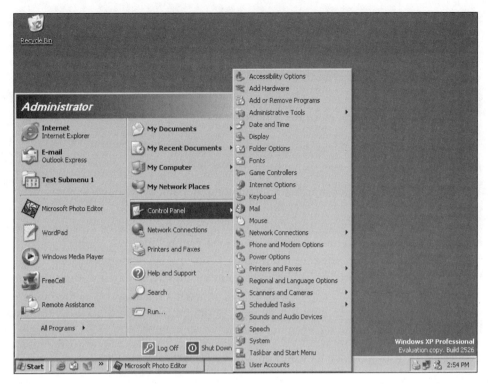

Figure 2.2
A modified Start menu in the Windows XP theme.

was switched to a menu, My Music and My Pictures were removed, and My Network Places was added, as were Network Connections, Printers, and Run.

Fonts and Colors

You know from the Themes and Appearance section that you can change not only the colors of the windows but also the font size used in them. You have other font and color options as well. For instance, if you are using a laptop computer or a desktop computer with a flat-screen monitor, you can change the appearance of the screen fonts from Standard to ClearType, resulting in clearer fonts for those particular types of screens. (If you choose this selection for a regular desktop computer with a standard screen, however, the fonts will look slightly blurry.) Other changes can be made as well, and those will be detailed in this section.

Using ClearType

To change from Standard to ClearType:

1. Right-click the desktop, and choose Properties.

2. Select the Appearance tab.

3. Choose Effects.

4. In the Effects dialog box, select Use The Following Method To Smooth Edges Of Screen Fonts.

5. Select ClearType in the list. Choose OK.

Note

For ClearType to work correctly, you'll need a monitor and a video card that support at least 256 colors.

Color Quality

You'll get the best video performance for your computer and the applications you run if you choose the highest color quality performance that your computer supports. Performance is measured using screen resolution and color quality. Screen resolution is related to the number of pixels shown on the monitor display. As the number of pixels shown increases, the size of the information on the screen decreases. Color display settings are chosen based on how many colors are to be used when information is displayed on the monitor. Although choosing the highest possible color display setting offered would give you the best display possible for your machine, doing so can cause a drain on your system. If performance is hindered using the highest setting, choose a lower color quality choice.

To view and possibly change the color quality that is set for your computer and monitor:

1. Right-click the desktop, and choose Properties.

2. Select the Settings tab.

3. Under Color Quality, select the highest quality that suits your particular situation and hardware capabilities. The highest value at the writing of the book is Highest (32-bit) or True Color.

Setting Font Size

Although you can change the font size for icon names and other screen elements by using the Appearance tab to create or modify a theme, you can also change the font size through the Settings tab of Display Properties. Changing the font size through the Settings tab applies the changes to all user-interface elements, not just to windows and icon names.

Figure 2.3 shows a screen as a result of changing the font size to large from the Settings tab (explained shortly). Figure 2.4 shows the screen as a result of changing the font size to large by using the Appearance tab to modify a theme using large fonts (as described in previous sections).

There are several differences in the two screens shown in these figures. Notice the difference in the size of the Display Properties dialog box itself. Also notice the size of the text labels in both shots. Those are not the only differences. In fact, when you change the font size by using the Settings tab, everything is larger, including the size of warning boxes, dialog boxes, and buttons and tabs.

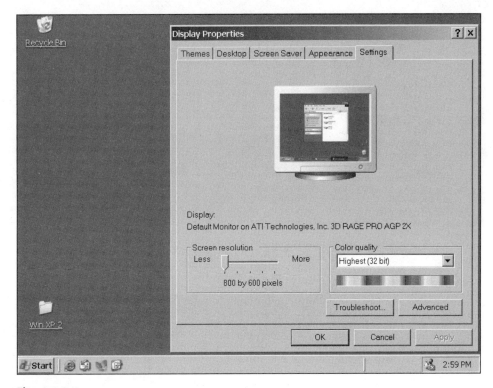

Figure 2.3
Large fonts set from the Settings tab.

To use the Settings tab to change fonts to large:

1. Right-click the desktop, and choose Properties.

2. Select the Settings tab.

3. Choose the Advanced button.

4. In the Font Size drop-down list, select Large. You can also select Other and create a size that is 75, 100, 125, 150, or 200 percent of the normal size.

5. Choose OK. You might be asked to install new fonts, use existing installed fonts, or even restart your computer. It is usually recommended that you accept the defaults and restart the computer if needed.

The Fonts Folder

The Control Panel includes a Fonts folder. This folder (introduced in Chapter 1) can be used to delete, add, or otherwise manage the fonts on your computer. You can hide the different variations of fonts, such as bold and italic, or preview fonts you might want to use.

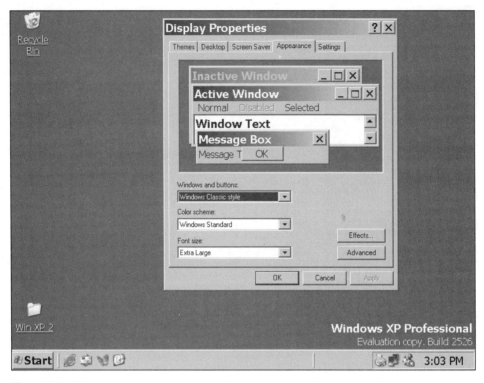

Figure 2.4
Large fonts set from the Appearance tab.

Changing Fonts and Colors In Internet Explorer

Internet Explorer comes with Microsoft Windows XP Professional and is used to access the Internet, also called "the Web." Using Internet Explorer Tools and Internet Options, you can change several things, including font size and hyperlink color. If you haven't configured an Internet connection yet, you can still configure these settings by opening Internet Explorer and choosing Work Offline.

Note

A bit about font size—many Web sites ignore personal font-size settings and use their own preferences. There is a way to override this behavior, however, by selecting Ignore Font Sizes Specified On Web Pages from the Tools|Internet Options|General tab and then clicking the Accessibility button.

To change the fonts and colors in Internet Explorer:

1. Open Internet Explorer by using the Internet Explorer icon on the desktop, by choosing Start | Programs | Internet Explorer, or by choosing Start | Internet Explorer (depending on what theme you're using).

2. Choose Tools | Internet Options.

3. Choose the Colors button.

4. Uncheck the Use Windows Colors checkbox.

5. To change any color, click on that color and pick a new color from the palette offered. When you're finished, choose OK.

6. Choose the Fonts button.

7. Select a Web Page Font and a Plain Text Font. Choose OK.

8. Choose OK.

To change the size of the text shown in Internet Explorer:

1. Open Internet Explorer.

2. Choose View | Text Size.

3. Select the font size you prefer.

Screen Resolution

You can also change the screen resolution. Screen resolution has to do with the number of pixels that are used when displaying the desktop. Increasing the screen resolution makes the desktop feel larger because the items on it are smaller. There are several resolution settings; the smallest and largest both depend on the type of video card that is installed in your computer and on the type of monitor you have. Generally, you'll have choices (in pixels) such as 640×480, 800×600, 1028×768, 1152×864, and 1280×1024. The shots you'll see in this book come from a screen using a resolution of 800×600 pixels.

To change the screen resolution:

1. Right-click the desktop, and choose Properties.

2. Select the Settings tab.

3. In the Display section, move the slider to the resolution you want, and choose OK.

4. Once the screen resolution changes, you'll have 15 seconds to accept the change. Click Yes to accept or No to reject. If you do not choose anything, the screen will revert to its previous setting.

Keyboards and Mice

You can change the keyboard and mouse settings through the Control Panel. Depending on the type of keyboard and mouse you have, the options will vary. For instance, on my workstation, I have a standard 101/102-key keyboard, and the Keyboard Properties dialog box has only two tabs. However, on my desktop PC, I have a wireless keyboard, so the Keyboard

Properties dialog box has three tabs. The same is true of different types of mice. In this section, I'll describe what the options are for standard keyboards and mice.

Keyboards

Only a few things can be adjusted for a keyboard because there is really only one thing that the keyboard is used for: inputting data. Basically, you can change the repeat delay (how long the computer waits before repeating a key that you're holding down) and the repeat rate (how fast the pressed key repeats). You can also adjust the blink rate of the cursor. This is all accessed from the Keyboard icon in the Control Panel.

Another option that can be configured is the input language of the keyboard. You can switch to a different keyboard or use the one that is installed to type data in other languages. Although the keys might not match what is actually typed on the screen, this option can be used with Windows XP.

To change the input language of the keyboard:

1. From the Control Panel, open Regional And Language Options.

2. On the Languages tab, choose Details.

3. Under Installed Services, choose Add.

4. Select a language to add, make sure the correct Keyboard Layout/IME is selected, and choose OK.

5. Choose the Language Bar button, and make any changes you want in the Language Bar Preferences.

6. Choose the Key Settings button, and note how to switch between languages.

7. Choose OK twice.

Mice

You can change several mouse settings, and you can access these options by clicking the Mouse icon in the Control Panel. However, keep in mind that your mouse settings might be drastically different from the ones listed here. You'll have all of the following options, but you could have more depending on the mouse you have installed. The standard options are:

♦ Switching the functions of the left and right buttons on the mouse

♦ Setting the double-clicking speed

♦ Turning on ClickLock, which allows you to highlight or drag without holding down the mouse button

♦ Changing the mouse pointer's theme, which changes how the mouse pointer is displayed while it's selecting items, working in the background, busy, and so on

♦ Selecting icons for the mouse pointer from a list of available cursors

♦ Adjusting how fast the mouse pointer moves

♦ Having the mouse pointer automatically "snap to" the default choice in dialog boxes

♦ Displaying pointer trails

♦ Hiding the mouse pointer while you're typing

♦ Showing the location of the pointer when the Ctrl key is pressed

♦ Viewing the name and type of mouse installed on the system

♦ Troubleshooting the mouse or installing a new driver

You can also change the number of mouse clicks required to open a file, folder, or program from two clicks to only one by changing the folder options through the Control Panel. (See Chapter 1.)

Changing How the Control Panel Looks

As with many other utilities, programs, and windows, you can change the way the Control P is lined up, and more. Most of the changes available here are also available in other, similar types of windows such as those for Windows Explorer, My Computer, and the Search utility.

By default, the Control Panel window has two toolbars: the Standard Buttons toolbar and the address bar. You can also add a Links bar, which can be configured with favorite places such as Web sites or intranetwork places. You can also add the status bar to the bottom of the Control Panel window; the status bar gives information about the selected icon. For instance, when Power Options is highlighted, the status bar says "Configures energy-saving settings for your computer."

You can choose to show the Explorer bar. The Explorer bar is shown on the left side of the screen and is not enabled by default. Figure 2.5 shows the Control Panel configured with the Explorer bar. You can show various things on the Explorer bar, and I've chosen Folders. The other options include:

♦ Search

♦ Favorites

♦ History

♦ Media

♦ Contacts

♦ Tip Of The Day

♦ Discuss

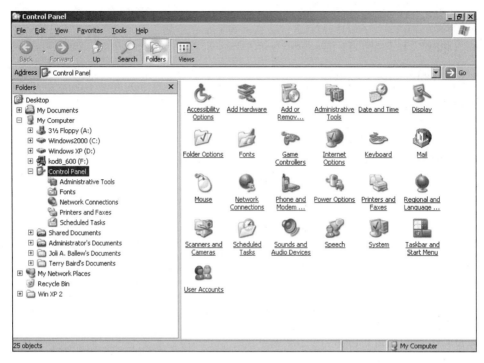

Figure 2.5
The Explorer bar in the Control Panel.

The icons shown in Figure 2.5 can also be changed. In fact, they don't have to be icons. They can be thumbnails (little pictures in boxes), tiles (larger icons in a horizontal list), a list of choices with very small icons, and a list of icons with very small icons with comments about each one.

Similar to arranging the icons on your desktop described earlier, you can also arrange the icons in the Control Panel. You can arrange the icons by name or comment, show them in groups, auto-arrange them, or align them to a grid. By default, they are arranged by name. When you arrange icons in groups, they are placed in an alphabetical list, displayed horizontally, with alphabetical separators between each of the groups of icons, and when you auto-arrange the icons, they are placed back in their default locations. Aligning the icons to a grid simply keeps them all nicely arranged, and they cannot be moved out of the grid.

To change the appearance of the Control Panel:

1. Open the Control Panel.

2. From the View menu, choose any of the following:

   ♦ *Toolbars*—This menu displays a checkmark next to each toolbar that is displayed. To select an additional toolbar, place a checkmark next to it by clicking it.

   ♦ *Status Bar*—To show the status bar, select it. This will place a checkmark next to it.

♦ *Explorer Bar*—To add an Explorer bar to the left side of the Control Panel, as shown in Figure 2.5, select the item you want to configure it with (Search, Favorites, History, etc.).

♦ *Arrange Icons By*—Choose Name or Comment, and either Show In Groups or Auto Arrange. You can also choose Align To Grid to keep the icons from being moved.

♦ *Thumbnails, Tiles, Icons, List, or Details*—Select the type of icon to be used for Control Panel objects.

3. The View menu will retract automatically as you choose options.

Customizing the Toolbar

You can choose which icons are shown on the toolbar in the Control Panel; choose View | Toolbars | Customize. The right side of the Customize Toolbar dialog box shows what the current toolbar buttons. The left side of this dialog box shows what can be added. See Figure 2.6.

To add an item, select it from the left side and choose Add. To delete an item, select it from the right side and choose Remove. In the Control Panel, many of these toolbar buttons aren't necessary, such as Cut, Copy, and Paste, which explains why they're not up there by default. However, you can use this knowledge to customize toolbars in other windows or programs and thus work more efficiently. By using the Move Up and Move Down buttons, you can organize the icons in the order that you prefer.

Notice in Figure 2.6 that you also have some text options. These options change the way the icons look on the toolbar. By default, the text is to the left of the icon, but you can place the text underneath the icon or remove the text entirely. You can also change the icons from large to small.

Sounds and Audio

Windows XP Professional includes some interesting and useful audio, and multimedia utilities that can be used for doing a lot more than just playing CDs while at the office. You can

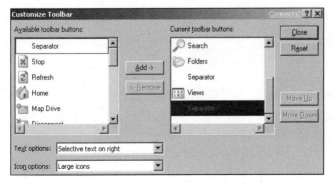

Figure 2.6
Customizing the toolbar.

also create a sound scheme for your computer, configure sound effects for specific events, create and mix your own sound recordings, play music stored on your hard drive, and more. Windows also includes some advanced utilities such as the Sound Recorder and Windows Media Player. In this section, I'll discuss some of these utilities and how they are used with the Media Player, and I'll even include some lessons on adding sound to documents and adding an echo to a sound file.

Keep in mind though, that making full use of these multimedia utilities requires a sound card, a microphone (for some features), speakers, and occasionally, an Internet connection. Additionally, if your computer has a revved-up sound card and some additional audio software, there will be some differences in the basic screens you'll see shown here. If there's no sound card installed on your computer, you won't be able to access these utilities at all.

Using Volume Controls

The first step in working with sounds on your Windows XP machine is to understand how to use the volume controls. To access the volume control, choose Start | (More)Programs | Accessories | Entertainment | Volume Control. The Volume Control window is shown in Figure 2.7.

To change the volume controls, move the sliders in each category. To change various display options in the Volume Control window, choose Options | Properties. You can use this Properties sheet to adjust the volume for Playback, Recording, or Other (Recording Control), and you can add or remove columns such as Volume Control, Line In, Microphone, MIDI, CD Audio, PC Speaker, Aux, and Wave. When adding these items or configuring existing ones, make sure that the Mute buttons aren't checked. The Aux Mute button is checked in Figure 2.7.

Displaying the Volume Control on the Taskbar
If you change the volume often, you might want to place the volume icon in the notification area of the taskbar so that the volume controls can be accessed more easily.

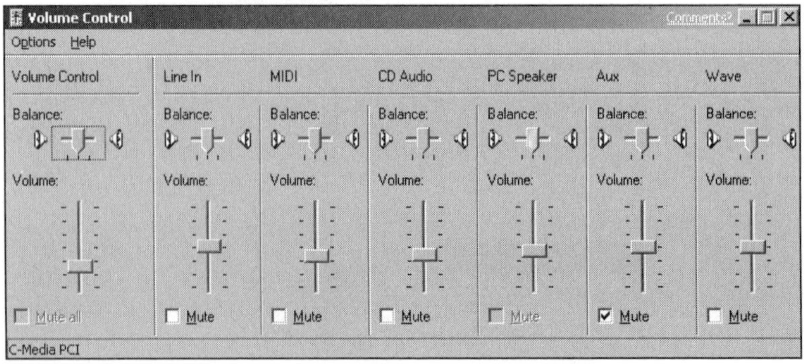

Figure 2.7
Basic volume controls.

To place the volume icon on the taskbar:

1. Open the Control Panel.

2. Choose Sounds And Audio Devices.

3. Select the Volume tab.

4. Check the checkbox Place Volume Icon In The Taskbar Notification Area.

5. Choose OK.

Customizing Sounds

There are several ways to personalize your computer with sounds and sound effects. In this section, I'll describe how to give system events specific sounds, how to create or use a sound scheme, and how to use sound effects.

Giving Events Their Own Sounds and Creating a Sound Scheme

Certain system and program events have their own unique sounds. For instance, when new mail arrives in your inbox, the computer issues a distinctive two-tone sound to alert you, and this sound is named, appropriately, Notify. When Windows XP starts, you hear the familiar Windows Logon Sound. You can probably recognize many more of these sounds (if you usually work with your computer's speakers turned on), but what you might not know is that you can change or remove these sounds to further personalize your computer.

To hear the sounds associated with specific events, to change or remove sounds related to events, or to add sounds to events:

1. Open the Control Panel.

2. Choose Sounds And Audio Devices.

3. Select the Sounds tab.

4. In the Sound Scheme drop-down list, select a sound scheme such as Windows Default or Utopia. Make sure that No Sounds is *not* chosen.

5. *To hear a default sound associated with an event*—Highlight Asterisk in the Program Events list box, and then press the forward arrow button at the bottom of the page to hear the sound associated with it. (Notice that no sound is associated with the next program event, Close Program.)

6. *To add a sound to an event that doesn't currently have one*—Highlight that event (I'll choose Incoming Call), click the down arrow for the Sounds drop-down list, and select a sound. (I'll choose Ringin.)

7. *To remove a sound associated with an event*—Highlight that event, click the down arrow for the Sounds drop-down list, and select None. Choose Yes when prompted to remove the sound.

8. *To see additional sounds not listed*—Highlight an event and choose Browse.

9. When you're finished configuring sounds, choose Save As and type a name for your new sound scheme. It cannot be saved over the Windows Default or Utopia sound scheme. Choose OK.

Using Sound Effects

If you have sound effects installed on your computer, through advanced sound card software, downloads, or some other method, you can add those sound effects through the Sounds And Audio Devices icon in the Control Panel.

To see if you have any installed sound effects and to configure those effects:

1. Open the Control Panel.

2. Choose Sounds And Audio Devices.

3. Select the Volume tab.

4. In the Speaker Settings area, choose the Advanced button.

5. In the Advanced Audio Properties dialog box, select the Effects tab.

6. Choose Add Effect.

7. Select the effect you want, and then choose OK.

8. To adjust the order of the effects, click the Move Up and Move Down buttons.

Note

If there are no effects listed, there are none installed on your computer. You can check Microsoft's Web site for downloads containing updates for these effects.

Using the Sound Recorder

Microsoft Windows XP Professional ships with a sound recorder that does a lot more than just record sounds. You can use the Sound Recorder to record, mix, play, and edit them as well. The Sound Recorder can also be used to link sounds to a document or insert them into a document. In this section, you'll learn how to use the sound recorder and perform some basic tasks associated with it. Remember, to use this utility you must have a sound card, a microphone, and speakers already installed and working properly.

Opening the Sound Recorder

To open the Sound Recorder, choose Start | Programs | Accessories | Entertainment | Sound Recorder. Although it isn't much to look at, it's a very effective utility. Figure 2.8 shows the Sound Recorder.

Adjusting the Volume

To prepare the Sound Recorder for use, you must first choose File | New and then verify that the recording and playback devices are configured properly and that their volume levels are set properly.

To prepare the recorder for its first use:

1. Open the Sound Recorder (choose Start | Programs | Accessories | Entertainment | Sound Recorder).

2. Choose File | New.

3. Choose Edit | Audio Properties.

4. Select the Audio Devices tab.

5. In the Sound Playback area, choose the Volume button for the default playback device.

6. Slide the volume bars to an appropriate level to verify that the settings for volume control, speaker control, and other controls are not muted and are loud enough.

7. Choose Options | Exit to return to the Audio Devices tab of the Audio Properties dialog box.

8. In the Sound Recording area, choose the Volume button for the default recording device.

9. Slide the volume bars to an appropriate level to verify that the settings for the Line In, Microphone, and other input devices are not muted and are loud enough.

10. Choose Options | Exit to return to the Audio Properties dialog box.

11. Perform the same tests for any additional default devices that are shown on the Audio Devices tab.

12. Choose OK.

Figure 2.8
The Sound Recorder.

Performing a Voice Test

Before doing any recording, do a voice test to make sure that all of the components needed to record on your system are working properly. You do the test through the Control Panel, and you need to do this only once to verify that everything is working.

To perform a voice test:

1. Open the Control Panel.

2. Open Sounds And Audio Devices.

3. Select the Voice tab.

4. If the Voice Playback or the Voice Recording areas are grayed out, then either the microphone or the speakers aren't installed or configured properly. If this is the case, you'll need to install those before continuing. If these areas are not grayed out, click choose the Voice Test button.

5. Choose Next to start the Sound Hardware Test Wizard.

6. After waiting for the wizard to test for available hardware, follow the on-screen instructions for testing the microphone, and choose Next.

7. For the speaker test, follow the on-screen instructions, and choose Next when finished.

8. After the tests are successful, choose Finish.

Recording

To learn how to use the basic controls and the Sound Recorder, you can make a simple recording of your voice and then manipulate that recording by using the Sound Recorder.

To record your voice:

1. Open the Sound Recorder.

2. Make sure the microphone is within a foot of you and that it is turned on.

3. Choose File | New.

4. Click the Record button (the red circle), and begin speaking into the microphone.

5. When you're finished, click the Stop button (the black rectangle).

6. Choose File | Save As.

7. Name the file, and choose Save. Notice that the Save As Type box saves this file as a .wav file by default and in PCM format. I'll discuss what this means and how to change it in another section of this chapter.

Tip

Note which folder the file was saved in. It is most likely the My Documents folder unless you have changed the default settings.

Don't close the Sound Recorder yet; you'll use it in the next section to play your recording.

Playing

There are many ways to play what you've recorded; you can use the Sound Recorder or another utility such as Windows Media Player. In this section, I'll describe both ways to play the file, and Windows Media Player will be further detailed in a later section.

To play the file you just recorded:

1. If you just completed the previous exercise, the Sound Recorder should still be open, and the file you recorded should still be loaded. (Otherwise, choose Start | Programs | Accessories | Entertainment | Sound Recorder. Then choose File | Open and select the file you recorded.)

2. Click the Play button (the right arrow) in the Sound Recorder window.

3. When the recording is done playing, close the Sound Recorder.

You can also play your recording in Windows Media Player, which also ships with Windows XP Professional.

To use Windows Media Player to play your recording:

1. Open the My Documents folder either from your desktop or from the Start menu. The location of this folder will vary depending on the theme you are using.

    (The file you just created should be in the My Documents folder. If you do not see the file there, choose Start | Documents and then the file name.)

2. Double-click the file. Windows Media Player should open and play the file. If it does not, then right-click the file you recorded, and choose Open With. Choose Windows Media Player. Check the checkbox Always Use This Program To Open These Files. Choose OK.

Converting to Another Format

When recording a file by using the Sound Recorder or any other recording utility, you can save that file in many formats. These formats are comparable to formats such as eight-tracks, LPs, and CDs. You can't play a CD in an eight-track machine, just as you can't play an MP3-formatted song in a program that only opens WAV files.

The format you save your file in determines not only which programs can be used to open it but also how much space you'll need to save it. A file saved as "telephone quality" takes up a lot less space on your hard drive than does a file saved as "CD quality." It's important to make sure you save the file correctly, so that you don't use unnecessary space to store it.

The Sound Recorder can be used to save files in many formats. Generally, the default format will work for your computer, but if the file is emailed or otherwise given to another user at another computer, the file might need to be converted to a different type. This can be done by changing the properties of the file itself.

To see which file formats are available and how much space each format takes up on your computer:

1. Open the Sound Recorder.

2. Choose File | Open, and select the file you recorded.

3. Choose File | Properties.

4. From the Format Conversion area, in the Choose From drop-down list, select All Formats. (Note that you can select Playback Formats or Recording Formats as well. The All Formats option lists both kinds.)

5. Choose Convert Now.

6. In the Sound Selection dialog box, in the Name drop-down list, choose Telephone Quality. Note the default settings for the Attributes box. Repeat this step for Radio Quality and CD Quality. Select an option, and choose OK.

Tip
The file I recorded uses 2,438,484 bytes of hard drive space when saved as CD quality. The same file saved as telephone quality uses only 152,400 bytes. That is a very large difference. Remember that the better the quality, the more disk space it will take to save it.

7. Choose OK to return to the Sound Recorder.

If you have saved the file in a different format and want to return to the previous one, choose File | Revert. You can use this command to revert to the last time the file was saved. This will negate any changes made since that time.

Changing the Sound Quality

Without an expensive sound card and speakers, there isn't a whole lot you can do to improve the quality of the sound except through the Sounds And Audio Devices Properties dialog box in Windows XP. From here, you can make a few changes in the quality of the audio and of voice recordings and playback. However, most of these changes require increased CPU usage that can affect computer response times for general operations. The computer will seem sluggish and unresponsive, so increase the sound quality only if recording is a top priority.

To enhance the default sound quality:

1. Open the Control Panel.

2. Open Sounds And Audio Devices.

3. On the Audio tab, under Sound Playback, choose the Advanced button.

4. In the Advanced Audio Properties dialog box, make sure that the correct speakers are selected in the Speaker Setup list on the Speakers tab.

5. Select the Performance tab.

6. In the Sample Rate Conversion Quality area, change the conversion quality from Good to either Improved or Best. Keep in mind that this will slow down response times for your computer.

7. Choose OK.

8. From the Audio tab, under Sound Recording, select Advanced and then the Performance tab In the Sample Rate Conversion Quality area, change the conversion quality from Good to either Improved or Best. Keep in mind that this will slow down response times for your computer.

9. Choose OK twice to apply the changes.

Mixing

You can mix one file with another if two or more recorded files are available. Record another voice file and save it as described previously. When both files are saved, do the following:

1. If the Sound Recorder isn't open, open it.

2. Choose File | Open, and select the first file you recorded.

3. Play the file for verification.

4. Choose Edit | Mix With File.

5. Select the second file you recorded in preparation for this exercise.

6. Click the Play button (the right arrow) to play both files at once.

Inserting a File into an Existing File

If you have two or more recorded files, you can insert one into the other at any point in the recording.

To insert a recorded file into a selected area of another file:

1. If the Sound Recorder isn't open, open it.

2. Choose File | Open, and select the first file you recorded.

3. Play the file for verification.

4. Stop the recording somewhere during the playing process by clicking the Stop button (the black rectangle).

5. Choose Edit | Insert File.

6. Select the recorded file to insert.

7. Play the selection from the beginning by sliding the bar all the way to the left and clicking the Play button (the right arrow).

Deleting Parts of a Recording

You can delete parts of any recorded file through the Edit menu as well. There are only two delete choices: Delete Before Current Position and Delete After Current Position.

To delete the beginning or end of a recorded file:

1. If the Sound Recorder isn't open, open it.

2. Choose File | Open, and select the first file you recorded.

3. Play the file for verification.

4. Stop the recording somewhere during the playing process by clicking the Stop button (the black rectangle).

5. Choose Edit | Delete Before Current Position or Edit | Delete After Current Position.

6. Play the selection from the beginning by sliding the bar all the way to the left and clicking the Play button (the right arrow).

Reversing the Recording

Not that you'd ever really need to do this other than just to have a little fun, but you can reverse a recording by using the Sound Recorder.

To see what your latest recording sounds like in reverse:

1. If the Sound Recorder isn't open, open it.

2. Choose File | Open, and select the first file you recorded.

3. Play the file for verification.

4. Choose Effects | Reverse.

5. Play the selection from the beginning by sliding the bar all the way to the left and clicking the Play button (the right arrow).

Adding an Echo to a Sound File

One last effect that can be added by using the Sound Recorder is the Echo effect.

To add the echo effect to your latest recording:

1. If the Sound Recorder isn't open, open it.

2. Choose File | Open, and select the first file you recorded.

3. Play the file for verification.

4. Choose Effects | Echo.

5. Play the selection from the beginning by sliding the bar all the way to the left and clicking the Play button (the right arrow).

Inserting a Sound File into a Word Document

It's possible to insert a sound file into a document. When the sound file is inserted, a sound icon is included in the document to represent the sound. This icon can be moved and resized as needed. When the reader of the document reads the file, he or she can also hear the sounds associated with it by clicking this icon.

To add a sound to a document:

1. If the Sound Recorder isn't open, open it.

2. Choose File | Open, and select a sound file.

3. Choose Edit | Copy.

4. Open a word processing program such as Microsoft Word.

5. Choose Edit | Paste.

Linking a Sound File to a Document

Finally, you can simply link a sound to a document. When the sound file is linked, an icon is included in the document to represent the link. This icon can be moved and resized as needed.

Linking the sound doesn't actually insert the sound file into the document; instead, it creates a path to the sound file. You can then edit the sound file where it is stored without having to reinsert it into the document to have the document reflect the change. By linking the sound file rather than embedding it, you keep the document file smaller.

To link a sound file to a document:

1. If the Sound Recorder isn't open, open it.

2. Choose File | Open, and select a sound file.

3. Choose Edit | Copy.

4. Open a word processing program such as Microsoft Word.

5. Choose Edit | Paste Special.

6. In the Paste Special dialog box, choose Paste Link.

7. Select Wave Sound Object.

8. Choose OK.

If you want to email the file to someone, put it on a floppy disk, or otherwise send it to someone else, make sure you don't insert the sound file as a link and that you do insert it by using Edit | Paste. The sound file must be available when the recipient of the file opens it. An exception to this rule occurs if the sound file is on a network server, and both you and the person receiving the file have access to the network server and the sound file on it.

Using Multimedia Utilities

Multimedia utilities consist of the CD players installed on your computer, any digital cameras or video cameras that you might have installed (and their software), plus the utilities that ship with Windows XP Professional. In this section I'll introduce the CD player and Windows Media Player. Windows Media Player can be used to manage and play your music and, if you have an Internet connection, to tune in to radio stations all around the world.

To use all of the capabilities of the media player, you'll have to have audio CDs, videos, sound clips, a microphone, a camera, a scanner, an Internet connection, and other similar items. If you don't have all of these items, don't worry. You can explore these utilities through their introductions and samples that are already stored on your hard drive. Windows XP comes with a sample playlist for Windows Media Player; you can use this playlist in these exercises if you don't have any music of your own.

Using the CD Player

One of the most basic pieces of multimedia hardware is the CD-ROM drive. Chances are good that you have a CD-ROM drive installed in your system. The newer models of CD-ROM drives play not only software CDs but also audio CDs.

To see what capabilities your computer has for playing audio CDs:

1. Place an audio CD in the CD-ROM drive.

2. Open My Computer.

3. Click on the CD-ROM drive's icon.

4. Select a track and click it. By default, Windows Media Player opens.

5. Click the Play button (the large right arrow in the bottom-left corner of the screen). See Figure 2.9.

Note

If this exercise didn't work, then your CD-ROM drive might not be capable of playing audio CDs. You should still be able to play music that is saved to your hard drive.

Using Windows Media Player

Now that you've seen Windows Media Player in action, let's take a better look at its capabilities. Windows Media Player is a terrific utility, and it's installed by default with Windows XP. Windows Media Player is also configured automatically as the default audio player, which is why it opens when you're choosing to play a CD.

Windows Media Player is a fully functional media utility that can do a lot more than just play your audio CDs. With Media Player, you can also listen to radio stations from all over the world, copy your CDs, download videos from the Internet, and create organized lists and groupings of your music and video files.

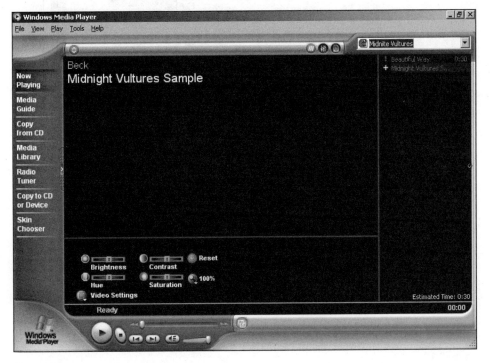

Figure 2.9
Windows Media Player.

General Controls

To work with the Media Player effectively, you'll need to understand how all of the controls work. You'll use these controls to perform such tasks as playing, stopping, and pausing music, seeking (fast-forwarding through CD music selections), muting or changing the volume, and choosing the previous or next tracks. You can also change from full mode to compact mode, and change the videos that play.

Figure 2.9 shows Windows Media Player. There are several buttons along the bottom of this screen. You can see what each of these buttons does by placing your mouse pointer over these buttons and hovering. (*Hovering* means that you do not select the choice, but just that you hold the mouse pointer over it.) After a second or two, a word will pop up to explain what each button does. Figure 2.10 shows these terms as well.

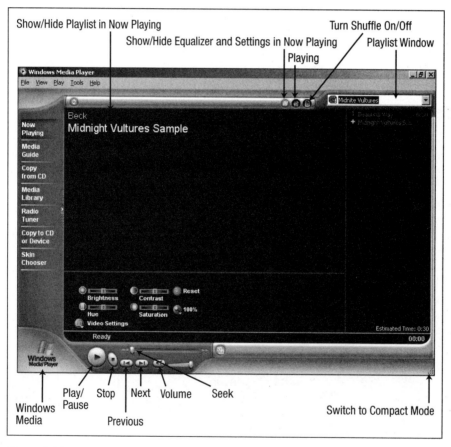

Figure 2.10
Windows Media Player buttons.

These buttons can be used to perform the following tasks.

- *Show/Hide Equalizer And Settings In Now Playing*—Displays the equalizer for bass and effects in the Now Playing window.

- *Show/Hide Playlist In Now Playing*—Removes the playlist from the window when music is playing.

- *Turn Shuffle On/Off*—Plays the audio tracks in random order (when set to On).

- *Playlist Window*—Shows what's playing or what is available to play.

- *Windows Media*—Connects the user to the WindowsMedia.com Web site. The first time this button is used, it will connect to an introductory Web page on WindowsMedia.com.

- *Play*—Plays the current selection.

- *Pause*—Pauses the selection that's playing.

- *Stop*—Stops playing the current selection.

- *Mute*—Continues to play the current selection but mutes the sound.

- *Volume*—Changes the volume.

- *Previous*—Plays the previous track or selection.

- *Rewind*—Rewinds from the present position in the selection.

- *Fast Forward*—Fast-forwards from the present position in the selection.

- *Next*—Plays the next track or selection.

- *Switch To Compact Mode*—Reduces the size of the Media Player screen.

- *Seek*—Moves through the CD selection when you use the sliding bar. This allows you to hear only a part of the song by fast-forwarding through it.

A few additional controls are available only when an audio clip is playing. Those controls have to do with selecting the *visualization* (video) that is shown while a piece of music is playing. These buttons, shown above the Play button, are named Select Visualization, Previous Visualization, and Next Visualization. Sometimes, depending on the visualization, you'll also see a button called View Full Screen. When this is selected, the visualization changes to full screen; you can turn this off by clicking the mouse button once.

Additional controls are accessible from the menu bar—in the File, View, Play, and Tools menus. Although many of the tools previously described as buttons are repeated in the menus, many tools are available only from the menus. For instance, from the File menu, you can import or export playlists, copy songs to a CD, and more. From the View menu, you can change how the player looks. (In the next section, I'll discuss how to customize your Media Player to suit your personal preferences.)

Playing a Song

Windows XP comes with some sample music that you can play when testing the Media Player.

To play a song in Windows Media Player:

1. Open Windows Media Player (choose Start | Programs | Windows Media Player).

2. Click the Now Playing button.

3. In the Playlist window, select All Audio.

4. Choose the Play button.

To play a song from a CD:

1. Open Windows Media Player.

2. Place a CD in the audio CD drive.

3. In the Playlist window, select the CD by its title.

4. Choose the Play button if the music doesn't start automatically.

To end the music, choose the Stop button.

Customizing the Player

There are several ways you can customize Windows Media Player. You can resize it, change the video settings, change the look of the player, and change the visualizations. Resizing the screen is the same as with any window; you can click the Restore button and drag from a corner to resize the entire window. However, the video screen can also be resized. You do this by moving the mouse pointer to the edge of the video screen until a two-headed arrow appears. Then just drag the line that separates the two panes to make the screen the length and width you'd like it to be.

To change the video settings for brightness, contrast, hue, and saturation, you can place these controls in the Media Player window. To do so, choose View | Now Playing Tools | Show Equalizer and Settings | Video Settings. (To remove them, choose View | Now Playing Tools | Show Equalizer And Settings.)

One thing that might surprise you is the Skin Chooser. The Skin Chooser button is available on the left side of the Media Player. A *skin* is a file that is used to change the appearance of Windows Media Player. A skin has a distinct appearance that usually incorporates basic Windows Media Player functions including play, previous, next, stop, and adjusting the volume. In many instances, you can also place certain audio files, view visualizations, or perform other activities based on the type of skin you apply to Windows Media Player. Skins can be chosen from Windows Media Player or downloaded from the Internet. Not all skins offer the same amount of functionality.

To see what skins are available:

1. Open Windows Media Player.

2. Click the Skin Chooser button on the left side of the window.

3. Notice that the default skin is the Windows Media Player Skin. Click other skins in the list to see what is available.

4. After selecting a skin, click Apply Skin.

5. Locate the Full Mode button on the new skin.

6. Select Windows Media Player Skin, and click Apply Skin again.

Finally, to change the visualizations while an audio clip is playing, you can use either of two utilities. Whichever one you choose, you'll need to have something playing in the Media Player.

To change the visualization:

1. Open Windows Media Player.

2. Choose the Now Playing button.

3. In the Playlist window, select All Audio.

4. Choose the Play button.

5. As the music plays, notice the video playing in the window. To change it, choose the Next Visualization button (above the Play button).

6. To change the type of visualization shown, choose the Select Visualization button (also located above the Play button). You can choose any of the visualizations.

Use the View menu to see a list of available visualizations. To date, approximately 50 visualizations are available within the Media Player. More can be downloaded from the Internet.

Downloading New Visualizations

Microsoft has provided even more personalization options on the Internet. These Internet options are included in Windows Media Player to make personalizing it to suit your tastes even easier. From one of Microsoft's Web sites, you can download new visualizations for your computer with just a few clicks of the mouse.

Note

To download an application such as a visualization from the Internet, you'll need an Internet connections as well as the appropriate permissions. If you are a home user, permissions are probably not an issue. However, if you are part of a network in an office or an organization, there might be restrictions in place to prevent you from doing this.

To see what other visualizations are available:

1. Open Windows Media Player.

2. Choose Tools | Download Visualizations.

3. After you have connected to the site (which is done automatically), select a visualization you like from the available options.

4. Choose Save This Program To Disk when prompted.

5. In the Save In box, browse to the My Documents folder.

6. Note the file name, and choose Save.

7. When the download is complete, choose Open. The visualization will be installed automatically. If it isn't installed automatically, simply click the file name to install the file.

8. Locate the new visualization in the View | Visualizations menu.

Copying Music from a CD

When you purchase a CD, you are also given a license to copy that CD and the tracks on it to your computer or to record it onto a portable device. You can copy tracks from CDs to your computer's hard drive and save them for listening to later. You can record these tracks to the hard drive while listening to the CD as well. The quality of the CD recording and the playback of the tracks will not be the same on all computers because the quality of the sound card and speakers plays a major role in this.

To copy a track from an audio CD to your computer and then play that track from your computer:

1. Open Windows Media Player.

2. Place an audio CD in the audio CD drive.

3. Choose the CD Audio button.

4. Uncheck all tracks but one. (You can record the entire CD, but for the purpose of this exercise, you should pick just one.)

5. Choose the Copy Music button.

6. Read the Copy Music Protection message that appears next, and either decide to protect the content so the music cannot be played on another computer, or choose not to protect the content. Protecting the content prevents unauthorized use of the recording of the CD track. Choose OK.

7. After the copy status has changed from Copying to Copied To Library, close the Windows Media Player.

8. Open the My Documents Folder.

9. Open the My Music Folder.

10. Open the folder that is named after the artist on your CD.

11. Open the folder that contains the song that you just recorded.

12. Click the song.

Using Error Control and Digital Playback to Enhance Audio Quality

You can use a couple of Media Player settings to enhance the quality of the audio you're downloading or copying. These settings have to do with error control and the type of electronic technology used: analog or digital.

When music is copied from one type of media to another, errors can occur; they are inherent in the technology. When you're using a modem to download music from the Internet, errors can be generated as the music is transmitted, when the analog signal is changed to a digital signal, and at many other points in the process. Error-checking devices are present in all areas of computing because errors occur all the time and must be discovered and resolved. When errors occur during the copying of music, the music can sound choppy or scratchy, even in the most advanced systems.

Windows XP addresses this concern by including its own error-correction utility. This utility can detect various types of errors and fix them automatically. The utility is not enabled by default; to enable it, use the Tools menu (see the next exercise).

You can also use the Tools menu to choose between analog or digital playback and copying. Digital communication is the newer technology; it's used now for TV cable service, some phone services, and satellite and fiber optic transmission. Analog technology is older and is used primarily in broadcast transmissions and basic telephone service. Digital communication occurs as a series of 1s and 0s, or ons and offs, while analog communication uses electronic signals of varying amplitude and frequency. A modem is used to convert the analog signals that are used in phone lines into the digital signals that are used by computers. Digital communication is faster than analog and provides better quality. If your computer supports it, you should use digital playback and copying.

Note

Using digital playback and copying instead of analog will work only if your hardware supports it. If, in the following procedure, Digital is grayed out or otherwise unavailable, your computer does not support digital playback or recording.

To enable error correction or to set digital playback and copying:

1. Open Windows Media Player.

2. Choose Tools | Options.

3. Select the Devices tab.

4. Highlight the device that is the audio CD, usually labeled D: or E:.

5. Choose Properties.

6. For Playback Settings, select Digital and Use Error Correction.

7. For Copy Settings, select Digital and Use Error Correction.

8. Choose OK twice.

Setting Options

Several options in Windows Media Player can be set differently from the defaults. For instance, the music that you save to your hard drive when using the Media Player is saved to the My Music folder automatically. You can change that folder to any other folder you like, or create a new folder for each artist whom you record. Other options are available as well. To see what is available for configuration, choose Tools | Options. Figure 2.11 shows the Player tab of the Options dialog box.

The Options dialog box has tabs for player options, music copying, devices, performance, the media library, visualizations, formats, and the network. The following are the options of most interest (arranged by their tabs) with descriptions of what you might consider changing:

♦ *Player*—The default settings usually work fine here, but you might want to have Windows Media Player check for updates weekly instead of monthly if you're waiting for an

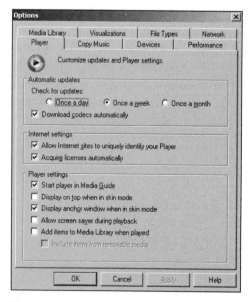

Figure 2.11
Tools | Options in Windows Media Player.

upgrade. You can also allow the player to download these updates automatically. If you use your computer as a stereo system, you might want to enable the screensaver to come on when music is playing.

♦ *Copy Music*—If you want to change the folder where your music is saved by default, you can do so here. Simply click the Change button and browse to another folder. You can also change the file format from Windows Media to MP3; do this if you plan to play music from an MP3 player instead of from the hard drive. You can also change the quality of the CD copy. Keep in mind, however, that the higher the quality, the more disk space the file will take up on your computer.

♦ *Devices*—This tab was detailed in the previous section, but in addition to setting the properties for audio devices, you can add them here. If you have an Internet connection, clicking the Add button takes you to the WindowsMedia.com Web site, where you can purchase additional devices such as personal audio players and handheld PCs. You can also access other areas of WindowsMedia.com (described later).

♦ *Performance*—You can change the connection speed, buffering speed, hardware acceleration, and digital video settings. The default settings are usually appropriate, but if you are knowledgeable in this area, you might be able to tweak the settings just enough to get a little more performance out of your system.

♦ *Media Library*—Set access rights to your media library and add purchased music to it. The default for the access rights of other applications is Read-Only, while the default for access rights of Internet sites is No Access. Unless you plan to share your files with other users on the Internet (a licensing no-no), you should leave these settings the way they are.

♦ *Visualizations*—View all of the current visualizations installed on your computer, add others, and view their properties. If you've downloaded any extra visualizations, you can remove them from here also. For a few of the visualizations, properties can be set for their screen size and off-screen buffer size.

♦ *Formats*—Windows Media Player supports several formats, including DVD video, CD audio, Movie File (MPEG), and MP3. All of the available formats are enabled by default, but you can disable them one by one.

♦ *Network*—To receive streaming media (music or video from the Internet or other networks), your computer must be configured to use the appropriate protocols. Protocols such as Multicast, UDP, TCP, and HTTP set rules for sending and receiving these types of data. The sender and receiver use the same protocols and agree on the same rules prior to transmitting. On this tab, you can review or change the protocols that are used; you can also configure proxy settings. If you are accessing the Internet from inside an organization, you probably have a proxy server configured here. A proxy server is a security measure that limits and scrutinizes which types of data pass through the organization to the Internet and back. The defaults are generally acceptable here.

Organizing Your Files

As you use Windows Media Player, you'll acquire lots of files that contain music from different artists, videos from different authors, and several playlists. These files are all accessed through the Media Library button. The Media Library has default sections called Audio, Album, Artist, Genre, Video, My Playlists, Radio Tuner Presets, and Deleted Items. These sections can also be accessed through the Playlist window. The music on your hard drive is listed in these categories.

To add new playlists, click the New Playlist button at the top of the screen. Once a new folder is created, you can right-click any music or video file, choose Add To Playlist from the file's context menu, and then choose the playlist you'd like to add the file to. Using these utilities, you can organize the files here in any way you'd like: by artist, by user, by genre, or any other way imaginable. In addition to creating folders, you can move songs up or down in the playlist by using the appropriate buttons.

You can also highlight a song in your Media Library and choose Media Details from the top of the screen. If you have an Internet connection, you'll be connected to **WindowsMedia.com**, where you can see what CD the music came from and read a short biography of the artists. In most instances, you can also buy the CD, download other music or videos by the same artist, and more. You return to the Media Library by clicking the Back button.

Using WindowsMedia.com

If you have an Internet connection, then when you launch the Windows Media Player and click the Media Guide button, you will be connected to the Microsoft Web site WindowsMedia.com. This Web site offers music, videos, downloads, radio stations, movies, Webcams, and sections on entertainment, lifestyles, business, news, sports, and more. You can sample the latest music and view the latest movie previews. There are also offerings to chat with celebrities, play games with others, and shop online.

Listening to the Radio

As long as you have a valid Internet connection, you can listen to radio stations all over the world by using the Radio Tuner included with Windows Media Player. To select a station and explore this part of the player, choose the Radio Tuner button.

The tuner has several preset stations, and you can find your own stations by searching by format, band (AM/FM), language, location, call sign, frequency, or keyword. In the Station Finder window, simply select the type of station you'd like to locate, and choose the Find button. You can then play your selection by double-clicking it.

To explore the radio presets:

1. Open Windows Media Player.

2. Choose the Radio Tuner button.

3. Under Presets, double-click a station.

4. Close any pop-up windows that appear. The radio station will play through the Media Player, so these windows are not needed.

To find other radio stations around the world:

1. In Windows Media Player, choose the Radio Tuner button.

2. Click the Station Finder drop-down list, and select a Find By criterion.

3. In the resulting window, select an appropriate criterion. (For instance, selecting Format from the Station Finder will open a new window called <Select Format>.)

4. When the stations appear that meet your requirements, double-click one to connect.

5. Close any pop-up windows that appear. The radio station will play through the Media Player, so these windows are not needed.

Configuring Radio Presets

Once you've found a station you like, you can save it as one of your presets so you can access it next time you want to hear it.

To add a station to your list of presets:

1. Open Windows Media Player.

2. Choose the Radio Tuner button.

3. Perform Steps 3 through 5 in the previous example to locate a station of your liking.

4. In the Presets window, change from Featured to My Presets.

5. Make sure the station you like is highlighted in the right pane, and click the left arrow in the middle section.

6. To remove a preset, highlight it in the left pane and click the right arrow.

Note
You can further edit these lists by choosing the Edit button and then following the on-screen directions.

Accessibility Options

There are several ways you can personalize the computer for users who have disabilities or special needs. Some of these options are useful even for people who do not have any special needs. One of my favorites is an up-and-coming technology having to do with speech and handwriting recognition. Windows XP offers several options for speech and handwriting recognition, including options for several languages such as English, Japanese, and Chinese. These utilities work with various programs, such as Word 2002 and Internet Explorer 5 or later, and with new input devices, such as a tablet and a pen stylus. You can also increase your workspace by installing multiple monitors if you have the necessary hardware. This section introduces these options and others, including the Accessibility Wizard, the Utility Manager, the Magnifier, Narrator, On-Screen Keyboard, and MouseKeys.

In this section, I'll detail how to configure the computer for all types of users, but keep in mind that many of these options might be used to improve your work area as well.

Speech and Handwriting Recognition

In the early days of personal computers, there were only two devices for entering data into a computer: the keyboard and the mouse. Later came the scanner and the digital camera, among other things, and now we have speech and handwriting hardware and software. Speech and handwriting technology is still in its infancy, but Windows XP does a good job of including it and allowing the OS to be compatible with input devices that will no doubt be available very soon.

To use these utilities, you'll of course need the required hardware and software. In this section, I'll introduce what you'll need to use both the speech and the handwriting utilities, and I'll provide a brief lesson on how to use them.

Speech Recognition

Speech recognition allows you to enter information into a program such as Word 2002 without typing the words. All you have to do is speak the words into a microphone, and they appear on the screen. You can also speak words such as "bold" and "underline" to perform those tasks with inputted data. The speech recognition utility isn't meant to be completely hands-free, though; it is best used along with the mouse or keyboard or both.

To use the speech recognition utility in Windows XP Professional, you'll need to install some hardware and software, and then "teach" the speech recognition utility to understand your voice and its characteristics. Here's an overview of what you'll need to have:

♦ A high-quality headset microphone with gain adjustment. *Gain adjustment* allows a microphone to modify its amplification so that the sound fed to the computer is constant. A USB microphone is recommended.

♦ At least 128MB of RAM installed on the computer.

♦ At least a 400MHz bus on the computer.

♦ Microsoft Internet Explorer 5 or later.

♦ The speech recognition engine, which is available in Microsoft Office XP.

Once the appropriate hardware has been acquired and Microsoft Office XP has been installed, you must add the speech recognition utility from the Regional And Language Options icon in the Control Panel.

To add speech recognition:

1. Open the Control Panel.

2. Open Regional And Language Options.

3. Select the Languages tab.

4. Under Text Service And Input Languages, choose Details.

5. Under Installed Services, choose Add.

6. In the Add Input Language dialog box, under Input Language, select an appropriate input language.

7. Check the Speech checkbox, and select an option from the list.

8. Choose OK twice.

If the Language tab doesn't have a Change button but does have a Details button, then the speech recognition engine has not been installed. To install it, open Microsoft Word 2002, and choose Tools | Speech. Speech recognition will now be available for all programs that have the capability to use it.

Handwriting Recognition

Handwriting recognition allows you to input data by handwriting it instead of typing it. There are several types of handwriting hardware you can buy, and the most popular at this time are graphics tablets and digital pens. These devices are installed like any other piece of hardware and come with accompanying software. The handwritten data can then be included in a document as either typed data or handwritten data.

To use the handwriting recognition utility available in Windows XP Professional, you'll need to install some hardware and software. Here's an overview of what you'll need to have:

♦ Although you can use your mouse, it is recommended that you have a handwriting input tool such as a graphics tablet and digital pen for inputting data. Preferably, this is a USB device.

♦ No additional RAM or increased bus speed is needed; any computer that can run Windows XP Professional can run the handwriting recognition utility.

♦ The handwriting recognition engine must be installed. This is included in Microsoft Office XP and can be used with this program and others that support handwriting recognition.

Once the appropriate hardware has been acquired and Microsoft Office XP has been installed, you must add handwriting recognition from the Regional And Language Options icon in the Control Panel.

To add handwriting recognition:

1. Open the Control Panel.

2. Open Regional And Language Options.

3. Select the Languages tab.

4. Under Text Services and Input Languages, choose Details.

5. In the Add Input Language dialog box, under Input Languages, select an appropriate input language.

6. Check the Handwriting Recognition checkbox, and select an option from the list.

7. Choose OK twice.

If Handwriting Recognition is not available as an option, then the handwriting recognition engine has not been installed. You must install the engine before adding the utility. Uninstall this option when it is not in use because it requires quite a bit of RAM and slows computer performance.

Multiple Monitors

If you have an additional PCI slot or AGP port on your motherboard, an extra video adapter card, and an additional monitor lying around the office, you can configure your computer to use multiple monitors. If you have a laptop and a desktop PC running Windows XP Professional, and you have a newer high-end display adapter, you can use a utility called DualView to view both screens by using only the hardware currently installed.

If you do set up two monitors, you can configure them so that both monitors contain a copy of the desktop or so that each is a continuation of the other. This way, you can work on multiple tasks at a time or stretch a single task, perhaps a large Excel worksheet, across the additional monitor.

To install an additional card or monitor, and to configure that new monitor to extend the desktop or copy it:

1. Turn off the computer.

2. Open the computer tower, taking the appropriate precautions with grounding to prevent ESD (electrostatic discharge) damage to the internal parts of the computer. Insert the new video adapter card into the appropriate slot. Close the computer case and fasten securely.

3. Plug the second monitor into the new card.

4. Turn on the computer, and let Windows XP detect the new monitor.

5. Install additional drivers if necessary.

6. Open the Control Panel.

7. Choose the Display icon.

8. Select the Settings tab.

9. Select the new monitor.

10. Check the checkbox Extend My Windows Desktop Onto This Monitor.

11. Choose OK twice.

In Step 11, the Extend My Windows Desktop Onto This Monitor option will not be available if your video card doesn't support multiple monitors. Also, selecting this checkbox is what allows you to drag items from one screen to another. By dragging the bottom of a window to resize it, you can drag that application to another monitor.

Once multiple monitors are installed, you can tell the computer how you want to drag items when moving them from one screen to another. For instance, if your monitors are sitting side by side, you'll probably pull items from left to right. However, if your monitors sit on top of one another, you'll want to configure dragged items by moving them up and down. You can do this through the Settings tab in the Display dialog box (accessible from the Display icon in the Control Panel).

DualView is a productivity enhancement for mobile users. Many of the newer laptops support two interfaces to a single display adapter. DualView allows these two interfaces (the laptop screen and a desktop PC screen) to display different outputs at the same time. A great use for this is for a presenter at a conference to use his or her own laptop for personal purposes, such as looking at notes or statistics, while showing another screen to attendees.

Whereas the previous three utilities, Speech, Handwriting, and Multiple Monitors, can be used and enjoyed by everyone, they can also be helpful for people who have disabilities. The utilities described next are generally designed to accommodate users with specific needs, such as the sight or hearing impaired or people with physical limitations that prevent them from typing or using the mouse as generally configured.

Magnifier

For users who are vision impaired, Windows XP includes the Magnifier utility. This magnifies what's on the screen so that it can be seen more easily. This provides a minimum level of functionality for users and, for the most part, is only a temporary application. You'll probably need a much better magnification utility for full-time employees who are sight impaired.

To turn on the Magnifier and see how it works:

1. Open the Magnifier (choose Start | Programs | Accessories | Accessibility | Magnifier).

2. Move the mouse around to see how the Magnifier works, and then choose OK in the Microsoft Magnifier introductory screen.

3. In the Magnification Level drop-down list box, select 5.

4. Leave Follow Mouse Cursor, Follow Keyboard Focus, and Follow Text Editing checked.

5. Check Invert Colors.

6. Notice that Show Magnifier is checked; if you uncheck it, you will not be able to see it at the top of the screen.

7. Choose Exit.

The next time that the Magnifier is used, it will retain these settings. Magnifier will open at the top of the screen to make reading portions of the screen easier.

Narrator

Narrator is a text-to-speech utility for users who are unable to read what is on the computer screen due to blindness or impaired vision. Narrator reads what is on the screen, including the menu options, the contents of the active window, and even the text that has been typed. As with the Magnifier, this utility provides only minimal functionality; for everyday use, a more functional program provided by a third party, and with more features, should be used.

Several items in Narrator can be configured and personalized. These include not only what is read aloud by the narrator but also the pitch and tone of the narrator's voice. You can even adjust the speed of the voice and have the mouse pointer follow the active item on the screen.

Narrator has a few basic requirements, the most important of which is a sound card that supports it. If Narrator will not open because of an incompatible sound card, then a new sound card will need to be installed. Additionally, Narrator will not open if your language is not supported; currently, the narrator speaks only in English. Updates to Narrator can be obtained from Microsoft's Web site.

To access the Narrator and configure the options:

1. Open the Narrator (choose Start | Programs | Accessories | Accessibility | Narrator).

2. Read the introduction, and choose OK.

3. In the Narrator dialog box, notice the four options:

   ♦ Announce Events On Screen

   ♦ Read Typed Characters

   ♦ Move Mouse Pointer To The Active Item

   ♦ Start Narrator Minimized

   Make the appropriate selections, and choose the Voice button.

4. From here you can change the voice speed, volume, and pitch. All can be configured on a scale of 1 to 9. Make the appropriate choices.

5. Choose OK and then Exit.

When checking and unchecking boxes in Narrator, you might have noticed that the Narrator also offers pressing the spacebar as a way to make a change and that the voice can be configured in many ways. Although this is a rather primitive accessibility option, it will certainly improve with time. Many other third-party options can be purchased from independent manufacturers.

On-Screen Keyboard

Another accessibility option for those who are mobility impaired is the On-Screen Keyboard. This utility is a virtual keyboard that is shown on the screen and that allows users to type words by using a joystick or other pointing device to form text and words. Three modes are available: clicking mode, scanning mode, and hovering mode. There are lots of other options, including displaying the keyboard in different views, using an enhanced keyboard with a numeric keypad, and using a click sound to verify that you've typed a key.

To open the On-Screen Keyboard:

1. Choose Start | Programs | Accessories | Accessibility | On-Screen Keyboard.

2. Open a word processing program such as Microsoft Word.

3. Click on the virtual keyboard and type a few letters with the mouse.

4. Keep the On-Screen Keyboard utility open while you read the rest of this section.

With the On-Screen Keyboard running, you can see that several menus are available that contain configurable options. The File menu allows you only to exit the program, but the Keyboard and Settings menus allow you to set various options.

From the Keyboard menu, you can:

♦ Switch back and forth between the enhanced and standard keyboards. The enhanced keyboard has a numeric keypad and other options.

♦ Switch back and forth between the regular layout and the block layout. The regular layout is the default and looks like a regular keyboard; the block layout uses more rectangular keys.

♦ Switch back and forth between 101-, 102-, and 106-key keyboard layouts.

From the Settings menu, you can:

♦ Choose that the keyboard always be on top of other programs. This means that the keyboard is shown in front of the application instead of behind it or minimized. On Top is the default.

- Choose to use a clicking sound when you're selecting keys from the virtual keyboard.

- Select the typing mode. You can choose between clicking to select, hovering to select, or using a joystick to select.

- Choose the font that will be displayed on the keyboard. This does not change the font that is typed in the application.

MouseKeys

For users who have trouble using a mouse, a utility called MouseKeys is available from the Accessibility Options. The MouseKeys utility enables you to use the keyboard's arrows and keys on the keypad to perform functions that are normally performed with a mouse. You can also drag items by using the Insert and Delete keys.

To turn on MouseKeys and configure the settings:

1. Open the Control Panel.

2. Open Accessibility Options.

3. Select the Mouse tab.

4. Check the Use MouseKeys checkbox.

5. Choose the Settings button.

6. Notice the defaults, and make a note of the shortcuts.

7. Choose OK twice.

Once MouseKeys is enabled, use the shortcut for MouseKeys, which is Left Alt+Left Shift+Num Lock to enable it. When the MouseKeys dialog box appears, choose OK to verify that you want to use MouseKeys.

When using MouseKeys, you'll need to remember a few keystrokes:

- To move the pointer up or down, or left or right, use the arrow keys on the numeric keypad.

- To move the pointer diagonally, use these keys: Home, End, Page Up, and Page Down.

- To change the MouseKeys settings, select the mouse icon in the notification window in the bottom-right corner of the screen.

Accessibility Wizard

Using the Accessibility Wizard is a great way to configure all of the accessibility options at once. Almost all of the options that can be configured here have been described in this section, in a previous section of this chapter, or in Chapter 1. The Accessibility Wizard brings them all together and even adds a few extra options, making the configuration tasks for special needs quite personal and easy to do. If you've forgotten what each item does, don't worry; it's described briefly in each page of the Accessibility Wizard.

Some configuration changes that can be made while using the Accessibility Wizard include the following:

♦ Default text size, including using Microsoft Magnifier

♦ Display settings such as font size and disabling personalized menus

♦ Microsoft Magnifier

♦ Scroll bar and windows border sizes

♦ Icon size

♦ High-contrast color settings

♦ Mouse cursor and cursor settings

♦ SoundSentry

♦ ShowSounds

♦ StickyKeys

♦ BounceKeys

♦ ToggleKeys

♦ Extra keyboard help

♦ MouseKeys

♦ Mouse button settings and mouse speed

♦ Automatic timeouts for accessibility options

♦ Making these settings the defaults or applying them to only the current user profile

To use the Accessibility Wizard:

1. From the previous list, decide which options you'd like to configure.

2. Choose Start | Programs | Accessories | Accessibility | Accessibility Wizard.

3. Work through the wizard, making changes where necessary.

4. When finished, select an option for applying the new options, either as a default for the system itself or for a specific user. Choose Finish.

Utility Manager

Utility Manager is a tool that is used by administrators to configure how and when users will utilize accessibility settings. The Utility Manager allows a user to check an Accessibility program's status and start or stop the program as needed. An administrator can configure accessibility options to start when a user logs on or when Utility Manager is started. Options can also be set to start after a computer's desktop has been locked and then unlocked. The programs (options) available have been discussed previously in this chapter; they are Magnifier, Narrator, and On-Screen Keyboard.

To start Utility Manager:

1. Press Windows+U (the Windows Logo key is between Alt and Ctrl).

2. The Narrator begins talking automatically. In the Utility Manager dialog box, select Magnifier in the top pane.

3. With Magnifier highlighted, make the appropriate selections. These include starting and stopping the service and choosing if and when the program will start automatically.

4. With Narrator highlighted, make the appropriate selections. These include starting and stopping the service and choosing if and when the program will start automatically.

5. With On-Screen Keyboard highlighted, make the appropriate selections. These include starting and stopping the service and choosing if and when the program will start automatically.

6. Choose OK when finished.

7. Right-click Narrator in the taskbar, and choose Close.

Wrapping Up

In this chapter, you learned how to personalize your computer by creating a desktop that was uniquely yours, personalizing sounds, and configuring accessibility options. Options for the desktop include icon arrangement, appearance and themes, smart menus, and more. For personalizing sounds, you learned about using the volume controls, playing and recording audio files, and using Windows Media Player. Finally, you learned about accessibility options, including Magnifier, Narrator, and configuring items such as multiple monitors and speech and handwriting recognition.

Chapter 3
Users and Groups

In this chapter, I'll introduce you to the basic tasks regarding users and groups, including using the built-in accounts Administrator and Guest, creating local user accounts, creating and managing passwords, configuring local groups, and using the default built-in groups for security. I'll also introduce you to user rights and privileges as well as to account and local policies.

User accounts and groups are generally used to make sure that a user's access to the computer or workgroup is secure. By creating a user account for each person who accesses the computer or its files, and by having each person use his or her account to log onto the computer or the workgroup, an administrator can make sure that users access only the files, folders, and programs that they are supposed to.

There are two general types of networks that a Windows XP Professional computer can be a member of, a domain or a workgroup. Domains are usually used in medium to large networks, and an administrator in the organization manages all of the users' computers and their respective user and group accounts. Large networks typically have several domains, and each domain has a computer serving as a domain controller. In contrast, a workgroup usually consists of 10 or fewer computers, and users share files and folders by using passwords and accounts. Windows XP Professional can be used on a standalone computer, such as a single computer in a small business or a family computer that everyone shares.

Because your domain administrator will manage domain accounts, this chapter will focus on creating and managing *local* user and group accounts; these are accounts that are configured for small workgroups and for standalone computers with multiple users. Local accounts can also be created for users who are in domains but who need access to a local computer that multiple users access, such as in a bank or restaurant. When these local accounts are used in domains, though, an administrator will still most likely be responsible for creating the domain users and groups. In addition, because domain security policies always override local policies, if the user and computer belong to a domain, then local policies will be overridden when that user is also connected to the network.

Note

The screenshots you'll see in the rest of this book are created on a Windows XP Professional machine using a Windows Classic look with a few minor changes. If you are using the Whistler theme, your screen will look different from the ones shown here. You might consider changing to the Windows Classic look while working through the exercises in this book.

Overview of User Accounts

As I just mentioned, user accounts can be configured for the local computer or for the domain. By creating local user accounts, you can limit each user's rights and privileges and make sure that users access only what you want them to. *Rights* are actions that can be performed by the user, such as backing up files or shutting down the computer. *Privileges* are associated with access to specific objects, such as printers or files and folders.

In a small business with only a few computers (a workgroup), you could set up local user accounts on each computer, and each user account would have an associated password. Each user could then use this account and password to log onto his or her computer or another computer in the company. The account's associated rights and privileges would then give the user access to only certain files, folders, and printers and would prevent the user from performing destructive tasks such as restoring data or changing the system time.

In contrast, a family or home business might have only one computer with multiple users. These users could be given user accounts and passwords for the same computer, and each user's access could be monitored and secured. This setup could prevent teenagers from downloading games or viruses from the Internet, for example, or prevent a temporary worker from accessing sensitive information.

In a network such as a domain with hundreds or even thousands of computers, a domain administrator is the one who configures domain user accounts. These domain accounts limit or allow access to domain servers, databases, company printers, sensitive information, and more. Local user accounts can be configured on users' computers in these types of situations, but a domain administrator manages even those local accounts. If local accounts are configured, they are overridden when domain accounts are also used. However, if a user is not logged on to the network, local user accounts can be useful in some situations.

In the following sections, I'll be talking about user and group accounts, rights and privileges, account policies, local security policies, and group policies. These topics will apply to workgroups and standalone computers, not necessarily to domains. In domains, domain rules override local rules and require much more administrative overhead and consideration. In domains, domain administrators are usually responsible for this work.

Built-In User Accounts

Your Windows XP Professional computer has two built-in, local user accounts: Administrator and Guest. On a scale of 1 to 10, with 10 being the most lenient (having the most access), an administrator is a 10, and a guest is a 1. Not everyone who accesses the computer needs to be an administrator, though, even in a home setting, and certainly most users need more access than the Guest account provides. Although these built-in accounts need to be introduced, you probably won't use them that often.

Administrator

The Administrator account is provided so that when Windows XP is installed, an account is available for accessing all parts of the system and for configuring it. Administrator privileges are intended for the person who is in charge of the system and who is responsible for installing programs, creating accounts, and accessing all of the files and folders on the computer. The administrator has full access to every part of the computer. An administrator can also do the following:

♦ Manage user accounts and passwords

♦ Change user accounts, passwords, rights, and privileges

♦ Rename the Administrator account

♦ Back up files and directories

♦ Debug programs

♦ Install and uninstall device drivers

♦ Manage auditing and security

♦ Profile system performance

♦ Take ownership of files and other objects

It's a good idea to limit how often the Administrator account is used, and you should consider creating a separate account with administrator privileges and using that account instead of the actual Administrator account most of the time. For even more security, you can disable the original Administrator account or rename it. Either way, you should log on with administrator privileges only when necessary. There are two main reasons for this. One reason is that if someone is trying to break into your computer and the Administrator account is available, all that person has to do is type "administrator" for the username and then figure out the password. If the password is the name of the family dog, a maiden name, the company name, or something similar, breaking into that account won't be too difficult for the right person. However, if the hacker has to figure out not only the password but also the name of the Administrator account, the job is a lot harder. Another reason the Administrator account should not be used often is the threat of viruses on the Internet. Some viruses can do more harm when downloaded or opened by a user with an Administrator account than with a more limited account because the limited account wouldn't have as much access to files and folders as an Administrator account would. The moral is this: Use the Administrator account sparingly, and not at all when possible.

Note

You can also log on as a standard user but use the Administrator account to run a program. This way, you are not logged on as an Administrator, and only that one program is run with the Administrator account. You can access the Run As command in Windows Explorer by pressing the Shift key and right-clicking the program to be run.

Guest

The Guest account is intended for users who have no configured account on the local computer but who need to access the computer briefly to check email or type a quick memo. The Guest account does not have a password, so these users can log on by typing "guest" as the username and leaving the Password box blank. When users log on using the Guest account, they receive the default profile of the local computer. This means that no personal settings—such as background, screensaver, shortcuts, or themes—are configured. In fact, logging on as a guest is similar to logging onto the computer for the first time. The installed programs are available, however, and the new user can access them.

Although guests can access the programs (such as Microsoft Word, Windows Media Player, and so on), they cannot access anyone else's personal files. If you log onto your computer as a guest, you'll see that there are no documents in the My Documents folder, no music files in the My Music folder, and no pictures in the My Pictures folder. Those files are private and belong only to the person who created and saved them. This could have been an administrator or a user (or you, when logged in as you), and they are not accessible by a guest. However, you still might not want just anyone to log onto your computer by using the Guest account, and because of that, it can be disabled and/or renamed.

While logged onto your computer, a guest can do only a few things, so most items in the following list describe what a guest can't do:

♦ Guests cannot change any attributes of the Guest account.

♦ Guests cannot install any software or hardware.

♦ Guests cannot make permanent changes to the computer settings. Desktop changes—for such items as shortcuts, screensavers, and backgrounds—are not saved for the next guest who logs on.

♦ When programs such as Windows Media Player are used, there are no saved Media Libraries or other personalized settings available.

To try out the Guest account and log on as a guest:

1. Close all running programs. (This isn't totally necessary, but it's always good practice. Windows XP will close all the programs for you, but you're better off saving your work and closing your programs.)

2. Choose Start | Shut Down.

3. From the What Do You Want The Computer To Do? drop-down list, choose Log Off <username>.

Warning
Remember the username you see here exactly as it is written. To log back on to this account, you must enter this username.

4. When the logon screen appears, type "guest" in the User Name box. Leave the Password box blank.

5. Choose OK.

6. After reviewing the Guest account, repeat Steps 1 through 3, and then log back on with your own user account.

It is a good idea to either disable the Guest account or rename it to prevent the unauthorized use of your computer. To disable or change password settings for the Guest account:

1. Log on as an Administrator.

2. Open the Computer Management console. (Choose Start | Programs | Administrative Tools | Computer Management. You can also access Administrative Tools from the Control Panel.)

3. Maximize the Computer Management window.

4. Expand the Local Users And Groups tree, as shown in Figure 3.1.

5. Select the Users folder, as shown in Figure 3.1.

6. In the right pane, double-click the Guest account.

7. To disable the account, check the Account Is Disabled checkbox.

8. To change the password properties, uncheck the checkboxes User Cannot Change Password or Password Never Expires, or both.

9. Choose OK.

To set a password for the Guest account (if the Computer Management console is still open, go directly to Step 5):

1. Log on as an administrator.

2. Open the Computer Management console.

3. Maximize the Computer Management window.

4. Expand the Local Users And Groups tree, as shown in Figure 3.1.

5. Select the Users folder, as shown in Figure 3.1.

6. In the right pane, right-click the Guest account, and choose Set Password.

7. Read the warnings, and choose Proceed.

8. Type the new password and confirm it. Carefully read the warnings in the Set Password For Guest box here. Choose OK when you're finished.

Note
You can rename both the Administrator and Guest accounts through the Local Security Settings console, which is described at the end of this chapter.

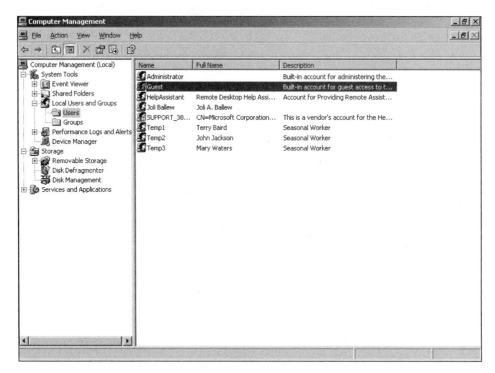

Figure 3.1
The Computer Management console.

Other Types of Accounts

Besides the Administrator and Guest accounts, which are considered built-in accounts, there are two other types of accounts that an administrator can configure for users. Those are standard accounts and limited accounts. Depending on the user for whom the account is being created, you should choose a type of account that matches what you'd like that user to access and have rights to do. While reading this section, consider the users for whom you'll need to create accounts, and decide what types of accounts you'll assign them.

Standard Accounts

A standard account rates around a 6 on the previously mentioned scale of 1 to 10, with 10 being the most lenient and represented by the Administrator account. Users with a standard account can make basic changes, such as installing software and hardware that don't change the restricted operating system files, and changing their account name, type, and password. Users with a standard account can personalize their computers with screensavers and backgrounds and generally take control of their computers when logged on under their accounts. These users can also use the programs installed on the computer and save and delete files and folders they've created.

Limited Accounts

A limited account rates around a 3 on the previously mentioned scale of 1 to 10, with 1 being the most restrictive and represented by the Guest account. Users with limited accounts cannot install software or hardware and cannot change their account names or type. They can, however, access the programs that are already installed on the computer, change their passwords and backgrounds, and somewhat personalize their computers. You'll learn how to create these accounts in the next section of this chapter.

The AT Service Account

The Task Scheduler uses the AT Service Account. It is a special account that must be set by the administrator or another user with appropriate permissions so that tasks can be viewed, modified, and run effectively. The AT Service account will be explained further in Chapter 5.

Creating and Configuring User Accounts

Now that you know a little about the different types of accounts, it's time to begin creating them. In this section, you'll learn how to add and delete user accounts, disable and enable them, modify and rename them, and change their passwords. Keep in mind that these are the basics, and there is far more you can do with accounts. Later, I'll introduce tasks such as creating groups and group policies, and I'll discuss local security policies. These can be used to further secure the computer and keep it out of harm's way.

> **Note**
>
> *As I mentioned earlier, these examples pertain to workgroups and standalone computers, not to domains. Domain administrators are in charge of domain accounts. For information on home-office workgroups and sharing resources between computers, see Chapter 10.*

Adding and Deleting User Accounts

To add a user account to your standalone computer:

1. Log on as an Administrator.
2. Open the Control Panel.
3. Double-click the User Accounts icon.
4. Under Pick A Task, choose Create A New Account.
5. Type a name for the new account. This name will appear on the Welcome page and the Start menu when you're using the Whistler theme. Choose Next.
6. Pick an account type: Computer Administrator, Standard, or Limited.
7. Choose Create Account.

> **Tip**
>
> *There is a second way to create a user account, and that way is generally preferred by administrators over the previous technique. Using the Computer Management console, you can create user accounts and assign passwords easily. The Computer Management console is discussed later in this chapter, but note that you can create user accounts in this console by selecting the Users folder and choosing Action|New User. The resulting dialog box is shown in Figure 3.10.*

To delete an account from your computer:

1. Log on as an Administrator.
2. Open the Control Panel.
3. Double-click the User Accounts icon.
4. Under the heading Or Pick An Account To Change, double-click the account to delete.

> **Note**
>
> *You cannot delete the Administrator or Guest accounts.*

5. From the What Do You Want To Change About <username>'s Account? list, select Delete The Account.

6. If the user whose account you are deleting has files and personalized desktop settings, you can automatically have Windows XP save them for you in a folder on the desktop. However, doing this does not save the user's email messages, Internet Favorites, or other settings. Choose Keep Files, Delete Files, or Cancel.

Disabling or Enabling a Local Account

Occasionally, you'll need to disable an account for a while and later enable it again. This might be necessary if a user has been laid off and then rehired, if an employee has been out of town or at another office for a long period of time, or if a family member has lost privileges and is not allowed to access the computer. Accounts are disabled through the Computer Management console mentioned earlier.

To enable or disable an account:

1. Log on as an Administrator.

2. Open the Computer Management console. (Choose Start | Programs | Administrative Tools | Computer Management. You can also access Administrative Tools from the Control Panel.)

3. Maximize the Computer Management window.

4. Expand the Local Users And Groups tree, as shown earlier in Figure 3.1.

5. Select the Users folder, as shown earlier in Figure 3.1.

6. Right-click the user account to be enabled or disabled (accounts are enabled by default), and choose Properties.

7. Select the General tab.

8. To disable an account, check the Account Is Disabled checkbox. To enable an account, uncheck the checkbox.

9. Choose OK.

Renaming a Local Account

To change the name of a local account:

1. Log on as an administrator.

2. Open the Control Panel.

3. Double-click the User Accounts icon.

4. Under the heading Or Pick An Account To Change, double-click the account to be renamed.

5. From the What Do You Want To Change About <username>'s Account? list, select Change The Name.

6. Type the new name, and choose Change Name.

Changing the Picture Associated with the Account

Each account has a picture associated with it, and you can see the picture next to the account name in User Accounts. To change this picture:

1. Log on as an administrator.

2. Open the Control Panel.

3. Double-click the User Accounts icon.

4. Under the heading Or Pick An Account To Change, double-click the account to be renamed.

5. From the What Do You Want To Change About <username>'s Account? list, select Change The Picture.

6. Either select an available picture, or choose Browse For More Pictures. (See the sidebar "Browsing for Other Files" for more information.)

7. Choose Change Picture.

Creating or Changing a Password for a Local Account

Creating a password for a new account is essential if the account is to be secure. Every user account should have a password so that no one else can use the account and so that the user can be held responsible for his or her actions while logged on. The password should not be shared. If User A and User B both have passwords, and User A knows User B's password, then User A can log on as User B and cause problems for both the user and the system.

To create a password, you can go through the User Accounts icon in the Control Panel or through the Computer Management console. Administrators will be more familiar with the

---

Browsing for Other Files

When given the option to browse for a file, such as a photo, you can search your computer, any shared files or folders on a workstation in your workgroup, or any files or folders available from anywhere on your company's network (if you have the appropriate permissions to access them). When browsing, click the down arrow next to the Look In box to search for the appropriate picture.

Figure 3.2 shows the Open box that you will see if you choose to browse for a picture. Notice that, in this example, the folder My Pictures on Desktop is highlighted. Also notice that the folder is not on the current computer but is located in a workgroup called Ballew. If the folder were on the local computer, it would be found under Local Disk (D:).

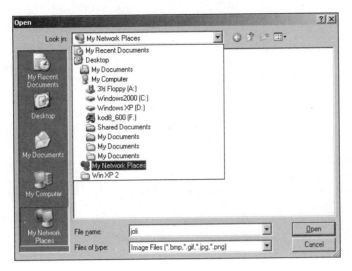

Figure 3.2
Browsing.

Computer Management way of doing things, while home users and small-business owners will most likely prefer the Control Panel.

To create and modify password properties by using the Computer Management console:

1. Log on as an Administrator.

2. Open the Computer Management console. (Choose Start | Programs | Administrative Tools | Computer Management. You can also access Administrative Tools from the Control Panel.)

3. Maximize the Computer Management window.

4. Expand the Local Users And Groups tree, as shown earlier in Figure 3.1.

5. Select the Users folder, as shown earlier in Figure 3.1.

6. To create or change a password for the user, right-click the username and choose Set Password.

7. Read the warnings, and choose Proceed.

8. Type the new password and confirm it. Carefully read the warnings in the Set Password For <username> box here. Choose OK when you're finished.

   The Computer Management console offers some options that are not available in the Control Panel. One of these options is to set the account so that the password can never be changed. To make this setting mandatory for a user, perform these two additional steps:

9. Right-click the user account, and choose Properties.

10. Check the checkbox User Cannot Change Password. Choose OK.

To create and modify password properties by using the Control Panel:

1. Log on as an Administrator.

2. Open the Control Panel.

3. Double-click the User Accounts icon.

4. Under the heading Or Pick An Account To Change, double-click the account to be modified.

5. From the What Do You Want To Change About <username>'s Account? list, select Create A Password.

6. Type the new password and verify it. Type a hint if you'd like to remind yourself what the password is if you forget it.

7. Choose Create Password.

User Rights, Privileges, and Permissions

As you are aware, users with Administrator accounts have more access to the computer than those with standard accounts, and those with standard accounts have more access than those with limited accounts. You are also aware that the Guest account is the most restrictive account on the computer. What makes these accounts different from one another are the rights and privileges that each specific user has. For instance, an administrator can install software and hardware, but a limited user cannot. And although an administrator can create and delete user accounts, no other user can, by default. These restrictions are based on the rights and privileges a user account has.

Before we get much further into user and group accounts, placing users in groups, and assigning those groups specific rights, privileges, and permissions, it is important to understand what these settings mean and how they can be used to allow or limit access to specific computer tasks and objects.

Introduction to User Rights

User rights can be assigned to specific users or to groups of users. In a very small company, one with only one or two users or computers, assigning rights directly to those users is generally fine. However, user rights are almost always applied to groups, with the groups containing the users who should have those rights. This is done because, as the number of users and groups grows, keeping up with individual accounts is much more tedious than keeping up with groups. There'll be more on groups later in this chapter.

Several rights can be configured. These rights define a user's capability at the local level and are often referred to as *logon rights*. These rights, which can be allowed or denied, are:

♦ Access this computer from a network.

♦ Log on locally.

♦ Log on as a batch job.

♦ Log on as a service.

Rights are used when the standard or limited accounts don't meet the needs of particular users. For instance, if your workgroup includes a group of users who will be denied the ability to access this computer from a network, you can create a group for those users and assign the appropriate logon rights.

Tip
Before creating your own groups, make sure you check out the built-in groups. You might find a group that meets your needs and that is already configured with the appropriate rights and privileges.

Introduction to User Privileges

Privileges can be assigned to specific users or to groups of users. Privileges are a form of user rights. In a very small company, one with only one or two users or computers, assigning privileges directly to those users is generally fine. However, privileges are almost always applied to groups, with the groups containing the users who should have those privileges.

Several privileges can be configured. The following privileges are the most commonly used and can be assigned to a user or a group of users:

♦ Add workstations to a domain

♦ Back up files and directories

♦ Force shutdown from a remote system

♦ Load and unload device drivers

♦ Manage auditing and security logs

♦ Restore files and directories

♦ Take ownership of files or other objects

♦ Remove a computer from the docking station

♦ Shut down the system

♦ Profile system performance

♦ Change the system time

There are several other privileges, which are used by processes (or applications), not by users. Privileges such as these include acting as part of the operating system, synchronizing directory service data, and creating permanent shared objects. Normally, you won't need to configure these types of privileges.

Privileges for users are configured when the standard or limited accounts don't meet the needs of particular users. For instance, if your workgroup includes a group of users who will back up files and folders, you can create a specific group for those users and assign them the privilege to do so. When additional users are added to this group, they'll also inherit that privilege.

Tip

Before creating your own groups, make sure you check out the built-in groups. You might find a group that meets your needs and that is already configured with the appropriate rights and privileges. A built-in group called Backup Operators can handle the aforementioned tasks.

Introduction to Permissions

Permissions are quite a bit different from user rights and privileges. Whereas logon rights refer to the logon abilities of the user, and privileges refer to what a user can actually do, a permission is a rule that is associated with an object to regulate who or what can gain access to a particular object, such as a printer or shared folder. For instance, if a printer is installed in a workgroup, and it is shared so others on the network can use it, permissions can be assigned to it and to users to regulate how the printer is used.

Figure 3.3 shows the Properties dialog box for a Lexmark 5700 printer that is shared in a workgroup. Notice that the Everyone group is highlighted and that this group has the permission to print documents but not to manage documents or printers. This means that users who are members of the Everyone group can print, but they can't change anything about the printer or what is scheduled to print. In contrast, a member of the Administrators group, as shown in Figure 3.4, does have the ability to do these things.

There are two important things to note here: these permissions can be changed for members of different groups, and permissions for objects are managed and changed by the object's owner (the person who created the object). The permissions shown in Figures 3.3 and 3.4 are default settings. Permissions can be set for printers, security descriptors, shared folders, and more, and special access permissions are also available.

Note

For more information on permissions and shared resources, see Chapter 4 and Chapter 10.

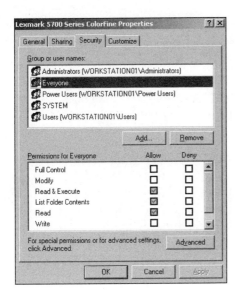

Figure 3.3
Permissions for the Everyone group.

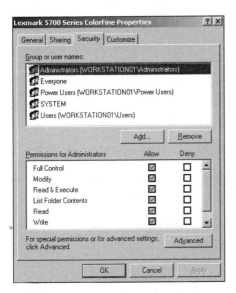

Figure 3.4
Permissions for the Administrators group.

Adding New Users to a Group

Users should be assigned to groups. Groups are used sort of like folders are; groups keep different types of users together the way the My Documents, My Music, and My Pictures folders keep different types of files together. It is important to create groups and use built-in ones because doing so makes managing users more efficient, just as grouping similar files together makes finding them easier.

To make a point about this, consider a network with three computers and three users. You can create three accounts on each of the three computers so that each user can log onto every computer, and you can share the folders, files, and printers as necessary and assign permissions for each user. Even though this scenario might work for a while (you can manage nine accounts), if the company grows and three more employees are added, the situation will become more difficult to manage. Additionally, if 10 or more employees are added, the entire system will need to be revamped.

Now consider the employees as members of groups. One employee is a member of the Administrators group, one is a member of the Backup Operators group and the Power Users group, and a third is a member of the Users group. The latter two employees have limits placed on them because of their group memberships. When additional employees are hired, they can simply be added to the appropriate group, and they will inherit all of the rights, privileges, and permissions of that group. Instead of your having to re-create all of those settings for each user, it is done automatically. To understand this concept better, let's look at the different types of built-in groups.

Built-In Groups

If a user is a member of a built-in group, that user has the ability to do what members of that group are allowed to do by default. This means that all members of the Administrators group have the rights, privileges, and permissions given to administrators, whereas members of the Guests group have only the abilities given to guests by default. Besides Administrators and Guests, which were explained earlier, several other built-in groups are available: Backup Operators, Power Users, Users, and Replicator.

Backup Operators

Members of the Backup Operators group can perform the following tasks:

♦ Back up files and folders on the computer regardless of the permissions assigned to those files

♦ Restore files and folders on the computer regardless of the permissions assigned to those files

♦ Log onto the computer locally

♦ Shut down the computer

♦ Bypass traverse checking (pass through folders for which they don't have permissions to access one for which they do).

Backup operators cannot change any security settings

Power Users

Members of the Power Users group can perform the following tasks:

♦ Create user accounts

♦ Modify and delete the accounts they create

♦ Create local groups

♦ Remove users from the local groups they've created

♦ Remove users from the Power Users, Users, and Guests groups

♦ Bypass traverse checking (pass through folders for which they don't have permissions to access one for which they do)

♦ Change the system time

♦ Remove a computer from a docking station

♦ Shut down the system

♦ Log onto the computer locally

Members of the Power Users group *cannot* do the following:

♦ Modify the Administrators group.

♦ Modify the Backup Operators group

♦ Take ownership of files

♦ Back up or restore directories

♦ Load or unload device drivers

♦ Manage security or auditing logs

Users

Members of the Users group can perform the following tasks:

♦ Run applications

♦ Use printers (network and local)

♦ Shut down the system

♦ Lock the workstation

♦ Create local groups

- Modify the groups they've created

- Bypass traverse checking (pass through folders for which they don't have permissions to access one for which they do)

- Remove a computer from a docking station

Members of the Users group *cannot* do the following:

- Share directories

- Share printers

Replicator

The Replicator group is used for directory replication functions and has only one member. This member is the domain user account used to log onto the Replicator services on the domain controller. Do not add any users to this group.

Warning
It is important to understand that administrators and members of the Administrators group have all of the rights and privileges mentioned in this section.

Adding Users to and Deleting Users from Built-In Groups

To add users to groups, you'll need to have administrator status. Once that has been achieved, consider the following scenario.

Scenario

Three new employees have just been hired in your small but up-and-coming organization. This brings the total number of employees to seven (including yourself). Currently, you don't have any groups configured. You are an administrator. You would like to make two of the three new employees users with standard user rights and privileges while also making one of them a backup operator. The other three employees are also users, and one of them needs to be able to create additional user and group accounts for other employees as they are hired. You would like to place these employees into their respective built-in groups to simplify management.

To summarize, you have the following employees:

- One administrator

- Six users who should be members of the Users group

- One user who should also be a backup operator (Backup Operators group)

- One user who should also be able to create user and group accounts (Power Users group)

To make these users members of their respective groups, you'll need to continue through the next example.

Adding a User to a Built-In Group

To add one of the users to the Users group:

1. Log on as an Administrator.

2. Open the Computer Management console.

3. In the left pane, expand Local Users And Groups, as shown in Figure 3.5.

4. In the left pane, double-click Groups, as shown in Figure 3.5.

5. Double-click the Users group in the right pane.

6. Choose Add.

7. In the Select Users dialog box, which is shown in Figure 3.6, type the name of the user account you have previously created, or type "administrator".

8. Choose Check Names.

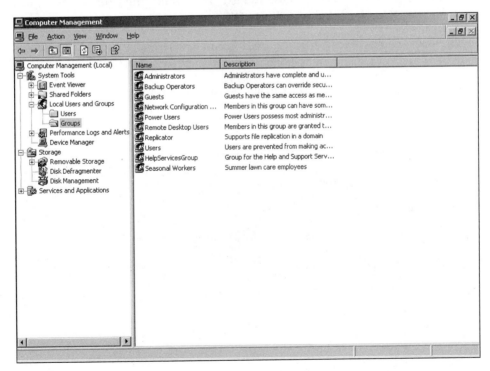

Figure 3.5
Local Users And Groups in the Computer Management console.

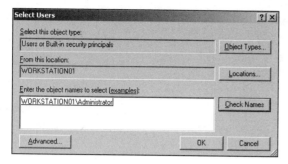

Figure 3.6
Adding users to a group.

Tip

If you get another dialog box stating that the user isn't found, make sure you've typed the name as it is shown in the logon screen.

9. Repeat Steps 7 and 8 until all employees who are to be users have been added. Choose OK twice.

10. To verify that the correct users were added, double-click the Users folder in the right pane again. Check the list, and choose OK.

To add a user who is a member of the Users group to a second group, you would perform these steps again using a different group name.

Besides using the Groups folder, you can also add a user to a group by using the Users folder. The next example walks you through this method. The result is the same, but you might prefer one way to the other.

To add a user to a group by using the Users folder:

1. Log on as an Administrator.

2. Open the Computer Management console.

3. In the left pane, expand Local Users And Groups, as shown in Figure 3.5.

4. In the left pane, double-click the Users folder.

5. Select the Member Of tab.

6. Choose Add.

7. Type the name of a group to which the user does not yet belong, such as Guest or Power Users.

8. Choose Check Names. Choose OK.

If you get an error here or are given an additional dialog box, make sure you've spelled the names of the groups correctly. For instance, typing "power user" instead of "power users" will bring up a Name Not Found dialog box, as shown in Figure 3.7.

9. From the <username> Properties dialog box, you can see the groups to which a user belongs. See Figure 3.8.

10. Choose OK.

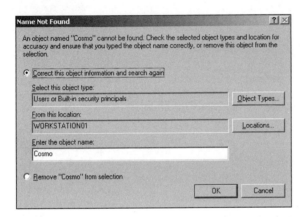

Figure 3.7
Name not found.

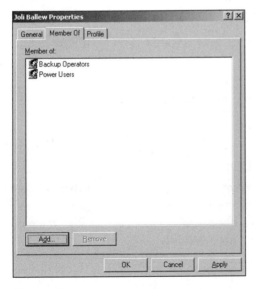

Figure 3.8
Member properties.

Deleting a User from a Built-In Group

Just as there are two ways to add members to groups, there are two ways to delete them from groups. You can delete members from groups by using the Groups folder in the Computer Management console or by using the Users folder in the Computer Management console.

To delete a group by using the Groups folder:

1. Log on as an Administrator.

2. Open the Computer Management console.

3. In the left pane, expand Local Users And Groups, as shown in Figure 3.5.

4. In the left pane, double-click Groups, as shown in Figure 3.5.

5. Double-click the group that has the member you want to remove from the group.

6. Highlight the user to remove in the Users Properties dialog box.

7. Click Remove and then click on OK.

To delete a group by using the Users folder:

1. Log on as an administrator.

2. Open the Computer Management console.

3. In the left pane, expand Local Users And Groups, as shown in Figure 3.5.

4. In the left pane, double-click the Users folder.

5. In the right pane, double-click the user whom you want to remove from a group.

6. Select the Member Of tab.

7. Highlight the group you no longer want the user to be a member of.

8. Click Remove and then click on OK.

Creating and Deleting Groups

One way to go about managing users is to create your own groups to put them in. Keep in mind that you can also place users in built-in groups as mentioned earlier, and using built-in groups reduces management tasks. However, if the built-in groups do not suit your purposes and needs, creating your own groups is certainly an option.

In the next example, you'll create a group called Seasonal Workers. The rest of this section will be based on this group and its members. To create a group:

1. Log on as an Administrator.

2. Open the Computer Management console.

3. In the left pane, expand Local Users And Groups.

4. In the left pane, double-click the Groups folder.

5. In the right pane, right-click an empty place in the pane, and choose New Group.

6. Type a name and description for the group. (I'll type "Seasonal Workers" for the group name.)

7. Choose Create.

8. Choose Close, and locate the new group in the right pane of the Computer Management console. (See Figure 3.9.)

There are a few rules for creating group names. A local group name cannot be the same as any other group name or username on the local computer, and the name cannot contain more than 256 characters. It also cannot include any of the following characters: ", /, \, [,], :, ;, |, =, +, *, ?, <, >. These characters should also not be used in usernames.

You can delete a group by right-clicking that group in the Computer Management console and choosing Delete. See Figure 3.9.

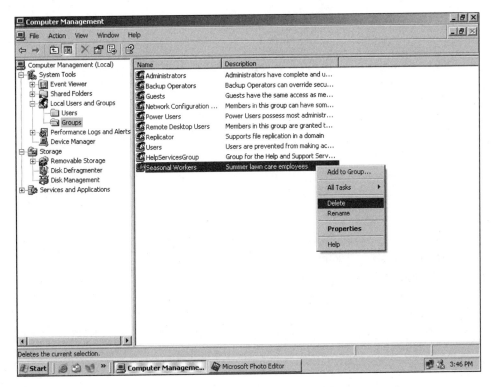

Figure 3.9
Deleting a group.

Adding Users to Personalized Groups

To make the group functional, you'll need to add a user (or users) to the group. In the following example, I'll introduce how to add users to a new personalized group. Before starting, you'll need to create three new user accounts named Temp1, Temp2, and Temp3, as well as a group called Seasonal Workers (or any names of your choice). You can create these user accounts through the Control Panel | User Accounts icon or through the Computer Management console. To create a user account from this console, see the sidebar.

To add new users to the group Seasonal Workers:

1. Log on as an Administrator.

2. Open the Computer Management console.

3. In the left pane, expand Local Users And Groups

4. In the left pane, double-click the Groups folder.

5. Double-click the group you want to add users to (in my case, Seasonal Workers).

6. Choose Add.

7. Type the names of the workers (the users), separated by semicolons, or type their usernames separated by semicolons.

8. Choose Check Names. If you made errors while typing the names, try again.

9. Choose OK.

Another Approach for Creating New User Accounts—Using the Computer Management Console

To create a new user account from inside the Computer Management console:

1. Log on as an administrator.

2. Open the Computer Management console.

3. In the left pane, expand Local Users And Groups.

4. In the left pane, double-click the Users folder.

5. Choose Action|New User, or, from an empty space in the right pane, right-click and choose New User.

6. In the New User dialog box, shown in Figure 3.10, type the username, full name, description, and password; confirm the password; and make the appropriate decisions for the password. (Only the User Name field is mandatory.)

7. Choose Create.

8. Repeat the process for all new users; then choose Close.

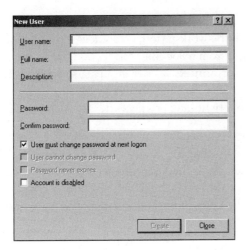

Figure 3.10
New User dialog box, opened from the Computer Management console.

10. As shown in Figure 3.11, notice the new employees now listed in the Seasonal Workers Properties dialog box. Choose OK.

Personalized Groups and Their Rights and Privileges

Now that you have created some user accounts and groups, and you have put those users into groups, how do you manage what those specific groups can do? If the users were placed in built-in groups, you don't have to do anything because those groups have automatic

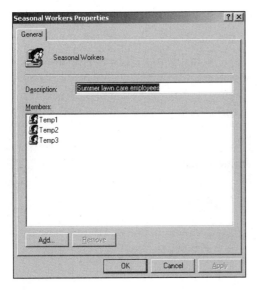

Figure 3.11
Adding members to a group.

limits placed on them. For instance, members of the built-in Users group can run applications, use printers, shut down the system, lock the workstation, create local groups, modify the groups they've created, remove a computer from a docking station, and bypass traverse checking, but they cannot share directories or printers. Other groups also have specific access privileges, as mentioned in previous sections. So what about a group that you've created, such as the Seasonal Workers group? What rights and privileges does its members have?

By default, the members of the Seasonal Workers group (or any other newly created group) are also members of the Users group. This means that the members of this group have the same rights and privileges that the regular users do. If the Users group offers more access to the computer than you'd like these employees to have, you have several options. One of the easiest options is to remove those users from the Users group and add them to a more restrictive group such as the Guests group.

To verify that the new users are indeed members of both the Seasonal Workers (or your personalized) group and the Users group:

1. Log on as an Administrator.

2. Open the Computer Management console.

3. In the left pane, expand Local Users And Groups

4. In the left pane, double-click the Users folder.

5. Double-click one of the users who is a member of the newly created group. In our example, this would be Temp1.

6. Select the Member Of tab of the user's Properties dialog box. Notice which groups the user is a member of. See Figure 3.12.

7. To remove the user from the Users group, you can highlight the Users group in this box and choose Remove. However, you'd have to perform this step for each temporary employee. There is a faster and more efficient way shown in the next example. Choose Cancel.

Changing a User's Group Membership

There are several ways to change a user's group memberships, and one way was introduced in the previous example. However, if you know which users belong to which groups, you can make these changes in a group's Properties dialog box, accessed through the Computer Management console.

To remove members of the Users group:

1. Log on as an Administrator.

2. Open the Computer Management console.

3. In the left pane, expand Local Users And Groups.

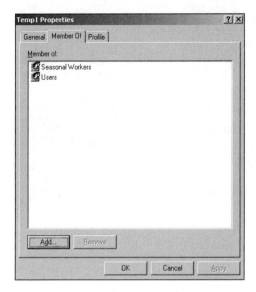

Figure 3.12
Group membership.

4. In the left pane, double-click the Groups tab.

5. Double-click the group that contains memberships that need to be changed. In this ongoing example, that is the Users group because members of the new group (Seasonal Workers) have also been placed in there.

6. Highlight the user who needs to be removed, and choose Remove. Repeat this step for all users who should be removed from this group.

7. Choose OK.

To place users in a group such as the Guests group:

1. Log on as an Administrator.

2. Open the Computer Management console.

3. In the left pane, expand Local Users And Groups.

4. In the left pane, double-click the Groups tab.

5. Double-click the group that contains memberships that need to be changed. In this ongoing example, choose the Guests group.

6. Choose Add.

7. Type the names of the users who need to be added to this group (in this example, Temp1, Temp2, and Temp3).

8. Choose Check Names, and make any necessary corrections.

9. Choose OK.

10. Notice that the new members are listed in the Guests Properties dialog box. Choose OK.

Verifying the Group Membership Change

You should, although this an optional step, make sure that the group membership change was applied correctly. For our continuing example, compare the group memberships shown in Figure 3.13 to those shown in Figure 3.12.

To verify that the membership was indeed changed:

1. Log on as an Administrator.

2. Open the Computer Management console.

3. In the left pane, expand Local Users And Groups.

4. In the left pane, double-click the Users folder.

5. Double-click one of the users who is a member of the new group. In our example, this user would be Temp1.

6. Select the Member Of tab. Notice which groups the user belongs to.

To sum up, when a new group is created, such as the Seasonal Workers group, and users are added to the group, those users are also added to the Users group. The Users group might be

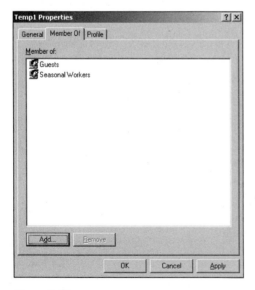

Figure 3.13
A successful membership change.

appropriate for the general user accounts added to a computer, but in the case of temporary workers, it was too lenient. To solve this problem, the temporary workers were removed from the Users group and added to the Guests group. Now these users have the rights and privileges of the more restrictive group, Guests. The opposite could also be true. If the new group were named Associate Administrators, you might want to add those users to the Power Users group as well as to the Users group so that they would have better access to their computers and to others.

As was mentioned earlier, changing a user's group membership is one of the easiest ways to limit a user's access. However, there are other ways. In the next section, you'll learn about group policies and local and account policies.

Group, Local, and Account Policies

In this last section, I'll introduce group policies, local policies, and account polices. Each of these policies performs different security functions. Let's start with group policies.

Group Policies

Group policies are configured by an administrator and are used to specify how users' desktops will look and what they will and will not contain. A group policy object—created by the administrator through the Group Policy snap-in—is the instrument for configuring these desktop settings. A *snap-in* is a tool that can be added to a Microsoft Management Console (see Chapter 1).

Administrators can create group policies to secure both domains and workstations. If your Windows XP Professional computer is a workstation in a domain, then your desktop probably has some limits placed there by a domain administrator and domain group policies. If that is the case, domain group policies will override local group policies, causing the configured local policies to be ignored. However, if you are in a workgroup, and/or multiple users access your computer or others, you can create a local group policy for security.

The Group Policy Snap-In
In Chapter 1, you learned how to create an MMC console and add snap-ins. To configure a group policy, you'll need to create an MMC console and add the Group Policy snap-in. When prompted to choose the group policy object, select Local Computer. Note that you can also choose Browse to select another computer in the workgroup. If you are an administrator in a workgroup, this can come in pretty handy. When you're finished, save the new console as "Group Policy Console".

With the Group Policy console created, you can now select settings to configure the users' desktops. In the following example, you'll see some of the group policy configuration options, and you'll see just how powerful a group policy can be. To begin, make sure you are logged on as an administrator.

In this example, you will create a group policy and save it to the Group Policy console. With this policy, you'll remove all icons from the desktop and change the title bar of Internet Explorer to include your name or your company's name. Then, you'll log on with the temporary account configured earlier (or any other user account) and see that there are no icons on the desktop. While logged on, you can also try to access the MMC and change the settings. Finally, you'll log back on as an administrator. You'll be able to see how the group policy can be used to regulate a user or group account.

Making Group Policies Work

In the next two exercises, you'll create a group policy and then verify that the policy has taken effect.

To create a group policy:

1. Log on as an administrator.

2. Open the Group Policy console by choosing Start | Programs | Administrative Tools | Group Policy Console. (This MMC console must be created using the Group Policy snap-in. For more information, see Chapter 1 and the previous few paragraphs.)

3. Expand the Local Computer Policy tree.

4. Expand the User Configuration tree.

5. Expand the Windows Settings tree.

6. Expand the Internet Explorer Maintenance tree.

7. Double-click the Browser User Interface folder as shown in Figure 3.14.

8. In the right pane, right-click the Browser Title folder and choose Properties.

9. Check the Customize Title Bars checkbox.

10. In the Title Bar Text checkbox, type your name or your company's name. Choose OK.

11. Expand the Administrative Templates folder, which is located at the bottom of the console tree.

12. Click the Desktop folder.

13. In the right pane, right-click Hide All Icons On Desktop.

14. Choose Properties.

15. Choose Enabled and then OK.

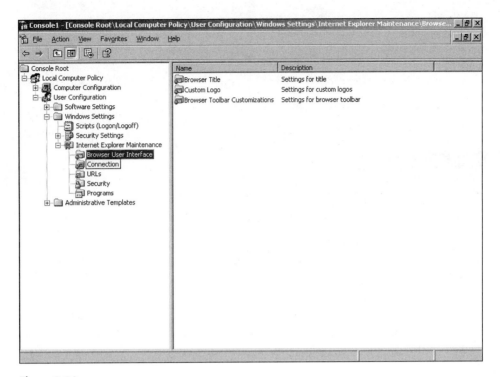

Figure 3.14
The Group Policy console.

If this is your first time seeing the Group Policy options, expand the other trees in the console's left pane, and read the options available for configuration in the right pane. You might find some other items to change for the Guest account.

16. Choose File | Save.

17. Close the Group Policy console.

To log on using the temporary account and verify that the group policy has taken effect:

1. Choose Start | Shut Down.

2. In the What Do You Want The Computer To Do box, select Log Off Administrator.

3. When logging back on, type "Temp1" for the User Name. If you've created a password for this account, type it in also. Choose OK.

4. Notice that the desktop has no icons. Choose Start | More Programs | Internet Explorer. Notice the title bar.

5. Try to access Administrative Tools from Programs. Notice that those tools aren't available.

5. Choose Start I Log Off, and log back on as administrator.

6. Notice that there are no icons on the administrator's desktop either.

7. Open Internet Explorer (choose Start I Programs I Internet Explorer). Notice the title bar.

8. Repeat Steps 2 through 17 in the previous example, changing Enabled to Not Configured to return the system to its previous state.

Note

When working through these steps, if you had logged on as a guest, you would have noticed that none of these changes took effect for that account.

Local Policies

Local policies are configured for computers. Any local policy that is configured affects every person who logs on to the computer. There are three types of configurable local policies: audit policies, user rights assignments, and security options. Although local policies have several good uses, an especially good one is to set strong local policies for computers that are accessed by the public or by several users or that are located in an open area such as a mechanic's garage or a mall. Local policies can be used to prevent disasters no matter who logs on or why.

Audit Policies

Auditing is a way to keep track of events that take place on the local computer. Several items can be audited, and in my experience, it is useful to audit at least a few of these so that when problems occur, you have a place to start when looking for a solution. Consider the following types of events that can be audited:

♦ Account logons

♦ Account management

♦ Directory service access

♦ Logon events

♦ Object access

♦ Policy changes

♦ Privilege use

♦ Process tracking

♦ System events

I would suggest auditing logon events (both successes and failures). If there is a high number of failed logon attempts, you might suspect that someone is trying to hack into your system.

Also, if these failed logon attempts occur when the office is closed, even more suspicions should arise. You can also audit policy changes. If there is only one administrator, any change to a policy that was not created by that administrator should be noted. Finally, you might choose to audit object access, especially if you suspect that some objects (such as printers) are being accessed too frequently.

As you can see, many auditing options are available, but understand that auditing too many items for too long will put a strain on the system, not only with CPU use but also with hard drive space. Choose your auditing carefully, and when you need to audit specific events for only a short period of time, turn the auditing of those events off when the problem is solved. You can view audit logs from Event Viewer in Administrative Tools. Event Viewer will be detailed in Chapter 12.

User Rights Assignment

Throughout this chapter, I've talked about user rights and privileges. You know, for instance, that only administrators can load and unload device drivers, and by default, no other group of users can do that. Although I would not suggest doing so, you can change which groups can perform what tasks through the User Rights Assignment area of Local Policies. Figure 3.15 shows most of the user rights that can be configured in this way.

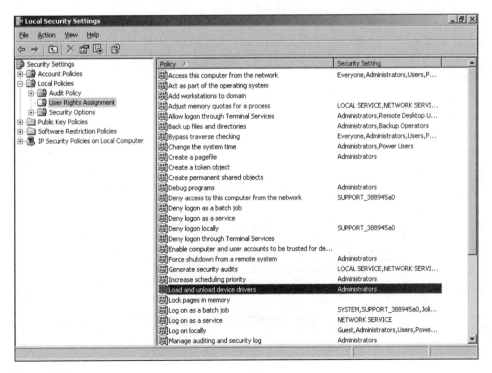

Figure 3.15
User rights assignments for local policies.

To configure a specific user right, simply double-click the right you want to change, choose Add from the Properties dialog box, and type the name of the user or group that you want to have this right. Again, let me stress that changing the default behavior of these user rights is *not* a good idea. It makes troubleshooting permissions problems more difficult, and it causes the system to act differently than it would normally. In addition, if you ever had to call Microsoft for help or hire an outside consultant, you'd have to make sure to inform them of this change or any others made here.

Security Options

You can also change security options for local policies, and doing so is far less disruptive to the system than changing user rights is. Figure 3.16 shows some of the security options and their default settings.

As you can see, Figure 3.16 shows one option highlighted: "Interactive Logon: Do Not Require CTRL+ALT+DEL." This is always the first thing I change when I get a new system because my network is safe from intruders and doesn't require such a measure. To change this setting so that you don't have to press Ctrl+Alt+Del each time you log onto your computer, double-click this setting and change it to Enabled. Figure 3.17 shows the resulting dialog box.

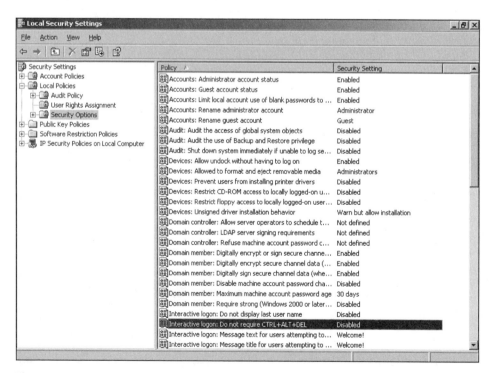

Figure 3.16
Security options for local policies.

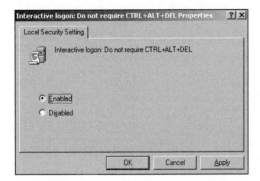

Figure 3.17
Changing a security setting.

Some other security options deserve a second look, and some you've seen before. For instance, the second option in the Policy column concerns the Guest account status. You can disable the Guest account from here. Other items of interest include:

♦ Rename the Administrator account

♦ Rename the Guest account

♦ Prevent users from installing printer drivers

♦ Do not display last user name (when multiple users log onto a single computer)

♦ Message text for users who attempt to log on (you can type in your own text)

♦ How soon to prompt a user for changes before the password expires

♦ Disconnect clients when logon hours expire

♦ Let Everyone permissions apply to anonymous users

♦ Allow automatic administrative logon

♦ Allow system to be shut down without logging on

Of course, many more options are available, as you can see from Figure 3.16, but generally, most of the defaults work fine and are appropriate.

Account Policies

Account policies are configured for users and user accounts. Account policies always affect users no matter what computer they log onto. In a domain, an administrator configures account policies for users in the domain, but on a Windows Professional workstation, the policy affects only the users who log onto the computer for which the policy is configured. If a local policy exists as well as a policy for an organizational unit or a domain, and if the policies conflict, the local policy will be overridden.

Password Policies

Six (and possibly seven) password policies can be configured for users who access the local computer. These policies are:

◆ *Enforce Password History*—Windows XP can remember up to 24 past passwords for a user account so that the old passwords cannot be reused.

◆ *Maximum Password Age*—Specify how many days a specific password can be used before it has to be changed by the user. This number can range from 1 to 999. A value of 0 can also be assigned so that the password never expires.

◆ *Minimum Password Age*—Specify how many days a specific password must be used before it can be changed. This number can range from 1 to 999, or a value of 0 can be set so that the password can be changed as often as desired.

◆ *Minimum Password Length*—Specify how many characters the password must contain. A password can have from 1 to 14 characters, or you can set this to 0 so that blank passwords can be used.

◆ *Password Must Meet Complexity Requirements*—If this setting is enabled (it isn't by default), the user's password cannot contain any part of the username, must be at least six characters long, and must contain uppercase and lowercase letters, at least one number from 0 to 9, and a non-alphanumeric character such as !, $, #, or %.

◆ *Store Password Using Reversible Encryption For All Users In The Domain*—By default, this setting is disabled for both local and domain users. Generally, the default setting should not be changed because doing so essentially stores the user's password as plain text.

◆ *Network Access: Force Network Logons Using Local Accounts To Authenticate As Guest*—Specify whether a local account that connects directly to a computer on the network must authenticate as a guest. If this setting is enabled, all local accounts that attempt to connect to the local computer are limited to Guest permissions. This policy is used only when a network is part of a domain.

Setting stronger policies than the defaults can further secure your computer. Defaults will differ depending on what type of network your Windows XP Professional machine is a member of. To see your defaults, follow the steps in the section "Changing Local or Account Policies."

Account Lockout Policies

Three account lockout policies are available. An account lockout is a security measure that monitors how many times a specific user tries to log on and fails. Depending on the settings, this user will be locked out either until an administrator intervenes or for a specific period of time. This security measure is designed to thwart hackers and password-breaking programs from repeatedly trying passwords to break into a computer. These programs can submit dictionary-type attacks in which all words in the dictionary are used, and they are very good at finding passwords when there is unlimited access.

The account lockout policies are:

♦ *Account Lockout Threshold*—Used to set how many bad password attempts can be made before the account is locked out. This can be a number from 1 to 999 or can be set to 0 to ensure that the account will never be locked out. Failed logons from password-protected screensavers or from intentionally locking the computer using Ctrl+Alt+Del do not count against this threshold number. By default, the setting is not configured.

♦ *Account Lockout Duration*—Used to set how many minutes the account will be locked out after the account lockout threshold has been met. The range is from 1 to 99,999 minutes. You can also set the account lockout duration to 0. This setting must be greater than or equal to the reset account counter (described next). By default, this setting does not have meaning because an account lockout value must be set for an account lockout duration to be needed.

♦ *Reset Account Lockout Counter After*—Used to set the number of minutes that must pass after a user is locked out of an account before the bad logon attempt counter is reset to 0. By default, this setting does not have meaning because an account lockout value must be set for the reset counter to be needed. The time configured here must be less than or equal to the account lockout duration, and it can be from 1 to 99,999 minutes. It can also be set to 0.

Kerberos Policies

Kerberos policies are available only to Windows XP Professional computers that are part of a domain. Kerberos policies are not available in workgroups. Kerberos is an authentication mechanism that is used to verify users and other entities, and it requires a domain controller. If you are a member of a domain, your domain administrator has configured a Kerberos policy for all users. These policies include the following:

♦ User logon restrictions

♦ Lifetime for a service ticket

♦ Lifetime for a user ticket

♦ Lifetime for ticket renewal

♦ Tolerance for computer clock synchronization

These settings are made domain-wide and cannot be changed by local policies or used in a workgroup.

Changing Local or Account Policies

To change the local or account policies on a local computer:

1. After logging on as an administrator, open the Local Security Settings console by choosing Start | Programs | Administrative Tools | Local Security Policy. (Or you can open Administrative Tools from the Control Panel.)

2. Expand the Account Policies tree.

3. Expand the Local Policies tree.

4. Choose the policy you want to change: Password, Account Lockout, Audit, User Rights Assignment, or Security Options.

5. Double-click the policy in the right pane.

6. Use the Properties dialog box to change the setting for the policy.

7. Choose OK.

8. Repeat Steps 4 through 7 until all policies you want to change have been configured.

9. Close the Local Security Settings console.

Wrapping Up

In this chapter, you learned how to create and modify user accounts and groups. You learned about the built-in user accounts and groups, how to use the built-in accounts safely, and how to place users that you've created into those built-in groups. You learned about the rights and privileges that come along with groups and special users, including administrators, backup operators, power users, users, and guests. You also learned how to use and apply group policies and local and account policies.

Although there is a lot more you can do with users and groups, this is a good start. As you work with the user accounts in your workgroup or those who access your computer, you'll see more and more things that you can do. To read more on the subject of permissions, shared folders, printers, and managing users and computers, skip to Chapter 10.

Chapter 4
Printing and Faxing

Whether you are the administrator of a standalone computer, a member of a small workgroup, or a member of a domain in a larger organization, you'll need to print. Printing is as essential as emailing or using a word processing program. In this chapter, I'll cover all of the aspects of printing that you'll need to know to survive in whatever situation you find yourself in.

The first section of this chapter covers installing a printer that is attached directly to the local computer, installing a printer that is shared in a workgroup, connecting a client to a shared workgroup printer, and installing and connecting to a network printer in a domain. These installations will include the physical installation as well as the printer software installation. In the second section, you'll learn how to configure and use the printer, from adding a new ink cartridge to troubleshooting printing problems. Finally, faxing will be covered. In this section, I'll assume you have a fax-modem or can access a physical fax machine locally or from a network.

Installing Printers

To use a printer, you must first have one installed. Printers of different models, such as Hewlett-Packard, Lexmark, or Canon, are all installed basically the same way. However, different *types* of printers are not. There are several ways to configure printers: local, shared, and network.

A *local printer* is a printer that is usually installed by plugging it into the back of a computer through the LPT1 or USB port. The printer is local to the computer, and if it is a standalone computer, the printer is used for only this computer and its users.

A *shared printer* is an extension of the local printer. When a group of computers are connected via a hub, as in a small home network or small business office, one or more computers in the workgroup can have locally connected printers. Those printers can be used by people who are not at the local computer (if they have the appropriate permissions to do so).

A *network printer* is a member of a domain, much like a computer is. A network printer is an entity that network users can access (again, with the correct permissions) to print documents. In a network, a printer is sometimes installed locally, but typically, it is connected to a print server or is part of a pool of printers. A large network can have many printers. These printers can be configured so that some users can print to certain printers, while others cannot. In very large organizations, a print operator is hired to maintain these printers.

Installing a Local Printer

Installing a local printer is the most basic type of installation. With Windows XP Professional, installing a printer is even easier due to the inclusion of many printer drivers, one of which will most likely match the printer you need to install. A *printer driver* is a piece of software that comes with the printer. The driver is located on an accompanying floppy disk or CD. This driver must be installed so that the operating system can work with the printer. After reading the manufacturer's instructions, perform the following steps:

1. Shut down the computer from the Start menu.

2. Plug the printer cable into the back of the computer. The cable might plug into the LPT1 port, a USB port, or another type of device. Follow the manufacturer's instructions.

3. Plug the printer's power cable into an outlet.

4. Turn the computer back on.

5. If the new printer is plug-and-play (and most everything is these days), you'll see a screen similar to that shown in Figure 4.1.

The next step is to install the driver for the printer. See "Driver Installation," next, or, if you did not see a screen similar to Figure 4.1, skip to "Troubleshooting Printer Installations" at the end of this section.

Driver Installation

There are several ways to install the printer driver, and this step is often performed automatically by Windows XP Professional. If Windows XP recognizes the new printer, then you'll see a screen telling you that. For example, Figure 4.2 shows the first screen displayed for a Lexmark 5700 printer.

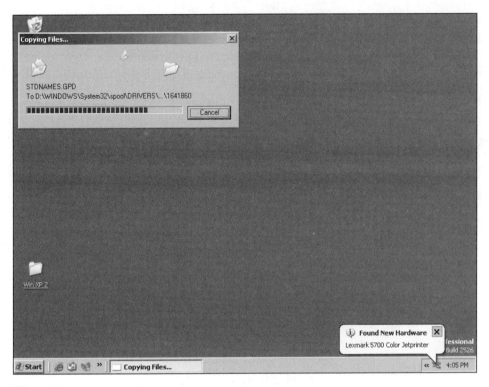

Figure 4.1
Found new hardware.

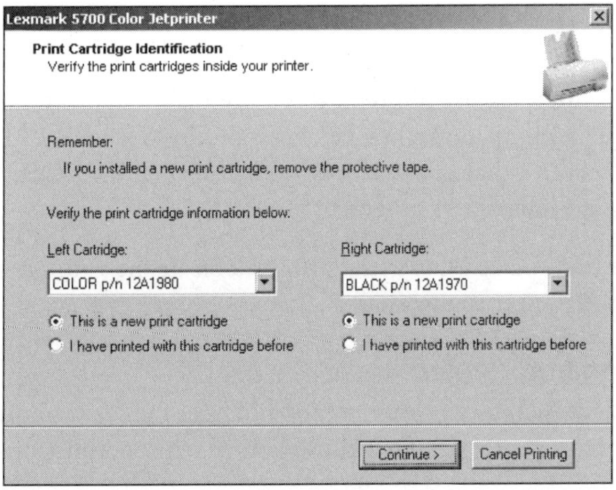

Figure 4.2
Sample printer installation.

The screen you'll see when you install a printer could be quite different from this one. Differences could arise if the printer is newer or older or if the printer is not supported in Windows XP. Some newer printers may simply have to have their ink cartridges aligned, and that's it. Work through these screens as they are offered to complete the driver installation.

If you were unable to load the driver because Windows XP does not support the printer, if drivers have to be installed from a floppy disk or CD-ROM, or if the driver is outdated or doesn't work properly, skip to the section "Troubleshooting Printer Installations."

Installing a Shared Printer

A shared printer that will be used in a workgroup is installed the same way a local printer is, except for the way it is configured. After the printer is installed, sharing it is as simple as right-clicking it and making it available to others in the workgroup. Then you can specify who you want to share the printer with and what permissions they have for accessing it.

To share a printer that has been installed locally to a Windows XP Professional machine that is part of a workgroup:

1. Log on as an administrator, or at least with rights and privileges to share a printer.

2. Open the Control Panel from either the Start menu or My Computer.

3. Double-click the Printers And Faxes icon.

4. Right-click the printer to be shared with others in the workgroup, and choose Sharing.

5. On the Sharing tab of the printer's property sheet, notice that the Not Shared option is selected by default. Select Share Name instead.

6. Type a name for the shared printer; for my printer, I'll use the name "Workstation01 Printer." Because this name is long, it might not be accessible from some MS-DOS workstations, as noted by the resulting dialog box. If your workgroup has MS-DOS workstations, consider a name of eight characters or fewer.

7. Notice that a hand icon has been placed under the printer icon in the Printers And Faxes folder, signifying that the printer is now shared.

Setting Permissions for the Shared Printer

When a workgroup shares an object such as a printer, folder, file, scanner, or other item, several default permissions are set automatically. For printers, the default permissions are as follows:

♦ All administrators in the workgroup can print documents, manage printers, and manage documents. Managing printers and their documents includes such tasks as installing new drivers for the printer, changing permissions for users who access the printer, and stopping, pausing, and deleting documents in the print queue.

- The CREATOR OWNER can manage documents.

- Everyone in the workgroup can print to the printer.

- Power users in the workgroup can print documents, manage printers, and manage documents.

Usually, the first thing you should do is remove the ability of everyone in the workgroup to print to the printer, and the same is true when files or folders are shared. The problem with everyone having the ability to print is that the printer isn't appropriately controlled. For example, you might not want to allow guests on the network to print, or, if more than one printer is installed, you might decide to allow one group to print to an inkjet printer while another group prints to a laser printer. Once the Everyone group has been removed, you can then add groups who can use the printer. You might choose to add a built-in group that contains users, or add personalized groups like the Seasonal Workers group created in Chapter 3.

To set permissions for your installed and shared local workgroup printer:

1. As an administrator, log onto the workgroup computer that has the printer installed locally and shared.

2. Open the Control Panel.

3. Open the Printers And Faxes folder.

4. Right-click the shared printer. Scroll down to Properties, but do *not* click Properties yet.

5. Press and hold the Ctrl key, and then choose Properties.

6. Select the Security tab.

Note
You won't be able to see the Security tab if you do not follow Steps 4 and 5 exactly. The Security tab is hidden unless you are also holding down the Ctrl key when choosing Properties.

7. Highlight the Everyone group, and choose Remove.

8. Choose Add.

9. In the Name box, type a username like "Temp1" or a group name like "Seasonal Workers" or "Users". For multiple entries, place a semicolon between each name.

10. Choose Check Names, and correct any mistakes.

11. Highlight Users; notice that they have the ability to print only. Highlight Seasonal Workers or Temp1 (or any other user or group added). Notice which permissions are allowed. For this example, we'll add the permission to manage printers, so highlight a user or group to whom you want to give this permission.

12. Check the Manage Printers checkbox for this user or group.

13. Choose OK.

Connecting to a Shared Printer in a Workgroup

After a printer has been installed and shared in a workgroup, other users can access the printer from other computers if those users have the correct permissions. If you accepted the default permissions for the printer, then everyone in the workgroup will at least be able to print. If you made changes, then only certain users will be allowed access.

To connect a Windows XP Professional computer to a shared printer installed in your workgroup:

1. As an administrator, log onto the computer that needs to be configured so that it can access a printer that is local to another computer.

2. Choose Start | Settings | Printers And Faxes | Add New Printer, or, from the Control Panel, open the Printers And Faxes folder and choose Add New Printer.

3. When the Add Printer Wizard appears, choose Next.

4. On the Local Network Or Printer page shown in Figure 4.3, select a Network Printer or A Printer Attached To Another Computer. Choose Next.

5. On the Specify A Printer page, choose Next to browse for a printer, or type the name of the printer in the form "\\computername\printername".

6. If you're browsing, select the printer that has been shared, and choose Next.

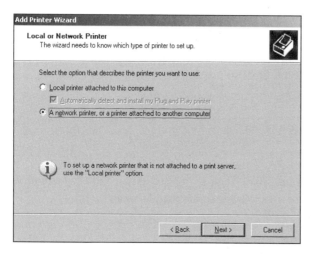

Figure 4.3
Local Or Network Printer page of the Add Printer Wizard.

7. On the Default Printer page, select Yes (or No) to make this printer the default printer (or not) for the local computer.

8. Choose Finish.

Installing a Network Printer in a Domain

Usually, a domain administrator or a print operator installs printers for a domain, and all the user has to do is connect to it through the network. Large networks install printers from print servers and configure them in printer pools. *Printer pools* are groups of printers that all use the same driver and are configured so that network clients can access them. *Print servers* are computers that are used to manage multiple printers from a single location. This type of physical installation probably won't be among your job duties.

However, if you are an administrator for a small domain, such as a domain for a home office or small business, you can still install a printer locally to the domain controller and then configure that printer for user access across your domain. In this section, we'll install a printer on a Windows 2000 server and then "share" it so that it can be accessed by the clients in the domain—in particular, Microsoft Windows XP Professional clients.

The Basics of Installing a Printer on a Domain Controller

If you are responsible for installing a printer on a domain controller and sharing it with clients on a network, the physical installation is the same as for a printer connected to standalone computer (described earlier). The differences in using a domain printer lie in sharing that printer and then connecting clients to it. When installing a printer on a domain controller, you are given the option of sharing the printer with others on the network. Choose Yes when prompted. Other scenarios, such as installing a printer via a print server or using a TCP/IP network connection, are beyond the scope of this chapter and book.

After the printer has been physically connected and appropriately shared, the members of the domain can access it to print documents if the permissions are left intact. Remember, when a printer is installed, everyone has permission to print.

Connecting a Client to a Network Printer

To connect a Windows XP Professional client to a printer installed locally on a domain controller or in a domain:

1. With rights and privileges to add printers and printer drivers, log onto the domain.

2. Open the Control Panel.

3. Open the Printers And Faxes folder.

4. Choose Add A Printer to launch the Add Printer Wizard. Choose Next.

5. Select A Network Printer Or A Printer Attached To Another Computer, and choose Next.

6. Choose Find Printer In The Directory, choose Next.

7. In the Find Printers dialog box, select the domain name from the In drop-down list. See Figure 4.4.

8. Choose Find Now, or type the name of the printer in the Name text box. See Figure 4.4. (The printer name must be written in this form: \\computername\printername.)

9. If you selected Find Now in Step 8, from the list of network printers shown in the resulting dialog box, select the printer to be added.

10. When prompted, specify whether this printer will act as the default printer for the local workstation. Choose Next.

11. Choose Finish in the Add Printer Wizard.

12. Print a test page. To do this, right-click the printer in the Printers And Faxes folder, choose Properties, and select Print Test Page from the General tab.

Note

Networks and network printers vary from model to model, and in some instances, you might be asked to download a printer driver from the network. This is usually very easy to do and must be done only once. If this is the case, follow the directions on your screen to install the new printer driver.

Troubleshooting Printer Installations

Several things can go wrong when a printer is first installed, and those problems usually stem from bad or outdated drivers or from older printers that Windows XP doesn't recognize as plug-and-play. When a printer is first installed, Windows XP displays the Found New Hardware bubble shown earlier in Figure 4.1. If this bubble isn't displayed, the printer has not been recognized and needs to be installed manually. Sometimes the Found New Hard-

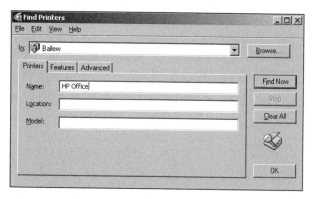

Figure 4.4
Add domain printer.

ware bubble is shown, but Windows XP does not have the driver for the printer in its driver database. In that case, you need to install the driver from the floppy disk or CD-ROM that came with the printer. In other instances, the driver supplied with the printer isn't new enough to work with Windows XP. For instance, a printer that was purchased with a Windows 95 machine more than a few years ago might not have come with a driver that will work with Windows XP. In those instances, you need to download an updated driver from the Internet.

Before moving forward with your troubleshooting efforts, go over the following checklist. Many times, the driver is not the problem; the physical connection is.

Have you:

♦ Plugged the printer into an electrical outlet?

♦ Made sure the electrical outlet is working?

♦ Connected the printer cable securely to the computer?

♦ Checked that the connections to the computer and printer are tight?

♦ Pushed in the USB connection firmly (if applicable)?

♦ Turned on the printer?

♦ Read all of the manufacturer's instructions?

♦ Put in the CD or floppy disk that came with the printer and waited for a program to run automatically?

♦ Rebooted your computer?

♦ Made sure you have permission to install a printer?

If you have checked all these things and still cannot get the printer installed, you'll need to move forward with your troubleshooting. The following three sections offer instructions to solve most printer installation problems. If you have not solved the problem after working through these suggestions, consider calling the printer manufacturer's help line.

Windows XP Did Not Detect Your Printer

If the Found New Hardware bubble isn't displayed after you physically install the printer, then Windows XP did not detect your printer. This is a common problem with older printers, although it happens less and less often with the newer Microsoft operating systems. If your printer was not detected automatically, then you'll need to install it manually.

To install a printer manually:

1. Log on as an administrator or at least with the permissions necessary to add a printer and install a printer driver.

2. Open the Control Panel.

3. Open the Printers And Faxes folder.

4. Choose Add Printer.

5. When the Add Printer Wizard appears, choose Next.

6. There are two choices for adding a printer; it's either a local printer or a network printer. Both scenarios have been detailed in this chapter. Network printers will be installed automatically in almost all instances, so in this example, I'll cover installing a local printer. Select the appropriate choice, and choose Next.

Note

If Windows XP did not find your locally installed printer when the computer was rebooted, the printer is not plug-and-play. The option Automatically Detect And Install My Plug And Play Printer can still be checked, though, and there is a slim chance that the printer could be detected this time.

7. When installing a printer locally, you'll see the Install Printer Software page shown in Figure 4.5. Select the appropriate manufacturer from the Manufacturers list box.

8. In the Printers list box, search for the model name and number of your printer. If it is listed, highlight it and choose Next. *If it is not listed, skip to the next section.*

9. Type a printer name. Select Yes if you want to make this printer the default printer.

10. On the Printer Sharing page, either select the option to share this printer, and type a name for the shared printer, or opt not to share the printer. Choose Next. The shared printer's name will be used to access the printer for other users on the network.

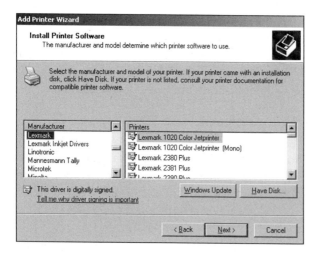

Figure 4.5
Installing printer software from within the Add Printer Wizard.

11. On the Location And Comment page, type optional information about the printer. Choose Next.

12. On the Print Test Page wizard page, choose Yes to print a test page.

13. After all the driver files have been copied, choose Finish.

Windows XP Prompts for a Driver from a Floppy Disk or CD-ROM

When you're manually installing a printer and printer driver, if the printer model isn't listed on the Install Printer Software page shown in Figure 4.5, you'll need to use the floppy disk or CD that came with the printer. If you've closed the Add Printer Wizard, perform Steps 1 through 8 again; otherwise, skip directly to Step 8.

1. Log on as an administrator or at least with the permissions necessary to add a printer and install a printer driver.

2. Open the Control Panel.

3. Open the Printers And Faxes folder.

4. Choose Add Printer.

5. When the Add Printer Wizard appears, choose Next.

6. There are two choices for adding a printer; it's either a local printer or a network printer. Both scenarios have been detailed in this chapter. Network printers will be installed automatically in almost all instances, so in this example, I'll cover installing a local printer. Select the appropriate choice, and choose Next.

7. When installing a printer locally, you'll see the Install Printer Software page shown in Figure 4.5. Select the appropriate manufacturer from the Manufacturers list box.

8. In the Printers list box, search for the model name and number of your printer. If it is listed, highlight it and choose Next. If it is not listed, choose Have Disk.

9. Place the floppy disk or CD into the correct drive, select the appropriate drive letter in the Copy Manufacturer's Files From dialog box, and choose OK.

10. On the Install Printer Software page, highlight the model of your printer, and choose Next.

11. Type a printer name. Select Yes if you want to make this printer the default printer.

12. On the Printer Sharing page, either select the option to share this printer, and type a share name, or opt not to share the printer. Choose Next.

13. On the Location And Comment page, type optional information about the printer. Choose Next.

14. On the Print Test Page wizard page, choose Yes to print a test page.

15. After the files have been copied, choose Finish.

No matter how hard you try, there will be times when the printer still won't install. Take a look at Figure 4.6. This is an error message you might see after choosing Finish from the Add Printer Wizard. I received this error message after trying to install an old printer with a Windows 95 driver.

When this happens, the driver you have won't work with Windows XP Professional. This doesn't necessarily mean that the printer won't work; it simply means that you'll need to get a newer driver.

Downloading New Drivers from the Manufacturer's Web Site

If you see the error message shown in Figure 4.6, and you've tried all of the troubleshooting tips listed in previous sections, you most likely need a new driver for your printer. There are many ways to obtain a more recent printer driver, and they range from calling the printer manufacturer's help line (if the manufacturer is still in business), to accessing the manufacturer's Web site, to finding a printer on the Internet from a third party such as **www.drivers.com**.

Of course, to access the Internet, you'll need to have an Internet connection configured. If you don't, you'll need to skip ahead to Chapter 9 to get this up and running. Your other option is to use a friend's computer to search for and download an appropriate driver. You can place this driver on a floppy disk or a Zip disk for transport.

After your computer is connected to the Internet, perform the following steps to search for a suitable driver:

1. Open Internet Explorer (choose Start | Programs | Internet Explorer).

2. Using the search engine of your choice—such as **www.yahoo.com**, **www.excite.com**, or **www.google.com**—type "printer drivers" in the search box.

3. Scroll through the search results, and look for your printer model. You can also type the name of your printer in the search box and go to the manufacturer's Web site. Either way, try to locate the manufacturer's Web site. Figure 4.7 shows the Lexmark Printer Drivers page.

4. Find the Drivers option or the Download option on the page, and fill in any required information (which sometimes includes registering with an email address or first and last name).

Figure 4.6
The "Unable To Install" error message.

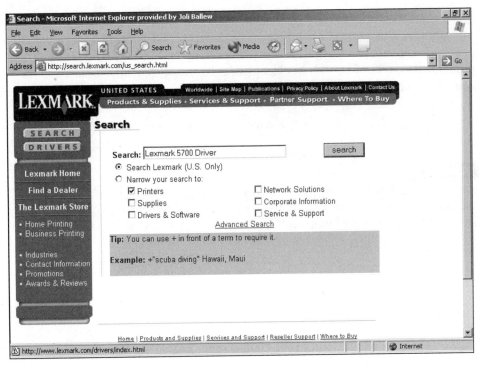

Figure 4.7
Downloading printer drivers.

5. Work through the pages (they'll differ depending on the site), and type the name and model number of your printer when prompted.

6. Choose the operating system when prompted.

7. Follow the steps to choose the driver. Then choose Download Now (or something similar), select Save To Disk, and note which folder the file is being saved in. (Sometimes you can specify the folder where you want to save the file.)

8. While the file is downloading, read the information on the Web site so that you can install the printer driver correctly. When the driver has finished downloading, choose Close. Then install the driver (see "Installing Downloaded Drivers").

Note

The printer driver for Lexmark 5700 is available in the Windows XP driver database, and this driver works correctly. This printer is used only as an example. You can also sign up to receive updated drivers from this Lexmark site when they are available.

Downloading a Driver from a Third-Party Site

I've found that if a suitable driver isn't available from the printer manufacturer's Web site, then a makeshift driver can usually be found from a third-party site. Although this is much riskier than obtaining a driver from the manufacturer's site, I've been pretty successful with these drivers. The purpose of third-party sites is to share information about drivers and the operating systems they work with. Sometimes a driver created for a fax-copier-scanner-printer will work just fine with an older piece of hardware that only prints. Also, these sites offer tips, such as noting that a certain printer and operating system work together only if the printer mode is ECP and is changed in the computer's BIOS. This can all get quite complex, as you can see, but there is a lot of information out there on the Internet, and it can be quite useful.

Warning

Don't install any third-party printer drivers on a computer that is critical to your welfare or business. Third-party drivers haven't been tested by Microsoft or the printer manufacturer, and they can bring a system down. Use third-party printer drivers only when there is no other option, and fully test them on a non-critical machine first.

To locate third-party driver sites and search for a printer driver:

1. Open Internet Explorer.

2. Using the search engine of your choice, type "drivers" in the search box; then look through the Web-page matches.

3. Look for well-established sites such as **www.WinDrivers.com**, **www.Drivers.com**, **www.DriverGuide.com**, and **www.DriverZone.com**.

4. Connect to a site, and type the name and model of your printer in its search box. Before deciding to download, read what others have said about the driver. Download the driver to a test machine, and install it.

Installing Downloaded Drivers

After you've downloaded the driver, you'll need to install it. If you've saved it to a floppy disk or a CD, you'll need to place that floppy disk or CD in the appropriate drive.

To install a printer using a downloaded printer driver:

1. Log on as an administrator or at least with the permission to install drivers.

2. In Windows Explorer or My Computer, open the folder in which you saved the downloaded printer driver. Make sure you've closed all open applications.

3. The driver might be saved in a self-extracting setup file. Double-click the application (printer driver).

4. If a screen appears with directions, follow them carefully.

5. Open the Control Panel.

6. Open Printers And Faxes.

7. Choose Add Printer.

8. Work through the Add Printer Wizard as described earlier. On the Install Printer Software page, choose Have Disk.

9. Choose the Browse button. Browse to the downloaded driver file. Highlight it and choose Open. Choose OK.

10. On the Install Printer Software page, highlight the printer name and model, and choose Next.

11. Continue through the rest of the wizard pages as described earlier.

Updating a Current Printer Driver

If a new driver becomes available after you've installed a printer, you can download the new driver from the Internet or obtain it from the manufacturer and install it from inside the printer's property sheet. You don't have to reinstall the printer; you just update its driver.

To update a driver for a locally installed printer:

1. Log on as an administrator or at least with permission to install a new driver.

2. Choose Start | Settings | Printers And Faxes, and right-click the printer name. Or open the Control Panel and Printers And Faxes, and right-click the printer name.

3. Choose Properties.

4. Select the Advanced tab. See Figure 4.8.

5. Choose the New Driver button. Choose Next when the Add Printer Driver Wizard appears.

6. Choose Have Disk.

7. Choose Browse, and locate the updated driver. Highlight the driver, and choose Open. Choose OK.

8. On the Install Printer Software page, highlight the printer name and model, and choose Next.

9. Continue through the rest of the wizard pages as described earlier. To print a test page to verify the installation, continue through Steps 10-11.

10. Select the General tab.

11. Choose Print Test Page.

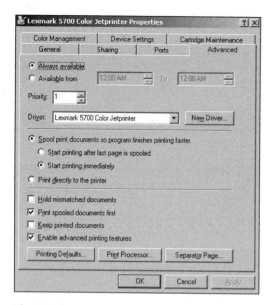

Figure 4.8
The Advanced tab of a printer's Properties dialog box.

Configuring and Using the Printer

After the printer has been installed, there are several options for configuring it. Because printing is such an integral part of business, it deserves a few pages dedicated to getting it set up correctly. In this section, I'll discuss how to add new printer cartridges, how to set printing preferences and defaults, how to pause, stop, and restart a printer, and how to troubleshoot printing problems. Configuration options also apply to domain (network) printers and can be set the same way. Keep in mind, though, that the majority of Windows XP Professional users in a domain will not have the permissions for managing a printer or managing documents and will be able only to print. Therefore, some of these options will not be available to network users.

Adding a Print Cartridge

One of the first things you will probably have to do when a new printer has been installed is add a new ink cartridge. This procedure varies from printer to printer. For some printers, changing the cartridge is just a physical task; for others, you also need to use the printer's Properties dialog box. When this is necessary, you can usually right-click the printer in Control Panel | Printers And Faxes to complete the task. These types of tasks include aligning the cartridges, cleaning the cartridges, and viewing the ink levels of the cartridges.

To install a new print cartridge for a locally installed ink jet printer, either follow the manufacturer's instructions or, if those are not available, perform the following steps:

Note

These instructions will vary depending on the type of printer that is installed. For best results, try to find and use the manufacturer's instructions.

1. Open the Control Panel.

2. Open Printers And Faxes.

3. Right-click the appropriate printer, and choose Properties.

4. Select the Cartridge Maintenance tab.

5. Choose Install/Change Cartridge.

6. Follow the directions on the screen. This task usually entails opening the printer cover and inserting the print cartridge. Make sure you remove the tape from the print cartridge before installing it.

7. Specify the cartridge installed, if necessary.

8. Choose Continue or OK.

9. Most ink jet printers will now print a test page for you to align the print heads. Follow the instructions on the screen.

10. Choose Finish or OK to verify the installation.

Setting Printing Preferences and Defaults

Several types of printing preferences and defaults can be set for your printers. Printing *preferences* are configured through applications such as Adobe Photo Deluxe or Microsoft Word. These preferences apply when those specific applications are used. Printing *defaults*, on the other hand, are configured for all users of the computer and apply unless printing preferences are set within an application. For instance, for a database application that is used only to print envelopes, you can set printing preferences to always print envelopes. The printer defaults for all of the users who access the printer can be set to print 8.5×11-inch paper. Of course, you'll need a printer with two trays to hold the different paper types!

Listed next are a majority of these printing preferences and defaults, with explanations of what each can be used to accomplish:

♦ *Portrait*—This is a paper orientation setting that prints vertically (from top to bottom) on the paper. This mode is typically the default.

♦ *Landscape*—This is a paper orientation setting that prints sideways (from left to right). This mode is often used to print spreadsheets, calendars, invoices, payroll, and such.

♦ *Page Order*—This setting allows the pages to be printed from front to back or from back to front. When you're printing large documents, consider printing them from back to front so that you don't have to place them in the correct order later.

♦ *Pages Per Sheet*—This setting is 1 by default, meaning that one page of a document will print on one piece of paper. For printers that can print more than one page per sheet, you can set this to 2 to print booklets or to conserve paper when you're printing rough drafts. When you print two (or more) pages side-by-side on one sheet of paper, the software automatically shrinks the pages to fit.

♦ *Paper Size*—Several paper sizes are usually available, including the standard letter size (8.5×11 inches), legal size (8.5×14 inches), A4 size (a European standard), and different envelopes, index cards, and postcards.

♦ *Print Quality*—Print quality is based on how many dots per inch (dpi) are used when printing a document or photo. The print quality will differ depending on the printer, but 300×300 and 600×600 resolutions are fairly common. The higher the print quality is set, the more ink or toner is used. To conserve on ink or toner, you can print at 300 dpi for rough drafts (some applications refer to the lower resolution as "draft output"), and save the higher resolution for final printouts.

♦ *Paper Source*—Some printers have several paper trays. If your printer has more than one tray, you can set the paper source to be selected automatically, always feed from the upper tray, or always feed from the lower tray. You can also choose to feed the paper through manually, if necessary. Sometimes, special papers such as transparencies or heat-transfer papers must be manually fed through the printer.

♦ *Media*—This refers to the type of paper. Generally, the medium is simply plain paper. But media can also be transparencies, glossy paper, iron-on or heat-transfer paper, coated paper, greeting card paper, banner paper, or even payroll papers or checks. If the printer you are configuring will be used to print only on transparencies, for instance, you can set this as the default.

♦ *Color*—The printer can usually be configured to print in black and white or (for color printers) in color.

♦ *Stapling, Collating, and More*—Depending, again, on the type of printer you have, you can specify how the printer will staple documents, collate documents, and more, from the appropriate dialog box tabs.

Changing Printer Defaults

You can change the printer defaults from the Control Panel | Printers And Faxes folder. These changes affect everyone who prints to the printer.

To change any of a printer's default settings:

1. Open the Control Panel.

2. Open Printers And Faxes.

3. Right-click the appropriate printer, and choose Properties.

4. On the General tab, select Printing Preferences.

5. Make changes as desired, and choose OK when you're done.

6. Choose Color Management (if available). Make changes as necessary.

7. Choose OK.

Changing Print Preferences from Inside an Application

You can change the print preferences from inside an application and override some (if not all) of the printing defaults mentioned earlier. Print preferences apply only to the application and do not permanently change the printer's default properties.

To change the printer preferences:

1. Open an application such as Microsoft Word or Internet Explorer.

2. Choose File | Print Preferences. Or, if the application does not have a Print Preferences command, choose File | Print.

3. In the Print dialog box, shown in Figure 4.9, select the appropriate printer from the Name drop-down list.

4. Choose the Properties button.

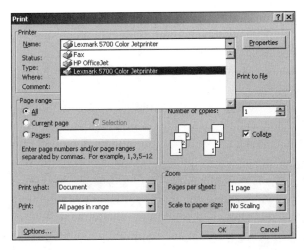

Figure 4.9
Print preferences.

5. Set the print properties for layout, page order, pages per sheet, stapling, collating, paper selection, quality settings, and color. Set print quality and document options as necessary. Choose OK.

6. In the Page Range area of the Print dialog box, select All, Current Page, or Pages; if you select Pages, type the numbers of the pages to be printed.

7. In the Print What drop-down list, select what is to be printed (typically, Document).

8. In the Print drop-down list, select an option for printing all pages, odd pages only, or even pages only.

9. In the Pages Per Sheet drop-down list, select how many pages will print on one sheet of paper. Select a scaling option if necessary.

10. Choose OK to print.

Depending on the application, some or all of these settings will be used the next time the Print command is used in the current work session. However, the settings will not be maintained with most applications once the application has been closed and then reopened, since printer settings override application settings. The application settings will not become the defaults for the local printer or for other users.

In addition to the settings shown in Figure 4.9, certain advanced print options can be set from inside an application. Figure 4.10 shows an example of these. The advanced settings for your printer might be more or less complex than the ones shown here.

Figure 4.10
Additional print preferences.

Pausing, Stopping, and Restarting Printers

If you have the job of managing the printers on your network, then you'll need to be able to pause, stop, and restart the printers. This can be done remotely from a Windows XP Professional machine or from a Windows XP server. For our purposes, I'll assume that you either have a locally installed printer or belong to a workgroup and manage printers for a group of users. Generally, a print operator or other domain member manages domain printers. However, even if you do belong to a domain and must perform these tasks yourself, they are performed in the same manner as the directions detailed next, except that you must first locate the printers in the domain using Windows XP's Active Directory and have the appropriate permissions in the domain to stop, start, or pause printing for all users.

Occasionally, a printer will need to be paused so that a paper jam can be cleared, paper can be added, or toner or ink cartridges can be replaced. Other problems can occur, of course, but these are the most common.

To open the Printer window for a printer:

1. Open the Control Panel.

2. Choose Settings | Printers And Faxes | *<printername>*.

It is through the print queues that printers are paused, stopped, and restarted. Other settings—such as printer sharing, default printer selection, and printer properties—can also be accessed through the print queues.

Pausing All Printing

If the print queue contains several documents waiting to be printed, you can pause printing for all jobs in the queue. Pausing a printer does not delete any print jobs in the queue; instead, pausing holds those documents until printing is resumed, restarted, or canceled.

To pause all print jobs in the queue, including the document currently being printed:

1. Log on with permissions to manage printers.

Note

You don't need to log on with manage printer permissions to pause, stop, restart, or resume your own document in the print queue; however, to pause, stop, restart, or resume other's documents, you must.

2. Open the Printer window. (Open the Control Panel, and choose Settings | Printers And Faxes | *<printername>*.)

3. Choose Printer | Pause Printing.

Pausing a Document

You can also pause printing for a single document. Figure 4.11 shows two documents in the print queue. The first document is printing, and the second document is paused.

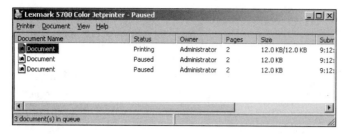

Figure 4.11
Pausing a print job.

Pausing the printing of a document does not delete the document from the queue. Instead, the document remains in the queue, as shown in Figure 4.11, until the job is resumed, restarted, or canceled.

To pause a document in the print queue:

1. Log on with permissions to manage printers (see note earlier).

2. Open the Printer window. (Open the Control Panel, and choose Settings | Printers And Faxes | <*printername*>.)

3. Highlight the document to be paused.

4. Choose Document | Pause.

Note

When all documents need to be paused, choose Printer|Pause Printing.

Resuming Printing

Once a document has been paused (or all print jobs have been paused), the document(s) will not print until the status has been changed to Resume, Restart, or Cancel. When resuming, the printer simply begins printing where it left off; it will begin in the middle of a document if that is where it was stopped.

Resuming is imperative to an administrator. Consider what would happen if a print administrator were printing paychecks and the printer needed a new toner cartridge. If that administrator could not change the toner cartridge and resume where he left off, all of the previously printed paychecks would need to be printed again. In addition to wasting time and resources, this would be a problem because many paycheck-printing programs do not allow the paychecks to be printed again for security reasons.

Once a print job or a printer has been paused, resume the printer's printing:

1. Log on with permissions to manage printers.

2. Open the Printer window.

3. Highlight the document that is paused. If more than one document has been paused (but not all of the documents in the queue), hold down the Ctrl key when highlighting the documents.

4. Choose Document I Resume.

Note

If all documents need to be resumed, choose Printer|Pause Documents to remove the check beside Pause Printing.

Restarting Printing

When a print job is paused and you want it to print, you can either restart printing (start the job over) or resume printing (continue the job where it left off). You would choose to restart printing if a paper jam caused the printed document to be unreadable so that it needed to be printed again from the beginning.

Once a print job has been paused, restart the printer:

1. Log on with permissions to manage printers (see note earlier).

2. Open the Printer window.

3. Highlight the document(s) to be restarted, and choose Document I Restart.

Canceling Printing

As with pausing, the documents in the queue can be canceled one by one or all at once. When a document is canceled, it is deleted from the queue. If the document canceled is already printing, it will cease printing and be deleted from the queue.

To cancel all documents in the queue:

1. Log on with permissions to manage printers (see note earlier).

2. Open the Printer window.

3. Choose Printer I Cancel All Documents.

To cancel a single document in the queue:

1. Log on with permissions to manage printers (see note earlier).

2. Open the Printer window.

3. Highlight the print job to be canceled.

4. Choose Document I Cancel.

Using Advanced Settings

If you are the administrator of the printers on your network, and you have several users, you can change some advanced features from the Advanced tab of a printer's Properties dialog box. These options are available from all Windows XP Professional machines, no matter what type of printer is used. You can use the Advanced tab to do the following:

♦ *Specify printer availability*—You can make the printer always available (the default) or available at only certain times of the day. You might need to limit availability to keep unwanted print jobs from being sent after you've left the office or to have certain jobs print only at night when no one is in the office.

♦ *Set a priority*—A priority setting is a number between 1 and 99 that can be set to manage documents and printers. The default priority is 1, and 1 is the lowest priority. Higher-priority documents print before lower-priority documents.

♦ *Spool documents*—When documents are sent to the printer, the documents are collected in the printer spool until they are ready to print. A spool holds documents on the hard drive of a computer until they are ready to print. To speed up printing when many documents are waiting, you can choose to start printing immediately, as soon as a page has been spooled. In contrast, you can also wait for the last page of a document to be spooled before the document starts printing.

♦ *Print directly to the printer*—Select this option only if printer spooling can't be used. This option does not spool the document, but instead sends it directly to the printer. Spooling requires space on the hard drive for holding documents; if no space (or not enough space) is available, spooling cannot be used.

♦ *Hold mismatched documents*—You can hold documents in the print queue (spooled) if the printer setup and the document setup do not match.

♦ *Print spooled documents first*—To increase the printer's efficiency, you can print the spooled documents first. When this option is chosen, a document's priority doesn't matter. When this option isn't chosen, the spooler sends documents to the printer based on priority only. This can slow down printing if a lower-priority document is ready to print but a higher-priority document is still being spooled.

♦ *Keep printed documents*—You can specify that the spooler should keep all queued documents even after they are printed. This ensures that documents can be resubmitted from the print queue instead of from the application. This option is not enabled by default.

♦ *Enable advanced printing features*—You can enable advanced features such as specifying page order, printing booklets, and selecting the number of pages per sheet. This option should be enabled when possible.

♦ *Specify a print processor*—You can specify a different print processor. A print processor is used to determine what type of data is being sent from the spooler to the graphics engine.

For instance, you might have a print processor that allows Macintosh clients to send postscript files to raster printers, or one that filters ASCII for use on a postscript printer. Generally, the default is fine.

◆ *Add a separator page*—When multiple users print to the same printer, documents can become hard to find and keep separate. If this is the case, you can specify that separator pages be printed between documents. The separator page can contain the user's name and document name. Separator pages use up paper and ink (or toner), so they should be used only when necessary.

To change these advanced print options:

1. Log on as an administrator.

2. Open the Control Panel.

3. Open Printers And Faxes.

4. Right-click the appropriate printer, and choose Properties.

5. Select the Advanced tab.

6. Make the appropriate changes. The Advanced tab of the Properties dialog is shown in Figure 4.8.

7. Choose OK.

Troubleshooting Printing Problems

Many things can happen to cause printing problems. These problems range from poor print quality to slow printing to the inability to print to a printer on your network or in your workgroup. In this section, I'll cover the most common problems and their solutions.

Documents Do Not Print

If a document doesn't print at all, several things could be going on. The document could be corrupted, the application you are printing from might not be compatible with Windows XP Professional, the print job might be too large for the computer to handle, or the printer might not be turned on or might be unplugged. One hopes that it's the latter problem, although it's somewhat embarrassing when discovered.

If a document won't print at all, try the following:

1. Make sure the printer is correctly installed, turned on, and plugged into a working outlet. Check that the printer icon is shown in the Printers And Faxes folder in the Control Panel. Check the connection from the printer to the computer or network.

2. Open the printer's Properties dialog box, and print a test document. If the document prints, then the printer is installed correctly, turned on, and plugged in, and the problem lies elsewhere.

3. Make sure the printer is online if it is a network printer. Online status is usually denoted by a green light on the printer. Ask an administrator if you're not sure.

4. Check to see if printing is paused. Resume or restart as necessary.

5. Make sure that you have selected the correct printer if more than one is available.

6. Print a test page from Notepad or WordPad. If a document prints from here but not from another application, the problem might lie in the application's compatibility with Windows XP Professional. Check Microsoft's Web site for compatible software.

7. Print a test page from the current application. If the test page prints, then the application is most likely compatible, and the problem lies with the size of the print job.

8. If the document is too large to print, your computer might not have enough RAM (random access memory). Memory plays a big part in handling a printed document while it is being printed. If the document was scanned or contains multiple colors or embedded graphics or equations, you might need to free up some memory by closing all other running programs and perhaps restarting your computer.

9. Try printing from a command prompt. If your printer is connected through an LPT port, type "copy con lpt1"; otherwise, type the port name in place of "lpt1." Then type "Test print" and press Enter. Press Ctrl+Z, and then press Enter again. If the printer prints a page with "Test print," the communication between the printer and computer is fine. For other types of printers, access Microsoft Troubleshooter from the Printer window shown earlier. Troubleshooters can be accessed from Start | Help and Support | Fixing a Problem | Printing Problems.

10. Consider reinstalling the printer driver and/or the printer.

11. Call the network administrator or the printer manufacturer's help line.

Printing Is Poor

Several things can cause a document to print poorly, including low ink or toner, incorrect print settings in print preferences, misaligned cartridges, and corrupted printer drivers. If you can print to the printer, but the print quality is poor, try the following:

♦ In the printer's Properties dialog box, make sure that the correct paper is chosen and that the print quality is set to something other than Draft.

♦ Check the printer for low ink in an inkjet printer using the printer's properties page, check the toner cartridges for laser printers, or check for physical problems with the printer. In a laser printer, the toner cartridge can be removed, inspected, and shaken gently if it is a sealed unit, or there might be a warning light on the printer itself indicating low toner.

♦ Check the page setup if the page is missing text or graphics around the edges of the page.

- Check page orientation and page size.

- Copy and paste the text from the current application into WordPad. If the document prints correctly from WordPad, there is most likely a problem with the application's compatibility with Windows XP Professional or the application's formatting.

- If the document is too large to print, your computer might not have enough memory. You might need to free up some memory by closing all other running programs and perhaps restarting your computer.

- Consider reinstalling the printer driver and/or the printer.

- Call the network administrator or the printer manufacturer's help line.

Printing Is Slow

Printing can be slow on a network because of an unusually high amount of traffic between users and printers. On workgroup computers or standalone computers, however, slow printing generally indicates other types of problems. If printing is unusually slow, try the following:

- If possible, restart the computer. Often, restarting solves problems painlessly.

- Make sure you have at least 120MB of free space on your hard drive so the computer can effectively send information to the printer.

- If the document is too large to print, your computer might not have enough memory. You might need to free up some memory by closing all other running programs and perhaps restarting your computer.

- Turn off print spooling to see if printing speed improves.

- Many problems can occur if the hard disk is excessively fragmented. Use Disk Defragmenter to see if your disk needs to be defragmented. (It's a good idea to back up your system, however, before defragmenting the hard drive.)

- The application could be the cause of slow printing. Try printing from another program and see if this solves the problem. If it does, the application might be incompatible with Windows XP Professional. Check Microsoft's Web site for a list of compatible software.

- Consider reinstalling the printer driver and/or the printer.

- Call the network administrator or the printer manufacturer's help line.

You Cannot Install a Printer

The inability to install a printer is often hardware-related. If the printer is new, there could be a problem with the printer's power supply, the driver, or even the cable that connects the printer to the computer. The first thing to do is to read the manufacturer's instructions. If the printer is not new, has been installed on another machine, and is now being moved to a

Windows XP Professional machine, check Microsoft's hardware compatibility list (HCL), accessed from the Microsoft Web site.

With both of these preliminaries out of the way, consider the following options:

♦ Make sure the printer driver is compatible with Windows XP Professional. If it's not, obtain an updated driver from the manufacturer's Web site.

♦ Try installing the printer again. On the Install Printer Software page of the Add Printer Wizard, choose one of the drivers that come with Windows XP Professional. (For my HP Office Jet 600, I installed the Windows XP driver for "HP Office Jet" because "600" was not available.)

♦ If possible, choose another printer to use with the Windows XP machine, or contact the manufacturer for the status of an updated driver.

♦ To rule out the chance that the printer port is not working at the local printer, try installing a different printer for the computer.

Printer Features Aren't Available

Most printers these days come with a multitude of options, but sometimes they don't work properly or are unavailable. The causes here can be the same as those listed in the section "Printing Is Poor." After making sure that you have the correct settings chosen, that advanced features are enabled, consider the following options:

♦ Make sure that the printer is on Microsoft's HCL and that the driver is the most up-to-date one available.

♦ Ask the manufacturer when a newer version of the driver will be available.

♦ Read the instructions that come with the new driver, if applicable. Some printers require BIOS changes such as using ECP or EPP port settings.

Fonts Are Not Printing Correctly

Different types of fonts are available—such as TrueType, OpenType, and PostScript fonts. TrueType and PostScript fonts print the same way on paper as they look on your screen. If the printed fonts do not look the same as those shown on your computer screen, make sure you have chosen a TrueType font (if your printer is not PostScript-compatible), and/or check that the font is installed. TrueType fonts are denoted with a double-T symbol, whereas either no symbol or another symbol denotes a non-TrueType font. PostScript fonts (also called *Adobe Type 1* fonts) might be indicated by a "P" symbol or an "a" symbol.

You can also run into problems with fonts that are installed automatically when various programs are installed on the computer. These fonts might not be TrueType fonts and might cause problems with certain printers.

In addition to different types of fonts, there are different types of printers. TrueType printers and PostScript printers are a couple of the most common. PostScript printers can also print TrueType fonts, but the reverse is not true. If you have a PostScript printer, it can be set to replace all TrueType fonts with PostScript fonts, and this replacement is called *font substitution*. You can turn this off if necessary.

As with other printing problems, if your fonts are not printing correctly, you should always suspect the printer driver above anything else. A corrupt, outdated, or otherwise bad printer driver can cause numerous problems. Look for an updated printer driver.

Access to the Printer Is Denied

The Access Denied message appears only if the appropriate permissions do not exist for the type of access you want with the printer. Remember, three basic printing-related permissions are available:

♦ *Print*—Users can print but cannot manage printers or documents. By default, everyone can print.

♦ *Manage Printers*—Users who have this permission by default are in the Power Users and Administrators groups. With the permission to manage printers, these users can pause and restart the printer, change spooler settings, share and set printer permissions, and change a printer's properties.

♦ *Manage Documents*—This is a limited permission given by default to members of the Creator-Owner group. These users can pause, resume, restart, and cancel documents submitted by other users but cannot do much more than that. For instance, members who have only the Manage Documents permission cannot send documents to the printer, control the status of the printer, or access documents in the print queue.

Make sure you have the appropriate permissions to access the printer in the manner you'd like. If you are an administrator, you can give these permissions to yourself; otherwise, you'll need to contact an administrator on your network.

Make Yourself a Power User

Before you go off assigning your own account or any other with permissions to manage printers, remember that assigning permissions directly to user accounts can become tiresome as the number of users on the network or in the workgroup grows. It is a better practice to assign users to groups, and then assign groups permissions. Recall that the Power Users group can fully access printers. It's better to make yourself a member of the Power Users group, with the ability to manage printers, than to assign specific print permissions to a user account. (For information on managing Users and Groups, see Chapter 3.)

For users who need the ability to manage printers but who should not be power users, consider making them members of another group that you create called Printer Managers or something similar.

If you are the only user of your computer or if you are in an extremely small workgroup, you might still want to assign specific account permissions to yourself (or another user) to manage printers. If you have administrator's status, perform the following steps to give the account appropriate access. By doing so, you can manage printers by using your own account instead of logging on as an administrator each time. It is best to log on as an administrator only when absolutely necessary.

To assign printing permissions to a user or group:

1. Log on as an administrator.

2. Open the Printer window.

3. Click Printer in the menu bar.

4. Hold down the Ctrl key while choosing Properties.

5. Select the Security tab of the Properties dialog box.

Note
If you don't see the Security tab, close the dialog box and perform Steps 4 and 5 again. Make sure you are holding down the Ctrl key when you click Properties.

6. Remember that it is best to assign permissions to groups, as mentioned in the sidebar. However, to add a user account and assign it the Manage Printers permission, choose Add. If the Group Or Users Names box already lists your account or the group you are in, skip to Step 10.

7. Type the name of the user or group to which you're assigning permissions.

8. Choose OK, and correct any errors as necessary.

9. Highlight the user or group to which you're assigning print permissions.

10. In the Permissions box, select the print permissions the user or group should have.

11. Choose OK.

Faxing

Faxing is the process of sending text or graphics over phone lines. This material can be scanned, can come from an email, or can be sent directly from the computer screen to the recipient without even so much as saving the information to the local computer. Even photos from digital cameras can be faxed directly to recipients by using the Fax Wizard discussed in this section.

Faxing is handled in many ways, the two most common being to use a fax-modem or use a separate fax machine. Even if you don't have a separate fax machine, almost all computers that have a modem can also send and receive faxes. This makes faxing from your Windows XP Professional machine possible.

Note

In this section, I'll assume that your modem is a fax-modem and capable of this task or that a fax machine is available.

Installing Fax Services

When Windows XP Professional is installed, the Fax Services component is not installed by default. To use the fax services available in Windows XP, you'll need the Windows XP Professional CD and the ability (or permissions) to add services.

To add the Fax Services component of Windows:

1. Open the Control Panel.

2. Open the Add Or Remove Programs window.

3. Choose Add/Remove Windows Components to launch the Windows Components Wizard.

4. On the Windows Components page, check the Fax Services checkbox, as shown in Figure 4.12.

5. Choose Next. If prompted, place the Windows XP Professional CD in the CD-ROM drive, and continue.

6. Choose Finish when done.

7. Close the Add Or Remove Programs window.

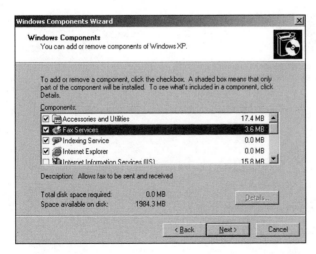

Figure 4.12
Installing Windows components.

Configuring the Fax Service

If you have a fax-modem, sending a fax is fairly straightforward. However, there are several housekeeping chores to take care of before that first fax can be sent. In this section, I'll cover how to compose and send a fax the first time and how to set up the fax service.

A fax can be composed in any application that can print to a printer, including word processing, graphics, and email programs. Composing a fax is the same as creating any document; just open the application, type a few words, and that's it. You can also create a document by scanning in a photo or text, by downloading a photo from a digital camera, or by obtaining information from a PDA or similar device. After creating your document, you use the Fax Wizard to send it.

The Fax Wizard

To use the Fax Wizard, you first need to have the fax composed and ready to send. To compose a basic fax and send it using the Fax Wizard:

1. Open an application such as Microsoft Word.

2. Type the message you want to fax.

3. Choose File | Send To | Fax Recipient.

4. The Fax Wizard appears, as shown in Figure 4.13. Choose Next.

5. On the Document To Fax page, make sure the document you want to fax is selected. (If you haven't saved this test document, it will be called "Document 1.") Accept the default option, With A Cover Sheet, and then click Next.

6. On the Fax Software page, select the program you want to use to fax the document. You can choose Microsoft Fax or a third party program that has been installed on the system.

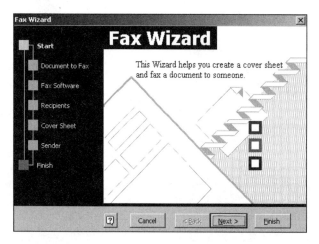

Figure 4.13
The Fax Wizard.

If you installed the Fax Services component as described in the previous section, choose Fax. (If not, return to that section and install Fax Services.) Choose Next.

Note

If Microsoft Fax is grayed out on the Fax Software page, then the Fax Services component has not yet been configured. For now, continue with the following instructions.

7. On the Who Should Receive This Fax page, type the name of the person to receive the fax, and type the phone number the way it should be dialed. If the name and fax number are listed in your Address book, you can get the number from there by choosing the Address Book button. Choose Next when finished.

8. On the Cover Sheet page, select the type of cover sheet you'd like to send along with the fax: Professional, Contemporary, or Elegant. Choose Next.

9. On the Sender page, fill in the information about the sender. Choose Next.

10. Choose Finish.

11. On the resulting cover page, make any changes necessary, including the date, number of pages, subject, and CC (courtesy copy) recipients.

12. Choose Send Fax Now.

Configuring the Fax to Send and Receive

The first time you send a fax, you'll need to configure the fax service. If an administrator has already done this, this won't be an issue. However, if you have just installed Fax Services component and are sending your first fax, the Fax Configuration Wizard will pop up before you send that first fax.

To work your way through the wizard and configure the fax:

1. When the Welcome page of the Fax Configuration Wizard appears, choose Next. (This page won't appear if the fax service has been configured by an administrator or is configured through a network policy.)

2. On the User Information page, type the appropriate information. Choose Next.

3. Select the device that will be used to send and receive faxes. This is generally a fax-modem installed in the computer.

4. On the Transmitting Station Identifier page, type your business name and fax number. This information will be used to identify the sending computer. This line can be left blank or left as Fax.

5. On the Specify Devices For Receiving Faxes page, select the device that will receive the incoming faxes. If no device is listed, or a device isn't checked, faxes cannot be received.

6. If a device is selected to receive faxes, choose how many times the fax's phone should ring before this device automatically answers. If you're working in a small office, and your phone and fax-modem share a line, make sure your phone is set to pick up after fewer rings than the fax-modem is.

7. Choose Next.

8. On the Called Station Identifier page, you can type your business name or fax number. When receiving faxes, the fax-modem uses this information to identify itself to the sending fax machine. Choose Next.

9. On the Routing Options page, select what you want to do when a fax is received. You can print it to a printer or copy it to a file, or both. Choose Next.

10. Choose Finish.

The Send Fax Wizard

The Send Fax Wizard assists you in sending faxes using the Microsoft Fax Service. The Send Fax Wizard assists you in sending faxes *only*, in contrast to the Fax Wizard, which assists you in configuring the Microsoft Fax Service the first time it is used.

When sending a fax, the Send Fax Wizard appears. To use the wizard, perform the following steps:

1. Choose Next to begin using the Send Fax Wizard.

2. On the Recipient Information page, type the recipient's name and fax number. Choose Next.

3. Select Send A Cover Page Template With The Following Information, and choose a cover page template from the list.

4. Type a subject in the Subject Line, and type a note if necessary. Choose Next.

5. On the Scheduling Transmission page, choose when to send the fax, and set the fax priority. Choose Next.

6. On the Delivery Notification page, select when and if you want a notification delivered when the fax has been sent. This notification can be a pop-up message on your computer or an email message. Choose Next.

7. Carefully review the summary page, and click the Back button if you need to make changes. Make sure the phone number will dial exactly as you want, and if two or more numbers appear, highlight the one you want to use before selecting Finish. Preview the fax if necessary.

The Fax Console

After the fax service has been installed and configured, you can use the Fax Console to view incoming, outgoing, and sent faxes. The console keeps track of the start time, the status, and the IDs of the faxes. It also records the number of pages sent or received and each recipient's name and fax number. In addition, you can change information for different users, change the cover pages, launch the Configuration Wizard, and access fax service administration features.

To view the Fax Console, choose Start | Settings | Printers And Faxes | Fax. The Fax Console is shown in Figure 4.14, and the Tools menu is pulled down to show the tools available from this console.

Notice the four folders available in the console: Incoming, Inbox, Outbox, and Sent Items. Keeping track of all faxes as they come in, the Incoming folder lists the time, current page, and size of each fax. The Inbox lists faxes that are waiting to be read or dealt with. The Outbox lists faxes that are waiting to be sent, and the Sent Items folder holds all faxes that were sent by the local computer.

From the File menu, you can send a new fax or exit the Fax Console. From the Document menu, you can view, print, save, email, pause, resume, restart, delete, and see the properties

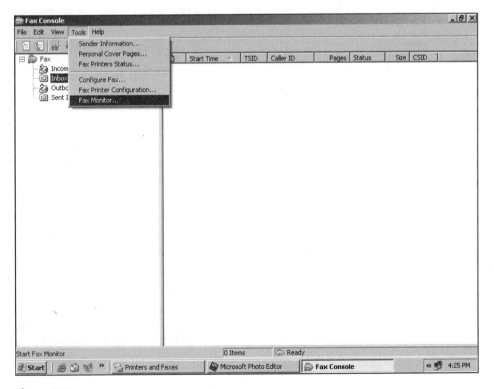

Figure 4.14
The Fax Console.

of any fax in any folder. From the Tools menu, you can change the information for a user, configure personal cover pages, see the server status, use the Configuration Wizard, and access service administration. Many items in the Tools menu—such as User Information—are pages that were used in configuring the fax service initially.

Cover Page Editor

One really neat tool is the Fax Cover Page Editor. To view this editor:

1. Open the Fax Console, and choose Tools | Personal Cover Pages.

2. In the Personal Cover Pages dialog box, choose New. You'll see the Fax Cover Page Editor, shown in Figure 4.15.

Using this editor, you can create personalized cover pages quite easily. From the Insert menu, you can choose to insert placeholders for recipient's name, recipient's fax number, sender's name, fax number, company, address, title, department, office location, and telephone numbers, and message note, subject, date and time, and page number. You can move these items anywhere on the page by dragging them to the appropriate spots. In Figure 4.15, I've started a personalized fax page. You can access your own completed fax page by choosing Tools | Personal Cover Pages in the Fax Console.

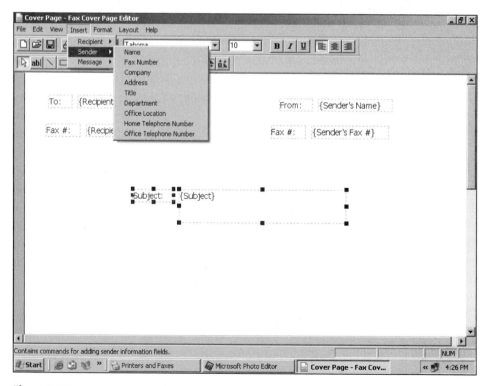

Figure 4.15
The Fax Cover Page Editor, showing the Insert|Sender options.

Using the Fax Service

With the fax service configured, sending a fax requires fewer steps than it did the first time. In fact, sending a fax is just a step up from printing.

To send a fax after the fax service has been set up:

1. Open an application such as Microsoft Word.

2. Type the message you want to fax.

3. Choose File | Print.

4. In the Name drop-down list, select Fax. Choose OK.

5. Choose Next to start the Send Fax Wizard. Type in the recipient's name and fax number. Choose Next.

6. Choose a cover page template, and type a subject line and a note. Choose Next.

7. Choose the fax time and priority. Choose Next.

8. Choose a delivery notification type. Choose Next.

9. Choose Finish.

To send a quick fax with only a cover page and a subject line and a note:

1. Open the Fax Console (choose Start | Settings | Printers And Faxes | Fax).

2. Choose File | Send A New Fax.

3. Choose Next to start the Send Fax Wizard. Type in the recipient's name and fax number. Choose Next.

4. Choose a cover page template, and type a subject line and a note. Choose Next.

5. Choose the fax time and fax. Choose Next.

6. Choose a delivery notification type. Choose Next.

7. Choose Finish.

After the computer has faxed the document, the document will move from the Outbox to the Sent Items folder. You can keep track of all sent faxes from this folder. The information here contains the recipient's name and fax number, the subject, the document name (if applicable), the number of pages, and the size of the document. This is essential information to have when a recipient claims not to have received the fax and that it was never sent.

Security Issues

You can share the fax service and set permissions for it just as with any other resource. Sharing a fax service can be beneficial in a small office where only one computer has a fax configured. If the fax is a separate device such as an all-in-one printer that is connected locally, or if the fax is simply a modem in one of the computers in the network, the fax service can still be shared and have permissions set.

To share and set permissions for the fax service installed in this chapter (the fax service that comes with Windows XP Professional):

1. Log on as an administrator.

2. Open the Control Panel.

3. Open Printers And Faxes.

4. Right-click the Fax to display its context menu.

5. While holding down the Ctrl key, choose Properties.

6. Select the Sharing tab.

7. If the Not Shared option is chosen, select Share Name and type "Fax". If the fax is already shared, continue with Step 8.

8. Select the Security tab.

9. Remove the Everyone group by highlighting it and choosing Remove.

10. To add groups that will need to use this fax, choose Add. Type the names of the groups, and choose OK.

11. Set permissions for the group as appropriate. Remember that the fax interprets these documents as print jobs, so users will at least need the ability to print.

12. Choose OK.

Wrapping Up

In this chapter, I discussed installing all kinds of printers, including local printers, shared printers, and network printers. Printer drivers play a large role in printers' functioning correctly, and drivers can be the source of many problems. Troubleshooting printers was also covered.

Configuring the printer is as important as installing it. Configuring includes adding printer cartridges, setting preferences and defaults, and managing print jobs. This chapter also covered faxing, including installing the fax service and configuring the service for the first use.

Chapter 5

Scheduled Tasks and Windows Update

One of the most important tasks a user or administrator has is keeping the computer in good working condition. Keeping the computer working properly and efficiently can be compared to maintaining a car. Every so many miles, you need to perform some maintenance. With a car, that means changing the oil, rotating the tires, and heeding dashboard warnings; with a computer, it means cleaning up the hard disks, obtaining the latest upgrades and fixes, and heeding system warnings. Windows XP includes many tools that can help you maintain your system, and two of them are Scheduled Tasks and Windows Update.

Both Scheduled Tasks and Windows Update can be used to keep the computer safe and up-to-date. Scheduled Tasks can be configured to run Disk Cleanup on your hard disks every day, week, or month, or it can be configured to run specific scripts, programs, or applications at any time that is most convenient. Windows Update can be configured to connect to and download the latest fixes and updates, and it can be used with or without Scheduled Tasks to perform these updates automatically.

In this chapter, I'll introduce both utilities and explain why and how they can be used to keep your system healthy.

Introduction to Scheduling Tasks

Scheduled Tasks is a utility accessed from the Control Panel. The Task Scheduler is the component of Scheduled Tasks that is used to configure the tasks you want to run. Task Scheduler starts each time you start Windows XP and runs in the background. Using Task Scheduler, you can do the following:

- Choose a task to run from the Task Scheduler list.

- Schedule a personalized script or program to run at a certain time.

- Schedule a document or application to open.

- Schedule a task to run daily, weekly, monthly, or at any given time.

- Change schedules for tasks; stop or pause tasks.

- Instruct Task Scheduler to notify you when a task doesn't run.

- Turn off all scheduled tasks.

- View a log of past scheduled tasks.

- Configure tasks while keeping power management options in mind.

The Scheduled Task Wizard can be used to configure many tasks. Many of those tasks are listed in the Scheduled Task Wizard because a user has installed the associated applications on the computer. For instance, WinZip, an application for compressing files before sending them and uncompressing files after receiving them, is listed in my Scheduled Task Wizard. If your computer doesn't have WinZip installed, it won't be shown. The applications in the Scheduled Task Wizard can vary from computer to computer, so I can't provide a complete list of what you might see.

The following list shows the most common tasks that can be scheduled, and these will be available on all Windows XP Professional machines. This is not a complete list, but it gives you a general idea of the uses for scheduling tasks:

- Accessibility Wizard

- Activate Windows

- Backup

- Command Prompt

- Disk Cleanup

- Fax Console

- Getting Started

- HyperTerminal

- Internet Explorer

- Magnifier

- MSN Explorer

- ◆ MSN Messenger Service

- ◆ Narrator

- ◆ NetMeeting

- ◆ Outlook Express

- ◆ Paint

- ◆ Synchronize

- ◆ System Information

- ◆ System Restore

- ◆ Utility Manager

- ◆ Windows Update

Basic Tasks

To configure scheduled tasks to run on your system, you must be familiar with the basics. These include creating a task, running a task, and modifying, removing, pausing, or stopping a task. Each of these jobs is detailed in the upcoming sections. Note that before you can run or modify a task, one must be created.

Creating a Scheduled Task

The first step in using Scheduled Tasks is to create a task. To create a scheduled task:

1. Open the Control Panel.

2. Open Scheduled Tasks.

3. Choose Add Scheduled Task to launch the Scheduled Task Wizard. Choose Next.

4. In the application list, highlight Outlook Express (or whatever application you want to schedule); then choose Next. (Note that you can browse to other programs or applications.)

5. Type a name for the task, or accept the default. Select when to perform this task: Daily, Weekly, Monthly, One Time Only, When My Computer Starts, or When I Log On. Choose Next.

6. Type the name and password of a user under whom the task will run. When choosing a user under whom the task will run, make sure to choose an administrator if the task can be run only by an administrator. If the task is to open Pinball, any user can run the task. Choose Next.

7. Choose Finish to end the wizard and return to the Scheduled Tasks console.

8. Choose View | Refresh. Notice the new task.

Run the Scheduled Task Wizard as often as you want, and configure as many tasks as you want. Remember, though, that running a task is like running an application, and it will use the computer's resources to do so. If you schedule CPU-intensive tasks, try to schedule them when the computer isn't in use.

Running a Task Immediately

After scheduling a task, you can run it at any time; just right-click it in the Scheduled Tasks console, and choose Run. Figure 5.1 shows the new task that was created, Outlook Express, and its context-menu choices.

Modifying a Scheduled Task

To modify a scheduled task, you right-click it and choose Properties. Look again at Figure 5.1, and notice that the last choice in the context menu is Properties. Figure 5.2 shows the Schedule tab of the Outlook Express task's property sheet. Outlook Express is scheduled to run at user logon, but you can select a different time from the Schedule Task drop-down list.

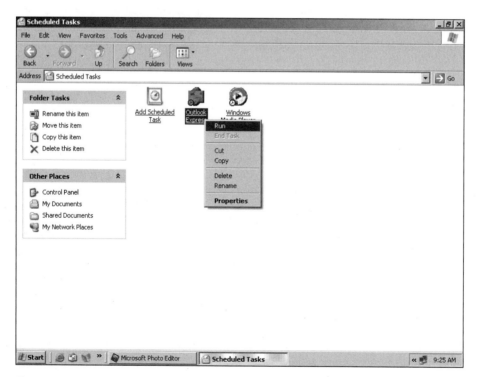

Figure 5.1
Run a task immediately.

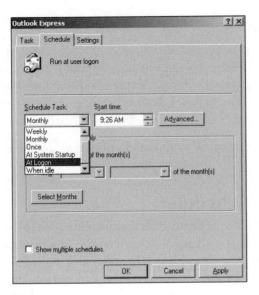

Figure 5.2
Modifying a scheduled task.

The Settings tab of a scheduled task's property sheet also includes items you can change for the task:

♦ If the task is not scheduled to run again, it can be deleted automatically after the task is finished.

♦ The task can be stopped if it runs for an inordinate amount of time, such as 72 hours (the default).

♦ The task can be configured to start only after the computer has been idle for a certain amount of time. This can guarantee that the task can run when the computer isn't being used.

♦ The task can stop automatically if the computer does not remain idle.

Removing a Scheduled Task

To remove a scheduled task, you right-click it and choose Delete. Figure 5.1 shows Run highlighted in the task's context menu, but Delete can be seen in the menu as well.

Stopping a Task That Is Running

To stop a task that is running, you right-click it and choose End Task. This might be necessary if the current task is no longer needed or if the task is using too much of the computer's resources.

Managing Scheduled Tasks

Scheduled tasks can be managed using the menu bar at the top of the Scheduled Tasks console. Figure 5.3 shows the Scheduled Tasks console, the Advanced menu choices, and four icons. Two of these icons are tasks I've created, Outlook Express and Windows Media Player, and the other two are default icons. (Remember, Scheduled Tasks is available in the Control Panel.)

Through the Advanced menu, several management options and utilities are available. In this section, I'll introduce each of these.

Stopping and Starting Task Scheduler

When Add Scheduled Task is chosen in the Scheduled Tasks console or when Windows XP boots up, the Task Scheduler automatically starts. To turn off the Task Scheduler, you can choose Advanced | Stop Using Task Scheduler. When the Task Scheduler is stopped, the scripts, programs, or other tasks will not run, and the Task Scheduler will not start automatically at bootup. The Task Scheduler will start again if Add Scheduled Task is chosen.

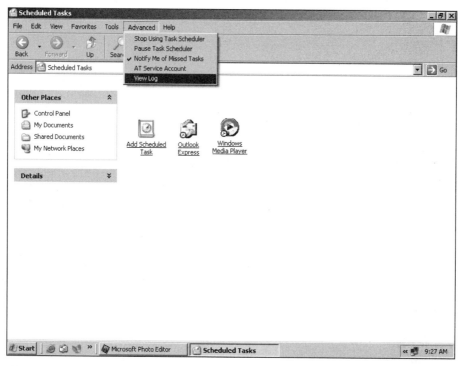

Figure 5.3
Advanced options.

Pausing and Continuing Scheduled Tasks

If you don't want to completely stop scheduled tasks from running, but you want to pause them to add new software or hardware or to perform routine maintenance, you can pause the service temporarily. In the Scheduled Tasks console, choose Advanced | Pause Task Scheduler. When you're ready to restart the service, choose Advanced | Continue.

Receiving Notification That a Task Didn't Run

To be notified when a scheduled task did not run, choose Advanced | Notify Me Of Missed Tasks in the Scheduled Tasks console. You must be an administrator to set this option.

Using the AT Service Account

In earlier versions on Windows, administrators used the AT command to configure scheduled tasks. In Windows XP, the AT command is still available and works with a new GUI. The AT service account can be configured to run tasks from a command line. This service account is similar to a user account, and it can be configured from inside Scheduled Tasks. The AT service account can be the system account or a specific account chosen by the administrator. If the system account is chosen as the AT service account, the schedB<ed task run using the default LocalSystem account, the tasks are the same as before: scripts, programs, and documents. However, some administrators prefer working from a command prompt and incorporating the tasks configured there with Task Scheduler. Listing 5.1 shows the syntax for the AT command, and Table 5.1 shows what switches are available and what each means. (This information is taken from a command prompt in Windows XP Professional.)

Note

Before running to use the AT command, make sure you really need to. The AT command and the AT Service Account are generally used by network administrators.

Listing 5.1   AT switches at a command prompt.

```
D:\>at /?
The AT command schedules commands and programs to run on a computer at
a specified time and date. The Schedule service must be running to use
the AT command.

AT [\\computername] [ [id] [/DELETE] | /DELETE [/YES]]
AT [\\computername] time [/INTERACTIVE]
    [ /EVERY:date[,...] | /NEXT:date[,...]] "command"
"command"  Is the Windows NT, or batch program to be run.
```

Tasks created using the AT command can be viewed and modified using Task Scheduler, but if they are modified in Task Scheduler, they are no longer available at the command prompt. All tasks that are created through the AT command must run in the same user

Table 5.1   AT switches.

Switch	Description
\\computername	Specifies a remote computer. Commands are scheduled on the local computer if this parameter is omitted.
Id	Is an identification number assigned to a scheduled command.
/delete	Cancels a scheduled command. If ID is omitted, all the scheduled commands on the computer are cancelled.
/yes	Used with cancel all jobs command when no further confirmation is desired.
time	Specifies the time when the command is to run.
/interactive	Allows the job to interact with the desktop of the user who is logged on at the time the job runs.
/every:date[,…]	Runs the command on specified day(s) of the week or month. If data is omitted, the current day of the month is assumed.
/next:date[,…]	Runs the specified command on the next occurrence of the day (for example, next Thursday). If date is omitted, the current day of the month is assumed.

account—either a specified user account or the system account. In contrast, tasks scheduled in Task Scheduler can use different user accounts.

To enable the AT command in Scheduled Tasks, choose Advanced | AT Service Account, and choose either to enter an account name and password, or to use the Service Account from the two options provided

Viewing a Log of Past Scheduled Tasks

To view a log of past scheduled tasks, choose Advanced | View Log in the Scheduled Tasks console. Depending on what types of tasks are scheduled and which of those tasks have run, the log can look quite complex. It is unlikely that two logs would ever look alike. Listing 5.2 shows part of a log for the tasks that have been configured in this chapter. Notice the information on Outlook Express and Windows Media Player starting.

Listing 5.2   Part of a task log.

```
"Outlook Express.job" (msimn.exe)
     Started 7/7/2001 12:40:59 PM
"Outlook Express.job" (msimn.exe)
     Finished 7/7/2001 12:40:59 PM
     Result: The task completed with an exit code of (0).
"IdleTask" (TaskId1)
     Started 7/7/2001 12:58:34 PM
"IdleTask" (TaskId1)
     Finished 7/7/2001 12:58:34 PM
     Result: The task completed with an exit code of (0).
"Help Services Scheduler.job" (HelpSvc.exe)
     Started 7/7/2001 1:00:06 PM
```

```
"Help Services Scheduler.job" (HelpSvc.exe)
     Finished 7/7/2001 1:00:06 PM
     Result: The task completed with an exit code of (0).
"Windows Media Player.job" (wmplayer.exe)
     Started 7/7/2001 1:29:40 PM
"Windows Media Player.job" (wmplayer.exe)
     Finished 7/7/2001 1:29:54 PM
     Result: The task completed with an exit code of (0).
"Windows Media Player.job" (wmplayer.exe)
     Started 7/7/2001 1:30:00 PM
"Windows Media Player.job" (wmplayer.exe)
     Finished 7/7/2001 1:30:03 PM
     Result: The task completed with an exit code of (0).
```

Because all of these tasks were completed successfully, they return with an exit code of
"(0)". Other error numbers and messages appear when tasks are not completed successfully.
In those error messages are specific reasons for the task's failure. See Listing 5.3.

Listing 5.3   Errors in the task log.

```
"Administrator's Desktop Cleanup monitor .job" (rundll32.exe) 7/6/2001 12:28:00
PM ** ERROR **
     The attempt to retrieve account information for the specified task
failed; therefore, the task did not run. Either an error occurred, or no
account information existed for the task.
     The specific error is:
     0x80070534: No mapping between account names and security IDs was done.
"Joli Ballew's Desktop Cleanup monitor .job" (rundll32.exe) 7/6/2001 2:13:00 PM
** ERROR **
     The attempt to retrieve account information for the specified task
failed; therefore, the task did not run. Either an error occurred, or no
account information existed for the task.
     The specific error is:
     0x8004130f: No account information could be found in the Task Scheduler
security database for the task indicated.
```

Monitoring these logs is important for anyone in charge of scheduling tasks and managing
a computer. To read more about viewing logs and using the AT command, open Task Sched-
uler in Windows XP Professional, and choose Help | Help Topics.

Tasks and Power Management

Sometimes it is best to schedule tasks to run at night or when the computer is idle. However, in many cases, the computer is not "awake" in the middle of the night and is on
stand-by or in hibernation. Perhaps the computer has been set to automatically power off
the monitor or the hard disks after a certain period of time. (These power settings can be
configured through the Control Panel for the specific computer; see the sidebar on page 11.)

However, when power management settings are mixed with Task Scheduler, decisions need to be made regarding what Task Scheduler will do if a task needs to be run but the computer is in stand-by or hibernation mode.

Because each task is configured to run at certain times, each task must be configured independently of the others when it comes to setting power management options. There are three power management options for a task. They are:

♦ Don't Start The Task If The Computer Is Running On Batteries

♦ Stop The Task If Battery Mode Begins

♦ Wake the Computer To Run This Task

As you can tell, the first two options relate directly to laptop or mobile computers. It is inefficient to run the task if the computer is running on batteries or if battery mode begins. Chances are good that the task would not be completed or would not be needed. For desktop PCs, though, you can decide if you want to wake the computer to perform a specific task.

To set power management options for a specific task:

1. Open the Control Panel.

2. Open Scheduled Tasks.

3. Right-click the task for which you want to set power management options.

4. Choose Properties.

5. Select the Settings tab.

6. Under Power Management, check the checkboxes for the options you want to enable. Uncheck any options you want to disable.

7. Choose OK.

Windows Update

Windows Update is an extension of Windows XP Professional that is available from Microsoft's Web Site. When Windows Update is used, it automatically connects to the Web site and checks for any updates or fixes that your Windows operating system needs. Windows Update then asks you if you'd like to download those updates to your computer. It is a great way for users to maintain the latest versions of drivers, applications, help files, and system files.

To use Windows Update, you'll need to log on as an administrator or have administrator status. If your computer is a member of a domain (network), even administrator status might not be enough. Corporate-wide networks usually have plenty of restrictions regarding downloading files from the Internet because downloading harmful files can destroy a computer or

Power Options in the Control Panel

To save on electricity and resources, you can configure your computer to turn off its monitor and hard disks after a certain amount of idle time. You can also configure the computer to go on stand-by after a certain period of time. Stand-by mode conserves electricity; turning off the monitor or hard disks saves both electricity and wear-and-tear on the system. It is a good idea to configure some power options here.

To configure power options for your computer:

1. Open the Control Panel, and choose Power Options.

2. On the Power Schemes tab of the Power Options Properties dialog box, select a power scheme from the Power Schemes drop-down list. (The options are Home/Office, Portable/Laptop, Presentation, Always On, Minimal Power Management, and Max Battery.)

3. In the Settings For *<power scheme>* Power Scheme area, make the appropriate selections for the following options:

   - Turn Off Monitor
   - Turn Off Hard Disks
   - System Standby
   - System Hibernates

4. Choose OK.

bring down a network, and downloading many types of material is forbidden. So, to use Windows Update, you'll need access to the Internet, administrator status, and permission to download files and applications.

Why Configure Automatic Updates?

I am a strong believer in using Windows Update to configure the computer with automatic updates from Microsoft's Web site. Microsoft updates its site often with new information for help files, updates to operating system files, bug and security fixes, and new drivers for hardware. Whether your computer is a laptop, desktop, or network computer, these files are almost always useful.

There are different types of updates; the most important to obtain are called "critical updates." Critical updates provide relief of known problems involving security vulnerabilities. These updates are also helpful in repairing bugs in Windows. These bugs can cause the computer to hang or freeze up.

Besides critical updates, there are several other types. These include:

♦ *Service packs and recommended downloads*—Improvements in Windows and Internet Explorer.

♦ *Management and deployment tools*—Utilities that provide performance enhancements, facilitate upgrades, and ease the load on system administrators in a variety of ways.

- *Internet and multimedia updates*—Upgrades for Internet Explorer, Windows Media Player, Movie Maker, and more.

- *Additional Windows downloads*—Updates for the desktop and other Windows features.

- *Multiple-language features*—Upgrades for dialog boxes, language support, and input methods for a variety of languages.

- *Hardware drivers*—Updates for hardware drivers.

You can always choose which of these downloads and updates you want. There are many ways to configure how Windows Update works. Windows Update can be configured to run automatically with Task Scheduler or through Microsoft's Web site. You can also configure automatic updates through the System icon in the Control Panel.

Using Windows Update with Scheduled Tasks

Because you're already familiar with Scheduled Tasks, I'll introduce using Windows Update with Scheduled Tasks first:

1. Open the Control Panel.

2. Open Scheduled Tasks, and choose Add Scheduled Task.

3. When the Scheduled Task Wizard starts, work your way through it, and select Windows Update from the list of applications or tasks. Decide when to perform a Windows Update, and choose a start time.

Windows Update will run at the scheduled time and day. It can be modified, stopped, deleted, or run from the Windows Update icon in the Scheduled Tasks console.

Using Windows Update from the System Icon in the Control Panel

Another way to configure Windows Update is to use the System icon in the Control Panel. To do this:

1. Open the Control Panel.

2. Open System.

3. Select the Automatic Updates tab of the System Properties dialog box.

4. Choose a Notification Setting:

   - Download The Updates Automatically And Notify Me When They Are Ready To Be Installed.

♦ Notify Me Before Downloading Any Updates And Notify Me Again Before Install-ing Them On My Computer.

♦ Turn Off Automatic Updating. I Want To Update My Computer Manually.

5. Choose OK.

Configuring Windows Update By Using the Internet

Finally, you can use the Microsoft Web site to specify what will be updated. To connect to the Windows Update site and personalize your updates:

1. Log on as an administrator.

2. Choose Start | Windows Update.

3. When connected to the Windows Update page as shown in Figure 5.4, click Personal-ize Windows Update. (The page is subject to change, so look for something similar if it doesn't look exactly like Figure 5.4.)

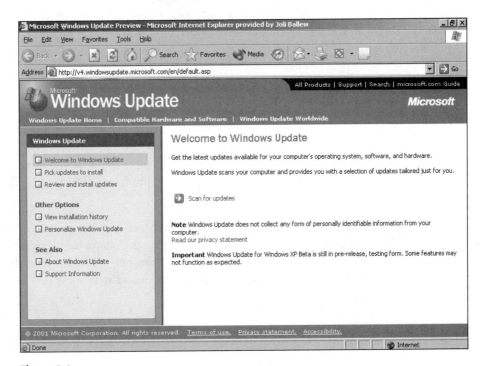

Figure 5.4
Windows Update Web site.

4. From the Personalize Your Windows Update Experience page, select the updates you'd like to receive.

Note

Do not log off or break your connection to the Internet yet; the next section assumes that you are connected to the Windows Update Web site.

Downloading the Latest Updates

Continuing from Step 5 in the previous instructions, click Welcome To Windows Update, or click the Back button to return to the Windows Update Home Page. Perform the following steps to download the latest updates:

1. Click Scan For Updates. Wait for the scan to finish.

2. If updates are available, you can select which ones you'd like to download, or you can choose to download all of the updates.

3. After making your selections, choose Download Now.

4. Select Save To Disk when prompted.

5. When the download is finished, you will be prompted to install the updates. Click Install Now. If you are not prompted to install, then locate the folder in which the update was saved, and double-click it or select Open Folder.

6. When the installation is complete, close all of the screens, and restart the computer if required.

Wrapping Up

In this chapter, you learned how to keep your computer up-to-date and running smoothly. Although Windows XP offers many tools for maintaining a computer, two of the most useful tools for periodic checks and the automatic completion of tasks are Windows Update and Scheduled Tasks.

Scheduled Tasks can be used to run specified scripts, programs, or documents once or any number of times. Personalized scripts can be helpful in keeping the computer running efficiently, and using programs such as Disk Cleanup regularly can help maintain hard disks and free up disk space. Using Windows Update with Task Scheduler can be especially useful in maintaining a system.

Chapter 6
Using System Restore

System Restore, an operating-system feature introduced in the Microsoft Windows Millennium Edition, is now available in Windows XP. System Restore monitors changes to your system and creates *restore points*, or records that can be used to revert the computer to a previous, stable state. System Restore allows you to undo something that was later found to have caused a problem.

System Restore does more than just restore your computer to a previous state, though. For instance, the restore process preserves personal files such as recent passwords, documents, and email messages, and it protects all files stored in the My Documents folder. Files with other extensions, such as .xls (Microsoft Excel file), also are protected, and any type of file can be saved if it is stored in the My Documents folder. Of course, the best defense is a good offense; System Restore is no substitute for using a backup utility daily or weekly for preserving important data and files.

Windows XP uses system restore points to create points of restoration. Depending on the amount of disk space configured for storing these points of restoration, a user can choose a restore point from the present date up to three weeks earlier. Several types of restore points are available, including driver restore points and system checkpoints. Additionally, any restoration is reversible, so you can undo unsatisfactory changes.

You can use System Restore only under the following conditions: you are an administrator; network policies do not prohibit its use; and the hard disk has at least 200MB of disk space available. If there isn't enough space when Windows XP is installed, System

Restore is installed but not enabled. It cannot be used until the disk space requirement has been met.

In this chapter, you'll learn how System Restore works, how to perform basic tasks, and how to restore system state data. You'll also learn how to free up disk space to make room for System Restore, if necessary.

Understanding System Restore

System Restore is automatic; Windows XP automatically creates and saves information for the user and makes it available when and if it is ever necessary. This feature provides the optimal safety net for all users of Windows XP Professional. System Restore can be used from safe mode as well as from normal mode, in case the computer won't boot properly.

Automatically Created Restore Points

The number of times that the system creates restore points is determined by the level of activity on the system. A computer with a lot of activity, such as adding programs or hardware, will have more restore points created than will a computer that rarely gets used. System Restore automatically creates restore points at specific times and for specific system events, including the following:

♦ *Initial System Checkpoint*—The first time a computer is booted after Windows XP is installed, the first restore point is created.

♦ *System Checkpoints*—A restore point is created every 24 hours of calendar time or every 10 hours that the computer is on. These restore points are created only when the system is idle (when no mouse or keyboard is in use).

♦ *Applications*—If the application uses System-Restore-compliant APIs (application programming interfaces), a restore point is created automatically before the application is installed. This restore point can be used if the program causes problems after installation.

♦ *Windows Update Installations*—When Windows updates are downloaded either automatically or by you, you are prompted with the opportunity to install the update. If you choose to install the update, Windows XP creates a restore point before doing so. Thus, if you want to remove the update, you can select this restore point.

♦ *Restore Operation*—If you try to restore the system but choose the wrong restore point, you can reverse the restoration and choose the right restore point. The restore operation creates its own restore point.

♦ *Microsoft Backup Utility*—Before the Backup Utility runs, System Restore creates a restore point. If the backup is unsuccessful or if something happens to the system during the backup, the system can be restored to the state it was in before the Backup utility was run.

◆ *Unsigned Driver Installation*—As drivers are installed for printers, scanners, hard drives, and more, the system checks whether these drivers are signed or unsigned. Unsigned drivers are not approved yet by Microsoft and might not be safe. For every unsigned driver that is installed, a restore point is automatically created. This makes it easy to revert to the previous state if the driver installation is unsuccessful.

Manually Created Restore Points

You can manually create restore points by using the System Restore Wizard, shown in Figure 6.1. This wizard is accessed through System Tools. Later in this chapter, I'll introduce how to use this wizard to create these restore points.

Although many restore points are created automatically, there are several reasons to create a restore point manually. Create a restore point at these times:

◆ Before installing new hardware

◆ Before making a risky change, such as downloading a game or screensaver from the Internet

◆ Before letting another user (especially a child or co-worker) have access to the computer

◆ Before installing any kind of driver

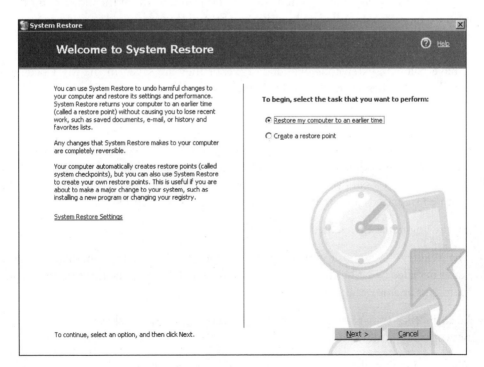

Figure 6.1
The System Restore Wizard.

- ♦ When the computer seems to be in its optimal state

- ♦ Before changing network or protocol settings

- ♦ Before cleaning up the computer by removing programs or files

- ♦ Before installing software (the software might not be System-Restore-compliant)

- ♦ Before using Disk Defragmenter

- ♦ Before performing any tasks at a command prompt

How System Restore Works

So, what makes System Restore work? Every time a restore point is created, System Restore takes a picture of the Registry data and other key files. System Restore then notes the date and time in the restore log and saves the information in a data archive located on the hard disk of the local computer. The archive is on the system disk and is hidden from users. As time passes, the number of restores grows, and when allotted disk space is used up, the old archives are deleted so that new archives can be saved. This is done on a first-in-first-out basis.

You can see the restore points in the System Restore interface and the System Restore Wizard. You can restore to any point available in the archive, from the oldest point to the newest. If a program is installed on Monday, and System Restore is used to revert to Sunday's state, that program might be uninstalled as part of the restore process. However, even if the program is removed, the data files created through that program will be preserved as long as they have common extensions like .doc or .xls or they are saved in the My Documents folder. To use the files again, however, you must reinstall the program.

What Is Restored?

Although the Registry and other key files and folders are replaced or restored with older versions of those files, many files and folders are left intact. This is done to ensure that recent information input by the user will not be lost. Listed next are some of the items that are restored (replaced) and items that are left the same (not restored).

The following items are restored:

- ♦ The Registry—Contains information about a computer's configuration, such as the programs installed, what hardware is on the system, which ports are being used, and settings for folders and program icons.

- ♦ Local profiles (not roaming profiles)—The settings for the desktop, screensaver, and network and printer connections.

- ♦ .dll (dynamic link library) files—Executable routines used by specific applications. These routines are stored in the library and are used only when called upon by the application itself.

♦ IIS (Internet Information Services) Metabase—Similar to the Windows Registry, the IIS Metabase stores information about IIS configuration settings.

The following items are *not* restored:

♦ Passwords

♦ Windows authentication information

♦ User data from user profiles

♦ Contents of redirected folders

♦ Documents (.doc files)

♦ Microsoft Excel, PowerPoint, Access, or Outlook files

♦ Non-Microsoft application files

♦ Email messages

♦ Internet Explorer history and favorites

♦ Anything stored in the My Documents folder, including the My Pictures and My Music folders

System Restore is not a backup tool. System Restore is used when there is a problem with the computer. To back up the My Documents folder or other personal data, you'll need to use the Backup and Restore tools introduced in Chapter 14 of this book. Additionally, if a program is installed and the computer experiences problems, System Restore can be used to recover from this problem. However, using System Restore does not take the place of uninstalling the program. To remove files associated with programs, you must use Add/ Remove Programs in the Control Panel.

Reversible Restorations

All restorations are reversible. There are two ways to reverse a restoration: by undoing the restoration or by choosing another restore point. After completing a restoration, System Restore provides the option to undo it. Choosing a restore point will be detailed later in this chapter.

Available Restore Points

You can choose from several types of restore points (see "Automatically Created Restore Points"). You have even more choices if you've created restore points manually. Because there are different types of restore points, it is sometimes difficult to know which point to choose when using System Restore. For small problems, the latest restore point will generally work fine, but depending on the problem or its perceived cause, other restore points might be better.

Listed next are the available restore points and when you should use them:

♦ *Initial system checkpoint*—Choose this restore point if the machine is new and if you've made several changes on it before rebooting it. If a printer, scanner, and camera are all installed consecutively the first day and problems ensue, it is easiest to restore the initial system checkpoint and start over. It is more difficult to trace the offending hardware or driver. As you're reinstalling the peripheral hardware, reboot and test the computer between each hardware addition.

♦ *System checkpoint*—Because these checkpoints are created automatically every 24 hours of clock time or every 10 hours the computer is turned on, use this checkpoint for restoring if the reason for the problem is unclear. Problems that occur with no obvious cause (such as a new software program or hardware device being added) are very hard to uncover.

♦ *Program installation restore point*—If you've installed a program using one of the latest installers, such as InstallShield 6.1 or higher, then a restore point is created automatically. If you encounter a problem immediately after installing a program, use this restore point. Remember, this will not remove the program files that were copied to the hard drive—that will have to be done through Add/Remove Programs—but it will restore the computer to a working point. If the program isn't installed using InstallShield, select the most recent restore point before the program was installed.

♦ *Automatic Update (Windows Update) restore points*—When an update starts to be installed, a restore point is created. In the rare instance that the download upsets the computer's stability, use this restore point to recover.

♦ *Restore operation restore points*—Use this checkpoint to reverse a restoration.

♦ *Unsigned-device-driver restore points*—If, after accepting the screen warnings, you install an unsigned device driver, use the unsigned-device-driver restore point to recover if problems occur.

♦ *Microsoft Backup utility recovery restore point*—If a problem occurs after or while you're using Microsoft's Backup utility, use this restore point to recover.

♦ *Manually created restore points*—Use these to return to an optimal computer setup or to return the computer to a state before you installed a program or downloaded something from the Internet.

Basic Tasks

Using System Restore is quite easy with the help of the System Restore Wizard. Before explaining how to use this wizard, though, I'll explain how to do some other tasks, such as turning System Restore off and on, manually creating a restore point, changing restore settings, and allocating more disk space for System Restore to use.

Turning System Restore Off and On

By default, System Restore is installed and enabled when Microsoft Windows XP is installed the first time. System Restore remains enabled unless it is turned off or unless available disk space for System Restore runs below 200MB. This space is needed to archive restoration information. If possible, leave System Restore enabled. You never know when you might need it.

To turn System Restore off or on:

1. Log on as an administrator.

2. Open the Control Panel.

3. Choose the System icon to open the System Properties dialog box.

4. Select the System Restore tab.

5. To disable System Restore, check the checkbox Turn Off System Restore On All Drives. Or, to enable System Restore, uncheck the checkbox.

6. Choose OK.

Making More Disk Space Available

If the hard disk doesn't have 200MB of free space for System Restore to use, you won't be able to enable it. Additionally, if disk space runs below 200MB after you've enabled the feature, monitoring of the drives will be suspended, and you will not be able to run the System Restore Wizard. You'll be informed of this with a Suspended status setting in the System Properties dialog box. If this is the case, you'll need to free up some disk space. Although this usually isn't an issue with the large hard drives available nowadays, your hard drive could still fill up, and there are several ways to solve the problem.

Removing Programs No Longer Used

If your computer has programs that you no longer use, remove them using the Add/Control Programs icon in the Control Panel. It is very easy to amass programs, especially if you are trying out several for a good fit. A professional artist, for instance, might install several illustration programs—such as Adobe Illustrator, Macromedia FreeHand, and Deneba Systems' Canvas—on the same computer. After a year or so, the artist might use only Illustrator. In this case, the other programs can most likely be uninstalled, thus freeing up disk space.

Note
For information on removing programs, skip ahead to Chapter 8.

Removing Music, Videos, or Pictures

Music files, videos, and pictures are hard-drive-space eaters. If you've downloaded videos from the Internet, saved music to your hard drive, or created movies using Windows Movie

Maker, chances are good that those files are the culprits for your hard-drive issues. To see a few samples, take a look at Figures 6.2 and 6.3.

Figure 6.2 shows the Properties dialog of the Windows Movie Maker Sample file that is included with Windows XP Professional. The file is 363KB but lasts only 29 seconds. Imagine how many KB of space a 5- or 10-minute movie would use.

Figure 6.3 shows some pictures saved to a Windows 2000 Professional hard drive. Notice the size of the files. If disk space were needed, these files could be moved to a Zip disk or compressed with WinZip or some other utility, and disk space would then be available. In this area alone, almost 16,200KB of space could be freed up.

Removing Components That Aren't Used

Windows XP Professional comes with many components that are installed automatically, including games, document templates, the Paint application, and wallpaper; these components can be uninstalled if they're not needed. Other items, such as Internet Information Services, might be installed initially but might never be used. IIS can be removed to release 16.1MB of disk space.

To see which Windows XP Components are installed on your computer, or to remove or add components:

1. Log on as an administrator and open the Control Panel.

Figure 6.2
Properties of a sample Movie Maker file.

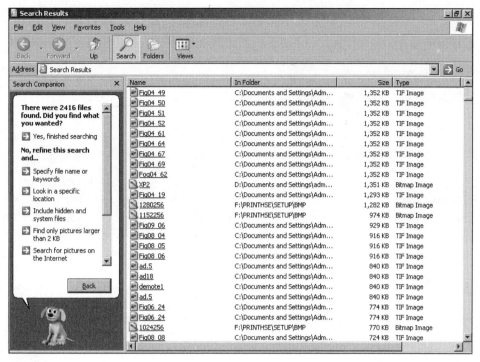

Figure 6.3
Preparing to free up disk space; notice the size of the graphics files.

2. Open Add Or Remove Programs.

3. Choose Add/Remove Windows Components.

4. Scroll through the list to see what is and isn't installed, and add or remove components as necessary.

5. Choose OK.

Using Disk Cleanup

Disk Cleanup is another utility, supplied with Windows XP Professional, that can be used to free up disk space and keep the computer running smoothly. After months of use, the computer retains unnecessary files, such as old program files or temporary Internet files. These files aren't needed by the user or the system and can be deleted.

Listed next are a few of the types of files that Disk Cleanup and the Disk Cleanup Wizard can delete or modify. (For more information on Disk Cleanup and similar utilities, see Chapter 12.) Disk Cleanup can remove or change the following types of files:

◆ Temporary Internet files

◆ Offline Web pages

- Files in the Recycle Bin

- Windows temporary files

- Unused Windows components

- Installed programs that are no longer in use

- Offline files

- Downloaded program files such as ActiveX controls or Java applets

You can launch Disk Cleanup by choosing Start | Programs | Accessories | System Tools | Disk Cleanup. You can also use Scheduled Tasks to set Disk Cleanup to run automatically at certain intervals. While running Disk Cleanup on my Windows XP Professional machine, I was able to free up almost 39,000KB of space. Of course, this number will differ depending on what's installed and how long it's been since the last disk cleanup.

Tip

A restore point is not created when running Disk Cleanup. You should manually create a restore point in case something goes awry during this process.

Creating a Restore Point

You can create a restore point manually by using the System Restore Wizard, available within System Tools. You should manually create a restore point any time you intend to replace a driver or software program or any time you download something from the Internet. Of course, you'll also use other security measures, such as running anti-virus programs and backing up your data, but you can never be too careful.

To create a restore point and see the graphical user interface for the System Restore Wizard:

1. Log on as an administrator.

2. Start the System Restore Wizard by choosing Start | Programs | Accessories | System Tools | System Restore.

3. The Welcome To System Restore page appears, as shown earlier in Figure 6.1. Select the Create A Restore Point option, and choose Next.

4. Type a description for the restore point—for instance, "Before Internet Download Screensaver 5" or "Before New Printer Driver". Choose Create.

5. On the Restore Point Created page, note the new restore point, the date and time, and the name of the restore point as listed. Choose Home to return to the System Restore Wizard, or choose Close to exit.

Changing System Restore Settings

System Restore has just a couple of settings. You can select which drives should be monitored, and you can set the amount of available disk space. By default, drive monitoring is enabled for all drives on a computer. In Figure 6.4, you can see that there are two disk drives on the computer. One drive is called Windows XP (D:), and the other is Windows 2000 (C:). On this computer, both drives are listed as monitored. Although both drives are listed, drive C: is not available for restoration because this particular drive uses Windows 2000 for its operating system.

You can change System Restore settings by using the System Properties dialog box or by using the System Restore Wizard. To use the System Properties dialog box:

1. Log on as an administrator, open the Control Panel, and open System Properties.

2. To turn off monitoring for *all* drives, select the System Restore tab, and check the checkbox Turn Off System Restore On All Drives.

   Or, to turn off monitoring for a *specific* drive, select the drive and choose the Settings button. In the Drive Settings dialog box, check the checkbox Turn Off System Restore On This Drive. This screen is shown in Figure 6.5.

3. Choose OK.

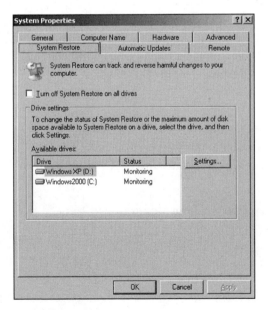

Figure 6.4
System properties.

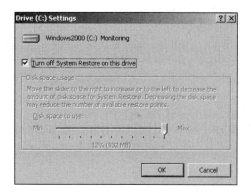

Figure 6.5
Allocating disk space for System Restore.

To use the System Restore Wizard to turn off monitoring for a specific drive:

1. Log on as an administrator.

2. Start the System Restore Wizard by choosing Start | Programs | Accessories | System Tools | System Restore.

3. The Welcome To System Restore page appears, as shown earlier in Figure 6.1. Choose System Restore Settings from the left side of the page.

4. System Properties opens and the System Restore tab is chosen as shown earlier in Figure 6.4. Highlight the drive for which you want to stop monitoring.

5. Check the checkbox Turn Off System Restore On This Drive.

6. Choose OK.

7. The resulting warning box states, "You have chosen to turn off System Restore on this drive. If you continue, you will not be able to track or undo harmful changes on this drive. Do you want to turn off System Restore on this drive?" Choose Yes to confirm that you want to stop monitoring.

8. Notice that the status of the drive has changed from Monitoring to Turned Off.

Note
The status of the drive will be Suspended if the amount of drive space is insufficient.

Allocating More Disk Space
As far as disk space goes, if enough disk space is present, Windows XP will automatically allot 12 percent of the hard drive's space to System Restore. Notice in Figure 6.4 that the minimum of 200MB is exceeded because 12 percent of the available disk space equals 622MB.

This number can be lowered if need be, but it's best left alone to provide maximum effectiveness when you're using System Restore.

To change the amount of disk space being used by System Restore:

1. Log on as an administrator.

2. Start the System Restore Wizard.

3. The Welcome To System Restore page appears, as shown in Figure 6.1. Choose System Restore Settings from the left side of the page.

4. Highlight the drive for which you want to change settings, and choose the Settings button.

5. Use the slider to increase or decrease the disk space that System Restore can use.

6. Choose OK twice.

Note
Twelve percent is the highest allotment possible. To make the space larger would require making the hard drive larger.

Restoring System State Data

System Restore is installed and configured automatically when Windows XP is installed, and System Restore can be used whenever necessary as long as the required disk-space minimum has been met. In this section, you'll learn how to use System Restore through the wizard to restore the system, how to undo a system restoration, and how to use System Restore when the computer will boot only in safe mode. Finally, you'll learn how System Restore compares to the Last Known Good Configuration (LKGC) option and which to choose when a system repair is needed.

Using the System Restore Wizard

The System Restore Wizard is available to walk you through the process of restoring your system to an earlier state. The wizard undoes harmful changes to the computer but does not remove or change any personal documents, email messages, or Internet favorites.

To use the System Restore Wizard to repair a system:

1. Log on as an administrator.

2. Start the System Restore Wizard.

3. The Welcome To System Restore page appears. Make sure that Restore My Computer To An Earlier Time is selected, and choose Next.

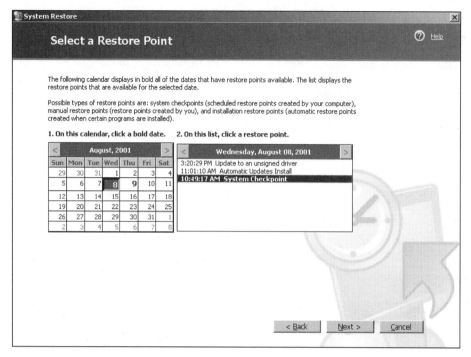

Figure 6.6
Selecting a restore point.

4. On the Select A Restore Point page, which is shown in Figure 6.6, click a date in the calendar to select an optimal restore point. The options available are in bold type. Choose Next.

5. On the Confirm Restore Point Selection page, confirm the information by choosing Next.

Note
The computer must reboot for the restore process to be completed. Make sure you close any open programs and save your work before choosing Next.

6. As the computer automatically reboots, you'll see the System Restore progress box. When the restoration is completed, the computer will be ready to use.

7. On the Restoration Complete page of the System Restore Wizard, you'll see confirmation that the computer was restored successfully. If it was not restored successfully, you can choose from the available options. Choose OK.

Undoing a System Restoration

If the system restoration does not solve the problem, there are a couple of options. The first option, to restore to a different date, restores the computer to another time and date. The second option, to undo the restoration, simply returns the computer to the state it was in before the restoration.

To undo the restoration:

1. Log on as an administrator.

2. Start the System Restore Wizard.

3. The Welcome To System Restore page appears, as shown in Figure 6.7. Select the Undo My Last Restoration option, and choose Next.

4. Save any changes in open documents and close any open programs before confirming the Undo command.

5. As the computer automatically reboots, you'll see the System Restore progress box. When the restoration is completed, the computer will be ready to use.

6. On the Restoration Complete page of the System Restore Wizard, you'll see confirmation that the computer was restored successfully. If it was not restored successfully, you can choose from the available options. Choose OK.

Note
Some files or folders might have been renamed during the restoration process. If this happened, Windows displays a note and a link so that you can see which files were renamed.

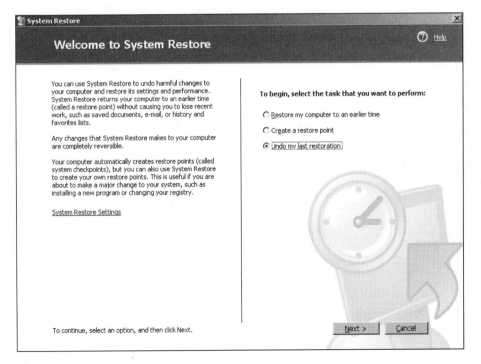

Figure 6.7
Undoing the last restoration.

Running System Restore in Safe Mode

If the computer has problems so bad that it is prevented from booting normally, you can try to boot into safe mode. You can achieve this by pressing F8, Please Select The Operating System To Start, and choosing Safe Mode from the list of available choices for booting.

As the computer boots, only minimal drivers are enabled to make troubleshooting easier. Figure 6.8 shows the Safe Mode Troubleshooter page that appears automatically as Windows XP boots to Safe Mode.

Note

If the computer won't boot to Safe Mode, there are other options for recovery in the Appendix, Troubleshooting.

To use System Restore in Safe Mode, perform the following steps.

1. Reboot the computer and press F8 when prompted to access other booting options, and when you see the Please Select An Operating System To Start choice(s).

2. Choose Safe Mode. Press No when prompted to use System Restore. Selecting Yes will proceed in Safe Mode without System Restore.

3. In the System Restore window shown in Figure 6.8, make the appropriate choice.

4. Work through the wizard as described earlier.

Comparing System Restore to the Last Known Good Configuration

Besides System Restore, there are other options for repairing a broken system. One of those options is Last Known Good Configuration (LKGC). LKGC is a little different from Sys-

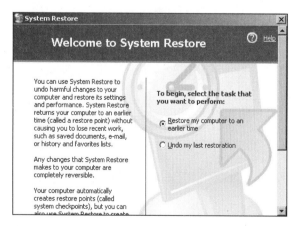

Figure 6.8
Welcome to System Restore.

tem Restore but can be useful if System Restore failed or if a bad device driver has been installed. LKGC is used mainly in cases of incorrect configuration.

LKGC reverts the system to an earlier state, as System Restore does, but the LKGC option won't save any changes to personal files, such as documents that were written, email messages that were sent or received, or favorites added to Internet Explorer. The LKGC is exactly that: the last good configuration that the system is aware of. When the system reverts to this state, any changes made to the system since then are lost.

Additional options are available. Many of these will be discussed in the appendix on troubleshooting. The LKGC option shouldn't be the first or second choice unless the computer problem stems directly from an incorrectly configured machine.

When System Restore Doesn't Work

Occasionally, System Restore will not solve the problem. This is usually due to a problem that the computer had when installed, such as the computer refusing to go on stand-by or into hibernation or not shutting down properly. When this type of problem occurs, there are other options to consider.

System Restore can also fail. In this case, after the restore process is complete, you'll receive a message that the restoration was unsuccessful. The first option at this point should be to pick an earlier restore point. If this is not satisfactory, or if the restoration fails again, there are other options to try.

Numerous things can cause a system to become unstable, and to list all of them would be impossible. However, Windows XP Professional does a good job of offering troubleshooting options, and this help is aimed especially at the novice user. There are two options I'd like to introduce here: troubleshooting in normal mode and using the Safe Mode Troubleshooter.

Troubleshooting in Normal Mode

Windows XP Professional includes many troubleshooting wizards, and if the problem seems to stem from a particular piece of hardware or a specific application, these troubleshooting wizards can be quite useful.

Listed next are most of the available troubleshooters. To launch these, choose Start | Help And Support Services, and then select Fixing A Problem on the Home page. These wizards walk through why a problem occurred, what caused it, and what can be done to repair it. In many cases, these troubleshooting wizards can solve the problems automatically. Here are most of the troubleshooters:

- Games And Multimedia Troubleshooter

- Sound Troubleshooter

- DVD Troubleshooter

- Microsoft Display Troubleshooter

- Internet Explorer Troubleshooter

- Outlook Express Troubleshooter

- Modem Troubleshooter

- Home Networking Troubleshooter

- Internet Connection Sharing Troubleshooter

- Drives And Network Adapters Troubleshooter

- Printing Troubleshooter

- Hardware Troubleshooter

- USB Troubleshooter

- System Setup Troubleshooter

- Startup And Shutdown Troubleshooter

These troubleshooters are very useful and can often be used in place of System Restore. Additionally, they are easy to use and understand.

Troubleshooting in Safe Mode

When booting to safe mode, there are several options to assist you with the troubleshooting process. One of these is the Help and Support Center. If System Restore and normal-mode troubleshooting tools are unable to solve the problem, this tool might help.

To use the Help and Support Center troubleshooters:

1. Restart the computer (or turn it on).

2. When prompted to access other booting options and when you see the "Please select the operating system to start" message, press F8.

3. Choose Safe Mode.

4. Choose Start | Help and Support Services.

5. Choose Fixing A Problem. In the Fixing A Problem window, select the type of problem you are having. For instance, you might choose Hardware and System Device Problems, or Startup and Shutdown Problems.

6. Choose a troubleshooter to use when prompted. Answer the questions in each window of the troubleshooter. The wizard will walk you through options for solving the problem you are having and advise proper procedure for solving the problem once found.

To help you decide what type of problem you are having and to choose the correct trouble-shooter, consider the following questions: How Did You End Up in Safe Mode?

- After you added new hardware, the computer booted into safe mode.

- During setup, the computer automatically and unexpectedly booted into safe mode.

- After you added new software, the computer booted into safe mode.

- A troubleshooter suggested starting in safe mode.

- You manually chose safe mode.

Depending on the type of problem, you'll have to guess at what type of troubleshooter you'll need. Most of them suggest restarting the computer as a first option. This often solves many problems related to hardware and software installations and even problems related to unexpected starts into safe mode. If restarting the computer doesn't solve the problem, then start the Help and Support Center again and try another option.

Using System Restore
If you've restarted the computer, the problem still exists, and the computer again boots into safe mode, the second option is usually to use System Restore. If System Restore didn't work the first time, however, it probably won't work now. If this is the case, skip this step and try something else.

If restarting the computer didn't work, try using System Restore in the following cases:

- After you added new hardware, the computer booted into safe mode.

- After you added new software, the computer booted into safe mode.

- You manually chose safe mode.

- You don't know how the computer got into safe mode.

Compatible Hardware and Software
Many problems are caused by incompatible hardware and software. If restarting the computer and using System Restore don't work, check Microsoft's hardware compatibility list, accessed through **www.microsoft.com/hcl**. If the hardware or software that is causing the problem isn't on Microsoft's HCL, then the problem most likely lies there. If the hardware or software is on the HCL, then the next step is to make sure that the software supplied with the hardware was installed properly through Add Or Remove Programs.

Disabling Startup Files
If, during startup, the computer boots unexpectedly into safe mode, or if the hardware and software are on the HCL and have been installed properly and problems are still apparent, the problem could lie in the startup files. When the startup files are not processed correctly or if they are corrupt or unavailable, they can be disabled temporarily to solve the problems.

To disable the startup files temporarily so you can see if the computer will boot normally:

1. In safe mode, choose Start | Run.

2. Type "msconfig" and choose OK to launch the System Configuration Utility.

3. On the General tab, select Selective Startup.

4. Clear the following options: Process System.ini File, Process Win.ini File, Load System Services, and Load Startup Items. Choose OK. See Figure 6.9.

5. Restart the computer when prompted.

If this step solves the problem, and the computer boots normally, then the problem lies with one of those startup files. To determine which file, start the computer with all of the files listed except one; when the offending file is found, leave its option checked on the General tab of the System Configuration Utility, and boot the computer without it. The file can then be replaced or left unchecked, and the computer can be booted normally.

Tip

Before attempting to disable startup files, you might try using an emergency repair disk (ERD) if one is available. These disks are discussed at the end of this chapter.

Another Troubleshooter Suggested Safe Mode

Only a few troubleshooters suggest that you restart the computer in safe mode. These are:

♦ Games And Multimedia Troubleshooter

♦ Hardware Troubleshooter

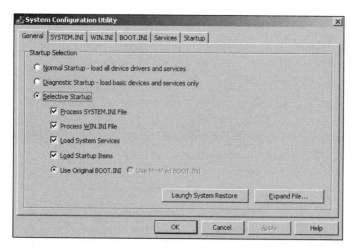

Figure 6.9
System Configuration Utility.

- Startup/Shutdown Troubleshooter

- System Setup Troubleshooter

- Internet Explorer Troubleshooter

- Video Display Troubleshooter

An Ounce of Prevention

At some point, every user will experience a problem with a computer. This problem can be one that causes the computer to boot into safe mode or requires a system restoration. Depending on System Restore and safe mode to provide protection from all computer problems is naïve, though. Your computer emergency kit should include several things, including good backups of personal files, a list of ID and product numbers for all installed software, help-desk numbers for hardware and software, an anti-virus program, and an ERD.

Creating backups is covered in Chapter 14. Organizing IDs, product numbers, and help-desk phone numbers is as simple as gathering all of the software and compiling a list. Anti-virus programs can be purchased online or from a computer store. Creating an emergency repair disk can be done through Windows XP Professional.

Creating an Emergency Repair Disk

An ERD is a disk, created using the Backup utility in Windows XP Professional, that contains information about how the current Windows operating system is set up. The ERD contains current system settings, and it can be used to start the computer if it won't boot to safe mode. The ERD can also be used to start and repair the computer if the system files are damaged or erased.

To create an ERD:

1. Choose Start | Programs | Accessories | System Tools | Backup.

2. Choose the Advanced Mode button.

3. Choose Automated System Recovery Wizard.

4. Choose Next to start the wizard.

5. Place a blank floppy disk in the floppy disk drive.

6. Choose Next.

7. Choose Finish.

Printing System Information

If System Restore doesn't work, safe mode doesn't work, and the ERD doesn't work, you'll most likely have to take your computer to an expert at a computer repair shop. If this ever happens, you should send a system summary of what the computer contains, including which version of Windows XP is installed, which drivers are installed, how much memory is installed, and so on.

To view and print a system summary report or to send the report to a floppy disk for archiving:

1. Choose Start | Help And Support Services.

2. Click Support at the top of the Help And Support Centerwindow.

3. Click Advanced System Information.

4. Select View Detailed Information in the Help And Support Services window, and then choose File | Print or File | Export from the System Information screen. If you choose Export, browse to the location where the file should be saved. Choose OK.

Wrapping Up

In this chapter, you learned about using System Restore, a utility that can return the system to a previous state without losing any of your personal data, such as documents, email messages, or Internet favorites. You learned how to perform basic and advanced tasks using System Restore and what to do if System Restore fails.

System Restore can also be used in safe mode, and this chapter discussed options such as troubleshooting in normal mode and using the Safe Mode Troubleshooter. Finally, you learned about creating ERDs and printing system information to use when System Restore won't solve the problem.

Chapter 7
Device Driver Rollback

After installing Windows XP Professional on a number of different machines, I can say with absolute certainty that Windows XP Professional has the largest device-driver library of any of the available Microsoft operating systems. This collection of drivers not only makes installing (or reinstalling) Windows XP easier, but also makes adding hardware devices, like Zip drives and digital cameras, easier.

Device drivers are the software programs that allow Windows XP to communicate with the hardware on your system. This hardware consists of a lot more than just printers and scanners or anything else considered an add-on. In Chapter 4, you learned about printer drivers and how to install them so that the printer functions correctly with your computer. Your system needs many other drivers, though, including the most basic driver, a video driver, which the computer needs to send information to the monitor.

In this chapter, you'll learn quite a bit about device drivers, driver signing, driver installation and updates, and Device Manager. You'll also learn about Device Driver Rollback, which now is an option in all of the driver Properties dialogs on the system. Driver Rollback allows you to recover from the installation of a driver that doesn't work or that causes the computer to hang or not start. Driver Rollback is a new feature available only in Windows XP operating systems, and it is, in my opinion, the best new feature in Windows XP Professional.

Introduction to Device Drivers

Drivers are an integral part of the system, for hardware outside and inside. Hardware that is outside the computer, such as a monitor or a scanner, must have a driver installed to run properly, while virtual device drivers are used internally to make hard drives and other internal computer hardware work properly. When you purchase a computer from a store or direct from a company, all of the necessary drivers are installed already and are working properly. When you're building your own computer, this is certainly not the case.

For the most part, you need be concerned with only the drivers for external hardware. The majority of hardware upgrades for a computer have to do with external additions, not internal ones. As hardware components are added, so are their drivers. Windows XP can install many of these hardware devices automatically from its library of available drivers. This library is quite large. However, not all drivers are available automatically from Windows XP's library and must be installed manually.

A common reason that a driver might not be available from Windows XP's library is that the hardware was created after Windows XP was released and before a service pack or Windows Update became available with the new driver. Another reason is that the hardware is so old that Windows XP no longer supports it. Finally, the hardware might not be plug-and-play (PnP), a capability that allows you to plug a device into a port and have the device be automatically recognized by the system. PnP devices are also called *plug-ins*, and many devices, including Zip disks and digital cameras, can be plugged in and used without even shutting down and restarting the system.

Note

Make sure to read the manufacturer's instructions, especially for zip disks. Some PnP devices should not be plugged into the machine while it is turned on or in hibernation. Doing so could harm the system.

Whatever happens, a driver must be installed for every new device added to the system, and all hardware on the system has a device driver. Drivers that are included automatically on many systems include drivers for the following hardware:

- Advanced Configuration and Power Interface (ACPI)
- Hard drives
- Display adapters (video cards)
- DVD, CD-ROM, CD-RW, and floppy disk drives
- Keyboards
- Mice
- Modems

♦ Monitors

♦ Network adapters (network connector cards)

♦ Communications ports

♦ The CPU (central processing unit)

♦ SCSI and RAID controllers

♦ Sound and media control devices

♦ Items on the system board, such as the PCI bus, the system timer, fans, and data processors

♦ USB root hubs and controllers

How Drivers Work

Device drivers work by allowing the operating system and the hardware to communicate. Without this communication, the device would not be able to act on your command, which is forwarded from you to the operating system and then to the device and back again. Because the computer and the hardware communicate in different languages, there must be a translator. The device driver is the liaison (or translator), so to speak, between the two, allowing them to communicate effectively.

The manufacturer must make hardware such as disk drives or video cards so that they can work with any operating system on the market. For instance, when you're buying a printer, the printer will include software (drivers) for several operating systems. These can include Macintosh OS, Novell NetWare, Linux, Windows 9x, Windows NT, Windows 2000, and Windows XP. Because each of these operating systems functions differently and communicates differently with devices, different drivers for each are needed.

Driver Problems

Problems can occur if the wrong device driver is installed. You can probably see why a Windows 98 driver installed on a Windows XP machine would cause problems. Windows XP and Windows 98 are two completely different operating systems and thus communicate with devices differently. These differences can be compared to two people speaking different languages. Although one might speak American English and the other might speak British English, and some similarities exist, they are still different enough to cause communication problems. Those bad drivers can cause problems such as intermittent communication lapses or no communication at all.

Other problems with drivers occur when the hardware isn't on Microsoft's hardware compatibility list (HCL). In my experience, it is always best to replace a device that is not on the HCL with one that is to avoid problems with installing and using the device. To see Microsoft's HCL, go to **www.microsoft.com/hcl**. If replacing the device that isn't on the list isn't an option, there are sometimes workarounds. (See the section "Obtaining Drivers from the Internet," or return to Chapter 4 for more information about downloading drivers.)

Another reason devices don't work is that they become corrupt or go out-of-date. If you suspect that the driver is corrupt or has somehow been damaged, you can replace or reinstall it through Device Manager. The symptoms of a corrupt device driver include the device performing oddly or not at all or any type of communication problem between the operating system and the hardware.

Out-of-date drivers are usually a problem when an older device is installed on a newer machine. For instance, say that a printer that was used with a Windows NT Workstation system will now be used with a Windows XP Professional computer. Although the printer is still in good working order, the driver that was used with Windows NT Workstation probably won't work with Windows XP. If the XP driver library doesn't have an updated version of the driver, one will have to be obtained from the manufacturer.

There are several ways to solve driver problems, and these will be discussed later in this chapter. There are very specific ways to avoid these problems, however, and one way is to use PnP devices.

Plug-and-Play Driver Support

Plug-and-play devices are hardware components that conform to specific standards—specifically, universal Plug and Play standards—that define how hardware and software will interact with each other. These standards are industry- and system-wide. They allow plug-and-play devices to be created by manufacturers so that users can add and remove devices dynamically, meaning that those devices need no manual installation of drivers.

The Plug and Play standard requires that the computer's BIOS, hardware, device drivers, and operating system all interact and combine resources and information. If the hardware in the computer is PnP-compatible, and the hardware and driver to be added are also PnP-compatible, then Windows XP Professional can perform all of the following tasks:

♦ Automatically installing new devices

♦ Recognizing changes to PnP hardware during system boot

♦ Responding to events such as plugging a device into a USB port or docking a laptop

♦ Installing device drivers

♦ Interacting with power management devices to awaken a computer or put it to sleep (in stand-by mode or hibernation)

♦ Providing partial support for many non-PnP devices

♦ Configuring the IRQ numbers

- Configuring DMA channels

- Configuring Input/Output addresses

- Configuring memory address ranges

The Plug and Play standard also makes sure that no two devices share any of these resources such that a conflict arises. Before Plug and Play, every device had to be configured manually. This caused many problems with device conflicts; if two devices used the same IRQ or the same memory ranges, problems ensued. With Windows XP, a PnP manager watches over all of the PnP devices to make sure these problems don't arise.

Conflicts can still occur, however, especially if non-PnP devices are installed. When this happens, and these devices are configured and installed manually, the PnP manager isn't consulted. Non-PnP devices are a drain on the entire system. If possible, it is best to stay away from non-supported devices.

Other facts about PnP:

- To install a plug-and-play device, you must be a member of the Administrators group or logged on as an administrator.

- Network policy can prevent even local administrators from installing devices and device drivers.

- Older PnP devices might have limited abilities.

- With many PnP devices, the computer doesn't even need to be restarted after installation.

Available Drivers

Windows supports many types of PnP hardware and provides drivers for multiple manufacturers. Although many products and manufacturers are supported, make sure to check the HCL before purchasing. The following is a list of the types of devices that are supported by Windows XP Professional; each device type is followed by a few of the manufacturers. "Supported" means that Windows XP Professional can install these devices. Keep in mind, though, that even though a specific make of device is supported, a particular model might not be. Here are device types and manufacturers:

- *Display adapters*—ATI Technologies, S3 Graphics, Silicon Motion, and SiS

- *Imaging devices*—Agfa, Canon, Casio, Epson, Hewlett-Packard, Kodak, Nikon, and Sanyo

- *Infrared devices*—AMP, Extended Systems, Parallax, VIA Technologies, Inc., and Vishay Telefunken

- *Modems*—Diamond Multimedia Systems, Digital Phone, Hayes, IBM, Microcom, Motorola, Panasonic, and TDK

- *Multiport serial adapters*—Digi International and Equinox

- *Network adapters*—3Com and Microsoft

- *PCMCIA adapters*—Compaq, Databook, Intel, and Vadem

- *Standard ports-* such as communications ports, printer ports, and communications ports

- *Printers*—Alps, Apple, AT&T, Brother, Canon, Citizen, Epson, Fujitsu, HP, IBM, Kodak, Konica, Lexmark, Minolta, NEC, Radio Shack, Samsung, Sharp, Texas Instruments, and Xerox

- *SCSI and RAID controllers*—Adaptec, Highpoint Technologies, Inc., and Mylex

- *Sound, video, and game controllers*—Creative Technology, Inc., ESS Technology, IBM, Microsoft, NeoMagic Corporation, ThrustMaster, and Yamaha

- *System devices*—Intel, Microsoft, and SCM Microsystems

- *Tape devices*—None as of RC2

Driver Signing

Microsoft digitally signs device drivers that pass the Windows Hardware Quality Lab (WHQL) tests. Only the drivers that pass are given a Microsoft digital signature. This digital signature is then associated with the driver package and is recognized automatically by Windows XP Professional systems.

Digital signatures ensure that the device driver has passed this level of testing and that the files have not been tampered with or modified since being tested. The knowledge that the driver to be installed is safe, or that its level of safety isn't known, can be used by the installer to determine if the file should be installed.

In this section, you'll learn how to use the File Signature Verification utility to see which files on your computer are unsigned and how to set file-signature verification options. You also see which warnings are shown when you install an unsigned driver. If a driver is signed, it will not be shown on this list.

File-Signature Verification

To see what files on your computer are unsigned (have not been digitally signed by Microsoft), use the File Signature Verification utility.

To use the File Signature Verification utility to view the files on your system:

1. Choose Start | Run.

2. Type "sigverif" in the Open box.

3. Choose OK.
4. Choose Start. When the process is complete, the Signature Verification Results window appears, as shown in Figure 7.1.

This information allows you to see which system files and device driver files have been overwritten or are unsigned. This log becomes useful when unsigned drivers have altered other files and caused instability in the computer. The Signature Verification Results window shows each file's name, location, modification date, type, and version number. The offending driver file can often be found here.

Installing an Unsigned Driver

Drivers are usually unsigned for a good reason. Installing an unsigned driver can cause system-wide or intermittent problems and can even cause a computer to "blue-screen." Blue screens have the nickname "Blue Screen of Death" because these errors are hard to get rid of and occasionally cause the computer's operating system to have to be reinstalled. A blue screen appears when the computer encounters a STOP error. Sometimes an error is so bad that the system cannot recover by itself, or even issue a STOP error. On occasion, a driver can completely freeze up a system. When this happens, the computer must be rebooted, sometimes by actually turning off, and then back on, the machine.

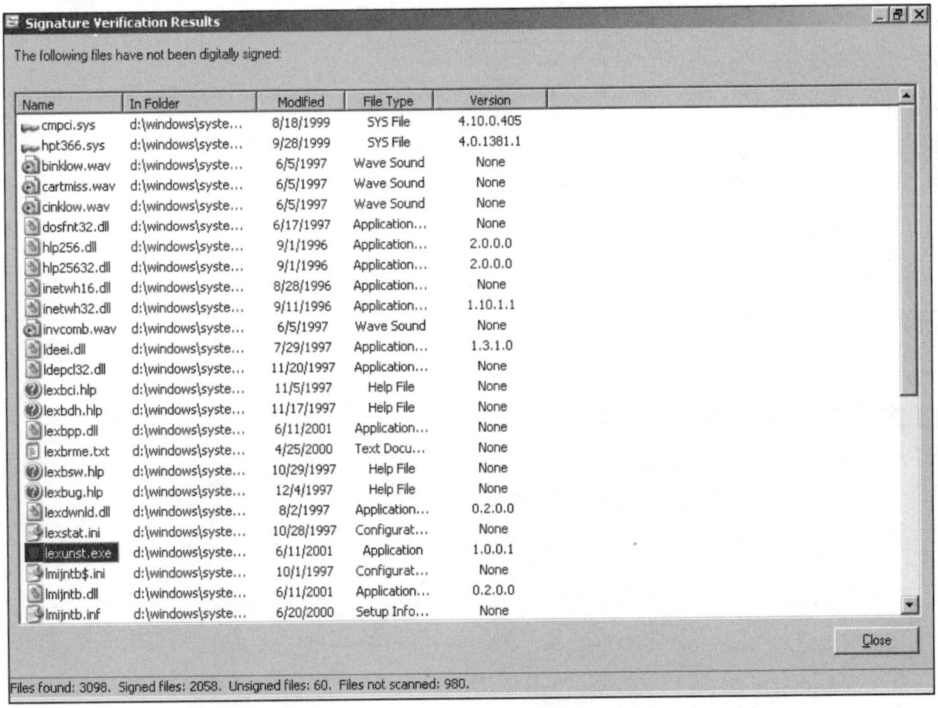

Name	In Folder	Modified	File Type	Version
cmpci.sys	d:\windows\syste...	8/18/1999	SYS File	4.10.0.405
hpt366.sys	d:\windows\syste...	9/28/1999	SYS File	4.0.1381.1
binklow.wav	d:\windows\syste...	6/5/1997	Wave Sound	None
cartmiss.wav	d:\windows\syste...	6/5/1997	Wave Sound	None
cinklow.wav	d:\windows\syste...	6/5/1997	Wave Sound	None
dosfnt32.dll	d:\windows\syste...	6/17/1997	Application...	None
hlp256.dll	d:\windows\syste...	9/1/1996	Application...	2.0.0.0
hlp25632.dll	d:\windows\syste...	9/1/1996	Application...	2.0.0.0
inetwh16.dll	d:\windows\syste...	8/28/1996	Application...	None
inetwh32.dll	d:\windows\syste...	9/11/1996	Application...	1.10.1.1
invcomb.wav	d:\windows\syste...	6/5/1997	Wave Sound	None
ldeei.dll	d:\windows\syste...	7/29/1997	Application...	1.3.1.0
ldepcl32.dll	d:\windows\syste...	11/20/1997	Application...	None
lexbci.hlp	d:\windows\syste...	11/5/1997	Help File	None
lexbdh.hlp	d:\windows\syste...	11/17/1997	Help File	None
lexbpp.dll	d:\windows\syste...	6/11/2001	Application...	None
lexbrme.txt	d:\windows\syste...	4/25/2000	Text Docu...	None
lexbsw.hlp	d:\windows\syste...	10/29/1997	Help File	None
lexbug.hlp	d:\windows\syste...	12/4/1997	Help File	None
lexdwnld.dll	d:\windows\syste...	8/2/1997	Application...	0.2.0.0
lexstat.ini	d:\windows\syste...	10/28/1997	Configurat...	None
lexunst.exe	d:\windows\syste...	6/11/2001	Application	1.0.0.1
lmijntb$.ini	d:\windows\syste...	10/1/1997	Configurat...	None
lmijntb.dll	d:\windows\syste...	6/11/2001	Application...	0.2.0.0
lmijntb.inf	d:\windows\syste...	6/20/2000	Setup Info...	None

Figure 7.1
Signature verification.

Of course, you know that System Restore can be used to revert the system to a previous state, even from safe mode, and many of these problems can be solved rather quickly, but unsigned device drivers still pose a risk. Even if an unsigned driver is installed and the computer doesn't blue-screen, you won't know if the computer is struggling. Later, when the CD-ROM drive quits working or the system hangs for no apparent reason, you might forget that the unsigned driver could be the culprit.

Figure 7.2 shows the Add Hardware Wizard and an unsigned-driver warning.

Driver Warnings

There will be times when you'll need to install drivers. In the following example, I was using a beta version of Windows XP Professional, and I needed to install a CD-RW drive whose driver wasn't appropriately tested at the time of the writing of this book. After I agreed to the license agreement and worked through the installation setup, Windows displayed the warning shown in Figure 7.3.

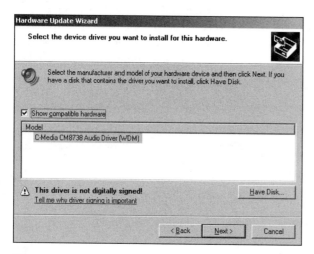

Figure 7.2
A warning about an unsigned driver.

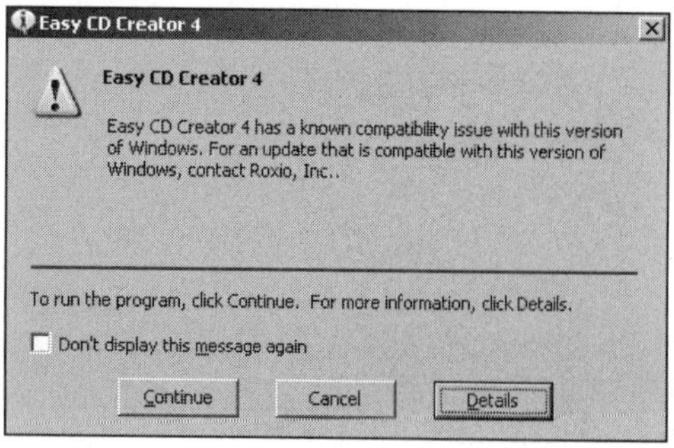

Figure 7.3
A compatibility warning.

I chose to run the program anyway. As I expected, the CD-ROM drive that was also installed on the computer couldn't be accessed and wasn't even listed in My Computer, and a week or so later, the CD-RW drive stopped working. During this time, intermittent problems occurred that may or may not have been related to the driver.

The point to remember is this: If Microsoft hasn't signed a driver, there is a reason, and if driver warnings are issued during installation, that's a red flag, too. If you must install an unsigned device and driver anyway, install it through Add/Remove Hardware, and install an update to that driver as soon as one is available.

Later in this chapter, I'll show you how to obtain an updated, and preferably signed, driver from the Internet.

Setting File-Signature Verification Options

When installing software such as device drivers, you can set rules for what can and cannot be installed. You then can apply these rules to anyone logging onto the computer. You have three file-signature verification options:

♦ *Ignore*—Installs all files regardless of the signatures

♦ *Warn*—Displays a message before installing an unsigned file (the default setting)

♦ *Block*—Prevents installation of unsigned files

To view or change your file-signature verification options:

1. Log on as an administrator.

2. Open the Control Panel.

3. Open System.

4. In the System Properties dialog box, select the Hardware tab.

5. Choose the Driver Signing button to open the Driver Signing Options dialog box.

6. Select the file-signature verification level that is appropriate.

7. Check the checkbox Make This Action The System Default.

8. Choose OK twice.

Installing Device Drivers (New Hardware)

To install a device by using the Add Hardware Wizard, you must be a member of the Administrators group or be logged on as an administrator. If the computer also is installed on a network, you'll need network permissions to install hardware and drivers. If the driver has already been installed, however, a user can add physical hardware to the system.

Chapter 4 explained how to install printers and printer drivers. Most times, other devices are installed the same way. Installations can differ, depending on whether the device is PnP or whether the device driver is digitally signed. Many scenarios for installing hardware were covered in that chapter and will be further detailed in Chapter 8. No matter what hardware is installed, though, a driver must be installed with it.

Before Installing a Driver

You can never be too careful when installing a new piece of hardware and a driver for it. Before installing a driver, there are a few safety measures to take. Make sure you have checked and/or performed the following items or tasks:

♦ Read the information about the driver carefully. Verify that it was written for Windows XP Professional.

♦ Examine any Read Me files associated with the driver. Some drivers have special requirements such as changing the BIOS settings or removing older copies of drivers.

♦ Check the device manufacturer's Web site for any known problems and their solutions.

♦ Back up your data.

♦ Create a restore point in System Restore.

♦ Close all running and open programs.

♦ Know how to recover from a blue screen by using safe mode and System Restore.

Installation

You can install drivers through the Control Panel—from Add Hardware, Gaming Options, Add Or Remove Programs, Printers And Faxes, Scanners And Cameras, or System—and/or from Device Manager. With PnP, installing a driver isn't an issue because the device will be installed automatically. It is only the drivers for non-PnP devices and devices that aren't supported in Windows XP Professional that need manual installation.

Installing non-PnP devices requires using one of the previously mentioned sources, usually Add Hardware and the Add Hardware Wizard. To use this wizard to install a new driver for a new piece of hardware:

1. Log on as an administrator.

2. Open the Control Panel.

3. Open Add Hardware.

4. When the Add Hardware Wizard starts, the first screen shown is the Installed Hardware page. This page shows all of the currently installed hardware on your system and is

available if you need to troubleshoot a piece of equipment. To add a new device and driver, highlight Add A New Hardware Device, as shown in Figure 7.4, and choose Next.

5. Wait while the wizard searches for the new hardware. If the hardware is found, either the hardware will be installed automatically because the driver is available in the Windows XP library or you'll need to skip to Step 10 to continue.

6. If the hardware isn't found, when prompted, answer if the hardware is connected or not. If you choose No, I Have Not Added The Hardware Yet, the wizard will end. If you choose Yes, I Have Already Connected the Hardware, it will continue.

7. Highlight the type of hardware you want to add, or choose Add A New Hardware Device, and choose Next.

8. Choose Install The Hardware That I Manually Select From A List (Advanced).

9. On the Common Hardware Types page, select the type of hardware you are installing (display adapter, modem, network adapter, etc.). Choose Next.

10. In the Manufacturers list box, select the manufacturer of the device. In the Model list box, select the device model. If the device's manufacturer and model aren't both listed, skip to Step 12; if they are, choose Next.

11. To start installing the hardware, choose Next and follow the resulting directions; then skip to Step 13. If a warning was issued that the driver selected doesn't match what is being installed, choose the Back button.

12. Choose the Have Disk button. Place the manufacturer's disk in the disk drive, or use the Browse button to browse to the driver files. These files could be in the floppy drive or in a folder of driver downloads from the Internet. Choose OK twice when done.

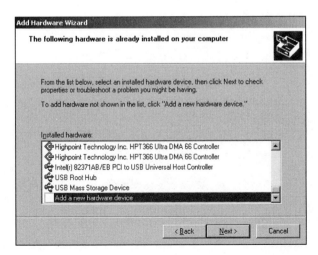

Figure 7.4
The Add Hardware Wizard's list of installed devices.

13. When the installation for the driver begins, one of three things will happen.

    ◆ The installation will go smoothly and finish without incident.

    ◆ The driver location you specified does not have any drivers, or those drivers are not compatible.

    ◆ The driver is not signed, and a warning is shown, as in Figure 7.5.

14. If the installation is completed, the hardware has been successfully installed. If the location you specified for the driver files doesn't have any compatible drivers, then find those drivers and save them to a floppy disk, Zip disk, CD-RW, or hard drive. If Windows displays the message shown in Figure 7.5, then the driver isn't digitally signed. Decide if you want to risk installing the unsigned driver or if you want to cancel the installation. If necessary, look for a different driver by contacting the manufacturer again or accessing driver websites.

Note

The warning shown in Figure 7.5 appears when default settings for file verification are used. If the setting has been changed to Ignore, the driver will be installed; if the setting has been changed to Block, no choice will be given, and the installation will abort. The screen in Figure 7.6 will be shown if the driver isn't installed.

Depending on what is being installed, after a successful driver installation, the Add Hardware Wizard will walk you though naming and sharing the device, typing a location for and comment about the device, and making additional configurations as necessary. This part of the hardware installation will be covered in more depth in Chapter 8.

Ignoring the Warnings

If you've chosen to install a driver that wasn't signed, as shown in Figure 7.6, or you install a driver that presented warnings, as was shown in Figure 7.3, chances are pretty good that

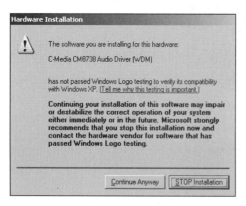

Figure 7.5
A warning for an unsigned (untested) driver.

Figure 7.6
Message that an unsigned driver was not installed.

you'll need to reverse, erase, or upgrade that driver installation at some point. The system might blue-screen, hang, or otherwise cause problems that are hard to trace. If you've ignored the warnings and installed anyway, fully check out the system before going much further. Interestingly, the device installed, as shown in Figure 7.6, works perfectly.

In the next few sections, you'll learn how to upgrade drivers, erase drivers, and use Device Driver Rollback to repair problems related to incompatible or unsigned drivers. You'll then learn how to download updated drivers from the Internet.

Warning
If you've just installed an unsigned driver and are currently having problems with it, skip to the section "Using Device Driver Rollback." Do not upgrade the device driver; rollback features can roll back only one driver installation, not two.

Upgrading Device Drivers (Existing Hardware)

When devices are installed with older drivers, or if the drivers are unsigned or present warnings, sometimes the hardware can still function minimally and occasionally even normally. When an upgraded driver is available, though, it should be installed as soon as possible. This is especially true if the driver is unsigned or if the computer has exhibited problem behaviors after the driver was installed.

Device Manager is the best place to install the updated driver. To upgrade a device driver by using Device Manager:

1. Log on as an administrator.

2. On the desktop, right-click My Computer, and choose Properties.

3. In the System Properties dialog box, select the Hardware tab.

4. Choose the Device Manager button.

5. Expand the tree that contains the hardware whose driver is unsigned or provides minimal support. You should have an updated driver handy on a floppy disk, the hard drive, an accessible network drive, or some other source. Double-click the hardware name. Figure 7.7 shows both the Device Manager and an unsigned driver that needs to be updated.

6. Select the Driver tab of the hardware's Properties dialog. See Figure 7.7 again.

7. Choose Update Driver.

8. The Hardware Update Wizard appears. Read the instructions carefully. If you have the updated driver on a CD-ROM or floppy disk, place it in the drive and choose Next. The installation will continue; skip to Step 11. If the updated driver is on the hard drive or network, check the checkbox Install From A List Or Specific Location (Advanced), and choose Next.

9. On the Please Choose Your Search And Installation Options page, make the appropriate choices to connect to the driver. The driver might be stored on a floppy or CD-ROM,

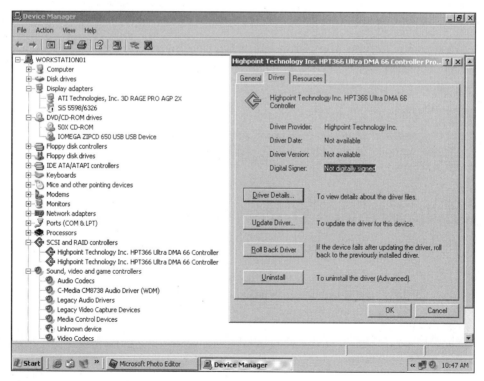

Figure 7.7
A hardware Properties dialog.

a network place, or a hard drive, or you can select from a list. If you know the location of the driver, browse to it and choose OK, then Next. Then, skip to Step 11. If you want to search for a driver, select Don't Search, I Will Choose The Driver To Install; choose Next.

10. Locate the driver to install, and choose Next.

11. After the updated driver is installed, you'll see a screen similar to Figure 7.8. Choose Finish. With Windows XP Professional, oftentimes this is all you need to do. Although, depending on the driver, you might have to reboot. Reboot if necessary.

Device Driver Problems

If, after you install the latest available disk driver, the computer remains unstable or blue-screens, and your attempts to resolve the issue fail, consider calling the driver manufacturer's technical-support line for information about where and when a new driver will be available or for information about any known problems with the driver or patches for those problems. Sometimes a driver update is available from the manufacturer even if the driver is a new one.

The following problems can indicate an inappropriate driver:

♦ The hardware doesn't work.

♦ The hardware has intermittent problems.

♦ A game doesn't recognize the controller.

♦ STOP errors occur.

♦ The computer hangs when a specific piece of hardware is used.

Figure 7.8
Successful installation of an updated driver.

- The computer reboots unexpectedly.

- The computer reboots in safe mode.

- The computer hangs when being shut down, or it doesn't shut down correctly.

- The computer hangs on boot-up.

- Error messages about the hardware are shown.

- The hardware has only minimal functionality.

- Other applications that have never had problems fail unexpectedly.

- The monitor flickers.

- CD-ROM drives, floppy drives, or DVD-ROM drives fail to work.

- Out-of-memory errors occur.

Device Driver Rollback

So, what if after all of these precautions and all of this information, you still install a driver that doesn't work? Well, it happens more often than you'd think, but thankfully, Windows XP Professional makes it very easy to recover from it. In all of the Properties dialogs for all of the drivers on the computer is a new button: Roll Back Driver. Figure 7.9 shows the Roll Back Driver button on the Driver tab of a modem's Properties dialog box.

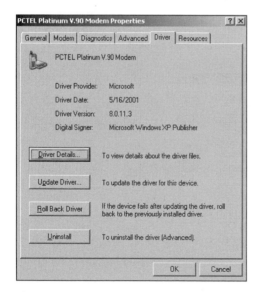

Figure 7.9
The Roll Back Driver button.

The Driver Rollback feature allows you to reverse damaging driver installations and revert to the previous driver. If no previous driver exists, as when you're installing a new piece of hardware, you'll see the following message: "No driver files have been backed up for this device. If you are having problems with this device you should view the Troubleshooter information. Would you like to launch the Troubleshooter?" A Yes response then launches the troubleshooter, and a No response cancels the driver rollback procedure.

If a device driver has been updated, then a previous driver does exist and is available. The message in the previous paragraph won't be shown, and the driver rollback procedure will begin.

Using Driver Rollback

To use Driver Rollback:

1. Log on as an administrator.

2. Right-click My Computer, and choose Properties.

3. In the System Properties dialog box, select the Hardware tab.

4. Choose the Device Manager button.

5. Expand the tree that contains the hardware with the faulty or out-of-date driver.

6. Double-click the device name to open the device's Properties dialog box.

7. Select the Driver tab.

8. Choose the Roll Back Driver button.

9. If the information page shown in Figure 7.10 is displayed, click Yes and work through the troubleshooter; if the troubleshooter doesn't solve the problem, skip to the section "If Driver Rollback Doesn't Work." If this page is not shown, continue with Step 10.

10. In the screen, Are You Sure You Would Like To Roll Back To The Previous Driver, choose Yes.

11. The driver rollback will occur automatically; when it's finished, choose Close.

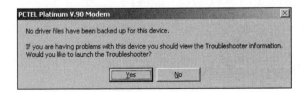

Figure 7.10
No rollback possible.

Note

If the driver you rolled back to doesn't work the way you'd like, you can run Driver Rollback again and revert to the previous driver.

Driver Rollback Limitations

There is one limitation of the Driver Rollback feature: It is a single-level rollback only. This is an important concept to understand. If an unreliable driver is installed, driver rollback can revert to the older, working driver. However, if a second driver is installed before the driver rollback is used, then the saved (backup) driver is the non-working one. To make sure this doesn't become an issue for you, always use Driver Rollback at the first sign of a driver problem.

If Driver Rollback Doesn't Work

Finally, if there isn't a previously saved driver, or if you installed a second driver before rolling back the first bad driver, other recovery options are still available. The first is System Restore, detailed in Chapter 6, and the second is Last Known Good Configuration (LKGC).

As a refresher, to use System Restore to revert the computer to a previous state:

1. Log on as an administrator.

2. Choose Start | Programs | Accessories | System Tools | System Restore.

3. Choose Restore My Computer To An Earlier Time, and choose Next.

4. Choose a checkpoint from before the driver installation, and choose Next.

5. Choose Next to confirm the restore point and to restore the system.

When you use the LKGC option, all changes made after the last known good configuration will be lost, including personal files. To use LKGC to revert to the last time the computer was working properly:

1. Reboot the computer.

2. At the Choose An Operating System To Start screen, press F8.

3. Choose Last Known Good Configuration.

Removing a Driver Completely

You can remove a driver completely and thus uninstall the driver and the hardware from the system. This is necessary if all other options to make the driver work have failed. This is usually done if the hardware's driver simply won't work with the current operating system.

Uninstalling a driver should be done from Device Manager. If a piece of hardware is simply deleted from a folder such as Printers And Faxes, the hardware's driver is not removed from the system. In Figure 7.11, you can see the Printers And Faxes folder (accessed through Control Panel) and the chosen printer with Delete highlighted in the context menu. Deleting this printer here will not remove the driver for the printer.

Using Add Or Remove Programs also doesn't work for removing hardware drivers. Only software programs can be removed from here. In some instances, a piece of new hardware also comes with a software program, like a graphics program or a user interface for the hardware. Although the software for the device can be removed, this again isn't the driver for the hardware. Remember, it is the bad driver that causes the system to be unstable.

To uninstall a driver from a system:

1. Log on as an administrator.

2. Right-click My Computer, and choose Properties.

3. In the System Properties dialog box, select the Hardware tab.

4. Choose the Device Manager button.

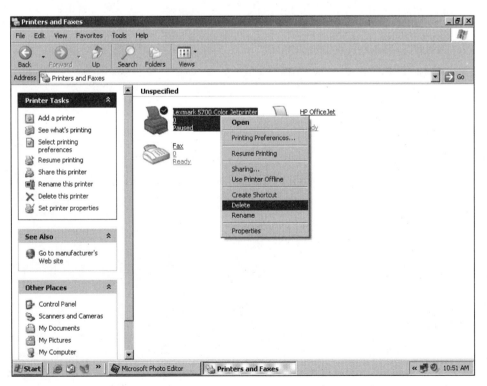

Figure 7.11
Deleting a printer, not the printer driver.

5. Expand the tree, and locate the device with the driver to uninstall; double-click it.

6. Select the Driver tab.

7. Choose Uninstall.

8. Choose OK in the warning box.

9. Notice that Device Manager refreshes and that the device is removed from the system. Close Device Manager and System Properties.

Device Manager

You can use Device Manager for other tasks besides rolling back, updating, and removing drivers. You can also get details about the driver for a particular device, including where the driver files are stored and what they are called. The file version is available as well as the copyright, provider, and digital signer.

Device Manager can also be used to disable a piece of hardware and its driver. Disabling a driver and uninstalling the driver are two completely different tasks. Uninstalling the driver removes it from the system. Disabling the driver leaves the driver on the system but temporarily prevents the driver from being used.

Disabling a Device Driver

To disable a driver for a device:

1. Log on as an administrator.

2. Right-click My Computer, and choose Properties.

3. In the System Properties dialog box, select the Hardware tab.

4. Choose the Device Manager button.

5. Expand the tree to locate the device in question.

6. Right-click the device name, and choose Disable.

7. Choose OK when prompted.

Obtaining Drivers from the Internet

If the driver installed for a device on your Windows XP Professional system isn't performing up to par, you might be able to get an updated driver from the Internet. There are several places to find these drivers, and some Web sites are more reliable than others. After using Windows Update to connect to Microsoft's site and to download the latest service packs, hot fixes, critical updates, and available drivers, and after performing a system restore, you can begin looking. The first place to look for a driver is the manufacturer's Web site.

Manufacturers' Web Sites

Accessing the manufacturer's web site is usually the best place to begin looking for new drivers. Within the Web site, the drivers are generally located in one of the following places:

♦ Drivers

♦ Support or Support | Drivers

♦ Downloads

♦ Tech Support

♦ Updates

After locating the Drivers page, type in the name, make, and model of the device, or choose this information from a list. Figure 7.12 shows an example of this from the Hewlett-Packard Web site.

You'll be prompted to give information about the operating system you are using and perhaps what type of computer you have. After you supply this information, you'll be directed to a place to download the driver you need—unless, of course, no driver is available. After

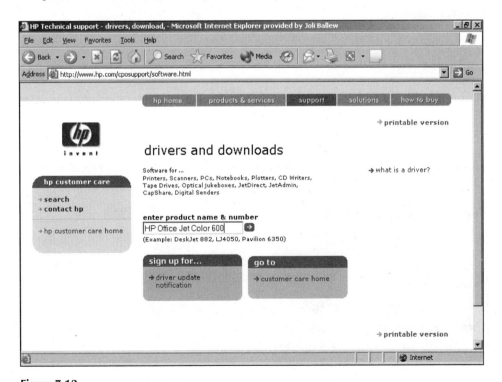

Figure 7.12
Searching for drivers.

locating the driver, choose Download. When prompted, choose Save To Disk. You can watch the progress of the download in the information box shown in Figure 7.13.

Use Device Manager and Update Driver to install the downloaded driver. Some drivers are created with their own setup program. You can run this setup program to install the new driver. Although this is an option, it is best to go through Device Manager anyway, just to be safe. Device Manager will inform you if the driver is unsigned, will offer driver rollback, and will walk you through the installation, as Windows XP expects it to be achieved. Using Device Manager will eliminate problems that might occur when using a driver's setup program.

Third-Party Drivers

Occasionally, the device manufacturer's Web site won't have an updated driver, but if you are the adventurous type, you still have a few other options. The Internet has multiple sites where people exchange information about drivers and where to find them. Several popular sites include:

♦ **windrivers.com**

♦ **driversplanet.com**

♦ **driverzone.com**

♦ **driverhq.com**

♦ **mrdriver.com**

Most of the drivers from these sites are shared among visitors and are not guaranteed to work. In the past, before Driver Rollback and System Restore, people were reluctant to try drivers from sites like these. However, now it's easier to restore your system if something goes wrong, and there is a multitude of information available on the Internet. Occasionally, a driver meant for one modem might work for another, or a driver meant for one sound card might work for another. It's worth a try if the driver you need isn't available.

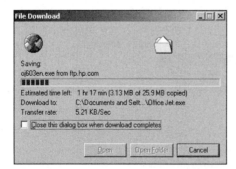

Figure 7.13
Downloading a file.

Drivers and Safe Mode

When problems arise with a driver, and the computer is restarted in safe mode by you or by the system, very few drivers are loaded. In fact, when safe mode is used, only the default settings for the VGA monitor are used, the Microsoft mouse driver is used, no network adapter drivers or printer drivers are loaded, and only the bare minimum system device drivers are loaded. By booting into safe mode, you can troubleshoot or remove troublesome drivers without harming the system any further.

Wrapping Up

There's a lot to know about drivers, how they work, why they're needed, how to install them, and what to do when the driver doesn't work or disturbs the system. In this chapter, you learned just about all you'll ever need to know about drivers and Windows XP Professional. All of these topics were covered in depth, including how to use Microsoft's newest offering, Driver Rollback. Besides this, though, System Restore can always be used to roll back the system to a previous state, and LKGC can be used when the problems are even more complex.

Chapter 8

Installing and Removing Software and Hardware

If you own a computer, sooner or later you'll need to install software and hardware. In this chapter, I'll cover installing many types of hardware, from cameras to multiple monitors, as well as software bought commercially or obtained from the Internet. I'll also discuss the many Microsoft Windows components, including Management And Monitoring Tools and Internet Information Services, that are not installed by default with Windows XP Professional.

Installing Hardware

Although there are hundreds, and perhaps thousands, of hardware manufacturers, the process of physically installing hardware doesn't vary much. For instance, with a scanner, you plug it into an electrical outlet, connect the scanner to the computer via a USB, SCSI, or parallel port, and turn on the computer and the scanner. Hardware comes with installation instructions, which should be followed precisely.

After the hardware is physically installed, the software and device drivers for the unit must then be added. As detailed in Chapter 7, a device driver can be installed manually from the manufacturer's disk or the Internet, or automatically if the driver is included with Windows XP's driver library. Because device drivers enable the hardware device and the computer to communicate with each other, you should understand how drivers are used before you install any hardware. If you haven't read Chapter 7 yet, you should do so before continuing.

In this section, I'll explain the installation of many kinds of hardware, including digital cameras, scanners, modems, wireless keyboards and mice, additional monitors, and all-in-one machines such as fax/scan/print/copy devices. With most hardware, the physical installation is fairly straightforward, and instructions are included with the devices. The more difficult tasks lay in installing the software and configuring the device itself. Later in this section, I'll also include a brief troubleshooting guide. If you run into a problem that the tips here do not solve, refer to the appendix, which provides more detailed troubleshooting information.

Digital Cameras

Digital cameras have gotten very popular in the past few years, and camera prices have come down dramatically. This makes purchasing one of these cameras easier for everyone, and plenty of people use these cameras at work. Using a digital camera and Windows XP Professional, a worker can take company photos and upload them to the organization's Web site, publish company newsletters, make user ID cards, and produce documents for meetings and presentations. These photos, once saved to the computer or accessed from the camera, can also be printed on virtually any type of paper from glossy paper to transparencies for overhead projectors.

Most digital cameras available when this book was written are installed through a USB port located either on the back panel of the computer or occasionally in the front. USB ports are included with most new or recently purchased computers, and these ports transfer pictures from the camera to the computer faster than do other types of ports. When a USB port is used on a Windows XP computer, you can plug in the camera without shutting down the computer.

Installing a Camera

You must be logged on as an administrator or as a member of the Administrators group to install a device by using the Add Hardware Wizard. If the computer is connected to a network, network policies might prevent you from installing devices even if you are logged on as an administrator. Always follow the manufacturer's instructions for physically installing the device, and if a disk has been included, read the directions for that, too.

The following instructions provide the general steps involved in installing a camera for your Windows XP Professional machine. Depending on the success or failure of each step, different actions will need to be taken. If a problem occurs during the installation, you'll be referred to the "Troubleshooting" section in this chapter.

To install a digital camera:

1. Log on as an administrator or as a member of the Administrators group.

2. If the manufacturer's instructions say to shut down the computer before physically installing the camera, do so.

3. Plug the camera's cable into the correct port on the back (or front) of the computer. Connect this cable to the camera itself as well.

4. Connect the camera to an electrical outlet or, preferably, to a power strip that is also a surge protector.

5. Turn the camera on, and turn on the computer if necessary.

6. Look at the digital camera and select the appropriate setting. This could be Setup or PC, or perhaps a camera icon. Check the manufacturer's instructions.

7. If Windows XP doesn't recognize the camera, restart the computer. If Windows XP does recognize the camera, continue.

8. If the camera came with a CD-ROM or floppy disk, place it in the appropriate drive.

Note

Some devices require you to install the software before connecting the hardware. Although this is not usually the case, make sure you follow the manufacturer's directions.

9. There are two ways the installation can go from here: either the camera was recognized, or it wasn't. If the camera was recognized, continue with these directions. If the camera wasn't recognized, skip to the "Troubleshooting" section in this chapter.

10. Some devices are recognized by Windows XP Professional and are installed automatically. This is the easiest scenario. If this happens, the device is installed and all you need to do is configure it with your preferences. If the hardware isn't installed automatically, the Found New Hardware Wizard opens. Choose what you'd like the wizard to do. You can install the software automatically, which is recommended, or you can install from a specific location, which is advanced. Select the automatic installation, and choose Next.

11. After the wizard has finished searching, the installation will again go one of two ways: The software will be installed automatically, or it will not be. If the appropriate driver was found on the manufacturer's CD-ROM or in the driver library on the computer, the installation files will be copied as shown in Figure 8.1.

12. If the wizard states that it could not find the software on your computer, choose the Back button, and select the Advanced option. Skip to the "Troubleshooting" section for more instructions.

13. If the wizard finishes and you see the screen shown in Figure 8.2, choose Finish and skip to the "Troubleshooting" section of this chapter.

14. After the software has been installed successfully, you can begin configuring the device.

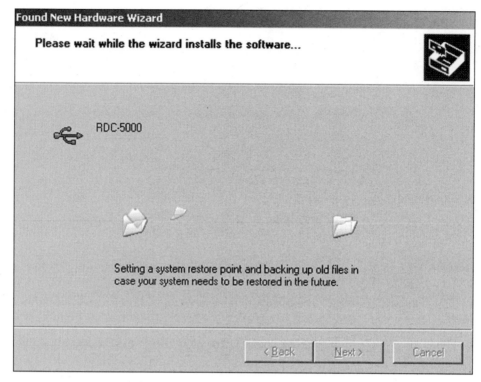

Figure 8.1
Successful installation.

Configuring a Camera

Once the camera has been properly installed, the Scanner And Camera Wizard appears the first time you use the device and/or immediately after its installation. You can either use the wizard to help you configure the device, or you can configure the device manually. If pictures are already stored on the camera, you'll see them in the Choose Pictures To Copy screen. Follow the directions on the screen to copy pictures to the hard drive of your computer; then choose Next.

As the wizard walks you through the configuration of the camera, accept the defaults, downloading the camera's pictures and placing them in the My Pictures folder. After the pictures have been saved to the hard drive, they can be manipulated, printed, and emailed. For more information on these tasks, consult the camera's documentation.

Some cameras are seen by the computer as an additional hard drive, and some can be accessed through the Digital Camera icon shown in My Computer. If this is the case, the Scanner And Camera Wizard might not appear. Figure 8.3 shows an example of how pictures can be viewed when the camera is seen as an additional hard drive instead of as a camera.

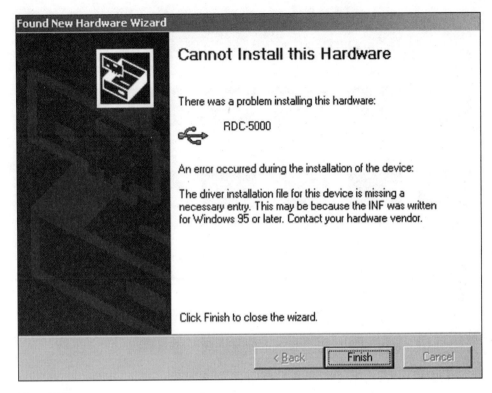

Figure 8.2
The page you'll see if the wizard cannot install the hardware's driver.

Scanners

Scanners and cameras are installed in a similar manner. Most scanners, like cameras, plug into a USB ports and can be configured automatically through the Add Hardware Wizard or through Cameras And Scanners in the Control Panel. In this section, I'll walk you through the installation and configuration of a scanner and offer troubleshooting tips where appropriate.

Installing a Scanner

You must be logged on as an administrator or as a member of the Administrators group to install a device by using the Add Hardware Wizard. If the computer is connected to a network, network policies might prevent you from installing devices even if you are logged on as an administrator. Always follow the manufacturer's instructions for physically installing the device, and if a disk has been included, read the directions for that, too.

The following instructions provide the general steps involved in installing a scanner for your Windows XP Professional machine. Depending on the success or failure of each step, different action will need to be taken. If a problem occurs during the installation, you'll be referred to the "Troubleshooting" section in this chapter.

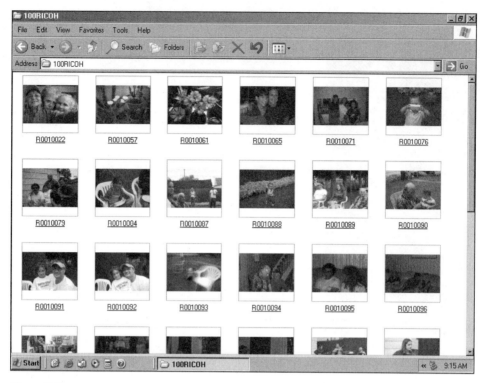

Figure 8.3
Selecting the photographs.

To install a scanner:

1. Log on as an administrator or as a member of the Administrators group.

2. If the manufacturer's instructions say to shut down the computer before physically installing the scanner, do so.

3. Plug the scanner's cable into the correct port on the back (or front) of the computer. Connect this cable to the scanner itself as well.

4. Connect the scanner to an electrical outlet or, preferably, to a power strip that is also a surge protector.

5. Turn the scanner on, and turn on the computer if necessary.

6. If Windows XP doesn't recognize the scanner, restart the computer. If Windows XP does recognize the scanner, continue.

7. If the scanner came with a CD-ROM or floppy disk, place it in the appropriate drive.

Note

Some devices require you to install the software before connecting the hardware. Although this is not usually the case, make sure you follow the manufacturer's directions.

8. There are two ways the installation could go from here: either the scanner was recognized, or it wasn't. If the scanner was recognized, continue with these directions. If the scanner wasn't recognized, skip to the "Troubleshooting" section in this chapter.

9. Some devices are recognized by Windows XP Professional and are installed automatically. This is the easiest scenario. When this happens, the scanner is installed and all you need to do is configure it with your preferences.

10. If the hardware isn't installed automatically, the Found New Hardware Wizard opens. Choose what you'd like the wizard to do. You can install the software automatically, which is recommended, or you can install from a specific location, which is advanced. Select the automatic installation, and choose Next.

11. After the wizard has finished searching, the installation will again go one of two ways. Either the software will be installed automatically, or it will not be. If Windows XP has an appropriate driver or finds one on the manufacturer's CD-ROM, the installation files will be copied.

12. If the software still doesn't install, choose the Back button, and select the Advanced option. Skip to the "Troubleshooting" section for more instructions.

13. If the wizard finishes and the software still didn't install correctly, choose Finish and skip to the "Troubleshooting" section of this chapter.

14. After the software has been installed successfully, you can begin configuring the device.

Configuring a Scanner

To configure the new scanner:

1. Open My Computer, and double-click the scanner icon. The Scanner And Camera Wizard opens.

2. Choose Next to continue. The wizard will walk you through choosing scanner preferences and configuring custom settings, and it will scan a picture automatically.

Modems and Other Internal Hardware

Some hardware must be installed internally, such as most modern modems, sound and video cards, network adapters, and USB ports. You install these pieces of hardware by opening the computer's case and inserting the card in the appropriate slot. Vacant slots inside the computer vary from manufacturer to manufacturer, and, depending on what types of cards you have installed, will cause the inside of your computer to differ from someone else's. Although it is best to have a qualified technician perform the physical installation, you can install the modem yourself if need be.

Once the hardware has been physically installed inside the computer, and the computer case has been closed up and the operating system restarted, the installation of the software for these devices is about the same as for any other device.

Installing a Modem

You must be logged on as an administrator or as a member of the Administrators group to install a device such as a modem. If the computer is connected to a network, network policies might prevent you from installing devices even if you are logged on as an administrator. Always follow the manufacturer's instructions for physically installing the device, and if a disk has been included, read the directions for that, too.

The following instructions provide the general steps involved in installing internal hardware for your Windows XP Professional machine. Depending on the success or failure of each step, different action will need to be taken. If a problem occurs during the installation, you'll be referred to the "Troubleshooting" section in this chapter.

To continue with the installation of an internal modem after it's been physically installed:

1. With the internal modem installed, turn the computer on, and log on as an administrator.

2. The modem will either be recognized or installed automatically, or it will need to be installed manually. If the modem is automatically installed, then no further action need be taken. If the modem must be manually installed, continue.

3. Open the Control Panel and then the Phone And Modem Options icon.

4. On the Modem tab, choose Add.

5. In the Install New Modem Wizard, choose Next. Make sure any CD-ROM or floppy disk supplied with the modem is in the appropriate drive.

6. The Add Hardware Wizard looks for PnP modems. If the modem is found, it will be installed automatically. If it isn't found, choose Next.

7. Look in the left and right panes of the Install New Modem page for the make and model of your modem. If it isn't there, browse to the location of the modem's driver by choosing Have Disk. Select the driver, choose OK.

8. Choose OK and continue with the installation. The modem will be installed.

If the modem wasn't installed, or if the installation caused errors described earlier, skip ahead to the "Troubleshooting" section later in this chapter.

Note

For internal hardware that is not a modem, install the hardware and then choose Add New Hardware in the Control Panel. Refer to Chapter 7 for information on the different types of hardware that can be installed and on how the Add Hardware Wizard can be used to install the drivers for the device.

Configuring a Modem

Modems can be configured through the Phone And Modem Options icon in the Control Panel or through Device Manager. Use the Modem Properties dialog box to do the following:

♦ *On the General tab*—Select the device type, manufacturer, physical slot location, and status of the device. You can also access the Windows troubleshooter from here or enable or disable the device.

♦ *On the Modem tab*—Adjust speaker volume, maximum port speed, and dial control.

♦ *On the Diagnostics tab*—Query the modem, and view the modem log.

♦ *On the Advanced tab*—Add extra initialization commands, configure advanced port settings, and change default preferences.

♦ *On the Driver tab*—View the driver details, update the driver, roll back the driver, and uninstall the modem.

♦ *On the Resources tab*—View the resource settings for the modem.

Usually the default settings are appropriate and work well. Changing the settings for ports and connection speeds haphazardly is not recommended. However, you can set some preferences for the modem here, such as setting the modem to automatically disconnect if the computer is idle for a certain period of time.

Wireless Keyboards and Mice

One of my favorite items to install with a new computer is a wireless keyboard and mouse. These hardware devices come with a transmitter that connects to the back of the computer either through the keyboard and mouse ports or through a USB port. The power for the keyboard and mouse is supplied with batteries, an important point to remember when one or the other device stops working. These devices run about $100 and are extremely easy to install.

Installing Keyboards and Mice

You must be logged on as an administrator or as a member of the Administrators group to install a device by using the Add Hardware Wizard.

To install a wireless keyboard and mouse:

1. Log on as an administrator or as a member of the Administrators group.

2. If the manufacturer's instructions say to shut down the computer before physically installing the devices, do so.

3. Remove the old keyboard and mouse. Plug the transmitting device into the correct port on the back (or front) of the computer. Place the transmitter within the required distance from the keyboard and mouse.

4. Install the batteries in the keyboard and mouse, and place the devices on the table or desk.

5. Turn the keyboard and mouse on (if necessary), and turn on the computer if it was shut down.

6. If the devices aren't recognized, restart the computer. If they are, continue.

Note

Some devices are recognized by Windows XP Professional and are installed automatically. This is the easiest scenario. If this happens, the device is installed and all you need to do is configure it with your preferences.

7. If the keyboard and mouse came with a CD-ROM or floppy disk, place it in the appropriate drive.

8. If the hardware isn't installed automatically, the Found New Hardware Wizard opens. Choose what you'd like the wizard to do. You can install the software automatically, which is recommended, or you can install from a specific location, which is advanced. Select the automatic installation, and choose Next.

9. After the wizard has finished searching, the driver should be installed automatically.

Because most wireless keyboards and mice are fairly new, Windows XP will most likely support them. If not, the software that comes with the device will be compatible. If the keyboard and mouse aren't installed easily, skip to the "Troubleshooting" section.

Configuring Keyboards and Mice

You can configure your new mouse and keyboard from the Control Panel and the Keyboard icon and/or the Mouse icon. Several configuration choices are available. Figure 8.4 shows configuration options for a wireless mouse; notice that this Mouse Properties dialog box has several additional tabs besides those in a generic mouse's property sheet.

Additional Monitors

If your computer's system board supports it, you can configure up to 10 monitors for your computer. For each, you'll need a video card, so the computer must have the available PCI

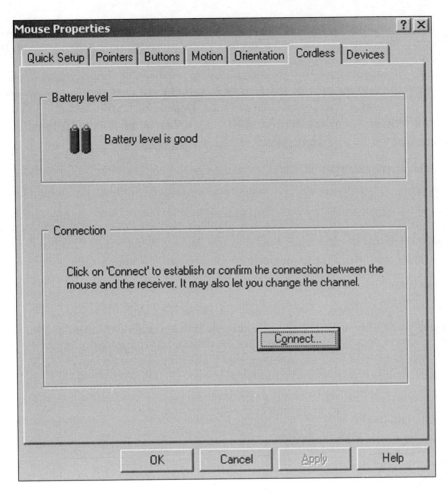

Figure 8.4
Properties for a wireless mouse.

or AGP slots to handle this, but if it does, you can set up quite a display center. Using multiple monitors, you can work on more than one task at a time, with each task shown on a different monitor, or you can move items from one monitor to another or stretch them across the monitors. You can also open a long document such as a database file and open the entire document over the multiple monitors.

One monitor is the primary monitor and will display the logon box when the computer is booted. The others are secondary monitors and are independent of each other. You can even set different screen resolutions and quality settings (such as color quality, DPI settings, screen refresh rate, and monitor color profiles) for each monitor.

Installing Multiple Monitors

You must be logged on as an administrator or as a member of the Administrators group to install a device by using the Add Hardware Wizard. If the computer is connected to a network,

network policies might prevent you from installing devices even if you are logged on as an administrator. Always follow the manufacturer's instructions for physically installing the device, and if a disk has been included, read the directions for that, too.

The following instructions provide the general steps involved in installing an additional monitor for your Windows XP Professional machine. Depending on the success or failure of each step, different action will need to be taken. If a problem occurs during the installation, you'll be referred to the "Troubleshooting" section in this chapter.

To install an additional monitor:

1. Turn off the computer.

2. Open the computer case, insert the new graphics card into the appropriate slot, and fasten it correctly. If the primary card is in the AGP slot, place a PCI card in the first slot on the board. Read the manufacturer's instructions for more details.

Warning

When handling internal expansion cards and system boards, make sure you are properly grounded. Any type of static electricity or shock to the component or the board can cause damage that is hard to repair and detect. Furthermore, adding internal components can void the manufacturer's warranty. It's best to have a qualified technician perform this part of the task.

3. Close the computer case, and connect the additional monitor.

4. Plug in the monitor, and turn it on.

5. Turn on the computer.

6. The primary (first) monitor will show the boot and login information.

7. Log on as an administrator.

8. The Found New Hardware bubble should appear in the bottom-right corner of the screen. This hardware is the new graphics card. If the card came with a CD-ROM, place it in the appropriate drive. If the hardware isn't installed automatically, continue. If the hardware was installed, skip to the next section.

9. Open the Control Panel.

10. Choose Add Hardware, and choose Next to begin the wizard.

11. Depending on the situation, either highlight the new video card in the Installed Hardware dialog box, or choose Next to select your hardware from the list. Browse to the location of the driver files if necessary. If the card is installed, skip to the next section.

12. If the new graphics card still isn't installed, and you've browsed to the CD that came with the card, the driver might not be digitally signed by Microsoft. To install the graphics card with an unsigned device driver or with a driver for another operating system, such as Windows NT 4, continue with these instructions. Close all application windows.

13. Right-click My Computer, and choose Properties.

14. In the System Properties dialog box, select the Hardware tab.

15. Choose Device Manager button.

16. Expand the Display Adapters tree.

17. Double-click the new display adapter.

18. On the Driver tab, choose Update Driver.

19. Select the option Install From A List Or Specific Location (Advanced), and choose Next.

20. Select the option Don't Search; I Will Choose The Driver To Install, and choose Next.

21. Choose Have Disk, and browse to the location of the driver that is unsigned (or perhaps located on a network drive or downloaded from the Internet).

22. Locate the driver, and install it. Once complete, close the wizard by choosing Finish.

Configuring the Additional Monitor(s)

After the graphics card and monitor have been installed, the new monitor must be configured to work with the older one. To configure the new monitor:

1. Open the Control Panel.

2. Open the Display icon.

3. Select the Settings tab.

4. Click the monitor icon that represents the monitor you want to use in addition to your current monitor.

5. Select Extend My Windows Desktop Onto This Monitor, and choose OK.

Troubleshooting Installations

Figure 8.5 shows Device Manager with two monitors installed and in working order. You can access Device Manager by right-clicking My Computer, choosing Properties, selecting the Hardware tab, and choosing Device Manager. If there are red xs or yellow exclamation points by the new monitor, it isn't working or installed correctly.

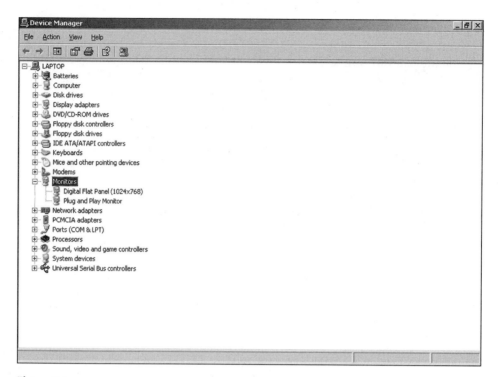

Figure 8.5
Two working monitors listed in Device Manager.

There are several reasons why a monitor and graphics card won't function correctly once installed. Here are some of them, with some possible solutions:

♦ *You're using an unsigned driver*—Search the Internet, and ask the manufacturer for an updated driver for Windows XP.

♦ *The monitor has no signal*—Restart the computer as a first step. If restarting doesn't work, open Device Manager, and uninstall and reinstall the card. See if an additional monitor is present. The monitor might not be supported.

♦ *The option Extend My Windows Desktop Onto This Monitor is not available*—The video card doesn't support multiple monitors; purchase and install one that does. If you are using Windows XP Personal instead of Professional, the option won't be available.

♦ *You're using Adobe Type Manager*—If you use Adobe Type Manager, you'll need to remove it for multiple monitors to function correctly.

♦ *The secondary monitor is not enabled in Control Panel | Display | Settings*—Enable the monitor as described earlier. (From the Display icon and the Settings tab, click the monitor icon that represents the monitor you want to use in addition to your current monitor, select Extend My Windows Desktop Onto This Monitor, and choose OK.)

◆ *You're using an ISA or EISA display card*—Only PCI and AGP cards are supported using multiple monitors.

◆ *The graphics card isn't on the hardware compatibility list (HCL)*—The secondary card must be listed on the HCL. The card must also support the options to disable VGA in the display driver or through a jumper on the card itself. Obtain an updated driver if possible.

◆ *The card is installed incorrectly*—The primary graphics card must be installed on the system board farthest from the ISA slot (the longest slot). If the primary display adapter is an AGP card, then the secondary card must be installed in the first PCI slot available next to that card.

◆ *The AGP card is in use as the primary display card*—If the AGP card is the primary display adapter, and a PCI card is secondary, then the computer's BIOS must support starting the AGP card before the PCI card when booting, or the PCI adapter must have the option to disable VGA functionality.

◆ *The monitor remains blank*—The monitor could be faulty; replace it if necessary.

Arranging Monitors

Once the additional monitor(s) are installed, you can arrange them physically as well as logically. If your monitors are on top of each other, they can be configured so that the logical display is shown vertically. If the monitors are side by side, they can be configured horizontally. Arranging the monitor icons in the Display Properties dialog box determines how you will move items from one monitor to another. The icon positions do not have to demonstrate how your monitors are physically arranged.

To configure the arrangement of your multiple monitors:

1. Open the Control Panel.

2. Open the Display icon.

3. Select the Settings tab.

4. Choose the Identify button to display a large number on each monitor.

5. Drag the monitor icons to the positions that show how you want them arranged. Choose OK.

Viewing the Same Desktop on All Monitors

To view the same desktop on each monitor that is installed:

1. Open the Control Panel.

2. Open the Display icon.

3. Select the Settings tab.

4. Check the checkbox Extend My Windows Desktop Onto This Monitor.

To resize a window among additional monitors, drag the window to the other monitor.

All-In-One Fax/Scan/Print/Copy

Installing an all-in-one unit such as a fax/scanner/printer/copier is very similar to installing a printer as described in Chapter 4. The only difference is the software that is installed with the hardware. As with any type of hardware, it might come with additional software other than the driver. With all-in-one machines, this is certainly true.

You must be logged on as an administrator or as a member of the Administrators group to install a device by using the Add Hardware Wizard. If the computer is connected to a network, network policies might prevent you from installing devices even if you are logged on as an administrator. Always follow the manufacturer's instructions for physically installing the device, and if a disk has been included, read the directions for that, too.

To install an all-in-one fax/scanner/printer/copier for your Windows XP Professional machine, refer to Chapter 4. After the device is properly installed, jump back here for troubleshooting information.

Note

Many other kinds of hardware can be installed, including tape devices, CD-R and CD-RW drives, and DVD drives. These devices are installed similarly to printers, faxes, scanners, and cameras, so instructions here would be redundant. However, you can follow the general instructions given in this section to install just about any kind of hardware you'd like.

Troubleshooting Hardware Installations

There are several reasons why a piece of hardware can't be installed. For instance, the device isn't a plug-and-play device, drivers cannot be found on the local machine or in local drives, you lack the permissions necessary to install devices, or the driver is not compatible with Windows XP. For each of these problems, you'll be prompted by Windows XP with some possible solutions for obtaining the appropriate software for the device and installing the hardware.

This section discusses what to do when a device isn't recognized after the computer is rebooted, what to do when automatic installation doesn't work, when to connect to the Internet and search for a driver, and what to do if the error message "Cannot Install This Hardware" is shown after you try to install a device.

Device Not Recognized

Even if a device isn't recognized, it can often be installed and used effectively. Many devices must be installed manually and are not automatically detected, whereas other devices must have their software installed before the hardware. If the device isn't recognized after the computer is rebooted, check the following:

♦ Is the device plugged into the computer correctly?

♦ Does the device have power?

♦ Is the device turned on?

♦ Is the electrical outlet working properly?

♦ Are the settings on the device configured properly?

♦ Do you also have to install a card in the computer? Is the card installed securely and firmly in the slot?

♦ Does the device, such as a wireless mouse, need batteries?

♦ Is the device recognized by any other Windows XP (optional) machines?

Once the questions above have been answered and dealt with accordingly, for a scanner or a camera, perform the following steps.

1. Log on as an administrator.

2. Open the Control Panel.

3. Open Scanners And Cameras.

4. Choose Add Device.

5. When the wizard appears, choose Next.

6. Look for the make of the scanner or camera in the left pane, and for the model in the right pane. If your device is listed, select it and choose Next. If it is not listed, choose Have Disk and browse to the location of the driver files.

Note
If there is no disk, and the make and model of the device aren't listed, choose Windows Update. There is a possibility that the appropriate information can be found there; if it is, it will be shown in the window in Step 6.

7. Select the driver file. Choose Open, and then OK.

8. If the correct software is found, it will be installed automatically. If not, proceed to the next section.

For other devices, such as modems, keyboards, and the like, you can also use the corresponding icons in the Control Panel to add them.

What to Do When Installing Automatically Doesn't Work

If Windows XP Professional has detected the new hardware, but the automatic installation doesn't work, you'll need to install the software manually. When given the installation choices in the Found New Hardware Wizard, select the second option, Install From A List Or Specific Location (Advanced). See Figure 8.6.

After choosing Next, you'll see the screen shown in Figure 8.7. If the software you need is located on a network or another drive, you'll need to browse for it. If this isn't an option, you can choose Don't Search. I Will Choose The Driver To Install. Sometimes, the latter option works well by offering software that is compatible and that might provide some functionality until you can find an updated driver.

If the hardware still cannot be installed, continue with the other troubleshooting options in this section.

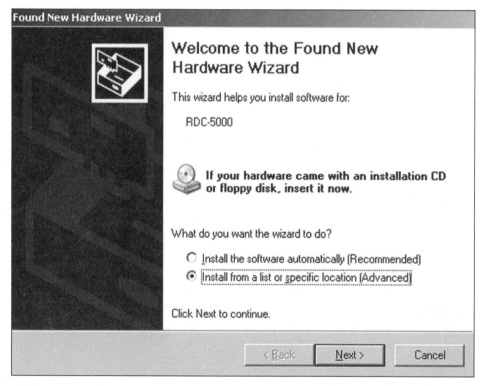

Figure 8.6
Starting a manual installation.

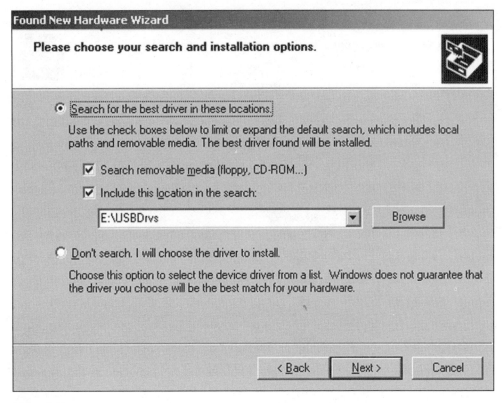

Figure 8.7
Installation options.

Connecting to the Internet for a Driver

You can also search for drivers on the Internet; this was discussed briefly in Chapter 3 and again in Chapter 7. To search for a driver in this way, select Yes, Connect And Search For The Software On The Internet when prompted by the Found New Hardware Wizard or the Add New Hardware Wizard. See Figure 8.8. You'll be able to look on the Internet for the latest drivers and software by going to the hardware manufacturer's site and downloading the information.

After a newer driver has been obtained from the Internet or another source, it can be installed in one of two ways. If the device was never installed, this driver can be used to install the hardware through the Add Hardware icon in the Control Panel. If the device was installed but doesn't work or doesn't work properly, it can be installed through Device Manager as an updated driver for the device.

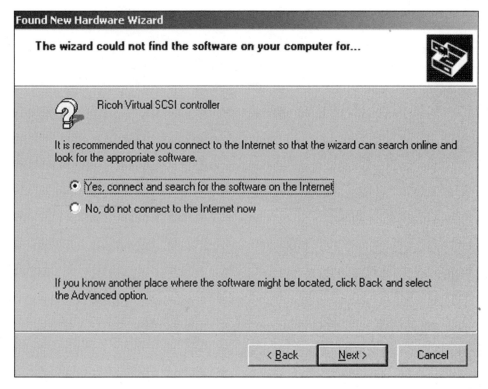

Figure 8.8
Choosing to search the Internet for drivers.

Using Device Manager

If the device was installed previously and updated drivers have been found for it, unzip the files if necessary, and then do the following:

1. Log on as an administrator.

2. Right-click My Computer, and choose Properties.

3. In the System Properties dialog box, select the Hardware tab.

4. Choose the Device Manager button.

5. In the Device Manager tree, locate the device that needs an updated driver or isn't working properly. See Figure 8.9; notice the exclamation point beside the RDC-5000 device.

6. Right-click the device in question, and choose Properties.

7. Choose the Reinstall Driver button.

8. In the Hardware Update Wizard, select Install From A List Or Specific Location (Advanced). Choose Next.

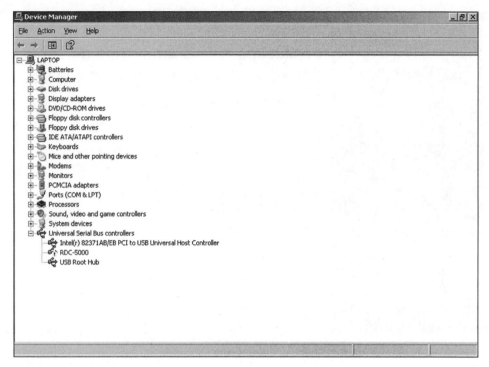

Figure 8.9
A non-working device listed in Device Manager.

9. Browse to the location of the downloaded or recently obtained drivers and choose Next.

10. The new drivers are installed automatically. See Figure 8.10. Choose Finish to complete the wizard.

When the Driver is Missing an Entry

If the message "Missing entry error—contact your hardware vendor" is shown, there isn't much you can do except hope that the company has released a newer driver. If you are daring, you can also explore third-party driver sites, where you might find that while the driver for your camera isn't available, another driver for a different model will work just fine. If you see the error page shown in Figure 8.2 (Cannot Install This Hardware), the driver is missing a necessary entry. You'll have to contact the hardware vendor.

Installing Software

Applications can be downloaded from the Internet, purchased from a computer store or catalog, supplied with your new computer, or included with a new piece of hardware. For instance, new printers often come not just with the printer drivers but with other programs as well, such as Adobe Acrobat Reader or a program that creates greeting cards. You might also have old programs that you want to use on your new computer.

Figure 8.10
Successful installation.

How these programs are installed depends on how old they are, what operating system they were originally designed for, and where you obtained them. For instance, an older application that isn't designed for Windows XP Professional will need to be manually installed in program compatibility mode, but programs from Microsoft's Web site are often installed automatically.

Installing Newer Commercial Applications

If you purchase an application from a computer store, the application will most likely be compatible with Windows XP Professional. The application's setup program will automatically start, and installation will occur with very little user intervention. This is the way it should work when you're installing new applications. With newer applications, either they start automatically (AutoPlay), or you must browse the CD to locate the setup.exe or install.exe file. (The files are not always named this, but the name will be similar to this.)

AutoPlay Installations

AutoPlay allows the application installation code to run automatically when the CD is placed in the CD-ROM drive. A Welcome screen generally appears to let you know about the program you're installing and to give you directions about what you'll need to do during the installation. Figure 8.11 shows a wizard that AutoPlay displays the first time you place this application's CD in the CD-ROM drive.

Installing the program generally consists of simply working through the installation wizard and either accepting the defaults or making custom changes. When given a choice between a typical installation and a custom installation, always choose the custom option. You do not have to make any changes, but you'll know what is being installed and where, and you can make changes if you think they're necessary.

Note
Don't make any changes from the defaults unless you fully understand what you are doing. For instance, in a dual-boot computer, you might need to choose the correct partition, but if you choose the wrong configuration, the program won't run properly.

While installing, you might be prompted to change the installation folder. If you run applications on a second disk or store your programs in a specific folder or partition, you should change the installation folder; otherwise, you should accept the defaults. Additionally, you might be prompted to choose what parts of the application to install. Sometimes, when installing software that doesn't check what's installed on your system, you might be prompted

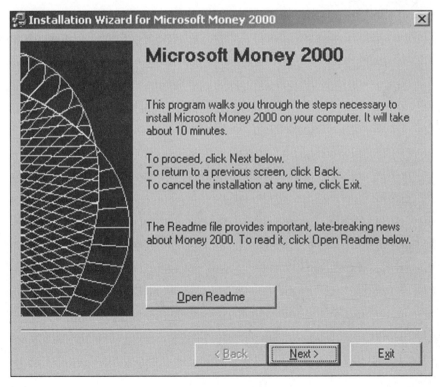

Figure 8.11
An installation wizard that starts automatically.

to install "bonus" software included on the CD. For instance, you could be running Internet Explorer 6, and then prompted to install Internet Explorer 5. If this happens, you should cancel that part of the installation. Finally, verify immediately that the program works correctly. If it does not, uninstall it and try again, or run the installation wizard again and choose to repair a recent installation.

Locating the Program Yourself

Sometimes installation programs do not start automatically. A program might not start automatically for several reasons, but it doesn't necessarily mean that the CD does not have AutoPlay configured. Not all programs have an AutoPlay feature, and your CD-ROM drive might be configured not to use AutoPlay. Whatever the reason, you'll need to locate the AutoPlay icon, the setup.exe program, the install.exe program, or some other folder that contains the installation files.

There are many ways to see what files are on the CD that you want to install. The best way (in my opinion) is to use Windows Explorer. (Right-click the Start button, and choose Explore.) Figure 8.12 shows Windows Explorer being used to browse what's on the CD that's in the CD-ROM drive (D:\). The right pane contains a Setup icon in the bottom-right corner. You can also see an AutoRun text file. To start the installation, simply double-click either icon.

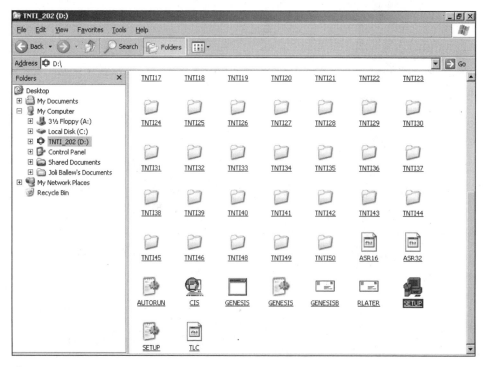

Figure 8.12
Manually locating setup.exe.

Note

Not all setup files are named setup.exe, but the name is fairly intuitive, and the file is generally represented by an icon such as the one shown in Figure 8.12.

Configuring the CD-ROM Drive to Use AutoPlay

If you notice an AutoRun or AutoPlay file when you're locating the setup files, but no installation program started automatically, your CD-ROM drive might be configured to not use AutoPlay. To check or change this setting:

1. Remove any CDs from the CD-ROM drive.

2. Open My Computer.

3. Right-click the CD drive, and choose Properties.

4. Select the AutoPlay tab.

5. From the content type drop-down list, select the content type: Music Files, Pictures, Video Files, Mixed Content, Blank CD, or Music CD.

6. Select the option Select An Action To Perform, and choose Play. Choose OK.

Using the Program Compatibility Wizard to Install Older Applications

Not all programs are compatible with Windows XP Professional specifically, programs written for Windows 3.1 or Windows 95. If you need to install an older program on your Windows XP Professional machine, and a manual installation does not work, consider installing the program in program compatibility mode. This mode allows you to install a program in the environment for which the program was written.

To install a program in program compatibility mode:

1. Place the application CD in the CD-ROM drive.

2. Choose Start | Programs | Accessories | Program Compatibility Wizard. Choose Next to start the wizard.

3. On the How Do You Want To Locate The Program That You Would Like To Run With Compatibility Settings page, select I Want To Use The Program In The CD-ROM drive. Choose Next.

4. On the Select A Compatibility Mode For The Program page, select the operating system that is recommended for the program. Choose Next.

5. On the Select Display Settings For The Program page, select any settings that are recommended for the program, and choose Next.

6. On the Test Your Compatibility Settings page, choose Next.

7. On the Did The Program Work Correctly page, leave this page alone, and do not do anything until after the program has been installed. (This page stays up while you complete the installation.)

8. Work your way through the installation. Then, if the program was installed correctly, select Yes, Set This Program To Always Use These Compatibility Settings. Otherwise, select No, Try Different Compatibility Settings or No, I Am Finished Trying Compatibility Settings. Choose Next.

9. If you want to, choose to send this information to Microsoft via the Internet. (When prompted with Would You Like To Send This Information To Microsoft, choose the Yes or No radio button, and then Next or Finish.)

Even when you use the Program Compatibility Wizard to install a program, you'll probably need to configure the program to run using compatibility settings. To do this:

1. Choose Start | Programs | Accessories | Program Compatibility Wizard. Choose Next to start the wizard.

2. On the How Do You Want To Locate The Program That You Would Like To Run With Compatibility Settings page, select either I Want To Choose From A List Of Programs, or I Want To Locate The Program Manually. Choose Next.

3. Either select the program, or browse to it, depending on your choice in Step 2. Choose Next.

4. On the Select A Compatibility Mode For The Program page, select the operating system that is recommended for the program. Choose Next.

5. On the Select Display Settings For The Program page, select any settings that are recommended for the program, and choose Next.

6. On the Test Your Compatibility Settings page, choose Next.

7. On the Did The Program Work Correctly page, leave this page alone and do not do anything until after the program has started and you have tested it fully. (This page stays up while you complete the installation.)

8. After testing, select Yes, Set This Program To Always Use These Compatibility Settings if the program was installed correctly. Otherwise, select No, Try Different Compatibility Settings or No, I Am Finished Trying Compatibility Settings. Choose Next.

9. If you want to, choose to send this information to Microsoft via the Internet. (When prompted with Would You Like To Send This Information To Microsoft, choose the Yes or No radio button and then select Next or Finish.)

Installing Programs from Microsoft's Web Site

You can download a variety of software, patches, fixes, and enhancements from Microsoft's Web site. To see some of these, simply point your Web browser to **www.microsoft.com** and choose Downloads from the All Products menu. Figure 8.13 shows the resulting page, also called the Microsoft.com Download Center.

At the bottom of this page, you can search for specific downloads by product name, operating system, title, and date. Once you've selected an application or other software to install, follow these steps:

1. Read the information on the Web page for the product you will download.

2. Make sure you are downloading the correct product for your operating system.

3. Choose the Download Now button.

4. In the File Download dialog box, choose the Save button.

5. In the Save As dialog box, browse to the location where you want to save the file. I'd suggest creating a folder on the desktop called Internet Downloads, and browsing to that.

6. Choose the Save button. After the download is completed, choose Open Folder in the Download Complete dialog box, or choose Close. If you choose Close, locate the saved

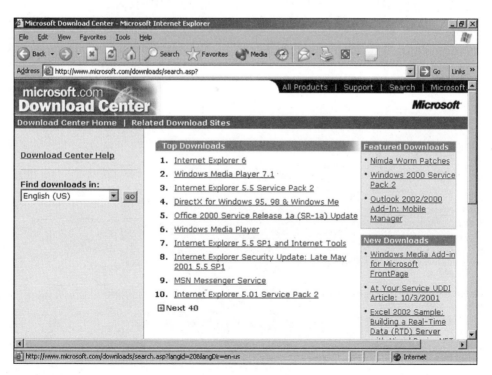

Figure 8.13
The microsoft.com Download Center.

file in the Internet Downloads folder or wherever you saved it. Double-click the file to begin the installation.

7. Depending on the application, the software might be installed automatically. Figure 8.14 shows a file download in progress.

Figure 8.14 shows the download for Office 2000 Service Release 1: Core Update.

Downloading and Installing Software from the Internet

You can obtain just about any type of software or application from the Internet, although the sites you download them from might be questionable. You should always download these applications to a test machine first, scan them for viruses, and install them on the test machine before risking the stability of your working computer. Because these applications are often not tested by a reliable source, they can harm your computer or cause it not to work properly if they aren't exactly compatible. However, there are many reliable sites and a good deal of free software available.

When you're downloading from sites other than Microsoft, the download process might work a little differently than installing from a CD or from Microsoft's Web site. Downloads can be harder to locate or install, and problems with file transfers can occur.

Software That Ships with Hardware Devices

Just because your hardware comes with a CD doesn't mean everything on that disc must be installed. Of all of the software on the disc, only the driver is generally necessary to run the hardware. Of course, there are exceptions to this rule, but most times, this additional software isn't necessary.

As an example, look at some of the software that came on the CD for an Epson Perfection 1200 U scanner:

♦ Epson TWAIN driver

♦ Adobe PhotoDeluxe Business Edition

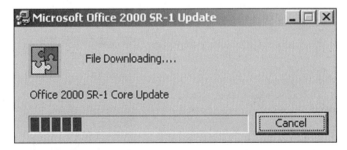

Figure 8.14
File download in progress.

♦ ArcSoft's PhotoPrinter Pro

As you can see, you might not need to install any of this software except the Epson TWAIN driver. Unfortunately, many users think that this software is required to make their hardware run, but this is not the case.

Here is another example. The CD that comes with Ricoh's 5300 digital camera includes the following software:

♦ ArcSoft Camera Suite

♦ Adobe Acrobat Reader 4

♦ USB drivers

♦ Twain drivers

♦ Camera utility

To use this camera, you need to install only one of these items: either the set of USB drivers or the set of TWAIN drivers.

It is worth mentioning however, that these programs can make using the hardware easier. For instance, the Camera utility offered by Ricoh can be used to obtain, edit, and print photos from the camera. Again, if you already have a program that you use for these tasks, you won't need this additional software.

Adding New Windows Components

Chances are good that not all of the available components were installed when Windows XP Professional was installed on your computer. You might need some of these components (such as Fax Services or Networking Services), and you can install them through the Control Panel.

In this section, I'll describe these optional components. After you know what components are available, you might decide to install or remove them. Adding new Windows components will be detailed at the end of this section.

Accessories And Utilities

Accessories And Utilities are installed by default with Windows XP Professional. The sub-components of Accessories And Utilities are:

♦ *Accessories*—Calculator, Character Map (lets you insert symbols into documents), Clipboard Viewer (enables you to use ClipBook), Desktop Wallpaper, Document Templates, Mouse Pointers, and Paint

♦ *Games*—FreeCell, Hearts, Internet Games, Minesweeper, Solitaire, and Spider Solitaire

Fax Services

The Fax Services component (not installed by default) allows faxes to be sent and received. With the Fax Services, you can create documents on your computer and fax them without ever having to leave your desk. You can also receive faxes at your computer and view them without printing, see what faxes have been sent and received, and view them without printing.

Indexing Service

This service is installed by default. It uses no hard disk space but does use lots of processing time. The Indexing Service is used to locate, index, and update documents to provide fast full-text searching. This allows the user to type in a keyword in the document, provide the document's properties, and more for finding a document on the computer or network.

Internet Explorer

Although Internet Explorer is installed by default on Windows XP Professional machines, selecting this component allows you to add or remove access to Internet Explorer from the Start menu and the desktop.

Internet Information Services

Internet Information Services is used to provide Web and FTP support for use with FrontPage transactions, Active Server Pages, and database connections. This support allows you to create Web-based transactions for users of the network. There are several subcomponents:

- *Common Files*—Installs the IIS program files

- *Documentation*—Installs documents on how to publish content and administer Web and FTP servers

- *FTP Service*—Provides support for uploading and downloading FTP files

- *FrontPage 2000 Server Extensions*—Enables the user to administer and create Web sites by using FrontPage and Visual InterDev

- *Internet Information Services Snap-In*—Installs IIS into an MMC console

- *SMTP Service*—Allows email messages to be sent and received

- *World Wide Web Service*—Uses the HTTP protocol to respond to Web client requests on the Internet or any TCP/IP network

Management and Monitoring Tools

These tools are not installed by default. These tools allow you to monitor and improve network performance. There are two subcomponents:

♦ *Simple Network Management Protocol*—Includes utilities that can be used to monitor network activity in hardware devices and report the information to a network console workstation.

♦ *WMI SNMP Provider*—Allows client applications to access static and dynamic SNMP information through WMI (Windows Management Instrumentation).

Message Queuing

Message Queuing is used to provide guaranteed delivery of messages to applications. This includes efficient routing and security and transactional support. There are four subcomponents:

♦ *Active Directory Integration*—Allows Message Queuing to work in a domain.

♦ *Common*—Provides basic messaging for local messaging services.

♦ *MSMQ HTTP Support*—Enables Message Queuing to send messages over HTTP lines, thus incorporating the Internet in Message Queuing.

♦ *Triggers*—Associates incoming messages with a queue of messages waiting to be delivered.

MSN Explorer

Similar to Internet Explorer, MSN Explorer can be used to surf the Web, read email, use Windows Messenger, and more.

Networking Services

You can install additional network services if you need specialized, network-related services and protocols such as those provided by these subcomponents:

♦ *RIP Listener*—Listens for routing updates that use the Routing Information Protocol version 1.

♦ *Simple TCP/IP Services*—Provides support for the following TCP/IP services: Character Generation, Daytime, Discard, Echo, and Quote Of The Day.

♦ *Universal Plug and Play*—Allows your computer to use PnP devices, including detecting and controlling those devices.

Other Network File and Print Services

Install this component when you need to support print services for Unix.

Update Root Certificates

Use this service to automatically download the most current root certificates for secure email, Web browsing, and software delivery.

Tip

If you aren't sure what these items are, it is best not to install them. Throughout the book, I'll explain how to use many of these components, including Message Queuing, MSN Explorer, Fax Services, Indexing Service, and Update Root Certificates.

Installing and Removing Windows Components

If you've decided to install some of these components, you can do so by performing the following steps:

1. Log on as an administrator.

2. Open the Control Panel.

3. Choose Add Or Remove Programs.

4. Choose the Add/Remove Windows Components button.

5. On the Windows Components page of the Window Components Wizard, check the checkbox for each component you want to add (or remove the check to remove the component). Choose Next.

6. Wait while the computer configures the components. Choose Finish when the process is completed.

Removing Software

You can remove software in several ways, such as using the Uninstall feature of the program itself or using the Add Or Remove Programs icon in the Control Panel. Less effective is manually removing the files yourself or using System Restore to revert your computer to an earlier state. In this section, I'll cover the only two good ways to remove programs: using Uninstall and using the Control Panel.

Using the Uninstall Feature of the Software

Figure 8.15 shows an application that has an Uninstall option. If the application you want to install has this option included, all you have to do is select the Uninstall option to remove the files. Occasionally, you'll need manually locate and delete the application folder and miscellaneous files, but with an application's uninstall feature, these are usually deleted.

Using the Add Or Remove Programs Utility

You can also use the Control Panel's Add Or Remove Programs utility to remove unused programs. Figure 8.16 shows this window. Notice that Microsoft Money 2000 Standard Edition is chosen.

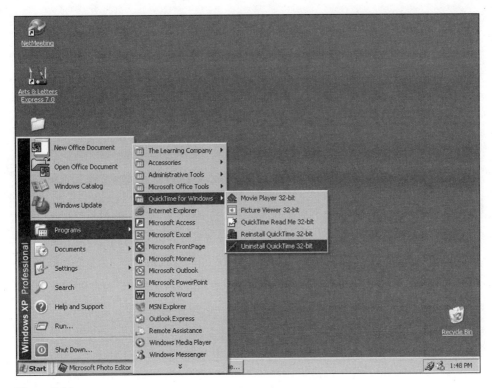

Figure 8.15
A program's Uninstall option.

To remove a program:

1. Log on as an administrator.

2. Open the Control Panel.

3. Choose Add Or Remove Programs.

4. Select the program you want to remove.

5. Choose the Change/Remove button to start the uninstaller.

Uninstalling Parts of Applications

Some software that you can purchase, such as Microsoft's Office XP, have multiple applications. For instance, Microsoft Office is actually a "suite" of applications. If you want, you can uninstall only specific applications and leave the other applications installed. Figure 8.17 shows the options for maintaining Microsoft Office 2000 on a computer that has the applications already installed. Notice there are three options: Repair Office, Add Or Remove Features, and Remove Office.

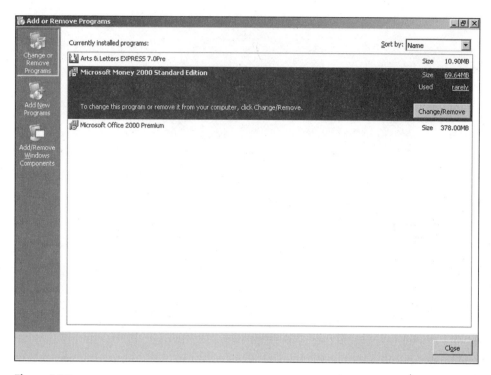

Figure 8.16
The Add Or Remove Programs window.

When you choose Add Or Remove Features, the Setup page appears and shows all of the items available for use:

♦ Microsoft Word For Windows

♦ Microsoft Excel For Windows

♦ Microsoft PowerPoint For Windows

♦ Microsoft Outlook For Windows

♦ Microsoft Access For Windows

♦ Microsoft FrontPage For Windows

♦ Office Tools

♦ Converters And Filters

To remove a component, you select it, and choose Uninstall, Remove, or Not Available (whichever is offered). Then, choose the Update Now or Next button to make the changes.

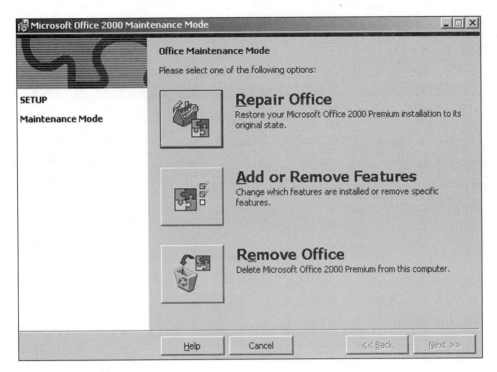

Figure 8.17
Add Or Remove Features.

Precautions and Warnings

When uninstalling programs, you might see warnings similar to that shown in Figure 8.18. The warning tells you that a component being uninstalled is needed by another component. Although you can choose Remove All or Remove, it is best to simply choose Remove None or Keep. Keeping these shared files won't take up very much room on your computer and will not cause problems, but deleting them could.

Other error messages you might receive can include references to dynamic link library (.dll) files. Windows XP Professional has a dynamic link library that contains files that are shared among multiple applications. Programmers write applications in such a way that they "borrow" these files as needed. This prevents the programmer from having to include all of these shared files in the application. However, problems can occur when a program is uninstalled and a .dll file is uninstalled that is needed by the system. If this happens, the computer will generate error messages for problems that are hard to locate and repair. To keep this problem from happening, always choose to keep all shared files, or to *not* uninstall them, when prompted.

Finally, don't simply browse to the program files and delete them. Although you are actually removing the files from your computer, you are not doing so in a good way. Figure 8.19 shows an example of an error message that is shown each time a computer boots up because

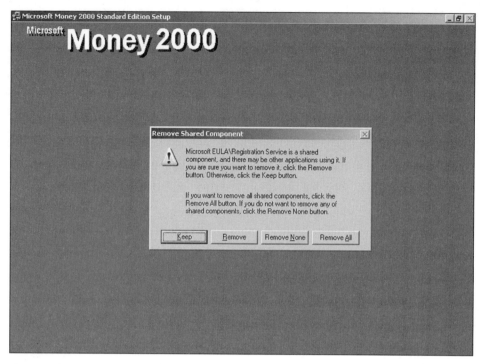

Figure 8.18
A warning about removing a shared component.

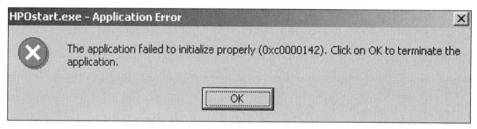

Figure 8.19
Application error.

the user deleted an application in this manner. Even though the application has been re-moved, the program still tries to start at bootup and fails. Software should be removed through an Uninstall option or the Control Panel, as described earlier.

Note
Right-clicking a program icon or name in the Start menu will remove the entry from the menu, but it will not uninstall the program.

Removing Hardware

As is true with software, simply right-clicking the icon for a piece of hardware and choosing Delete doesn't uninstall the hardware; it simply removes the link to the hardware from wherever you've deleted the icon. Similarly, unplugging a device from the wall and from the back of the computer doesn't uninstall it, either. And, as you would guess, removing a sound, network interface, or modem card won't uninstall the device, either. To uninstall a piece of hardware, you need to remove its reference in Device Manager.

Using Device Manager

To uninstall a piece of hardware through Device Manager:

1. Log on as an administrator.

2. Right-click My Computer, and choose Properties.

3. Select the Hardware tab.

4. Choose the Device Manager button.

5. Expand the appropriate tree to locate the device you want to uninstall.

6. Right-click the device, and choose Uninstall.

7. In the Confirm Device Removal dialog box, choose OK to verify that you want to uninstall the device. Close Device Manager, and choose OK.

8. Turn off the computer and physically remove the device from the computer by unplugging it from the back or removing it from the inside of the computer case.

What If the Device Isn't Listed in Device Manager?

Not all hardware is listed in Device Manager. Peripherals such as printers and scanners are not. To uninstall devices such as these, you usually delete the icon for the printer or other hardware device from the appropriate folder, and then uninstall any software that was installed with the device.

To remove a printer, scanner, or camera:

1. Log on as an administrator.

2. Open the Control Panel.

3. Open the appropriate folder, such as Printers And Faxes, or Scanners And Cameras.

4. Right-click the device you want to delete, and choose Delete.

5. Choose Yes in the dialog box to verify your choice.

6. Return to the Control Panel, and choose Add Or Remove Programs.

7. If there is a program installed for the device, highlight it and choose the Remove button.

Wrapping Up

In this chapter, you learned about installing and removing different types of hardware and software. Most hardware is physically installed by following the directions on the package and by then installing the software. In this chapter, you were given step-by-step instructions for installing cameras, scanners, printers, and more. You also learned about installing multiple monitors and troubleshooting all hardware installations.

Most software is installed from an AutoRun or AutoPlay file that is configured on the CD. If you have older programs to install, you can use the Program Compatibility Wizard for doing so.

You also learned how to install additional Windows components such as Fax Services, IIS, Message Queuing, and Networking Services. Finally, you learned how to uninstall both hardware and software.

Chapter 9
Internet and Email

Windows XP Professional is outfitted with many tools, utilities, and wizards to help users connect to the Internet, send and receive email, surf the Web, and connect to other computer users in a variety of ways. Included with Windows XP is Windows Messenger, a utility for sending and receiving instant messages; Outlook Express for sending and receiving email; NetMeeting for connecting to others using voice, video, and telephone; and MSN Explorer for connecting directly to the MSN Web site. There are many other options, too, and in this chapter, you'll learn about all of them.

You'll need a couple of things before starting. One, you must have a modem installed and in working order, or have another type of device to connect to the Internet. This can be a DSL (Digital Subscriber Line) modem, an ISDN (Integrated Services Digital Network) modem, or perhaps a shared Internet connection through a server at your office. Two, you'll need a working connection such as a phone line or DSL line and access to an Internet service provider (ISP). ISPs charge around $20 per month for basic service, and more for DSL lines or fiber optic cable.

Connecting to the Internet

If you are setting up an Internet connection at home, you'll most likely be connecting through a phone line and some type of modem. If you are connecting at an office, the same may be true; however, in an office, there is also the possibility that you already have an Internet connection through a server, or have a connection that is shared among other users. If the latter is the case, then the following information on choosing an ISP is not relevant.

No matter what type of Internet connection you'd like to make, there is a wizard available in Windows XP Professional for doing so. You can connect to the Internet through an ISP and a phone line, or use a shared connection on a local area network.

Selecting an Internet Provider

ISPs provide access to the Internet through their own network servers. These servers are connected to other servers around the world, and information is passed between them. It is these servers and the phone and cable lines that connect them that make the Internet work. To connect to the Internet, you must have an ISP to provide you with access to these servers. The largest ISPs (at the time this book was written) are AT&T, AOL, Earthlink, and MSN.

Selecting the right ISP is important. There are a few free ISP services, but these don't offer all of the advantages of paid services such as multiple email accounts, technical support, high speed access, and free web space. Most ISPs charge a monthly fee or charge by the hour. Some ISPs limit the number of hours you can use per month, while other ISPs offer unlimited access. The price difference between unlimited access and limited access is generally minimal, $5 a month or so, so you'll probably be better off with an unlimited-access account.

When you click the Connect To The Internet icon on the desktop to start the Internet Connection Wizard, you'll have some choices for Internet providers. If you haven't chosen a provider already, the wizard will connect you to a referral service that contains information about providers in your area. From there, you can see which service providers are available, and compare features and rates.

Using the Internet Connection Wizard

The Internet Connection Wizard is accessed through an icon on the desktop or through the Help and Support Center. This wizard is used only once, the first time you configure your Internet connection. When an Internet connection has been configured, this icon disappears. The wizard can still be accessed from the Help and Support Center, however. This section describes how to configure an Internet account, and the next section covers configuring an email account. On the last page of the wizard in each of the examples in this section, you'll be asked if you'd like to set up an email account now. If you want to set up this account, skip to the next section when prompted.

Signing Up with a New ISP

To use the Internet Connection Wizard to connect to the Internet and sign up with a new ISP:

1. Open the Internet Connection Wizard by clicking the Connect To The Internet icon on the desktop. If this icon is unavailable, open Start | Help and Support and search for Internet Connection Wizard.

Note

As noted in previous chapters, Classic view is being used.

2. On the Welcome page, choose Next.

3. On the Select An Internet Service Provider page, choose Next. The computer will dial automatically and connect you to the referral service for the service providers in your area. Figure 9.1 shows an example of this. If you want to choose one of these providers, highlight it and choose Next.

Note

If no services are listed, you'll need to choose Finish and select an ISP from the phone book or other reference.

4. Sign up with the ISP by providing information such as your name, address, city, state, and phone number. Choose Next.

5. After reading the billing information carefully, select a billing option. Choose Next.

6. Type in your credit card information. Choose Next.

7. The computer will dial the new provider, and you will receive a username, a password, and other information.

8. Continue by following the instructions provided by the service. Your computer will most likely be configured automatically. If it's not, then after obtaining the information, continue with the next example to complete the connection configuration.

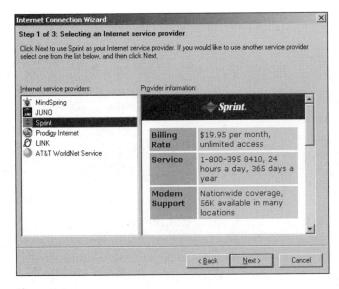

Figure 9.1
A sample list of available ISPs.

Getting Account Information from an Existing ISP Account

To use the Internet Connection Wizard to connect to the Internet and set up your Windows XP computer with an ISP account that you already have:

1. Open the Internet Connection Wizard by clicking the Connect To The Internet icon on the desktop. If this icon is unavailable, open Start | Help and Support and search for Internet Connection Wizard.

2. On the Welcome page, select the second option, Get My Account Information From My ISP, and choose Next.

3. If the Select Internet Provider page lists your provider, highlight it and choose Next. Otherwise, choose My Internet Service Provider Isn't Listed.

4. Follow the on-screen instructions provided by the ISP, if available; otherwise, skip to the next example for configuring the connection manually.

Manually Connecting Through a Phone Line

To use the Internet Connection Wizard to connect to the Internet and connect to an ISP manually:

1. Open the Internet Connection Wizard.

2. On the Welcome page, select the third option, Set Up A Connection Manually Or Through A Local Area Network. Choose Next.

3. On the Setting Up Your Internet Connection page, select I Connect Through A Phone Line And A Modem. Choose Next.

4. On the Internet Account Connection Information page, type the telephone number of your ISP. Choose Next.

5. On the Internet Account Logon Information page, type the username and password given to you by your ISP. Choose Next.

6. On the Configuring Your Computer page, type a name for the connection. Choose Next.

7. In the Completing The Internet Connection Wizard screen, place a in the checkbox To Connect To The Internet Immediately, Select This Box And Then Click Finish. Test the connection.

Manually Connecting Through a Local Area Connection

For you to use the Internet Connection Wizard to connect to the Internet through a local area network (LAN), at least one computer on the network must be connected to the Internet, and Internet Connection Sharing must be enabled. To set up Internet Connection Sharing on a computer in your LAN, refer to Chapter 10.

To connect to the Internet through a LAN:

1. Open the Internet Connection Wizard.

2. On the Welcome page, select the third option, Set Up A Connection Manually Or Through A Local Area Network.

3. On the Setting Up Your Internet Connection page, select I Connect Through A Local Area Network (LAN). Choose Next.

4. On the Local Area Network Internet Configuration page, accept the defaults. Choose Next, then Finish.

5. If Internet Connection Sharing is set up appropriately on a working LAN, you'll be connected to the Internet after choosing Finish.

Viewing and Editing Internet Connections

All configured Internet connections are viewed and edited through the Control Panel and Network Connections. (The Network Connections utility is not the same as the My Network Places utility that is located on the desktop.) Figure 9.2 shows the Network Connections window for a computer that has two Internet connections: one connected by a modem, and

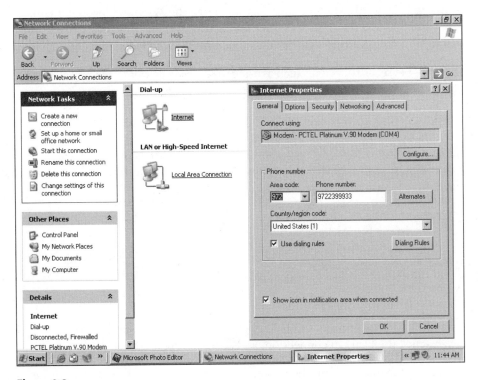

Figure 9.2
Properties window for a dial-up connection.

the other through a LAN. By right-clicking a connection and choosing Properties, you can edit or reconfigure these connections if they're not working properly. The Properties dialog for the Internet-via-modem connection is shown in Figure 9.2 also.

One of the more common problems when you're setting up an Internet connection using a modem is configuring the dialing rules correctly. If these rules are set up incorrectly, the modem will dial a "1" or will dial an area code that isn't needed. This setup and more can be changed from a connection's Properties dialog.

Editing the Dial-Up Connection

The Properties dialog box for a dial-up Internet connection has five tabs: General, Options, Security, Networking, and Advanced. The General tab, shown in Figure 9.2, shows what modem is used to dial the connection, what phone number is dialed when connecting, and whether dialing rules should be used. If there is a problem with the way the number is dialed when you're connecting, it can be changed here. By clicking the Dialing Rules button on the General tab, you can see how the connection is dialed. If it is being dialed incorrectly, you'll need to uncheck the Use Dialing Rules checkbox.

Other tabs can be used for the purposes listed next:

♦ *Options*—Set dialing options, such as displaying progress while dialing, prompting for names and passwords when connecting, including the Windows logon domain, setting redial attempts and the time between them, setting the idle time before the connection is dropped, and specifying whether the connection should redial if the line is dropped.

♦ *Security*—Set security options, such as using unsecured passwords, requiring a secure password, and using smart cards to log on. You can also use this tab to require data encryption, configure security protocols, and configure interactive logon and scripting.

♦ *Networking*—Specify the type of dial-up server the modem calls, and specify which networking components will be used during that call. The ISP generally sets up these items automatically, and/or the defaults usually work fine. (The last third of this book includes much more information on protocols and networking.)

♦ *Advanced*—Configure a firewall, set up and configure Internet Connection Sharing, and access the Home Networking Wizard.

To change any of these settings:

1. Open the Control Panel.

2. Open Network Connections.

3. Right-click the Dial Up connection, and choose Properties.

4. Select the tab that contains the options needing to be changed, and make the appropriate changes. Choose OK when finished.

Editing the Local Area Connection

The Properties dialog box for a local area connection has three tabs: General, Authentication, and Advanced. A competent network administrator should be the only person to configure the options on these tabs. The tabs are detailed in the following three bullets:

♦ *General*—Allows the administrator to add, remove, and configure protocols such as Internet Protocol (TCP/IP), as well as configure options for Client For Microsoft Networks, File and Printer Sharing for Microsoft Networks, and more. There is also an option to show an icon in the notification area when the local area connection is made.

♦ *Authentication*—Allows the administrator to enable network authentication controls such as authenticated access using smart cards or other security measures.

♦ *Advanced*—Allows the administrator to enable an Internet Connection Firewall to protect the computer and network by limiting access to and from the Internet.

To view any of these settings:

1. Open the Control Panel.

2. Open Network Connections.

3. Right-click the LAN connection, and choose Properties.

4. Select the tab that contains the options needing to be changed, and make the appropriate changes. Choose OK when finished.

Outlook Express

Outlook Express is the email program included with Windows XP Professional; the current version is Outlook Express 6. Outlook Express can be used for more than sending and receiving email messages, though; it can be used with newsgroups and directory services as well.

In this section, you'll learn how to set up an email account, use the various features of the program, compose and send email, organize your email, send and open attachments, import an address book, protect your computer from viruses, add users, and configure accessibility options. The first step, of course, is to sign up for an email account.

Setting Up an Email Account

If you pay for an ISP each month, that ISP will most likely give you an email account or two. Some ISPs offer as many as 10 (or more) accounts. These accounts can be configured through the Internet Connection Wizard or through Outlook Express (or other email programs). If you've just used the wizard to configure your Internet service, you can configure an email account by choosing Yes, Configure An Email Account Now when the choice is offered. If you have already closed the wizard, you can open Outlook Express and configure the account from there.

Setting Up an Email Account from an ISP

To configure an email account with information from an ISP, perform the following steps. If you are working from inside the Internet Connection Wizard, perform only Steps 5 through 8.

1. Open Outlook Express by choosing Start | Programs | Outlook Express. The first time you open Outlook Express, you might be prompted to make it your default browser and import addresses from another email account.

2. Choose Tools | Accounts.

3. In the Internet Accounts dialog box, select the Mail tab.

4. Choose Add | Mail.

5. The Internet Connection Wizard opens at the Your Name page. When you send email, a name is shown in the display window of the recipient's screen. Type the name you'd like these recipients to see. This name does not have to be your username. Choose Next.

6. Type the email address that your ISP assigned to you. An example is **Joli_Ballew@Admin911.com**. Choose Next.

7. On the Email Server Names page, choose the type of server that your ISP uses to hold your email for you. Type the names of the incoming and outgoing mail servers as well. You'll have to obtain this information from your ISP. Choose Next.

8. On the Internet Mail Logon page, type the account name and password for your email account as assigned by your ISP. Choose Next, then Finish.

9. If your cursor is inside Outlook Express, choose Close.

Setting Up a Free Hotmail Account with Hotmail.com

To set up a free account with MSN and Hotmail.com, perform the following steps.

1. Connect to the Internet and go to **www.microsoft.com**.

2. From the Subscribe menu, choose Free Email Account.

3. Click Sign Up For A Free E-Mail Account.

4. Fill out the required information. Once finished, open Outlook Express.

5. Click Tools | Accounts.

6. Click the Add button, then choose Mail.

7. Type in the name that you want people to see when they receive an email from you. Click Next.

8. Type in your new Hotmail account in the Internet Email Address screen. Click Next. On the following screen, accept the defaults and click Next again.

9. In the Internet Mail Logon screen, type in the password you used to created the account. Click Next, then Finish.

Reading, Composing, and Sending Email

If you don't want to go through the Start menu to open Outlook Express, you can create a shortcut for it on your desktop. To do this, choose Start | Programs, *right-click* Outlook Express in the Programs menu, and choose Create Shortcut. Figure 9.3 shows this process using the Windows Classic theme. The process is basically the same for the Windows XP theme.

When Outlook Express is first opened, it looks like Figure 9.4. Composing and sending email is as simple as clicking the right button and typing the information. To compose and send an email:

1. Open Outlook Express.

2. Choose Create A New Mail Message.

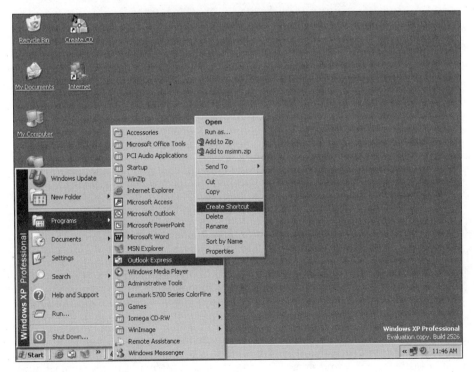

Figure 9.3
Creating a shortcut for Outlook Express.

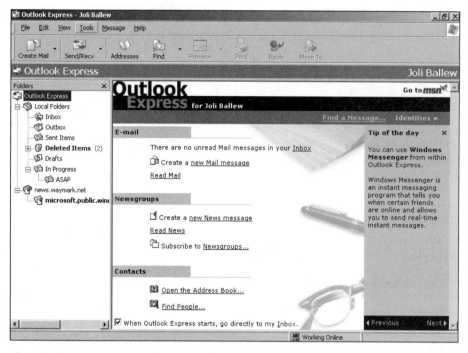

Figure 9.4
The Outlook Express application window.

3. In the To box, type the recipient's email address in the form "name@serviceprovider.xxx". Type a subject and your message.

4. Choose the Send button.

To read email from the screen shown in Figure 9.4, simply click Read Mail, or click the Inbox in the left pane. (Notice the Contacts section; you can also open up your address book from this screen.)

Organizing Email and Creating New Folders

Outlook Express has five folders in the left pane for organizing your email. As messages come in, they are automatically placed in the Inbox folder. When you're sending messages, they automatically go to the Outbox folder. After the messages are sent successfully, they go to the Sent Items folder. The Deleted Items folder holds deleted messages, and the Drafts folder can be used to hold unfinished messages. If you are using Hotmail, you'll have two additional folders: Bulk Mail and MSN Announcements.

You can also create your own folders. Creating your own folders can be helpful when you do a lot of work through email and you need to save messages for future reference. For instance, by creating a folder named In Progress, you can move and hold emails that require further work. Other folders you might consider are folders named Personal, To Keep, or Clients, or you might want to create a folder for each client.

You can also configure Outlook Express to place incoming messages into selected folders using Tools | Message Rules. Rules can be configured to place incoming emails in a folder, delete the message, forward the message, highlight it, flag it, mark it as read, reply with a message, do not download from the server, and delete from the server, using any of the following as the criteria:

♦ When the From line includes a certain person

♦ When the Subject line contains certain words

♦ When the message body contains specific words

♦ When the To line contains certain people

♦ When the CC line contains certain people

♦ When the message is marked high priority

♦ When the message is from a certain account

♦ When the message size is larger than a specific number

♦ When the message has an attachment

♦ When the message is secure

♦ For all messages

To set a message rule, do the following:

1. Open Outlook Express.

2. Open Tools | Message Rules | Mail.

3. Select the condition for your rule.

4. Select the action for your rule.

5. In the Rule Description area, click on any highlighted words to type in the words or people to add to this rule. Click OK twice when finished.

Creating Folders

To create a new folder and subfolder in Outlook Express:

1. Open Outlook Express.

2. In the Folders pane, right-click Local Folders, and choose New Folder.

3. Name the folder, and choose OK. Notice that the new folder has been created in the Local Folders folder and is shown last.

4. Right-click the new folder, and choose New Folder.

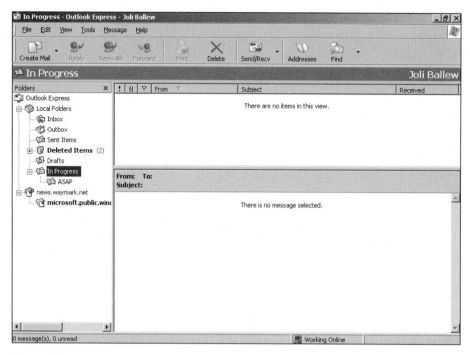

Figure 9.5
Folders and subfolders.

> 5. Type a name for the folder, and choose OK. This new folder is now a subfolder of the first new folder. Figure 9.5 shows a new folder named In Progress and a subfolder named ASAP.

You can delete folders by right-clicking them and choosing Delete.

Warning
Deleting a folder will delete all messages stored in it as well as any subfolders created under it.

Moving an Email Message

To move an email message from one folder to another, click the message and drag it to the folder you'd like to store it in.

Email Attachments

Outlook Express can also be used to send attachments to email messages. These attachments are actually files, usually photos, documents, data files, or something similar. For instance, you might need to send an Excel spreadsheet or a Word document to a colleague to work on and later return. With an Excel file, for instance, when the recipient opens the attachment, it opens automatically in Excel and can be modified immediately.

When you receive an attachment, Outlook Express displays a small paperclip beside the message in the Inbox, and displays another paperclip in the upper-right corner of the message itself. You view the attachment by clicking this paperclip.

As you're opening the attached file, a warning message will appear, informing you that this attachment could contain a virus. This is a standard warning, but it is best to open attachments only from friends or coworkers and *only when you are expecting the attachment*. Some viruses can get into address books and send themselves out to everyone in the address books, so just because an attachment comes from someone you know doesn't mean it's safe. In addition, you should open only files you are familiar with, such as .doc files (Word documents), .xls files (Excel documents), .ppt files (PowerPoint presentations), and .jpeg, .tif, .bmp, and other photo and graphics files. However, even these files can contain viruses. Opening files that end in .vbs (Visual Basic files) or .bat (batch files) is strongly discouraged because viruses can be sent easily through these formats. The I Love You virus and others were in the form .vbs. If you're in doubt, do *not* open an attachment.

Sending an Email with an Attachment
When a file needs to be sent from the local computer to an email recipient, that file can be sent as an attachment. To send a file as an attachment:

1. Open Outlook Express.

2. Create a new email message by choosing the Create Mail button or Create A New Mail Message. Type your message.

3. In the New Message window, choose Insert | File Attachment.

4. In the Insert Attachment dialog box, use the Look In drop-down list to select the folder containing the file you want to attach.

5. In that folder's list of files, highlight the file to attach, and choose Attach. You can attach multiple files by holding down the Ctrl key while selecting files.

6. Notice the Attach text box in the New Message window. This box contains the name of the file you are attaching. The email message is ready to send after you type the recipient's name in the To box.

Sending a Photo
Sending a photo is exactly the same as sending any other file attachment. In the New Message window, choose Insert | File Attachment or Insert | Picture. The Insert | File Attachment command will include the picture as an attachment, and the Insert | Picture command will include the picture in the message itself and as an attachment. In Windows XP, pictures are stored by default in the My Pictures folder. This folder is located inside the My Documents folder, making pictures easy to locate when you're adding email attachments.

The Address Book

The Outlook Express address book is an electronic equivalent of a paper-based address book or rotary file, but the Outlook Express address book can hold much more information. In the Outlook Express application window, you'll see the Addresses button in the toolbar. To open the Address Book application, simply click the Addresses button.

Using the Address Book, you can add contacts, groups, and folders, and configure properties. You can also import an address book from another computer or a floppy disk, create a profile, find people, and organize email addresses. Email addresses are added to the address book by default each time you reply to an email message.

Adding a Contact

To add a contact to the Address Book:

1. Open Outlook Express, and click the Addresses button, or, on the Welcome screen, under Contacts, choose Open The Address Book.

2. Maximize the window. Choose the New button and select New Contact from the drop down list.

3. In the Properties dialog box, type as much information as you know (or want to store) about the new contact. Figure 9.6 shows the Properties dialog for the contact. Choose OK when you're finished.

The Contacts Properties dialog box contains several tabs. You can see the Name tab in Figure 9.6, and this tab contains the only required information: the email address. From the other tabs, many options are available. My favorites are listed here.

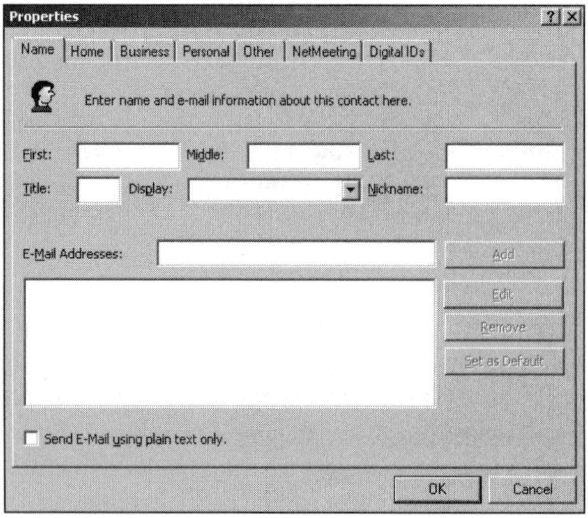

Figure 9.6
The Contacts Properties dialog box.

- *Home tab*—Address, phone number, fax number, mobile number, Web page address, and a View Map button

- *Business tab*—Address, job title, department, office location, phone number, fax number, pager number, IP phone (for a computer's IP address), Web page address, and a View Map button

- *Personal tab*—Spouse's name, children's name, and contact's gender, birthday, and anniversary

- *Other tab*—Notes, group membership, and folder location

- *NetMeeting tab*—Conferencing server and address

- *Digital IDs tab*—Digital IDs associated with the user

Adding a Group

You can use groups to manage contacts so that you can send messages to a group instead of having to select each recipient separately. The members of a group can be chosen from the address book, added as a new contact to both the group and the address book, or added as a contact that belongs to the group but is not added to your personal address book.

To create a mailing group:

1. Open Outlook Express, and click the Addresses button, or, on the Welcome screen, under Contacts, choose Open The Address Book.

2. Maximize the window. Choose New | New Group.

3. Choose the Select Members button to add existing contacts, or choose the New Contact button to add a new contact.

4. After selecting members or adding a new contact, choose OK.

5. Type a name for the group. Choose OK.

Creating a Personal Identity

You can create a personal identity for yourself and use it as a business card that can be sent with all outgoing messages. You can also create additional identities for other users; this will be covered later.

To create a main identity profile for yourself:

1. Open Outlook Express, and open the Address Book.

2. Choose Edit | Profile.

3. The default option—Create A New Entry In The Address Book To Represent Your Profile—should already be selected. Choose OK.

4. Fill in as much information as you'd like, and then choose OK.

Importing an Address Book

Often, an address book will already exist on another computer and will need to be copied to a new one. You can import the address book into your Windows XP address book. (The imported address book does not have to be an Outlook Express address book.)

To import an address book from a Windows 2000 computer to a Windows XP Professional computer:

1. Place a floppy disk in the older computer, a Windows 2000 Professional computer in this example.

2. From the Windows 2000 computer, export the address book by performing the following steps:

   a. Open Outlook Express.

   b. Choose File | Export | Address Book.

   c. Select Text File (Comma Separated Values), and choose the Export button.

   d. Browse to the floppy drive, A:\, choose Save, and choose Next.

   e. Select the fields to export to the new computer's address book, and choose Finish.

3. Remove the floppy disk from the Windows 2000 computer's drive and place it in the Windows XP computer's drive.

4. Open Outlook Express on the Windows XP computer.

5. Open the Address Book.

6. Choose File | Import | Other Address Book.

7. Choose Text File (Comma Separated Values) from the list, and choose the Import button.

8. Browse to the floppy drive, A:\.

9. Highlight the address book, and choose Next.

10. Verify the fields to be imported, and choose Finish.

11. Close the dialog box.

Of course, there are other operating systems and various types of address books, but the steps involved are virtually the same. This type of import works with just about any type of address book or operating system version.

Outlook Express Options

Outlook Express provides several ways to customize the program to meet your specific needs. The main place for such configuration changes is the Options dialog box (choose Tool | Options to open it). The Options dialog box is shown in Figure 9.7.

The Options dialog box has 10 tabs. You should take the time to work your way through all of these tabs and familiarize yourself with all of the options. Although I won't spend the time here to discuss each of them, I will introduce the ones I find of most interest, as well as the ones most often changed:

◆ *General tab*—The options here include having Outlook Express display the Inbox folder instead of the main screen when you start the program, automatically logging onto Windows Messenger, playing sounds when new messages arrive or are sent or received at startup, specifying how often to check for new messages, and specifying when the computer should connect to check messages.

◆ *Read tab*—These options include specifying when to mark messages as read, specifying whether messages should be automatically downloaded in the preview pane, and changing the default font for messages. International settings can also be configured here.

◆ *Receipts tab*—A receipt is verification that the recipient has received an email message. You can request a read receipt for all of the messages you send or for only specific ones. When people request a receipt from you, you can use this tab to configure how you want to handle that. By default, you will be notified if a sender requests a receipt from you.

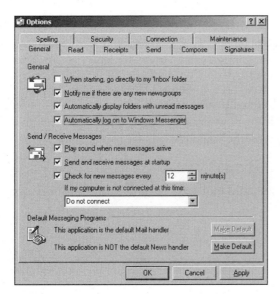

Figure 9.7
The Options dialog box in Outlook Express.

◆ *Send tab*—Here you can specify what to do with messages you send. These options include saving copies of your messages in the Sent Items folder, sending messages immediately, automatically adding to the Address Book the addresses of people you reply to, automatically completing email addresses as you type them, and including the original message in the reply. You can also set the format for sending mail and news: HTML or plain text.

◆ *Compose tab*—Use these options to set the font, font size, and font color for your outgoing messages. You can select stationery, download more stationery, and create stationery. Finally, you can include a business card with all outgoing email. The business card you choose can be based on the main identity you created earlier.

◆ *Signatures tab*—A signature is text that is added to either all outgoing email or just new email, not including replies and forwards. Signatures can include whatever text you like; many people use their name and business address, and sometimes phone and fax numbers as well. To create a signature, choose New and type the appropriate information.

◆ *Spelling tab*—Use this tab to configure spelling checks. These checks can be done on all words or only in specific cases.

◆ *Security tab*—This tab offers options for virus protection, such as specifying how restrictive Internet Explorer should be with the sites it connects to, warning you if applications try to send email, and configuring Outlook Express not to open attachments that could be dangerous. There is also a place to configure secure email and encrypt or digitally sign all outgoing messages.

◆ *Connection tab*—Use this tab to configure the connection and specify whether it should automatically hang up after sending and receiving, or prompt you before switching dial-up connections. The automatic hang-up option can be useful for laptop users who must dial a long-distance number to get email.

◆ *Maintenance tab*—Specify how the Deleted Items folder will be used, whether messages should be compacted, and when to delete newsgroup messages. You can also use this tab to clean up the downloaded messages on the computer.

Changing Compose Options

As an example, to set the font, font size, and font color, and to select stationery for all outgoing messages:

1. Open Outlook Express.

2. Choose Tools | Options.

3. In the Options dialog box, select the Compose tab.

4. Choose the first Font Settings button (the one for Mail).

5. In the Font dialog box, select a font, a font style, and a font size.

6. Select a color for the font. Choose OK.

7. In the Stationery section of the Options dialog box, check the Mail checkbox, and choose the Select button.

8. In the Select Stationery dialog box, select the stationery you want to use. Choose OK.

9. Choose OK to close the Options dialog box.

10. In the application window, choose New Mail, and type a few words to see the new Compose settings.

Personalizing Outlook Express

There are many ways to personalize Outlook Express by configuring the layout of the screen, the look of the windows, and what is shown when Outlook Express is opened. These configurations will change the appearance of the program, so what you'll end up with won't look exactly like the screenshots shown in this book. However, personalizing the program is important so that it's functional and efficient for you.

To personalize how Outlook Express looks when it's opened:

1. Open Outlook Express.

2. Choose View | Layout.

3. In the Window Layout Properties dialog box, check the checkboxes for the components you want to display, such as the status bar, the toolbar, and so on. (To get the screen shown in Figure 9.8, I checked all the boxes.)

4. Choose the Customize Toolbar button.

5. *To add toolbar buttons*—Scroll through the Available Toolbar Buttons list box, select a button you want to add, and choose the Add button. Do this for each button you want to add. (To get the screen shown in Figure 9.8, I added the Preview, Print, Reply, and Move To buttons.)

   To remove toolbar buttons—Scroll through the Current Toolbar Buttons list box, select the button you want to remove, and choose the Remove button. Do this for each button you want to remove.

6. Choose Close and OK to return to the application window.

7. *To have Outlook Express open directly to your Inbox*—Choose Tools | Options. On the General tab, check the checkbox When Starting Go Directly To My Inbox Folder. Choose OK.

8. Close Outlook Express and open it again. The changes are shown in Figure 9.8.

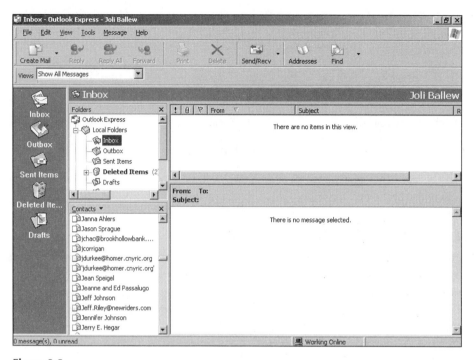

Figure 9.8
A different layout for the Outlook Express application window.

There are several other ways to personalize Outlook Express, and they are quite simple. For instance, by clicking the words From, Subject, or Received in your Inbox, you can arrange the messages in a different order based on who they're from, what they're about, or when they were received. This is useful when you're looking for a particular message sent on a specific day or from a specific person.

More Features of Outlook Express

Before we leave the subject of Outlook Express, a few other features are worth noting—specifically, the ability to create and switch identities when using Outlook Express, giving each user his or her own address book and personal settings. This is important when more than one person is using the computer to send and receive email in Outlook Express.

Also important is the ability to block certain senders from sending you email. As time goes by, many undesirable people obtain your email address for the purpose of selling you stuff, offering you "hot" tips on stocks, and sending many other questionable proposals. These senders can be blocked from sending any future email messages to your computer.

Another topic not yet covered is the ability to join newsgroups. Newsgroups are a collection of messages posted by users just like you. Newsgroups exist on virtually any subject and can be quite interesting. Finally, accessibility options are available for people with disabilities such as those involving hearing, sight, or mobility.

Creating and Switching Identities

If more than one person uses your computer to send and receive email, you can configure an account, or an identity, for each of those users. Each user will then have his or her own address book, contact list, and personal settings, and these user identities can be switched back and forth without going offline or disconnecting.

To create a new identity in Outlook Express:

1. Open Outlook Express.

2. Choose File | Identities | Manage Identities.

3. In the Manage Identities dialog box, double-click the identity named Main Identity.

4. In the Identity Properties dialog box, type your name. If a password should be used to log on with this identity, check the Require A Password checkbox.

5. Choose OK.

6. In the Manage Identities dialog box, choose New.

7. In the New Identity dialog box, type the name of another person who will use Outlook Express to retrieve and send email. If a password should be used to log on with this identity, check the Require A Password checkbox. Choose OK.

8. When asked if you want to switch to the new identity now, choose No. Choose Close.

To switch and manage identities:

1. Open Outlook Express.

2. Click File | Switch Identities.

3. In the Switch Identities dialog box, select the identity to switch to. Choose OK.

4. When using the new identity for the first time, set up the email account that this identity will use. These steps are similar to those for creating email addresses, described earlier.

5. Continue working through the Import Wizard to import messages or address books if applicable; if not, choose Do Not Import At This Time.

The new identity's Outlook Express configuration is the default and is not the same as the configuration of the first identity.

Block Sender

As I mentioned earlier, after a while, many companies, organizations, and other businesses (and probably some scam artists) obtain your email address through various tactics. When you share your email address with people on the Internet either through Web sites or other means, the address gets passed around and sold to others. As time passes, the amount of junk email (often called *spam*) in your Inbox every morning can become annoying. To prevent these users from emailing you again, you can use the Block Sender option in Outlook Express. When you block senders, they can no longer email you using that particular address. When they do, their messages are sent directly to the Deleted Items folder and never reach your Inbox.

To use Block Sender:

1. Open Outlook Express.

2. Click any folder that contains email.

3. Highlight the email from the sender you want to block.

4. Choose Message | Block Sender. Choose Yes to remove all of the previous messages from this sender. Choose OK.

Newsgroups

Newsgroups are a free and easy way to obtain information on just about any subject you can imagine. For you to subscribe to a newsgroup, your ISP must have a newsgroup server. The server name is usually in the form ***news.servername.xxx***. Once the newsgroup settings have been set up through Outlook Express, you can choose which newsgroups to subscribe to. Subscribing to a newsgroup means that you'll receive messages in Outlook Express as they are posted to the newsgroup. You'll also be able to post responses to the group.

To connect to your ISP's newsgroup server and subscribe to a newsgroup:

1. Open Outlook Express.

2. Choose Tools | Accounts.

3. In the Internet Accounts dialog box, select the News tab.

4. Choose Add | News to launch the Internet Connection Wizard.

5. Type your name as you'd like it to appear in the group. Many people use aliases and not their real names. Choose Next.

6. On the Internet News E-Mail Address page, type your email address. Choose Next.

7. On the Internet News Server Name page, type the name of the news (NNTP) server that your ISP supplied you with. Check the checkbox if the news server requires you to log on. Choose Next and then Finish.

8. In the Internet Accounts dialog box, choose Close.

9. Choose Yes to download newsgroups from the new account. This will take a few minutes depending on the newsgroups available. See Figure 9.9.

10. With the list of newsgroups available, scan through to see what interests you, and choose a newsgroup to join. Choose Subscribe, then Go To.

   The files download, and there is a new folder in the left pane.

Posting (or writing) to the newsgroup is the same as sending an email message. To respond to a group entry, highlight the entry and choose Reply Group. To compose a new entry for the group, choose New Post.

Accessibility Options

A few things in Windows Outlook Express can be considered accessibility options, in addition to the built-in options in the operating system itself. These options are:

♦ Sound notifications when email messages arrive

♦ Resizable folder lists and message panes

♦ Toolbars that can be customized

These options can be changed using the View and Tools menus discussed earlier.

Instant Messaging

Instant messaging has gotten very popular in the last year or so, and the Windows Messenger Service is included in Windows XP Professional. Instant messaging is similar to sending email except that the message is sent and received immediately between two or more persons. All parties involved in a conversation using Windows Messenger must have a "passport" from Microsoft, which is obtained at no cost over the Internet.

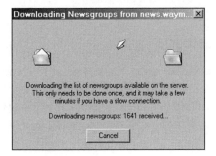

Figure 9.9
Downloading newsgroups.

In this section, I'll introduce Windows Messenger Service, explaining how to get a passport, add contacts, send a message to another Windows Messenger user, and personalize the service with fonts, colors, and emoticons. You can also use Windows Messenger to make phone calls over the Internet and to send or receive pages.

Signing Up for a Passport

To use the Windows Messenger Service, you'll need a passport. To get a passport:

1. Use Internet Explorer to go to **http://messenger.msn.com/download**. (When first using Windows Messenger, you might be linked to the site automatically.)

2. Click the Get A Passport button.

3. The easiest way to complete the passport process is to sign up for a Hotmail account. Earlier in this chapter, you may have gotten one of these accounts when setting up Outlook Express. Either way, simply fill in the appropriate information, and click Sign Up. In less than a minute, you'll be ready to use Windows Messenger.

To sign in to the service:

1. While remaining logged onto the Internet through your ISP, choose Start | Programs | Windows Messenger.

2. At the sign-in screen, type your sign-in name and password.

3. Once logged in, you'll need to accept the terms of use. You'll then receive an email from MSN welcoming you to the service and outlining the available features.

Figure 9.10 shows a brand new account with Windows Messenger; this is how the interface will look the first time Windows Messenger is used.

Adding Contacts

To add a contact, you'll need to know someone else who has a passport and uses Windows Messenger. With that little detail out of the way, the steps are simple:

1. In the Windows Messenger Service window, click Add.

2. If you know the person's email address and/or sign-in name, click Next at the Add A Contact window. Just type in the person's name, and that person will be notified that you are adding him or her to your contact list. If that person accepts you into his or her contact list, you'll see the person's name in the Windows Messenger window.

Messaging

Once you've added a contact, you can send a message to that person anytime he or she is online; just double-click the person's name in the Windows Messenger window. You can see

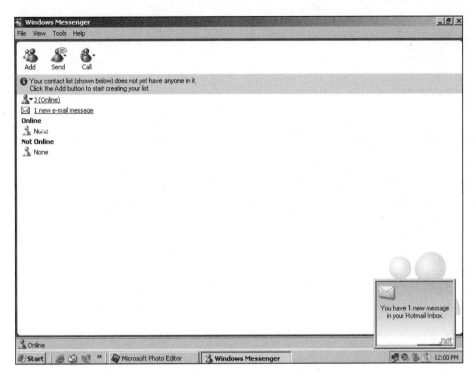

Figure 9.10
Windows Messenger.

who's online and who isn't by looking in the window. Figure 9.11 shows the Windows Messenger Service window with one person online and several others who aren't.

Personalizing Windows Messenger

There are several ways to personalize Windows Messenger. From the window shown in Figure 9.11, you can do all of these things:

♦ *From the File menu*—Change the status of your MSN connection from Online to Busy, Be Right Back, Away, On The Phone, or Out To Lunch, or you can be listed as offline.

♦ *From the View menu*—Change the layout of the Windows Messenger Service window by adding or removing toolbars, or configuring Windows Messenger to remain on top of all other applications.

♦ *From the Tools | Options dialog box*—Change your display name, edit your public profile, change the fonts and colors used for messaging, set up mobile devices and phone numbers, and specify which alerts will be shown when your contacts come online or send you an instant message, which contacts can see you when you're online, and which senders, if any, should be blocked.

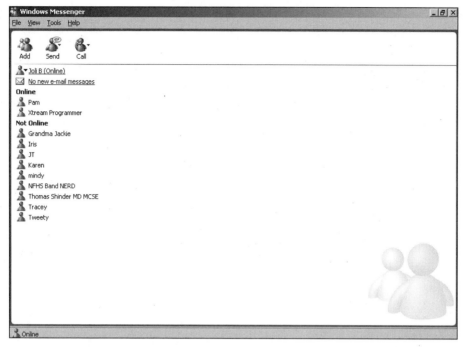

Figure 9.11
Contacts in Windows Messenger.

To configure the Windows Messenger Service by using the Options dialog box:

1. Open Windows Messenger by choosing Start | Programs | Windows Messenger.

2. Sign into the service.

3. Choose Tools | Options to open the Options dialog box.

4. On the General tab, change your display name. Notice that Figure 9.11 shows display names such as Xtream Programmer and Mindy. This name has no bearing on your passport name or how you log in; it can be anything you like.

5. Also on the General tab, click Edit Your Public Profile. You'll be connected to the Web site **http://profiles.msn.com**. Here you can create a profile for other users to see with information about yourself, your spouse, and your occupation.

6. Finally, on the General tab, choose Edit Font. Change your font in the Set My Message Font window. You can also change the color, size, and effects. Choose OK. Leave the checkbox Show Graphics (Emoticons) In Instant Messages checked. For more on emoticons, see the sidebar.

Emoticons

Emoticons are graphics you can add to instant messages by typing certain sets of characters. For instance, typing a left parenthesis, a "c," and a right parenthesis—(c)—while using Windows Messenger will show a coffee cup on the screen. Here are some others:

- (p) is a camera.
- (y) is a thumbs-up sign.
- (g) is a gift.
- (K) is a kiss.
- (s) is a moon.
- (i) is a light bulb.

More emoticons are shown in Figure 9.12.

---

7. On the Preferences tab, check the Run This Program When Windows Starts check-box to change settings for how the program will be started, and configure when the service will show you as "away" from the computer. Also select which sounds will be played and when.

8. Explore the other tabs, and choose OK when finished.

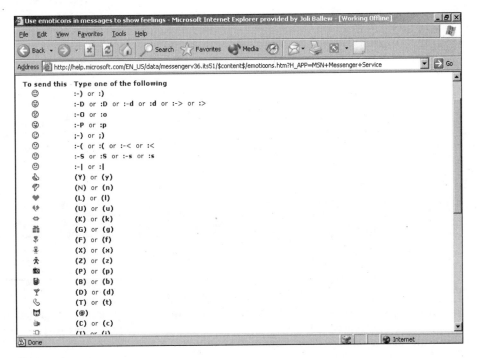

Figure 9.12
Emoticons.

Phone Calls and Pages

Windows Messenger can also be used to place phone calls via the Internet. When phone calls are made through your ISP, there are often no long-distance charges. This can be quite useful if you have the hardware to make such calls. You must have a microphone and speakers to place calls through Windows Messenger.

Windows Messenger can also be set up to send and receive pages to wireless devices. This is done through the Internet via wireless technology. If you have a wireless phone or pager that is capable of receiving these pages and is set up with an email address, you can configure it here.

Windows Messenger Phone Options

To use the phone available in Windows XP Professional and Windows Messenger, you need to install speakers and a microphone before continuing with these instructions. (You can find information on installing hardware in Chapter 8.) For Internet calls, Windows Messenger is used with Net2Phone and charges $.02 a minute. The first time you make a call, you'll need to fill out an application with Net2Phone before continuing.

To set up the phone and place a call:

1. Start Windows Messenger, and log onto the service.

2. Choose Tools | Audio Tuning Wizard, and set up your microphone and speakers by working through the wizard.

3. Choose Tools | Options, and select the Phone tab.

4. Type your phone number, and select the appropriate country. Choose OK.

5. In the Windows Messenger Service window, choose Tools | Call | Dial A Phone Number.

6. In the Windows Messenger Phone dialog box, choose a call destination country.

7. Type the phone number, and choose Dial.

8. Click Go To My Net2Phone Account. Close any advertising windows that appear.

9. Fill out the information at the Net2Phone Web site. After the account is set up, you can continue with the call. See the sidebar for free calling options.

Free Calling Options

Net2Phone currently has free service for calls in the U.S. that are under five minutes. Information is available at the Web site **www.net2phone.com**. Other free services include **www.isfree.com**, **www.freewebcall.com**, **www.bigredwire.com**, and **www.go2call.com**. Free Internet calling is an option if you look hard enough. Try using your Web browser to search the Web for "free Internet phone calling," and then compare the options before signing up with any one provider.

Paging Options

With a wireless pager or telephone that accepts text messages over the Internet, you can set up the Windows Messenger Service to work with your device. You can do this by clicking the Page button in the Windows Messenger Service window. You'll be connected to **http://mobile.msn.com**, where you will need to fill out information about your wireless device, get an authorization code, and then configure the settings.

Internet Explorer Version 6

In most cases, Windows XP Professional comes with Internet Explorer version 6. If your computer didn't, you can get Internet Explorer from Microsoft, or you can use MSN Explorer, detailed in the following section. In this section, you'll learn about this version of Internet Explorer, including how to use it to surf the Web, what the address bar is and how to use it, what cookies are, and how to make sure your identity remains secure and private while you're on the Web. You'll also learn about personalizing Internet Explorer, controlling access to Web sites, configuring fonts and colors, setting options, and protecting your computer from viruses.

Internet Explorer Features

To use Internet Explorer, you must have a working connection to the Internet. Then you can use Internet Explorer by clicking the icon on the desktop or by choosing Start | Programs | Internet Explorer.

Internet Explorer is a Web browser that is used to connect you to the information on the Internet. There are several ways to locate this information, from typing search words in the address bar to using the Search button on the toolbar. Once you've located a Web page you like, you can access similar information by using the Show Related Links feature.

There is also a place to add shortcuts to favorite Web sites and a Favorites list that can be configured as well as additional folders for organizing those sites. You can also select a personal home page to view each time Internet Explorer is started, change Web fonts, and change the appearance of the browser itself. Security levels can be set to protect your computer from unwanted access; Web pages can be printed or used offline; and sending and receiving information over the Web is secure and safe. In this section, you'll learn about these features and more so that you can get the most out of the Internet.

Surfing the Web

Being able to traverse the Internet is, of course, the main purpose of having a Web browser like Internet Explorer. This application allows you to connect to the Web sites you choose and to access all aspects of the Internet. Surfing the Web starts with logging onto the Internet and opening Internet Explorer.

The Internet Explorer Interface

Figure 9.13 shows the Internet Explorer interface. Internet Explorer has the File, Edit, View, Tools, and Help menus that you've seen in many other applications, plus a Favorites menu. Each of these menus offers different types of configuration information. Internet Explorer also has a toolbar with Back, Forward, Stop, Refresh, Home, Personal, Favorites, and History buttons.

All of these menus and buttons are here to enhance your Internet experience. However, most of the tasks associated with surfing the Internet are done not through these menus but rather through the Web sites themselves or the Back, Forward, Search, and Favorites buttons. The most-used buttons are described next:

- *Back*—Returns you to the last Web page you viewed during a browsing session. The Back button can be used as often as needed and has a long list of previously viewed sites.

- *Forward*—Returns you to the last Web page you viewed *before clicking the Back button* during a browsing session.

- *Stop*—Stops the page from loading—useful when the page is taking too long to load or when you chose the wrong link.

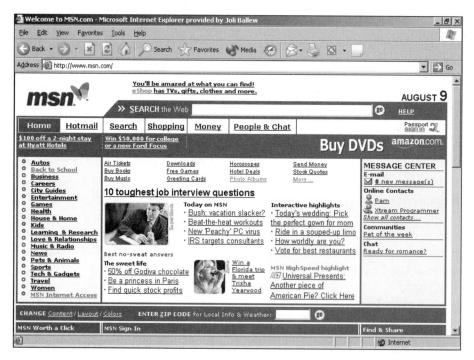

Figure 9.13
The Internet Explorer application window.

- *Refresh*—Redisplays the content on the current page. This is useful on pages where content changes often, such as news pages or stock pages.

- *Home*—Opens the page configured as a user's home (starting) page. The home page by default is **www.msn.com**; to change it, choose Tools | Internet Options, select the General tab, and type the address of the home page you want to use.

- *Media*—The media button opens a pane on the left side of the browser window that can be used to access Media Places such as My Music, My Videos, More Media, and Radio Guide.

- *Search*—Adds a pane that can be used to search the Internet for specific information. This pane is aptly named the Search Companion, and it lists matches related to your query. This pane is displayed on the left side of the browser window and replaces any existing pane.

- *Favorites*—Lists Web sites designated as favorites. Some are included by default, such as MSN.com, the Radio Station Guide, and more. You can also add your own favorites to this list and create folders for organizing them.

- *History*—Enables you to view pages that you visited two weeks ago, last week, or on previous days of the current week. This is useful when you need to return to a site but can't remember its name or location.

Each of these toolbars can be personalized to meet the needs of any user. You can use the View menu to add other toolbars and to add buttons to or remove them from the Explorer bar. The Explorer bar is the one added to the left pane when a specific button is chosen. Also, you can choose View | Text Size to change the size of the text displayed on a Web page. This might not take effect on some Web sites, depending on the rules set out for each.

Using the Address Bar

The address bar is where the address of the Web site is located and/or typed in. In Figure 9.13, the address bar holds the address **http://www.msn.com**. You can use the address bar to type in a known address, such as **http://www.ask.com** or **http://www.spca.org**. You can also use the address bar as a search mechanism. As an example, typing "computers" in the address bar brings up a list of over 14,000 sites about computers. These are listed 15 at a time, and any of these sites can be accessed through the links listed in the browser.

Cookies

Some Web sites you visit will store a small text file called a *cookie* on your hard drive. There are lots of different types of cookies, and you can choose whether you want them to be stored on your computer. Cookies are seen as both good and bad, but generally, no harm comes from allowing cookies to be stored on your computer. Cookies are what enable you to visit a Web site and automatically obtain information such as news or weather for your specific part of the country, or to have a Web site remember your name or personal preferences. Cookies also help companies serve you better by remembering what banner ads have already been displayed and what types of books or music you generally prefer.

If you choose not to allow cookies, you won't be able to view some Web sites, and the sites you do visit can't be personalized. However, some people view cookies as a violation of privacy and do not want to allow them.

To change the preferences for how cookies are handled on your computer:

1. Open Internet Explorer.

2. Choose Tools | Internet Options.

3. Select the Security tab.

4. Click Custom Level.

5. For the different types of cookies, choose Enable, Prompt (to be prompted for approval for each one), or Disable.

6. Choose OK twice.

Security and Privacy

Besides cookies, several other issues concerning privacy and security are of concern. Many of these issues revolve around what information is sent over the Internet and what happens to that information once it gets there. All companies post (or should post) their privacy policies. It is always a good idea to read these policies if you are concerned that the information you plan to send will be sold or transferred to a third party.

Other precautions to take when using the Internet include the following:

♦ Use secure Internet sites when performing transactions on the Web. Secure sites are those that have **https://** instead of **http://** in front of their Web addresses. Banks, Internet stores, and any other site that receives sensitive information from you should have a secure site for doing so. Sending private information over non-secure sites is risky because others could obtain that information fairly easily.

♦ For extra security, obtain a personal security certificate from a third party. This certificate is like an electronic identity card. You can use this card to encrypt and decrypt data safely on the Internet. Most users won't need such security, but if you do a lot of business over the Web, getting a certificate is recommended.

♦ Before sharing information with anyone, ask yourself if you would share this information over the phone with a complete stranger. This is in essence what you are doing. If a site you've never heard of asks for your Social Security number or credit card number, beware! In fact, I'll add here that I can't think of any reason to give out your social security number over the Internet.

♦ Security levels can also be set for different types of Internet access. In a highly secure environment, the setting should be set to High; in a non-secure or experimental environment, the setting could be Low. (These settings are covered later in this chapter.)

♦ When downloading applications, screensavers, or any executable files from the Internet, make sure they are from a company or Web site you trust. Windows XP will warn you if the executable you are tying to run is unsigned.

♦ Use Content Advisor to control Internet access from your computer. Settings can be configured for language, nudity, sex, and violence.

Personalizing Internet Explorer with the Internet Options Dialog Box

Internet Explorer can be personalized through the Tools | Internet Options dialog box. There are multiple options here for specifying exactly how you want Internet Explorer to perform, setting security levels, customizing privacy settings, and more. In this section, I'll go through the dialog box tabs separately to help you choose which options you want to configure for your personalized Internet Explorer browser. To follow along and make these changes, open Internet Explorer and choose Tools | Internet Options.

Note

These same options are available in Outlook Express. Choose Tools|Options, select the Connection tab, and choose Change.

General Tab

You can use the General tab of the Internet Options dialog box to change the home page from the default **www.msn.com** to any other Web page. The easiest way to do this is to browse to the site that you want to use as your home page, choose Tools | Internet Options, select the General tab, and choose Use Current from the Home Page options.

You can also use this tab to delete the temporary files created when you surf the Internet, such as cookies and other temporary Internet files. You can delete these without harming any permanent files on the computer. Internet Explorer stores these temporary files on your hard disk to increase the speed with which frequently visited pages are displayed. Use the Settings button to configure how these temporary files are refreshed—specifically, how often to check for newer versions of stored pages and how large to make the Temporary Internet Files folder.

After you've surfed the Web a bit, you'll have a large number of temporary files on your computer. To view these files, choose the Settings button on the General tab, and choose View Files. To delete these files, return to the General tab and choose the Delete Files button. To also delete the cookies stored on your computer, also choose the Delete Cookies button.

In the History section of the General tab, you can specify how many days to keep a Web page in the History folder. The default is 20 days. You can also clear the History folder by choosing the Clear History button.

Finally, the colors, fonts, languages, and accessibility options for Internet Explorer can be changed from the default. To change these options, simply click on the appropriate button and make the desired changes. Figure 9.14 shows the General tab of the Internet Options dialog box.

Security Tab

Use the Security tab of the Internet Options dialog box to configure security zones. Four zones are available: Internet, Local Intranet, Trusted Sites, and Restricted Sites. Each zone level can be configured with its own level of security, using either the provided settings or a custom level. The provided levels are Low, Medium-Low, Medium, and High, or you can set a custom level of security based on what should and should not be allowed for each zone.

The Internet zone contains all of the zones that haven't already been manually configured as Trusted Sites, Restricted Sites, or Local Intranet Sites. The Internet zone's default setting is Medium, meaning that safe browsing is enabled, a prompt is issued before you download unsafe content, and unsigned ActiveX controls cannot be downloaded. This setting is suitable for most Internet sites.

The Local Intranet zone is set to Medium-Low by default. Less restrictive than the Medium setting, the Medium-Low setting does not prompt you when dangerous downloads are occurring. It is appropriate for most intranets.

The Trusted Sites zone has a default setting of Low. Sites can be added through the Sites button, and all sites listed here are treated differently than in any other zone. With a setting of Low, there are minimal safeguards, no warning prompts are sent, and all ActiveX content

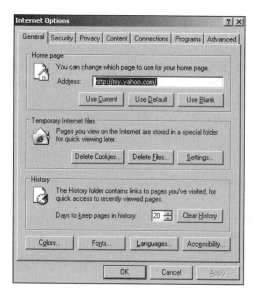

Figure 9.14
The General tab of the Internet Options dialog box.

can be run. This level is safe for only those sites that are absolutely trusted by the company or the user.

Finally, there is the Restricted Sites zone. The default here is High; it is the safest way to browse the network but is the least functional. Cookies are disabled, and many sites will not run under this setting.

Privacy Tab

Use the Privacy tab of the Internet Options dialog box to set a privacy level. By default, that setting is Medium. With a Medium setting, Internet Explorer checks Web sites for privacy policies, compares the policies to the preferences chosen here, allows all Web sites to use cookies, does not allow third-party sites to use cookies, and is compatible with most Web sites. This setting can be changed to Low or High, but Medium is the most functional. Additional custom privacy preferences can be imported as well.

Content Tab

Use the Content tab of the Internet Options dialog box to enable the Content Advisor. This utility enables the administrator of the computer to restrict the types of sites that can be accessed from this computer; restrictions are based on the usage of language, nudity, sex, and violence. A slider is available to move from the default level of 0 to the highest level of 4. Each level is more restrictive than the previous one and bases its judgment on how explicit each category of offense is. A supervisor of the computer can also be named, and a password can be used to configure these settings, preventing other users from changing them.

Certificates can also be used, as mentioned earlier, to provide a means to positively identify yourself to others and them to you. These certificates can be imported, exported, or removed, and a list of trusted publishers will be listed.

Finally, personal information can be configured through the My Profile button. My Profile uses the Microsoft Profile Assistant to store your personal information. This information can then be shared when a Web site requests it from you to make purchases or apply for services. AutoComplete is available as well to automatically complete typed information for Web addresses, forms, usernames, and passwords.

Connections Tab

Using the Connections tab, you can launch the Internet Connection Wizard, add dial-up settings, and configure LAN settings. Most of these options were covered earlier in this chapter. The Network Connection Wizard is also available here; it will be discussed in Chapter 10.

Programs Tab

To use the Internet, you can use several other browsers and email programs besides Internet Explorer and Outlook Express. In addition, to create Web pages, you can use other HTML editors besides Microsoft FrontPage; for a calendar and contact manager, you can use other programs besides Microsoft Outlook. To change the default programs used when you use email, newsgroups, Internet calls, a calendar, or a contact list, or when you create a Web page, you'll need to make those changes here.

If you've added a Hotmail account, then Hotmail is one of the options available under Email. To switch between Outlook Express and Hotmail, simply make the choice here. The default Web settings can also be applied here if changes have been made and the default is desired.

Advanced Tab

The Advanced tab is generally used by more advanced users; it can be configured such that very specific changes are made to the browser. Although there are approximately 60 choices up for grabs here, the most common ones to change are the following:

♦ Automatically check for Internet Explorer updates (not checked by default).

♦ Enable install-on-demand (not checked by default).

♦ Enable personalized Favorites menus. These personalized menus hide favorites that aren't accessed often (checked by default).

♦ Notify you when downloads are completed (checked by default).

♦ Show friendly URLs (not checked by default).

♦ Always show the Internet Explorer radio toolbar (not checked by default).

♦ Warn if you're switching between secure and non-secure mode (not checked by default).

You can also restore all default settings by using the Restore Defaults button.

Example: Controlling Access to Web Sites

To change security options in Internet Explorer:

1. Open Internet Explorer.

2. Choose Tools | Internet Options.

3. In the Internet Options dialog box, select the Security tab.

4. Select the Trusted Sites zone, and choose the Sites button.

5. Type "**https://www.microsoft.com**" or your company's secured home page.

6. Choose Add, then OK.

7. In the Internet Options dialog box, click Default Level if it isn't grayed out. Notice that the Trusted Sites setting is Low. Change it to Medium-Low or Medium if you want to. Choose OK to accept this change, or Cancel to quit.

Protecting Your Computer from Viruses

Windows XP Professional can't protect your computer from viruses without help from you. Earlier I discussed the importance of taking on some of these responsibilities by opening email only from people you know and opening only those attachments you trust. What's most important, never open a file that ends in .vbs or .bat unless you are sure of the file's origin. Other file extensions to watch out for are .exe (executable files) and .com files.

There are other precautions you can take. For one, when downloading a program from the Internet, always save the program to a disk first (a floppy disk, Zip disk, or hard drive). This allows you to run an anti-virus program on it before using or installing it. Two, save all of your work and close all programs before running any installation program. Three, make sure you have disconnected yourself from any local area network before running any installation program.

Other tips include purchasing a third-party anti-virus program, configuring it to run daily and to download updates automatically, and setting the security zones on your computer to the highest functional level. Make sure to keep yourself up-to-date on the latest viruses through a newsgroup or magazine. Watch for warning signs of viruses as well, including weird error messages, uncommon program behavior, decreased system performance, and missing data. By keeping all of this in mind and being just a little careful, you can minimize your chances of having your computer catch a virus.

MSN Explorer

I really like MSN Explorer. It is included with Windows XP Professional and is accessed through Start | Programs | MSN Explorer. MSN Explorer is a Web browser that can be personalized to meet any user's needs. This browser that comes with Windows XP Professional is free to use, however, signing up with MSN as an Internet service is not. Be careful not to sign up for anything you don't need. When you start the browser, a voice says "Good Afternoon! or Good Morning, depending on the time of day," and an extremely friendly graphical user interface appears. You must log onto MSN Explorer with your Hotmail passport, so if you haven't gotten one yet, you'll have to do that before logging on. This is a great browser, and the trip through this section will be well worth your time.

Signing In or Adding a User

To use MSN Explorer, you'll be asked to log in using your Hotmail passport. Earlier in this chapter, I discussed how to obtain one of those. With your passport ready, start MSN Explorer by choosing Start | Programs | MSN Explorer. If there is another user already configured on the computer, or if you aren't prompted immediately for your logon information, select Add User from the top-right corner of the Welcome screen. Once the user has been added, that user can log on after that simply by clicking on his or her sign-in name, as shown in Figure 9.15.

Figure 9.15
The Welcome screen of MSN Explorer.

If this is the first time you've used MSN Explorer, you'll be asked to type in your Hotmail account or password. Just follow the instructions on the screen; Microsoft will walk you through the process.

Taking the Tour

The first time MSN Explorer is run, you are invited to take the MSN Explorer tour. To take the tour from this prompt, click Take The Tour. If you don't have time during your first logon, you can access the tour by typing the word "tour" in the Go box.

MSN Explorer Features

MSN Explorer has so many features that it would be difficult to introduce all of them here. However, the majority of them can be seen from the screenshot in Figure 9.16, and I've personalized this page just a little bit to suit my own needs. When you log in, MSN knows where you're from, and it places in the top-left corner of the screen a guide to your local news, weather, and entertainment. This information is obtained from the information you typed in when getting your passport or Hotmail account; if you don't want them to know, leave this information blank when signing up. You can further personalize these items by clicking their links.

The toolbar at the top of the window contains icons for Home, Email, Favorites, Online Buddies, People And Chat, Money, Shopping, and Music. These icons all perform functions similar to those described in the Internet Explorer section or are self-explanatory. By clicking the Shopping button, for instance, you are connected to MSN eShop, where you can purchase anything from apparel to toys. The People And Chat button connects you to

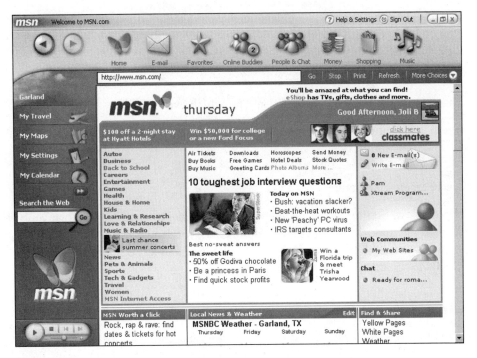

Figure 9.16
The MSN Explorer application window.

a page where you can search for subjects that interest you and join email communities, chats, or other groups if applicable. You'll need to download the chat software, but it is done automatically and takes only two minutes.

You can also personalize the MSN interface to suit your tastes. In the following section, these options will be detailed.

Personalizing MSN Explorer

In the top-right corner of the MSN Explorer window is a welcome message stating "Good Afternoon" or "Good Morning" followed by the user's logon name. To the right of that is a picture. Click the picture to personalize your picture settings. Other settings can be accessed from More Choices | Settings.

From the More Choices | Settings page, many changes can be made, and they are made quickly without your having to wait for the page to refresh each time. From here, you can do all of the following:

- Get Help

- Change your password

- Customize home-page content

- Add users

- Change connection settings

- Choose a new picture for the account

- Change which sounds are generated and for which events

- Personalize content for My Stuff

- Block spam

- Create an email signature

By choosing All Settings from this menu, you can also personalize or change your nickname, personal information, or public profile, create a calendar, clean up your Web space, organize favorites, connect to a mobile device, change email settings, configure online rules, and view MSN's privacy statement.

NetMeeting

NetMeeting is included with Windows XP Professional but is not installed by default. By installing NetMeeting, you can open doors not previously available. NetMeeting provides a way to communicate with others via telephone lines and the Internet to exchange not only voice data but video data as well. With NetMeeting, users can participate in company meetings, see and speak with grandchildren across the country, and share information over a company intranet.

NetMeeting uses address books and directories stored on your local computer to locate the people you want to communicate with. There are many ways NetMeeting can be used; you can exchange diagrams or other graphics on an electronic whiteboard, use the chat area for real-time typed conversations, use audio and video communications, and collaborate on shared documents. Chat conversations can be encrypted to ensure privacy, and program sharing can allow several users to work on the same project simultaneously.

Installing NetMeeting

To open NetMeeting, choose Start | Programs | Accessories | Communications | NetMeeting. Before using NetMeeting, though, you need to install it. When the first NetMeeting screen appears, read the information shown and choose Next. This process begins the installation.

To continue installing NetMeeting:

1. Fill in the information for name and email address, and optionally a location and comments. Choose Next.

2. Select the Microsoft Internet Directory as the default directory when logging on with NetMeeting. Optionally, list your name in the directory. Choose Next.

3. Select the speed of your modem or connecting device, and choose Next.

4. Choose to place a shortcut on the desktop (it can be removed later) and optionally on the Quick Launch bar. Choose Next.

5. Choose Next to start the Audio Tuning Wizard.

6. Test the playback by using the Test button, and choose Next.

7. Configure the Microphone settings, and choose Finish.

Basic Conferencing

There are several ways to place a call using NetMeeting. You can type an email address, a computer name, a telephone number, or an IP address. This is typed in the address bar in the Phone Dialer, as shown in Figure 9.17. The address bar in this figure is blank, and it is located under the menu options Call, View, Tools, and Help. Figure 9.17 also shows a connection in progress between two users on different computers. The receiving computer does not have to have NetMeeting installed to answer the call or participate in the chat.

With the appropriate dialing information typed in the address bar, simply click Place Call to begin the connection. If NetMeeting can't call automatically, then the Place A Call dialog box opens, and you'll need to select a connection type. Once connected, the users connected can talk through microphones and hear through speakers, and if they have video cameras hooked up, they can view each other as well.

Figure 9.17
NetMeeting in a call.

Using the Whiteboard

With a connection in progress, users can share a whiteboard to exchange ideas and graphics. A sample whiteboard is shown in Figure 9.18; two people are using NetMeeting, and both are typing on the same whiteboard. During a call, you can open the whiteboard by clicking the marker and whiteboard icon at the bottom of the NetMeeting screen, as shown in Figure 9.18.

Other Features

Several other features are available in NetMeeting. You can ask other people to join the conversation, find people by using the Find Someone utility, place secure calls, and share applications with those in the meeting. Remote desktop sharing is also possible, as is sharing files and folders.

Phone Dialer

Another Windows XP Professional accessory that allows you to make telephone calls and video calls is Phone Dialer. In Phone Dialer, you can make a voice call using the recipient's phone number, IP (Internet Protocol) address, or DNS (Domain Name System) name. You can use Phone Dialer with a modem, over a network, or while connected to a LAN. All you need are a microphone and speakers. To receive a call, Phone Dialer must be running.

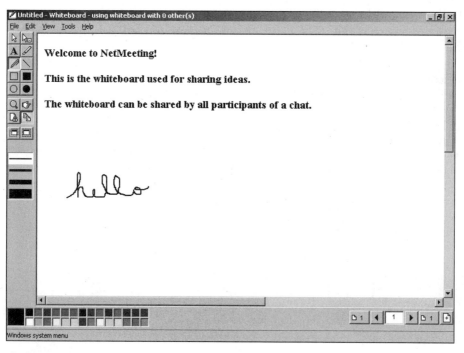

Figure 9.18
The NetMeeting whiteboard.

To make a call:

1. Open Phone Dialer by choosing Start | Programs | Accessories | Communications | Phone Dialer.

2. Choose Phone | Dial.

3. In the Dial As dialog box, select the type of call you want to make: Phone Call or Internet Call.

4. Choose Place Call.

It is equally easy to place a conference call to multiple users. Instead of choosing Phone | Dial as in the previous example, choose Phone | New Conference. Type a name and description for the call, and type a call time. Send all prospective participants email telling them when the call is scheduled or asking them to join the call while it is in progress.

HyperTerminal

HyperTerminal is a utility that is used to connect to other computers that belong to Telnet sites, bulletin board systems, online services, and the like. This connection can be made through a modem, a null modem cable, or an Ethernet connection. This is less common than it used to be, and HyperTerminal isn't used very much these days. However, in certain circumstances, it can prove useful.

HyperTerminal can be used to troubleshoot connections, and this is useful because HyperTerminal records the messages that are passed between computers. This information can then be used to solve connectivity problems. HyperTerminal can also be used to send large files from one computer to another or to help debug code from a remote terminal.

When using HyperTerminal, you create and save configured connections. Each of these connections can be different, but you can have only one connection open during a HyperTerminal session. HyperTerminal does not automatically save passwords or login names for any of these connections.

Games on the Internet

Windows XP Professional comes with several games installed, and many of them can be played on the Internet with other users of Windows XP Professional. Although your boss probably won't appreciate your playing games at work, it can be a nice stress-reliever at lunchtime.

Games included with Windows XP Professional include the following:

♦ FreeCell

♦ Hearts

- ◆ Minesweeper

- ◆ Pinball

- ◆ Solitaire

- ◆ Spider Solitaire

- ◆ Internet Hearts

- ◆ Internet Backgammon

- ◆ Internet Checkers

- ◆ Internet Reversion

- ◆ Internet Spades

Playing these games over the Internet is as simple as clicking the game you want to play. To get started:

1. Connect to the Internet.

2. Choose Start | Programs | Accessories | Games, and select the game you want to play.

3. Choose Play in the dialog box.

4. Play begins. Use the mouse to participate. Some games, such as Internet Checkers, include a chat area. See Figure 9.19.

While connected to the game, you are also connected to **www.zone.com**. You can get help on any game from the Help menu. Checkers, for instance, offers Help | Checkers On The Web. From the Web site, you can choose whom to play against and at what level of play, chat with your opponent, participate in worldwide tournaments, and access dozens of other games. You can also pick a nickname, download game software, and play single-player games. Some single-player games include the following:

- ◆ Blackjack

- ◆ Celebrity Trivia

- ◆ Pop Trivia

- ◆ Sports Trivia

- ◆ Bejeweled

- ◆ Alchemy

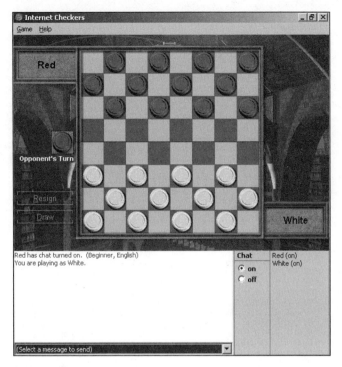

Figure 9.19
Internet Checkers.

Wrapping Up

Windows XP Professional has a lot to offer when it comes to the Internet and email. In this chapter, you learned how to establish a connection to the Internet by using the Internet Connection Wizard, how to use Outlook Express to read, write, and send email and to send email attachments, what Internet Explorer 6 has to offer, and even a little about MSN Explorer.

This chapter also covered making surfing on the Web safe, as well as deciding whether to accept cookies, protecting your computer from viruses, and protecting your privacy. NetMeeting, Phone Dialer, HyperTerminal, and Internet Games were briefly introduced, along with tips on how to make free Internet phone calls. In the next chapter, you'll learn how to set up a home network, and you'll learn more about the Internet, including Internet Connection Sharing.

Chapter 10
Small-Office Networks

There are two ways to set up a small-office network: by configuring the computers in a workgroup, and by setting up the computers in a domain. Workgroups and domains are different in many ways, and the requirements for configuring and administering them are entirely different. Windows XP Professional can be used to set up a workgroup in a small office, but it cannot be used to set up a domain. Windows XP Server (not Professional) is the "lead" computer in a domain and is required to configure a domain. However, if a domain is configured, Windows XP Professional machines can be domain members.

Because this book is written for Windows XP Professional, I'll focus solely on that operating system. In this chapter specifically, the focus will be on setting up a small network by using a workgroup. I'll also cover configuring Internet connection sharing (ICS), managing users and computers, sharing resources, and managing workgroup permissions. I'll cover both share and NTFS permissions as well as advanced permissions, and I'll talk a little about protocols at the end of the chapter. If you are a member of a domain and you work in a corporate environment, the first part of this chapter won't apply to you. However, the information on NTFS permissions, FAT and NTFS file systems, and protocols is relevant for all readers.

Workgroups

Using workgroups is the simplest way to share resources such as computers, printers, scanners, and files and folders. Workgroups are also referred to as *peer-to-peer networks* because computers communicate with each other directly and do not require a server to manage resources and permissions for those resources. These peers, or participating computers and their users, are equals on the network, share resources with each other, and can transfer information among themselves. The security of these resources is determined by each user and is protected by permissions and passwords. Sharing allows users to access other users' resources, including printers, scanners, and files and folders. Workgroups in the past were suggested for offices containing 10 or fewer computers, but My Network Places offers support and will automatically create shortcuts for a workgroup that contains between 2 and 32 computers. Although a workgroup of 32 computers is most likely unmanageable, it is certainly possible.

Note
Servers are used in domains to accept client requests for access to resources. The server either fulfils a request or denies it based on the client's (user's) permissions for that resource. Domains always use NTFS permissions (more on that later).

Advantages of Configuring a Workgroup

Configuring your office's computers as a workgroup provides several advantages. With a workgroup, you no longer have to take information from computer to computer on a floppy disk or other removable media. Because the computers are physically connected, that information can be transferred "across the wire," or over the connection the computers share. Other advantages include the following:

♦ All users on the network can share a single Internet connection.

♦ User accounts on the network can be added and deleted, preventing unwanted local access to the computers.

♦ Users can be placed in groups and given specific access to resources, further securing the network.

♦ Multiple user accounts can be configured for a single computer and can be managed by the administrator of the computer.

♦ Computers and other resources can be added to the workgroup easily.

♦ Printers, scanners, files, folders, cameras, and more can be shared among users easily.

♦ Both share and NTFS permissions can be set for resources; these permissions include Read, Write, Change, Modify, Full Control, and Take Ownership.

♦ One computer can be assigned to serve as a firewall to secure the network and protect your Internet connection.

♦ A user on a computer in one office can work on a file on another computer in another office, and users can collaborate on projects.

♦ Users can play multiplayer games across the network.

In this chapter, you'll learn how to install and configure a small network and perform all of the tasks just mentioned. There are several ways to set up a small network, the most common being with a local area connection using an Ethernet hub and network adapters.

Local Area Networks

A *local area network (LAN)* is a network that is configured for the office (workgroup); this network includes only the workgroup itself; it is not part of the Internet. A LAN can also be connected to the Internet. In a workgroup, this connection to the Internet is generally shared. One computer is the *host*, and the other computers access the Internet through this host. These days, it is almost mandatory to have Internet access, not only for emailing, but also for faxing, ordering products online, and getting information.

There are really only two secure ways to configure a workgroup with a shared Internet connection. One way is to use an Ethernet hub, a modem for the host computer, and network interface cards for connecting the computers; the other way is to use a residential gateway. A third option isn't so secure, and that is allowing each computer on the workgroup to have its own Internet connection.

Internet Connection Sharing (ICS)

Figure 10.1 shows an example of how a local area network might be configured using a shared Internet connection and an Ethernet hub.

This type of network is used more often than other types because it is fairly easy to set up and manage, and it isn't as expensive as other options. With Windows XP's firewall placed between the local area network and the Internet, the workgroup is secure from outsiders, too. All users can share the Internet connection, and the entire network can be controlled using the host computer. The only disadvantage of this configuration is that the host computer must be on for others to access the Internet through it.

Residential Gateway

A configuration using a residential gateway is very similar to the setup shown in Figure 10.1. However, the residential gateway is used when a DSL (Digital Subscriber Line) or cable modem is used instead of a simple telephone modem. The residential gateway is a hardware device that is set up between the DSL or cable modem and the local area network. These types of connections are more expensive than others and require more time to configure. However, with a residential gateway, the host computer does not have to be on for others to access the Internet, as it does with a shared Internet connection.

Individual Internet Connections

If the Internet connection uses a DSL or cable modem, the modem can be used to offer connectivity for each user on the network. With this setup, no computer has to be on for others to access the Internet. However, there are serious security problems with this type of configuration. Instead of a single computer acting as the firewall for the network and pro-

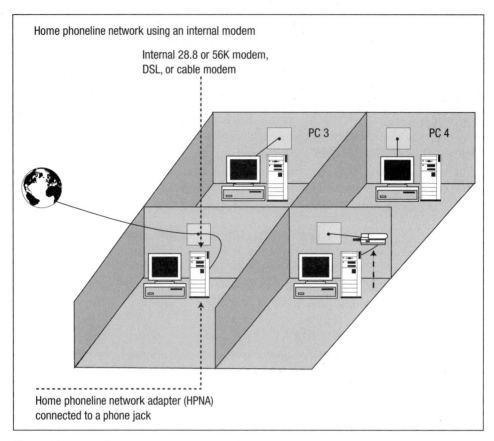

Home phoneline network using an internal modem

Internal 28.8 or 56K modem,
DSL, or cable modem

PC 3

PC 4

Home phoneline network adapter (HPNA)
connected to a phone jack

Figure 10.1
A local area network with an Ethernet hub and a shared Internet connection.

tecting it from outsiders, security has to be maintained on each computer that connects to the Internet on its own. If each computer isn't configured with its own firewall, Internet users can access files and folders on it.

How Workgroups Differ from Domains

So, what makes a domain so much different from a workgroup? There are several differences, and the main differences have been touched on already: A domain should be used when there are more resources than can be managed effectively (fewer than 32 computers), and you'll need a Windows XP server for running and managing it. However, there are many other differences.

In a workgroup, the users decide what is to be shared and what isn't. The users also decide who can access their files and resources and who can't. These resources are controlled by passwords and permissions. To locate another resource in a workgroup, you simply find it by using My Network Places or the Search Companion and typing in the appropriate password. In a domain, the process isn't that simple.

Domains use *domain controllers* which are servers that are used to control who can access what and when. Microsoft Windows XP Server is the latest offering, but Microsoft Windows 2000 Server and Microsoft Windows NT 4 can be used as well. The domain controller doesn't use the Search Companion or My Network Places for managing resources; instead, it uses Active Directory. Active Directory is a component of Windows 2000 Server and Windows XP Server that manages user access to the network, including logging on, getting authentication, accessing the shared resources, and accessing the directory itself. The directory stores information about all of the resources on the network and makes this information available to all of the users on the network. Active Directory also allows users to use one logon to control access to all resources. (This is not true of workgroups, where several passwords might need to be remembered.) The directory is hierarchical and tree-like, separating resources into groups and making user management possible. This hierarchical structure also allows users to search for specific resources based on their attributes, such as a full-color scanner or a printer that can print envelopes.

If you are currently a member of a large organization, you are most likely a member of a domain. Chapter 11 focuses on using Windows XP Professional in a domain.

Setting Up a Small-Office Network

Figure 10.1, shown earlier, gives you a good example of what a small-office network or local area network might look like. The network includes computers and users, printers, scanners, an Internet connection, and a host computer. For the most part, workgroups are configured this way, with one computer acting as the host computer and offering Internet access, while the others are part of the workgroup and are peers. An administrator is in charge of what type of users and groups are configured, and this administrator can have basic control over the network. Users then share files, folders, and other resources as necessary. In this section, this type of network will be detailed. If you're using a cable or DSL modem, the setup is almost exactly the same, with the exception of installing and configuring the modems.

Planning

One of the most important tasks in setting up a new office network is proper planning. Before starting any installations or making any connections, make sure you perform the tasks in Table 10.1 in the order in which they are presented. The following sections will help you in making these decisions and will give you more information about each task as needed. As you complete each task, check it off the list, make notes about what needs to be purchased, and complete drawings of how the network should look when finished. You can print this table from the CD included with this book.

Table 10.1 Worksheet for planning the network.

Task	Notes	Completed
Draw the physical layout of the office(s).		
Show each computer and printer and in what room they should be located.		
List the hardware for each computer.		
Determine if existing hardware is on Microsoft's hardware compatibility list (HCL).		
Locate updated drivers as necessary (don't forget drivers for printers, scanners, and other hardware).		
List what is needed for each computer (network interface cards, modems, etc.).		
Choose the host computer if Internet connection sharing is to be used.		
Decide on a network type: wireless, Ethernet, home networking with existing phone lines, or other.		
Determine the network topology: bus, star, ring, or mesh.		
Make a list of hardware to purchase, and verify that it's on the HCL.		
Purchase the hardware.		
Install network adapters.		
Install hubs, routers, or other connectivity devices.		
Install other hardware devices, and make sure they are working properly before sharing them on the network.		
Read all pertinent information in Microsoft Help files.		
Read all pertinent information from manufacturers' instructions.		

Hardware for a Small Network

To create a workgroup for a local area network, you need several components. You need at least two computers, of course, and they must have the necessary hardware installed. To function on a network, a computer must have a component that can connect to the network. In almost all cases, this component is a *network interface card* (NIC), but sometimes it is a converter that uses a USB port to connect to an Ethernet hub. Also popular are home-phone-line network adapters that use existing phone lines in the home to connect the network.

When a NIC is used, it is installed in an available PCI slot; the NIC uses a connector and line similar to a telephone line and telephone cord. Physically connecting the computers with NICs is just about as easy as plugging a telephone into a wall jack. A home-phone-line adapter is easy to install; it simply plugs into the home's existing phone jack and the computer to be networked. USB-to-Ethernet connectors plug into USB ports and connect to an Ethernet hub on the network.

A *hub* is used to connect all of the computers in the network together. Figure 10.2 shows a sample hub configuration, and this type of configuration is referred to as a *star* configuration. (Using a hub is currently the most-used way to create a small network, but there are other options. Those options are detailed later.)

Cables connect the computers, converters, and hubs. The configuration shown in Figure 10.2 is an Ethernet network, which requires Ethernet cables. These cables look like telephone cables but are larger. They are referred to as UTP (unshielded twisted-pair) and STP (shielded twisted-pair) cables; they are also called RJ-45 cables.

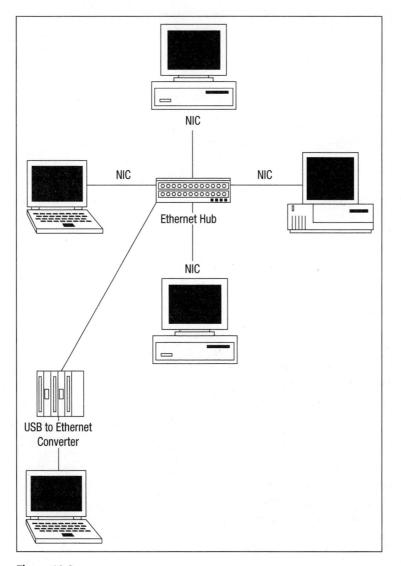

Figure 10.2
Example of a star configuration.

A modem is necessary for the computer that will be connected directly to the Internet and sharing that connection. Any other computer that will connect directly to the Internet will also need a modem, but those connecting via the shared connection do not. The modem needs to be at least 28.8Kbps, but it can also be a 56Kbps modem, a wireless modem, or an ISDN, DSL, or cable modem. If the modem requires a NIC to connect, then the host computer will need two: one for the Internet connection, and another for the local area connection. The host computer must also be running Windows XP Home or Professional editions, but other computers on the network can be running almost anything else. The Network Setup Wizard, however, can be used only on computers using Windows 98, 98SE, Millennium, Windows XP Home, or Windows XP Professional.

Other Hardware Options

There are many other ways to physically install a small network, but the hub/computer scenario is currently the least expensive and easiest to configure. The cables are easy to work with, and the hubs are easily installed and configured. Other options include the following, but for small offices I would not recommend the majority of them:

♦ Two computers can be physically connected using a serial port and a null modem cable.

♦ Wireless modems can be used to reduce the cabling requirements.

♦ A *bus* topology—in which each computer connects to a central communications cable— can be used. Each computer or resource has a unique address on the network and passes data to others using the appropriate addresses.

♦ A *ring* topology—in which each computer is connected in a circular fashion—can be used. Data can be passed by a computer only when it is that computer's "turn" to do so.

♦ A *mesh* topology can be used. This is applied effectively in only two networks—the Internet and the public telephone system.

♦ If the appropriate hardware is installed, additional cable types can be used, including coaxial cable and fiber optic cable. Coaxial cable consists of a center wire surrounded by insulation and then a grounded shield of braided wire; coaxial cable is used for cable TV and some cable Internet access. Fiber optic cable consists of a bundle of glass threads, each of which carries data as light impulses. Both of these cabling options are difficult to employ in a small network.

♦ A home-phone-line network adapter (HPNA) can be used. This is an ideal way to configure a home network and is easy to use. Each computer on the network needs a HPNA, which must be plugged into the existing phone jacks in the home or office. The data is then sent from computer to computer via the phone lines in the home office.

♦ Completely wireless networks can also be configured; in a wireless network, NICs connect via high-frequency radio waves rather than by physical cables.

Choosing the Computer That Will Be the ICS Computer

Before getting underneath the desks, connecting all of the hardware together, and using cabling ties to make everything nice and neat, make sure you've properly considered the role and location of each computer in your network. One computer in particular that requires extra thought is the one that will serve as the ICS (Internet connection sharing) computer. If you aren't going to configure a computer for ICS on the local area network, skip this section. However, Microsoft recommends that, for this type of network, one computer be configured to provide Internet access to all of the other computers in the workgroup.

To choose the proper computer as the ICS host, make sure the following are true:

♦ The computer is running Windows XP Professional or Windows XP Home Edition.

♦ The computer can be turned on and left on for long periods of time. When this computer is turned off, others will not have access. Do not configure the ICS computer as a laptop or dual-boot machine that isn't always online.

♦ If DSL or cable access to the Internet is available, and if one computer has a DSL or cable modem, use this computer as the ICS host.

♦ If a shared printer is planned, make sure that it can be installed on this computer and that appropriate drivers are available.

♦ Because this computer is the host, make sure it has extra RAM (random access memory) and a fast bus speed. This computer will be working a little harder than the others.

♦ No other computers are currently set up to perform ICS for the network.

Verifying Hardware Requirements

Before physically connecting the computers, printers, scanners, and the like, verify that each computer has the necessary hardware installed. Listed next are some final thoughts on different configurations and necessary hardware requirements.

Table 10.2 refers to Ethernet configurations, Table 10.3 refers to wireless configurations, and Table 10.4 refers to home-phone-line connections.

Table 10.2   Hardware requirements for an Ethernet network.

Component	Number Needed	Notes
Network adapters	One for every computer	An extra adapter is needed on the ICS host computer if it connects to the Internet using a NIC. Make sure you get Ethernet adapters, and check Microsoft's HCL before purchasing and installing them.

(continued)

Table 10.2 Hardware requirements for an Ethernet network *(continued)*.

Component	Number Needed	Notes
Hub	One	The hub needs one connection for each computer on the network. See Figure 10.2. If the network has seven computers, buy a 10-port hub.
RJ-45 cables	One for every computer and a few extra in case of cable failure	Make sure the cables purchased are long enough to reach from the hub to the computers.
Modem	One for the ICS host computer	

Table 10.3 Hardware requirements for a wireless network.

Component	Number Needed	Notes
Wireless network adapters	One for each computer on the network	These are often called *transceivers*.
Adapter software	Installed on all computers as needed	Check Microsoft's HCL before purchasing.
Modem	One for the ICS host computer	

Table 10.4 Hardware requirements for a network using a home-phone-line network adapter.

Component	Number Needed	Notes
HPNA	One for each computer	Make sure the adapters are on Microsoft's HCL.
Telephone cables	One for each computer	These are not RJ-45 cables; they are regular telephone cables.
Modem	One for the ICS computer	

Microsoft's HCL

A lot has been said about checking hardware against Microsoft's hardware compatibility list. This is important for many reasons, including ensuring that the hardware will work correctly and that it's supported for Windows XP by both Microsoft and the hardware manufacturers. The HCL can be accessed in the Windows XP Help services (under Find Compatible Hardware And Software For Windows XP) or at **www.microsoft.com/hcl/default.asp**.

Physically Connecting Computers

After a topology has been decided on, hardware has been purchased, and all hardware has been verified on Microsoft's HCL, physical installation can begin. Before opening a single computer case and installing network interface cards or any other internal hardware, make sure you are aware of the following points:

♦ Electrostatic discharge (ESD) is static that is passed from the installer to the computer component, almost always unknowingly. ESD can cause numerous problems for computers and their components. Before attempting any installation, take the precautions described in this list.

♦ Damage done by unknowingly shocking a computer part might not become obvious initially, and the delay could make finding the cause of a problem later almost impossible.

♦ Low humidity, improper grounding, poor connections, and movement in machines or people most often cause ESD.

♦ A shock that cannot be felt by a human can destroy a sensitive electrical component.

♦ To ensure proper grounding when you're installing a new component, touch the computer chassis *before* removing the component from the system or installing a new one. The computer must be plugged into a grounded outlet.

♦ Remove components from their antistatic bags only when they are ready to be installed. Make sure you are properly grounded.

♦ Buy an antistatic wrist strap, and wear it properly before installing any new components. Do not, however, wear such a strap when you're working on high-voltage components such as monitors or power supplies.

Installing Network Adapters

With the proper precautions taken, begin the network adapter's installation by first reading the information that came with the card. This can't be stressed enough; often, the card must be placed in the first or last slot, or jumpers (physical settings) on the card itself must be configured.

To install a network adapter:

1. Turn off the computer, open the computer case, and ground yourself appropriately.

2. Locate an open slot on the motherboard. Most new adapter cards fit into PCI slots, which are the smaller, white ones.

3. Remove the screw and cover for the open slot.

4. While grounded, remove the card from the antistatic bag. Hold the card by its edges, and do *not* touch any components on the card itself.

5. Place the card firmly in the appropriate slot. If the manufacturer requires any special jumper settings on the card, make those changes now.

6. Use the screw that was removed in Step 3 to secure the card.

7. Close the case, and turn on the computer.

The next steps involve installing the software for the card. This software is a driver, which is installed as detailed in Chapter 7. (Note that the previous instructions also work for other types of network connectors, such as wireless networking components and home-phone-line adapters. It is always best to follow the manufacturer's instructions.)

Connecting Hubs and Cables

If you've decided to go with an Ethernet hub and a star configuration, as shown in Figure 10.2, you'll need to connect the hub and cables. In some instances, the hub might need to have software installed as well. This is unlikely with a simple hub, but you should be aware of this circumstance. Besides hubs, there are routers and bridges, depending on the network that can be installed in place of the hub.

To connect the computers and the hub, place the hub in a central location. Run an RJ-45 cable from the back of each computer's NIC to the hub itself. Make sure you understand which ports are available—one port is usually reserved for stacking another hub on top of the present one. When all of the computers are physically connected via a twisted-pair cable, continue with the next section.

If home-phone-line adapters are used, the same rules apply. The additional telephone cables will need to be run from the phone jacks to each computer's NIC. The NICs in this case are the home-phone-line network adapters that are installed either internally or externally for each computer. This type of configuration eliminates the need for a hub. Although this is a great way to configure a home network, it isn't ideal for small-office networks with more traffic than home networks.

Tip

Resist the urge to tuck away these cables and hide the hub before testing the network. If problems occur, hidden equipment makes troubleshooting more difficult.

Connecting Other Equipment

With the hubs and computers connected, continue setting up the network by connecting hardware such as printers and scanners to the computers to which those devices will be connected. For several reasons, this is an important task to complete *before* running the Network Setup Wizard. First, it is best to have these devices in working order before sharing them. Second, with these devices connected and installed, the Windows XP Network Setup Wizard can determine if these devices will work with Windows XP or if there will be compatibility problems. Many times, older printers (or other hardware) with outdated drivers that are working okay on a Windows 98 machine will not function correctly when Windows XP users try to use the equipment. Third, some hardware you'd think would work just fine, like some Adaptec CD-RW drives, don't work at all and will cause the system to reject the hardware and disable it. These surprises are better dealt with before running the Network Setup Wizard than after.

The Network Setup Wizard

To use the Network Setup Wizard, you must be logged on as an administrator or be a member of the Administrators group. If the computer is currently connected to a network, you might not be able to continue with this setup because of network settings. You should run the wizard on the computer that is the ICS (host) computer on your network.

When running the wizard, you can do multiple tasks, including:

♦ Naming the computer and providing a description

♦ Configuring all of the computers to use a single Internet connection

♦ Enabling a firewall

♦ Enabling a network bridge (if multiple adapters are installed)

After the host computer has been set up and the wizard run, the Network Setup Wizard must be run on other computers on the network.

Setting Up the Host Computer

Before starting the Network Setup Wizard, do the following:

1. If you do not have a connection to the Internet from the host computer, return to Chapter 9 and set one up.

2. Log on as an administrator.

3. Connect to the Internet.

4. Make sure that all of the computers on the network are turned on and that printers, scanners, and other hardware have been installed on their respective machines and are powered up.

5. Verify that the hardware and computers are correctly connected to hubs and/or telephone jacks.

6. Disable ICS on any other computers offering it.

7. On the host computer, start the wizard from Network Connections in the Control Panel. From the Network Tasks pane, choose Set Up A Home Or Small Office Network. You can use the Network Setup Wizard for four tasks, as shown in Figure 10.3.

Note
You can also start the Network Setup Wizard from within the New Connection Wizard by choosing Set Up A Home Or Small Office Network on the appropriate page.

8. On the Before You Continue page of the Network Setup Wizard, double-check that you've done the prerequisite tasks; then choose Next to begin.

Figure 10.3
The Network Setup Wizard.

9. Select the first option, which states, "This computer connects directly to the Internet. The other computers on my network connect to the Internet through this computer." Select the second option if you're using a residential gateway on the host computer. (If neither option suits your needs, choose Other and skip to the section entitled "Other Connection Settings," later in this chapter.)

10. Select the Internet connection from the list of connections. (If no connections are present, return to Step 1, connect to the Internet, and begin again.)

11. Type a description for the host computer, and type a computer name.

12. On the next page of the Network Setup Wizard, type a workgroup name. Make sure you remember the workgroup name.

13. After verifying the changes, choose Next to allow the Network Setup Wizard to apply the changes to the network. Depending on the number of computers and hardware, this process could take a few minutes. See Figure 10.4.

14. The next page of the Network Setup Wizard asks what you'd like to do about the other computers on your network. For each computer, you'll need to run the Network Setup Wizard. If those computers run Windows XP, it will be easy. For computers not running Windows XP, you have four options:

   ♦ Create A Network Setup Disk

   ♦ Use The Network Setup Disk I Already Have

   ♦ Use My Windows XP CD

   ♦ Just Finish The Wizard; I Don't Need To Run The Wizard On Other Computers

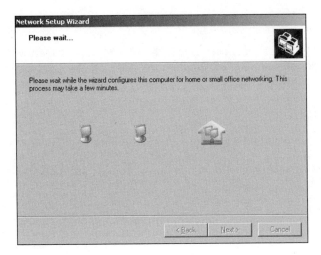

Figure 10.4
Finalizing the network setup.

Select the appropriate option, and choose Next. If you choose to create a network setup disk, you'll need to continue with the directions next. If not, skip to Step 16.

Tip
If you think you'll need a setup disk for a computer, make it now. If you don't and you decide you need it later, you'll have to go through these steps again.

15. To create a setup disk, place a disk in the floppy drive, and continue. Format the disk, if necessary.

16. On the last page of the wizard, read the directions for configuring the other computers on the network. Detailed instructions will follow here. Choose Finish to close the wizard.

17. Restart the computer.

Running the Network Setup Wizard on a Windows XP Professional Client Computer

After the host computer has been set up, you can begin setting up the client computers. For each client computer, you must run the Network Setup Wizard, use the setup disks, or use the Windows XP CD to add them to the network.

To configure a Windows XP Professional client computer to join the new network:

1. Log on as an administrator.

2. Open the Control Panel.

3. Open Network Connections.

4. From the Network Tasks pane, choose Set Up A Home Or Small Office Network.

5. Start the wizard by choosing Next twice; then select the second option as shown in Figure 10.5. (If this option doesn't suit your needs, choose Other and skip to the section entitled "Other Connection Settings," later in this chapter.)

6. Type a computer name and description.

7. Type the workgroup name that you used when configuring the host computer earlier.

8. Wait as the settings are applied, and then choose Just Finish The Wizard; I Don't Need To Run The Wizard On Other Computers.

9. Choose Finish, and restart the computer.

Note

If the wizard returns with a notice that the setup was unsuccessful, make sure that you are connected to the Internet, that all hardware and software are installed and connected properly, and that other prerequisites have been fulfilled.

Using a Setup Disk to Add a Client Computer

If you need to add a non-Windows-XP computer to the network, you'll need to run the Network Setup Wizard on that computer to add it to the network. I hope that you made the necessary network-setup floppy disks when prompted earlier or that you have the Windows XP CD handy. If not, you'll have to run the Network Setup Wizard again and enter the same information; then when the page appears that offers the option to make a disk, you can do so.

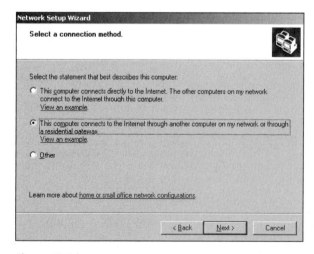

Figure 10.5
Setting up a client computer.

As I stated earlier, the only computers that can be added using the network setup disks are computers running Windows 98, Windows 98 SE, Windows Millennium Edition, or Windows XP. (If the client computers use Windows 2000, see "Adding a Windows 2000 Professional Computer.")

To add a non-Windows-XP or non-Windows-2000 computer to the network:

1. Log onto the computer as an administrator.

2. Place the network setup floppy disk in the floppy drive.

3. Browse to the floppy disk.

4. Select Netsetup.

5. An information box will appear stating that the computer may need to restart after the wizard has begun. Save and close any folders or applications before continuing.

6. After the computer restarts (if applicable), start the Network Setup Wizard by choosing Next twice; then select the second option, as shown in Figure 10.5.

7. Type a computer name and description.

8. Type the workgroup name you used when configuring the host computer earlier.

9. Complete the wizard, choose Finish, and restart the computer.

Using the Windows XP CD to Add a Client Computer

Computers can also be added using the Windows XP Professional installation disk. To add a Windows XP computer to the network by using this disk:

1. Log on as an administrator.

2. Place the Windows XP Professional CD in the CD-ROM drive.

3. From the What Do You Want To Do? screen, choose Perform Additional Tasks.

4. Choose Set Up A Home Or Small Office Network.

5. Choose Yes when prompted to begin.

6. Work through the wizard as described in earlier sections.

Adding a Windows 2000 Professional Computer

You might have noticed that Windows 2000 operating systems were not included in the list of computers that can be configured using the setup disks or the Windows XP CD. This is because Windows 2000 has a compatible setup program for getting connected to the new network.

Note

As I stated earlier, the only computers that can be added using the network setup disks, including the CD-ROM, are computers running Windows 98, Windows 98 SE, Windows Millennium Edition, or Windows XP.

To add a Windows 2000 Professional computer to the network:

1. Log on as an administrator.

2. Right-click My Computer, and choose Properties.

3. In the System Properties dialog box, select the Network Identification tab.

4. Choose the Properties button.

5. In the resulting Identification Changes dialog box, type a computer name and the name of the workgroup to join. See Figure 10.6.

6. Choose OK. When the computer has been added to the new workgroup, you'll be prompted to restart your computer.

Verifying Communication on the New Network

After all computers have been added using the Network Setup Wizard or by other means, use My Network Places to verify that the computers are communicating:

1. Open My Network Places.

2. From the Network Tasks pane, choose View Workgroup Computers.

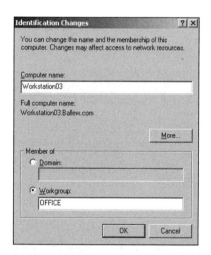

Figure 10.6
Adding a Windows 2000 Professional computer to a workgroup.

3. Verify that all of the computers have been added. If no computers are shown, or if a computer is missing that should be there, ski6¿to "Troubleshooting the Small Network" later in this chapter. Figure 10.7 shows a workgroup called Office with three computers successfully added to the network.

4. From each client computer, use Internet Explorer to verify that the client can access the Internet through the shared connection.

Other Connection Settings

You might have noticed that the Network Setup Wizard page shown in Figure 10.5 contains one other option for connecting a computer to a network or creating a network from a host computer. This option is called Other. Figure 10.8 shows the other Internet connection methods available.

The first option should be used if your network setup is configured such that each computer is physically connected to a hub, which in turn is physically connected to the Internet. This is not the same as a network that simply has a hub and uses ICS. Figure 10.9 shows such a configuration. Most of these configurations also involve a DSL or cable modem, which is external to the host computer.

The second option is for a single computer that connects directly to the Internet, with no network currently configured. The third option is used for a network that does not have an Internet connection at all.

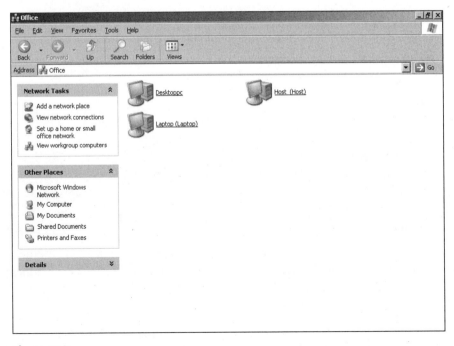

Figure 10.7
Successful network installation.

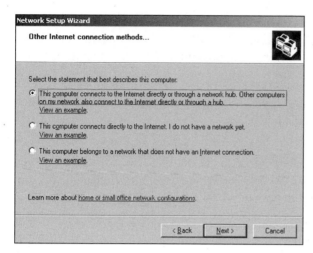

Figure 10.8
Other Internet connection methods.

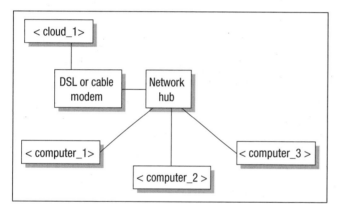

Figure 10.9
A network hub.

After choosing the correct option, continue through the wizard as previously described: Select an Internet connection to use, enter a computer name and description, and create a workgroup name.

Advanced Network Setups

There are a couple of advanced setups that don't generally apply to most small-office networks but that are worth mentioning. These options are located in the New Connection Wizard, not in the Network Setup Wizard. These options are Set Up An Advanced Connection and Connect To The Network At My Workplace.

Setting up a connection that connects to your workplace allows you to dial into or connect using a virtual private network (VPN) so that you can work from home, from a field office, or while out of town. Advanced connections allow you to connect directly to another computer using a serial cable, a parallel cable, or an infrared port. Advanced connections also allow you to configure the computer so that others can connect to it.

Setting Up a Connection That Connects to Your Workplace

To configure your computer to connect to a computer at your workplace:

1. As an administrator, log onto the computer that needs to connect to a workplace computer.

2. Open the New Connection Wizard by choosing Start | Programs | Accessories | Communications | New Connection Wizard.

3. On the Network Connection Type page, select Connect To The Network At My Workplace.

4. On the Network Connection page, select the type of connection that you want to configure: Dial-Up Connection or Virtual Private Network Connection.

5. On the Connection Name page, type the name of the connection.

6. On the Phone Number To Dial page, type the phone number of the connection.

7. Check the checkbox to place a shortcut to this connection on the desktop, and then finish the wizard.

To see if the connection works properly:

1. Double-click the shortcut for the connection on the desktop.

2. Type your user name and password. (You'll need appropriate permissions from your network administrator and a configured account.)

3. Choose Dial.

Figure 10.10 shows two dial-up connections: one named Work Connection and one named Waymark.net. This configuration is on the host computer. The Waymark.net connection is the shared Internet connection for the network, and the Work Connection is the dial-up connection created in the previous example. In this particular example, the computer has only one modem installed, and that's why the shared Internet connection is currently disconnected. This figure shows a successful dial-up session with another computer.

Setting Up an Advanced Connection

The New Connection Wizard also allows you to create advanced connections. As I stated earlier, these are connections that allow a computer to accept incoming connections or to connect physically to another computer by using a direct connection through a port on each machine.

The first example explains how to configure a computer to accept incoming connections. The second example explains how to connect directly to another computer.

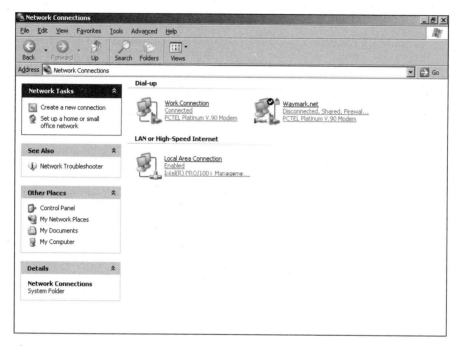

Figure 10.10
A successful dial-up to a workplace computer.

To allow your computer to accept incoming connections from others:

1. Log on as administrator, and start the New Connection Wizard.

2. On the Network Connection Type page, select Set Up An Advanced Connection.

3. On the Advanced Connection Options page, select Accept Incoming Connections.

4. Choose the modem that will be used to accept the incoming connections. If no choices are offered, the connection cannot be configured.

5. Choose either to allow or disallow VPN connections. Allowing VPN connections will modify the firewall currently configured. Read the information on this page carefully before making a decision.

6. On the User Permissions page shown in Figure 10.11, check the box for each user who'll be allowed to connect to your computer. You can also add users as necessary.

7. On the Networking Software page, make sure the required protocols are checked (more on protocols later), and install TCP/IP if necessary. Choose Finish.

To verify the connection, open Network Connections from the Control Panel. See Figure 10.12; it shows that one user is connected, and that user is Mary Anne Cosmo.

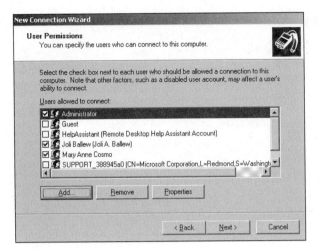

Figure 10.11
User permissions.

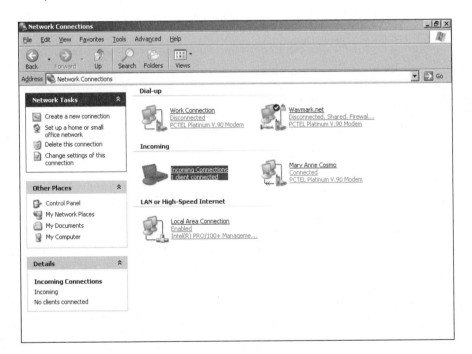

Figure 10.12
Incoming connections.

When you're configuring a computer to accept incoming connections on specific types of networks, problems can occur while connecting; these problems might be caused by the calling computer's IP address and the local network's configuration. Although this concept is beyond the scope of this chapter, steps can be taken to solve specific problems related to these types of errors.

If the connection doesn't work properly or if the remote computer terminates the session and informs you of a *protocol* or *IP address* problem, do the following:

1. Log on as an administrator.

2. Open the Control Panel and Network Connections.

3. Right-click the Incoming Connections icon, and choose Properties.

4. Select the Networking tab.

5. Highlight Internet Protocol (TCP/IP).

6. Choose the Properties button.

7. Check the checkbox Allow Calling Computer To Specify Its Own IP Address.

8. Choose OK twice.

Troubleshooting the Small Network

If you are having problems locating the other computers on your network, or if you are receiving errors stating that other computers cannot be found or accessed, you will need to do a little bit of troubleshooting. Other common problems include the inability to access shared files or printers and the inability to access the Internet through the LAN, the shared Internet connection, or the modem. In this section, you'll learn how and in what order to find and repair these types of problems.

Common Problems

Oftentimes, the next few simple tricks work when computers can't be found on the network. First, make sure that the computer names on the network are unique. You'll need to check each computer's name. While you're at it, also verify that the workgroup name has been spelled correctly and is located in the workgroup (not domain) window. If you find any computers with identical names, correct them. See Figure 10.13.

To view or change a computer's name:

1. Log on as an administrator.

2. Right-click My Computer, and choose Properties.

3. Select the Computer Name tab.

4. Note the computer description, computer name, and workgroup name. Make sure that the computer name is not duplicated on the network and that the workgroup name is spelled correctly.

5. If a change is needed, choose the Change button.

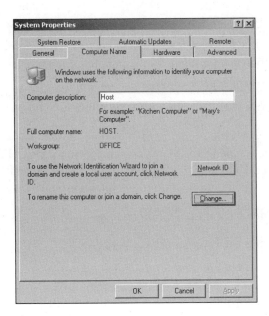

Figure 10.13
The Computer Name tab in System Properties.

6. In the Computer Name Changes dialog box, type the correct computer name or workgroup name. If the computer belongs to a domain and not to a workgroup, change this also. Choose OK twice to close the dialog boxes.

7. Reboot the computer if changes were made.

Note

If the computer belongs to a domain, domain policies might prevent you from making these changes.

Another option to try is to run the Network Setup Wizard again on all of the computers. Do this one computer at a time, starting with the host computer. Let each computer reboot before you run the wizard on another computer. For each computer, check My Network Places | View Workgroup Computers to see whether the computer was added.

Specific Troubleshooting

With small-office networks composed of workgroups, you'll typically find three main types of problems: the Internet connection or ICS isn't working for the host and/or the clients; file or printer sharing isn't working; or problems with modems or dial-up connections are occurring. In each of the following sections, I'll introduce the most common problems relating to these three aspects, and discuss how they can be solved.

Basic Do's and Don'ts

ICS has some very specific rules that must be followed for it to work correctly. If ICS didn't install properly, or if, after installation, there are problems with computers communicating properly on the network, read the following important points:

♦ Do not use ICS on an existing network with Windows 2000 or Windows XP domain controllers.

♦ Do not use ICS on a network that relies on DNS (Domain Name System) or DHCP (Dynamic Host Configuration Protocol) servers for name resolution and/or IP address allotment.

♦ Do not use ICS on a network configured with static TCP/IP addresses.

♦ Do enable ICS on the computer that has the Internet connection.

♦ Do log on as an administrator when installing ICS.

Cannot Receive Email on a Client Computer

With ICS, a number of things can go wrong for both the host computer and the clients who use the connection. A common problem is that the client computer cannot receive email through the shared Internet connection. This problem is generally caused by a previous Internet connection configuration. To receive email through a shared Internet connection, the client computer on an ICS network must be set up to receive email from the LAN and not from a modem. The following directions work for Windows XP and Windows 2000 computers:

1. Log onto the client computer as an administrator.

2. Open Outlook Express.

3. Choose Tools | Accounts.

4. On the Mail tab, highlight the email account. (If more than one email account exists, perform these steps for each account.)

5. Choose the Properties button.

6. Select the Connection tab.

7. As shown in Figure 10.14, check the box Always Connect To This Account Using, and choose the local area network.

8. Choose OK and Close.

Cannot Browse the Internet from the Host Computer

When the host computer cannot connect to the Internet, neither can any client that is configured to use that computer for Internet access. The solutions for these types of problems differ depending on the type of dial-up access you have. For dial-up modems or

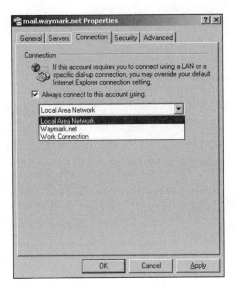

Figure 10.14
Using the local area connection.

connections involving network interface cards, the problem sometimes occurs because there aren't enough NICs to go around. When a computer is configured for ICS, that computer must have separate cards (or have a modem and a NIC) to enable access for users. The first card or the modem connects to the outside world (the Internet), while the second NIC connects to the internal network. If this is the problem, install another NIC in the computer, and configure the network again.

Another common problem occurs when older, unidirectional NICs are used. This type of NIC can only send or only receive data, not both. Some modems are also unidirectional and can cause similar problems. Check your manufacturer's information to determine if this is the problem.

If the host computer has two NICs, make sure that the NIC that is to be used for the Internet is the one connecting to the Internet and that the NIC that is to be used for the intranet is configured for the intranet. Crossing these two will cause the network not to work. You can check these connections through Network Connections by right-clicking the local area connection and choosing Properties. The Connect Using tab lists which adapter is used for which purpose.

Finally, the problem might not be caused by the modem or the NIC but might be caused by Internet Explorer itself. You can try the Internet Explorer Troubleshooter, located in Help, to self-diagnose this problem.

Cannot Browse the Internet from the Client Computer

If a client cannot browse the Internet, the simplest solution is to see if the host computer is turned on and connected to the Internet. Problems can also occur if the host computer is in hibernation or on stand-by. If this isn't the problem, work through the options for host computers in the previous section.

Cannot Log Onto the Network

When a user can't log onto the network, the problem is often that the user's name and password have been entered incorrectly. If this is determined not to be the problem, several other things can be checked. In a new network, the problem can be the computer name. If a duplicate name exists on the network, the computer will not be able to log on. To repair this, see the "Common Problems" section earlier in this chapter.

If this is not the problem, perhaps the NIC is installed incorrectly or not at all. You can use Device Manager to see if there is a NIC installed and if there is a problem with it.

To access Device Manager and view the NIC's properties:

1. Log on as an administrator.

2. Right-click My Computer, and choose Properties.

3. Select the Hardware tab.

4. Choose the Device Manager button.

5. Expand the Network Adapters section by choosing the + sign.

6. Highlight the adapter. If there isn't a network adapter listed, the network adapter isn't installed. If there is a yellow or red icon next to the network adapter, it isn't working properly. If this is the case, continue with the following steps; if the adapter is installed and working properly, stop here.

7. Right-click the NIC, and choose Uninstall.

8. Reboot the computer, and reinstall the NIC.

If this doesn't solve the problem, the NIC could be seated incorrectly or could be faulty. Try reseating the card. This involves turning off the computer, opening the computer case, grounding yourself properly, and then removing and replacing the card.

Cannot Locate a Shared Folder

If a shared folder cannot be located, there are several things to check. First, make sure you are connected to the network if this is necessary. Second, verify that the folder is still shared by the owner of the folder. Third, verify that the Network Setup Wizard has been run on the local computer and that the computer is part of the network. Finally, check the network hardware, and make sure everything is properly connected. This includes hubs, computers, printer cables, and so on. Try using the Hardware Troubleshooter, located in the Help files, to investigate the problem.

Error Message When Dialing with a Modem

When you're connecting with a modem, two error messages are common:

♦ The protocol is not configured.

♦ A dial-up connection could not be established.

If you receive a protocol error, ask your ISP or network administrator which protocols are necessary, and then remove any unnecessary ones from your computer. Install the correct protocols if they aren't already installed. More information on protocols is provided at the end of this chapter, but for now, it is sufficient just to check on the protocols and add or remove them.

To check protocols on the computer, and add or remove them:

1. Log on as an administrator.

2. Open the Control Panel.

3. Open Network Connections.

4. Right-click the dial-up connection, and choose Properties.

5. Select the Networking tab.

6. Uncheck any unnecessary protocols, and choose Uninstall.

7. If the required protocol isn't checked or isn't listed, check it and choose Install, or choose Install to add one that isn't listed. See Figure 10.15.

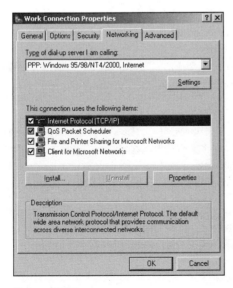

Figure 10.15
Checking protocols for a dial-up connection.

8. If the required protocol isn't listed, you'll see the Select Network Component Type box. Choose the Protocol button, and then click Add.

9. Select the required protocol, and choose OK.

10. After the necessary protocols are added, reboot the computer if prompted.

If dial-up connections fail because they could not be established, as in the second error-message example, do the following steps, checking all items listed next:

1. Log on as an administrator.

2. Open the Control Panel.

3. Open Network Connections.

4. Right-click the dial-up connection, and choose Properties.

5. Select the Networking tab.

6. In the Type Of Dial-Up Server I Am Calling drop-down list, select PPP for an ISP connection, or select SLIP for a Unix connection.

7. Highlight Internet Protocol, and choose Properties. For most ISPs and networks, you need to choose Obtain An IP Address Automatically. If you need a static IP address configured, verify the address with your network administrator.

8. On the General tab, verify that the phone number is typed in correctly. Choose OK.

Using the Networking Troubleshooter

If you still can't solve the problem, the Network Troubleshooter can help you find and repair problems with your network. The troubleshooter can be accessed in many ways; the easiest is from the Help and Support Center. Choose Start | Help, and type "list trouble-shooters" in the Search box. Choose the Home Networking Troubleshooter, which is listed as the Networking Troubleshooter or the Network Problems Troubleshooter in other places in Windows XP.

The first page of the troubleshooter asks you to characterize the problem as an Internet problem, a sharing problem, or a dial-up problem. From there, the wizard offers advice and solutions. In several places, the troubleshooter allows you to select Investigate, or to allow Windows XP to troubleshoot the problem for you. Figure 10.16 shows such a screen.

Several troubleshooters are available, and occasionally, what might seem like a network problem may really be a hardware problem. If the Network Troubleshooter doesn't solve the problem, try another troubleshooter. Listed next are the available troubleshooters:

♦ Printing

♦ File And Print Sharing

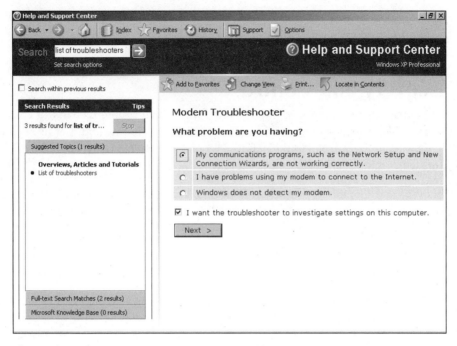

Figure 10.16
The Help and Support Center.

- ◆ Outlook Express
- ◆ Internet Explorer
- ◆ Internet Connection Sharing
- ◆ Modem
- ◆ Sound
- ◆ USB
- ◆ Drives And Network Adapters
- ◆ Input Devices
- ◆ Digital Video Discs
- ◆ Multimedia And Games
- ◆ Display
- ◆ Startup/Shutdown
- ◆ System Startup

Note

For more troubleshooting information, see the Appendix.

ICS Discovery and Control

If you've set up a new network using Windows XP Professional as described in this chapter, you have most likely already configured Internet connection sharing and thus have access to ICS Discovery and Control. However, if ICS is not set up during network configuration, this feature will be unavailable. ICS must be set up for you to use ICS Discovery and Control.

ICS Discovery and Control is a utility that allows a client to monitor and manage the shared Internet connection from any computer on the network. All clients can use this tool to get information about the shared connection, as well as to control it when necessary. With ICS Discovery and Control, any user can:

♦ Access, monitor, and control the shared Internet connection through an icon displayed in the notification area of the toolbar.

♦ Use the shared connection to connect to and disconnect from the ISP.

♦ View the status of the shared connection.

♦ View basic statistics about the shared connection.

It is up to the administrator of the host computer to enable this feature for the network's client computers. With ICS Discovery and Control enabled, the clients will have control of the connection. Even if this utility is not enabled, though, users still can view the statistics and the status of the connection.

Setting Up ICS

ICS is set up using the Network Setup Wizard described earlier in this chapter. If ICS isn't already configured, return to the section "The Network Setup Wizard," and perform the steps listed in the subsection "Setting Up the Host Computer."

Setting Up ICS Discovery and Control

After ICS is set up on the network, you can use the connection's property sheet to configure how much control users can have. Figure 10.17 shows this property sheet on the host computer.

To use this computer as the ICS host, you must check the Allow Other Network Users To Connect Through This Computer's Internet Connection checkbox. To allow any client on the network to force the host computer to connect to the Internet at any time, you must check the Establish A Dial-Up Connection Whenever A Computer On My Network Attempts To Access The Internet checkbox. Finally, to allow clients to disconnect, disable,

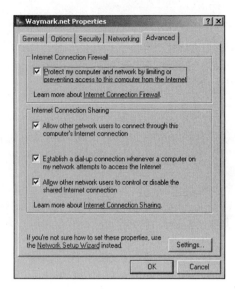

Figure 10.17
Properties dialog box for a shared Internet connection on the host computer.

and thus control the Internet connection, you must check the Allow Other Network Users To Control Or Disable The Shared Internet Connection checkbox.

To enable ICS Discovery and Control:

1. Log onto the host computer as an administrator.

2. Open the Control Panel.

3. Open Network Connections.

4. Right-click the Internet connection, and choose Properties.

5. Select the Advanced tab.

6. Make the appropriate choices.

7. Choose OK.

When ICS Discovery and Control is enabled on the host computer, any user on a Windows XP or Windows 2000 client computer can place an icon in the notification area of the taskbar by following these steps:

1. Log onto the client computer as an administrator.

2. Open the Control Panel.

3. Open Network Connections.

4. Right-click the Internet connection, and choose Properties.

5. Select the General tab.

6. Check the checkbox Show Icon In Notification Area When Connected. See Figure 10.18.

7. Choose OK.

Figure 10.18 shows a Windows XP Professional client computer with several connections configured. This screenshot shows the Properties dialog box for the shared Internet connection on the host computer.

Non-Windows XP/2000 Clients

For computers not running Windows XP or Windows 2000 operating systems, configuring ICS Discovery and Control is a little trickier. To enable ICS Discovery and Control on Windows 98, Windows 98 SE, or Windows Millennium Edition computers, you must run the Network Setup Wizard from the floppy disk or the Windows XP CD. In addition, Internet Explorer version 5 or later must be installed.

If you use the CD, choose Perform Additional Tasks, and choose Set Up A Home Or Small Office Network. From the floppy disk, choose Netsetup. Both start the Network Setup Wizard and can be used to install ICS and thus enable ICS Discovery and Control.

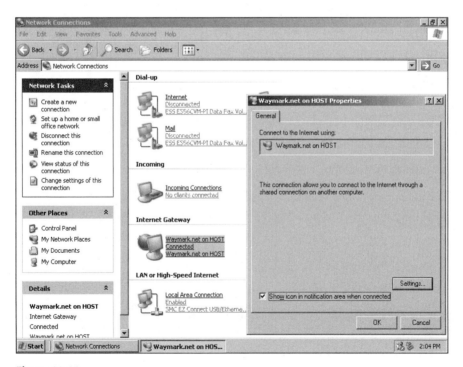

Figure 10.18
The General tab of a connection's property sheet.

ICS Discovery and Control Components

With the icon in the taskbar, the user on the client computer can access and control the connection very easily; all the user has to do is double-click the icon. Figure 10.19 shows the Status dialog box that the user sees when ICS Discovery and Control is enabled.

This Status dialog box has several sections:

♦ *Title bar*—Displays the name of the shared connection. Notice that Figure 10.19 shows several available connections. This particular connection is to Waymark.net, which is an ISP, and the connection travels through the computer, HOST, to connect to the ISP.

♦ *Status*—Shows the status of the connection from the host computer to the ISP. The status is displayed as Connected or Enabled, or Disconnected or Disabled.

♦ *Duration*—Shows how long the host computer and the ISP have been connected. This number is updated in real time and is displayed in days, hours, minutes, and seconds.

♦ *Speed*—Shows the speed of the connection between the host and the ISP in Mbps (megabits per second).

♦ *Shared Connection (Activity)*—Shows the activity between the host, the ISP, and the local computer. Activity refers to the number of packets sent and received by each.

♦ *Disconnect button*—Allows users to disconnect a shared dial-up connection or to disable a DSL or cable modem connection. Disconnect is used for dial-ups; Disable is used for high-speed DSL or cable connections.

Users and Computers

When you have a small network that is configured as a workgroup, chances are you have multiple users and computers. Even if it's a home network, you probably have accounts

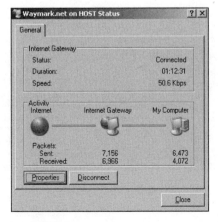

Figure 10.19
Status of a shared Internet connection.

configured for the different members of your family. Managing these accounts is pretty simple in a small network, but in larger workgroups (up to 32 computers and users), it can get fairly complex.

Chapter 3 introduced user accounts and passwords, along with adding members to groups and configuring some basic permissions and rights. In this section, you'll learn more about user accounts, groups, and computers, including how to use the Computer Management console to administer those objects. This section also covers adding computers, using Network Places, and recovering a user's password.

Managing Users

From Chapter 3, you should already know how to add, delete, and modify user accounts, as well as how to put those users into groups. After you create user accounts, however, there is more to consider, including how to manage users who share computers, how to manage passwords, and how to use the Computer Management console to simplify administration.

Fast User Switching

When two or more users share a computer, repeatedly having those users log off and log back on when a switch needs to be made can become quite tedious. Windows XP Professional offers Fast User Switching for users in a workgroup. With Fast User Switching, users can switch from one identity to another easily, without having to close programs or save work before doing so. For instance, if one user is logged onto the computer and working on an Excel spreadsheet, and another user needs to log on to retrieve some information from his or her address book, the first user can log off and leave Excel running. When this user logs back on again, the Excel program is still running and does not have to be reopened.

To enable Fast User Switching:

1. Log on as an administrator.

2. Open the Control Panel.

3. Open User Accounts.

4. Under Pick A Task, choose Change The Way Users Log On Or Off.

5. In the Select Logon And Logoff Options dialog box, check the checkboxes Use The Welcome Screen and Use Fast User Switching. Choose the Apply Options button.

Note
I had to restart my computer for Fast User Switching to be enabled. There is currently no prompt to remind you to do this.

There are some limitations when using or enabling Fast User Switching. These include the following:

♦ Fast User Switching cannot be enabled if Offline Files is also enabled. If Offline Files is enabled, an error message will appear. Choose OK to change Offline Files settings.

♦ Fast User Switching cannot be enabled while multiple users are logged onto the computer.

♦ When Fast User Switching is enabled, the Administrator account is not shown on the Welcome screen by default.

♦ You can identify the current user by choosing Start | Log Off <*name of users*>.

♦ Fast User Switching slows down the computer for its users because all programs remain running.

♦ SerialKeys will not work while Fast User Switching is enabled.

♦ Only workgroups, not domains, can enable Fast User Switching.

To switch users without logging off:

1. Choose Start | Log Off.

2. Choose Switch User.

3. Choose the user to switch to.

Forgotten Passwords

Passwords are the first security roadblock that a hacker or unwanted guest has to get past before doing any harm to your computer. Passwords should be "strong," containing a mixture of letters and numbers and not forming any words, children's names, or other familiar features. One problem with using a strong password is the need to write it down, which is risky, or to try to remember it, which can also be dangerous. If a password is forgotten, though, there are a couple of ways to get logged back on.

When a user forgets a password, and the password hint doesn't help, that user can use a password-reset disk to create a new password. This disk can be created through the Forgotten Password Wizard. If this disk hasn't been created, an administrator will have to reset the password for the user. The steps for creating and using the password-reset disk are different for users of a domain and users of a workgroup.

To create a password-reset disk in a workgroup:

1. Log onto the computer.

2. Open the Control Panel and then User Accounts.

3. If you are an administrator, double-click your account, and choose Prevent A Forgotten Password from the Related Tasks pane. If you are a limited user, this option will be located on the left side of the screen in the Related Tasks pane.

4. Choose Next to begin the Forgotten Password Wizard. Place a blank floppy disk in drive A:.

5. On the next page of the wizard, type the current password, and wait for the disk to be created. Choose Finish.

To create a password-reset disk in a domain:

1. After logging on, press Ctrl+Alt+Del to open the Windows Security dialog box.

2. Choose Change Password.

3. Choose Backup to start the Forgotten Password Wizard.

4. Choose Next. Place a blank floppy disk in A: drive.

5. On the next page of the wizard, type the current password, and wait for the disk to be created. Choose Finish.

To use the password-reset disk in a workgroup:

1. After a failed logon attempt, the Logon Failed dialog box appears and asks if you want to reset the password by using the password-reset disk or if you want to try again. Choose Reset to use the disk.

2. Choose Next to start the Password Reset Wizard, and place the reset disk in the floppy drive.

3. Type a new password, and confirm it; then type a new password hint.

4. After the wizard finishes, type the new password in the Log On To Windows screen. Create a new password-reset disk immediately.

To use the password-reset disk in a domain:

1. At the Welcome screen, press Ctrl+Alt+Del.

2. After a failed password attempt, the Logon Failed dialog box is displayed. Choose Reset to use the password-reset disk.

3. Choose Next to start the Password Reset Wizard, and place the reset disk in the floppy drive.

4. Type a new password, and confirm it; then type a new password hint.

5. After the wizard finishes, type the new password in the Log On To Windows screen. Create a new password-reset disk immediately.

If a user has forgotten his or her password and does not have a password-reset disk, an administrator will have to change the password. The administrator cannot recover the password, only change it.

To change the password as an administrator in a workgroup:

1. Open the Control Panel and then User Accounts.

2. Select the user account whose password needs to be changed.

3. Choose Create A Password.

4. Type in the new password and confirm it; then type in a password hint.

5. Tell the user to change the password and to create a password-reset disk the first time he or she logs onto the computer.

Note

If you are a member of a domain and are not an administrator, you'll need to contact your administrator if no reset disk has been made.

Using Computer Management for Users and Groups

Computer Management is a preconfigured Microsoft Management Console (MMC) used mainly by administrators for the purpose of managing the users, the computers, and the applications and services available to users on the network. Computer Management is separated into three sections: System Tools, Storage, and Services And Applications. In this section, I'll introduce using the Computer Management console to manage users and groups on the network. These accounts are accessed through the System Tools section. Later you will learn about other aspects of this console.

The Computer Management console is one of the many Administrative Tools available in Windows XP Professional. Administrative Tools is an icon in the Control Panel, but it is not listed on the Start menu by default. To place Administrative Tools on the Start menu:

1. Right-click the taskbar, and choose Properties.

2. In the Taskbar And Start Menu Properties dialog box, select the Start Menu tab, and choose the Customize button. In the Customize Start Menu dialog box, you can add Administrative Tools to the Start menu. See Chapter 1 for more information on configuring the taskbar.

To open the Computer Management console and view users and groups connected to a local or remote computer:

1. Open Administrative Tools either from the Control Panel or by choosing Start | Programs | Administrative Tools.

2. Choose Computer Management.

3. Expand the System Tools folder.

4. Expand the Local Users And Groups folder.

5. Highlight the Users folder in the left pane.

6. Highlight the Groups folder in the left pane.

   As you learned in Chapter 3, you can add, remove, delete, and modify user and group accounts from within these folders. Several other tasks can also be performed. One task of particular importance is connecting to another computer on the network. To connect to another computer:

7. In the left pane of the Computer Management console, highlight Computer Management (Local).

8. Choose Action | Connect To Another Computer.

9. In the Select Computer dialog box, type the name of the computer to connect to, or choose Browse.

10. Choose OK when finished, and choose OK again to connect.

11. Expand the System Tools folder.

12. Expand the Local Users And Groups folder.

13. Highlight the Users folder in the left pane.

14. Highlight the Groups folder in the left pane.

Notice that the users and groups are different for the second computer. From the local computer, you can manage users and groups on a remote computer or on the local one. This usually makes going to a specific desk or another office unnecessary.

Using Computer Management to Send a Console Message

In addition to managing users and groups, you can use the Computer Management console to send messages, called *console messages*, to users on other computers. These console messages come in handy when you need to send a quick message to another user on the network or when you need to notify all users of something. Figure 10.20 shows such a console message.

Figure 10.20
A sample console message.

To send a console message to a remote computer:

1. Open the Computer Management console.

2. Highlight Computer Management (Local).

3. Choose Action I All Tasks I Send Console Message to open the Send Console Message dialog box.

4. In the Message box, type a message.

5. The Recipients box lists who will receive this message. If you want to add people to or remove people from the Recipients box, use the Add or Remove buttons.

6. Choose Send.

Using Computer Management to View Connections

The Computer Management console provides other options having to do with users and groups on a network. For instance, you can find out who is logged onto the host computer, which folders are being shared and the number of clients connected to it, which files are open, and who is using these files. An administrator can even disconnect a user from a session. Figure 10.21 shows the Sessions folder from a host computer in a workgroup. Two users are logged onto the host computer. The first user is an administrator working from a

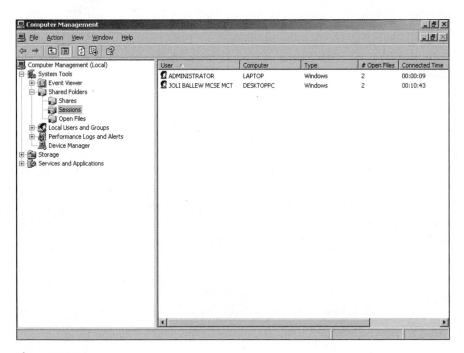

Figure 10.21
The Sessions folder in the Computer Management console.

laptop; the other is me on the computer DesktopPC. From the Sessions folder, an administrator can disconnect anyone connected to any computer by right-clicking the user's name and choosing Close Session.

The Shares folder—shown as the Sessions folder in Figure 10.21—shows the shared folders on the local computer. Other information includes the shared folder's path, the number of client connections, and any comments regarding that folder. Using the shared folder, you can right-click any resource and stop sharing. The Open Files folder, underneath the Sessions folder, shows which files are being accessed on the local computer and who is accessing them. An administrator can close any open file by right-clicking the file and choosing Close Open File.

To see which folders are being shared, which files are open, and who is using these files:

1. Open the Computer Management console.

2. Highlight Computer Management (Local).

3. Expand System Tools.

4. Expand Shared Folders.

5. Highlight Shares, Sessions, or Open Files.

6. Right-click any share, session, or open file and choose Stop Sharing to discontinue the connection.

You can also view these folders on other computers on the network as long as you have administrators' rights. To view shares, sessions, or open files on any other computer on the network, just choose Action | Connect To Another Computer before performing the previous steps.

Adding and Managing Computers

Once the network is running, computers are hooked up and connected to each other appropriately, and either ICS is working or you've verified that all computers can communicate, you can add new computers to the network and/or managing existing ones. Each computer and its users have to be able to connect to other computers and access shared files and folders on the network. In this section, I'll introduce how to add a computer, locate a computer, and use My Network Places.

Adding a Computer

Adding a computer to an existing, functioning network is very similar to setting up a new network, and it's usually done with the Network Setup Wizard. Before adding a computer, however, make sure you have decided what role the computer will play on the network. If the new computer is the most powerful computer on the network or has a faster modem than the current host computer, the new computer should be configured as the host computer, if possible. If the new host computer has a DSL or cable modem instead of a telephone modem, performance on the network will improve for ICS clients. If the new computer is a laptop or a less powerful computer, however, it shouldn't be set up as the host computer. Finally, the new computer should use Windows 98 or higher because other operating systems can't be added to the network automatically with the Network Setup Wizard.

To add a new computer to the network:

1. Physically connect the computer to the network, and turn the computer on.

2. If this computer will be the new host computer, turn off ICS sharing on the current host computer. Log on as an administrator.

3. If the computer uses Windows 98, Windows ME, Windows XP Home Edition, or Windows XP Professional, then use the Network Setup Wizard described earlier in this chapter. This wizard can be run from the CD or the setup disk.

   If the new computer uses Windows 2000, then right-click My Computer, choose Properties, select the Network Identification tab, choose the Properties button, and type the name of the workgroup to join. If this computer is going to be the host, configure the computer to use ICS. See Windows 2000 Help for specifics on this task.

Locating a Computer

Once the network is physically connected and you know that ICS is working for all of the computers, then you also know that the computers are communicating properly. If you are *not* running ICS, then follow these steps to verify that all computers on the network are connected properly or to locate a computer on the network:

1. Open My Network Places.

2. In the Network Tasks section in the left pane, select View Workgroup Computers.

3. To connect to a computer and access its shared folders, double-click the computer's icon. Figure 10.7, shown earlier, gives an example of this. You must have a username and password for the computer you are connecting to. Type the username and password, and choose OK.

4. In this window, you can also view the Shared Documents folder and the Printers And Faxes folder in the Other Places pane.

My Network Places for Administrators

My Network Places stores all of the shortcuts to the shared folders on your computer. The folders that you should add to My Network Places are resources that you need to access that are configured or connected to other computers on the network. Figure 10.22 shows an example of a My Network Places folder.

For you to add a folder to My Network Places, that folder must be shared, and you must have the appropriate permission to access it (administrator, in this case). For instance, a host

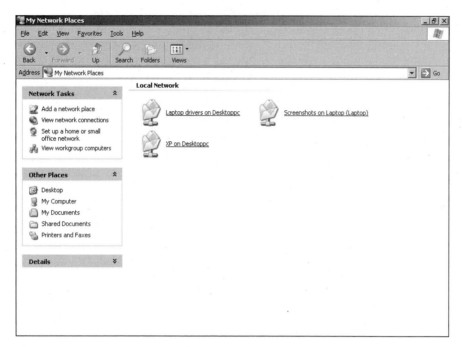

Figure 10.22
My Network Places.

computer might have two shared folders: one called General and another called Secret. The Secret folder is shared but is restricted to administrators only. The General folder is also shared, but it is placed in the Shared Documents folder and can be accessed by anyone on the network. If a network user tries to add the shared folder to My Network Places and does not have the appropriate permission to add it, an error message appears (see Figure 10.23). Also, if you're not logged on as an administrator, the folder won't appear as available when you're adding a network place.

Configuring and using a shared folder requires the administrator to choose Add A Network Place from the My Network Places window and select the appropriate folder. In the next section, you'll learn how to do this as well as how to share your own resources.

Before leaving this section, notice that Figure 10.22 shows many options for getting to other places quickly, including the desktop, My Computer, My Documents, Shared Docu-

Figure 10.23
Access denied from a Windows 2000 machine.

ments, and Printers And Faxes. Shared Documents is the folder used by members of the network who are not logged on as administrators. Limited users move files here for sharing. More on all of this in the next section.

Sharing Resources

In a workgroup, there is no central server or domain controller that holds all of the data, and there is no single network administrator who determines who can access what. In a workgroup, sharing resources is up to the people who are the "owners" of those resources. The owner shares files and folders only as needed. This type of sharing is the backbone of a workgroup.

In this section, you'll learn how to share files and folders, as well as how to assign some basic permissions so that you can control access to your resources. You'll also learn how to share hardware such as printers and scanners, how to connect to another user's shared resources, and how to map a network drive.

Note

This section is devoted entirely to workgroup and computer administrators. If you are not the administrator of your computer, or if you belong to a domain and have access to only the Shared Documents folder, you will not be able to perform the tasks as detailed in this section.

FAT vs. NTFS

There are two types of file systems: FAT and NTFS. FAT stands for *file allocation table*; NTFS stands for Windows NT Filing System and is sometimes referred to as New Technology File System. FAT is the simpler of the two file systems. Depending on who configured your computer, it could use either system.

To see which file system your computer uses:

1. Log on as an administrator.

2. Open the Computer Management console by choosing Start | Programs | Administrative Tools | Computer Management. (If you don't see Administrative Tools, open it from the Control Panel.)

3. Expand the Storage folder.

4. Highlight the Disk Management folder. (If this can't be accessed, you aren't logged on with the appropriate permissions. Limited users cannot access this utility.)

5. From Disk Management, locate the drive of your computer. Under the File System column, see if your computer is configured as FAT or NTFS.

When you're configuring permissions for your network, there are two types to choose from (or both can be used). You can use shared-folder, or *share*, permissions and/or NTFS permissions:

♦ Share permissions are used primarily with the FAT file system. There are three share permissions: Full Control, Read, and Change. These permissions are applied to shared folders to restrict a shared resource's availability over the network to only certain users. Share permissions work only when users access the resource over the network. They do not apply if the user is sitting at the computer that offers the resource. Share permissions are applied to entire folders, not to individual files.

♦ NTFS permissions are used with the NTFS file system. These permissions include Full Control, Modify, Read And Execute, List Folder Contents, Read, Write, and several special permissions. NTFS permissions work both over the network and when a user is sitting at the computer that offers the resource. NTFS permissions can be applied to any folders or files.

In a home network, FAT (share) permissions are adequate; in an office environment, I'd suggest using NTFS permissions.

The NTFS file system has a few restrictions. You can't use NTFS permissions unless the hard drive is formatted as NTFS. You can't use NTFS permissions on a drive formatted as FAT. You can, however, use share permissions on either a FAT drive or an NTFS drive. If your hard drive uses FAT, you can convert to NTFS without losing any data. You *cannot* change from NTFS to FAT, however, without formatting the drive and losing all data.

How do you know if you should use FAT or NTFS? NTFS offers more security than FAT does and should be used when any level of security is necessary. FAT is a simpler file system to handle in terms of assigning permissions, and it doesn't require much management once configured. In most cases, though, you should use NTFS.

Converting FAT to NTFS

If your computer is configured as FAT, and you'd like to use advanced NTFS permissions, you'll need to convert your file system. Doing so will not harm the system, but the conversion is irreversible. If you decide later that you want to use FAT, you'll have to reinstall Windows. Keep in mind, though, that share permissions can be used even on an NTFS drive, and the computer can be configured to use simple file sharing as described later in this chapter.

To convert a FAT file system to NTFS:

1. Log on as an administrator.

2. Open a command prompt by choosing Start | Programs | Accessories | Command Prompt.

3. Type the following: "CONVERT *<drive letter>*: /FS:NTFS", where *<drive letter>* is the drive letter of the volume.

4. Type the name of the volume. If you don't know, open the Computer Management console again, and in the Disk Management section, obtain the name of the volume. If you do this, close the Computer Management console before continuing.

5. After entering the drive letter, you might receive a warning that the drive is not mounted or that it is currently in use by another program. If you get this warning, choose Yes (press Y) to confirm that you want to convert the file system on the next reboot.

6. Reboot the computer. As the computer starts back up, the file system will be changed. You won't notice any difference except for the new Security tab when you're sharing a file.

Files and Folders

Sharing is different for administrators and for limited users. Administrators have free rein to create files and folders and to share them on the network. Limited users, however, must move their shared resources to the Shared Documents folder. The Shared Documents folder is preconfigured with specific permissions so that any folder or file placed there is secure. This system allows limited users to share files and folders without allowing the users to assign permissions themselves.

Note

In this section, I'll be referring to administrators again and discussing how administrators share files and folders. If you are not the administrator of your computer, skip to "Using the Shared Documents Folder" later in this section.

To share a file or a folder on your computer with others on the network:

1. Log on as an administrator.

2. Use Windows Explorer to locate the folder, if necessary. Right-click the folder, and choose Sharing and Security.

3. Select either the Share This Folder option or the Share This Folder On The Network option. (One or the other will be shown, depending on the current computer settings.) Type a share name.

4. Choose OK.

By default, the folder has certain permissions already configured. The share permissions are shown in Figure 10.24. Share permissions are used in workgroups to secure the resources being shared. In Figure 10.24, notice that the group Everyone has permission to read what's in the folder. These permissions can be changed as described in the next section.

Using Computer Management to Add a Shared Folder

Shared folders can also be configured from the Computer Management console. Remember, Computer Management can be opened from Administrative Tools in the Control Panel,

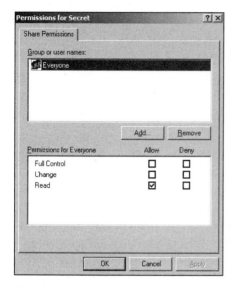

Figure 10.24
Share permissions for a folder.

but Windows XP does not list Administrative Tools in the Start menu unless you've specifically configured it that way.

Note

Before continuing, determine whether you are using simple file sharing. In Windows Explorer, choose Tools\Folder Options. On the View tab, scroll down to the last choice, Use Simple File Sharing (Recommended). Clear the checkbox, and choose OK. For more information, see the sidebar on the following page.

To share a folder from the Computer Management console:

1. Log on as an administrator. If you are not an administrator, skip to "Using the Shared Documents Folder" later in this section

2. Open the Computer Management console.

3. Expand System Tools and Shared Folders.

4. Highlight the Shares folder.

5. In the right pane, right-click an empty space, and choose New File Share. If you don't see this option, your computer is configured to use simple file sharing. You'll need to change this to continue. Return to the beginning of this procedure, and make the change.

6. Browse to the location of the new shared folder. Choose OK.

7. Type a share name and a description. Choose Next.

Simple File Sharing

By default, Windows XP Professional is configured to use simple file sharing. Simple file sharing is just that—a simple way to share files and folders in a workgroup. This might work for small home networks, but for an office, I'd suggest turning it off. Simple file sharing is available on both FAT and NTFS file systems. Look at the difference in the two figures shown next; each figure shows the property sheet displayed after right-clicking a folder and choosing to share.

In Figure 10.26 and Figure 10.27, the Sharing tabs differ. In Figure 10.26, with simple file sharing enabled, there is no option to set permissions for the folder, and there is no Security tab. In Figure 10.27, there is a Permissions button and a Security tab. (Figure 10.24, shown earlier, shows the dialog box displayed when this Permissions button is chosen and simple file sharing is disabled.) Additionally, you can use the Security button to designate the users and groups who can access the folder, and you can change permissions for those users. You won't see the Security tab if you are using the FAT file system. (This tab is available only on NTFS volumes. If you do not see the Security tab, you should convert your file system to NTFS as described earlier in this chapter.)

For instance, by default, the Everyone group can read a file and see what's in the folder. You can change this and give Everyone the permission to write to the file if necessary. Although this isn't generally a good practice, it does show how many more options are available when simple file sharing is disabled.

For reference once more: To disable or enable simple file sharing, open Windows Explorer, and choose Tools|Folder Options. On the View tab, scroll down to the last choice, Use Simple File Sharing (Recommended). To enable this, check the checkbox. To disable it, clear the checkbox.

---

8. On the Create Shared Folder page, select the basic share permissions that users who access this folder should have. See Figure 10.25.

9. Choose Finish, and choose either to create another shared folder or to quit.

10. In the Computer Management console, notice the new share in the right pane. To change permissions, double-click the folder.

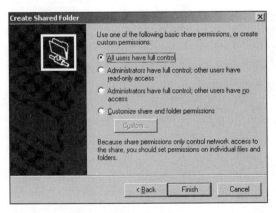

Figure 10.25
Creating a shared folder.

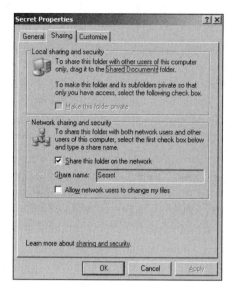

Figure 10.26
Simple file sharing is enabled.

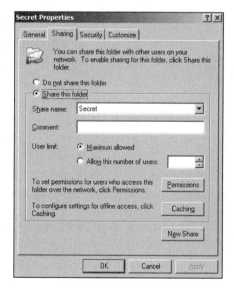

Figure 10.27
Simple file sharing is disabled.

Shared-Folder Permissions

After creating a shared folder, you might decide that you don't want *everyone* to be able to access it. This was discussed briefly in Chapter 3; you can strengthen the security of a file or folder by removing the Everyone group and adding only the groups and users to whom you want to give access. By default, *everyone* has access to what's in the folder, and the material could be private and shouldn't be accessible by all users.

You can change permissions from inside the Computer Management console or by right-clicking the folder itself. Share permissions can be set on the Sharing tab, and NTFS permissions can be set on the Security tab. (If you have your computer set for simple file sharing as in described in the sidebar earlier, you won't see these options. To disable this feature, follow the directions in the sidebar.) There are only three basic share permissions: Read, Change, and Full Control.

Read

The Read permission is the most restrictive permission. The Read permission allows the user to do only the following:

♦ View the file names and subfolder names in the folder

♦ Traverse to any subfolders in the folder

♦ View data in the folder's files

♦ Run any program files in the folder. (This permission is also called Execute.)

Change

The Change permission is the Read permission plus a few extra perks. The Change permission allows the user to do the following:

♦ View the file names and subfolder names in the folder

♦ Traverse to any subfolders in the folder

♦ View data in the folder's files

♦ Run any program files in the folder. (This permission is also called Execute.)

♦ Add files and subfolders to the folder

♦ Change the data in the files and save the changes

♦ Delete any files or subfolders in the folder

Full Control

The Full Control permission is the default when you're creating a new share and it is applied to the Everyone group. Full Control allows the user unlimited access to the file or folder, including the permissions given for Read and Change. The Full Control permission allows the user to do the following:

♦ View the file names and subfolder names in the folder

♦ Traverse to any subfolders in the folder

♦ View data in the folder's files

- Run any program files in the folder. (This permission is also called Execute.)
- Add files and subfolders to the folder
- Change the data in the files and save the changes
- Delete any files or subfolders in the folder
- Change permissions (NTFS files and folders only)
- Take ownership of the share (NTFS files and folders only)

Disadvantages

Remember that share permissions apply only if the user is accessing the resource over the network. If the user sits down at the computer that stores and offers the resource, the share permissions do not apply. It is best to use NTFS either alone or with share permissions to secure a network.

Share permissions also apply to the entire contents of the folder. For instance, a folder called General could have two subfolders: Private and Public. The Private and Public folders would have the same permissions as the General folder. This is not true of NTFS permissions. See Figure 10.28.

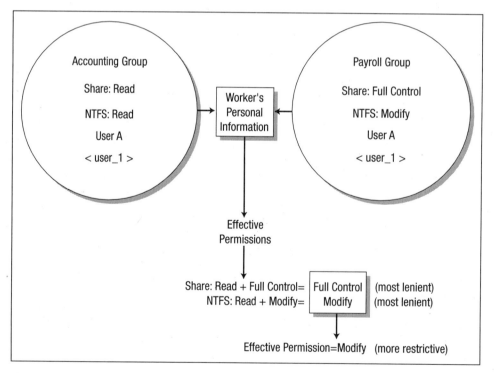

Figure 10.28
Share permissions.

Assigning Share Permissions

To assign share permissions for a folder:

1. Log on as an administrator.

2. Use Windows Explorer to browse to the Shared folder.

3. Right-click the folder, and choose Sharing And Security.

4. Choose the Permissions button.

5. Highlight the Everyone group, and choose Remove.

6. Choose the Add button.

7. Type the name of the group to whom you want to give access to this folder. Separate multiple groups by semicolons. (You can also type in specific user names, although this isn't recommended. To add a specific user, you should place that user in a group first and then add the group here.) Choose OK.

8. If you want to change the share permissions, check or uncheck the boxes for Full Control, Change, and Read. Choose OK twice.

File and Folder (NTFS) Permissions

NTFS permissions are more secure than share permissions and offer a wider variety of configuration options. NTFS file and folder permissions are Full Control, Modify, Read And Execute, List Folder Contents, Read, and Write. Table 10.5 shows what each of these file and folder permissions allows, and each permission is made up of a group of the following special permissions.

> **Note**
>
> *The number listed by each permission is for reference in Table 10.5.*

Table 10.5   File and folder permissions.

Permission	Full Control	Modify	Read & Execute	List Folder Contents	Read	Write
1	X	X	X	X	-	-
2	X	X	X	X	X	-
3	X	X	X	X	X	-
4	X	X	X	X	X	-
5	X	X	-	-	-	X
6	X	X	-	-	-	X
7	X	X	-	-	-	X
8	X	X	-	-	-	X
9	X	-	-	-	-	-

(continued)

Table 10.5   File and folder permissions *(continued)*.

Permission	Full Control	Modify	Read & Execute	List Folder Contents	Read	Write
10	x	-	-	-	-	-
11	x	x	-	-	-	-
12	x	x	x	x	x	x
13	x	-	-	-	-	-
14	x	x	x	x	x	x

(1) Traverse Folder/Execute File

This permission is different for folders and for files. For folders:

♦ Even without having permission for a folder, a user can move *through* it to reach other files or folders.

♦ This permission takes effect only if the user is not granted Bypass Traverse Checking permission. By default, the Everyone group has Bypass Traverse Checking permission.

For files:

♦ Execute File allows the user to run program files inside the folder.

♦ Setting Traverse Folder permissions does not automatically set the Execute File permission on all files that are in that folder.

(2) List Folder/Read Data

The List Folder/Read Data permission allows users to view file names and subfolder names inside the shared folder. This permission applies only to folders.

(3) Read Attributes

Attributes of a file can be read-only, hidden, ready for archiving, compressed, encrypted, and indexed. Users with the Read Attributes permission can view these attributes but cannot change them.

(4) Read Extended Attributes

Extended attributes vary by program, but users with the Read Extended Attributes permission can view these extended attributes.

(5) Create Files/Write Data

The Create Files/Write Data permission allows users to do the following:

♦ Create files within shared folders.

♦ Make changes in the file and save those changes.

♦ Overwrite data in the files.

(6) Create Folders/Append Data

The Create Folders/Append Data permission allows users to do the following:

♦ Create folders within the shared folder.

♦ Add changes to the end of the file.

Users cannot overwrite data in or delete data from the file.

(7) Write Attributes

The Write Attributes permission allows users to change the attributes of a file or folder. Users cannot write data to the file.

(8) Write Extended Attributes

The Write Extended Attributes permission allows users to change the extended attributes of a file or folder. Users cannot write data to the file.

(9) Delete Subfolders And Files

The Delete Subfolders And Files permission allows users to delete subfolders and files within the folder. The Delete permission does not have to be granted on the subfolder or the file if this permission is given.

(10) Delete

The Delete permission allows a user to delete the file or the folder.

(11) Read Permissions

The Read Permissions permission allows a user to see which permissions have been granted on the file or folder.

(12) Change Permissions

The Change Permissions permission allows a user to change the permissions on the file or folder.

(13) Take Ownership

The Take Ownership permission allows a user to take ownership of the file or folder. Remember, though, that ownership can only be taken, never given.

(14) Synchronize

The Synchronize permission is only used by multithreaded, multiprocess programs. It allows different threads (or pieces of the program) to synchronize with files or folders involved with the program.

Planning for NTFS Permissions

When assigning permissions for the first time, you should do some planning first. There are several de facto standards that will work in almost any scenario. For instance, permissions should be given to and set for groups of users instead of for individuals. There are several reasons for this, but the main one is that a group of users is much easier to manage. Consider this scenario: If the network has 30 users, and 10 are temporary workers, 15 are data-entry workers, three are salespeople, and two are administrators, it is much easier to create and maintain 4 groups than it is to manage 30 individual accounts and the permissions for them. In this example, the four groups can be called Temp, Data, Sales, and Admins. Therefore, when you need to change permissions for all workers in the Data group, you need to make that change only one time instead of 15.

Try to use preconfigured permissions for the groups on your network. Don't change the default groups unless it's absolutely necessary. For example, the Guest group has the Read share permission by default but does not have Change or Full Control permissions. In addition, the Guest group has NTFS permissions Read And Execute, List Folder Contents, and Read by default. If you change the Guest group's permissions for a particular folder, you'll be confused when problems arise because the permissions for the Guest group are different from the defaults. Instead of changing the Guest group's share permissions, create a new group called New Guest or Temp Guest, and assign the appropriate permissions to that group.

Assigning NTFS Permissions

Assigning NTFS permissions is similar to assigning share permissions, except that more permissions are available. To assign NTFS permissions:

1. Log on as an administrator.

2. Use Windows Explorer to browse to the Shared folder.

3. Right-click the folder, and choose Sharing And Security.

4. Select the Security tab.

5. Highlight a group or a user whose permissions you want to change.

6. In the Permissions For box, check or clear checkboxes as necessary. Choose OK twice.

Effective Permissions

If both share and NTFS permissions are being used, figuring out what permissions a user actually has for a resource can be a little tricky. If only share permissions or only NTFS permissions are used, the resulting permission—the *effective* permission—is the combination of all permissions for a file or folder and is the least lenient of the choices. For instance, say that a user belongs to a Temp group and a Data group; the Temp group has Read permission for a file, but the Data group has Change permission for the file. In this case, the user has the effective permission to Change the file. Change is the combination of Read and Change and is the more lenient of the two.

The same is true for NTFS permissions. If a user belongs to the Sales and Finance groups, for example, and if the Sales group has Modify permission and the Finance group has Full Control, then the user will have the most lenient of the two, which is Full Control. In many cases, though, both share and NTFS permissions are involved.

When Share and NTFS Permissions Are Both Assigned

When both share and NTFS permissions are assigned, the calculation is a little more complicated. Effective permissions are calculated by first figuring out what the effective share permission is (the combination of all share permissions), then figuring out what the effective NTFS permission is (the most lenient or the combination of all NTFS permissions), and finally taking the most restrictive of the two permissions. Figure 10.29 shows an example.

User A is a member of two groups: Accounting and Payroll. The file named Worker's Personal Information has all the workers' data, such as Social Security numbers, home addresses, and tax information. For this file, the Accounting group has the share permission Read and the NTFS permission Read. The Payroll group has the share permission Full Control and the NTFS permission Modify.

The more lenient share permission is Full Control. The more lenient NTFS permission is Modify. The more restrictive of the two is Modify. The user can modify the file.

Denying Permissions

Although using Deny, as shown in Figure 10.30, isn't suggested as the best way to secure the network, it is possible. The best way to deny a user access to a particular resource is to place that user in a group that is not given any type of access.

If Deny is set when effective permissions are calculated, the user does not have access to the resources. In the previous example, User A is denied access to the file Worker's Personal Information. User A will not be granted access even though he belongs to two other groups who do have access to the file. Deny always means deny.

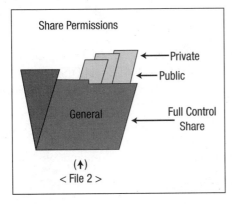

Figure 10.29
Calculating effective permissions.

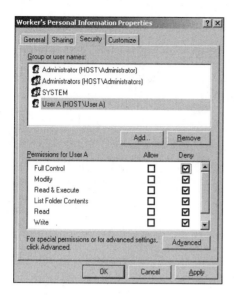

Figure 10.30
Denying permissions.

Letting Windows XP Calculate Effective Permissions

By clicking the Advanced button shown in Figure 10.30, you can let Windows XP calculate effective permissions. This is a much easier and more precise way of calculating effective permissions. Not only can you see if a user can read or modify a file, but also you can see whether each of the 14 permissions detailed earlier is enabled or disabled.

To view effective permissions for a shared file or folder:

1. Log on as an administrator.

2. Using Windows Explorer, browse to a file or folder that is shared, preferably one that has users configured to access it with permissions assigned.

3. Right-click the folder, and choose Sharing And Security.

4. In the folder's property sheet, select the Security tab. If you can't see the Security tab, read the sidebar on simple file sharing and the section on FAT vs. NTFS.

5. Choose the Advanced button.

6. In the Advanced Security Settings dialog box, select the Effective Permissions tab.

7. Choose the Select button. Type the name of the object to select, and choose OK.

8. The Effective Permissions box lists the effective permissions. See Figure 10.31.

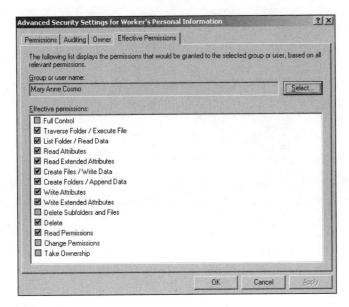

Figure 10.31
Effective permissions.

Printer Permissions

When a printer is installed on the network, default permissions are applied to the printer. These default permissions allow users to print and allow print operators and administrators to manage the printers and print jobs. There are three printer permissions: Print, Manage Printers, and Manage Documents. As with share and NTFS permissions, when a user belongs to multiple groups, the least restrictive permissions apply. Again, the Deny permission is available and can be used to prevent certain groups from accessing the printer if necessary.

Print

The Print permission is the most restrictive of all three printer permissions. When given the Print permission, a user can connect to the printer and print documents. The members of the Everyone group have the Print permission by default. This allows all users on the network to send documents to the printer and to manage their own documents. Also, the owner of a document can delete the job, make multiple copies, and read permissions for the document. The following groups are assigned the Print permission by default: Administrators, Everyone, Power Users, Print Operators, and Server Operators.

Manage Documents

The Manage Documents permission allows a user to do the following:

♦ Pause, resume, restart, and cancel any document waiting to be printed.

♦ Change the order of the documents waiting to be printed.

- ◆ Read and change permissions.

- ◆ Take ownership.

The user cannot print to the printer or do any tasks related to managing the printer, as described in the next section. The following groups are assigned the Manage Documents permission by default: Administrators, Creator-Owner, Power Users, Print Operators, and Server Operators.

Manage Printers

The Manage Printers permission allows users to do all of the things that users with the Print permission can do, plus have complete control of the printer. This means the user can do all of the following:

- ◆ Pause the printer.

- ◆ Restart the printer.

- ◆ Change print spool settings.

- ◆ Share printers.

- ◆ Change printer permissions.

- ◆ Read and change printer properties.

The following groups are assigned the Manage Printers permission by default: Administrators, Power Users, Print Operators, and Server Operators.

Setting Printer Permissions

Printer permissions are set by right-clicking the printer and choosing either Sharing And Security or Properties. Printer permissions differ from previous permission-setting examples in that there are not share and NTFS choices; there are only the three basic permissions described in this section. The printer permissions are located on the Security tab of the printer's Properties dialog box.

To set printer permissions for users or groups:

1. Log on as an administrator, print operator, server operator, or power user.

2. Open the Control Panel.

3. Open Printers And Faxes.

4. Right-click the printer for which you're setting permissions, and choose either Sharing or Properties.

5. On the Sharing tab, verify that the printer is shared on the network. If it isn't, share it now.

6. On the Security tab, notice which groups are already included by default. (If there's no Security tab, see the sidebar.) The Administrators and Power Users groups have full control of the printer, with all three permissions checked; the Create-Owner group has the Manage Documents permission checked; and the Everyone group has the Print permission checked. See Figure 10.32.

   ♦ To remove a group or user, highlight that group and choose Remove.

   ♦ To add a group or user, choose Add and type the name of the group to add.

   ♦ To change the permissions for any group or user, highlight the group and add or remove checkmarks for the permissions you want to change.

   ♦ To see the effective permissions for a group or user, choose the Advanced button and then select the Effective Permissions tab.

7. Choose OK.

Tip

Remember that it's always best to add groups and not specific users. To add a user and assign permissions, first put that user in a group, and then add the group in Step 6 of the previous procedure.

Connecting to a Shared Folder—Administrator

Users have several ways to connect to a shared folder or resource. Connecting to a resource in a workgroup and connecting to a resource in a domain are done differently. In this section,

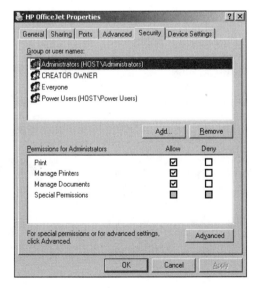

Figure 10.32
The Security tab of the Printer Properties dialog box.

I'll discuss the process for connecting to a shared resource as an administrator in a workgroup. In the next section, I'll cover connecting to a shared resource as a limited user or non-administrator in a workgroup.

Using My Network Places

As I mentioned earlier, My Network Places can be used to view network connections, view workgroup computers, and set up a small-office network. Administrators can also use My Network Places to add shortcuts to shared resources on the network.

To connect to a shared resource by using My Network Places:

1. Log on as an administrator.

2. Open My Network Places.

3. From the Network Tasks pane, choose Add A Network Place. Choose Next to start the Add Network Place Wizard.

4. On the Where Do You Want To Create This Network Place page, select Choose Another Network Location.

5. On the What Is The Address Of This Network Place page, choose Browse.

6. On the Browse For Folder page, expand Entire Network, Microsoft Windows Network (if it's appropriate from the choices listed), the workgroup name, and finally the name of the computer that holds the resource.

7. From the list of shares underneath the computer name, select the resource to connect to. Choose OK. Choose Next to continue.

8. On the What Do You Want To Name This Place page, type a name or accept the default, and choose Next. Choose Finish to close the wizard.

   By default, the resource or folder opens immediately.

The next time you want to connect to this resource, simply open My Network Places and double-click the folder.

Viewing Workgroup Computers

Administrators can also connect to resources by using View Network Connections from My Network Places. To connect to a resource this way:

1. Log on as an administrator.

2. Open My Network Places.

3. From the Network Tasks pane, select View Workgroup Computers.

4. In the list of computers, double-click the computer that holds the resource you want to connect to.

5. From the icons available, select the resource you need to use or connect to. Double-click it to connect.

Mapping a Network Drive

Administrators can also access resources on the network by mapping a network drive. Mapping a network drive allows you to assign a drive letter to a network computer or to a folder on the computer. This drive letter appears in My Computer along with the local drives on the computer. Drive mapping makes drives on other computers easy to access.

To map a network drive:

1. Log on as an administrator.

2. Open My Network Places.

3. In My Network Places, choose Tools | Map Network Drive.

4. On the Map Network Drive page, select a drive letter from the Drive drop-down list.

5. Choose Browse to locate the folder or drive to which you want to connect.

6. On the Browse For Folder page, expand Entire Network, Microsoft Windows Network (if it's appropriate from the choices listed), the workgroup name, and finally the name of the computer that holds the resource.

7. From the list of shares underneath the computer name, select the resource to connect to. Choose OK. Choose Next to continue.

8. Choose Finish to close the wizard.

    By default, the resource or folder opens after you close the wizard.

To view the new drive, open My Computer. This window will now have an extra section called Network Drives, which will have an icon for the new network drive.

Using the Shared Documents Folder

The Shared Documents folder can be used to share documents among users of the same computer or with other users in the workgroup. With a single computer, using this method of sharing is quite simple; in a workgroup, it's a little more complex. (In a domain, the Shared Documents folder is not available.)

Creating a Shortcut on the Desktop

Before using the Shared Documents folder to share data with users who all use a single computer, create a shortcut on the desktop if the folder isn't there already:

1. Open Windows Explorer.

2. Browse to *<drive letter>*\Documents And Settings\All Users.WINDOWS\Shared Documents.

3. Right-click the Shared Documents folder, and choose Create Shortcut.

4. Choose Yes to create a shortcut on the desktop, or drag the folder to the desktop yourself.

Repeat this procedure for all users of the shared computer.

Using the Shared Documents Folder on a Single Computer

To place a document in the Shared Documents folder:

1. Use the My Documents folder or Windows Explorer to locate the file or folder that you want to share.

2. Drag the file or folder to the desktop shortcut for the Shared Documents folder.

3. Open the Shared Documents folder to verify that the file or folder was moved. If you want to, drag the folder again to the Shared Music or Shared Pictures folder inside the Shared Documents folder.

When a user places a document or any other item in the Shared Documents folder, all users who log onto that computer can access that item. By default, the Everyone group has Full Control. Consider changing these permissions if necessary, or use simple file sharing and let Windows XP Professional do the work of assigning permissions.

Using the Shared Documents Folder in a Workgroup

You can also use the Shared Documents folder in a workgroup, but the folder must be set up and shared like any other folder, as described earlier. To share and use the Shared Documents folder in a workgroup:

1. Browse to your Shared Documents folder.

2. Right-click the folder, and choose Sharing And Security.

3. On the Sharing tab, select the option to share the folder.

4. If the Share This Folder On The Network checkbox is available, check it.

5. To allow others on the network to change the files in your shared folder, check the checkbox Allow Other Users To Change My Files.

Connecting to a Shared Folder

Connecting to a shared folder is the same as connecting to any other shared folder. Just open My Network Places, choose Add A Network Place, browse to the Shared Documents folder, and follow the procedure described earlier in this section.

Connecting to Other Shared Resources

To connect to other shared resources on the network, the procedure is the same as connecting to a shared folder. However, in many instances, you'll need the name and password of an administrator, or you'll need to belong to a certain group and have specific permissions to access the resource. Figure 10.33 shows the error you'll receive when trying to add a network place that you do not have permission to access.

Mapping a Network Drive

Drive mapping can be used configure My Network Places. Mapping a network drive allows you to assign a drive letter to a network computer or to a folder on the computer. This drive letter appears in My Computer along with the local drives on the computer. Drive mapping makes drives on other computers easy to access.

To map a network drive:

1. Log on either as an administrator or as a limited user.

2. Open My Network Places.

3. In My Network Places, choose Tools | Map Network Drive.

4. On the Map Network Drive page, select a drive letter from the Drive drop-down list.

5. Choose Browse to locate the folder or drive to which you want to connect.

6. On the Browse For Folder page, expand Entire Network, Microsoft Windows Network (if it's appropriate from the choices listed), the workgroup name, and finally the name of the computer that holds the resource.

7. From the list of shares underneath the computer name, select the resource to connect to. Choose OK. Choose Next to continue.

8. Choose Finish to close the wizard.

   By default, the resource or folder opens after you close the wizard. If you do not have appropriate permissions to access the resource, an access-denied message will appear.

As I mentioned earlier, sharing files and folders doesn't work the same when the computer is connected to a domain. Chapter 11 covers how files and folders are shared in a domain.

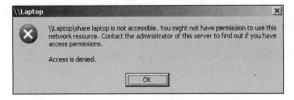

Figure 10.33
An access-denied message.

Advanced Access Control for Administrators

Administrators can take advantage of some advanced access-control options in Windows XP Professional. These options include taking ownership of a resource, setting, viewing, changing, and removing special permissions, and changing the behavior of inherited permissions. In this section, you'll learn how to further tweak the network with these advanced options.

Taking Ownership of Files or Folders

An administrator can take ownership of any file or folder on the network at any time. For security reasons, however, the administrator cannot grant ownership. A resource owner who is not an administrator can grant permission for other users to take ownership at any time, but beyond that, non-administrators are not allowed to take ownership of any files or folders but their own.

Taking Ownership

To take ownership of a file or folder:

1. Log on as an administrator. Use Windows Explorer to locate the file or folder that you want to take ownership of.

2. Right-click the resource, and choose Properties.

3. Select the Security tab.

4. Choose the Advanced button, and then select the Owner tab.

5. In the Change Owner To box, select the new owner.

6. If you want also to change the owner of all subcontainers and objects, check the Replace Owner On Subcontainers And Objects checkbox.

Granting Others the Permission to Take Ownership

If you are the owner of a file or folder, you can allow others to take ownership of that resource. To grant others the permission to take ownership:

1. Right-click the shared file, and choose Sharing And Security.

2. On the Security tab, choose the Add button.

3. In the Select Users Or Groups text box, type the name of a user or group to whom you're granting permission to take ownership of the file or folder. Choose OK.

4. In the Properties dialog box, highlight the newly added user or group.

5. Choose the Advanced button.

6. In the Advanced Security Settings dialog box, make sure the newly added user or group is highlighted, and choose the Edit button.

7. Scroll down to the last permission in the Permissions box, and check the Allow checkbox beside Take Ownership.

8. If you want the settings to apply to objects or containers within the folder, check the checkbox Apply These Permissions To Objects And/Or Containers Within This Container Only. See Figure 10.34.

9. Choose OK three times.

Setting, Viewing, Changing, and Removing Special Permissions

There are several other special permissions besides Take Ownership. These were discussed earlier in the section "File and Folder (NTFS) Permissions." Any of these special permissions can be changed using the same procedure as in the previous example.

Explicit vs. Inherited Permissions

There are two types of permissions: explicit and inherited. *Explicit* permissions are those permissions that are created automatically when the object is created; for example, a shared folder gives the Everyone group Full Control of the objects in it. Explicit permissions are also those permissions that are assigned by an administrator or by the owner of the resource. When special permissions are set, those permissions are explicit.

Inherited permissions are just what you'd expect. Their parent folder—the folder in which they are stored—gives these permissions automatically to the objects inside them. Permissions

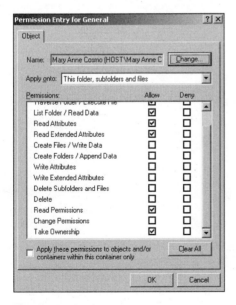

Figure 10.34
Special permissions.

are configured this way by default to make permissions management easier and to ensure that permissions are assigned in a consistent manner.

Generally, inherited permissions are a help and not a hindrance. However, in some instances, you'll want to prevent inherited permissions from being applied to certain files and folders, or you'll need to change permissions on an object that has inherited its permissions. There are several scenarios, each covered in the following sections.

Disabling Permissions Inheritance

To prevent a folder from propagating permissions inheritance to the files and folders it contains:

1. Right-click the shared folder, and choose Properties.

2. Select the Security tab.

3. Choose the Advanced button.

4. On the Permissions tab, choose Edit.

5. In the Apply Onto drop-down list, select This Folder Only. Figure 10.35 shows an example.

Note

If the permissions are grayed out, the permissions are inherited from another folder. Skip to the section "Changing Inherited Permissions."

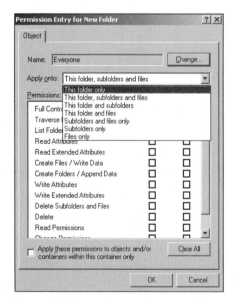

Figure 10.35
Applying permissions to this folder only.

Preventing Specific Files and Folders from Inheriting Permissions
To disable permission inheritance for a specific file or folder (a child object) in a shared folder:

1. Right-click the file or subfolder, and choose Properties.

2. Select the Security tab.

3. Choose the Advanced button.

4. Clear the checkbox Inherit From Parent The Permission Entries That Apply To Child Objects. Include These Entries Explicitly Defined Here.

5. In the Information box, select Copy, Remove, or Cancel to copy the previously applied permissions, remove the previously applied permissions, or cancel them, respectively.

Changing Inherited Permissions
You can change inherited permissions in a number of ways. You can change the permission of the parent folder; you can override Allow or Deny by selecting the opposite permission from the list; or you can clear the checkbox as described in the previous section. To change permissions for the parent folder, simply browse to that folder and change the permissions as described earlier.

To select the opposite permission of Allow or Deny:

1. Right-click the shared folder or file, and choose Sharing And Security.

2. Select the Security tab.

3. Choose the Advanced button.

4. Check the boxes for which you want to change permissions. Choose OK three times.

A Little About Protocols

A *protocol* is a set of rules and conventions for sending data over a network. When data is sent from one computer to another, those computers have to agree on a number of things, including content, format, timing, sequencing, and error control. The most commonly used protocol is TCP/IP (Transmission Control Protocol/Internet Protocol). TCP/IP is the protocol (actually, a suite of protocols) on which the Internet is based, and all computers that access the Internet must have this protocol installed and configured.

Different types of networks use different protocols, including IPX/SPX (Internetwork Packet Exchange/Sequence Packet Exchange), which is used on Novell NetWare networks. These networks still use TCP/IP to connect to the Internet, though. NetBEUI (NetBIOS Extended User Interface) is another common protocol. It is a Microsoft networking protocol that can be used in small LANs (those with 200 or fewer clients). NetBEUI is easier to use than TCP/IP, but NetBEUI cannot be routed and is therefore unsuitable for larger networks. The only type of routing that NetBEUI networks can use is Token Ring source routing. Token Ring is a network configuration in which computers take turns sending data out on the network.

A common protocol used in many networks is the Dynamic Host Configuration Protocol (DHCP). When you configure a home network by using the Network Setup Wizard, this is the protocol used; it is a subset of the TCP/IP protocol.

Viewing the Protocols Installed on Your Computer Network

To see which protocols are used on your computer after you've set up a home network with the Network Setup Wizard:

1. As an administrator, log onto the host computer with ICS enabled.

2. Right-click My Network Places, and choose Properties.

3. Right-click the Local Area Connection, and choose Properties.

4. In the Local Area Connection Properties dialog box, notice the protocols listed. They most likely include Client for Microsoft Networks, File and Printer Sharing for Microsoft Networks, and Internet Protocol (TCP/IP). Select TCP/IP.

5. Choose the Properties button. Notice the IP address. Choose OK twice.

6. In the Network Connections window, right-click your Internet connection and choose Properties.

7. Select the Networking tab.

8. In the Internet Connection Properties dialog box, notice the protocols listed. They most likely include QoS Packet Scheduler and Internet Protocol (TCP/IP). Choose OK.

9. Choose Install, then Protocol, and then Add. Notice the protocols that can be added. Choose Cancel three times.

10. Log onto an ICS client computer on your network. Perform Steps 1 through 5 again. Notice that the client computer has no "static" IP address; instead, Obtain An IP Address Automatically is selected.

What this all means is that the ICS host computer uses TCP/IP as the protocol and has a specific IP address that it uses to identify itself on the local network. The ICS clients obtain their addresses automatically. Having the clients obtain their addresses in this manner reduces management tasks for administrators. Most larger networks use TCP/IP and DHCP to manage their networks and enable communication between computers.

It is not necessary for you to understand exactly how data is sent from one computer to another in order to use Windows XP Professional or be a member of a network. A little knowledge of protocols can't hurt, though. If any error messages appear that contain the word "protocol," you'll at least know that it has to do with how your computer is communicating with others on the network or the outside world.

Wrapping Up

In this chapter, you learned how to set up a small-office network. You learned about workgroups and domains and the difference between the two. A small-office network is a local area network in which computers, printers, files, folders, and other resources can be shared among all of its users.

Setting up a home network consists of obtaining the correct hardware, physically connecting the computers and peripherals, installing network adapters, hubs, and cables, and running the Network Setup Wizard. Within this LAN, you can configure Internet connection sharing so that all users can benefit from a single Internet connection.

With the network up and running, you learned how to manage the users on your network, how to configure Fast User Switching for multiple users on a single computer, and how to use the Computer Management console to administer not only users and groups but also computers, shares, and sessions.

The remainder of the chapter detailed the heart of any network: sharing resources. Sharing works differently for administrators and for limited users. Limited users can share files easily through the Shared Folders folder.

Finally, some advanced access controls were introduced, including taking ownership of a file or folder, configuring special permissions, and working with explicit and inherited permissions. A short introduction to protocols was also included to help you understand how data is sent to and from computers on the network.

Chapter 11

Corporate Networks

There are two types of networks: those that are workgroups, as explained in Chapter 10, and those that are domains, which are explained here. Domains differ from workgroups in that domains have a domain controller that verifies all user logons and allows users to connect to the resources they need. A network administrator runs the network using Windows XP servers, Windows 2000 servers, or Windows NT 4 servers. The users on the domain network use a workstation operating system, such as Windows 98, Windows NT 4 Workstation, Windows 2000 Professional, or Windows XP Professional, and users must log onto the domain to gain access to the resources on it. Domains offer a much higher level of security than workgroups do, and domains are used in just about every corporate network that has more than 200 users or 32 computers. (These numbers vary.)

This chapter is geared mostly toward the Windows XP Professional user—the user who logs onto the network each day in a corporate environment to access the resources on it and to share information and data. A few sections, however, are geared toward administrators, too. In all instances, the domain user should understand these concepts, including how to access a server by using remote-access technologies, how remote storage plays a part in the network, how wireless networking is set up and used, and how an administrator can troubleshoot your computer by using Remote Assistance and Remote Desktop utilities. The user must also understand how Windows XP Professional works in a domain, how users and groups are categorized to prevent unauthorized access, how the network is protected from intentional or unintentional harm, and why limits are placed on a domain user's access.

More About Domains

In a domain, a user's account operates differently than it does in a workgroup. For this reason, in this section, I'll reintroduce user accounts and NTFS permissions and discuss what role the local security policy plays in a domain environment. Besides permissions, there are also privileges and rights associated with user accounts and groups; these privileges and rights will be discussed along with how they differ from the permissions you've already been introduced to.

Overview of User Accounts

The user account is a record configured to allow a user to log onto a workgroup or a domain and to access resources. In a domain, the network administrator (working on a domain controller) configures the user account. The user must be a member of at least one group, and each user is a member of the Domain Users group by default when the network administrator creates the user account. The user account is generally configured so that the user can log on, create files and folders, run programs, and save files. Users cannot usually add users to groups, change user passwords, manage remote computers, modify their own system settings, or set permissions for other users. The user can be assigned to multiple groups, though, and each group can have different access permissions. By adding a user to another group, an administrator can grant that user more permissions to access resources. A user who is a member of the Users group and who is then added to the Power Users group has much more freedom and access to resources than he or she did before the addition.

Consider User A, a member of the Domain Users group, which by default has specific permissions to files and folders. User A, because he is a member of this group, can access the shared file or folder and read its contents, among other things. The user also has Full Control permissions for any folder he creates. From Chapter 10, you know that both share and NTFS permissions can be assigned for a file or folder and that effective permissions are the result of calculating all group memberships and their permissions.

To view your effective permissions for a particular file or folder:

1. Log onto the domain with your user account.

2. Open Windows Explorer.

3. Browse to the folder for which you want to view effective permissions.

4. Right-click the folder, and choose Properties.

5. On the Security tab, choose the Advanced button.

6. In the Advanced Security Settings dialog box, select the Effective Permissions tab.

7. Choose the Select button.

8. Type your username, and choose OK.

9. View your effective permissions for the folder.

When using the network to access a shared folder that they did not create and are not the owners of (unless specific permissions were applied later), users also have the following permissions by default:

♦ Traverse Folder/Execute File

♦ List Folder/Read Data

♦ Read Attributes

♦ Read Extended Attributes

♦ Read Permissions

♦ Read

♦ Read And Execute

Built-In User Accounts

There are only two built-in user accounts: Administrator and Guest. The Administrator account is set up when Windows XP Professional is installed, and it's the first account an administrator uses to access the new operating system. This account cannot be deleted or disabled, although administrators usually create accounts for themselves for security reasons and do not log on with the default Administrator account.

People who need to log onto the network only rarely can use the Guest account and do not have or need a user account. Although the Guest account is disabled by default, an administrator can enable it quite easily. The problem with the Guest account stems from its not having a password configured by default; that is a security risk.

The network administrator creates all of the other accounts on the network domain. Your account was manually created, and it became a member of the Users group. You might also have been placed in other groups, such as the Power Users group or a group specific to the company, such as Finance, Sales, or Management. Your effective permissions are calculated as described in Chapter 10; they are a combination of all of the NTFS and share permissions applied to your account for a specific resource.

Overview of Built-In Groups

An administrator does not generally assign specific permissions to a specific user. Instead, the administrator places user accounts into local groups. The administrator then places the local groups into global groups and assigns permissions. This type of assignment keeps the management of users and groups as simple as possible. By assigning users with similar needs to a single group, an administrator can manage all those users through the group's permissions.

Several built-in groups are available in a domain. Each group has preconfigured permissions and user rights, and when a user account is added to one of these groups, the user automatically has the rights and permissions associated with the group. The following sections explain each built-in group. To determine which groups you are a member of, ask your administrator.

Note

Although built-in groups were introduced in Chapter 3, the information is worth repeating here in a domain context with the general user's understanding of these concepts in mind.

Administrators

The Administrators group is the least restrictive group available. Administrators have full control of the computer, the network, and user accounts. Only a few users should be in this group, and they should be chosen carefully. Even when users are in the Administrators group, they should log on as an administrator only when necessary. Otherwise, they should log on as a power user or a user. This guideline is important because certain viruses, when attacking through an administrator's account, can cause many more problems than they can when attacking through a more restricted account. Besides this, there are security risks involved with leaving an administrator's computer unattended or with others' obtaining access.

Members of the Administrators group can do almost anything with the computer, but following are some of the more common administrative tasks not generally assigned to most other groups. Administrators can:

♦ Take ownership of files and folders.

♦ Back up and restore system data.

♦ Audit the network and manage audit logs.

♦ Set policies—such as password policies or logon policies—for network users.

♦ Install service packs and Windows Updates.

♦ Perform upgrades.

♦ Perform system repairs.

♦ Install device drivers and system services.

Backup Operators

Backup operators are necessary in large organizations. Users who are members of this group can back up and restore users' files and folders, as well as system-state files and other critical operating system files. As a precautionary measure, a common practice is to give these users permission to either back up or restore, but not both. A user could do a great deal of harm by backing up, changing, and restoring harmful data to the network. Backup operators also have permissions that allow them to access user files and to read and write to those files. Administrators should put group policies in place to prevent these users from having this type of access.

By default, backup operators can do the following:

♦ Back up and restore data

♦ Shut down the computer

Power Users

The Power Users group sits between the Administrators group and the Users group in terms of permissions and rights. Power users can do what any user can do, plus the following:

♦ Modify computer-wide settings

♦ Run non-certified Microsoft applications (programs not accepted by Microsoft as fully compatible with Windows XP)

♦ Run legacy applications

♦ Install applications that do not modify operating system files or add system services

♦ Customize Control Panel options, such as date, time, and power options

♦ Customize network printers

♦ Create local user accounts and local groups

♦ Manage local user accounts and local groups

♦ Stop and start system services that do not start by default

Users

The Users group is what many network users belong to in larger organizations. The Users group is very secure because its users don't have very many permissions or rights and therefore have a smaller chance of causing a problem. A user's account, if hacked into, also offers very little access to sensitive network resources and data. Members of the Users group can do the following:

♦ Shut down their workstations

♦ Create local groups

♦ Manage the local groups they create

♦ Run programs installed by administrators, but only if the programs are certified by Microsoft as compatible

♦ Retain full control over anything they create

Users cannot perform any of the tasks listed above for previous groups, such as modifying operating system settings, backing up and restoring network data, installing programs or device drivers, or stopping and starting system services.

Guests

Members who log on as guests are members of this group. Guests can run programs on the workstation and shut it down, but they have very few permissions and rights beyond that. The Guests group is the most restrictive.

Replicator

The Replicator group is not for adding users. This group is designed for directory replication functions and is used by a domain user account to log onto the Replicator service on the domain controller.

Permissions vs. Privileges and Rights

Previous sections have referred not only to permissions but also to user rights and privileges. These terms have been used loosely so far in this section, but rights and privileges are different from permissions. Rights and privileges are used in domains to control access by users and to secure the network. Permissions are used when referring to objects such as files and folders. The permissions Read, Read And Execute, and Write all refer to what a user can do with the file or folder. A user right, however, refers to a specific action that a user can take, such as logging on locally or remotely, adding workstations to a domain, or changing the system time. A *permission* is given for an *object*, while a *right* is given to a *user*.

There are two types of user rights: privileges and logon rights. As with similar management tasks, administrators assign privileges and logon rights to groups rather than to individual user accounts. Multiple privileges and rights are available for administrators to grant to users. The next two sections discuss the privileges and rights that pertain mostly to users and power users.

Privileges

The list shown next is not a complete one; there are many privileges that can be assigned to users. However, some of the privileges, such as Create A Token Object, refer mainly to processes and are not assigned to any user group by default. The following list contains the privileges that are important to domain users and power users:

♦ *Add A Workstation To A Domain*—This privilege is not granted to any group by default. It allows the user to add computers to a specific domain. This right might be necessary for lab workers, junior administrators, or network technicians. A user with this privilege can add up to 10 workstations to the domain.

♦ *Back Up Files And Directories*—This privilege is granted to the Administrators and Backup Operators groups by default. Users with this privilege can back up the system even though they do not have specific access to files and folders located on the system. This works only when the backup process is achieved through an NTFS backup application programming interface.

♦ *Bypass Traverse Checking*—This privilege is granted to the Administrators and Power Users groups on workstations. This privilege allows the user to travel through a folder on the way to a shared folder even though the user does not have specific permissions to access the folder that is in the path. The user cannot see what else is in the folder being passed through.

♦ *Change The System Time*—This privilege is granted to the Administrators and Power Users groups on workstations. This privilege allows the user to change the system time on the local computer.

♦ *Force Shutdown From A Remote System*—This privilege is granted to the Administrators group on workstations. This privilege allows the user to shut down a computer from a remote location.

♦ *Load And Unload Device Drivers*—This privilege is granted to the Administrators group on workstations. Device drivers are necessary to run hardware, such as printers and cameras, and installing incorrect drivers can bring down a system. Only administrators should have this privilege.

♦ *Remove A Computer From A Docking Station*—This privilege is granted to the Administrators, Power Users, and Users groups. This privilege allows the user of a laptop to undock the computer when necessary.

♦ *Take Ownership Of Files Or Other Objects*—This privilege is granted to the Administrators group but can be useful in a domain if a single document is shared among several trusted users.

♦ *Shut Down The System*—This privilege is granted to the Administrators, Backup Operators, Power Users, and Users groups on all workstations. It allows the user to shut down the local computer.

Logon Rights

The list shown next is not a complete one; there are many logon rights that can be assigned to users. Some logon rights are specifically for services and other operating system tasks. For instance, Log On As A Batch Job is not a necessary logon right for a user or power user. Listed next are the most common user logon rights:

♦ *Access This Computer From A Network*—This privilege is granted to the Administrators, Power Users, Users, and Backup Operators groups by default. It allows a user to connect to a computer over the network.

♦ *Log On Locally*—This privilege is granted to the Administrators, Power Users, Users, Guests, and Backup Operators groups by default. It allows a user to log onto the computer locally, meaning by sitting at the computer and using the computer's own keyboard.

♦ *Deny Access To This Computer From The Network*—This privilege is not granted to anyone by default. It prohibits a user or a group of users from connecting to a specific computer on the network.

♦ *Deny Local Logon*—This privilege is not granted to anyone by default. It prohibits a user or a group of users from connecting to a local computer directly, through the computer's keyboard.

Local Security Policy in a Domain

Local security policies are generally created when users are in workgroups and when multiple users access the same computer. The *local security policy* controls who uses the computer, how much access they have to the computer and its resources, and more. In a domain, if you're attempting to create a new local security policy, and you don't have the privileges needed to do this, an error message might appear, as shown in Figure 11.1. If a local security policy does exist, it is subject to strict rules of precedence.

By default, each computer installed with Windows XP Professional has one group policy configured. Local group policies were introduced in Chapter 3. In a workgroup, these polices are very influential; in a domain, they are not.

Local security policies are the lowest in the hierarchy of security. In a domain, security settings are created from a list of security policies in the following order (from lowest precedence to highest):

♦ *Local security policy*—The policy configured for the local computer

♦ *Site policy*—The policy created for the local network or subnet

♦ *Domain policy*—The policy created for the entire domain

♦ *Organizational unit policy*—The policy created for the organizational unit that holds the domain

If conflicts arise, the highest security policy that exists is used. A group policy almost always is created for the domain. In the next section, you'll learn about these policies and how they affect you.

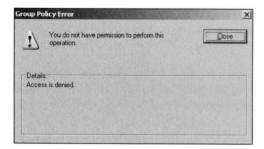

Figure 11.1
Permission to create a local security policy is denied.

Group Policies in a Domain

Because you are a member of a domain, your work environment is no doubt influenced by a domain group policy. Created by domain administrators, domain group policies are used to manage the users' desktop environment, including which programs users can access, what the Start menu looks like, and sometimes even what screensaver or wallpaper is used. These group policies don't just apply to users, though; they also apply to domain controllers and other servers on the network.

Group policies are most often configured to create a more secure and more easily managed environment than would exist without such a policy. For instance, when users save their work in their My Documents folders, that data can be redirected to a corresponding My Documents folder on a network server. With this achieved, the administrator can back up all users' data with one fell swoop; he or she just uses a backup utility that copies their files.

An administrator can also use group policies to run logon or logoff scripts. These scripts are used for a multitude of administrative tasks, such as running virus programs or informing users of a specific event in the future. Scripts can be run easily and quickly from the domain controller, and users will receive these updates as they log on or off during the workweek. An administrator can also manage applications by publishing, assigning, updating, or re-pairing applications that users need through the Software Installation utilities. These can be used to install service packs, install new applications, or install any non-Microsoft pro-grams that are needed.

To determine which policies have been applied to your computer:

1. Choose Start | Help And Support.

2. Under Pick A Task, choose Use Tools To View Your Computer Information And Diag-nose Problems.

3. From Tools, choose Advanced System Information.

4. From Advanced System Information, choose View Policy Information.

Windows XP and the Domain

When Windows XP Professional is part of a domain, logging on is a little different, permis-sions are generally more restrictive, and even saving files can be different from the way it's done in workgroups. In some instances, if you are the administrator of your computer, you might even switch from a workgroup to a domain when necessary. In this section, you'll learn how to configure your computer to be part of a domain when it was in a workgroup previously, how logon procedures work, how to view network resources in the new do-main, and how to recover your password if it's lost. You'll also learn how removable and remote storage play a part in the domain and why Internet connection sharing doesn't work in a domain.

Switching from a Workgroup to a Domain

Administrators whose computers are configured as part of a workgroup can change their computers' membership to join a domain. Even if you are the administrator of your computer, you'll need an administrator's name and password in the new domain you are joining. In the following example, the computer is currently a member of the OFFICE workgroup, and its membership will be changed to the BALLEW domain. A computer cannot be a member of both a workgroup and a domain at the same time.

To switch a computer's membership from a workgroup to a domain:

1. Log on as an administrator.

2. Right-click My Computer, and choose Properties.

3. Select the Computer Name tab.

4. Choose the Change button to open the Computer Name Changes dialog box.

5. In the Member Of box, select the Domain option, and type the name of the domain to join. See Figure 11.2, and notice that the workgroup name OFFICE is grayed out. Choose OK.

6. In the resulting dialog box, type the username and password of someone who has permission to join this domain. See Figure 11.3. Choose OK.

7. After Windows checks the username and password, an information box appears that says "Welcome to the _____ domain." Choose OK three times, and restart the computer.

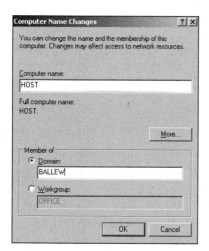

Figure 11.2
Switching a computer's membership from a workgroup to a domain.

Figure 11.3
Administrator's name and password.

Logon Procedures

After the computer becomes a member of the domain, the logon screen has an extra choice. You can choose to log onto the computer and not log onto the domain, or you can choose to log onto the domain through the network. If you log onto the domain, you are subject to all rules and regulations in the domain. If you log onto the local computer only, the local security settings apply.

After logging onto the domain, you receive the desktop of a new machine—the desktop that is required by group policies. The desktop does not look like the desktop you receive when logging onto the computer only. Figure 11.4 shows how group policies can be set up

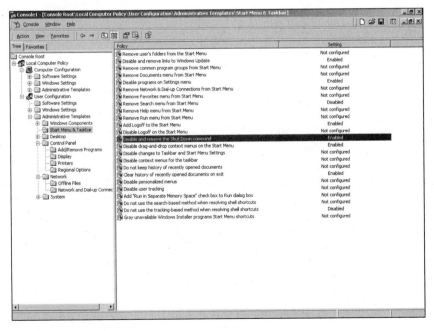

Figure 11.4
Group policy restrictions.

(by an administrator) from a domain controller on the network. Notice all of the choices available just for configuring the Start menu and the taskbar.

As you can tell, multiple restrictions can be placed on users who log onto the network. In this example, users cannot use Windows Update, the Settings menu, or the Shut Down command, among a variety of other restrictions. Other settings can be configured for the desktop, the Control Panel, the network, and more. Thus, when users log onto the network and receive these security settings, it is obvious why users receive a different desktop and different permissions than they would if they were members of a workgroup.

Viewing Network Resources

This section is for all users of the network domain, not just administrators. Administrators can access just about anything they want, and users are much more restricted. For the following examples, the user is a member of a domain. Depending on the user's permissions and group membership, the user may or may not be able to perform the tasks described here.

In a domain, network resources are made available by a domain controller and Active Directory (in Windows 2000 and XP Server editions). Active Directory is a database that maintains a list of all resources on the network, including users, computers, printers, scanners, files, folders, and shares. Users can access what's listed in Active Directory through My Network Places or by choosing Start | Search. In the My Network Places window, the Network Tasks section has three options: Add A Network Place, View Network Connections, and Search Active Directory. (Adding a network place is covered in the section "Sharing Documents and Resources.")

To simply view resources on the network, you can use any of four distinct methods. You can use Active Directory from My Network Places, use View Network Connections from My Network Places, use the Search Companion from the Start menu, or use the Computer Management console. This last method is much more restricted than the others.

Active Directory and My Network Places

To use Active Directory in My Network Places, open My Network Places and choose Search Active Directory from the Network Tasks section. To use this method to access files and folders on other computers, you must have the appropriate permissions. Once Active Directory has been selected, the Find Users, Contacts, And Groups window will be opened, as shown in Figure 11.5.

Active Directory stores its information in groups, including the following, which are available in the Find drop-down list shown in Figure 11.5:

♦ Users, Contacts, And Groups

♦ Computers

♦ Printers

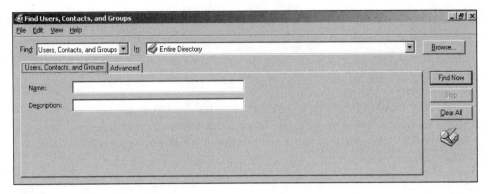

Figure 11.5
Searching Active Directory.

♦ Shared Folders

♦ Organizational Units

You can also use a custom search, using criteria from each of these objects.

To locate a particular object, select the type of object you want to search for from the drop-down list, and choose Find Now. If the network is large, you'll also want to type in other search criteria. For each of the objects just listed, you can use the following criteria to limit the search:

♦ *Users, Contacts, And Groups*—Name and/or description

♦ *Computers*—Name, owner, and/or the role of the computer (workstation, server, domain controller, or any)

♦ *Printers*—Name, location, and/or model

♦ *Shared Folders*—Name and/or keywords

♦ *Organizational Units*—Name

In addition to, or instead of, typing in criteria, you can select a different domain if more than one domain exists. This is done through the In drop-down list, also shown in Figure 11.5.

To use My Network Places and Search Active Directory:

1. Open My Network Places.

2. From Network Tasks, choose Search Active Directory.

3. From the Find drop-down list in the Find Users, Contacts, And Groups window, select the type of object you want to find.

4. From the In drop-down list, select the domain, or leave the default selection to search the entire directory.

5. Type any information you know about the object, such as its name, description, or keywords.

6. Choose Find Now.

The Find Users, Contacts, And Groups window also has an Advanced tab for doing advanced searches. Using this tab, you can use the Field button to add criteria that match the object you want to find. These criteria can include information about the location, model number, name, comment, whether a printer supports collating or stapling, and so on.

Figure 11.6 shows an Active Directory search for the computers on the network. Notice that no criteria were specified and that the role of the computers searched for is listed as Workstations And Servers.

Note

Network settings might prevent you from performing this task or other tasks described in this section.

View Network Connections and My Network Places

To view all of the connections from your computer, choose View Network Connections from Network Tasks in My Network Places. Several types of network connections can be configured, as described in previous chapters. There might be dial-up connections for remote servers, incoming connections from other users, LAN connections for the local intranet, and high-speed Internet connections that pass through the network.

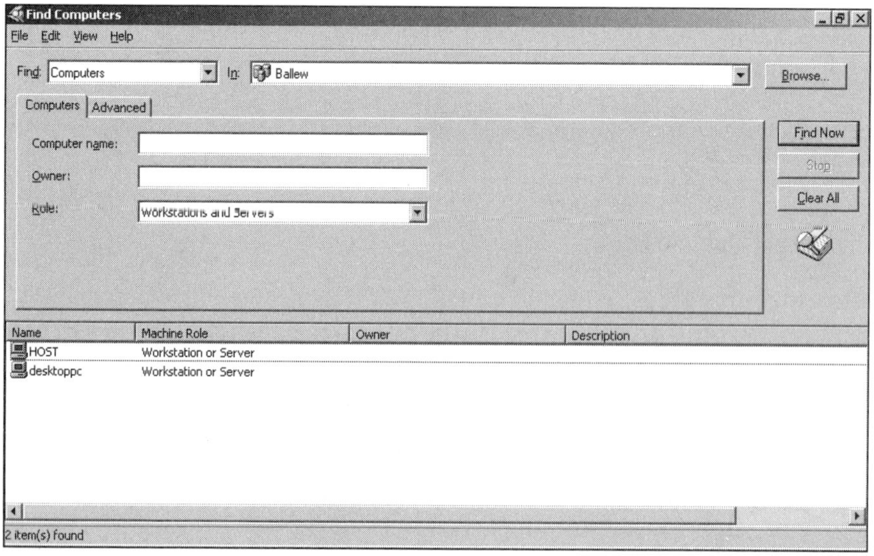

Figure 11.6
Finding computers.

To view information about any of these connections, right-click the connection and choose Properties.

The Search Companion from the Start Menu

You open the Search Companion by choosing a command from the Start | Search flyout menu. The Search Companion makes it easy to locate files, folders, printers, people, and computers on the network, as well as information located on the Internet. When searching for files and folders, you can search by options such as size, date, or location, and when searching for a printer, you can search by listing the printer's name or location. Many other options are available when you're using the Search Companion, but for now, let's just focus on finding resources on the domain. I prefer using the Search Companion to using My Network Places and finding files by using Active Directory. The Search Companion can be personalized, and it can be used to locate any resource in a user-friendly manner with a nice graphical user interface.

The Start | Search menu provides the following options:

◆ For Files Or Folders

◆ On the Internet

◆ Find Printers

◆ For People

◆ Using Microsoft Outlook (or a similar program, depending on the programs installed)

If you choose For Files Or Folders from the Search flyout menu, the Search Companion also offers the other options, so this choice is a good one to use as an example. Figure 11.7 shows the Search Companion. Notice the options available on the left.

Note

If you don't see this window as shown in Figure 11.7, choose View|Explorer Bar|Search.

To use the Search Companion to locate a resource:

1. Choose Start | Search | For Files And Folders if you haven't already done so.

2. From the What Do You Want To Search For options, select All Files And Folders. If you don't see the Search Companion window, as shown in Figure 11.7, see the note accompanying Figure 11.7.

3. In the text boxes provided, type either all or part of the file name, a word or phase in the file, or both.

4. In the Look In drop-down list, select the local hard drive (or whichever drive you want to search). You can also choose to browse to the resource. See Figure 11.8.

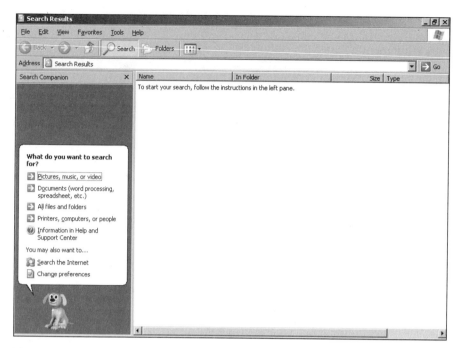

Figure 11.7
The Search Companion.

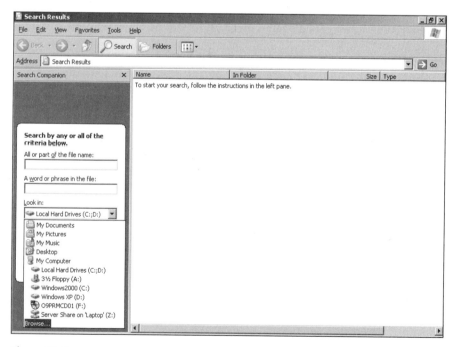

Figure 11.8
The Look In drop-down list.

5. After the search is complete, select one of the following options: Yes, Finished Searching; Look In More Locations; Start A New Search; or Back. For instructional purposes, choose Start A New Search.

6. In the What Do You Want To Search For pane, choose Printers, Computers, or People.

7. Select either A Printer On The Network, A Computer On The Network, or People In Your Address Book. Depending on the choice, you'll either type a name for the resource or simply choose Find Now or Search. For this example, choose to search for a computer.

8. Highlight a computer, and choose Search This Computer For Files. As the Search Companion starts again, repeat Steps 1 through 6. If you are an administrator, you'll be amazed at how many files there are. If you are a user, only specific files will be shown.

Personalizing the Search Companion

There are several ways to personalize the Search Companion. Listed next are the preferences that can be changed and descriptions of how each can be changed:

◆ *Without An Animated Screen Character*—By default, an animated character is shown at the bottom of the Search Companion window. This character can be disabled. The questions will still be the same, though, and nothing else related to the Search Companion will change.

◆ *With A Different Character*—Several characters are available, including a miniature computer robot, a red smiley face, Einstein, a globe, Merlin the magician, and a cat.

◆ *With Indexing Service (For Faster Searches)*—When the Indexing Service is enabled, the files on your computer are indexed so that you can perform faster searches in the future.

◆ *Change Files And Folders Search Behavior*—The standard behavior, selected by default, is what has been described previously; it's a step-by-step procedure for locating files. An advanced option is available and includes options to enter search criteria manually.

◆ *Change Internet Search Behavior*—The default behavior provides suggestions and automatically sends you to other search engines. The Classic Internet behavior allows you to select the default search engine.

◆ *Don't Show Balloon Tips/Show Balloon Tips*—Use this option to turn on or off balloon tips while searching.

◆ *Turn AutoComplete Off/On*—Use this option to disable or enable AutoComplete, a feature that finishes words as you are typing them when you're searching for objects that the Search Companion knows about.

To change preferences for the Search Companion:

1. Choose Start | Search | For Files And Folders.

2. Choose Change Preferences.

3. From the How Do You Want To Use Search Companion options, select the preference you want to change.

Using the Computer Management Console

Administrators have the most access to Computer Management console functions and can use the console to see shared folders, sessions in progress, and a list of open files. Members of the Users group cannot do these things. However, both administrators and users can access the Local Users And Groups part of the Computer Management console to view the users and groups on the local computer.

As a user, you can access the console and view members, but you cannot add, remove, or modify any user settings. In addition, you cannot change password properties or any other security settings. From the Groups folder, you can view who is a member of what group, but again, you cannot add, delete, or otherwise modify a group or its membership. Even though you cannot change the user accounts or groups, viewing a list of group members can sometimes be useful.

Removable Storage

Removable storage is the term used for storage media that are not permanently installed, such as CD changers, hardware libraries containing jukeboxes, and smaller media such as tape drives and Zip drives. The Removable Storage service is used with Microsoft Backup or other backup programs and allows you to manage the hardware from a single location. Remote Storage is a data management service used to move data that is not used often from local storage to remote storage. When the data is needed again, it is retrieved. This service allows the computer to perform better in various ways. In this section, I'll introduce removable storage.

To see what removable storage is available on your computer, open My Computer and view Devices With Removable Storage. The items you see here can be local or non-local. Look at Figure 11.9. The computer shown is logged onto a domain. The Devices With Removable Storage section shows two devices: a floppy drive and a CD-RW drive. The Network Drives section shows a mapped network drive to E On Desktoppc, which is a removable Zip drive. The Server Share On Laptop is another removable media device. In a domain, a network administrator can configure removable storage that can be accessed by all users.

If you are an administrator, do the following to add users allowed to have access to the Removable Storage service:

1. Open the Control Panel.

2. Open Administrative Tools.

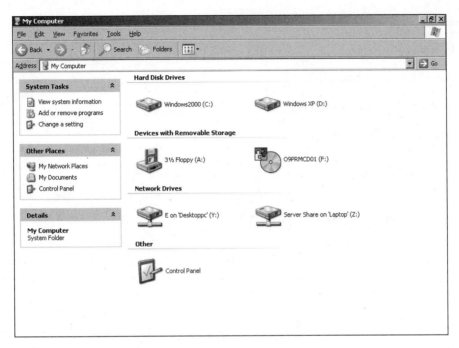

Figure 11.9
Removable storage.

3. Open the Computer Management console.

4. Expand Removable Storage.

5. Right-click the removable storage medium to which you want to allow access, and choose Properties.

6. On the Security tab, choose Add.

7. In the Name box in the Select Users, Computers, Or Groups dialog box, choose the users and groups to add. Choose OK.

Removable media are accessed the same way that any network resource is. This can be through any of the aforementioned processes, or the user can map a network drive to the resource. Mapping a network drive will be covered shortly.

Password-Reset Disks

Password-reset disks were also discussed in Chapter 10, but the information is worth repeating here. To avoid the possibility that you will forget your password and either get locked out of your account or need to have an administrator create another password, you can create a password-reset disk. This disk can be used to change the password on your computer even though you don't know the password to log on.

To create a password-reset disk in a domain:

1. After logging on, press Ctrl+Alt+Del to open the Windows Security dialog box.

2. Choose Change Password.

3. Choose Backup to start the Forgotten Password Wizard.

4. Choose Next. Place a blank floppy disk in drive A:.

5. Type the current password on the next page of the wizard, and wait for the disk to be created. Choose Finish.

Internet Connection Sharing

You might have noticed that Internet connection sharing (ICS) isn't used in your domain or that if ICS is configured, it either doesn't work properly or causes interruptions in network communication. This occurs because ICS configures the network's TCP/IP addresses to suit its own needs. You can think of a TCP/IP address as a phone number; when a computer wants to talk to another computer, it uses that number. In a domain, TCP/IP addresses are required, and they allow communications to occur between computers. When ICS is used in a domain, address conflicts occur because ICS changes the addresses on the client computers.

When ICS is enabled, the following changes take place:

♦ The host computer is given the address 192.168.0.1.

♦ The DHCP allocator is started, and it gives clients on the network addresses in the range of 192.168.0.x.y.

♦ The DNS proxy is enabled.

The problem with these changes taking place is that in a domain, either a DHCP server exists that gives clients their IP addresses, or each address on every client computer is manually input. Either way, every client has an individual IP address that it uses to communicate with others on the network. If these numbers are changed, problems occur. Of course, it's a little more complicated than that, but for our purposes here, suffice it to say that in a domain, ICS cannot be used.

Sharing Documents and Resources

You can share your own documents on the domain, connect to shared folders and resources on the domain, and map a network drive to a resource by using My Network Places. These tasks are done differently in a domain than in a workgroup because domains do not have built-in folders named Shared Folders, Shared Pictures, or Shared Music. In this section, you'll learn how to use My Network Places and the folder itself to share resources.

Before you can share your information with others, though, you'll need to know where on the network you are allowed to place shared documents. The administrator of the domain will configure this for you on the network server.

Sharing a Folder by Using Web Publishing

The Web Publishing Wizard is available to help you make your files and folders available to others on your network. This wizard walks you through the steps required. After an administrator has created a shared folder on the network, you can share your files or folders by doing the following:

1. Create a folder on your local computer, and place the documents in it that you want to share.

2. Locate the folder by browsing to it in Windows Explorer, from the desktop, or by other means. The easiest way to work with this if you are a first-timer is to create a shortcut to it on the desktop.

3. Open the folder. From the File And Folder Tasks section, choose Publish This Folder To The Web. Choose Next to start the Web Publishing Wizard. See Figure 11.10.

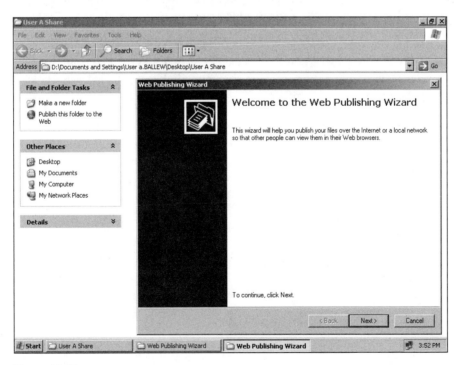

Figure 11.10
The Web Publishing Wizard.

4. On the Change Your File Selection page, check the boxes next to all of the files that you want to share with others. Choose Next.

5. If you receive the error message "No available services. The wizard could not find any service providers in your area, please try again later," double-click that error message to continue.

6. On the Specify A Location page, choose the Browse button to specify where the shared file should be stored, or type the name of the folder in the form "\\computer name\share name". (You'll need to obtain this information from your administrator.) Choose OK and Next to continue.

7. Type a share name for this network place.

8. Choose Next to copy the files to the shared folder.

Sharing a Folder by Using My Network Places

Another way to share a folder or file is to use My Network Places. As with the previous example, you must know the name of the network folder that you can use to house your shared files. Then you can create a network place in the My Network Places folder and drag and drop the files and folders you want to add to this share.

In the following example, the folder User A's Share has been created on the desktop and contains two files. The folder Management Share—where User A can share his files and folders—is located on one of the servers on the network. Figure 11.11 shows the layout of User A's computer and the network server.

To create a shortcut in My Network Places on User A's computer (your computer) to the shared folder on the network server (Management Share):

1. While logged onto the domain, open My Network Places.

2. Choose Add A Network Place, and start the wizard.

3. Choose Next and then the Browse button.

4. On the Browse For Folder page, browse to the folder, or type the name of the folder in the form "\\computer name\share name".

5. Highlight the folder, and choose OK.

6. Choose Next, and type a name for the new network place.

7. Continue, and choose Finish.

The new share—in this case, it's called Management Share—now has a shortcut to it in My Network Places. To place any files or folders in that folder so other users can access it, simply drag those files or folders to this location. See Figure 11.12.

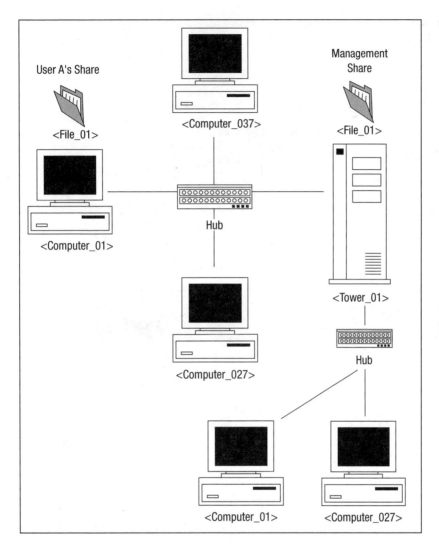

Figure 11.11
A network share.

Now, any user who has access to the share (Management Share) on the server can also access User A's Share, which has been moved to that folder.

Sharing Is Easier for Administrators

To create a shared folder by using My Network Places while logged on as a member of the Administrators group:

1. Create a folder on your local computer, and place the documents in it that you want to share.

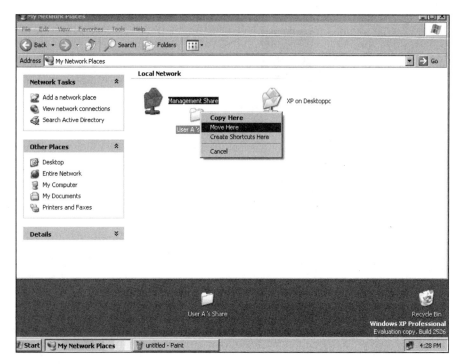

Figure 11.12
A new folder in My Network Places.

2. Locate the folder by browsing to it in Windows Explorer, from the desktop, or by other means.

3. Right-click the folder, and choose Sharing And Security.

4. Select Share This Folder, and type a share name.

5. From the Security tab, add (or delete) users and groups who should (or should not) access this folder from the network.

6. Choose OK.

Any network user who has permissions to access this folder can do so through My Network Places.

Connecting to a Shared Folder

After folders are shared and stored on the network server, any user on the network who has the appropriate permissions to access the shared folder can do so. Just as there were several ways to share a folder on the network, there are several ways to connect to a shared folder. This section discusses a few of these ways.

Automatic Searches

From Folder Options in the Control Panel, you can configure the computer to automatically search for shared files and folders on the network. When this is done, all of the shared folders on the network are automatically listed in My Network Places. In a large network with thousands of shared folders, this would not be effective. However, in a smaller network, it can be quite helpful.

To configure your computer to automatically place links to all shared folders on the network in the My Network Places folder:

1. Open the Control Panel.

2. Choose Tools | Folder Options.

3. On the View tab, check the checkbox Automatically Search For Network Folders And Printers.

Using My Network Places

You can add shared folders by using Add A Network Place in My Network Places. This is done similarly to adding a network place when you're in a workgroup.

To add shared folders by using My Network Places:

1. Open My Network Places.

2. From Network Tasks, select Add A Network Place.

3. Use the Add Network Place Wizard to browse to the shared folder, or type the name of the folder in the form "\\computer name\share name".

4. Highlight the folder to add, and choose OK. Complete the wizard.

Using the Search Companion

You can also use the Search Companion to connect to shared folders on the network. The Search Companion has been explained already, but Figure 11.13 shows what can happen when you're using the Search Companion (or any other searching tool) to locate a shared folder on another computer when you do not have the appropriate resources to retrieve files from the computer.

After obtaining a username and password to access this computer and choosing OK, you can drag the share to My Network Places.

To locate and connect to a shared folder by using the Search Companion and to create an icon for the folder in My Network Places:

1. Log on as a user or power user.

2. Open the Search Companion by choosing Start | Search | For Files Or Folders.

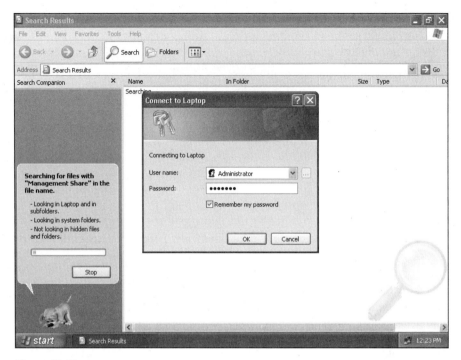

Figure 11.13
Connecting to a resource by using the Search Companion.

3. Choose All Files And Folders.

4. In the Look In drop-down list, choose Browse, and highlight My Network Places.

5. In the Browse For Folder window, browse to the shared folder. If the folder is in the window, simply highlight that folder and choose OK. The shared folder will automatically be shown in the Search window. If this is the case, you are finished.

   If the folder is not in that window, expand the Entire Network tree to locate it, and continue.

6. In the Search criteria windows, insert as much information as possible, and choose Search. You can browse to the computer name and type the file name, or set advanced search criteria, such as when the file or folder was last modified or what size it is. Choose Search when finished. Figure 11.14 shows a generic search from My Network Places with no file name, search word or phrase, or advanced options specified.

7. Choose the file, folder, or resource to connect to, and double-click it. If you have permission to access the resource, it will be opened for you automatically. If you do not have permission, you'll receive an access-denied message or a message that the file cannot be opened.

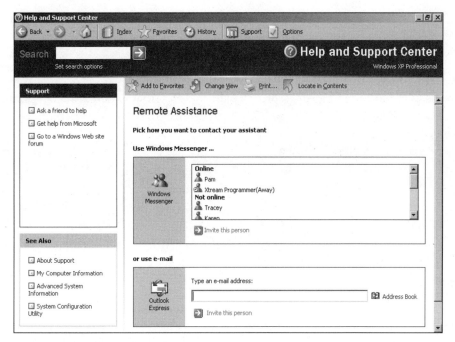

Figure 11.14
Shared files.

8. Copy the file to your My Network Places folder by dragging the file from this list to the My Network Places icon on the desktop.

Using Active Directory

Connecting to shared folders by using Active Directory is useful if you have the appropriate permission to access the folder on another computer and from the shared folder. To use Active Directory in this case, do the following:

1. Open My Network Places.

2. From Network Tasks, choose Search Active Directory.

3. In the Find Users, Contacts, And Groups window, select Shared Folders.

4. From the In drop-down list, select the domain, or leave the default to search the entire directory.

5. Type any information you know about the object, such as its name, description, or keywords.

6. Choose Find Now.

7. Double-click the folder to open it.

8. Copy the file to your My Network Places folder by dragging the file from this list to the My Network Places icon on the desktop.

Connecting to Other Shared Resources

Of course, there are other shared resources besides folders. Other resources include printers, scanners, and digital cameras. The easiest way to connect to these network resources in a domain is through Active Directory, as described earlier. You can also access them by choosing Start | Search | For Printers And Faxes or by opening the Search Companion and choosing Printers, Computers, Or People. This is achieved the same way as described in the previous sections; you can use My Network Places, Active Directory, or the Search Companion.

Mapping a Network Drive

As with a workgroup, members of a domain can map a network drive to a specific resource, computer, file, or folder so that the resource acts and looks like an additional drive in My Computer.

When My Computer is first used after Windows XP Professional is installed, there are usually only two sections: Hard Disk Drives and Devices With Removable Storage. By mapping a network drive to a resource, you can create a new section, entitled Network Drives.

To create a network drive:

1. Open the Control Panel.

2. Choose Tools | Map Network Drive.

3. On the Map Network Drive page, select a drive letter to represent the new network drive you are creating.

4. Choose the Browse button to locate the resource.

5. Choose Finish.

A network-drive icon and a shortcut to the resource will be created in My Computer. This will happen even if you do not have access to the resource itself. To delete the drive, simply right-click it and choose Disconnect.

Remote Assistance

Remote Assistance is a new feature from Microsoft that allows you to ask someone else who is running Windows XP to help you solve a problem on your computer. Remote Assistance can be used to chat with others, let others view your computer screen, and even let others work on your computer from their desktops if you allow it.

In this section, I'll introduce Remote Assistance, the requirements for it, and ways to ask for help or give help to others. It's also important that you have defenses for maintaining password security and for preventing others from taking control of your computer if that is not what you want.

Requirements

For Remote Assistance to be used, both of the computers involved (the one involved in asking for help and the one involved in giving help) need to be running a compatible operating system. At this time, the only compatible operating system is Windows XP. In addition to this requirement, both computers also need to be using MSN Messenger or a compatible email account such as Microsoft Outlook or Outlook Express.

Remote Assistance takes place over the Internet, so both computers involved must be connected. This is true even if both are on the corporate intranet, and if this is the case, network firewalls might prevent Remote Assistance from being used. Microsoft has made giving and receiving remote assistance as secure as possible by encrypting all sessions and making them password-protected.

Using Remote Assistance to Ask for Help

The easiest way to get started with using Remote Assistance is to get together with a friend who also runs Windows XP Professional and ask him or her for assistance through the Help and Support Center of your computer.

To start Remote Assistance and ask an assistant to help you with a problem on your computer:

1. Choose Start | Help And Support.

2. From the Help and Support Center, choose Ask For Assistance and Invite A Friend To Connect To Your Computer With Remote Assistance. You can also launch Remote Assistance by clicking the Support icon on the toolbar and choosing Ask A Friend To Help.

3. When Remote Assistance starts, you must either sign into MSN Messenger or type your email address. Note that you must be using a MAPI-compliant email program such as Outlook or Outlook Express.

4. Choose the person whom you want to help you. This can be a person in your list of online contacts in MSN Messenger, or you can type an email address for a person who is not online with MSN Messenger. Figure 11.15 shows the options for a user who asked for assistance using an MSN Messenger account.

5. Choose Invite This Person.

6. In the next screen, either you will see the page Remote Assistance–Email An Invitation, or MSN Messenger will attempt to contact the person by using the messenger service. If the contact is made through Messenger and the person is available, the connection will be made as soon as the receiving party accepts. If this is the case, skip to Step 11.

   If the contact is made through email, you'll need to fill out some contact information.

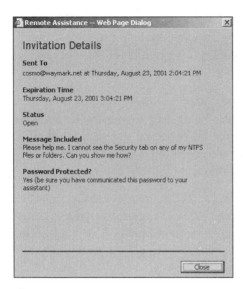

Figure 11.15
Remote Assistance.

7. On the Remote Assistance–E-mail An Invitation page, type your name in the From box, and type a message in the Message box. Choose Continue.

8. Next, set an expiration date for the invitation to lessen the chance that someone other than the invitee can access your computer. The default is one hour.

9. On the same page, configure a password, and leave the box checked that requires the recipient to use the password when connecting. Choose Send Invitation.

10. After the invitation has been sent, the Remote Assistance screen will inform you of this. From here, you can send another invitation or view the invitation status.

11. On the page View Or Change Your Invitation, select the email address of the person you chose, and click the Details button. Figure 11.16 shows an example of an invitation details page.

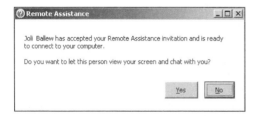

Figure 11.16
Remote Assistance details.

12. After the recipient of the invitation accepts and is connected, you will be asked if you want to let this person connect to the computer and contact you. Choose Yes to accept. See Figure 11.17.

Using Remote Assistance to Give Help

After you've been asked for assistance through email or MSN Messenger, you must decide to accept the invitation before continuing. Microsoft warns that you should accept invitations only from people you know and that you should read the precautions at **http://Windows.Microsoft.com/RemoteAssistance/RA.asp** before accepting any invitation.

From an Email Invitation

When the email program announces that someone is trying to send you an invitation to assist him or her by using Remote Assistance, a message box will appear to ask if you want the message to be sent. Choose Send to accept the email message.

With that out of the way, do the following:

1. Open the email message and the attachment.

2. Open the file attached to the email message. Make sure the file is of the type MsRCincident. If prompted to open or save it, choose to open it.

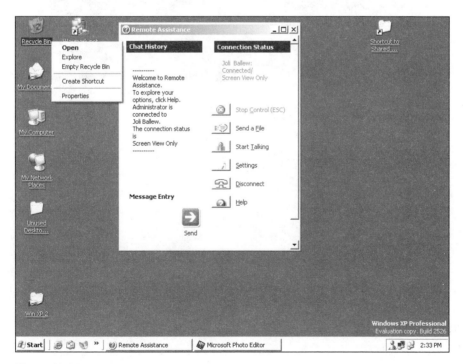

Figure 11.17
Remote Assistance invitation accepted.

3. If a password is required, obtain the password from the sender. Type the password, and choose Yes to accept the invitation.

4. Once connected to the user's computer, you will need to log on. You will not be asked for another password.

From an MSN Messenger Invitation

After you've been contacted to give assistance through MSN Messenger:

1. After receiving the message from MSN Messenger, choose Accept to accept the invitation.

2. Once connected, proceed to the next section, "Using Remote Assistance After Being Connected."

Using Remote Assistance After Being Connected

Once the connection has been made using Remote Assistance, the assistant on the remote computer can see anything the end user does on his or her computer. To understand this concept, look at Figures 11.18 and 11.19. Figure 11.18 is the view from the end user's computer (the one who asked for help), and Figure 11.19 is the view from the assistant's computer (the one who will give help). In these examples, the end user is right-clicking the Recycle Bin.

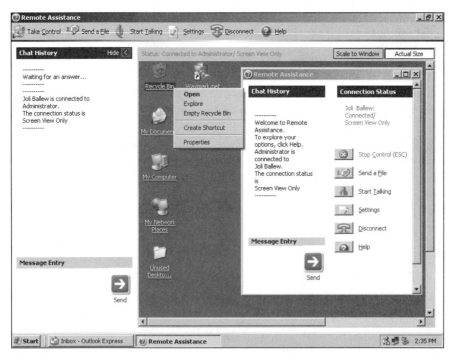

Figure 11.18
End user's computer screen.

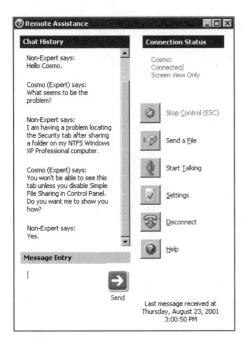

Figure 11.19
Assistant's computer screen.

Notice that the assistant can see this right-clicking, the end user's choices, and everything else on the end user's computer screen.

There are lots of options when you're using Remote Assistance: Send A File, Start Talking, Settings, Disconnect, and Help. You can also send and receive instant messages by using the Message Entry area and Chat History. In the following sections, many of these will be detailed.

Send and Receive Messages

If you've ever used MSN Messenger, then you are familiar with instant messaging. ICQ, Yahoo! Messenger, AOL Instant Messenger (AIM), and PeopleLink Instant Messaging are also instant messaging programs. Sending and receiving messages by using Remote Assistance works exactly like these programs. Figure 11.20 shows two people connected and using the Message Entry box to communicate. Notice that the conversation is also held in the Chat History area of this window.

To use the chat feature, simply type what you'd like to say in the Message Entry area of the Remote Assistance screen. Choose Send when finished. The person you are connected to will receive this message and will respond in the same manner. In the conversation shown in Figure 11.19, notice that the Expert is planning to "show" the Non-Expert how to solve his computer problem. The Expert can take control of the Non-Expert's computer and

Figure 11.20
Communicating with an assistant.

physically manipulate it from his remote computer by using his own mouse and keyboard. This will be detailed later, in the "Remote Control" section.

Send a File
The end user, or Non-Expert can send the assistant, or Expert, a file if necessary. To send a file, choose the Send A File button (shown in previous figures). In the resulting window, choose Browse. After locating the folder, choose the Send button. The recipient then receives a message that includes the name of the file and asks if the recipient wants to accept it.

Start Talking
When either user wants to initiate spoken conversation, he or she chooses the Start Talking button. If both computers have the required hardware and software, and if they are configured for use, conversation can be started.

Settings
To configure the computer to use the highest quality possible for sending and receiving audio and video data, choose the Settings button and make the appropriate changes. An Audio Tuning Wizard is available to assist you with setting up your audio hardware.

Disconnect
Use the Disconnect button to end the session and disconnect from the other person's computer.

Remote Control

Remote Control is a feature of Remote Assistance that allows an Expert user to assist a Non-Expert user by taking control of his computer. When this happens, the Expert can use his own mouse and keyboard to use the Non-Expert's computer remotely. In a corporate environment, Remote Control can save time and money by saving an administrator a trip to the user's computer. In the example shown in Figure 11.19, the Expert user offers to show the Non-Expert how to disable simple file sharing.

To do this, all an Expert has to do is choose Take Control from his computer. Take Control is not available from the end user's computer. To see the Expert's computer again, look at Figure 11.19. After the Expert chooses the Take Control button, the end user receives a message stating: "<Expert name> would like to share control of your computer to help solve the problem. Do you wish to let <Expert name> share control of your computer?" The end user can choose Yes or No.

If the end user chooses Yes, the Expert can then click anywhere on his computer's screen to access the remote computer. At this point, whatever the Expert does within the end user's window is applied not to the Expert's computer but to the end user's. In this manner, the Expert can show the user how to do a task, fix a problem, or search for files or folders. The Expert has full control of the computer. The Expert can end his remote-control session by pressing the Escape key.

The Importance of Password Security

When using Remote Assistance with another user whom you will invite via email, you can check the box that requires the assistant to use a password to connect. This is not an option when an assistant is chosen from the MSN Messenger list of contacts. Microsoft assumes that the people who are your contacts are trusted friends and coworkers.

It is important to require a password when you're sending an invitation by email. Suppose that the recipient of the email message isn't the one who opens the email, or suppose that the message has been intercepted and is in the hands of another user. You could be giving control of your computer to a complete stranger. It is also important that you do *not* type the password in the body of the email message. Doing so defeats the purpose of requiring one. When sending an invitation via email, require a password, and communicate this password to your would-be assistant in another manner. This can be through a phone call or by having a previously agreed upon password. Whatever the case, requiring a password is strongly recommended.

Preventing Remote Control

You can prevent others from gaining remote control of your computer. To do this, either choose No when the user asks for permission while in a Remote Assistance session, or use other means. If more than one person uses the computer, you might choose to make this a permanent configuration.

To make sure that remote control is never given on your computer:

1. Open the Control Panel.

2. Open System.

3. In the System Properties dialog box, select the Remote tab.

4. Choose the Advanced button.

5. Clear the checkbox Allow This Computer To Be Controlled Remotely.

   In this dialog box, you can also set how long an invitation can be active (open). The default is 30 days. To change this setting, continue with Step 6.

6. Under Invitations, set the maximum amount of time that invitations can remain open.

Remote Desktop

Remote Desktop is like the old Terminal Services in previous Microsoft operating systems. Remote Desktop can be used to access a work computer from home and to connect to an office computer from another office or branch location on the network. Remote Desktop can even be used with multiple users on a single computer.

Remote Desktop works when you leave your office computer turned on and logged on and then connect to it from another computer. This connection allows you to access anything on the office computer—including all of the computer's files, folders, programs, and even network resources—from anywhere. While connected using Remote Desktop, the office computer is automatically locked and can be accessed only by you upon your return to the office. To unlock the computer, you press Ctrl+Alt+Del and type your password. While connected using Remote Desktop, it seems like you are actually sitting at the office computer.

Remote Desktop vs. Remote Assistance

Remote Desktop is much different from Remote Assistance. Although the same technology is used—including using the Internet and controlling another computer—the reasons for using each feature differ. With Remote Desktop, you are accessing your own computer from a different location. With Remote Assistance, however, you are allowing a second person to be involved. An assistant is allowed to access your computer while you are sitting at it yourself. The assistant then can take control of your computer and perform tasks on it if you have given the assistant permission.

Requirements

Because Remote Desktop is a Windows XP feature, the computer that is the office computer (or the one to which you'll connect) must be running Windows XP Professional. This computer—the host—must also have a connection to either the Internet or a LAN. The remote connection can be made through either.

The connecting computer (the computer that is at home, or a laptop that is used on the road) must have the Remote Desktop Connection client software installed. This was called the Terminal Services Client in previous Microsoft operating systems. Installing the Remote Desktop Connection software will be detailed later in this section.

Finally, the second computer must have access to the first one through an Internet connection or a LAN. This can also be a VPN (virtual private network) connection for added security. The user of the connecting computer must have appropriate permissions from the office computer and the network administrator to connect through a LAN. Appropriate permissions must also be configured when you're connecting through the Internet.

Configuring the Office (Host) Computer

Before getting started with Remote Desktop, verify that others can access the computer by using Remote Desktop. To perform this test or to enable Remote Desktop:

1. Log onto the host computer as an administrator, and open the Control Panel.

2. Open System.

3. In the System Properties dialog box, select the Remote tab.

4. If it's not already checked, check the All Users To Connect Remotely To This Computer checkbox. Choose OK.

You must also verify that you have permission to access your own computer by using Remote Desktop. To do this, you must be the administrator of your computer, a member of the Administrators group, or a member of the Remote Desktop Users group on your computer or in your network. If you are not an administrator or a member of this group, ask your network administrator to place your account in the Remote Desktop Users group before continuing.

After you're armed with the required permissions, you must decide who can access your computer by using Remote Desktop. Perhaps the only person you want to access the computer is you. However, perhaps you have a different logon name for accessing remotely, or maybe you would like to add other users. Before continuing, decide to whom you want to give remote access.

To choose which users can access the computer by using Remote Desktop:

1. Log on as an administrator, a member of the Administrators group, or a member of the Remote Desktop Users group.

2. Open the Control Panel on the host computer.

3. Open System.

4. In the System Properties dialog box, select the Remote tab.

5. Click Select Remote Users.

6. Choose Add.

7. As described in previous chapters, select the user or users you want to add. Choose OK.

Note

Even if you remove the Administrators group and any listed administrators from this list, any member of the Administrators group can access your computer through Remote Desktop at any time. Remote Desktop can be disabled.

Installing Remote Desktop Connection on Other Computers

Any computer that will be used to connect to the host computer through Remote Desktop must have the Remote Desktop Connection client software installed. Because there are various versions of Windows, the procedures vary for enabling them to connect. The Remote Desktop Connection software is located on the Windows XP Professional CD, which is used to install this utility for almost any Microsoft operating system. Three types of Windows operating systems can be installed: 32-bit versions, which include Windows 9x, Windows NT 4, and Windows 2000; 16-bit versions, which include Windows for Workgroups; and computers running Windows NT 3.51.

Installing Remote Desktop Connection on 32-bit Systems

To enable a Windows 95, Windows 98, Windows NT 4, or Windows 2000 computer to connect to the host computer by using Remote Desktop, install the Remote Desktop Connection client software:

1. Log onto the connecting computer as an administrator.

2. Place the Windows XP Professional CD in the CD-ROM drive.

3. On the Welcome screen, choose Perform Additional Tasks.

4. Choose Set Up Remote Desktop Connection.

5. Choose Next to start the InstallShield Wizard. Accept the Licensing Agreement.

6. Type the customer information required.

7. Choose Install to begin the installation.

8. Choose Finish, then Exit.

Installing Remote Desktop Connection on 16-bit Systems

To enable a Windows for Workgroups computer to connect to the host computer by using Remote Desktop, install the Terminal Services Client software:

1. On a computer running either Windows 2000 Server or Windows XP Server, share the client setup folder:

    a. Using Windows Explorer, browse to *<drive>*\Windows\System32\Clients\Tsclient.

    b. Right-click the Tsclient folder, and choose Sharing.

    c. Share the folder, and accept the name Tsclient.

2. From the Windows for Workgroups computer, connect to the LAN where this server is connected, and log on as an administrator.

3. Connect to the shared folder Tsclient.

4. In the Tsclient\Win16 folder, open Setup.exe.

5. Follow the directions that appear on the screen.

Installing Remote Desktop Connection on Windows 3.51 Systems

To enable a Windows 3.51 computer to connect to the host computer by using Remote Desktop, install the Terminal Services Client software:

1. On a computer running either Windows 2000 Server or Windows XP Server, share the client setup folder:

    a. Using Windows Explorer, browse to *<drive>*\Windows\System32\Clients\Tsclient.

    b. Right-click the Tsclient folder, and choose Sharing.

    c. Share the folder, and accept the name Tsclient.

2. From the Windows 3.51 computer, connect to the LAN where this server is connected, and log on as an administrator.

3. Connect to the shared folder Tsclient.

4. In the \Win32\Acme351 folder, open Setup.exe.

5. Follow the directions that appear on the screen.

Configuring Remote Desktop

On any Windows XP computer, you can find the Remote Desktop utility by using the Search command. In most cases, the utility is located under Start | Programs | Accessories and in the Communications folder. You can create a shortcut on the desktop for faster access.

Several options can be set from the client computer. In Figure 11.20, the Remote Desktop Connection dialog-box tabs shown are on a Windows 2000 Professional computer, but the options and the look are the same as on a Windows XP Professional computer. You must choose the Options button to see the entire page as shown in this figure.

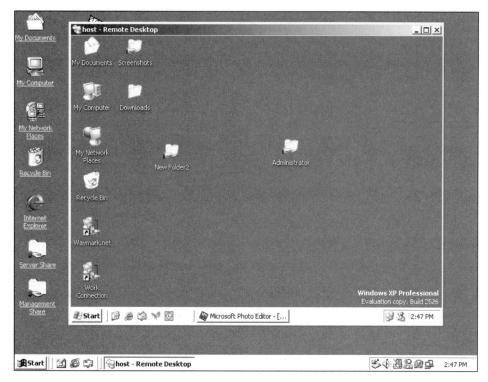

Figure 11.21
The Remote Desktop Connection dialog box.

The General Tab

On the General tab of the Remote Desktop Connection dialog box, you can type the name of the computer you want to connect to, your username, your password, and the domain name. (You can also select a computer from the Computer drop-down list.) In addition, once a connection has been made, you can save that connection configuration by choosing Save As, or you can open a previously saved configuration by using the Open button, as shown in Figure 11.21.

The Display Tab

The Display tab of the Remote Desktop Connection dialog box lets you configure the size of the remote desktop and the number of colors used; you can also choose whether to display the connection bar when in full-screen mode. Figure 11.22 shows an active connection. The connection has been configured from the Display tab so that the remote desktop does *not* appear in full-screen mode. The inside square is the host computer (office computer), and the background system is the laptop computer connecting to it. The user can work on both computers simultaneously and easily by using this configuration.

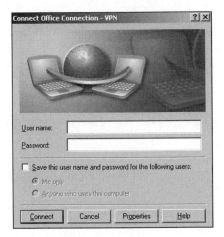

Figure 11.22
An active remote connection.

The Local Resources Tab

On the Local Resources tab of the Remote Desktop Connection dialog box, you can configure how sounds are to be managed and whether Windows key combinations such as Alt+Tab should be used. You can also specify what types of devices the connecting computer should have access to: disk drives, printers, and serial ports. Only the Printers option is chosen by default.

The Programs Tab

On the Programs tab of the Remote Desktop Connection dialog box, you can select a program that is to be run when the connection is made. You must enter the name of the program and the path to it, as well as configure the order in which those programs should run.

The Experience Tab

On the Experience tab of the Remote Desktop Connection dialog box, you must choose the speed of the connection. The following choices are available:

♦ Modem (28.8 Kbps)

♦ Modem (56 Kbps)

♦ Broadband (128 Kbps to 1.5 Mbps)

♦ LAN (10 Mbps Or Higher)

♦ Custom

You can also choose to allow or disallow the following:

♦ Desktop background

♦ Showing the window contents while dragging

- ◆ Menu and window animation
- ◆ Themes
- ◆ Bitmap caching

These options are often not needed, and they will slow down transmission times between the host and the connecting computer. If you're using a slow link between the two, consider disabling these items.

Connecting Through a LAN

To start a remote desktop session through a LAN:

1. Make sure the host computer is turned on and connected to a LAN.

2. Log off the host computer, and leave the Log On To Windows screen up. This will protect the computer from any unauthorized access while you are away from it.

3. On the connecting computer, open the Remote Desktop Connection. (Use a desktop shortcut, if you've made one, or choose Start | Programs | Accessories | Communications.)

4. Expand Options to show the full dialog box.

5. On the General tab, type the computer name or select it from the Computer drop-down list. Next, type a username and a password that give you permission to log onto the remote computer. Type the domain name (although on a LAN, this isn't always necessary.)

6. On the Display tab, choose a remote desktop size and the number of colors you want to use.

7. On the Local Resources tab, choose sound and keyboard settings.

8. On the Experience tab, choose LAN (10Mbps Or Higher).

9. Return to the General tab, and choose Save As.

10. Type a name for this connection, such as "Office Connection – LAN". Choose Save.

11. Choose Connect.

12. Log onto the remote desktop the same way you would log onto it if you were sitting at the host computer. Use your name and password.

You can now work on your computer as if you were actually sitting in front of it. See Figure 11.22. The computer at the office will not be accessible by any other user without a proper name and password. If someone logs onto your office computer, the session with the connecting computer will be terminated automatically.

Connecting through the Internet

To start a remote desktop session over the Internet:

1. Make sure the host computer is turned on and connected to the Internet.

2. If possible, log off of the host computer, and leave the Log On To Windows screen up. This will protect the computer from any unauthorized access while you are away from it. (You might not be able to log off of a standalone computer or a computer in a workgroup and still maintain an Internet connection.)

3. On the connecting computer, open the Remote Desktop Connection as described earlier.

4. Expand Options to show the full dialog box.

5. On the General tab, type the public IP address or the URL address of the computer. Next, type a username and a password that give you permission to log onto the remote computer. Type the domain name.

6. On the Display tab, choose a remote desktop size and the number of colors you want to use.

7. On the Local Resources tab, choose sound and keyboard settings.

8. On the Experience tab, choose the type of connection you have. Do *not* choose LAN (10 Mbps Or Higher).

9. Return to the General tab, and choose Save As.

10. Type a name for this connection, such as "Office Connection – Internet". Choose Save.

11. Choose Connect. If prompted with multiple Internet connections, choose one.

12. Log onto the remote desktop the same way you would log onto it if you were sitting at the host computer. Use your name and password.

You can now work on your computer as if you were actually sitting in front of it. See Figure 11.22. The computer at the office will not be accessible by any other user without a proper name and password. If someone logs onto your office computer, the session with the connecting computer will be terminated automatically.

Using Remote Desktop

After you've established a connection, using the remote desktop is pretty easy. The remote computer's desktop is shown in its own window, and you can perform tasks on the remote computer through this interface. (See Figure 11.22 earlier.) You can cut and paste items from the remote computer to the local one with almost any recent version of Windows. The computers must be able to use clipboard sharing for this to work properly, and cutting and pasting work the same way between computers as they do between documents. Just locate the data on the remote computer, right-click, and choose Copy. Locate a local file on the local computer, right-click, and choose Paste.

You can end a session in two ways. You can either disconnect from the session without ending it, or you can simply log off and end the session entirely.

To end a session without disconnecting from it:

1. In the Remote Desktop window, choose Start | Shut Down.

2. In the Shut Down Windows dialog box, choose Disconnect.

To end a session and completely disconnect:

1. In the Remote Desktop window, choose Start | Shut Down.

2. In the Shut Down Windows dialog box, choose Log Off *<username>*.

Disabling Remote Desktop

You can disable Remote Desktop on your computer and thus not allow anyone to access the computer remotely. You should do this if you do not plan ever to access your computer remotely or if you are in a highly secure environment. You can also prevent administrators from accessing the computer remotely even when they are not on the Remote Desktop Users list.

To disable Remote Desktop:

1. Log on as an administrator.

2. Open the Control Panel.

3. Open System.

4. In the System Properties dialog box, select the Remote tab.

5. Clear the checkbox Allow Users To Connect Remotely To Your Computer. Choose OK.

Troubleshooting Remote Desktop

The majority of problems that come about when you're using Remote Desktop are of two types: either the physical connection itself is not working or the Remote Desktop configuration (including permissions) is wrong. Other error messages can appear when the licensing for Terminal Services is invalid or when the license was not renewed or upgraded properly. Licensing problems occur on domains and are the responsibility of the network administrator. In this section, I'll detail the types of error messages you'll most likely receive as an end user.

Sessions End Unexpectedly

When sessions end unexpectedly, you should first try to reconnect. An unexpected session end to your session can be caused by many things beyond your control. Often, the problems have to do with security breaches such as data encryption breaking down or a user being connected to the session longer than the allotted logon time. Another very common reason for a session to end unexpectedly is that the network administrator is working on the network. If reconnecting doesn't work immediately, wait a few minutes and try again.

Time-Out Errors

Time-out errors can occur for many reasons as well. The server expects a response with your logon name and password in a specific amount of time, and if you do not respond within that time limit, you'll receive a time-out error. You can also receive a time-out error through no fault of your own, though. In cases of heavy network traffic, the time-out error will occur because the information could not get to the server in the allotted amount of time. As with other errors, try to log on again, or connect at a later time.

User Errors

User errors—typing errors, specifically—are the most common, but the error messages don't ever say "You typed it wrong" or "You forgot to log on." Instead, these error messages come in the form of the following:

- The computer name contains invalid characters. Please verify the name and try again.

- The specified remote computer cannot be found. Verify that you have typed the correct computer name or IP address, and then try connecting again.

- Because of a security error, the client could not connect to the remote computer. Verify that you are logged onto the network, and then try connecting later.

Low-Memory Errors

There are several errors that indicate problems with memory. Memory, also called random access memory (RAM), is usually 64, 128, or 256MB. It is used to store information temporarily until a document is saved, a picture is printed, or a program is closed. If you don't have enough RAM in your computer, you'll receive errors related to RAM. When you see these messages, close as many open programs as you can, and try again. Also print or close any documents that have scanned pictures, or send or close large documents that are being prepared to be printed. If this still does not solve the problem, empty your Recycle Bin, delete temporary Internet files, and/or move some of your data to another drive.

Errors Your Administrator Should Know About

Many of the error messages you receive should be reported to your network administrator, especially if the errors prevent you from using Remote Desktop and happen frequently. Some of these errors will occur the first time you try to use Remote Desktop. Any error related to licensing should be reported immediately. The most common error messages include the following:

- Client and server versions do not match. Please upgrade your client software and then try connecting again.

- Because of an error in data encryption, this session will end. Please try connecting to the remote computer again.

- The remote session was disconnected because another user has connected to the session.

- The connection was ended because of a network error. Please try connecting to the remote computer again.

- The client could not connect to the remote computer. Remote connections might not be enabled or the computer might be too busy to accept new connections. It is also possible that network problems are preventing your connection. Please try your connection again later.

- Because of a protocol error (error_code), the remote session will be disconnected. Please try connecting to the remote computer again.

Remote Access

Remote Access is a Windows service that enables a user to connect from a client computer (such as a laptop) to a remote-access server or domain controller that is configured to accept incoming connections. (On a Windows 2000 Professional machine, you can set up Remote Access by configuring a connection that allows incoming connections.) The Remote Access Service is similar in many ways to the Remote Desktop and Remote Assistance technologies, but it is far more encompassing. Although users might use a remote-access server to connect to the network and then log onto their desktops remotely, many users use the remote-access server only to log onto the network.

Remote access has become more popular in the past few years because many users prefer to work at home or need to work while traveling. Remote-access servers are set up on the network to allow these clients to call in. This service allows the user to access everything on the network, including printers and other hardware and all files and folders stored on the servers. In this section, I'll introduce the basic remote-access concepts, including what is required, how logging on is done, how authentication works, and how resources are accessed.

Requirements

To set up remote access, a network administrator will install and configure a remote-access server or will configure another server on the network to perform the remote-access duties. The administrator will also set permissions for your user account so that you can log on remotely. When you are away from the computer that physically connects to the network, such as your office computer, you will then dial into (connect to) the remote-access server and connect to the network.

To dial in, you must have a computer that is connected to the Internet, you must be running software compatible with the servers on the network, and you must have a remote connection configured on the computer with which you will be connecting. You must also have a username, a password, and the appropriate permissions on the network.

Remote-access connections occur through the Internet. However, some remote-access connections occur through the Internet by way of a VPN (virtual private network). VPNs are more secure than regular Internet connections.

Acceptable Remote-Access Clients

Computers with the following operating systems or related software can connect to a Windows XP computer configured with an incoming connection:

♦ Windows XP

♦ Windows 2000

♦ Windows NT 4

♦ Windows NT 3.1, 3.5, and 3.51

♦ Windows Millennium Edition

♦ Windows 95 and 98

♦ Windows for Workgroups

♦ MS-DOS and LAN Manager

♦ Any non-Microsoft PPP client using IPX or TCP/IP

The newer the operating system, the more security and protocol options are available, along with technologies such as Multilink. It is best to use the newest operating system possible for maximum productivity and efficiency.

Configuring the Connection

Before you can connect to a network remotely, you must have a connection configured to do so. As I mentioned earlier, there are two types of remote-access connections; one is a simple connection through the Internet, and the other is a connection through the Internet by way of a VPN. Both connections are configured using the New Connection Wizard.

To configure a remote-access connection for a simple Internet connection:

1. Open the Control Panel.

2. Open Network Connections.

3. Under Network Tasks, choose Create A New Connection. Choose Next to start the New Connection Wizard.

4. On the Network Connection Type page, select Connect To The Network At My Workplace.

5. On the Network Connection page, select Dial-up Connection.

6. On the Connection Name page, type a name for the connection.

7. On the Phone Number To Dial page, type the phone number of the remote-access server. Type the number exactly how it should be dialed.

8. On the Connection Availability page, choose to create the connection for anyone who uses this computer or to create the connection only when you are logged on.

9. As the wizard completes, check the checkbox Add A Shortcut To This Connection To My Desktop, if you like, and choose Finish.

To configure a remote-access connection through the Internet and a VPN:

1. Open the Control Panel.

2. Open Network Connections.

3. Under Network Tasks, choose Create A New Connection. Choose Next to start the New Connection Wizard.

4. On the Network Connection Type page, select Connect To The Network At My Workplace.

5. On the Network Connection page, select Virtual Private Network Connection.

6. On the Connection Name page, type a name for the new connection.

7. On the Public Network page, select the connection that should be used to connect to the Internet.

8. On the VPN Server Selection page, type the host name or the IP address of the computer to which you want to connect.

9. On the Connection Availability page, choose for whom to create the account: anyone who logs on to this computer or only you.

10. Finish the wizard. In the Initial Connection dialog box that follows, there are two options. You can choose Yes to connect to your Internet connection now, or you can choose No to connect at a later time. Choose Yes to connect now.

11. A logon box will appear. Type a username and a password to log on using the VPN connection.

Logging Onto the Network

After the connection has been configured and connection requirements have been met, the next task is to connect to the remote network. You do not have to be an administrator to connect; you just need to have the proper permissions. Even when you have those permissions, the network administrator must also enable remote access for you. To do this, the network administrator chooses Allow Remote Access on the Dial-In page of your user account's Properties dialog box.

To use remote-access technology to log onto a remote network via the Internet:

1. Log onto the local computer. In the Log On To Windows dialog box, type your username and password, and choose the correct domain to log onto.

2. Check the checkbox Log On Using Dial Up Connection.

3. Select the connection that is configured for your office or remote-access server.

4. Type your username and password, and choose Dial.

5. When the connection is established, an information bubble will appear in the notification area of the taskbar.

The Authentication Process

When you connect to the Internet, you are using a remote-access server. Your ISP requires a logon name and password, which you enter, to log onto one of its servers. After you log on, the ISP grants you access to the Internet. While connected to the Internet, you might be asked for additional credentials to log onto specific Web sites or to purchase something from an online store.

The same type of authentication happens when you log onto a remote-access server at your office. First, you must log onto the local computer either at home or on the road (wherever you're working). Then, you must log onto the network server at your place of business. These credentials are generally not the same as for logging onto the local computer. When you're logged onto the corporate network, the resources that you want to access might also ask you or your computer for credentials. As with the Internet, some of these resources might require a different set of credentials. Although in many instances, all three sets of passwords can be the same, many times they aren't.

Network administrators usually configure the remote-access server to accept the same credentials as the domain controller (or logon server), and administrators allow one password to work for all of the resources on the network. This setup is called Single Sign-On (SSO), and it's the most efficient way to configure a network and manage passwords. However, when users are remote-access clients, they log onto their local machines (such as a laptop) before attempting to log onto the network. This local logon is usually different.

Configuring Windows XP to Remember Passwords

Windows XP Professional can remember lots of passwords by using the Stored User Names and Passwords feature. This is specifically designed for situations like the one described earlier in which users must remember multiple passwords. Stored User Names and Passwords keeps a database of the server name, domain name, computer name, and the passwords associated with each, and it will look through this list for a match when challenged. This is not recommended if you share your computer with another user.

To have the computer remember your passwords, simply check the checkbox Remember My Password every time you are prompted for a password. Eventually, all passwords will be stored, and you will not have to provide a username and password anymore.

Wireless Networking

Wireless networks are the latest from the technological community and are gaining popularity very quickly. Wireless networking isn't just office computing without the wires, though; it has become the core of most types of communications over the past few years. Wireless networks range from data networks to telephone communications over long distances, to walkie-talkies, infrared light devices, and radio frequencies for short distances. The onslaught of cell phones, pagers, personal digital assistants (PDAs), handheld computers, and the call for wireless Internet usage has made wireless networking almost commonplace.

Microsoft and other companies take the demand for wireless networking seriously because of the need for more wireless networks and networking capability and because customers insist on having it. Windows XP Professional ships ready for the future challenges of wireless networking.

Note

Because there are so many different manufacturers and ways to physically install the wireless network, I will assume in this section that you've followed the manufacturer's instructions and have all of the hardware installed properly. The steps included in this section are for configuring the network after it's physically installed.

Types of Wireless Networks

There are several types of wireless networks. The largest wireless networks are those that are wide area networks (WANs). These networks cover large areas and use both public and private networks to transmit communications. These connections are used with cell phones and pagers and for wireless Internet access on handheld computers and PDAs. These services are made available from wireless service providers, and the communications travel through satellites and antenna sites maintained by them. When you use this type of network, you pay the provider either a monthly fee or a per-use fee as agreed upon by you and the service provider. Three other types of networks are available that can be controlled at varying levels by private businesses and corporations. These are metropolitan area, local area, and personal area networks.

Metropolitan Area Networks

Metropolitan area networks (MANs) are much smaller than WANs and do not maintain any satellites or antennae hardware. MANs are typically created to connect multiple offices within the same city or to connect different buildings in a university campus. Wireless networks are often better in the long run in these situations because buying and maintaining personal wireless equipment is cheaper and easier than laying fiber-optic lines or copper cables. Creating a wireless network can also be more cost-efficient than leasing lines in a long-term situation.

Companies also use these types of wireless networks as backups for their digital or cable networks, which can be unreliable if leased. These wireless connections generally use infrared light or radio waves to transmit data.

Local Area Networks

LANs can also benefit from using wireless technologies. When a company leases a building and cannot install the cabling needed, a wireless LAN might be the only choice. Wireless LANs reduce physical cabling needs and restrictions and offer a newer, more versatile way to connect computers. The users of these computers can move to other areas of the building and other offices, and use access points for connecting to the network. An *access point* is a physical piece of hardware that connects the user to the corporate network. Users can also gather in a small physical area and connect in a peer-to-peer fashion without a physical access point. As wireless technologies improve, more and more of these networks will begin to emerge.

Personal Area Networks

A personal area network is configured for a single user and is defined by a personal area of 10 meters or fewer. Individuals can configure these networks to allow their PDAs to communicate with their laptops, or WANs can be used to allow a user to connect to another user with a cell phone or pager.

Requirements

To create a wireless network in your office, there are several requirements. One of the most important is the network adapter. Each computer that will access the network via wireless technologies must have a network adapter that supports wireless networking. In a domain, the network administrator will select and configure this hardware, but if you are setting up a wireless network either at home or in your workgroup office setting, setup will be up to you.

When selecting a network adapter, make sure it is on the Windows XP hardware compatibility list. The adapter must also support the Wireless Zero Configuration service. Information about this service should be on the outside of the adapter's box, or you can contact the manufacturer of the adapter. A transceiver is used to connect the computer to the network in order to transmit and receive signals. The transceiver converts signals in parallel and serial form.

There are two ways to set up a wireless network. You can either connect to an existing wireless network, or you can configure a new wireless network. Both of these types of networks have two options for setting up the network. Wireless networks can be set up using access points, which connect the computers to the network backbone, or they can be set up in a peer-to-peer configuration, in which computers communicate directly with one another.

Connecting to an Existing Wireless Network

To set up your network to connect to an existing wireless network, make sure you know the wireless network key (it's sort of like a password and is obtained from your administrator). Then log onto the host computer or domain controller as an administrator, and do the following:

1. Open the Control Panel.

2. Open Network Connections.

3. Right-click Wireless Network Connection, and choose Properties.

4. Select the Wireless Networks tab.

5. If you are using third-party wireless software or you want to configure all aspects of the wireless networking configuration manually, clear the Use Windows To Configure My Wireless Network Settings checkbox. To have Windows XP assist you in this task, leave this box checked. By leaving the box checked, you can do the following:

    ♦ Connect to an existing wireless network.

    ♦ Change connection settings.

    ♦ Create a new wireless connection.

    ♦ Specify preferred wireless networks.

    When you have Windows configure your wireless network settings, Windows XP does the following automatically:

    ♦ Notifies you when new wireless networks become available

    ♦ Automatically configures your wireless adapter for the chosen network

    ♦ Attempts to connect

6. Under Available Networks on the Wireless Networks tab, choose either to connect using an existing access point or to connect to an existing computer. If the network you want to connect to is not listed here, then choose Add under Preferred Networks. In Wireless Network Properties, specify the name of the network and any key settings.

7. If you're connecting to an existing access point, choose Configure. In the Wireless Network Properties dialog box, specify the network key settings, or check the checkbox The Key Is Provided For Me Automatically.

8. If you're connecting to an existing computer, select the network name under Available Networks, and choose Configure. In the Wireless Network Properties dialog box, specify the network key settings, or check the checkbox The Key Is Provided For Me Automatically. If the access point and the computer are within range of your computer, choose the Advanced button, and choose Computer-To-Computer (Ad Hoc) Networks Only.

9. Close all dialog boxes to apply the settings.

Setting Up a New Wireless Network

To set up a new wireless network, make sure you know the wireless network key (it's sort of like a password and is obtained from your administrator). Then log onto the host computer or domain controller as an administrator, and do the following:

1. Open the Control Panel.

2. Open Network Connections.

3. Right-click Wireless Network Connection, and choose Properties.

4. Select the Wireless Networks tab.

5. If you are using third-party wireless software or you want to configure all aspects of the wireless networking configuration manually, clear the Use Windows To Configure My Wireless Network Settings checkbox. To have Windows XP assist you in this task, leave this box checked. By leaving the box checked, you can do the following:

   ◆ Connect to an existing wireless network

   ◆ Change connection settings

   ◆ Create a new wireless connection

   ◆ Specify preferred wireless networks

   When you have Windows configure your wireless network settings, Windows XP does the following automatically:

   ◆ Notifies you when new wireless networks become available

   ◆ Automatically configures your wireless adapter for the chosen network

   ◆ Attempts to connect

6. On the Wireless Networking tab, choose Add.

7. In the Wireless Network Properties dialog box, specify the network name and the wire-less network key settings as required.

8. If this connection is not going to use access points and will instead use computer-to-computer communications, check the checkbox This Is A Computer-To-Computer (Ad Hoc) Network; Wireless Access Points Are Not Used.

9. Close all dialog boxes to apply the settings.

Changing Preferences

You can change the order in which connection attempts are made for connecting to a wireless network. You can also change the preferences for each connection through its Properties dialog. Finally, you can remove connections and configure automatic connections.

To see or change wireless network connection options:

1. Log on as an administrator, and open the Control Panel.

2. Open Network Connections.

3. Right-click Wireless Network Connection, and choose Properties.

4. Select the Wireless Networks tab.

5. To change the order in which connection attempts will be made, under Preferred Net-works, use the Move Up and Move Down arrows.

6. To change a setting for any of the preferred networks, select the network you want to change, click it, and select the Properties tab.

7. To remove a network from the preferred networks list, click it, and choose Remove.

8. To update the list of available networks, choose Refresh.

Connecting Clients to Any Available Wireless Network

When you use a cell phone, the cell phone automatically looks for the closest satellite or service provider to connect your call. The same is true of a pager. If you make a phone call from your car in one city, then drive for a few hours and make another call from the same phone, you can use two different satellites or wireless networks. In doing this, you do not have to manually select a network provider for the area.

Wireless networks in offices are similar, and client computers can be configured to look for available networks the same way that cell phones do. Say, for instance, that a laptop user is a wireless network client who accesses the network at the office and at home. The user's computer can be configured with several preferred networks so that whichever wireless network is available can be used. The laptop user only looks at a list of preferred networks and chooses the one he or she wants.

To connect to a wireless network:

1. Open the Control Panel.

2. Open Network Connections.

3. From Connect To Wireless Network, choose Available Networks. Select the wireless network you want to use.

4. Provide the network key if required, and choose Connect.

License and Registration, Please!

One bone of contention for network administrators and users alike is the new activation rules that Microsoft has put in place to protect against unauthorized use of its product. Before Windows XP, Microsoft had no way to prevent users from borrowing a copy of an operating system from a friend and burning a copy to install on their computer. When Windows XP Professional is purchased and installed, it is intended for a single computer, just as other operating systems have been. Hundreds of thousands of users ran their computers on the newest operating system by borrowing or copying the software, and Microsoft lost billions of dollars.

To solve this problem, Microsoft created Windows Product Activation. This is often referred to as "the registration worm," requiring a user who installs Windows XP to have it activated by Microsoft within 30 days of its installation. If the user does not activate the software, it will stop working until this is done.

Activation

During installation, the Setup Wizard asks for a product key. This is a 25-character alphanumeric code that is located on the software package, and Windows will not install until this code is typed in correctly. After Windows is installed, you are prompted to register this number with Microsoft through the Internet. Basically, a snapshot is taken of the computer and its hardware, including machine-specific identifiers. This information is referred to as a *hardware identifier*; it's used with the product ID number to create a unique picture of the computer and software. Microsoft claims that this process is totally anonymous and that no personal information is sent to Microsoft.

When your Windows installation is activated, Microsoft has a very good idea of what your computer should look like, should you ever have to reinstall Windows XP. If you try to install Windows XP on another home machine, a friend's machine, or your office computer, the product will install but cannot be activated. When the snapshot is taken of the computer and sent to Microsoft for activation, Microsoft knows that the computer having Windows installed is not the original computer for which the CD was purchased. You will be prompted to call Microsoft and explain the situation and ask for a new product ID number.

This is too much for many users, and it has caused anxiety among computer manufacturers and those who install operating systems on thousands of computers each year. However, Microsoft will make allowances here and there to ease the process for these users. Microsoft is well within its rights to protect its software from unauthorized use, to require activation, and to keep an eye out for those who would install the operating system on multiple computers, however unhappy its users are about the change.

If you ever lose or forget your product ID number, it is listed in the Properties tab of the System Properties dialog box. You can access this by right-clicking on My Computer and choosing Properties.

Registration

While the software is being activated, and this takes only about a minute, users are also prompted to register with Microsoft. Registration is optional. If you register with Microsoft, you'll be prompted for your name, address, ZIP code, and other personal information. You can choose to allow Microsoft to contact you with promotions and information if you'd like to. Registration is different from activation because registration is not required. Do not register if you want to remain totally anonymous with Microsoft.

Microsoft says that if you register your software, you'll receive the following perks:

♦ You can get the latest files and drivers through Windows Update.

♦ You'll receive better customer support.

♦ You can get up-to-date information about upgrades and new products.

♦ Your registration is effective immediately, and if you register online, you don't have to mail the yellow registration card.

If you do choose to register with Microsoft, Microsoft will also:

♦ Make your name and address available to Microsoft and all its subsidiaries

♦ Share information about the ownership and purchase of the product with Microsoft subsidiaries

♦ Take inventory of your system, and ask you if you want to submit this information

♦ Process and store the information in the U.S. and in your country of residence

♦ Ask for information, such as where the computer will be used, the home or business address, phone number, and information about the type of job you do, and then share the information with others

Licensing

When Windows XP is installed, you must agree to the licensing agreement. If you do not, the operating system will not be installed. The licensing agreement states that you will install the product on only one machine and that you will not lease, rent, or otherwise loan the software to another individual. The agreement also explains how you can create a copy of the software as a backup.

Temporary and Seasonal Domain Users

One of the problems in a large corporation is managing temporary and seasonal workers. These workers need to use network computers and access resources on the domain. The network administrator is in charge of setting restrictive permissions for those users, but you might be in charge of training them or getting them set up in their departments. When these temporary workers have no experience with Windows XP Professional, how do you introduce them to the new operating system as quickly and efficiently as possible?

These users can use the tours and tutorials available in Windows XP to familiarize themselves with the product. These tours are also very helpful for new users, new hires, and even experienced users who have not had a chance to work with XP. If you or anyone in your domain or on your network needs a crash course, consider the tours and tutorials in the following sections.

Windows XP Tour

The Windows XP Tour give a general overview of Windows XP's features in the introduction and then allows you to choose from a list of tours. These tours include:

♦ Best For Business

♦ Safe And Easy Personal Computing

♦ Unlock The World Of Digital Media

♦ The Connected Home And Office

♦ Windows XP Basics

If you don't select a tour from this list, Windows automatically starts at Best For Business and continues through the remaining four tours. In the Windows XP Basics section, topics covered are the Windows Desktop, Icons, Taskbar, Files and Folders, Windows, and Control Panel. This section will prove extremely useful to new users. When the animated option with voice narration is chosen, the entire tour takes about 20 minutes.

To start the Windows XP Tour:

1. Choose Start | Help And Support.

2. Under Pick A Help Topic, choose What's New In Windows XP.

3. Choose Taking A Tour Or Tutorial.

4. Choose Take The XP Tour.

5. Choose Next to take the tour. You can choose to play the animated tour that features text, animation, music, and voice narration, or play the non-animated tour that features text and images only.

6. You can manually choose a tour to take by clicking it, or you can let the entire tour series run.

Note

For training new users or temporary workers, allow them the time to watch the entire video. When finished, end the session by clicking the X in the bottom-right corner of the screen. Otherwise, the video will continue to play again from the beginning.

Personalizing Your PC Tutorial

Another helpful tool for new or temporary domain users is the Personalize Your PC tutorial. This tutorial teaches users how to customize the desktop, change mouse settings, make startup faster, and more. In general, a user will need about an hour to work through all of the related tutorials.

To see the Personalize Your PC tutorial:

1. Choose Start | Help And Support.

2. Under Pick A Help Topic, choose What's New In Windows XP.

3. Choose Windows XP Articles: Walk Through Ways To Use Your PC.

4. Choose Personalize Your PC from the list of walkthroughs.

5. From the Personalize Your PC section, work through the four tutorials offered.

Sharing Your PC Tutorial

If multiple users do their work from the same PC, have each user work through the Sharing Your PC tutorial. This tutorial teaches users how to use user accounts, protect accounts with passwords, switch users, and more. In general, a user will need about a half hour to an hour to work through all of the related tutorials.

To start the Sharing Your PC tutorial:

1. Choose Start | Help And Support.

2. Under Pick A Help Topic, choose What's New In Windows XP.

3. Choose Windows XP Articles: Walk Through Ways To Use Your PC.

4. Choose Sharing Your PC from the list of walkthroughs.

5. From the Share And Share Alike section, work through the four tutorials offered.

Windows Media Player Tour

If users need to access the Media Player, a tour is available to get them started. The Media Player does a lot more than just play CDs; in fact, it can be used to organize digital media files on the computer or Internet, locate digital media, copy files from a CD, listen to radio stations from all over the world, copy digital media to a CD, and more.

To start the Windows Media Player Tour:

1. Choose Start | Help And Support.

2. Under Pick A Help Topic, choose What's New In Windows XP.

3. Choose Taking A Tour Or Tutorial.

4. Choose Take The Windows Media Player Tour.

5. You can manually choose a tour to take by clicking it, or you can let the entire tour run.

Note

For training new users or temporary workers, allow them the time to watch the entire tutorial and the optional movies included. These movies show the physical steps involved in performing tasks. When finished, end the session by clicking the X in the top-right corner of the screen.

Other Tutorials

There are some other tutorials available, including Making Music and Digital Photos, that might interest users new to Windows XP. You can view these additional tutorials from the Help and Support Center, as with the other tutorials. All are similar in the way they are used, and they are easily accessed. The Help and Support Center also provides overviews of just about any Windows subject imaginable, including keyboard shortcuts, the desktop, Windows components, and tools.

Wrapping Up

In this chapter, you learned what a domain is and how Windows XP participates in a domain. User accounts, permissions, privileges, and rights were discussed, as were local and group security policies. Domain network administrators configure these security features.

As a member of a domain, you must know how to log on, how to view network resources, and how to create and share folders and other resources with other users on the network. These tasks were covered, as was getting help by using Remote Assistance. You can use

Remote Assistance when you need help from an administrator or trusted friend, and it can save an administrator a trip to your computer.

Another feature of Windows XP, Remote Desktop, was also introduced. Remote Desktop allows you to log onto your office computer from home or from a laptop computer, and access the office computer's files, folders, programs, and network resources just as if you were sitting physically at the host computer.

This chapter also covered Remote Access, including how to configure a Remote Access connection, log on remotely, and access resources. Wireless networking was detailed next, and finally, you learned a little about licensing and registration, and got a few tips for training temporary or new users in the domain.

Chapter 12
Disk and Computer Management

Computers are basically made of four types of hardware: data-input devices, such as keyboards and mice; data-output devices, such as monitors and printers; the components, such as CPUs, necessary to perform calculations on the data; and the components, such as disk drives, required to store the data. Maintaining these resources properly can extend the life of the computer, maintain the integrity of the data, and improve the performance of the machine.

Although maintaining the keyboard and mouse isn't a high priority, maintaining the hard disk drive is. After all, it is the responsibility of this drive to store the data you save on your computer. There are many physically different types of drives, including floppy disk drives, hard disk drives, CD-ROM drives, and tape drives. This chapter focuses on different types of hard disk drives and their management.

You can do several things to keep your disk drives running smoothly. Windows XP Professional offers Disk Cleanup, Disk Defragmenter, disk compression utilities, and the ability to manage remote disks on other computers. There are also many ways that disks can be configured, including basic and dynamic, simple, spanned, striped, and mounted. These types of configurations are covered in this chapter.

Adding a new disk is often necessary when a computer runs out of space or when you need to configure some form of fault tolerance. Adding a new disk involves several steps, including choosing a disk type, having Windows XP detect the new disk, and creating partitions or logical drives. Disk quotas can also be configured to limit how much disk space a user can have access to.

Besides the management of the disk drives, this chapter also covers different aspects of computer management. Several utilities are available to assist you in enhancing performance or finding problems such as bottlenecks; these utilities are Event Viewer, Performance Logs And Alerts, and Device Manager. Performance can be enhanced in many areas, including processor performance, memory performance, and video performance. All of these aspects of performance are covered here. Finally, programs can be run in program compatibility mode when legacy programs are needed.

Note
Throughout this chapter, the terms disk, hard disk, disk drive, drive, and volume will be used interchangeably and will refer to the local computer's hard disk drive(s).

Disk Management

Because your computer has a hard disk already installed and in use, the logical place to start is with keeping this disk healthy and running smoothly. Over time, a disk can become cluttered, especially if programs have been added or removed, or if lots of data has been saved and then deleted. This clutter makes performance suffer, and simply cleaning up the disk a little can make a noticeable improvement. For problems related to low disk space, you can use Disk Cleanup to delete temporary files, uninstall unused programs, compress a drive, and more.

Tip
The most important thing, though, is the security of the disk drive itself and of the data stored on it. Before starting this chapter, if you are still using FAT as your file system, consider converting to NTFS. See "FAT vs. NTFS" in Chapter 10. Many of the following utilities (such as compression) are not available on FAT volumes. In these sections, you can assume that the utility works for both FAT and NTFS unless otherwise noted.

Disk Cleanup

After time, your hard disk becomes cluttered with unnecessary files. Some of these files are used only temporarily to perform an installation or a process, and others are temporary Internet files no longer needed. You might also have Windows components installed, such as Internet Information Services (IIS), that you've never used. You can create more space on your hard drive and clean up these unnecessary files and components by using Disk Cleanup. Although Disk Cleanup was mentioned briefly in Chapter 2, it is worth mentioning again here.

Disk Cleanup can be used to do the following:

♦ Remove temporary Internet files.

♦ Remove downloaded program files, such as ActiveX controls and Java applets obtained from the Internet.

♦ Empty the Recycle Bin

♦ Remove Windows temporary files

♦ Remove Windows components that you are not using, such as IIS

♦ Remove installed applications that you no longer use

♦ Compress old files

♦ Remove catalog files for the Content Indexer

I would suggest running Disk Cleanup about once a month or more. You can run Disk Cleanup as a Scheduled Task, and configure it to run automatically at certain intervals.

To run Disk Cleanup now:

1. Choose Start | Programs | Accessories | System Tools | Disk Cleanup. (If you are in Classic View, choose All Programs.)

2. If more than one logical or physical drive exists on your computer, select the drive you want to clean up. Choose OK.

3. In the Disk Cleanup dialog box, select which file types you want to delete.

4. Check the Compress Old Files checkbox to compress files that haven't been used in 50 days or more. You can change this number by selecting the Options button while Compress Old Files is highlighted and checked.

5. Choose OK, and choose Yes to confirm that you want to perform these actions.

Disk Defragmenter

When data is stored on your local hard drive, it is stored starting on the outside of the volume and working inward. When data has been stored on the disk sequentially, the data might then be erased, leaving blank spaces on the disk drive. See Figure 12.1. The next time data is saved, the computer tries to write the data to the hard disk, starting at the beginning of the disk again, and working outward. It is possible, and it happens a lot, that the next set of data saved won't be saved to the disk sequentially. Instead, the data will be stored across three or four physical locations on the drive.

When data is stored in different places on a drive, the data is considered *fragmented*. Because the data is not stored together in a single place and is not stored sequentially, the hard drive has to work harder to retrieve the data. Therefore, the Disk Defragmenter utility should be run to place these sets of data together on the hard drive.

Disk Defragmenter begins by analyzing the disk to determine how fragmented it is and to get a clear picture of what data needs to be moved. Once the data has been analyzed, defragmentation begins. To defragment your hard disk, you might need to be logged on as

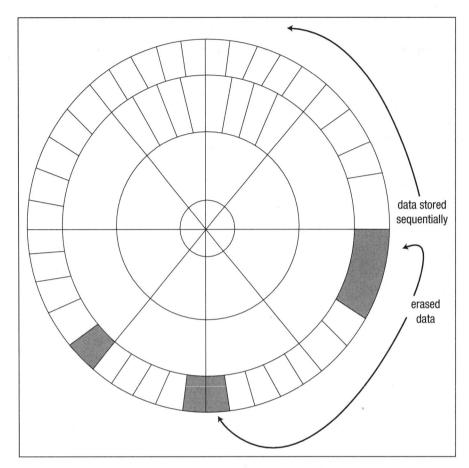

Figure 12.1
The hard disk.

an administrator if you're on a network. Disk defragmenting can take quite some time depending on how fragmented the data on the disk is.

To defragment a disk:

1. Log on as an administrator.

2. Back up crucial data.

3. Close any open programs.

4. Choose Start | Accessories | System Tools | Disk Defragmenter.

5. If the computer has more than one disk or partition, choose the disk (also called a volume) that you want to defragment.

6. Choose Defragment.

You can also make the Disk Defragmenter part of any Microsoft Management Console that you create. Just choose Start | Run, type "mmc", and follow the instructions in Chapter 1. Disk Defragmenter is also available from the Computer Management console. Figure 12.2 shows this console.

Freeing Up Disk Space

Another way to maintain hard disks is to keep them free of unnecessary data. There are several ways to free up disk space, and Disk Cleanup and Disk Defragmenter work well as a start. If, after using these utilities, you still find that you are getting hard drive space errors, or you do not have enough hard drive space to burn a CD or install a program, you'll need to take a more aggressive approach.

Some other options are listed next, and a few of them are expanded on later. The other options include (in no particular order):

♦ Compressing an NTFS disk drive

♦ Zipping up unused files and folders

♦ Removing unnecessary programs

♦ Removing disk space hogs, such as music and picture files

♦ Removing unused Windows components

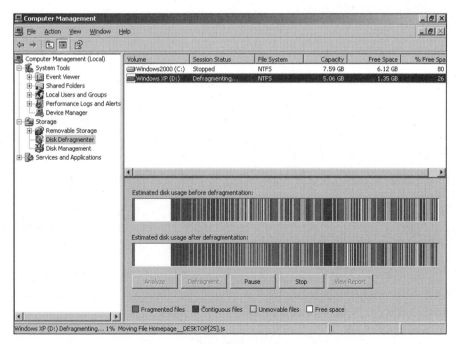

Figure 12.2
The Computer Management console and Disk Defragmenter.

Compressing an NTFS Folder or Drive

When disk space is limited, you should consider compressing the disk drive or at least some of the files, folders, and programs stored on it. Compression decreases the amount of space that the data takes up on the hard drive, leaving more room for additional data. Windows XP Professional offers two types of compression: NTFS compression, detailed in this section and zipped folders, detailed in the next.

Compressing files and folders works only if you are using NTFS on your hard drive. Compression has many features and limitations that you need to be aware of before continuing, including the following:

♦ Files, folders, or entire drives can be compressed.

♦ NTFS compressed files can be edited without being decompressed first. Decompression is automatic when the file is opened and is transparent to the user. The act of decompressing these folders can slow down performance.

♦ Compressed files can be shown in a different color so that they are easily recognizable.

♦ If you move or copy a compressed folder from an NTFS drive to a FAT drive, compression is lost.

♦ If you move or copy any file to a compressed folder, it is automatically compressed.

♦ If you move a file from one NTFS drive to a compressed folder on another NTFS drive, the file is automatically compressed.

♦ If you move a file from the same NTFS drive into a compressed folder, the file retains its original state, compressed or not.

♦ Compressed files cannot be encrypted, and encrypted files cannot be compressed.

♦ Compression is not available in the Windows XP Home Edition or the Windows XP 64-bit Edition.

To compress a file or folder on an NTFS drive:

1. Use Windows Explorer or My Computer to locate the file or folder you want to compress.

2. Right-click the file or folder, and choose Properties.

3. In the Properties dialog box, select the General tab.

4. Choose the Advanced button.

5. In the Advanced Attributes dialog box, check the Compress Contents To Save Disk Space checkbox, as shown in Figure 12.3.

6. Choose OK twice. If a Confirm Attributes Changes dialog box appears, choose how you want the compression to be applied (to this folder only, or to subfolders and files also), and choose OK.

Figure 12.3
Advanced attributes.

To compress an NTFS drive:

1. Log on as an administrator (network polices might still prevent you from completing this procedure if you are a member of a domain).

2. Open My Computer.

3. Right-click on the drive you want to compress, and choose Properties.

4. On the General tab, select the Compress Drive To Save Disk Space checkbox, and choose OK.

5. In the Confirm Attribute Changes dialog box, choose how you want the drive to be compressed (the drive only, or subfolders and files also). Choose OK.

Note

For a drive, the process of compressing can take quite a bit of time and slow down the computer immensely. In my case, it took 20 minutes.

To display compressed files, folders, and drives in color:

1. Open the Control Panel.

2. Choose Tools | Folder Options.

3. On the View tab, check the checkbox Show Encrypted Or Compressed NTFS Files In Color. Choose OK. Figure 12.4 shows compressed files in a lighter color than uncompressed files.

Zipping Up Folders

Another way to create extra disk space is to compress files and folders by using the zip compression technique. This is a different type of compression than the method just discussed, and it's also available in Windows XP Professional. You have probably heard of

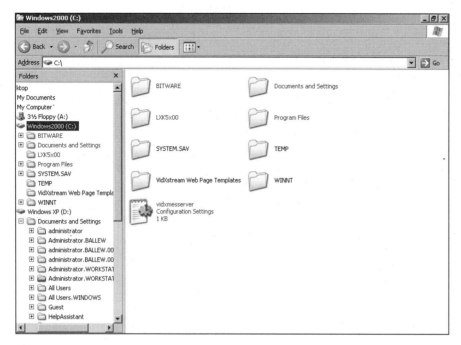

Figure 12.4
Compressed files and folders shown in color.

zipping programs such as WinZip; these have always been available only from third-party manufacturers. Now, however, this technology is included with Windows XP.

Note

Zip compression is not the same as a Zip disk. A Zip disk is a physical medium; zip compression is a software utility or technology.

Zipping up data such as large files and folders not only saves room on the local hard drive but also allows you to transfer the data to other computers quickly. Zip compression is most often used when you're sending large files over the Internet and when you're storing a large file on removable media for transfer. Once zipped, the folder (and zipped files and folders are held in a folder) has a zipper icon associated with it, and the files must usually be unzipped (extracted) before they can be used. (Some programs, however, can run directly from zipped folders without extracting the files, as long as the zipped files are not dependent on any other files that are not included.)

There are a few major differences between NTFS compression and zip compression. First, files and folders that are compressed using the zip technique can be compressed on either FAT or NTFS disk drives, while NTFS compression works only on NTFS drives.. Second, zipped compression does not decrease the computer's performance as NTFS compression does. Finally, you can protect zipped files with passwords, while NTFS folders are protected by NTFS permissions.

Using Zipped Compression

To create a new zip compression folder:

1. Open My Computer.

2. Double-click the file or folder you want to compress.

3. Choose File | New | Compressed (Zipped) Folder. (You can also right-click the file or folder and choose this option if you are using a third-party zip utility.)

4. Type a name for the folder, and press Enter. If you are sharing these files with other computer systems, do not use more than eight characters in the name for backward compatibility.

Note

If you have already downloaded or purchased a third-party zip utility, the option to choose File|New|Compressed (Zipped) Folder will not be available; instead, the compression utility you purchased will be in the list. For instance, File|New| WinZip File.

After you've created the compressed folder, all you need to do to add files or folders to the compressed folder is to drag them to the folder. To extract files from a compressed folder, simply right-click the folder and choose Extract All.

Uninstalling Programs

One of the best ways to free up disk space is to uninstall programs that are never used. Chapter 8 covered installing and removing both hardware and software, but briefly, programs should be uninstalled using the Add Or Remove Programs icon in the Control Panel.

To uninstall a program that is no longer being used:

1. Open the Control Panel. (You can open Windows Explorer or My Computer as well.)

2. Open Add Or Remove Programs.

3. In the Change Or Remove Programs window, highlight the program you want to uninstall.

4. Choose the Change/Remove button.

5. In the Information dialog box, choose Yes to continue with the uninstall.

6. Depending on the application, either the program will be uninstalled automatically, or you'll need to walk through a Windows Uninstaller procedure. This consists of choosing Next or OK to continue with the uninstall. Occasionally, the computer will need to be restarted.

7. Choose Close to exit the Add Or Remove Programs window.

Note
Using System Restore after installing a program that fails does not remove the program. The program must be uninstalled using the Control Panel.

Uninstalling Windows Components

You can uninstall unused Windows components through Disk Cleanup or through Control Panel. To uninstall these components by using the Control Panel:

1. Log on as an administrator and open the Control Panel.

2. Open Add Or Remove Programs.

3. Choose Add/Remove Windows Components.

4. In the Windows Components Wizard that appears, clear the checkboxes for the unused Windows components. These might be Fax Services, Indexing Service, Internet Information Services, or Management And Monitoring Tools, just to name a few.

5. Choose Next to begin the process; then choose Finish and Close.

Removing Picture and Music Files

Two of the biggest space hogs on any computer are the music and picture files. If you've been saving these files in the My Music and My Pictures folder, then deleting them is as simple as right-clicking the files and choosing Delete. However, not all users are quite this organized, and files or folders with this data could be scattered around the entire hard drive. You can find these files and folders by using the Search Companion.

To locate music and pictures stored on your computer:

1. Choose Start | Search | For Files Or Folders.

2. From the What Do You Want To Search For options, select Pictures, Music, Or Video. (If you do not see the Search Companion, choose View | Explorer Bar | Search.)

3. From the Search For All Files Of A Certain Type, Or Search By Type And Name box, select either Pictures And Photos, Music, or Video, or just click the Search button to locate all of these types of files.

Note
If you install a clean copy of Windows XP Professional and search for all pictures, photos, music, and video, you'll come up with over 1,000 files. These files are included by default and take up lots of room on the hard drive. You can delete some of these files, especially the music files, and create some extra hard drive space on your computer.

4. After the search is complete, you might want to refine the search by using the Search Companion, or choose View | List to see a list of all of the files instead of icons (the default).

5. When you've located a file or folder you want to delete, simply right-click it and choose Delete.

Managing a Remote Disk

Administrators of Windows 2000 Professional computers can manage hard disks that are connected to other computers. These computers are considered remote, and the administrator of the local computer must be an administrator on both the local computer and the remote computer to perform these tasks. The user account and both the local and remote computers must be either in the same domain or in trusted domains.

Other requirements for remote administration of disks include the following:

♦ Certain types of disks, such as mirrored volumes and RAID 5 volumes, can be configured only on specific operating systems, such as Windows 2000 Server or Windows 2000 Advanced Server. You cannot configure a mirrored volume or a RAID 5 volume on a Windows 2000 Professional or Windows XP Professional machine. (The next section provides more information on these disk types.)

♦ Windows XP Professional can manage a Windows 2000 Professional or Server computer, and vice versa.

Remote Disk Tasks

Having the ability to connect to another computer's hard drive and view its configuration has quite a few advantages. By connecting to the remote computer through the Computer Management console, an administrator can perform the following tasks:

♦ Use Event Viewer to view the remote computer's event logs, including application logs, security logs, and system logs

♦ View shared folders on the disk, and see how many users are accessing those shares

♦ View the local user accounts and groups configured on the remote computer

♦ View performance logs

♦ View Device Manager on the remote computer and make changes

♦ View removable storage

♦ View the partitions, volumes, and file systems on the remote computer

♦ Change the drive letters and paths, and convert a basic disk to a dynamic disk

♦ View the services running on the remote computer, and stop, start, or pause services

To connect to a remote computer, manage its disks, and view its Computer Management console information:

1. Log on as an administrator of both the local and remote computers.

2. Open the Control Panel and Administrative Tools.

3. Open the Computer Management console.

4. In the left pane, highlight Computer Management.

5. Choose Action | Connect To Another Computer.

6. In the Select Computer dialog box, type the name of the computer, and choose OK.

7. Expand the Storage Tree, and highlight Disk Management. If necessary, type a username and password.

8. Right-click on Disk 0 or Disk 1, and look at the choices. Depending on the computer accessed, the choices will differ. Figure 12.5 shows the options from a Windows 2000 Professional machine that is being used to remotely manage a Windows 2000 Server.

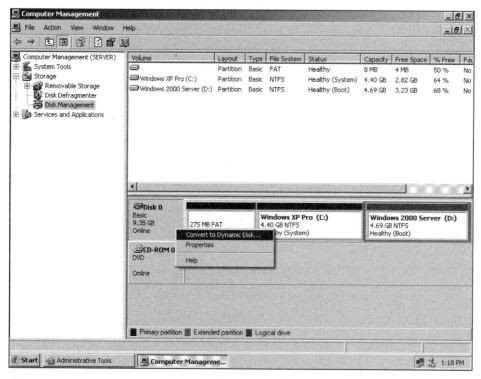

Figure 12.5
Disk options.

Notice that the Windows 2000 server is a dual-boot configuration and that the disk partitions are basic. The file systems for the three partitions are FAT, NTFS, and NTFS.

Before changing the disk type, however, let's get up to speed on what types of disks are available.

Types of Disks (Drives)

There are many types of disk drives; there are hard disk drives, floppy disk drives, tape drives, and CD-ROM drives. As mentioned earlier, this chapter focuses on the hard disks in a computer. These disks (also referred to as *drives*) can be configured in lots of ways. They can be basic or dynamic, and spanned, striped, or mirrored. Not all versions of Windows XP offer all of these disk configurations as options, but you might be asked to manage these configurations remotely at some point. In this section, you'll learn about different disk types and the terms used to describe them.

Partitions

To understand how disks are created and used, you first need to understand the different types of partitions that can be configured. *Partitions* are portions of the disk that act like separate physical disks.

When a computer is purchased from a computer store, the computer is almost always configured with only one partition, and is configured with a basic disk. A basic disk is a hard disk that contains a primary partition, and possible extended partitions and logical drives. The basic disk and its primary partition holds the operating system that came installed with the system. Figure 12.6 shows a computer with only one partition configured for its single hard disk. This partition is Windows (C:). Drive C: holds the operating system files on this computer and is the hard disk drive, drive E: is a removable Zip disk, and there is also a CD-ROM drive.

This computer is not a dual-boot system; this computer has only one operating system on it. Disk 0 is the local hard drive; Disk 1 is a removable Zip drive. (If it had a second operating system installed, there would be a second disk named D: with a different name and separate graphic in Computer Management.) The single hard drive is the norm for most office computers. Even with only one partition and one physical hard disk, the partition can be one of several different types.. Listed next are a few of these partition types.

Active

An *active partition* is the partition the computer boots from, and it's usually the floppy disk drive. This can be changed as the computer boots up, though, and the active partition can be the hard disk, a CD-ROM drive, or a Zip drive. You can change the active partition by pressing keys such as Del or Ctrl+Tab during start up and entering the computer's BIOS settings.

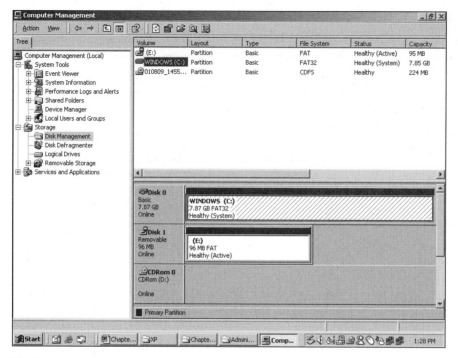

Figure 12.6
Disk with a single partition.

The BIOS (Basic Input/Output System) is used to configure how the computer boots. This partition has to be a primary partition when the disk is configured as a basic disk.

Primary

A *primary partition* is used when a basic disk is configured, and it is the disk from which the computer boots. You can have one, two, three, or four primary partitions, or three primary partitions and one extended partition. Primary partitions cannot be subpartitioned.

Extended

An *extended partition* is part of a basic disk that can contain logical drives. You configure logical drives when you want to use more than four partitions on the basic disk. The extended partition can be configured to hold logical drives within the extended partition. Only one of the partitions can be extended.

Partition Characteristics

In Figures 12.5 and 12.6, you can see that these partitions are also classified as system and boot. The *system partition* contains the files needed to load Windows XP. This partition can also be the boot partition, but it doesn't have to be. The *boot partition* holds the Windows XP operating system files. The boot partition can also be the system partition but, again, doesn't have to be. Note that the boot partition holds the system files, and the system partition holds the boot files.

Note

These partitions and logical drives are configured while the operating system is being installed. If you've purchased a computer and want to configure different partitions and logical drives, you'll either have to format the entire computer and start over, or purchase a third-party utility such as PartitionMagic.

Logical Drives

After an extended partition has been created, logical drives can be created within it. Logical drives can be configured only on basic disks because logical drives are derived from within an extended partition. These logical drives can be formatted and assigned a drive letter such as E:, F:, or G:; they are used to separate data on the hard disk and to further partition the extended drive. Logical drives are listed in the Computer Management console. When logical drives are listed, not only are the extended partitions shown, but so are any floppy drives, CD-ROM drives, or removable disks.

Basic Disks

A basic disk is the default configuration when an operating system is installed on a computer. A *basic disk* is a physical disk that can contain primary and extended partitions as well as logical drives. Basic disks can also be used to create other types of configurations, such as spanned, mirrored, striped, and RAID 5 volumes. Basic disks can be accessed by MS-DOS and are backward-compatible with Windows NT volume sets, striped sets, mirrored volumes, and disk striping with parity. All versions of Windows, including 9x and NT, can use basic disks because this technology is an industry standard. Basic disks can be converted to dynamic disks without data loss, but the reverse is not true.

Basic disks should be configured for portable computers or when multiple operating system are to be installed on a single computer. You can do the following when using a basic disk:

♦ Create and delete primary and extended partitions

♦ Create and delete logical drives within an extended partition

♦ Format any partition, and make it an active partition

♦ View disk capacity, available space, label, type, and file system

♦ Change drive-letter assignments for removable drives and other storage devices

♦ Convert the basic disk to a dynamic disk

♦ Share volumes and partitions if the disk is formatted with the NTFS file system

♦ Extend the volume with contiguous space at the end of the same physical disk

Dynamic Disks

Dynamic disks offer features that basic disks do not, such as the ability to extend the volume to span multiple disks instead of extending it to include extra space at the end of only the one physical disk. With a dynamic disk, you can also create fault-tolerant volumes that will protect your data if one of the physical disks fails. Fault tolerance using mirrored and RAID 5 volumes is available only in Windows XP Server and higher, though, and is not available in Windows XP Professional. An administrator can configure these disk types on a Windows 2000 or XP server from a Windows XP Professional machine. Dynamic disks do have their limitations, though, and both advantages and disadvantages will be listed here.

Advantages

When a dynamic disk is used, you can do the following tasks within the Computer Management console:

♦ Create and delete simple, spanned, striped, mirrored, and RAID 5 volumes

♦ Extend simple or spanned volumes

♦ Remove a mirrored volume, or split the volume into two parts

♦ Reactivate missing or offline disks

♦ View disk capacity, available space, label, type, and file system

♦ Change drive-letter assignments for removable drives and other storage devices

♦ Share volumes and partitions if the disk is formatted with the NTFS file system

Limitations

Dynamic disks have the following limitations:

♦ Dynamic disks cannot be used on laptops or on detachable disks that use USB, FireWire, or SCSI ports to connect to the computer

♦ Dynamic disks cannot be used on dual-boot computers

♦ Windows XP Professional can be installed on only simple and mirrored dynamic volumes (in addition to basic disks). You cannot install Windows XP Professional on a striped volume

♦ Changing from a dynamic disk to a basic disk causes data to be lost

Converting a Basic Disk to a Dynamic Disk

You have to have a dynamic disk configured to create simple, spanned, striped, mirrored, and RAID 5 volumes. In Windows XP Professional, the only options after Windows XP has been installed and a dynamic disk has been configured are dynamic simple, spanned, and striped volumes. For Windows 2000 Server and Window XP Server, the options also include dynamic mirrored and RAID 5 volumes. If you want to use any of these types of disks, you'll have to convert them from basic to dynamic. This is very simple to do, but remember, you can't go back.

To convert a disk from basic to dynamic:

1. Log on as an administrator.

2. Open the Computer Management console (from Administrative Tools), and then highlight the Disk Management tree.

3. Right-click in the Disk 0 or Disk 1 box, as shown earlier in Figure 12.5. Choose Convert To Dynamic Disk.

4. Choose OK.

5. In the Disks To Upgrade dialog box, highlight the disk you want to upgrade. Choose the Upgrade button.

6. In the Disk Management information window, choose Yes after reading the warnings.

    The system will reboot, and the changes will be made.

Simple Dynamic Disks

Once a dynamic disk has been configured, managing the disk is a little different from managing a basic disk. With a simple dynamic disk, you cannot configure partitions or logical drives, and simple dynamic disks can be accessed only by Windows 2000 or XP operating systems. When using a simple dynamic volume, you can increase the size of the disk by allocating space from an empty area of the same disk or a different one. However, the disks must be formatted with NTFS or converted if necessary. When a simple volume is extended to include space on a different dynamic disk, it becomes a spanned volume. Simple volumes can be mirrored, but spanned volumes cannot. Simple dynamic disks are not fault tolerant; if the disk fails, all of the data on it will be lost.

Spanned Disks

Spanned volumes contain free space from multiple physical disks. The amount of free space on each of these disks does not have to be the same. Spanned volumes cannot be mirrored. They are written to until each disk is full, and then the next disk is written to. Spanned volumes are a good way to use multiple physical disks that have little space on each. If any one of the disks on a spanned volume fails, all of the data on the spanned volume is lost.

Striped Disks (RAID 0)

RAID stands for Redundant Array of Inexpensive (or Independent) Disks. Several levels of RAID are available. RAID 1 and RAID 5 offer fault tolerance in case of a disk failure. Striped disks (RAID 0) do not offer fault tolerance. In a striped volume, data is written to multiple disks at the same time, making disk reads and writes faster than other types of disk configuration. The data that is written to the disks is written in blocks, and the data is distributed to the disks evenly. These volumes cannot be mirrored, and they should be configured on hard disks that are the same size, model, and manufacturer. Striped disks are used when fast performance is crucial, such as when you're collecting data from databases, when information is needed (such as stock market quotes) that must be updated frequently, or when streaming media applications are being used.

Mirrored Disks (RAID 1)

Mirrored disks are just that; they are used when data is crucial and always need to be available, no matter what. The configuration is made of two disks, and every time data is written to one disk, it is also written to the other. This setup provides fault tolerance because if one disk crashes, the other is right there to provide data and information to users. Reconstructing the mirror is as simple as replacing the disk and re-creating the mirror configuration.

Mirrored volumes are slow to write to, though, and the cost is just about double what you'd have to pay for any other configuration. In terms of wasted disk space, you lose half of what you purchase. Mirrored volumes are not available on Windows 2000 Professional computers but are available in Server versions. A Windows XP Professional computer can be used to manage or create mirrored volumes on these other computers, though, and you might be asked to perform this task at some point. Both system and boot partitions can be mirrored.

Disk Striping with Parity (RAID 5)

Disk striping with parity is like disk striping except that an extra disk is configured to hold parity information about the data. This parity information can be used to reconstruct the data should one of the disks crash. (Parity is a value that is calculated based on the number of ones and zeros that makes up the data being saved.) Basically, disk striping with parity works like this: data is written to the disks in chunks simultaneously. If the RAID 5 set has five disks, then four of them get data written to them, while the fifth gets the parity information. If one of the disks fails, the data can be re-created using the parity information. These volumes have better read performance than mirrored volumes do, but when a disk is missing or has failed, the read performance suffers tremendously until the volume is repaired. RAID 5 is not available on Windows XP Professional machines but can be used in Server editions.

Converting from Dynamic Back to Basic

You can convert a dynamic disk to a basic disk by using the Computer Management console *as long as you back up all of the data first.*

Warning

During the conversion, the disk is reformatted, and all data is erased.

To convert from a dynamic disk back to a basic disk:

1. Log on as an administrator.

2. Back up all data on the dynamic disks.

3. Open the Computer Management console.

4. Highlight Disk Management.

5. Right-click in the Disk 0 or Disk 1 box, as shown earlier in Figure 12.5. Select the disk you want to convert, and right-click it. Choose Delete Volume.

6. Do this for each volume on the dynamic disk.

7. Right-click in the Disk 0 or Disk 1 box, and choose Convert To Basic Disk.

Mounted Drives

A *mounted drive* is a hard disk, a floppy disk, a CD, or any other type of disk that is assigned a name instead of a letter. Members of the Administrators group can create mounted drives. A mounted drive is configured using an empty folder on an NTFS volume. The mounted drive is used the same way any other drive is used, except that the mounted drive's name is a path instead of a drive letter as with other drives. When a volume is made into a mounted drive, you can create more than 26 drives on your computer (you won't be limited by the 26 letters of the alphabet). Mounted drives make data more manageable by allowing you to assign each folder a disk quota to limit disk usage by the users who access the drive.

Creating a Mounted Drive

To create a mounted drive:

1. Log on as an administrator, and create an empty folder on the desktop or in My Computer.

2. Open the Computer Management console, and then expand the Computer Management (Local) tree.

3. Select Disk Management and right-click the volume you want to mount, and choose Change Drive Letter And Paths.

4. To mount a volume, choose Add.

5. Browse to the location of the empty folder. (Disk Management will assign a path to the drive automatically.)

Master-Boot-Record Disks and GPT Disks

There are two types of partitioning technology: MBR and GPT. When an IBM/Intel/X86 computer is used, the partitions on the disk are organized using a master boot record (MBR). The MBR is the first sector on the hard disk and is used to boot the computer. The MBR knows where the first bit of code is that is required for the computer to start up. The MBR also knows how the partitions on the disk are configured.

If the computer is running Windows XP 64-bit Edition, a GUID partition table must be used (GPT) instead of a MBR; a GUID is a globally unique identifier. With GPT, the computer does not use a BIOS but instead uses Extensible Firmware Interface (EFI). These GPT partitions are supported only on computers running the 64-bit edition of the software. For more information on these partition types, open the Computer Management console, choose Help, and search for "GPT disks."

Performing Tasks on Basic Disks

If you are using a basic disk, you might need to do specific tasks, such as changing a drive letter, marking a partition as active, formatting the volume, creating a logical drive, or extending a basic volume. These are fairly straightforward tasks; for many, you can simply right-click the volume and choose the correct option.

To change, assign, or remove a drive letter:

1. Log on as an administrator.

2. Open the Computer Management console.

3. Highlight Disk Management.

4. Right-click the partition, logical drive, or volume, and choose Change Drive Letter And Paths.

5. To assign a drive letter, choose Add. In the Add Drive Letter Or Path box, choose the new drive letter to assign and press OK. (You can also choose Mount In The Following Empty NTFS Folder here.)

6. To change a drive letter, choose Change. In the Change Drive Letter Or Path box, select the new drive letter and click OK. You'll be prompted to verify this is what you want to do. Choose OK.

7. To remove a drive letter, click Remote in the Change Drive Letter Or Path box. Highlight the drive to remove and choose OK. You'll be prompted to verify this is what you want to do. Choose OK.

To mark a partition as active:

1. Log on as an administrator.

2. Open the Computer Management console.

3. Highlight Disk Management.

4. Right-click the partition, logical drive, or volume, and choose Mark Partition As Active.

Note

Logical partitions cannot be marked as active, and only one active partition is allowed on an MBR disk.

To format a volume:

1. Log on as an administrator.

2. Open the Computer Management console.

3. Highlight Disk Management.

4. Right-click the partition, logical drive, or volume, and choose Format.

5. Confirm that you understand that formatting the volume erases all data on it.

Note

You cannot format the system or boot partitions.

To create a partition or logical drive:

1. Log on as an administrator.

2. Open the Computer Management console.

3. Highlight Disk Management

4. Right-click a part of the disk that is unallocated, and choose New | Partition, or right-click some free space in an extended partition on the disk, and choose New Logical Drive.

5. The New Partition Wizard appears. Choose Primary Partition, Extended Partition, or Logical Drive. The wizard will walk you through the steps necessary to complete this process.

To extend a basic volume:

1. Log on as an administrator.

2. Open a command prompt. (Choose Programs | Accessories | Command Prompt.)

3. Type "diskpart" and press Enter.

4. Type "list volume" and press Enter.

5. Note the volume you want to extend. This is the basic volume. Type "select volume" followed by the volume number. Press Enter.

6. At the diskpart prompt, type "extend [size=n]" where n is the size in MB.

> **Note**
>
> *For you to extend a volume, it must be an NTFS volume, and the extra space must reside on the same disk as the volume you want to extend.*

To delete a partition or a logical drive:

1. Log on as an administrator.

2. Open the Computer Management console.

3. Highlight Disk Management.

4. Right-click the partition, logical drive, or volume, and choose Delete Partition.

5. Confirm that this is what you want to do.

Performing Tasks on Dynamic Disks

If you are using a dynamic disk, you might need to do specific tasks, such as changing a drive letter, formatting the volume, deleting a logical drive, or creating a spanned, striped, mirrored, or RAID 5 volume. A few are fairly straightforward tasks, which you can do by right-clicking the volume and choosing the correct option. Other tasks require locating additional disks or even installing them.

To assign, change, or remove a drive letter:

1. Log on as an administrator.

2. Open the Computer Management console.

3. Highlight Disk Management.

4. Right-click the partition, logical drive, or volume, and choose Change Drive Letter And Paths.

5. To assign a drive letter, choose Add. In the Add Drive Letter Or Path box, choose the new drive letter to assign and press OK. (You can also choose Mount In The Following Empty NTFS Folder here.)

6. To change a drive letter, choose Change. In the Change Drive Letter Or Path box, select the new drive letter and click OK. You'll be prompted to verify this is what you want to do. Choose OK.

7. To remove a drive letter, click Remote in the Change Drive Letter Or Path box. Highlight the drive to remove and choose OK. You'll be prompted to verify this is what you want to do. Choose OK.

Note

Be careful when changing drive letter assignments because older programs could refer to those drive letters and cease to function correctly. Remember that you cannot change the drive letter of a system or boot volume.

To format a volume:

1. Log on as an administrator.

2. Open the Computer Management console.

3. Highlight Disk Management.

4. Right-click the partition, logical drive, or volume, and choose Format.

5. Confirm that you understand that formatting the volume erases all data on it.

Note

You cannot format the system or boot partitions.

To create a spanned or striped volume:

1. Log on as an administrator.

2. Open the Computer Management console.

3. Highlight Disk Management.

4. Right-click some unallocated space on a dynamic disk, and choose New Volume.

5. When the New Volume Wizard appears, choose Next. Then select Spanned or Striped. Because disk configurations vary from computer to computer, follow the specific instructions in the wizard.

To create a mirrored or RAID 5 volume:

1. Log on as an administrator.

2. Open the Computer Management console.

3. Highlight Computer Management.

4. Choose Action | Connect To Another Computer.

5. Connect to either a Windows 2000 server or higher or a Windows XP server or higher.

6. Right-click the unallocated space on one of the dynamic disks, and choose New Volume.

7. When the New Volume Wizard appears, choose Next. Then select either RAID 5 or Mirrored. Because disk configurations vary from computer to computer, follow the specific instructions in the wizard.

To reactivate a dynamic volume:

1. Log on as an administrator.

2. Open the Computer Management console.

3. Highlight Disk Management.

4. Right-click the volume that is marked Failed, and choose Reactivate Volume.

Adding a New Disk

Even when you use Disk Cleanup and Disk Defragmenter and you uninstall unused programs and components, there will probably come a time, especially on a server, that the available disk space has been used up. When this happens, you have three choices: buy a new computer with a larger hard drive; replace the disk on the existing computer; or add a second (or third, perhaps) hard drive to the existing computer. Adding a new disk drive is much less expensive and takes less time than configuring a new computer.

In this section, you'll learn how to add a disk to a computer, determine what disk type to use, create partitions and logical drives, and format the new disk in preparation for data. The first step is physically installing the new disk.

Installing the New Disk

New hard disk drives are usually installed internally. Replacing an old disk is fairly simple, but in a desktop computer, adding a second disk is more complicated. A cable connects the new drive to the old drive and the hard drives are usually installed in a piggyback fashion. Piggybacking is a way to connect two drives where the cable from the back of the new drive is connected to the back of the second drive. The new drive is physically installed in an extra slot inside the computer, either directly above or below the old drive. The old drive remains connected to the system board. When you're adding a second disk to a computer, make sure that the jumpers for the first disk are set to Master and that the settings for subsequent disks are set to Slave. In older computers, you might have to connect the new hard drive directly to the system board, or there might not be an option to piggyback the hard drives. If this is the case, installing a new (or second) drive will be a little different from what's been described here. In this instance, refer to your system's manual. With more powerful workstations, the drives might connect to a SCSI, USB, or FireWire interface. With network servers, drives can be installed in several ways, both internally and externally, but this is a job for your network's A+ technician.

When a new drive is installed, it is electronically blank. This means that there is nothing on the drive at all; the drive cannot be used until it is set up and formatted correctly. In most newer computers—specifically, those that can be used to run Windows XP Professional— the computer detects the drive automatically during the computer's CMOS setup. The drive manufacturer typically performs the low-level format, marking off the hard drive into cylinders and sectors, so users no longer need to do this. Users are responsible for partition-ing the drive, performing the high-level format, and placing the data or the operating system on the drive.

Having Windows XP Detect the New Disk

There are two types of disk installations: Either the disk is a new disk and is the only disk in the computer, or the disk is a second disk being added to create more disk space, and it is a spanned, striped, mirrored, or RAID 5 volume. If the disk is new and is the only disk in the computer, you'll need to install Windows XP Professional on it. If this is the case, you'll need to configure the computer from scratch. This task is beyond the scope of this book. However, if the disk is being added to a computer that already has a disk, then after the new disk is physically installed, Windows XP Professional can be used to detect it.

To have Windows XP detect the newly installed disk:

1. Log on as an administrator.

2. Open the Computer Management console.

3. Expand the Device Manager tree.

4. Choose Action | Scan For Hardware Changes.

5. Highlight Disk Management.

6. Choose Action | Rescan Disks.

7. If the new disk appears and is not initialized, restart the computer.

To initialize a new disk:

1. Log on as an administrator.

2. Open the Computer Management console.

3. Highlight Disk Management.

4. Right-click the disk that needs to be initialized, and choose Initialize Disk.

5. In the Initialize Disk dialog box, select the disk(s) to initialize. Choose OK.

The disk is initialized as a basic disk. Now you need to choose a disk type and create partitions or logical drives from the unallocated space. With a basic disk configured, cre-ate the partitions and logical drives you want by following the guidelines in the previous sections. Depending on what the new disk is being used for, you might not even want to configure the disk with partitions or logical drives, especially if the drive is only to be used for storing data.

Choosing the Disk Type

As you know, there are several ways to configure multiple disks. You'll need to decide which configuration you'd like to use. Here are some suggestions to help you decide whether you should use basic or dynamic disks and, if you're choosing dynamic, whether you should use simple, spanned, and striped disks. These are the only options for Windows XP Professional computers. If you are configuring a new disk for a Window XP or 2000 server, there are also suggestions for dynamic mirrored and RAID 5 volumes. All dynamic volumes must be formatted with the NTFS file system. Basic disks can either be FAT or NTFS.

Use basic disks if:

♦ You don't know which type to choose. (You can always convert to dynamic later.)

♦ You want to use primary and extended partitions and logical drives.

♦ You have a large disk with extra space, and you want to extend the disk space with this same disk at some later time.

♦ A dual boot is necessary, and the other operating system is MS-DOS, Windows 9x, Windows ME, Windows NT 4, or Windows XP Home Edition.

♦ You are using a laptop.

♦ The disks are removable, detachable, or connected to SCSI buses, FireWire interfaces, or USB interfaces.

♦ You are using the FAT file system.

♦ You do not require fault tolerance.

Use dynamic disks if:

♦ You want to create volumes that extend to other physical disks that are formatted with the NTFS file system.

♦ You want to create spanned, striped, mirrored, or RAID 5 volumes.

♦ You want to extend simple or spanned volumes.

♦ An earlier operating system—such as MS-DOS, Windows 9x, Windows ME, Windows NT 4, or Windows Home Edition—does not need to access this volume.

Use simple dynamic disks if:

♦ You have only one physical dynamic disk, and it is formatted with the NTFS file system.

♦ You want to mirror the volume to another disk.

♦ You plan to extend this volume within the same disk or onto another disk.

♦ You do not require fault tolerance.

Use spanned dynamic disks if:

♦ You want to use disk space on more than one physical disk, and those disks are formatted with the NTFS file system

♦ You do not need to mirror the disk

♦ You have at least two dynamic disks to work with

♦ You do not need to stripe the disk

♦ You do not require fault tolerance

Use striped dynamic disks if:

♦ You want to use disk space on more than one NTFS-formatted physical disk

♦ You have at least two dynamic disks to work with

♦ You do not require fault tolerance

♦ You need fast read and write performance

♦ You do not need to mirror or extend the disks

Use mirrored dynamic disks if:

♦ You are configuring the disk for Windows XP Server or Windows 2000 Server or higher

♦ The disks are formatted with the NTFS file system

♦ You require fault tolerance

♦ You do not require fast read or write performance

♦ You want to mirror an existing simple dynamic volume

♦ You do not need to extend or stripe the volume

Use RAID 5 dynamic disks if:

♦ You are configuring the disk for Windows XP Server or Windows 2000 Server or higher

♦ The disks are formatted with the NTFS file system

♦ You require fault tolerance

♦ You have at least three NTFS dynamic disks available

♦ You do not need to extend or mirror the disks

♦ You want good read and write performance

Formatting the New Disk

With the new disk configured, the disk now needs to be formatted. Earlier I mentioned that a low-level format is the responsibility of the manufacturer, but the high-level format is the responsibility of the user. High-level formats involve configuring the disk to accept data. Formatting the disk is easy after the disk has been initialized and a disk configuration has been decided on.

To format a basic or dynamic disk:

1. Log on as an administrator.

2. Open the Computer Management console.

3. Highlight Disk Management.

4. Right-click the disk that needs to be formatted, and choose Format. Choose OK.

Disk Status Descriptions

When using the Computer Management Console, you'll see several disk-status descriptions. I hope that most of the time, the description is "Online." Any other disk-status description spells trouble. In this section, I'll explain the disk-status descriptions you'll see most often, what they mean, and what to do about these errors.

Foreign

The Foreign status icon is displayed when a dynamic disk is moved to the local computer from a different computer that runs Windows 2000 or Windows XP. This icon can also appear when a computer that is running Windows XP Home Edition is configured to dual-boot with another operating system that uses dynamic disks. Dynamic disks are not supported in the Home Edition.

To configure the computer to access the data on this disk on a Windows 2000 Professional machine:

1. Log on as an administrator.

2. Open the Computer Management console.

3. In the console tree, highlight Disk Management.

4. Right-click the foreign disk, and choose Import Foreign Disks.

5. Choose Action | Rescan Disks.

Initializing

While you are converting a basic disk to a dynamic disk, the status is changed from Basic to Initializing. When the initialization is complete, the disk's status should become Online and Healthy.

Missing

When the Missing status icon appears, the computer is unable to locate the dynamic disk. This can happen for many reasons, but the most likely reasons are that the disk has been disconnected or turned off, is corrupted, or has crashed. If the Missing status is shown, first try to reactivate the disk by right-clicking it and choosing Reactivate Disk. If this doesn't work, locate the physical disk connections to the power supply and the system board or other hardware, and verify that those connections are good. Try again to reactivate the disk.

If this doesn't work, and if the disk is considered unusable and must be replaced, right-click the disk and choose Remove Disk. You'll lose any data stored on the disk, but you can recover that data from backups as needed.

Not Initialized

If a disk's status is Not Initialized, then the disk is not properly installed. After installing a new disk, you must initialize it by right-clicking it and choosing Initialize Disk. This writes an MBR (master boot record) and allows you to create partitions on the disk.

Online and Online (Errors)

Online is the best status available. Online means that the disk is installed properly and is working fine. There is no need for any user action until the status of the Online disk changes to Online (Errors). Errors can mean a number of things, but often, this status has to do with errors that are detected on a portion of the disk. Most times, the Error status can be removed simply by reactivating the disk. You can do this by right-clicking the disk and choosing Reactivate Disk. You might also try using the Disk Cleanup and Disk Defragmenter utilities.

Offline

Generally, an otherwise healthy disk will change to Offline status because the disk is temporarily unavailable. Either that disk has been physically turned off or removed, or it is being serviced by a network technician. The disk can also be corrupted or disconnected. As with other disk problems, verify that the disk is connected, powered on, working, and available. Then right-click the disk, and choose Reactivate Disk.

Unreadable or Failed

A basic disk or a dynamic disk can become unreadable if it has had a hardware failure such as a read/write head failing, is corrupt, which can occur after certain viruses or other similar hazards, or has physical errors on the disk as when the computer has been jarred and the read/write device has physically touched the hard disk. Additionally, the disk's database or MBR might be corrupted. Often, these are not recoverable errors. Verify that all connections are working, that disks are turned on, and that there is power to the disks. You can try to rescan the disks as described earlier to see if the status changes. However, you will often need to replace the disk.

Healthy

This is another good status. If a disk is Healthy, it is working properly and requires no user intervention.

Healthy (At Risk)

If a disk is Healthy but also At Risk, it usually also has the Online (Errors) status. At Risk can mean a number of things, but it often has to do with errors that are detected on a portion of the disk. Most times, you can remove the At Risk status simply by reactivating the disk. (Right-click it, and choose Reactivate Disk.) You might also try using the Disk Cleanup and Disk Defragmenter utilities. Consider backing up the data and replacing the disk as soon as possible if this message appears again.

Unknown

When a basic or dynamic disk's status is Unknown, the boot sector for the volume is probably corrupt because of a virus or because the disk was not installed and initialized properly. If this is a new disk, initialize it by right-clicking it and choosing Initialize Disk. If the disk is not new, it might be corrupt. This could be because of a virus. Run virus-checking software on the volume, and repair from backups if the disk's status cannot be brought back to Healthy.

Data Incomplete

This status appears only after some, but not all, of the disks in the volume have been moved to another location. Data on the Data Incomplete volumes will be deleted unless the disks that make up this volume are moved, and the entire volume is imported together. You cannot move some of the disks at one time and some at a later time. All disks must be moved at the same time.

Mirrored Disk Problems

Mirrored disks are available only on Windows 2000 Server and Windows XP Server computers or higher. However, you can manage these computers from a Windows XP Professional machine. There are several errors specific to mirrored disks: Data Not Redundant, Failed Redundancy, and Stale Data. Redundancy means that both of the mirrored disks are working. Any errors relating to redundancy, then, imply that there is a problem with one of the mirrored disks.

Data Not Redundant and Failed Redundancy

If the Data Not Redundant status is shown, it means that one of the mirrored disks was imported, but the other has not been imported yet. The non-imported disk will have a status of Failed Redundancy or Missing until the second disk is successfully imported. You can import all disks at the same time to avoid these problems. You can also receive these messages while removing a mirrored disk. Once one of the disks has been successfully removed, the remaining disk returns to Healthy status.

With Failed Redundancy status, you know that one or both of the mirrored disks (or volumes) has failed. The failed disk should be replaced at once.

Stale Data

When you're importing disks that contain a mirrored volume, make sure that their status is Healthy before doing so. If the status is not Healthy, then you might receive the Stale Data status after the disks are imported. Stale means that the data is not up-to-date and will not be of value. To correct this problem, put the disk back in the original computer, bring its status to Healthy, and try again.

RAID 5 Problems

RAID 5 status errors are the same as those for mirrored disks, but RAID 5 configurations use at least three disks, whereas mirrored configurations use only two.

Data Not Redundant

These errors occur when some but not all of the disks in the volume were moved. The disks in the volume must be moved together to avoid this status.

Failed Redundancy

As with mirrored volumes, this status indicates that one or more of the disks in the RAID 5 volume has failed and needs to be replaced. The disk should be replaced as soon as possible.

Stale Data

As with mirrored volumes, this status indicates that the disks that were imported weren't healthy at the time of the import. Move the disks back where they came from, repair them to a healthy status, and then bring them back.

Disk Quotas

Disk quotas allow administrators to limit how much disk space users of the computer have access to for saving their files and other data. Disk quotas are available only on NTFS volumes. You can set varying levels of warnings and cutoffs for the quotas. You can set how much of the hard drive the user can use, and you can have a system event logged in Event Viewer when a user exceeds a specified warning level. You can decide what should happen if a user exceeds his quota limit (you can specify whether that user should be allowed to save his data or not). Disk quotas are quite useful for both administrators of single computers and network administrators. In this section, you'll learn how to configure disk quotas on local disks, export those quotas to other volumes, and configure disk quota settings.

Disk Quota Settings

Before setting quotas, take a look at the different types of settings that can be configured. There are basically two types of settings: disk quota limits and disk quota warning levels. Limits refer to exactly how much space a user can have on the hard drive for personal files and folders. For example, you might first grant a user 1GB of space. This number is as much space as the user can have. The second setting is the warning level. A warning level is a number that is set automatically when quotas are enabled, but can be changed as needed. Warning levels are used to inform users they are nearing their quota limit and to log entries regarding quota levels in the System log. In this example, the warning level can be set for 0.75GB. At this level, you can configure disk quotas to write an event to the system log.

You can enable quotas on any NTFS volume, including a local volume, a network volume, and even removable storage. These volumes have to be shared, of course, so that users can access them.

Quota Limits

Setting quota limits seems easy, but you must take into account how much space each user realistically needs for his or her files and folders. A graphic artist, for instance, needs more space than a data-entry employee, and a photographer needs more space than those two combined. Although you should make sure you provide enough space, when first starting, consider setting fairly strict limits; it is always better to give more later than to take away previously configured space. Each user should be given at least 10MB of disk space, but more realistically, at least 500MB.

After deciding on the limit, settle on what to do when a user exceeds that limit. There are several options:

♦ Make users delete files or folders to make room for what they want to save.

♦ Allow users to save the files and folders even though the users have exceeded their limit.

♦ Do not configure disk quotas at all; just track a user's disk usage.

♦ Decide if you will log an event to the system file when a user exceeds his or her warning level.

Quota Warnings

Depending on your needs, you can choose to log an event when a user nears the disk quota limit and reaches the warning level. By default, an event is written to the system log on the local computer whenever a user exceeds the quota limit but not when the user reaches the warning level. You can view these events in Event Viewer. They are recorded every hour by default, and this can be changed as well. More on Event Viewer later.

Configuring Disk Quotas on a Local Disk

Once you've decided to use disk quotas, they must be enabled. To enable disk quotas on a local disk:

1. As an administrator, log onto an NTFS volume.

2. Open My Computer.

3. Right-click the disk for which you want to enable disk quotas, and choose Properties.

4. Select the Quota tab, and check the Enable Quota Management checkbox. See Figure 12.7.

5. To deny disk space to users who exceed their quota limits, check the checkbox Deny Disk Space To Users Exceeding Quota Limit.

6. To limit disk usage, check the Limit Disk Space To checkbox. Choose a level of disk space for each user. The default is 100MB.

7. In the Set Warning Level To text box, set a warning level. This should be less than the disk-limit level.

8. To log events for quota limits and warning levels, check the checkboxes Log Event When A User Exceeds Their Quota Limit and Log Event When A User Exceeds Their

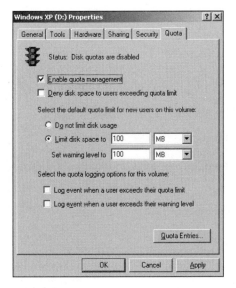

Figure 12.7
Enabling disk quotas.

Warning Level. Steps 9 through 11 are optional. If you do not have any specific users to add, choose Apply and skip to Step 12.

Note

When quotas are configured, they are applied after the user writes to the disk the first time. If you want to quotas to be applied for a user or group before they write to the disk the first time, perform Steps 9 through 11.

9. Choose the Quota Entries button to add a specific user or group now. Notice that the BuiltIn\Administrators group is not configured with a quota limit or a warning level. To add a new user or group to which these quota settings will apply, choose Quota | New Quota Entry.

10. From the Select Users window, enter the user or group names that this quota will apply to. Choose OK.

11. In the Add New Quota Entry box, set the limits and warning levels. Choose OK, and close the Quota Entries dialog box. In the disk's Properties dialog, choose Apply.

12. In the warning box that appears, stating that this process could take several minutes, choose OK.

Exporting Quota Settings to Another Volume

Once disk quotas are configured for the local hard drive, they can be exported to additional volumes. The volumes must also be formatted with the NTFS file system, and you must be an administrator to export the settings.

To export your settings to another volume:

1. As an administrator, log onto the local computer with disk quotas configured.

2. Open My Computer.

3. Right-click the disk that has quotas already set, and choose Properties.

4. In the Properties dialog box, select the Quotas tab.

5. Make sure that the Enable Quota Management checkbox is checked, and then choose the Quota Entries button.

6. Highlight the entries you want to export. See Figure 12.8.

7. Choose Quota | Export.

8. In the Export Quota Settings dialog box, browse to a location where you want to save or apply the file, and choose Save.

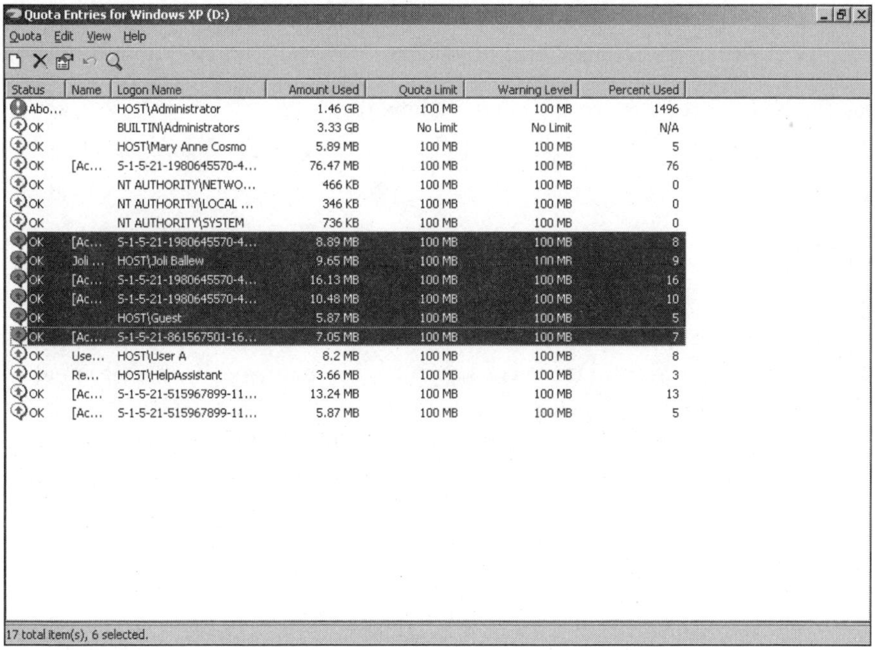

Figure 12.8
Exporting quotas.

Creating Quota Reports

Setting quotas and warnings won't do you any good if you don't know how to use Event Viewer to read them or if you don't create reports for others to view. In the next section, "The Computer Management Console," you'll learn all about Event Viewer, but for now, I'll concentrate on creating some reports.

To create a quota report:

1. Log on as an administrator.

2. Open My Computer.

3. Right-click the disk for which you'd like to create a report (one that has disk quotas configured), and choose Properties.

4. Select the Quota tab, and choose the Quota Entries button.

5. Minimize the Quota Entries window.

6. Open the program and document in which you want to create the report, such as Microsoft Excel or Microsoft Word.

7. Maximize the Quota Entries window, and highlight the users you want to include in your report. Resize the window so that you can see the document you just opened.

8. Drag the highlighted rows to the open document.

The information for the users selected will be placed neatly in the document.

The Computer Management Console

The Computer Management console helps administrators perform the tasks necessary to manage their shared computers and to manage remote computers in their workgroup or domain. The Computer Management console combines many of the most common Windows XP tools into a single interface. In previous chapters, you learned about a few of these tasks, including creating and managing local users and groups, and managing shared folders, including who uses them and for how long. This section introduces some other Computer Management options. The System Tools tree contains Event Viewer, Performance Logs And Alerts, and Device Manager. The Services And Applications tree contains Services, WMI Control, and the Indexing Service. Some of these tools are best viewed from other consoles, but all can be accessed from Computer Management.

Event Viewer

Event Viewer offers three kinds of logs: application, security, and system. As you learned earlier, disk quota overruns are recorded in the system log. Event Viewer lets you gather and record information about various system events, including those having to do with hardware and software problems or more complex system problems. By default, all users can view the application and system logs, but only administrators can modify the system logs.

The application log records events that are caused by applications running on the computer. For example, a program might log an event when a user tries to delete a file but can't, when a user tries to log onto a domain controller but can't, or when a program tries to locate a file, but it isn't there.

The security log isn't started by default. It is used to audit specific events, such as successful logons or logoffs, successful creation of files and folders, successful resource access, or failure of any of these tasks.

The system log records events caused by Windows XP itself. These events have to do with system components. Examples include:

♦ Information balloon pop-ups that tell the user that something has happened, such as a scheduled event not running

♦ When a service such as Terminal Services begins

♦ When the browser cannot locate a list of servers on the network

♦ When no domain controllers are found

In the following sections, I'll detail how to perform tasks and configure the Event Viewer logs to suit your needs. The application and system logs run on their own, so many events are already recorded on your computer. If you don't know anything about Event Viewer, you should start by viewing some events that have already been recorded.

Viewing Events

To view application and security logs:

1. Open the Computer Management console, and expand the System Tools tree.

2. Click Event Viewer in the left pane, as shown in Figure 12.9.

3. Select the application log.

4. In the right pane, double-click any event in the log. See Figure 12.10.

From the Event Properties dialog box, you can use the up and down arrow keys to view the event before or following the selected event. You can also view the date, source, time, category, type, event ID, users, and computer involved in this event. A description of the event is also included and can assist you in deciphering what the event means.

Interpreting Events

In Figure 12.10, notice that the type of event is Error. There are three types of events: Errors, Warnings, and Information. Information events are simply that: information.

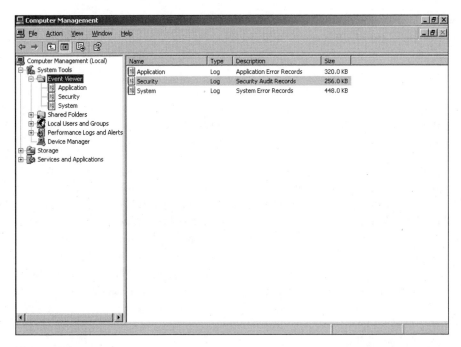

Figure 12.9
Event Viewer.

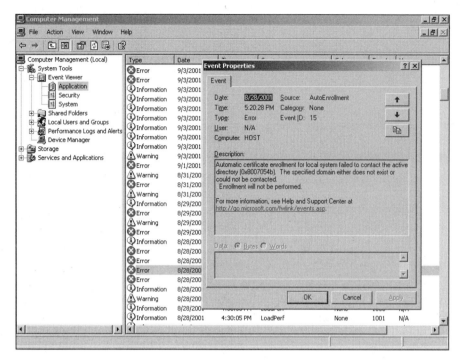

Figure 12.10
Event Properties.

These events record such things as services starting and stopping successfully and data being recorded successfully. Warnings indicate that something might go wrong in the future; warnings include services that fail to start, a server that cannot be found, or system hardware trying to write to an illegal address. Although the system can deal with these events on its own, they could signal future problems. Finally, errors are events that can and do harm the system either now or in the future. Errors include programs attempting to read from illegal addresses, failures to contact Active Directory on a server, or failures to obtain the domain control name for the computer on the network.

The Description box provides information about the type of problem and the application or component involved in the event. You can get a general idea of the problem from this information, but you can get more detailed information from the Help and Support Center by clicking its link in the Description box. Clicking this link immediately connects you to the site if you have a working Internet connection. If you decide to connect to this Web site, you'll be asked to verify that it is okay to send the information related to this event over the Internet. When the connection is established, the Windows XP Help and Support Center will open automatically, and you'll receive information about the event you've selected.

Archiving Log Files

When log files get full or when you want to save log files for future reference, you can archive them by completing the steps listed here:

1. Open Event Viewer.

2. In the left pane of the console tree, highlight the log you want to save.

3. Choose Action | Save Log File As.

4. In the File Name box, type a file name. Select a log file type.

If you save the log as a text (.txt) or comma-delimited (.csv) file, you can open the file in other programs, such as database or word processing programs. However, the files do not retain their binary data. If you save the logs in a log-file format (.evt), you can open them again in Event Viewer. These logs do retain their binary data.

5. Choose Save or Save As.

Creating a New Log View

You can add a new log view in Event Viewer. The additional view is simply a copy of the log itself. You might want to create another view of the log (a copy) so that one of the views can be configured to show only the warnings, while another view shows all events. These additional views appear in the console tree and can be managed and customized the same way as the default logs in Event Viewer.

To create an additional view:

1. Open Event Viewer.

2. Select the log for which you'd like to add another view.

3. Choose Action | New Log View.

4. A copy of the log will be placed in the console tree in Event Viewer with the log name followed by a (2), (3), (4), etc., depending on the number of log views created. You can rename the log to make it representative of what the log view has been created for, such as Application (Errors).

Finding a Specific Event

If you need to locate a specific event for troubleshooting or to show it to a network technician, you can locate the event in Event Viewer. To locate a specific event:

1. Open Event Viewer.

2. Highlight the log you want to search.

3. Choose View | Find. For Steps 4 through 11, input as much information about the event as possible.

4. In the Event Types area of the Find In dialog box, check or uncheck the boxes for the types of event you want to find: Information, Warning, Error, Success Audit, and/or Failure Audit. By default, all are checked.

5. In the Event Source drop-down list, select an event source, such as Spooler, Security, or Security Account Manager. The default is All.

6. In the Category drop-down list, select a category if any are available, or select All.

7. If you know the Event ID, type it in the Event ID box.

8. If you know the user's name, type it in the User box.

9. If you know the computer name, type it in the Computer box.

10. If you know any words in the description of the event, type them in the Description box.

11. Choose whether the search should move up the list or down it. Choose Find Next and then Close. You'll see all listings that match your criteria in the Event Viewer window.

Sorting and Filtering Event Logs

If you need to locate more than a single event, you can sort and filter the events in the event logs. You can sort event items to arrange them by date (from newest to oldest), by type, by source, by category, by event, by user, or by computer. If you want to see all of the events related to a specific person, for example, you can sort the log by user; you'll also still be able to see the remaining events. You can filter the logs when you want to see only certain types of events, such as errors or warnings, certain event IDs, or specific users or computers. In this instance, not all of the events in the log are shown; only the ones matching the filter requirements are shown.

To sort events in the log:

1. Open Event Viewer.

2. Highlight the log you want to sort.

3. Choose one of the column headings—Type, Date, Time, Source, Category, Event, User, or Computer—and click it.

Figure 12.11 shows a system log sorted by users. Users are sorted alphabetically.

To filter events in the log:

1. Open Event Viewer.

2. Highlight the log you want to filter.

3. Choose View | Filter.

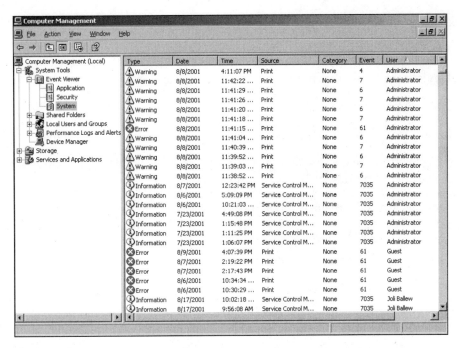

Figure 12.11
Sorting events by users.

4. In the Properties dialog box, check or uncheck the boxes for the types of event you'd like to see or not see in Event Viewer. Fill in any other information, such as source, category, event ID, user, computer, and/or the dates and times of the events. Choose OK.

Clearing, Opening, Refreshing, and Freeing an Event Log

You can perform multiple tasks on an event log by right-clicking it and choosing the option you want. Right-clicking an event log offers the following choices (not all of the options are listed if they have been mentioned previously):

♦ *Open A Log File*—Choose this to open any saved log file.

♦ *Clear All Events*—Choose this to remove all events from the log file.

♦ *Rename*—Choose this to rename a log file.

♦ *Refresh*—Choose this to refresh the data in the log file. Refreshing updates the data in the log file and shows events that have occurred since the file has been open.

Setting Event-Logging Options

Because event logs collect so much data, it is important that you understand what the default event-logging options are. Depending on the importance of these logs in your organization, you might want to save them, change the log size, or choose not to overwrite logs as they get full.

To see and set the event-logging options:

1. Open Event Viewer.

2. Highlight the log for which you want to configure options.

3. Choose Action | Properties.

4. On the General tab, in Display Name, type a new name for the log (if you want to).

5. In Log Size, change the amount of hard drive space that should be dedicated to the log file. The default is 512MB. Adjust this number as necessary.

6. Specify what to do if the maximum log size is reached:

    ♦ Overwrite Files As Needed.

    ♦ Overwrite Files Older Than _____ Days (this is the default choice, and the default number of days is 7).

    ♦ Do Not Overwrite Events (Clear Log Manually). Selecting this option requires an administrator to clear the logs manually before the computer can be used again.

7. Choose OK.

Enabling the Security Log

As I mentioned previously, the security log isn't enabled by default. This is because an administrator must choose which events to monitor and must determine how much disk space should be allotted to this task. Auditing takes up system resources and uses quite a bit of disk space, so it must be configured properly. Auditing is configured through an MMC console configured with the Group Policy snap-in. If you already have a Group Policy console configured, begin the next procedure at Step 8.

To enable the security log and begin auditing events:

1. Log on as an administrator.

2. Choose Start | Run, and type "mmc" in the Run dialog box.

3. Choose File | Add/Remove Snap-In.

4. In the Add/Remove Snap-In dialog box, choose the Add button.

5. In the Add Standalone Snap-In dialog box, select Group Policy. Choose the Add button.

6. In the Select Group Policy Object page, select Local Computer; then choose Finish.

7. Choose Close and OK.

8. In the Group Policy console, highlight Local Computer Policy.

9. Expand the tree Local Computer Policy\Computer Configuration\Windows Settings\Security Settings\Local Policies\Audit Policy. See Figure 12.12.

Figure 12.12 shows some audit policies already set. All of your security settings should be set to No Auditing.

10. To set up auditing, double-click any policy and check the Success or Failure checkbox. Choose OK. Auditing will begin on those events.

11. When you close the console, save the changes.

Deciding What to Audit

If you turned on all of the auditing available, the security log would fill up so quickly that either it would be useless because the data would be overwritten so quickly, or you would be overwhelmed with saving the files as they filled up. It is important to carefully select the events you want to audit so neither of these things happen.

On a Windows XP Professional machine, the nine events listed next can be audited for successes, failures, both, or neither. Checking the Success box records a successful event, and checking the Failure box records a failed attempt for the event. For instance, for Account Logon Events, a success is a completed logon, and a failure shows that someone tried

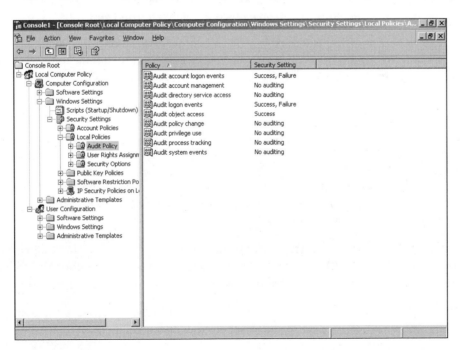

Figure 12.12
Setting audit policies.

to log onto the local machine but failed. After each item, I'll put in my two cents' worth about which audits are necessary. You can audit these types of events:

♦ *Account logon events*—Events that coincide with successful or failed logons to the local computer. You should log both successes and failures, especially when you suspect that others are logging onto your computer without your permission, or if you suspect that someone is trying to log on and failing. You do not need to audit these events if your computer is physically secure, or if you are sure that no other users are trying to log on.

♦ *Account management events*—Events related to changes made in accounts, such as creating, modifying, or deleting user or group accounts, renaming, disabling, or enabling existing accounts, or setting or changing passwords. You should audit both successes and failures when you suspect a user or users of performing these tasks without the proper permissions.

♦ *Directory service access events*—Events that have to do with a user accessing an Active Directory object. Active Directory objects are resources in domains, so logging isn't necessary for computers in workgroups. In domains, this logging is usually configured on the domain controller.

♦ *Logon events*—Events that coincide with successful or failed logons to a local computer when these logon attempts are made over a network. You need to log these events only if you are a member of a network, and you believe people are trying to access your workstation from their computers. Successes and failures can be audited at all times, though, just for security. There shouldn't be too many records related to this event.

♦ *Object access events*—Events occurring when a user accesses an object, such as a file or folder, a Registry key, a printer, and so on. You should consider monitoring failures of these events occasionally to verify that users are not trying to access forbidden resources.

♦ *Policy changes*—Events related to changes in users' rights assignments, audit polices, and trust policies. Only administrators should be able to make these changes. If you suspect that others are making these changes when they shouldn't be, audit these events.

♦ *Privilege use*—Events having to do with user rights. User rights include adding workstations to a domain, creating a paging file, logging on locally, and many more. Log these events only when necessary because multiple entries could be written to the logs every few minutes even on a small network.

♦ *Process tracking events*—Events related to processes, such as those occurring when a program activates or exits. Only system administrators need to log this information when they are looking for problems related to programs running on the local computer.

♦ *System events*—Windows events, such as those occurring when a user shuts down or restarts a computer or when something happens that affects the system security or security logs. Log these events on an as-needed basis.

Using Event Viewer on a Remote Computer

You can log onto a remote computer through the Computer Management console and use Event Viewer on your local computer to view and manage logs on the remote one. You can connect to another computer by highlighting Computer Management and choosing Action | Connect To Another Computer as described earlier. Once connected, you can view the other computer's application, security, and system logs just as if you were sitting at the computer locally.

Performance Logs And Alerts and System Monitor

Another Computer Management console utility is Performance Logs And Alerts. You can also access this utility from the Performance console in Administrative Tools. You can use Performance Logs And Alerts with System Monitor to monitor what's happening on the local or remote computer in terms of workload, resource availability, and more. With Performance Logs And Alerts, you can also set alerts based on specific thresholds, and have the computer notify you when those thresholds are met.

You can save this information in a SQL database, view it using System Monitor, or export the data to a spreadsheet program. Then, you can use this data to analyze a computer's performance. You can also view the data as it is being collected, and set stop and start times for data collection. No user needs to be logged onto the computer for data to be collected.

Before working with this utility, make sure you are logged on as an administrator to avoid any local or remote permissions problems. Then do the following:

♦ Before performing any monitoring tasks, stop any screensaver programs.

♦ Stop any services that do not need to be monitored.

♦ When logging, note that any logging activity will slow down the local system. If logging is producing too much of a strain on the system, increase the intervals in which samples are taken.

♦ Log enough information initially to create a baseline so you can get a general feel for how the computer performs most of the time.

Objects and Counters

The components that are inside your computer can be polled for performance data. The data that is collected from components in your system are referred to as *performance objects*. For instance, the Memory object obtains information about RAM performance, while the CPU object obtains information about processor performance. Each of these performance objects has related counters. The Memory object has counters such as Pages Per Second, Write Copies Per Second, Available Bytes, Page Faults, Page Reads, Page Writes, and dozens more. How to determine which objects and counters you should collect information about could fill an entire book in itself. In the following sections, I'll introduce the basics about Performance Logs And Alerts and get you started with some basic performance logging.

Viewing a Sample Counter Log

To view a sample counter log and get an idea of what the log looks like:

1. Open Performance Logs And Alerts from Administrative Tools | Performance. If you don't see Administrative Tools on the Start menu, open it from the Control Panel.

2. Expand the Performance Logs And Alerts tree, and highlight Counter Logs.

3. In the right pane, right-click the System Overview log, and choose Start.

4. In the left pane, highlight System Monitor to view the log in action. Notice what is being logged in the window at the bottom of the screen.

5. In the left pane, highlight Counter Logs again, right-click the System Overview log, and choose Stop.

Selecting Objects and Counters

Deciding which objects and counters you should use can be quite confusing. Because there are so many objects and counters available, it is quite difficult to understand when and why to use each one. The objects that you can choose to monitor are listed here along with brief descriptions. You can view more information about any object or counter through the Add Counters dialog box by selecting the object or counter and choosing Explain. This process is shown later.

Here are the most common objects and counters for workstations:

♦ *Memory*—These counters are related to the physical RAM and virtual memory (called a *paging file*) on the hard disk. When physical memory runs out of room for data, the data is paged to and from the RAM to the physical disk (paging file). This transfer of information slows down the computer's performance. RAM and paging files can be monitored to determine problems in this area.

♦ *Physical Disk*—These counters are related to the computer's hard disk. Data that is saved to, read from, or written to the computer are placed here. If there seem to be problems with the hard drive, consider monitoring this object.

♦ *Processor*—The processor is the computer's CPU. It is the hardware that is the heart of the system, performs all of the needed calculations on data, and sends data to printers and other peripherals. In some instances, a computer's slow performance has more to do with an overworked processor than it does with a lack of necessary memory or hard drive space.

♦ *System*—These counters include File Data Operations Performed Per Second, and related file read, write, and operations per second. These counters are used by more advanced administrators to determine if a particular system counter is causing problems for the computer.

♦ *Cache*—These counters refer to the amount and performance of cache on the system. A *cache* is an area of memory that stores frequently used data, such as program code or computer instructions, so it can be accessed quickly. Sometimes a cache is RAM, but in newer computers, it is a separate chip such as an L1 or L2 cache.

♦ *Print Queue*—These counters are used to display statistics about how well the print queue is performing.

To view more information about any object or counter offered by Performance Logs And Alerts:

1. Open Performance Logs And Alerts from Administrative Tools | Performance. If you don't see Administrative Tools on the Start menu, open it from the Control Panel.

2. Expand the Performance Logs And Alerts tree, and highlight Counter Logs.

3. In the right pane, right-click a blank area, and choose New Log Settings. Name the log.

4. In the Log Properties dialog box, choose Add Objects.

5. In the Add Objects dialog box, highlight the performance object for which you want more information, and choose the Explain button. Choose Close.

6. In the Log Properties dialog box, choose Add Counters.

7. In the Performance Object drop-down list, select the performance object that relates to the counter for which you want more information.

8. In Select Counters From List, highlight the counter for which you'd like more information, and choose the Explain button. Choose Close and Cancel.

Table 12.1 sums up what you should monitor if you are aware that a certain problem exists, such as a memory bottleneck or a processor bottleneck. A bottleneck happens when lots of

Table 12.1   Discovering problems.

Suspected Source of Problem	Counters to Select	What to Look For
Print Queue	For the Print Queue object: Bytes Printed/Sec; Job Errors/Sec; Jobs Spooling/Sec	Low values for Bytes/Sec and high values for Job Errors/Sec.
Processor	For the Processor object: Interrupts/Sec; %Processor Time/Sec. For the System object: Processor Queue Length	Interrupts/Sec should be around 1000/sec; %Processor Time should be around 85%.
Memory	For the Memory object: Available Bytes; Pages/Sec	Available Bytes should be less than 4MB; Pages/Sec should be around 20.
Disk	For the Physical Disk object: %Disk Time; Disk Reads/Sec; and Disk Writes/Sec. For the Logical Disk object: %Free Space	%Disk Time should be around 90%; %Free Space should be around 15%; other counters depend on the disk manufacturer.
Paging File	For the Paging File object: %Usage	Should be above 70%.

data is sent to an object, and the object can't handle the load. A bottleneck is analogous to a traffic jam; when four lanes of a highway suddenly drop to only two lanes, traffic backs up and cars must wait their turn to get through. Even if you aren't sure what type of problem you have, by trial and error and by using these tips, you can probably figure it out.

Many of these values also depend on the manufacturer of the hardware and on the expected performance and workload. If you see out-of-range numbers on multiple occasions, perhaps your computer or its components are not capable of the load that it's under. It might be time to upgrade to a faster processor, more RAM, or a larger hard drive.

Creating Counter Logs for a Local Computer

After you've decided what to log, open the Computer Management console and create a log. To create a counter log:

1. In the Performance console, expand the Performance Logs And Alerts tree.

2. In the left pane, highlight Counter Logs.

3. In the right pane, right-click an empty area of the screen, and choose New Log Settings.

4. Type a name for the new log, and choose OK. (I named mine Processor because I intend to monitor the processor of my system.)

5. The Log dialog box opens, as shown in Figure 12.13. Choose Add Objects.

6. In the Add Objects dialog box, choose to use local computer counter objects.

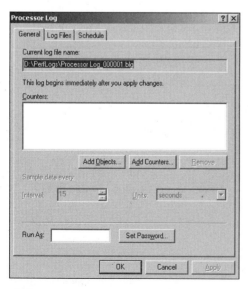

Figure 12.13
The Log dialog box.

7. Scroll down through the objects in the Performance Objects window of the new Log file's Properties dialog box, and select ProcessorPerformance. Choose the Add button and then the Close button.

8. Back in the Log dialog box, shown in Figure 12.13, choose the Add Counters button.

9. In the Add Counters dialog box, select %Processor time, and choose Add.

10. In the same dialog box, select %User Time, and choose Add again.

11. Choose Close and then OK. In the right pane, notice the new log. If the icon is green, then the log has started; if the icon is red, right-click the log and choose Start.

Note

To add counters for remote computers, choose Select Counter Objects From Computer, and select the computer you want to monitor from the drop-down list.

12. To view the activity for this log, click System Monitor in the left pane of the Performance console.

A default log is configured to run when System Monitor is chosen, even if no logs have been configured. Figure 12.14 shows this log.

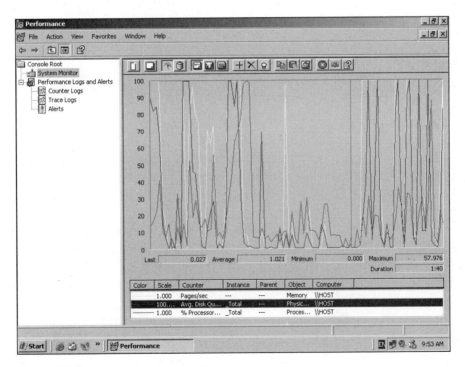

Figure 12.14
Sample performance log.

Counter Log Options

There are several tasks that you can configure while using a counter log. Some of the tasks, such as adding objects and counters, have already been introduced. Other options can be configured, though; you can see them by right-clicking the log and choosing Properties.

On the General tab of a log's Properties dialog box, you can change the sample interval. Different counters have different default intervals. In the last example, the Processor object and the %Processor Time counter defaulted to a data sample every 15 seconds. For general performance and troubleshooting purposes, the defaults will work best. Experienced network administrators often change these defaults to locate hard-to-find problems, but for workstation-related tasks, stay with the defaults for now.

On the Log Files tab, you can select a log file type, such as binary file (the default), text file, binary circular file, and SQL database file. To export the data to Excel or another spreadsheet program, choose the Text File format. To open the file in System Monitor, accept the default format. To export and save the data using SQL, select the SQL format.

You can configure the log file's size by choosing Configure on the Log Files tab of the Log Properties dialog box. Figure 12.15 shows both the Log Properties dialog box and the Configure Log Files dialog box. Notice the default location of the log files and the file name. You can limit the size of the file in the Configure Log Files dialog box also.

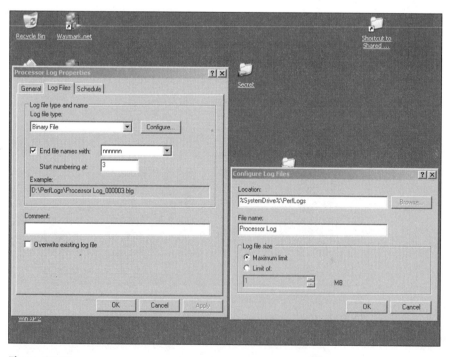

Figure 12.15
The Processor Log Properties and Configure Log Files dialog boxes.

On the Schedule tab, you can specify dates and times for when the log should start and stop. You can configure a command to run when the log gets full—perhaps a command to save the file to a specific folder.

Saving the Log

You can save any log while it is running or after it has been stopped by choosing File | Save As. However, do not accept the default while saving; choose a different name from the one offered. "Perfmon" is the default name, and if you save to this file, you'll permanently alter it.

Trace Logs

Trace logs are generally used by developers of applications and computer systems to provide logs of specific events such as input/output errors or page faults. In contrast to performance logs, trace logs record data when an event occurs instead of at configured intervals. Trace logs give the application designers an opportunity to see when and how errors occur within their applications and systems.

Creating Trace Logs

As with performance logs, you should log on as an administrator to avoid any potential permissions problems while accessing the local or remote computer.

To create a trace log:

1. Open the Performance console.

2. Expand Performance Logs And Alerts, and then highlight Trace Logs.

3. Right-click in the right pane, and choose New Log Settings.

4. Type a name for the new log.

5. In the Trace Log dialog box, on the General tab, select the events to log.

6. On the Log Files tab, select the Log File type.

7. On the Schedule tab, choose when to start and stop the log.

8. On the Advance tab, change the buffer size as needed. *Buffers* are places in memory where the information is stored until it is transferred to the log file. The defaults are usually fine. Choose OK.

9. In the Performance console, right-click the trace log, and choose Start. After a period of time, right-click again and choose Stop to stop the log.

Configuring Alerts

You can configure the Performance console and Performance Logs And Alerts to send you an alert when a specific counter (or counters) reaches a certain threshold. This alert could be a number related to processor usage, paging file usage, print queue jobs or errors, or any other counter available from the Performance console.

To configure an alert for any of these objects:

1. Log on as an administrator to avoid any permissions problems with the local or remote computer.

2. Open the Performance console.

3. Expand the Performance Logs And Alerts tree, and highlight Alerts.

4. In the right pane, right-click and choose New Alert Settings.

5. Type a name for the alert you want to configure. Choose OK.

6. In the alert dialog box that appears, on the General tab, choose the Add button to add a counter.

7. In the Add Counters dialog box, choose the local computer or a remote one, and then select a performance object. Choose Add.

8. Select any other counters you want to include in this alert. Choose the Close button.

9. In the Alert When The Value Is _____ drop down list, choose Over or Under.

10. In the Limit text box, type a number. For instance, you could select Processor_Total for the counter, and then specify Over 98.

11. In the Sample Data Every section, choose the Interval and the Units. For instance, select the interval to be 5 and the units to be seconds.

12. On the Action tab, choose what you want to have happen when this threshold is met. The choices are:

    ♦ Log An Entry In The Application Event Log

    ♦ Send A Network Message To

    ♦ Start Performance Data Log

    ♦ Run This Program

13. On the Schedule tab, specify when you want the log to start and stop. Choose OK.

If you choose to send a network message to someone when a threshold is met, the recipient will see a message similar to the one shown in Figure 12.16.

Analyzing Data

The system overview log that is included with Windows XP Professional is a good place to start monitoring. This log, after manual startup, collects information every 15 seconds until the maximum size of the log has been met. You can then analyze this data to see just how healthy the system is.

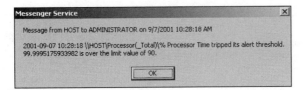

Messenger Service

Message from HOST to ADMINISTRATOR on 9/7/2001 10:28:18 AM

2001-09-07 10:28:18 \\HOST\Processor(_Total)\% Processor Time tripped its alert threshold.
99.9995175933982 is over the limit value of 90.

OK

Figure 12.16
Message that an alert threshold has been met.

You can view this data by using a graph, especially when you're watching real-time monitoring. You can also view the data by using a histogram, but it is more useful to record data as a report and save it to a file for analysis. Once the data is saved, you can export it to a database, such as SQL, and use the application to analyze and query results by using various parameters. You can use this information as a baseline to determine if and when a system needs to be upgraded with memory, processors, and hard drives, as well as with network-specific hardware such as redirectors, which send data out onto the network. Generally, a network administrator performs this type of monitoring. However, if it is your job, you can find much more information about analyzing data from the Windows XP Help and Support Center and from Microsoft's Web site.

More About System Monitor

Once a log has been created (on a workstation, this is probably a counter log), you can use System Monitor to add more counters, delete counters, and manipulate the log in a number of other ways. You can also use System Monitor to connect to a remote computer without returning to the counter log itself in Counter Logs in the Performance console. System Monitor also has a Properties dialog box that can be used to change the color, look, and feel of System Monitor itself.

Figure 12.17 shows System Monitor in action. I've right-clicked the graph to open the screen you see here. The Add Counters dialog box shown in this figure is the same as the Add Counters dialog box shown from inside Counter Logs. Simply right-clicking inside the graph and choosing Add Counters opens this screen. Notice that you can use the Select Counters From Computer drop-down list to connect to the local computer or to a remote one.

System Monitor Properties

When using System Monitor, you can do more than just view the data in graph form with the default fonts and colors that you've seen in this chapter. You can view the data as a histogram or a report, and change the GUI of System Monitor entirely. To make these changes, right-click the graph itself, and choose Properties. You'll see the screen shown in Figure 12.18.

On the General tab, you can change the view, the display elements, and the report and histogram data that is shown. You can also change the appearance from 3D to flat, and place a border around the GUI. You can change the sample rate and allow duplicate counters to be monitored.

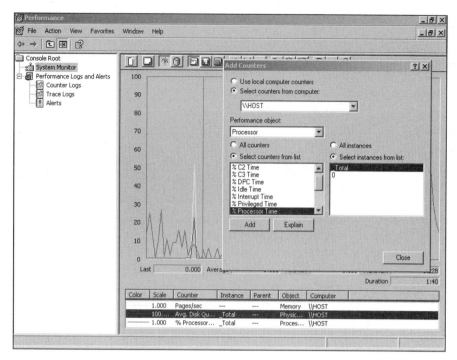

Figure 12.17
System Monitor and Add Counters.

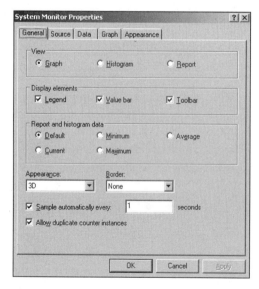

Figure 12.18
System Monitor Properties.

On the Source tab, you can select a different data source. By default, it is the current activity, but you can open a saved log file to view it as well. On the Data tab, you can add or remove counters and change the color of each counter that is defined. The scale, width, and style can be changed as well. On the Graph tab, you can type a title and name for the vertical axis, and show a grid. Finally, on the Appearance tab, you can choose a graph background and change the font. Figure 12.19 shows a graph that has been changed dramatically from the default.

Device Manager

Device Manager has been briefly introduced a few times for updating device drivers, adding or replacing hardware, and viewing device information. However, using the Computer Management console, you can access Device Manager while using the other console tools in a single place for easier management. Device Manager is a tool that you can use to determine which components of your system are not working properly and to solve those problems. You can also change the device settings, disable, enable, and uninstall devices, and print a summary of what's on your computer. To use Device Manager to its fullest, you must have permissions to add and remove device drivers and to write settings to the Registry. To avoid any potential permission problems, it is best to log on as an administrator when you're using Device Manager.

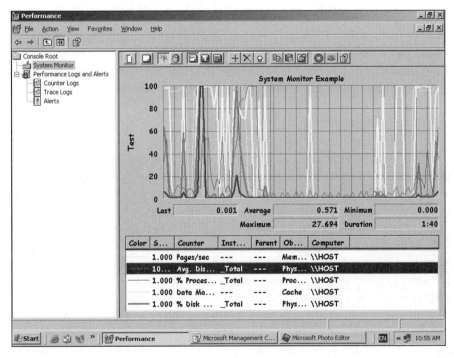

Figure 12.19
System Monitor after it has been customized.

Because you already know how to add and remove drivers and how to view the system summary from Device Manager, I'll move on here to more complex tasks, such as configuring non-PnP (non-Plug-and-Play) devices and creating hardware profiles. First, you need to understand the different views of Device Manager.

Device Manager Views

There are several options for viewing the hardware listed in Device Manager. From the View menu, you can select different options for showing the devices:

- *Devices By Type*—This is the default view; it lists the computer's hardware components alphabetically.

- *Devices By Connection*—This setting lists the devices—such as audio, video, and media devices—by connection.

- *Resources By Type*—When shown by type, the devices are listed under four categories: Direct Memory Access (DMA), Input/Output (I/O), Interrupt Request (IRQ), and Memory.

- *Resources By Connection*—Similar to Resources By Type, this setting lists the devices under four categories: Direct Memory Access, Input/Output, Interrupt Request, and Memory.

- *Show Hidden Devices*—This setting shows devices that are usually hidden from the user, such as kernel components.

When you need to install a non-PnP device, you'll need to configure the device's IRQ number, the DMA channel, and the I/O address, and you'll need to allot memory space for the device to run in. If you need to see which IRQ numbers are free, you can do so by viewing Resource By Type. You can also view all of the other information you need as well.

Installing Non-PnP Devices

When a PnP device is installed on a computer, the computer automatically assigns the device an IRQ, a DMA channel, an I/O address, and a memory address range. Each device then uses these resources to communicate with the processor and other components to work with the system. When a device is not PnP, though, these numbers and addresses might not be configured correctly. If two devices are configured to use the same IRQ or other resource, a *device conflict* will occur. Device conflicts occur because the two components try to use the same path through the computer to reach the processor. When the processor receives mixed signals, a conflict occurs. For instance, if a camera and a scanner are configured to use the same resources, when the processor receives the message to use one of these devices, it might send out instructions for the camera when the scanner instructions are really needed. In this case, sometimes the device will receive the correct instructions, and sometimes it won't. This situation can cause intermittent errors. Other times, neither device will work at all. Some resources can be shared, though, which makes installing non-PnP devices even more difficult.

When you're installing a non-PnP device, the driver that comes with the hardware will automatically configure the resources. If there is a conflict, the device will need to be configured manually. You can view conflicts in Device Manager.

To see if there are any conflicts on your computer:

1. Log on as an administrator.

2. Open the Computer Management console.

3. Expand Performance Logs And Alerts, and highlight Device Manager.

4. Look for any devices with yellow exclamation points or red X's beside them.

5. Double-click one of these devices.

6. The dialog-box tabs will differ depending on the device chosen. If there is a Resources tab, select it.

7. The Conflicting Device List section will list any conflicts for this device.

If you do find conflicts, you'll need to locate the instructions that came with the device, or call the manufacturer's help line to find out what should be done about this conflict. If that isn't possible, you can try to repair the problem yourself. This is not recommended, though, and could cause multiple problems that would be hard to locate and repair. However, if you must, you can uncheck the checkbox Use Automatic Settings and then choose Change Setting. You can make manual changes here.

To decide what settings to use, view devices by connection and make a note of any free resources, such as IRQs, I/O addresses, and the like. Then go through each device to verify that no other conflicts have arisen due to your recent changes.

Hardware Profiles

A *hardware profile* is a set of instructions that tells your computer what to do when the computer boots up. Hardware profiles are especially important for laptops because they will probably be used in multiple hardware settings. For instance, a user might configure one hardware profile for the office, a second hardware profile for use on the road, and a third hardware profile for working at home. The office profile could include a printer, a scanner, and a network connection; the mobile profile could include a portable printer and a telephone network connection; and the home profile could include the family's printers and Zip drives and a Remote Desktop connection.

With hardware profiles, then, you don't have to deal with unnecessary items on the computer or with unnecessary resources being taken up when they're needed for something else. In profile 1, IRQ 3 could be configured for a network printer, for profile 2, a portable printer, and for Profile 3, an inkjet printer.

To configure a second hardware profile for your computer:

1. Log on as an administrator.

2. Open the Control Panel.

3. Open System.

4. In the System Properties dialog box, select the Hardware tab, and choose Hardware Profiles.

5. Highlight Profile 1, and choose Copy.

6. Name the new profile, and choose OK.

7. If this is a portable computer, choose Properties.

8. In the Profile Properties dialog box, check the checkbox This Is A Portable Computer. Check the appropriate box if the computer is currently docked, if its state is unknown, or if the computer is undocked.

9. In the Hardware Profiles Selection area, check the checkbox Always Include This Profile As An Option When Windows Starts if you want this profile to be shown as an option on boot-up. Choose OK.

10. Back at the Hardware Profiles dialog box, select one of these options: Wait Until I Select A Hardware Profile or Select the First Profile Listed If I Don't Select A Profile In (30) Seconds. Choose OK twice.

11. Restart the computer, and select the new profile.

12. Add any new printers, scanners, cameras, or network configurations, and set the power options.

13. In Device Manager, double-click the device you do not want to use when logged on with this profile.

14. On the General tab, in the Device Usage drop-down list, select Do Not Use This Device In The Current Hardware Profile. See Figure 12.20. Choose OK.

Services

The Computer Management console also provides a collection of services. A *service* is a program that runs in the background while you work on your computer. Services perform such tasks as maintaining the system time, maintaining network connectivity, enabling a user to configure scheduled tasks or use themes, allowing a user to enable support for specific protocols such as TCP/IP, and connecting to different types of servers. Without these services, most of the work you do on your computer wouldn't be possible.

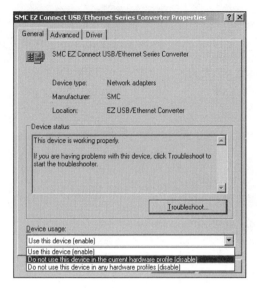

Figure 12.20
Disabling a device for the current profile.

Occasionally, you might have to stop, start, pause, or resume a service on either the local computer or a remote computer, or specify what to do if a particular service fails. You can also disable unneeded services for different hardware profiles.

Most services are started automatically and are necessary for the computer to function properly either as a standalone computer or as a member of a network. Other services must be started manually and are used only when needed.

Some of the services started automatically include:

♦ Automatic Updates

♦ Computer Browser

♦ DHCP Client

♦ DNS Client

♦ Error Reporting

♦ Event Log

♦ Help And Support

♦ Internet Connection Firewall

♦ Messenger

- Plug and Play

- Print Spooler

- Themes

- Workstation

Some of the services started manually include:

- ClipBook

- Fast User Switching

- Indexing Service

- Internet Connection Sharing

- NetMeeting Remote Desktop Sharing

- Performance Logs And Alerts

- Remote Access Connection Manager

- Routing And Remote Access

- Smart Card

- Terminal Services

- UPS

- Utility Manager

To view more information about each service and to view additional services:

1. Log on as an administrator.

2. Open the Computer Management console.

3. Expand the Services And Applications tree.

4. Highlight Services.

5. Double-click any service to view its description. Figure 12.21 shows the Computer Management console, the Services window, and the Fax Service Properties dialog box.

To configure how a service is started:

1. Log on as an administrator.

2. Open the Computer Management console.

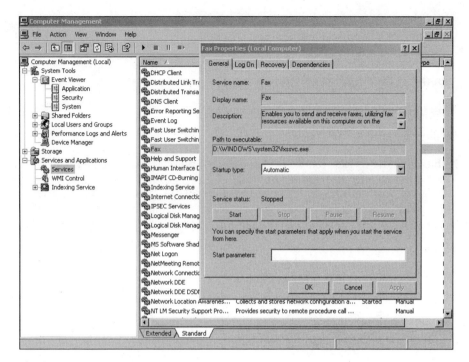

Figure 12.21
A service description.

3. Expand the Services And Applications tree.

4. Highlight Services.

5. Double-click any service to view its description. Figure 12.21 shows the Computer Management console, the Services window, and the Fax Service Properties dialog box.

6. On the General tab, select a startup type from the Startup Type drop-down list. The choices are Automatic, Manual, or Disabled. Choose OK.

To pause, stop, start, or resume a service:

1. Log on as an administrator.

2. Open the Computer Management console.

3. Expand the Services And Applications tree.

4. Highlight Services.

5. Right-click any service, and use its context menu to stop, start, pause, or resume it, or use the Fax Services Properties dialog box as shown in Figure 12.21.

To specify what action to take if the service fails:

1. Log on as an administrator.

2. Open the Computer Management console.

3. Expand the Services And Applications tree.

4. Highlight Services.

5. Double-click the service you want to configure, and select the Recovery tab.

6. Select what you want to do if the service fails for the first, second, and subsequent failures. The choices are:

   ♦ Take No Action

   ♦ Restart The Service

   ♦ Run A Program

   ♦ Restart The Computer

7. Choose OK.

WMI Control

WMI (Windows Management Instrumentation) Control is a tool that allows you to manage different aspects of a local or remote computer. By default, no WMI controls are set initially. Using WMI Control, you can perform the following tasks:

♦ Set permission levels for users and groups

♦ Authorize users and groups

♦ Turn on or off error logging, and configure it to log errors in different ways

♦ Back up the database that is accessed through WMI

♦ Change the namespace for WMI scripts

The topic of using WMI controls is beyond the scope of this book. However, to view the options available, right-click WMI Control in the Computer Management console, and choose Properties. From the tabs available in this Properties dialog box, you can do the following:

♦ *General*—View system information, including processor type, operating system, Service Packs installed, and more

♦ *Logging*—Enable or disable logging, and set the maximum log size and its location

♦ *Backup/Restore*—Manually back up and restore WMI databases to specified files

♦ *Security*—Select a namespace for which you want to specify user access permissions. You can set permissions for groups and users by clicking the Security button on this page

♦ *Advanced*—Select default namespace scripting

The Indexing Service

The Indexing Service must be configured before it can be made available for users. Once configured, this service provides expanded search offerings, including searching by file name, by author, or even by specific words. This service also automatically creates the index, updates the index, and has computer-failure recovery options in place. The Indexing Service doesn't require much maintenance, although it does use the computer's resources and can slow down a system. To start the Indexing Service, right-click it in the Computer Management console, and choose Start.

As the service runs, it gathers information about the files and data on your computer. You can place a query by using the Indexing Service Query Form. To display this form, expand the following trees in the Computer Management console: Services And Applications\Indexing Service\System. Then highlight Query The Catalog. This form is shown in Figure 12.22.

When a query is typed in, the files located can be listed by Rank, Title, Path, Size, or Modified, and they can be placed in ascending or descending order.

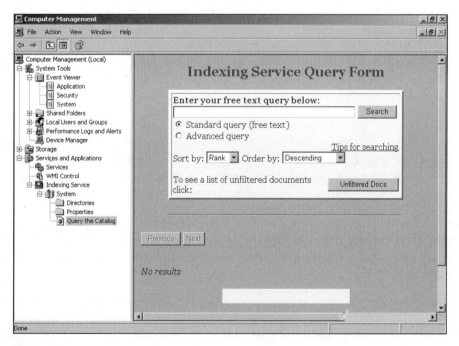

Figure 12.22
The Indexing Service Query Form.

Enhancing Performance

Using all of the tools introduced in this chapter can help you find any weak spots that your system might have. These can include weaknesses having to do with memory, processors, and hard drives, or weaknesses stemming from device conflicts. You can cause your own weaknesses by over-monitoring or setting too many alerts, but you can also locate bottlenecks and potential problems. Upgrading the computer or relieving some of the strains placed on it can solve many of these problems. Other times, you can configure your computer differently to reduce the load. For instance, you can reduce the number of colors shown on the display from the highest setting of 32-bit to 256 colors. You can also use hardware profiles to make a laptop run more efficiently when running on batteries. There are many ways to lighten a computer processor's load.

In this section, I'll cover two other options for enhancing performance: System Properties and Program Compatibility Mode.

System Properties

The System icon is located in the Control Panel. The System Properties dialog box has seven tabs; many of these tabs can be used to enhance system performance. You are familiar with the General tab, the System Restore tab, and the Automatic Updates tab, but the other tabs have not been detailed yet. On the Advanced tab, you can configure performance settings, user profile settings, and startup and recovery settings.

The Advanced Tab

To follow along here, open the Control Panel, open System, and select the Advanced tab. The Advanced tab is shown on the left in Figure 12.23. Choose the Performance button to see the screen on the right.

After selecting the Advanced tab and clicking the Performance area's Settings button, you can configure the computer to let Windows choose what's best for the computer, adjust the settings for best appearance, adjust the settings for best performance, or create a custom setting. When you choose to adjust for best performance, all of the boxes become unchecked.

On the Advanced tab of the Performance Options dialog box, you can configure options for processor scheduling, memory usage, and virtual memory. For processor scheduling, you can adjust the processor to spend more time on the performance of either the programs or the background services. For memory usage, you can select either programs or system cache. For virtual memory, you can change the size of the paging file.

Back in the System Properties dialog box, the User Profiles area's Settings button opens a dialog box where you can change or delete user profiles stored on the local computer. On a network, user profiles can be changed from local to roaming, meaning that the user's default profile settings follow him or her to other computers on the network.

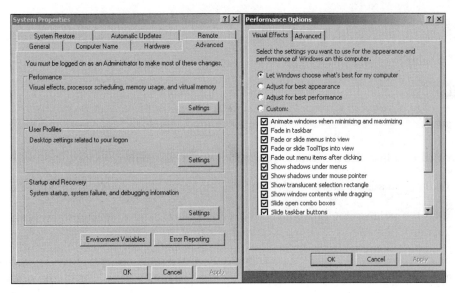

Figure 12.23
The System Properties and Performance Options dialog boxes.

Finally, from the System Recovery section, you can choose a default operating system if the computer is configured to dual-boot, specify how long the list of operating systems should be displayed before one is chosen automatically, and specify how long recovery options should be shown during startup if they're needed. You can also decide what to do when the system fails: write an event to the system log, send an administrative alert, and/or automatically restart the computer. Finally, you can configure how and when debugging information should be written when startup or shutdown fails.

Automatic Updates Tab

As mentioned previously, automatic updates should be configured to update automatically or at least should be set so that you are notified when updates are available. Using these updates allows your computer to obtain necessary files as they are available.

Program Compatibility Mode

Although most newer programs will run just fine with Windows XP Professional, there is always the chance that you have an old favorite lying around that you'd still like to use. I have a program like that, and the manufacturer hasn't upgraded it since Windows 95 was the predominant operating system. Because of this problem, Microsoft has created program compatibility mode and the Program Compatibility Wizard.

Program compatibility means that older programs, like the one just mentioned, can still be run on the Windows XP Professional machine. All you have to do is install the program and run the Program Compatibility Wizard once to configure the program. In addition, if the program cannot be installed because of compatibility problems, you can configure the wizard for the program's setup program so that even the installation runs in program compatibility mode.

Note

You should not run anti-virus programs, system programs, or backup programs in this mode.

To configure an installed program to run in program compatibility mode:

1. Log on as an administrator.

2. Open the Program Compatibility Wizard by choosing Start | Programs | Accessories | Program Compatibility Wizard. Choose Next to start the wizard.

3. Decide how you will locate the program: from a list of programs, from the CD-ROM, or manually. Choose Next, and highlight or browse to the program. Choose Next again.

4. Select the operating system for which the program was originally written. The choices are Windows 95, Windows NT 4.0, Windows 98/ME, or Windows 2000. Choose Next.

5. Select the display settings that the program supports. If the program isn't limited to a specific number of colors or a specific resolution, leave these items unchecked, and choose Next.

6. Choose Next to test the program. Close the program once you've finished testing.

7. Answer the questions regarding how the program performed. You can indicate that the program worked fine or that you want to try a different setting. Make your choice, and complete the wizard.

If the program won't install at all, you can use the Program Compatibility Wizard to assist you in this process.

To install a program while using program compatibility mode:

1. Log on as an administrator.

2. Browse to the application's setup program on the CD or floppy disk, and take note of the location of this file.

3. Start the Program Compatibility Wizard. Choose Next.

4. Select the option I Want To Locate The Program Manually. Choose Next.

5. Choose the Browse button, and locate the setup (or installation) file. Choose Next.

6. Select an operating system for the compatibility mode. Choose Next.

7. Select the display settings that the program supports. If the program isn't limited to a specific number of colors or a specific resolution, leave these items unchecked, and choose Next.

8. Choose Next to test the settings. If they work, install the program. If not, return to Step 4, and select either I Want To Use The Program In The CD-ROM Drive or I Want To Choose From A List Of Programs.

9. Choose Next to install the program. Close the program when you've finished testing it.

10. Answer the questions regarding how the program performed. You can indicate that the program worked fine or that you want to try a different setting. Make your choice and complete the wizard.

The program will begin to install in the mode for which it was written.

Wrapping Up

In this chapter, you learned all about disk and computer management. Disk management consists of using the NTFS file system rather than FAT, if you can, and maintaining your disks by using Disk Cleanup and Disk Defragmenter. You can also keep disks healthy by freeing up disk space; for instance, you can remove unused programs and files and compress folders and drives.

Several types of disks can be configured; these include logical drives, partitions, spanned disks, striped disks, and simple dynamic disks. You learned how to configure an extra disk and assign disk quotas to users.

In this chapter's section on computer management, you learned about Event Viewer, Performance Logs And Alerts, Device Manager, and more. To enhance performance, Windows XP offers extensive system tools and a Program Compatibility Wizard.

Chapter 13
Security

One of the most important tasks that computer users have to do is to ensure the security of the computers for which they are responsible. This is not just an administrator's job; in fact, the workstation or domain user can play an important role, too. If the workstation users are part of a workgroup, securing their own computers becomes even more important because there are no domain controllers or administrators to manage the security of the network by using server security techniques.

There are several ways that users and administrators can secure their systems. Windows XP Professional offers several options. The security features detailed in this chapter include the following utilities and options: applying access controls; auditing security events; using digital certificates; utilizing Encrypting File System (EFS); using smart cards, security templates, and security configuration and analysis tools; adding security settings extensions to group policies; configuring a local security policy; using the command-line tool Secedit; applying anti-virus protection; using Windows Management Instrumentation (WMI) control; understanding Kerberos; and using built-in firewalls.

This chapter is organized into three main sections: "Security for Users," "Security for Administrators," and "Additional Security Features." There is some overlap, though—such as the information on anti-virus protection, Internet Connection Firewall, and uninterruptible power supplies (UPSs)—that will benefit both users and administrators. Not all of these security options need to be used in every network configuration, so choose the utilities and options that are right for your organization.

Security for Users

A domain user or workgroup user can do several things to help secure the local computer. Although domain users might not have the permissions needed to use all of the options described here, these users will probably be able to apply a few of them. Workgroup users, on the other hand, will most likely be able to apply all of these features, especially if the users are the administrators of their own computers.

Some of the topics featured in this section include securing files and folders in a workgroup, using the security features of Internet Explorer 6, using the built-in Internet Connection Firewall utility, using EFS, configuring anti-virus programs, and using a UPS. There is also another brief look at local and group policies because they are two of the most effective ways to secure a computer (for a more thorough explanation, see Chapters 10 and 11).

Securing Files and Folders in a Workgroup

When your computer is a member of a workgroup, keeping other users from viewing your files is important. You already know how to share files and folders, but what about making sure that no one can access them? You can make several folders private, including subfolders and files, so that no other user of the computer can access them. These folders are My Documents, the Desktop, Start Menu, Cookies, and Favorites, and they are part of your user profile on the local machine.

If you choose not to make your folders private, then anyone who logs onto the computer— even a limited user—can use Windows Explorer to access the folders in your user profile. If you make these folders private, users trying to access them from accounts other than yours will receive an access-denied message.

For you to make a folder private, your drive must be formatted with the NTFS file system. If it is, do the following:

1. Log on as the administrator of your computer.

2. Open My Computer.

3. Double-click the C: drive (or whatever drive holds your system files). If you can't see the contents of this drive, then, under System Tasks, click Show The Contents Of This Drive.

4. Double-click the Documents And Settings folder.

5. Double-click your user folder.

6. Right-click any folder in this folder, and choose Properties.

7. On the Sharing tab of the Properties dialog box, check the Make This Folder Private checkbox. See Figure 13.1.

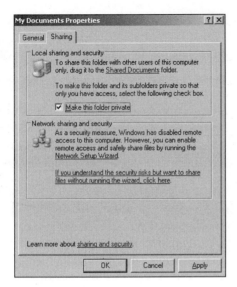

Figure 13.1
Making a folder private.

8. If you do not have a password for your account, a warning box will appear, informing you that even though the folder is now private, you'll need a password to finish this task. Create a password if necessary.

After performing the previous steps, if you want to verify that no one else can view the folders made private on your computer, log on as another user and do the following:

1. Right-click the Start menu, and choose Explore All Users.

2. Click the minus sign next to All Users to close the tree.

3. Locate your user name in the Documents And Settings tree, and open your folder.

4. Double-click the folder that was configured as private. Notice the access-denied message. Double-click a folder that is not configured as private, and notice that your non-private folders can be accessed by any other user of the computer.

Security Features of Internet Explorer 6

You can use Internet Explorer 6 to protect your computer and its users from problems that can occur when accessing the Internet. Internet Explorer 6 provides several types of settings, including privacy settings, privacy alerts, certificates, Authenticode settings, zones, and privacy reports. This section focuses on making Internet access safe for both you and the users of your computer. Security problems can arise from a number of sources other than the usual virus scares; these sources range from giving out information such as credit card numbers on non-secure sites to allowing access to users and giving information to questionable Web sites.

Privacy Settings

Privacy is a major concern of many users who access the Internet to find information, make purchases, or conduct business. Because of this concern, most Web sites offer privacy policies that tell you what kind of information the site will collect from you and how that information will be used. Contrary to what some people believe, a Web site cannot gain much information without your permission. For instance, a Web site cannot find out what your email address is unless you supply it. In addition, the Web site cannot find out your name, home address, telephone number, or credit card numbers without your inputting that information either manually or by using the Profile Assistant (described later in this chapter).

However, if you visit a Web site such as **www.amazon.com**, log on using a logon name (usually your email address) and password, and browse through the merchandise, Amazon.com can (and does) collect information about what types of items you are interested in. The next time you access this site, the company has an idea of what you might want to look at, and it places related items in your browser's window. For instance, if you usually search for computer books, then at the bottom of the Web page you access, Amazon will list some computer books, offering those that it thinks you might enjoy. This practice isn't illegal, and it can be quite helpful for users who visit the same site often. These bits of information are called *cookies*, are saved on your hard drive, and are used each time this Web site is accessed. See Figure 13.2.

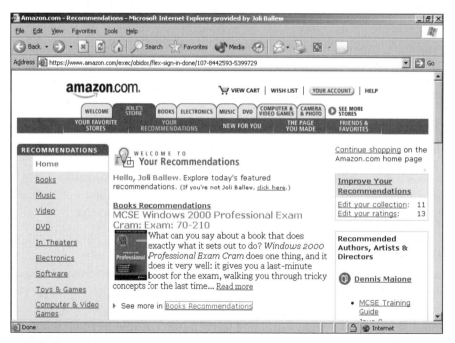

Figure 13.2
Example of the use of cookies.

Sites such as these usually offer privacy statements. (See Figure 13.3.) Many sites also offer a Platform for Privacy Preferences (P3P) privacy policy, which can be used by IE6 to see if a site's policy matches the privacy settings configured for your computer. If it doesn't, then the site will not be displayed in the browser window or will not be displayed with all of the site's features enabled.

Just by visiting a site where a privacy notice is offered, you are accepting the practices described in the notice. These practices can include the following:

♦ Obtaining information about you from other sources and adding it to your account information. This information can come from shipping companies, other Web sites that have obtained information from you, and more.

♦ Giving or selling your information to other retailers.

♦ Giving your information to companies involved in getting products to you, such as delivery companies, the post office, marketing assistance companies, and credit card companies.

♦ Sending email messages to you regarding promotions or sales offered by this company or its affiliates.

♦ Collecting information automatically without your written consent. This information includes your IP address, browser type and version, operating system, purchase history, and products you've viewed.

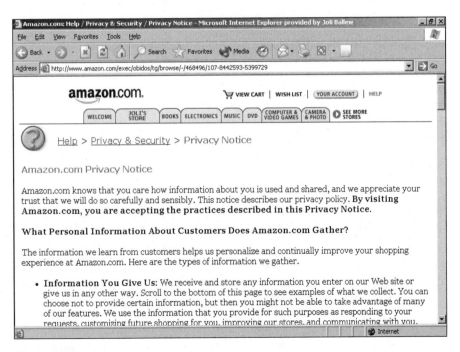

Figure 13.3
A sample privacy notice.

You can monitor and change the settings regarding what information you'll allow to be taken automatically from your computer and what types of cookies you'll allow to be placed on your hard drive. In Internet Explorer, you can choose Tools | Internet Options to place restrictions on cookies. The Privacy tab has several settings, which you configure by using a sliding bar, starting at Accept All Cookies and ending at Block All Cookies. The following list describes these settings:

♦ *Accept All Cookies*—All cookies will be saved to your computer, and all cookies on your computer can be used by the Web sites that created them.

♦ *Low*—Cookies from third-party sites without privacy policies that can be read by Internet Explorer will be blocked. If cookies from these same sites use information from your computer that was not explicitly given, those cookies will be deleted when you exit Internet Explorer.

Note

This section discusses two types of sites: first-party sites and third-party sites. A first-party site is the site you are viewing, and third-party sites are sites that service the first-party site. For instance, an advertiser might be a third-party site and might use cookies.

♦ *Medium*—This setting contains all of the restrictions in the Low setting plus one more: Cookies from first-party Web sites that use your information without your consent will be deleted from your computer when you exit Internet Explorer.

♦ *Medium High*—This setting contains all of the restrictions in the Medium setting plus one extra: Cookies from first-party Web sites that use your information without your consent will be blocked.

♦ *High*—Cookies from all Web sites without computer-readable privacy policies will be blocked, and cookies from all Web sites that use your personal information without your consent will be blocked.

♦ *Block All Cookies*—All cookies are blocked, and any cookies already on your computer cannot be read by any Web site.

Some Web sites require cookies, so if your settings are more restrictive than the Web site's requirements, you might not be able to access the site. In addition, these privacy settings affect only those Web sites configured in the Internet zone. There are four zones: Internet, Local Intranet, Trusted Sites, and Restricted Sites. (These are explained in more detail, later in this section.)

Finally, you can configure settings for specific sites, or create custom settings for all Web sites that you visit. Next, you'll learn how to change the settings for cookies on your computer, how to configure custom settings for all Web sites, and how to configure settings for a single site.

Note

Note that if you are a member of a domain, you might be prevented from completing the following tasks.

To configure privacy settings for general use:

1. Log on as an administrator.

2. Open Internet Explorer from the taskbar or from the Start menu.

3. Choose Tools | Internet Options.

4. Select the Privacy tab.

5. Move the slider to the appropriate setting—anywhere from Accept All Cookies to Block All Cookies. Choose OK.

To configure privacy settings for all Web sites:

1. Log on as an administrator.

2. Open Internet Explorer.

3. Choose Tools | Internet Options.

4. Select the Privacy tab, and choose the Advanced button.

5. In the Advanced Privacy Settings dialog box, check the Override Automatic Cookie Handling checkbox.

6. Select how you want to handle cookies for both first-party cookies and third-party cookies. See Figure 13.4. Choose OK twice. Notice that the Internet Options dialog box now lists Custom in the Settings area instead of Low, Medium, High, or other default options.

Figure 13.4
Advanced privacy settings.

To configure privacy settings for a single Web site:

1. Log on as an administrator.

2. Open Internet Explorer.

3. Choose Tools | Internet Options.

4. Select the Privacy tab.

5. In the Web Sites area, choose the Edit button.

6. In the Per Site Privacy Actions dialog box, type the address of the Web site you want to manage, and choose Allow or Block (to allow or block cookies) for this particular site. Choose OK.

Note

You can also import security settings by using the Import button on the Privacy tab, or return to default settings if needed.

Privacy Alerts

When you access a site that doesn't meet your criteria for privacy as configured in the previous section, Internet Explorer alerts you to this fact. When you choose Block All Cookies, and you go to sites that you've previously logged into automatically, you'll have to type your username and password to gain access. Once logged in, you can still access the site as you used to, but you won't be able to access others that contradict your security settings.

Privacy Reports

You can view a Web site's P3P (Platform for Privacy Preferences) policy by using Internet Explorer to find out if the site contains information provided by a third-party Web site. You can also see if Internet Explorer blocked or restricted cookies from the site you are visiting.

To view this policy report:

1. Using Internet Explorer, log onto the Internet and access a Web site.

2. In Internet Explorer, choose View | Privacy Report.

3. In the Privacy Report dialog box, highlight the site for which you want to view privacy settings, and choose the Summary button. See Figures 13.5 and 13.6.

In the Privacy Report dialog box shown in Figure 13.5, you can choose the Settings button to view the settings for any of the sites visited. The Settings button opens the Internet Properties dialog box, where these settings can be modified if necessary. This is the same dialog box as the Tools | Internet Options dialog box described earlier.

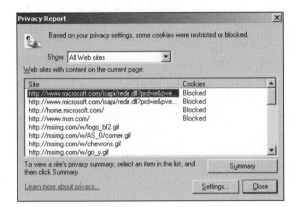

Figure 13.5
A privacy report.

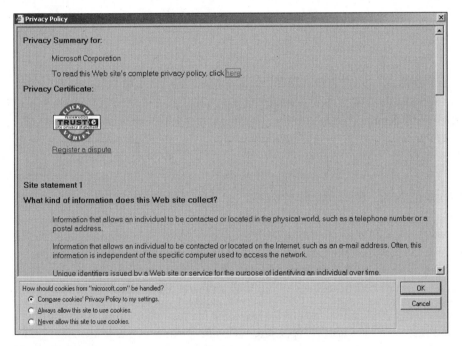

Figure 13.6
A privacy summary report.

Profile Assistant

If you do a lot of shopping on the Internet or if you join lots of groups or communities, you probably get tired of typing your name, address, phone number, email address, and the like every time you are asked for this information. Windows XP Professional comes with a secure "assistant" for helping you with this process. The Profile Assistant can enter this information for you by storing it on your hard drive for use when needed. No one else can obtain this information from your computer without your permission, and this information cannot be shared with others unless you specifically state that it is to be used.

The Profile Assistant doesn't give all of the information it has when you decide to use it, though. It first tells you the name of the site requesting information (or the site you've decided to give information to), what information is requested, and how this information is to be used. If you do not want to give all of the requested information, you can pick and choose what to give. You can also see if the site has a secure connection, and verify the site's certificate if it does. The data that you send over the Internet can be encrypted as well, further securing the information sent.

To configure the Profile Assistant:

1. Open Internet Explorer. (You do not have to be connected to the Internet to configure the assistant.)

2. Choose Tools | Internet Options.

3. Select the Content tab.

4. In the Personal Information area, choose the My Profile button.

5. In the Properties dialog box that appears, type all of the information you want to add on these tabs: Summary, Name, Home, Business, Personal, Other, NetMeeting, and Digital IDs.

6. Choose OK.

Certificates and Digital IDs

Previous chapters mentioned certificates and digital IDs but did not cover actually obtaining a certificate and understanding a Web site's certificate. Certificates are used to identify people and Web sites on the Internet so that a visitor can verify the security of a business or individual. A *certificate* is a statement that verifies that an entity is who it says it is. There are several types of certificates, including Web server, server, wireless server, and personal.

Personal certificates allow people to verify their identities to secure Web sites, whereas Web-site certificates are just the opposite. Web-site certificates are designed for businesses that need to identify themselves to people. Web-site certificates ensure that your personal information will be dealt with in a secure manner and that the business is genuine and secure.

Certificates work by using public and private keys. Each certificate corresponds to a public key, and only the owner knows the corresponding private key. The certificate owner uses his private key to encrypt data that will be sent to others over the Internet. When people receive the data, they also receive the certificate with the public key. The recipients can decrypt the data by using the public key, and encrypt the data on its return trip to you. When the owner receives it again, he uses his personal private key to decode the data.

To obtain your own security certificate, you must contact a Certificate Authority, such as Microsoft, VeriSign, Entrust, Netscape, or any other Certificate Authority. Figure 13.7 shows a valid certificate from VeriSign.com.

Web-server certificates are digital certificates that allow a Web server to establish Secure Sockets Layer (SSL) sessions with browsers such as Navigator and Internet Explorer. These certificates are automatically trusted by these browsers, making the Internet security features transparent to the user. At the Entrust.com Web site at the time of the writing of this book, Web-server certificate pricing ranged from $349 to $900 a year in the U.S., depending on the type chosen.

Microsoft Authenticode

Microsoft Authenticode is an industry standard for verifying the security of files downloaded from the Internet. Downloading programs, even something as simple as screensavers, can be disastrous if the programs are not verified by a reliable source. Microsoft offers this verification to all users of Internet Explorer. As program files are downloaded, Internet Explorer checks that the program has a valid certificate and that the publisher matches the name on the certificate. Microsoft Authenticode is not responsible for how well the program works; it guarantees only that the program is safe for download and is made available by a known and reliable source.

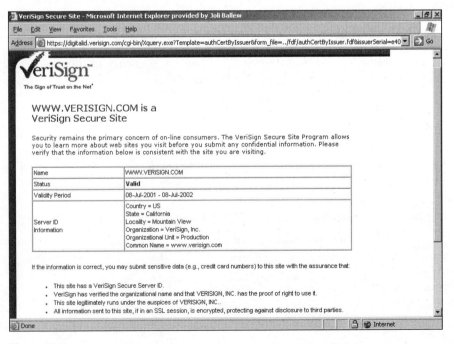

Figure 13.7
A valid VeriSign certificate.

You can change settings related to the types of prompts you'll receive when downloading material from the Internet or from a corporate intranet. For instance, in a highly secure environment, you might need to insist that nothing is downloaded; on a test computer in a lab, you might want to be able to download anything without any warnings or prompts. These settings are applied to different "zones" configured for Internet Explorer. There are four zones: Internet, Local Intranet, Trusted Sites, and Restricted Sites. For Internet sites, the default downloading rules are to enable file download and font download and to prompt before installing desktop items. Other zones have other default settings, which you can change. Table 13.1 defines some of the default settings for downloading files and installing desktop items.

Note

ActiveX controls and Java applets are the files and programs typically downloaded to your computer so that all of the features are displayed on the Web page. ActiveX controls are similar to Java applets in that they are small programs, used by Web sites to offer animations and small applications for users.

To configure these download settings:

1. Log on as an administrator.

2. Open Internet Explorer, and choose Tools | Internet Options.

3. Select the Security tab.

4. Choose the Default Level button to use default settings for zones, or choose the Custom Level button to configure settings manually. See Figure 13.8.

Zones

As mentioned in the previous section, there are four zones: Internet, Local Intranet, Trusted Sites, and Restricted Sites. Figure 13.8 shows these zones and their respective icons. When you visit a site, the bottom-left corner of the Internet Explorer application window displays an icon denoting which zone you are in.

Table 13.1   Default download settings.

Setting	Internet	Local Intranet	Trusted Sites	Restricted Sites
Download Signed ActiveX Controls	Prompt	Prompt	Enable	Disable
Download Unsigned ActiveX Controls	Disable	Disable	Prompt	Disable
File Download	Enable	Enable	Enable	Disable
Font Download	Enable	Enable	Enable	Prompt
Installation Of Desktop Items	Prompt	Prompt	Enable	Disable

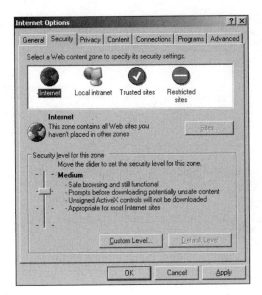

Figure 13.8
Zones.

The four zones are briefly described next:

♦ *Internet*—This zone covers all of the sites you'll visit that are not listed as trusted sites or restricted sites. It also does not include anything configured as residing on the local intranet. The default setting is Medium.

♦ *Local Intranet*—Any site configured on your local intranet that does not require passing through a proxy server is considered the local intranet zone. These sites can be network paths, mapped network drives, or My Network Places. The default setting is Medium.

♦ *Trusted Sites*—These are sites that you trust. Often, when downloading a program, you'll first receive a dialog box that asks you if you want to always trust this site. If you answer Yes, the site becomes a trusted site. The default setting is Low.

♦ *Restricted Sites*—These sites are manually configured by adding specific URLs to the list. These are sites you don't trust—sites that you think can cause harm to your computer if downloads are allowed. The default setting is High.

You can configure each zone to suit your organization's specific needs. As you work on a network, be it the Internet or the local intranet, the settings will be applied for each zone as it is accessed. For instance, when in the Internet zone (connected to the Internet), you might be prompted before downloading material, or the downloading capability might be disabled. However, on the same computer, while connected to the local intranet, downloading may be enabled and no prompt will be shown. You can configure each zone manually or accept the default. The default settings for each of the four zones are shown in Table 13.2. If

Table 13.2 Default settings for security zones.

Setting	Internet	Local Intranet	Trusted Sites	Restricted Sites
Initialize And Script ActiveX Controls Not Marked As Safe	Disable	Disable	Prompt	Disable
Run ActiveX Controls And Plug-Ins	Disable	Enable	Enable	Disable
Script ActiveX Controls Marked Safe For Scripting	Enable	Enable	Enable	Disable
Java Permissions	High Safety	Medium Safety	Low Safety	Disable Java
Access Data Sources Across Domains	Disable	Prompt	Enable	Disable
Allow Meta Refresh	Enable	Enable	Enable	Disable
Display Mixed Content	Prompt	Prompt	Prompt	Prompt
Don't Prompt For Client Certificate Selection When No Certificate Of Only One Certificate Exists	Disable	Enable	Enable	Disable
Drag And Drop Or Copy And Paste Files	Enable	Enable	Enable	Prompt
Launching Programs And Files In An IFRAME	Prompt	Prompt	Enable	Disable
Navigate Sub-Frames Across Different Domains	Enable	Enable	Enable	Disable
Software Channel Permissions	Medium Safety	Medium Safety	Low Safety	High Safety
Submit Nonencrypted Form Data	Enable	Enable	Enable	Prompt
Userdata Persistence	Enable	Enable	Enable	Disable
Active Scripting	Enable	Enable	Enable	Disable
Allow Paste Operations Via Script	Enable	Enable	Enable	Disable
Scripting Of Java Applets	Enable	Enable	Enable	Disable
Logon	Automatic Logon Only In Intranet Zone	Automatic Logon Only In Intranet Zone	Automatic Logon With Current User Name And Password	Prompt For User Name And Password

you need more information about these settings, contact your administrator or use the Windows XP Help and Support Center. Usually, for the office user, the default settings work well.

Secure Internet Sites

When you give information such as your name and address or a credit card number to an Internet site, Internet Explorer and other browsers compare the site's digital certificate to current security protocols and personal settings, and the browsers warn you if the credentials are suspect. You can tell if you are in a secure site by checking the URL or the site page; the URL should start with "Https" instead of "Http," and an icon of a lock should appear at the bottom of the screen. If the site is not secure, you will be warned before any information is sent. You should not send information such as credit card numbers to any non-secure site. In addition, in my opinion, unless you're applying for a credit card or a home loan online, I can see no reason *ever* to send your social security number over the Internet or at the request of any email received.

Built-In Internet Connection Firewall (ICF)

Windows XP Professional comes with its own built-in firewall, which can be used to protect the network or the standalone computer from Internet hackers and intrusions. A *firewall* is a security measure that acts like a proxy server between your network and the Internet. You can use firewalls to specify what can and can't move from the Internet to the local network and vice versa.

Firewalls can be composed of hardware, software, or a combination of both, to provide security, and they are configured either by network domain administrators or by workgroup administrators. If you are a member of a domain, you will most likely not be able to perform the tasks described in this section.

Planning for the Windows XP Firewall

There are several items you should understand and consider before setting up Internet Connection Firewall (ICF). If the computer is a standalone computer, you can simply follow the instructions in the next section to enable ICF. If the computer is part of a network or is the Internet Connection Sharing (ICS) host, however, there are a few restrictions and suggestions.

If your computer is part of a workgroup (intranet) in a small office, you can use ICS to allow everyone on your network to use the same Internet connection to save money. If your network is using ICS, the Internet Connection Firewall should be enabled on a computer that is the ICS host, and ICF should be enabled on the shared Internet connection.

ICF works by monitoring what comes in through the ICF gateway (host computer). ICF reads all of the message and data headers to verify that the destination computer or recipient is on the local network. This step prevents unsolicited data, such as hacking attempts and viruses, from entering the network. The data is discarded as it comes in, but information is stored in a log (described later in this section).

Here are some suggestions for using ICF:

♦ ICF should be configured on a computer that connects directly to the Internet. If ICF is configured on a client computer, data sent through the local network will be interrupted or disabled.

♦ ICF isn't needed in domains, where administrators configure proxy servers or other firewall configurations.

♦ ICF can protect you from only the connection that accesses the Internet. If ICF is set up on the host computer, but a client logs onto the Internet by using a private modem, the client's computer will not be protected.

♦ ICF logs can be configured to record permitted and/or rejected traffic.

♦ Do not configure ICF on virtual private network (VPN) connections because ICF will interfere with file and printer sharing.

Enabling the Firewall

You can enable or disable the Internet Connection Firewall through Network Connections:

1. As an administrator, log onto the standalone computer or the ICS host computer.

2. Open the Control Panel and then Network Connections.

3. Highlight the connection you want to protect, and in the Network Tasks section, click Change Settings Of This Connection. You can also right-click the connection and choose Properties.

4. Select the Advanced tab.

5. Check the Protect My Computer And Network By Limiting Or Preventing Access To This Computer From The Internet checkbox. Choose OK.

Note
Disabling the ICF on a computer is as simple as clearing this checkbox.

Configuring the Firewall

Although the firewall works automatically once enabled, you should look at the default settings and configure the firewall to suit the needs of your network.

To view the advanced firewall settings:

1. As an administrator, log onto the standalone computer or the ICS host computer.

2. Open the Control Panel and Network Connections.

3. Highlight the connection you want to protect, and in the Network Tasks section, click Change Settings Of This Connection. You can also right-click the connection and choose Properties.

4. Select the Advanced tab.

5. Choose the Settings button to open the Advanced Settings dialog box.

6. On the Services tab, the Security tab, and the ICMP (Internet Control Message Protocol) tab, configure the settings as needed:

   ♦ *The Services tab*—Figure 13.9 shows the Services tab of the Advanced Settings dialog box, used for configuring ICF. Here, you can select the network services that Internet users can access. By checking these boxes, you are allowing an Internet user or entity to contact a service, a computer, or a user on your private network.

   ♦ *The Security Logging tab*—Figure 13.10 shows the Security Logging tab. Here, you can choose whether to log all dropped or successful connections originating from either the Internet or the local network. You can also see the log file options and change the size of the log.

   ♦ *The ICMP tab*—Figure 13.11 shows the ICMP tab. Here, you can allow computers to share information related to errors and status. Listed are the type of requests that can be sent and received. Checking these boxes will allow computers to respond to these requests by others. For more information about each type of request, highlight it and read the Description section.

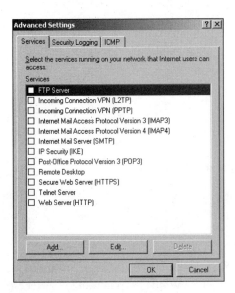

Figure 13.9
The Services tab.

Figure 13.10
The Security Logging tab.

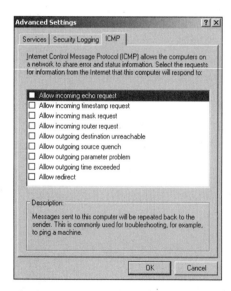

Figure 13.11
The ICMP tab.

Viewing and Understanding ICF Security Logs

On the Security Logging tab of the Advanced Settings dialog box, choose Browse to locate the log file. The default file name and location is <root>:\Windows\pfirewall.log. After browsing to this file, right-click it and choose Open. Figure 13.12 shows an example of a log file.

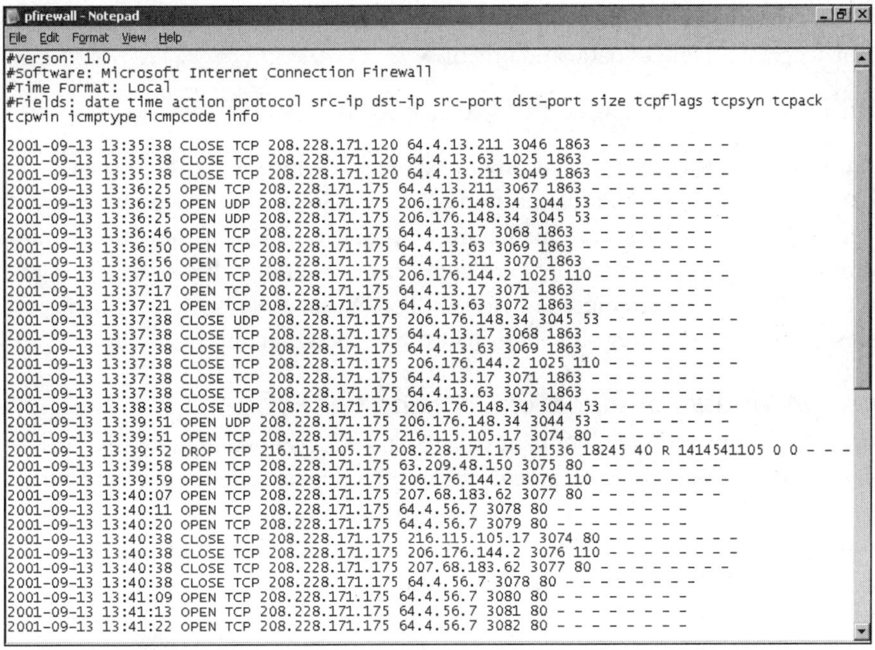

```
pfirewall - Notepad
File Edit Format View Help
#Verson: 1.0
#Software: Microsoft Internet Connection Firewall
#Time Format: Local
#Fields: date time action protocol src-ip dst-ip src-port dst-port size tcpflags tcpsyn tcpack
tcpwin icmptype icmpcode info

2001-09-13 13:35:38 CLOSE TCP 208.228.171.120 64.4.13.211 3046 1863 - - - - - - - -
2001-09-13 13:35:38 CLOSE TCP 208.228.171.120 64.4.13.63 1025 1863 - - - - - - - -
2001-09-13 13:35:38 CLOSE TCP 208.228.171.120 64.4.13.211 3049 1863 - - - - - - - -
2001-09-13 13:36:25 OPEN TCP 208.228.171.175 64.4.13.211 3067 1863 - - - - - - - -
2001-09-13 13:36:25 OPEN UDP 208.228.171.175 206.176.148.34 3044 53 - - - - - - - -
2001-09-13 13:36:25 OPEN UDP 208.228.171.175 206.176.148.34 3045 53 - - - - - - - -
2001-09-13 13:36:46 OPEN TCP 208.228.171.175 64.4.13.17 3068 1863 - - - - - - - -
2001-09-13 13:36:50 OPEN TCP 208.228.171.175 64.4.13.63 3069 1863 - - - - - - - -
2001-09-13 13:36:56 OPEN TCP 208.228.171.175 64.4.13.211 3070 1863 - - - - - - - -
2001-09-13 13:37:10 OPEN TCP 208.228.171.175 206.176.144.2 1025 110 - - - - - - - -
2001-09-13 13:37:17 OPEN TCP 208.228.171.175 64.4.13.17 3071 1863 - - - - - - - -
2001-09-13 13:37:21 OPEN TCP 208.228.171.175 64.4.13.63 3072 1863 - - - - - - - -
2001-09-13 13:37:38 CLOSE UDP 208.228.171.175 206.176.148.34 3045 53 - - - - - - - -
2001-09-13 13:37:38 CLOSE TCP 208.228.171.175 64.4.13.17 3068 1863 - - - - - - - -
2001-09-13 13:37:38 CLOSE TCP 208.228.171.175 64.4.13.63 3069 1863 - - - - - - - -
2001-09-13 13:37:38 CLOSE TCP 208.228.171.175 206.176.144.2 1025 110 - - - - - - - -
2001-09-13 13:37:38 CLOSE TCP 208.228.171.175 64.4.13.17 3071 1863 - - - - - - - -
2001-09-13 13:37:38 CLOSE TCP 208.228.171.175 64.4.13.63 3072 1863 - - - - - - - -
2001-09-13 13:38:38 CLOSE UDP 208.228.171.175 206.176.148.34 3044 53 - - - - - - - -
2001-09-13 13:39:51 OPEN UDP 208.228.171.175 206.176.148.34 3044 53 - - - - - - - -
2001-09-13 13:39:51 OPEN TCP 208.228.171.175 216.115.105.17 3074 80 - - - - - - - -
2001-09-13 13:39:52 DROP TCP 216.115.105.17 208.228.171.175 21536 18245 40 R 1414541105 0 0 - - -
2001-09-13 13:39:58 OPEN TCP 208.228.171.175 63.209.48.150 3075 80 - - - - - - - -
2001-09-13 13:39:59 OPEN TCP 208.228.171.175 206.176.144.2 3076 110 - - - - - - - -
2001-09-13 13:40:07 OPEN TCP 208.228.171.175 207.68.183.62 3077 80 - - - - - - - -
2001-09-13 13:40:11 OPEN TCP 208.228.171.175 64.4.56.7 3078 80 - - - - - - - -
2001-09-13 13:40:20 OPEN TCP 208.228.171.175 64.4.56.7 3079 80 - - - - - - - -
2001-09-13 13:40:38 CLOSE TCP 208.228.171.175 216.115.105.17 3074 80 - - - - - - - -
2001-09-13 13:40:38 CLOSE TCP 208.228.171.175 206.176.144.2 3076 110 - - - - - - - -
2001-09-13 13:40:38 CLOSE TCP 208.228.171.175 207.68.183.62 3077 80 - - - - - - - -
2001-09-13 13:40:38 CLOSE TCP 208.228.171.175 64.4.56.7 3078 80 - - - - - - - -
2001-09-13 13:41:09 OPEN TCP 208.228.171.175 64.4.56.7 3080 80 - - - - - - - -
2001-09-13 13:41:13 OPEN TCP 208.228.171.175 64.4.56.7 3081 80 - - - - - - - -
2001-09-13 13:41:22 OPEN TCP 208.228.171.175 64.4.56.7 3082 80 - - - - - - - -
```

Figure 13.12
A sample log file.

The information in this file is best viewed and dealt with by an advanced network administrator, but I'll provide a brief description here. There are several fields, most of which are listed here:

- *Time*—Time of the transaction, in hours, minutes, and seconds
- *Date*—Year, month, and day of the transaction
- *Action*—The type of transaction: open, close, drop, or info-events-lost
- *Protocol*—TCP, UDP, or ICMP
- *Source IP address*—The IP address of the sending computer
- *Destination IP address*—The IP address of the destination computer (not necessarily the receiving computer)
- *Source Port Address*—The port number (from 1 to 65,535). Only TCP and UDP return valid entries; all others are denoted by a dash
- *Destination Port Address*—The port number of the destination computer (from 1 to 65,535). Only TCP and UDP return valid entries; all others are denoted by a dash
- *Size*—The size of the packet in bytes

- *TCPFlags*—A list of the flags in the header packet of the data. These flags include acknowledgement, end of data, and urgent.

- *ICMP Type*—The number associated with the ICMP type.

Each of these fields provides information on each message logged. This information can be used to troubleshoot network problems, find out how many packets were rejected and how many successful connections were made, and find out from whom they came and where they were going. An experienced network administrator can use this information to manage the firewall and view attempted intrusions. For the small network, logging is probably not necessary because the firewall will protect the general user automatically.

Information for Administrators of Domains

If you are the administrator of a domain, you won't want other computer administrators to have the ability to enable ICF, because doing so on a domain client computer will impair that computer's ability to send and receive information on the local network. Although general users will not have this ability, you should consider restricting this through group policies. When setting up the domain group policy, choose the option to Prohibit Use Of Internet Connection Firewall.

Encrypting File System

Encrypting File System (EFS) is another security technique that can be used by the general user on a network. When a file is encrypted, its contents are converted into a form that only the file owner and the network administrator can decrypt. *Decryption* is the process of converting the file back to its original form. Users can encrypt data as they store it on an NTFS disk as long as that data is not also compressed or is a system file.

Encrypting files and folders protects users from unauthorized attacks on their data. If a user gains access to the computer or network and is able to browse to an encrypted file, that user cannot open the file, and an access-denied message is displayed. The network administrator can decrypt the file, though, because this is necessary when an employee is let go or moves. Encrypting does not prevent users or hackers from deleting files; it prevents them only from reading the files.

There are several other advantages of EFS. Encrypting is transparent to the user, and users of files and folders can work with the data as though it were not encrypted at all. Also, encryption can be performed on remote computers, although when the data is in transit from one computer to another, it is not encrypted through EFS. There are other encryption methods available for this purpose, including security protocols such as Single Socket Later/ Transport Layer Security (SSL/TLS) and Internet Protocol Security (IPSec). These protocols do allow for security of the data while it is being sent, and can be used with encryption to make transporting data across the Internet or intranet secure.

Suggestions for Encryption

EFS is a great way to secure sensitive data and should be used whenever it's deemed necessary. Because encryption is best configured at the folder level, encrypting folders such as the My Documents folder is a good idea for all users.

It's also a good idea to create a System Restore Point immediately after encrypting the folders. This ensures that if a failure occurs, the restored data is also encrypted.

On a domain, encrypt the files stored on the domain server, and use IPSec or any other available network protocol to ensure that the data is safe as it is transmitted to other network locations. Also, encrypt files stored on the local computer, and make sure the data is backed up often.

By far, the most important type of computer on which to encrypt data is the mobile computer. Even if the computer is stolen, a hacker cannot decrypt the data unless he can log on with your username and password. Data cannot be taken from the hard drive or decrypted without the encryption key.

Encrypting and Decrypting Data

To encrypt or decrypt a file or folder on a local computer:

1. Open Windows Explorer on an NTFS-formatted computer.

2. Browse to the file or folder you want to encrypt.

3. Right-click the file or folder, and choose Properties.

4. On the General tab, choose the Advanced button.

5. To encrypt the data, check the Encrypt Contents To Secure Data checkbox. Choose OK. See Figure 13.13. To decrypt a file, clear the checkbox.

Figure 13.13
Encrypting data.

6. In the Confirm Attribute Changes dialog box, choose either Apply Changes To This Folder Only or Apply Changes To This Folder, Subfolders, And Files. Choose OK twice.

If you are a member of a domain, and you want to encrypt the data on it, you'll need to ask your administrator if the server is set up to accept remote encryption requests. This capability is enabled through the server's Active Directory Users and Computers console and by selecting the Trust Computer For Delegation checkbox. This checkbox is also accessed by right-clicking on the server and choosing Properties. The checkbox is located on the General tab. When this feature is enabled on the server, you can remotely encrypt files and folders there.

To encrypt a file on a remote computer:

1. Open Windows Explorer or My Network Places.

2. Locate the folder on the remote server on which you want to encrypt data.

3. Right-click this folder, and choose Properties.

4. On the General tab, choose the Advanced button.

5. To encrypt the data, check the Encrypt Contents To Secure Data checkbox. Choose OK. See Figure 13.13. To decrypt a file, clear the checkbox.

6. In the Confirm Attribute Changes dialog box, choose either Apply Changes To This Folder Only or Apply Changes To This Folder, Subfolders, And Files. Choose OK twice.

Copying and Moving Encrypted Files and Folders

You can copy and move encrypted files and folders in the same way that you copy and move compressed files and folders. You can use the Cut, Copy, and Paste commands, or you can drag and drop the files and folders. If you right-click when you drag a file, you can choose to move it or to copy it. Depending on whether the file is moved or copied, and on what type of file system the folder is sent to, different results will occur.

If a file is copied or moved from an NTFS volume to one that is not NTFS, the file's encryption is lost unless you are copying to a Web Distributed Authoring and Versioning folder on a domain server. If a file is copied or moved to another NTFS volume, encryption remains, as it does when an encrypted file or folder is moved within the same NTFS volume.

Backing Up the Encryption Keys

When files are encrypted, a key is used to decrypt the data. This key is also encrypted to further enhance the security of the data. The key is associated with the user's EFS certificate and should be backed up onto a floppy disk as soon as the first files are encrypted.

To back up your default recovery keys to a floppy disk:

1. Log on as an administrator.

2. Choose Start | Run, and type "mmc" in the Open text box. Choose OK.

3. In the Microsoft Management Console (MMC), choose File | Add/Remove Snap-In.

4. Choose Add. In the Add Standalone Snap-In dialog box, choose Certificates.

5. In the Certificates Snap-In dialog box, select My User Account (the default), and choose Finish.

6. Choose Close and OK.

7. Expand the Certificates–Current User tree and the Personal tree, and highlight Certificates.

8. In the right pane, right-click the certificate, and choose All Tasks | Export.

9. When the Certificate Export Wizard appears, choose Next to begin.

10. On the Export Private Key page, select Yes, Export The Private Key, and choose Next.

11. On the Export File Format page, accept the defaults and choose Next.

12. Type a password to maintain the security of this floppy disk. Choose Next.

13. Browse to the floppy disk, and type a name for the file. Choose Save, Next, and Finish.

Recovery Agents in Domains

When an employee with encrypted files and folders on his computer leaves the company, those files can be decrypted only by recovery agents. Recovery agents are administrators who have special certificates and private keys that allow the encrypted data to be decrypted. Recovery agents are added to domains when an administrator adds their certificates to the existing recovery policy. This task is performed on the domain controller.

Recovery Agents on the Local Computer

Recovery agents on local or standalone computers are the administrators of those machines. However, you can configure additional recovery agents for your local computer if you have met some prerequisites. To configure a recovery agent in a workgroup or for a local computer, you'll need to do the following first:

♦ Configure a group policy

♦ Have the user who is to be the recovery agent publish a recovery certificate

With these requirements met, do the following:

1. Log on as an administrator.

2. Open the Group Policy console.

3. Expand the tree Local Computer Policy\Computer Configuration\Windows Settings\Security Settings\Public Key Policies.

4. In the right pane, right-click on Encrypted Data Recovery Agents. Choose Add Data Recovery Agent, and work your way through the wizard.

Recovering Encrypted Files and Folders

There are two ways to recover encrypted data: either you are a recovery agent for a workgroup or domain, or you are the administrator of the local or standalone computer. If you are the administrator of your local computer, you can use the floppy disk created earlier to recover files. If you are a member of a domain and are not the administrator of your computer, you'll have to ask an administrator to help you recover the data.

To recover an encrypted file or folder by using your floppy disk:

1. Log on as the administrator of your local computer.

2. Open the MMC console with the Certificates snap-in created earlier.

3. Expand the Certificates–Current User tree and the Personal tree, and highlight Certificates.

4. In the right pane, right-click the certificate, and choose All Tasks | Import.

5. When the Certificate Import Wizard appears, choose Next to begin. Follow the steps in the wizard to import the key.

If you are not the designated recovery agent and you do not have a file encryption certificate, you'll need to access a backup of the folder in question and send that folder to your administrator. The recovery agent can then use his or her recovery certificate to decrypt the file and send it to you.

Local and Group Policies

Several local and group policies can be used to secure the computer. Policies related to passwords and auditing have been discussed in depth, but we haven't yet discussed the options under the Security Options folder. Some of the most important local and group policies to put in place for security are listed in this section.

To access local policies, open the Control Panel and then Local Security Policy. To access group policies, choose Start | Run, type "mmc", and add the Group Policy snap-in.

Local Policies in a Workgroup

Regarding security, several important policies can be enabled or disabled to prevent users from harming the computer or accessing objects they shouldn't. Listed here are some of the policies that relate to a workgroup or standalone computer. To access these, choose Start | Programs | Administrative Tools | Local Security Policy, expand the Local Policies tree, and choose Security Options. Here are some of the policies for a workgroup or standalone computer:

- *Administrator account status*—Enable/disable

- *Guest account status*—Enable/disable

- *Limit local account use of blank passwords to console logon only*—Enable/disable

- *Rename administrator account*

- *Rename guest account*

- *Audit the use of the Backup and Restore privilege*—Enable/disable

- *Shut down system immediately if unable to log security audits*—Enable/disable

- *Allow undock without having to log on*—Enable/disable

- *Allow to format and eject removable media*—Administrators only

- *Prevent users from installing printer drivers*—Enable/disable

- *Restrict CD-ROM access to locally logged-on user only*—Enable/disable

- *Restrict floppy access to locally logged-on user only*—Enable/disable

- *Unsigned driver installation behavior*—Silently succeed; warn but allow installation; or do not allow installation

- *Do not display last user name*—Enable/disable

- *Do not require CTRL-ALT-DEL*—Enable/disable

- *Message text for users attempting to log on*—Leave blank, or type any message

- *Message title for users attempting to log on*—Leave blank, or type any title

- *Allow system to shut down without having to log on*—Enable/disable

- *On shutdown, clear virtual memory pagefile*—Enable/disable

There are other policies as well, but for the workgroup or standalone computer, these will suffice if changes to the defaults are needed. Assess carefully what changes need to be made prior to making any changes.

Local Policies for Domain Members

When a local computer is a member of a domain, the local computer's security policy is the least important and the first one overridden, but you can set security policies in case other policies are not in use. Several policies are available; to access these, choose Start | Programs | Administrative Tools | Local Security Policy, expand the Local Policies tree, and choose Security Options. (A few of these policies are also useful in workgroups.)

For domain members, the following security settings can be useful:

- *Allow server operators to schedule tasks*—Enable/disable

- *Refuse machine account password changes*—Enable/disable

- *Digitally encrypt or sign secure channel data (always)*—Enable/disable

- *Digitally encrypt secure channel data (when possible)*—Enable/disable

- *Digitally sign secure channel data (when possible)*—Enable/disable

- *Disable machine account password changes*—Enable/disable

- *Require strong (Windows 2000 or later) session key*—Enable/disable

- *Prompt user to change password before expiration*—From 0 to 999 days

- *Require domain controller authentication to unlock workstation*—Enable/disable

- *Smart card removal behavior*—No action, lock workstation, or force logoff

Local Policies for a Microsoft Network and/or Network Access

Several policies can be set for members of Microsoft networks and for those users requesting general network access. These policies are:

- *Digitally sign communications (always)*—Enable/disable

- *Digitally sign communications (if server agrees)*—Enable/disable

- *Send unencrypted password to third party SMB server*—Enable/disable

- *Amount of idle time before suspending session*—From 0 to 99,999 minutes

- *Disconnect clients when logon hours expire*—Enable/disable

- *Let Everyone permissions apply to anonymous users*—Enable/disable

- *Shares that can be accessed anonymously*—COMCFG, DFS$

- *Sharing and security model for local accounts*—Classic (local users authenticate as themselves), Guest only (local users authenticate as Guest)

- *For the Recovery console: Allow automatic administrative logon*—Enable/disable

- *For the Recovery console: Allow floppy copy and access to all drives and folders*—Enable/disable

- *For shutdown: Clear virtual memory pagefile*—Enable/disable

Group Policies

You can set just about any policy by using an MMC console with the Group Policy snap-in. Most of these settings have been discussed in previous chapters. However, for security purposes, certain settings should definitely be considered. In the Group Policy console, expand the trees for Computer Configuration and User Configuration. Under the Computer Configuration tree, the security settings are related to IP Security policies, which will be discussed later in this section. Other settings are also available here.

Within the Group Policy console, in the Computer Configuration\Administrative Templates\System folder, consider changing these settings:

Note
Beside each policy setting is its respective System folder. See Figure 13.14. Not all options are displayed in this list.

♦ *Turn off Autoplay*—System

♦ *Do not automatically encrypt files moved to encrypted folders*—System

♦ *Wait for remote user profile*—User Profiles

♦ *Maximum retries to unload and update user profile*—User Profiles

♦ *Only allow local user profiles*—User Profiles

♦ *Don't display the Getting Started welcome screen at logon*—Logon

♦ *Always use classic logon*—Logon

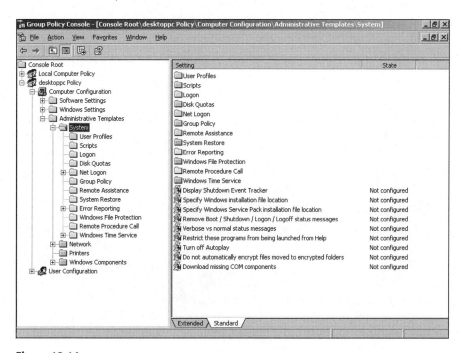

Figure 13.14
The Group Policy console.

- *Run these programs at logon*—Logon

- *Always wait for the network at computer startup and logon*—Logon

- *Enable disk quotas*—Disk Quotas

- *Enforce disk quota limit*—Disk Quotas

- *Expected dial-up delay on logon (in seconds)*—Net Logon

- *Solicited Remote Assistance*—Remote Assistance

- *Offer Remote Assistance*—Remote Assistance

- *Turn off System Restore*—System Restore

Within the Group Policy console, in the User Configuration\Administrative Templates folder, consider changing these settings:

- *Remove links and access to Windows Updates*—Start Menu And Taskbar

- *Do not keep history of recently opened documents*—Start Menu And Taskbar

- *Don't save settings on exit*—Desktop

- *Hide Internet Explorer icon on desktop*—Desktop

- *Hide specific Control Panel applets*—Control Panel

- *Prohibit access to the Control Panel*—Control Panel

- *Prohibit TCP/IP advanced configuration*—Network | Network Connections

- *Prohibit access to the New Connection Wizard*—Network | Network Connections

There are literally hundreds of other options to change inside these folders. I've tried to list those that a user of a small network or workgroup might need. Some of these policies can be quite useful even on a standalone unit. All you need to do to change a policy is double-click it and change its setting.

Protecting Computers from Viruses

Viruses are an unfortunate byproduct of our reliance on the Internet and software. Viruses are pieces of programming code that cause a computer to do things it normally wouldn't. This behavior can range from playing a simple piece of music or flashing an inappropriate message to destroying all of the data on your hard drive. The virus is generally hidden in an email attachment or on a floppy disk, but viruses can also be acquired from CD-ROMs or from files downloaded from the Internet. Most viruses tend to attack the computer immediately, but some wait for a particular date and time.

There are several ways to protect your computer from viruses, and the best way is to know what programs you are installing and who created them. You should also *never* open an email attachment from anyone you don't know. Adhering to this rule can be nearly impossible in the workplace, though; it is difficult to get workers to comply with this rule. Recently, a virus was released through an email message, and the subject line was "Per Your Request." In a large organization, many users would open this file automatically, even if properly warned about viruses previously. Some users have even been quoted as saying "I knew it was a virus, I just wanted to see what would happen." This was a common occurrence with the I Love You virus of 2000.

Anti-virus programs can help you protect your computer better than you can by yourself. Some of these programs are free, but your best bet is to purchase a program from a well-known and well-trusted manufacturer, such as McAfee or Symantec. After purchasing one of these programs, configure it so that it automatically downloads the latest patches and code from the manufacturer's Web site. This can be done daily or weekly and even at specific times of the day. Figure 13.15 shows the window used in Norton AntiVirus 2000 to schedule when anti-virus scans should be done or when updates should be made. In this case, scans are scheduled for every Friday night at 8:00.

Make sure you configure the anti-virus program to check all email messages before they are opened. Sometimes this behavior isn't the default when a program is installed. Carefully install the program, and choose Custom if it's available. Then, while installing the program, choose to protect as much as possible for your system.

Suggestions for Avoiding Viruses

There are several things that you can do as a user or an administrator to protect your computer(s) from infection. Some obvious protection comes from keeping the computer up-to-date by using Windows Update and installing service packs from Microsoft as they

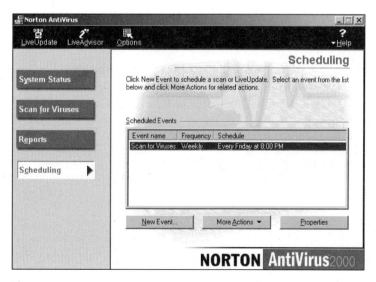

Figure 13.15
Scheduling a weekly anti-virus scan.

become available. Besides updates for Windows XP, you should also keep an eye out for updates to any office or browser programs you are using. Microsoft offers updates for its Internet Explorer browser occasionally, and those updates should be installed as soon as possible.

Because many viruses are sent as Visual Basic files or VBScript files, you can remove the registered file-name extension so that double-clicking a .vbs file to open it would require choosing a program for doing so. This might be enough to stop some users from opening these types of files. However, this is not an option if you regularly use .vbs files on your computer or network. Another option is to delete Windows Script Host (.wsh) settings files. Again, there are known vulnerabilities with these files and viruses.

To disable .vbs or .wsh files from opening automatically when selected:

1. Log on as an administrator.

2. Open My Computer.

3. Choose Tools | Folder Options.

4. Select the File Types tab.

5. Scroll down the Extensions list until you see VBS. Highlight it, and choose the Delete button. You can also delete the WSH (Windows Script Host) file settings if you are not part of a domain using this type of file. Contact your administrator for information about this setting.

Another helpful hint is to allow your anti-virus program to scan for viruses daily or every time you log onto the computer. This practice ensures that your computer is virus-free at the beginning of each workday. Finally, use your anti-virus software to scan any floppy disk you receive before installing any file from it onto your computer.

Virus Hoaxes

If you receive more than 5 or 10 email messages every day, chances are good that a few of them are virus warnings from well-intended friends and coworkers. Although a handful of the warnings I've received were valid, with an educated guess I'll say that 95 percent of them were not. There are several Web sites that keep up-to-date lists of the latest viruses and virus hoaxes. These sites include the following:

- **http://www.symantec.com/avcenter/hoax.html**

- **http://vil.mcafee.com/hoax.asp**

- **http://www.datafellows.com/news/hoax.htm**

- **http://hoaxbusters.ciac.org**

- **http://www.virusbtn.com**

Although it is good to be vigilant, passing on virus hoaxes only perpetuates problems. Consider checking the sites above before passing on any email messages regarding viruses, and instead send the hoax-page links to the person who sent you the message about the virus.

Logging On as an Administrator

You should not log onto your computer as an administrator unless you have some administrator's duties to take care of. Instead, you should make yourself a member of the Power Users group and log on using that account. The problem with running your computer as an administrator is that the system is more vulnerable to Trojan horse viruses and other system weaknesses. A *Trojan horse* virus is a program that looks like any other program when it asks the computer for information. However, the information it asks for can be usernames and passwords, or email address lists, and this information can be used to perpetuate viruses or to break into the system later. Internet sites can have Trojan horse virus codes also, and this code can be downloaded to your system and executed.

If you log on as a member of the Power Users group, anyone or anything accessing the information on your system can retrieve only the information that a power user could retrieve, thus lessening the destruction that can be done. Power users can run programs, install programs, install printers, and have a high level of control over the computer. Then, while logged on as a power user, you can use the Run As command to run any program as an administrator without having to log off and on again to do so. To start a program as an administrator, you hold down the Shift key while right-clicking the program icon; then choose Run As, and enter the username and password for the administrator's account.

Uninterruptible Power Supply

An *uninterruptible power supply (UPS)* is a hardware device that keeps your computers running even when power to the computer has been interrupted. This interruption can be caused by a blackout or power failure, and the UPS device will keep the computers running on batteries until the power is restored or at least until the computers can be shut down properly. UPS devices provide protection against power surges and brownouts as well.

There are several items to configure and manage when installing and using a UPS. In the following sections, I'll explain how to install and configure a simple UPS device and how to test the installed device.

Installing a UPS Device

To physically install the UPS device, follow the instructions that came with the device. Then log on as an administrator, and follow these steps:

1. Open the Control Panel, then Power Options.

2. Select the UPS tab.

3. In the Details area, click the Select button.

4. On the UPS Selection page, select the manufacturer of the device, the port the device is installed on, and the model of the device. Choose Next.

5. On the UPS Interface Configuration page, choose Finish.

If the device installs without a problem, continue to the next section. If necessary, open Device Manager and look for the UPS device or for a device with a yellow exclamation point or red X beside it. Either uninstall and reinstall the driver, or search for a newer driver that will work with Windows XP Professional. Make sure the device is installed properly before continuing.

Configuring a UPS Device

Once the device is correctly installed, you can configure it through the Control Panel and Power Options. Figure 13.16 shows the UPS Configuration dialog box for a generic UPS device. Notice that there are settings for enabling notifications, specifying how many seconds to wait between the power failure and the first notification, specifying how many seconds to wait between subsequent notifications, and specifying what to do when the UPS battery is low or almost exhausted or after a specific amount of time that the computer has been on battery power.

To configure the UPS:

1. Log on as an administrator. Open the Control Panel, then Power Options.

2. Select the UPS tab.

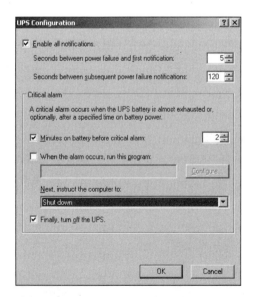

Figure 13.16
UPS configuration.

3. In the Details area, choose the Configure button.

4. Make the necessary changes, and choose OK twice.

Removing a UPS Device

If you need to remove a UPS device, you can do so from the Control Panel and Power Options, as described in previous sections. After selecting the UPS tab, click the Select button. In the UPS Selection dialog box, under Select Manufacturer, click None.

Testing the UPS Device

You should always test new equipment after installing it, and in the case of a UPS, you should check it every week or so to verify that it is working properly. You can test the UPS simply by disconnecting the power supply from the computer and seeing if it works. Of course, just in case of a failure, make sure you don't have any programs or important documents open that haven't been saved.

After the battery has had a chance to use some of its resources, make sure the computer shuts down as it is supposed to, or restore power to the computer and recharge the battery. You can then check your system logs to verify that no errors occurred.

Security for Administrators

There are several ways to apply security settings to both domains and workgroups. You've already learned about local and group policies and about changing default settings related to passwords, account lockout, and auditing. You also know that domain administrators set policies for entire networks and that you can belong to groups with special permissions, rights, and privileges. However, there is another, more powerful, enterprise-wide way to configure security for a network. That is by using security tools such as the Security Configuration And Analysis console, Security Configuration Manager, security templates, the Security Settings extension of the Group Policy console, and Secedit, a command-line tool for administrators.

Whereas domain members and administrators use or are affected by the majority of these tools, administrators of workgroups and standalone computers—as well as domain administrators—can use Security Configuration And Analysis. In this section, you'll learn about all of these tools and how to use them. The first subsection, "The Security Configuration And Analysis Console," is appropriate for all readers.

The Security Configuration And Analysis Console

You can use the Security Configuration And Analysis console to analyze and configure the local security policy on your computer, and you can use the tools provided with this console to export that policy to any other computers in your workgroup or domain. Any local security policies will be overridden by any domain network policies, but if you are a member of a workgroup or you share a standalone computer, this tool and preconfigured policies can ease security administration tasks.

The Security Configuration And Analysis console can help you review your current security settings and determine if they are working as you'd like. This tool can also detect security flaws that occur but go unnoticed by users, and then suggest ways to correct these flaws. The Security Configuration And Analysis console can also be used to import security templates to the local computer and configure the computer with the security settings you need. Because there are more complex tools available for domains, this tool is often used for standalone computers and workgroups, whereas group policies and the Security Settings extension are used by domain administrators.

Planning for the Security Configuration

Before configuring security for your network, you should figure out just how tight you want security to be. You also need to verify that the systems affected are formatted with NTFS. Most of these security options have been described in earlier chapters, and some in this chapter, too. Security encompasses all of the following:

♦ Using account and local policies

♦ Configuring restricted groups

♦ Setting permissions for files and folders

♦ Setting permissions for Registry keys

♦ Using the event log and auditing

♦ Setting logon rights and privileges

Once you are sure what you want, you must create an MMC console with the Security Configuration And Analysis snap-in and decide which security template to import.

Introduction to Security Templates

Using security templates is the best way to start when you're configuring security for a single computer or for computers in workgroups or domains. After a security template is chosen and customized, it can be used on hundreds and even thousands of computers in your network. The template can then be exported to or imported from the Security Configuration And Analysis console or through the Local Security Policy console. You can also apply the settings to multiple machines by using the Security Settings extension of the Group Policy snap-in.

Before setting up any automatic security configuration through a template, you need to choose a security template that most closely matches your needs. Several security templates are available, and each offers a different level of security. The first template is the Default Security template (security.inf). This template has all of the default settings that are configured when the computer is first installed. This is a good template to configure if you've been experimenting with the default settings and you don't remember what they were, or if you want to start with a clean slate. This template's policy should never be applied through the Group Policy console because this template is computer-specific and applies default settings each time the policy is applied.

The second template is the Compatible template (Compatws.inf). Understanding why this template was created and why it would be used requires a little background information. Basically, there are three types of domain users: administrators, power users, and users. Power users have more privileges than users do. Power users can run applications that are not certified for regular users to run, specifically, those applications that are not members of the Certified for Windows Program. Because regular users probably need to run those programs, you can either add these users to the Power Users group (which is usually unacceptable), or apply the Compatible template. You should not use the Compatible template on domain controllers; use it only on workstations.

The third template is the Secure template (Secure*.inf). This template applies higher levels of security than the first two templates do, while still allowing users to work with non-Windows-certified applications. The increased security settings are applied to stronger password requirements and lockout, as well as to audit settings. Templates are available for both workstations and domain controllers.

The fourth template is the Highly Secure template (Hisec*.inf). More secure than the Secure template, this one restricts the level of encryption used, the types of computers that have access to the domain controllers, and the protocols that can be used. Some clients that cannot be used with this security setting are Windows NT clients prior to SP 4, Windows for Workgroups computers, and Windows 95 and 98 computers that do not have the DS Client Pack installed. Templates are available for both workstations and domain controllers.

A fifth template is the System Root Security template (Rootsec.inf). This template can be applied when the root directory's permissions need to be reapplied. This is necessary if the permissions have been changed or need to be returned to their defaults.

Once you've decided on a template that most closely matches your security ideal, you can modify it by using the Security Templates snap-in. You can also view these templates from <root drive>\Windows\Security\Templates. You can view these templates by double-clicking them.

Creating the Security Configuration And Analysis Console

The Security Configuration And Analysis tool is a snap-in that must be added to an MMC console. To create a new console just for this purpose, or to add this snap-in to an established MMC console:

1. Log on as an administrator.

2. Either choose Start | Run, type "mmc" in the Open text box, and choose OK, or open an existing personalized console.

3. Choose File | Add/Remove Snap-In. In the Add/Remove Snap-In dialog box, choose Add.

4. Highlight the Security Configuration And Analysis snap-in, and choose Add. Then choose Close, then OK.

5. Choose File | Save As, name the console, and choose Save.

When you've got the console ready, you can do several things. You can analyze the security settings you have already configured to see if there are holes in your settings, and then repair them; you can configure security from scratch; or you can simply apply a new template over your current settings. If you like the settings as they are currently configured, skip to the section "Analyzing Security." If you are planning to configure security from scratch or replace what you already have, continue with the following section.

Configuring the Security Console and Importing a Template

When you're using the Security Configuration And Analysis console for the first time, the screen will look like the screen shown in Figure 13.17. To use the console, you'll need to either open an existing security template database or create a new database. If your computer has security features configured, either you can skip to the "Analyzing Security" section, analyze what's configured, and then return here to continue, or you can apply the default security template (Setup security.inf). The latter option applies all of the default settings to the computer. In this section, I'll describe how to create a new database and import a security template.

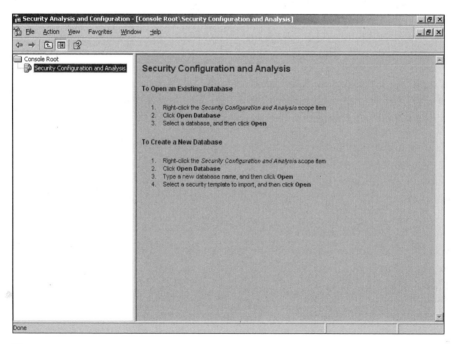

Figure 13.17
The Security Configuration And Analysis console.

Tip

The security templates will override your existing settings; thus, it is important to import a security template to a machine that doesn't already have security features configured.

To create a new database and configure a security policy for the first time:

1. Log on as an administrator.

2. Open the Security Configuration And Analysis console created earlier through the Start | Programs | Administrative Tools menu.

3. In the left pane, right-click Security Configuration And Analysis, and choose Open Database.

4. The Open Database dialog box will be empty. Type a name in the File Name text box, and choose Open.

5. In the resulting Import Template dialog box , select an appropriate template. I'll select the Compatible template in this example. If you are reverting to default settings, you'll select the Default Security template (Setup security.inf).

6. The right pane of the console will change from what is shown in Figure 13.17. In the right pane will be information about configuring the new console. Right-click the Security Configuration And Analysis icon, and choose Configure Computer Now.

7. In the Configure System dialog box, choose OK to accept the default location of the error log file.

8. Right-click Security Configuration And Analysis again, and this time choose Analyze Computer Now. In the Perform Analysis dialog box, choose OK to verify the Error Log File path.

The console will now look like Figure 13.18.

Creating Your Own Template

The default templates are not the end-all answer to all security needs or all organizations. Because of this, you can alter the default settings for the template that has been configured. To do this, you'll need to add the Security Templates snap-in to the existing console or to a new one. You do this the same way that you added the Security Configuration And Analysis snap-in earlier, but this time, choose Security Templates.

After you've added the Security Templates snap-in to an MMC console, change the default settings by doing the following:

1. Log on as an administrator.

2. Open the MMC console that contains the Security Templates snap-in.

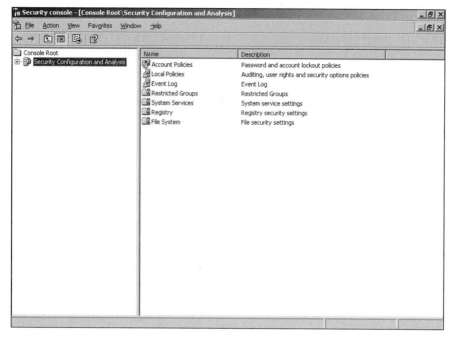

Figure 13.18
The completed Security Configuration And Analysis console.

3. Expand the Security Templates tree and the console-root templates tree below it.

4. Expand the tree of the security template that you want to change.

5. Change the template as necessary. Changes are made here the same way they are made in the Group Policy console; simply double-click the setting and make the necessary changes. See Figure 13.19.

6. Right-click the policy you've changed, and choose Save As. Type a name other than the default name, and choose the Save button.

The new policy will be saved in the Security Templates folder with the other templates. The template can then be imported into the local computer or a remote computer or be exported to any computer.

Applying a Template to a Local Computer Policy

If you've created a new template by changing an existing template, as shown in the previous section, you can now import that template to the local machine and apply it to the computer. The template can also be imported from remote machines.

To import a policy to the local machine by using the Security Configuration And Analysis console:

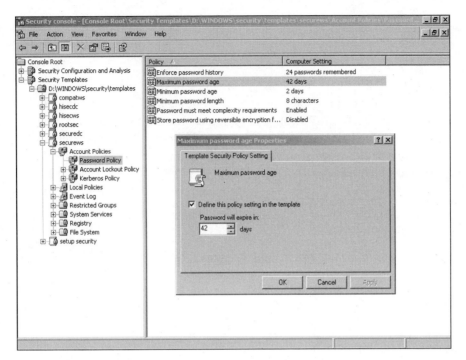

Figure 13.19
Changing default settings for a security template.

1. Log on as an administrator.

2. Open the MMC console that contains the Security Configuration And Analysis snap-in. Right-click Security Configuration And Analysis, and choose Open Database. Choose the database to open.

3. Right-click Security Configuration And Analysis, and choose Import Template.

4. Locate the template you recently created, and choose Open.

5. Right-click Security Configuration And Analysis, and choose Configure Computer Now. Choose OK when prompted.

6. Right-click Security Configuration And Analysis, and choose Analyze Computer Now. Choose OK when prompted.

Analyzing Security

There are several reasons you might want to analyze the security settings on your computer. You'll need to analyze the system after first configuring the imported template. You can also analyze your security settings before changing them to determine if your current settings are working well. You should also analyze the settings occasionally to determine if any changes have occurred that do not match your proposed level of security. After analyzing the security settings, the Security Configuration And Analysis console will show you where your security settings do not match required security levels, and it will state what can be done to improve security.

When a template is first imported, configured, and analyzed, there are no discrepancies between what you've stated you want in a security policy and what is actually configured on the computer. However, security settings will not remain static for long, and changes occur for many reasons. Sometimes, a higher level of security must be configured temporarily, or other security templates are added and the resulting combination of templates leaves things in a state of uncertainty.

To analyze your computer's security settings:

1. Log on as an administrator.

2. Open the Security Configuration And Analysis console.

3. Right-click Security Configuration And Analysis, and choose Open Database. Select the database you want to analyze, and choose OK.

4. Right-click Security Configuration And Analysis, and choose Analyze Computer Now. Choose OK when prompted.

5. Expand the trees for Account Policies, Local Policies, and Event Log to view discrepancies.

So, what do all of those red X's, green checkmarks, and other icons mean? Table 13.3 describes what types of icons you might see and what each icon represents.

Figure 13.20 shows a sample analysis. There are three red X's, two green checkmarks, and one item with nothing beside it at all.

Table 13.3 Analysis icons.

Icon (Flag)	Description
Red X	The entry is defined, but the security setting of the computer does not match the security setting in the Security Configuration And Analysis database that has been configured.
Green checkmark	The entry is defined in the database and on the system, and the entries match.
Question mark	The entry is not defined in the database, and the setting was not analyzed. Sometimes entries are not analyzed because the person analyzing the data doesn't have the correct permissions. Always log on as an administrator.
Exclamation point	The entry is defined in the database, but the entry does not exist on the system.
Nothing	The entry is not defined in the database or on the system.

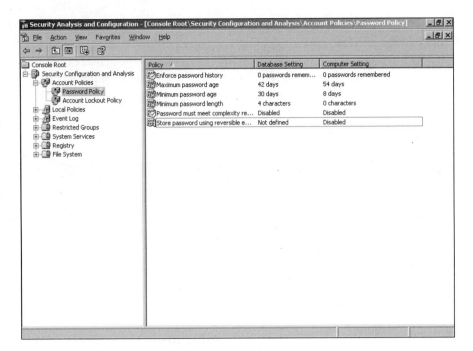

Figure 13.20
Analyzing security settings.

Correcting Discrepancies Found While Analyzing

If, after analyzing the data, you notice several red X's or other notifications, you should (in most cases) correct those discrepancies. There are several ways to do this, but the easiest way is to reconfigure the entries with the red X's or other icons beside them. You can do this by editing the analysis database as follows:

1. Log on as an administrator.

2. Open the Security Configuration And Analysis console.

3. Right-click Security Configuration And Analysis, and choose Open Database. Select the database you want to analyze, and choose OK.

4. Right-click Security Configuration And Analysis, and choose Analyze Computer Now. Choose OK when prompted.

5. In the details pane, double-click the entry you want to edit.

6. Check the Define This Policy In The Database checkbox, and select a new setting for the entry. Choose OK. (You can compare the database setting to the computer setting in the right pane.)

7. Repeat Steps 5 and 6 until all discrepancies have been resolved.

If you think things are so messed up that the original settings should be applied, you can re-import the security template, reconfigure the computer, and re-analyze the settings on a standalone computer or on multiple computers; however, you'll have to make these changes on all of the computers involved. Reapplying the template is the best choice when multiple computers are involved, such as in large workgroups or domains. To reapply the template, return to the previous sections and follow the directions there.

Reapplying Default Settings

You can reapply the default settings for any computer by applying the following security template as described here:

1. Log on as an administrator.

2. Open the Security Configuration And Analysis console.

3. In the left pane, right-click Security Configuration And Analysis, and choose Open Database.

4. In the Import Template dialog box, choose the Setup Security template.

5. Right-click the Security Configuration And Analysis icon, and choose Configure Computer Now.

6. In the Configure System dialog box, choose the OK button to accept the default location of the error log file.

7. Right-click Security Configuration And Analysis again, and this time choose Analyze Computer Now. In the Perform Analysis dialog box, choose OK to verify the error log file path.

The Security Settings Extension of the Group Policy Snap-In

When configuring security for a domain, administrators apply group policies to all users instead of traveling to each computer and physically configuring their security settings through the consoles described earlier. For an administrator to use security templates for domain members, he or she must first configure the policy as described earlier, and then link it to a group policy object.

If you are working on a workstation or a server that is a member of a domain, you can import a security template into a group policy object stored in the domain. Remember, a group policy object is simply a set of group policy settings for domain groups.

To apply a security template to a group policy object in a domain from a workstation or a server in the domain:

1. Log on as an administrator.

2. Choose Start | Run, type "mmc" in the Open text box, and choose OK.

3. Choose File | Add/Remove Snap-In.

4. In the Add/Remove Snap-In dialog box, choose Add. Select Group Policy.

5. In the Select Group Policy Object Wizard page, choose Browse.

6. On the Browse For A Group Policy Object page, select the policy object you would like to modify, and choose Finish.

7. Choose Close and OK.

8. In the Group Policy console tree, expand Computer Configuration \ Windows Settings \ Security Settings.

9. Right-click Security Settings, and choose Import Policy.

10. From the Templates folder in the Import Policy From dialog box, select the template you want to add. Do not import Setup Security (Security.inf) into a group policy object.

> **Note**
> *Security settings are refreshed only every 90 minutes on a workstation or server and every 5 minutes on a domain controller.*

The Secedit Utility

You can analyze your security settings and compare them to specific templates from a command line as well as from inside the Security Configuration And Analysis console. Comparing settings from a command prompt requires the use of the Secedit utility. There are four main **secedit** commands, and they are listed along with their syntax requirements in Table 13.4.

Following are the parameters for the **secedit** commands:

♦ **/db** *filename*—This parameter is required; it specifies both the path and the file name of the database that is configured for the computer. If *filename* is a new database, then the **/cfg** parameter is also required.

Table 13.4   Secedit commands.

Secedit Command and Switch	Syntax and Parameters
secedit /analyze	secedit /analyze /db *filename* [/cfg *filename*] [/log *filename*] [/quiet]
secedit /configure	secedit /configure /db *filename* [cfg *filename*] [/overwrite] [/areas *area1 area2...*] [/log *filename*] [/quiet]
secedit /export	secedit /export [/mergedpolicy] [db *filename*] [cfg *filename*] [/areas *area1 area2...*] [/log *filename*] [/quiet]
secedit /validate	secedit /validate *filename*

♦ **/cfg** *filename*—This parameter specifies the path and file name for the security template that will be imported into the database and analyzed. This parameter must be used with the **/db** parameter unless you want to compare the *filename* against what is already configured in the database.

♦ **/log** *filename*—This parameter specifies the path and file name of the log file This parameter is not required; if no log file is specified, the default log file will be used.

♦ **/quiet**—This parameter performs the analysis without showing anything on the screen or in the log output. You can view the results in the Security Configuration And Analysis console.

♦ **/overwrite**—If the **/cfg** parameter is used, this parameter can be used also. By choosing to overwrite, you are allowing the computer to overwrite any template that is stored in the database instead of appending the results to it.

♦ **/areas** *area1 area2 . . .*—This parameter specifies which security areas are to be applied to the system. By default, all areas are applied to the system. The areas are: **SecurityPolicy**, **Group_Mgmt**, **User_Rights**, **RegKeys**, **FileStore**, and **Services**.

♦ **/mergedpolicy**—This parameter is used when you want to merge and export domain and local policy security settings.

Additional Security Features

While all administrators can certainly benefit from the security tips offered in the first two sections, several other tools are available to administrators. These include security hosts, smart card support, IP Security policies, the Resultant Set of Policy (RSoP) console, and software restriction policies.

Although domain administrators will configure the more complex security measures, such as security hosts and smart cards, some measures can also be employed for standalone computers or workgroups. In this section, I'll introduce some of the additional security features of Windows XP Professional and, when applicable, discuss how the domain end user will be affected and how to use these features for standalone and workgroup computers.

Security Hosts

Security hosts are authentication devices that validate whether a computer and user are authorized to connect to a remote-access server in the domain. A remote-access server is a computer that is running the Routing and Remote Access Service (RRAS) and is configured to allow computers to dial into it and access information. One popular security host is the RADIUS (Remote Authentication Dial-In User Service) server. It uses the RADIUS security protocol, which authenticates users for dial-up and tunneled network access for ISPs, corporate networks, and small domains. RADIUS is the most widely used protocol and dial-up server at this time.

A security host is a physical computer that sits between your computer and the remote access server. When you dial into a remote access server, the security host must verify your credentials before access is granted to the remote access server. Even after access is granted, that server must still validate you as well. This extra bit of security is certainly necessary when you are allowing users to dial into your servers and domain.

Smart Card Support

Smart cards are credit-card-size devices that are used basically the same way that a bank card is used at an ATM. The card is used to store your sign-in credentials, such as a password, your public and private keys, and other information, including which floors, offices, or buildings you are allowed access to. You must not only have the card but also use a personal identification number (PIN) to verify your identity. The smart card is used mostly in domains for the purpose of logging onto computers and obtaining access to domain resources or email. In a large network, the smart card is the best method of providing portable security solutions for those workers who move around the organization a lot or who access multiple computers. These cards are nearly impossible to hack into, and they offer additional support for Microsoft's Public Key Infrastructure (PKI), described later.

The smart card works well as a hacking deterrent because the hacker must have not only the card but also the PIN. This PIN does not have to be a series of numbers; it can also contain letters. This makes using common attacking tools, such as dictionary attacks (where every possible word is tried as a password), obsolete. In addition, smart cards are configured to fail after a specific number of unsuccessful logon attempts, and the owner of the card will notice its disappearance at some time in the near future.

For users, logging on with a smart card is as simple as sliding the card through the card reader and typing in the PIN. The user doesn't even need to press Ctrl+Alt+Del.

IP Security Policies

IP Security (IPSec) policies can be used in both domains and workgroups to offer security when users are communicating over Internet Protocol (IP) networks. The IPSec protocol protects networks from Internet and other attacks by using encryption standards that are open standards. Open standards allow different manufacturers and telecommunication companies to use IPSec without having to develop standards of their own. The IPSec protocol provides secure communications between workgroups, LANs, domain clients and servers, and physically remote offices.

Note

IPSec is used with Layer 2 Tunneling Protocol (L2TP). IPSec encrypts the data and L2TP creates the secure tunnel it travels through.

There are many ways a hacker can try to attack a network. Hacking attempts can occur through email attachments, as downloads from Web sites, by eavesdropping on the unencrypted data passing through the network cables, by modifying data, by trying multiple passwords, through denial-of-service attacks (where the network is flooded with requests), and by hundreds of other methods. Using IPSec on the network can greatly reduce the impact of these attacks, if not prevent them entirely, if IPSec is used with anti-virus programs and other security measures. The administrator of your domain will configure IPSec policies, which require a great deal of planning and configuring; to the general user, these security measures will seem transparent.

IPSec for Workgroups

You can employ IPSec policies on your local computer and on computers in a workgroup. However, IPSec is not enabled by default and is not necessary on computers that do not deal with sensitive data. If you want to secure traffic between specific computers and you have the time to devote to installing and configuring IPSec on your local computer, continue with this section. Using IPSec will require some administration, however, so make sure it is necessary before starting.

To add the IP Security Policies snap-in to an MMC console:

1. Log on as an administrator.

2. Choose Start | Run, type "mmc" in the Open text box, and choose OK.

3. In the new MMC console, choose File | Add/Remove Snap-In. Choose Add.

4. Select IP Security Policy Management, and choose Add. Choose Local Computer when prompted.

5. Select IP Security Monitor, and choose Add. (This is optional, but you'll need it to monitor IP Security later.)

6. Choose Finish, Close, and OK. Save the new console as "IPSec".

Tip

You can also access IP Security policies on the local computer from the Local Security Policy console in Administrative Tools, but because this is a preconfigured console, you won't be able to add IP Security Monitor.

Defining IPSec Policies, Rules, and Settings

When defining IPSec policies, rules, and settings, you can either work from an existing policy or create a new one. There are three predefined IPSec policies that can be used in most instances. These policies can be accessed from the IPSec folder in the previously created MMC console. In this section, you'll learn how to create a new policy.

To create a new IPSec policy:

1. Log on as an administrator, and open the console created in the previous section.

2. Highlight IP Security Policies On The Local Computer, and choose Action | Create IP Security Policy.

3. Choose Next to start the IP Security Policy Wizard. On the IP Security Policy Name page, type a name (and optionally a description) for the new policy.

4. On the Requests For Secure Communication page, accept the default to Activate The Default Response Rule (described on this wizard page), and choose Next.

5. On the Default Response Rule Authentication Method page, select the default (Active Directory Default) unless you have a certificate from a certification authority. Choose Next.

6. Choose Finish to close the IP Security Policy Wizard, and make sure the checkbox is checked to Edit Properties when the wizard is closed.

7. In the new IP policy's Properties dialog box, verify that the information is correct, and make changes as needed. Choose OK when finished.

Assigning and Managing the Policy

To assign the new IPSec policy to the local computer, you must "activate" the policy from a Group Policy console.

To activate a new IPSec policy:

1. Log on as an administrator.

2. Open the Group Policy console.

3. Expand the tree Local Computer Policy\Windows Settings\Security Settings, and highlight IP Security Policies On Local Computer. See Figure 13.21.

4. In the right pane, right-click the policy you want to assign, and choose Assign.

If you need to unassign the policy in the future, first unassign the IPSec policy in this Group Policy console, wait 24 hours, and then delete the IPSec policy or the group policy object from the computer. This will prevent any problems with the policy remaining active after it has been unassigned.

IPSec is a service that might need to be stopped, restarted, or paused. You do that through the Services console, as with other computer services. You can also export or import policies to other computers, or define policies for multiple computers. If you look closely at Figure 13.21, you can see that two computers are configured with IPSec policies. The first is the local computer, which is highlighted, and the other is IP Security Policies On \\desktoppc, located at the bottom of the second tree. To review how to manage other computers in your workgroup, return to Chapters 10 and 11.

Monitoring IPSec Policies and Activities

You can monitor IPSec activity through the IP Security Monitor snap-in mentioned earlier. If you followed the instructions for adding the IP Security Policies snap-in, you also added

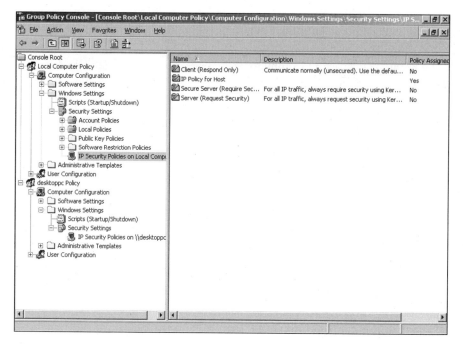

Figure 13.21
Assigning IPSec policies.

the IP Security Monitor snap-in. After adding this snap-in, you must add computers to it to define which computers should be monitored.

To add a computer to the IP Security Monitor snap-in:

1. Log on as an administrator.

2. Open the IPSec console created earlier or an existing MMC console that contains the IP Security Monitor.

3. Right-click IP Security Monitor, and choose Add Computer.

4. If you want to add a remote computer, browse to it in the Add Computer dialog box, or choose Local Computer.

Figure 13.22 shows the IP Security Monitor with two computers added. The red X next to the desktoppc indicates that the remote computer is unavailable, does not have the IPSec Monitor service started, or is incompatible with IPSec Monitor. For computers running Windows 2000, the IPSec policies must be configured through resources in the Windows 2000 Server Resource Kit.

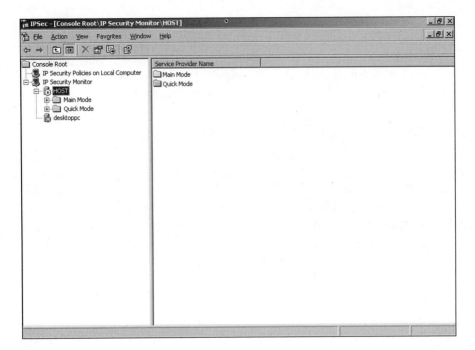

Figure 13.22
IP Security Monitor.

To monitor IP security statistics:

1. Log on as an administrator.

2. Open the IPSec console created earlier, or open an MMC console that contains the IP Security Monitor.

3. Right-click a computer name, and choose Statistics.

In the Statistics window that opens, you can view statistics of parameters such as the following:

♦ Acquire failures

♦ Receive failures

♦ Negotiation failures

♦ Invalid packets received

♦ Active tunnels

♦ Confidential bytes sent

♦ Confidential bytes received

♦ Key update failure

There is enough information concerning IPSec policies, managing those policies, adding specific filters, and adding generic filters to fill an entire book all by itself. If you need to apply specific filters or configure IPSec in a way that is more complex than its default, you should acquire more information on this subject from Microsoft's Web site, Microsoft Help, or books on the subject.

The Resultant Set of Policy Snap-In

The Resultant Set of Policy (RSoP) snap-in is used with the Group Policy console to allow an administrator to check security policies at different levels of domains to see if any policies conflict. RSoP is a query engine that polls all policies that are used to troubleshoot hard-to-diagnose problems. Administrators often run into problems because a group of computers in an organizational unit might have particular policies while users of a specific site might have other policies. If these users are in both groups, conflicts will arise between policies. Of course, there is an order of precedence among these levels, but sometimes problems still occur. Domain administrators can use RSoP in many ways, but for the general user, RSoP can be applied to verify changes made after importing a security template and to edit those changes using the Group Policy console.

Viewing policy settings and discovering conflicts are very useful tasks, which you can do by using the logging mode of RSoP. RSoP provides another mode, called *planning mode*, which allows you to simulate a policy change or implementation to see how it would affect your network. Both logging mode and planning mode will be discussed in this section, but first, you should install the RSoP snap-in, and make sure you have local and group policies configured.

Installing RSoP (Logging Mode)

RSoP is a snap-in to an MMC console. To add the snap-in, you must use the RSoP Wizard.

To install the RSoP snap-in:

1. Log on as an administrator.

2. Choose Start | Run, type "mmc" in the Open text box, and choose OK.

3. Choose File | Add/Remove Snap-In. In the Add/Remove Snap-In dialog box, choose Add.

4. Scroll down to Resultant Set Of Policies, select it, and choose Add.

5. Choose the Next button to start the Wizard. Notice that you can choose either Logging Mode or Planning Mode. If your computer is a member of a workgroup and not a domain, the Planning Mode option will be grayed out. At this time, choose Logging Mode. Choose Next.

6. On the Computer Selection page, select This Computer or Another Computer. If you choose Another Computer, you'll need to browse to it.

7. On the User Selection page, select a user from the list, or choose Current User. See Figure 13.23. Choose Next.

8. On the Summary Of Selections page, choose Next. Choose Finish when prompted.

9. In the Add Standalone Snap-in dialog box, highlight Resultant Set Of Policy again, and work through Steps 5 through 7 again.

10. Figure 13.24 shows what the Add/Remove Snap-In dialog box should look like after users have been added. Choose OK.

Logging Mode

After a security template has been applied using the Group Policy console, you can use RSoP to verify the changes that have been made regarding security. In the RSoP console, simply expand each tree to see what changes have been applied to which users. In logging mode, you can right-click any folder that contains information, and choose Properties to obtain more data. This data includes group policy objects (GPOs) and filtering status, scope of management, and revision information (see Figure 13.25). You can edit this information by clicking the Edit button, which opens the Group Policy console so that the settings can be modified. Although this is a great way to quickly edit a user's group policy settings, there is a better way to view the information.

Through the Help and Support Center, you can view, in HTML, the information obtained from RSoP. It is easily readable but not editable.

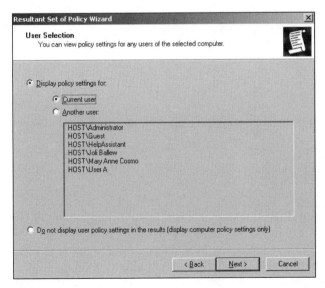

Figure 13.23
The User Selection page of the Resultant Set Of Policy Wizard.

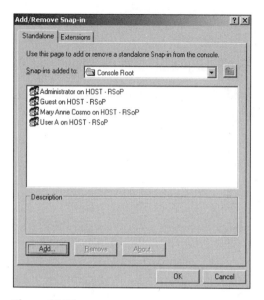

Figure 13.24
The RSoP console.

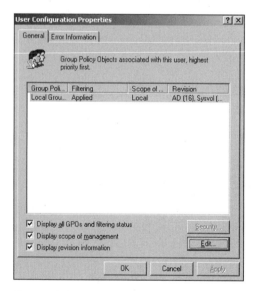

Figure 13.25
User Configuration Properties.

To view the information logged:

1. Choose Start | Help And Support.

2. In the Pick A Task section, choose Use Tools To View Your Computer Information And Diagnose Problems.

3. In the Tools section, choose Advanced System Information.

4. In the right pane, choose View Group Policy Settings Applied.

After the information has been collected, it will be displayed as shown in Figure 13.26.

You can also scroll down to the bottom of the screen shown in Figure 13.26, and choose Run The Resultant Set Of Policy Tool. The RSoP console will open, where you can see the folders related to the GPO.

Planning Mode

For you to use planning mode, the computer must be a member of a domain, and the server or computers in the domain must be running Windows XP Server or higher. You can install the RSoP snap-in and choose Planning Mode when prompted. You'll need at least one domain controller and two Windows XP Professional machines to make this work. (As this book was being written, Windows XP Server was not available yet.)

To add the RSoP snap-in in planning mode:

1. Log on as an administrator to your domain. (You cannot install RSoP in planning mode in a workgroup.)

2. Choose Start | Run, type "mmc" in the Open text box, and choose OK.

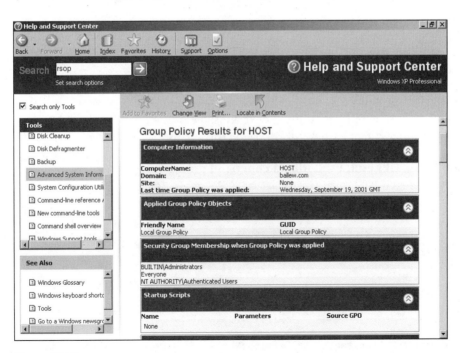

Figure 13.26
Group policy information.

3. Choose File | Add/Remove Snap-In. In the Add/Remove Snap-In dialog box, choose Add.

4. Scroll down to Resultant Set Of Policies, select it, and choose Add.

5. Choose Next to start the Resultant Set Of Policies Wizard. Choose Planning Mode.

6. On the Computer Selection page, select This Computer or Another Computer, type the name of the computer, and choose Next.

7. Work through the wizard; it is similar to the logging-mode wizard described earlier.

The GPResult Utility

GPResult is a command-line tool that can be used to display group policy settings and RSoP settings for a user or a computer. GPResult provides information about the operating system, the user, and the computer. GPResult also provides information such as the last time the policy was applied, the folders that have been redirected, disk quota information, and IPSec settings.

To see how GPResult works:

1. Log on as an administrator.

2. Open a command prompt by choosing Start | Programs | Accessories | Command Prompt.

3. Type "gpresult /z>*filename*.txt" and press Enter.

4. After the information has been acquired, type "notepad *filename*.txt" and press Enter to open the file.

Viewing the Results

The results file is quite long, so listed next are some of the items you'll find in your file. Sections of interest are highlighted. Following this is a list of what was not included here.

Listing 13.1   GPResult used from a command prompt.

```
RSOP results for HOST\Administrator on HOST:Logging Mode
----------------------------------------------------------------


OS Type:Microsoft Windows XP Professional
OS Configuration:Member Workstation
OS Version:5.1.2600
Domain Name:BALLEW
Domain Type:WindowsNT 4
Site Name:Default-First-Site-Name
Roaming Profile:
Local Profile:D:\Documents and Settings\Administrator.WORKSTATION01.000
Connected over a slow link?: Yes
```

```
COMPUTER SETTINGS
------------------

Last time Group Policy was applied: 9/19/2001 at 1:41:52 PM
Group Policy was applied from:Laptop.Ballew.com
Group Policy slow link threshold:500 kbps
```

Applied Group Policy Objects
```
----------------------------
Local Group Policy
The computer is a part of the following security groups:
----------------------------------------------------------

BUILTIN\Administrators
NT AUTHORITY\Authenticated Users
Resultant Set Of Policies for Computer:
```

USER SETTINGS
```
---------------
Last time Group Policy was applied: 9/19/2001 at 2:56:09 PM
Group Policy was applied from:N/A
Group Policy slow link threshold:500 kbps
```
Applied Group Policy Objects
```
----------------------------
Local Group Policy
The user is a part of the following security groups:
--------------------------------------------------------

None
Everyone
BUILTIN\Administrators
Remote Desktop Users
BUILTIN\Users
LOCAL
NT AUTHORITY\INTERACTIVE
NT AUTHORITY\Authenticated Users
Resultant Set Of Policies for User:
-------------------------------------
```

Software Installations
```
----------------------
N/A
Public Key Policies
-------------------
N/A
Administrative Templates
------------------------
N/A
Folder Redirection
-------------------
```

```
N/A
Internet Explorer Browser User Interface
------------------------------------------
GPO: Local Group Policy
Large Animated Bitmap Name:N/A
Large Custom Logo Bitmap Name:N/A
Title BarText:Joli Ballew
UserAgent Text:N/A
Delete existing toolbar buttons: No
Internet Explorer Connection
--------------------------
HTTP Proxy Server:N/A
Secure Proxy Server:N/A
FTP Proxy Server:N/A
Gopher Proxy Server:N/A
Socks Proxy Server:N/A
Auto Config Enable:No
Enable Proxy:Yes
Use same Proxy:No
Internet Explorer URLs
----------------------
GPO: Local Group Policy
Home page URL:http://www.swynk.com/friends/ballew
Search page URL:N/A
Online support page URL: N/A
Internet Explorer Security
--------------------------
Always Viewable Sites:N/A
Password Override Enabled: False
GPO: Local Group Policy
Import the current Content Ratings Settings:No
Import the current Security Zones Settings:No
Import current Authenticode Security Information:No
Enable trusted publisher lockdown:No
Internet Explorer Programs
--------------------------
GPO: Local Group Policy
Import the current Program Settings: No
```

Items not included in this list are:

◆ Software installations

◆ Startup scripts

◆ Shutdown scripts

- Account policies

- Audit policy

- User rights

- Security options

- Event log settings

- Restricted groups

- System services

- Registry settings

- File system settings

- Public key policies

- Administrative templates

GPResult Syntax

Other switches and parameters can be used with the GPResult command-line utility. In the previous example, only the **/z** switch was used. The **/z** switch allows you to print the results to Notepad for easier viewing. The full syntax options are:

```
gpresult [/s computer [/u domain\user /p password]] [/user target user name]
[/scope {user|computer}] [/v] [/z>filename.txt]
```

Each of these switches is described next:

- **/s**—This switch is used to specify the computer's name or IP address. The default is the local computer, but when you're naming a remote computer, type **/s *computer name*** without the usual **** in front of the computer name.

- **/u**—When the GPResult utility is run, it is run under the user who is currently logged onto the computer. However, you can use this switch to specify the account permissions of another user under whom this utility should be run. The syntax is **/p *user*** or **/p *domain\user***.

- **/p**—When specifying a different user for the utility to run under, you also need to specify that user's password. This switch is used only when the **/u** switch is used.

- **/user**—This switch specifies a user whose RSoP data is to be collected and displayed.

- **/scope**—This switch displays either the user or computer results. If this is not added, both user and computer results are displayed, as in the previous example.

◆ **/v**—This switch sends the information to the command-prompt window instead of to a text file. This switch cannot be used when the **/z** switch is used.

◆ **/z**—This switch allows the information to be printed as a text file to be opened and viewed in Notepad.

Software Restriction Policies

Software restriction policies allow administrators to control which software can run on the local computer, thus protecting the computer from unintentional harm done by inappropriate programs, programs that aren't certified, or programs that aren't compatible with Windows XP Professional. Some applications can damage a computer's dynamic link library (.dll) files, causing problems that are difficult to track. You can also protect your computer or others from email attachments that can carry viruses or untrusted code downloaded from Internet sites.

Generally, organizations, businesses, workgroups, and users of shared standalone computers rely on a few specific programs to do their work. Because these applications are standard company applications, they need to be used by everyone. An administrator can prevent other programs from being used or installed.

In this section, you'll learn how to configure software restriction policies on your local computer and how to apply different rules for restriction. There are four types of rules: hash, certificate, path, and Internet zone. These rules can be configured with two types of security levels: Unrestricted and Disallowed. Each of these rules is configured with different purposes in mind, and if several rules exist, they are processed in this order: Hash, Certificate, Path, and Internet Zone.

Before I get into rules and security levels, though, you should open the folder where these software restriction policies will be created:

1. Log on as an administrator to the local computer.

2. Open the Local Security Settings console by choosing Start | Programs | Administrative Tools | Local Security Settings.

3. Expand the Security Settings tree (if applicable), and highlight the Software Restriction Policies folder. See Figure 13.27.

Hash Rules

You can create a hash rule in a software restriction policy so that the hash rule will override the default security settings on the computer. A *hash rule* is created by a hash algorithm, which is composed of data, such as a session key or a piece of code that uniquely identifies a program or a file. You can configure the hash rule so that users cannot run a specific file or application.

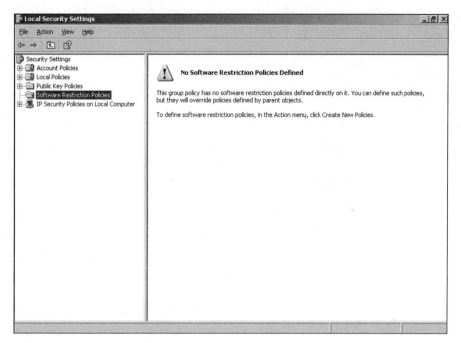

Figure 13.27
Software Restriction Policies.

To create a hash rule:

1. Log onto the computer as an administrator.

2. Open the Local Security Settings console, and expand the Software Restriction Policies folder.

3. Right-click the Additional Rules folder, and choose New Hash Rule.

4. In the New Hash Rule dialog box, choose Browse to select the file you want to hash.

5. Choose Open. In the Security Level drop-down list, select either Disallowed or Unrestricted. See Figure 13.28.

6. Type a description, if needed, and choose OK. The new hash rule will appear in the right pane of the Local Security Settings console.

Certificate Rules

A *certificate rule* identifies files and applications by their digital certificates. These rules are applied only to scripts and Windows Installer packages; these rules cannot be used with executable files or dynamic link library files. Certificate rules can be configured for trusted sites and trusted domain units to allow users to access applications there without being prompted, as would be the default in most cases.

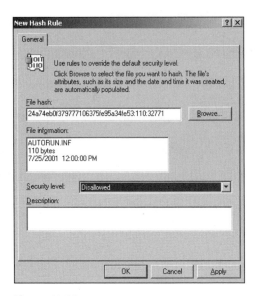

Figure 13.28
Creating a new hash rule.

To create a certificate rule:

1. Log onto the computer as an administrator.

2. Open the Local Security Settings console, and expand the Software Restriction Policies folder.

3. Right-click the Additional Rules folder, and choose New Certificate Rule.

4. Choose the Browse button to select a certificate. If you do not have any certificates, you will not be able to create this rule. To search for a certificate, use the Help and Support Center, and type "*.cer" in the search box.

5. After locating the certificate, choose Open. In the Security Level drop-down list, select either Disallowed or Unrestricted.

6. Type a description, if needed, and choose OK. The new certificate rule will appear in the right pane of the Local Security Settings console.

Path Rules

Path rules are not created from hashes or from certificates, but rather are created from the path of the folder itself. Common paths are those related to users and directories, such as the path to the user profile or the Programs folder. The path rule does not follow a file if it is moved from this path to another; the rule is good only for the specific path indicated. Path rules are processed after hash and certificate rules, but before Internet-zone rules.

To create a path rule:

1. Log onto the computer as an administrator.

2. Open the Local Security Settings console, and expand the Software Restriction Policies folder.

3. Right-click the Additional Rules folder, and choose New Path Rule.

4. Choose the Browse button to select a file.

5. Choose Open. In the Security Level drop-down list, select either Disallowed or Unrestricted.

6. Type a description, if needed, and choose OK. The new path rule will appear in the right pane of the Local Security Settings console.

Internet-Zone Rules

Internet-zone rules apply only to Windows Installer packages. Windows Installer is a utility that allows administrators to install and run software from various places on an intranet and to define rules during the installation process. As a domain member or workgroup member, you will not likely be assigned tasks related to Windows Installer. However, you might want to restrict software from specific Internet zones assigned in Internet Explorer. An Internet-zone rule can identify software from Internet sites, and installations can be restricted for users who access specific Web pages.

To create an Internet-zone rule:

1. Log onto the computer as an administrator.

2. Open the Local Security Settings console, and expand the Software Restriction Policies folder.

3. Right-click the Additional Rules folder, and choose New Internet Zone Rule.

4. From the Internet Zone drop-down list, select the Internet zone; then set the security level. For instance, for the Trusted Sites zone, you might choose Unrestricted. For the Restricted Sites zone, you might choose Disallowed.

You can configure only one rule at a time, though, so to create one for the Trusted Sites zone and one for the Restricted Sites zone, you must complete Steps 3 and 4 again.

Applying Policies to Everyone Except the Administrator

Although you'd probably like to configure some of these rules, as an administrator, you'll need to exclude yourself from these sweeping software restrictions so that someone on the network can install and run applications of any type. Because of this, there is an easy way to apply these policies to everyone on your network except you, the administrator.

To exclude the administrator from software restriction policies:

1. Log on as an administrator.

2. Open the Local Security Settings console, and highlight the Software Restriction Policies folder.

3. In the right pane, double-click Enforcement.

4. In the Enforcement Properties dialog box, in the Apply Software Restriction Policies To The Following Users section, select the All Users Except Local Administrators option. Choose OK.

Adding or Removing Specific File Types in Software Restriction Policies

You might need to add a specific file type that isn't defined by default or remove a file type that is used often by the organization so that your software restriction policies work as well as possible. If your company often uses Visual Basic (.vbs) files in its work, you would not want any of the software restriction policies to apply to those files.

To add files to or remove files from software restriction policies:

1. Log on as an administrator.

2. Open the Local Security Settings console, and highlight the Software Restriction Policies folder.

3. In the right pane, double-click Designated File Types.

4. In the Designated File Types Properties dialog box, highlight any file extension you want to remove, and choose the Remove button. To add a file extension, type it in the File Extension text box. Choose OK.

Changing Default Software Restriction Policy Settings

Although I wouldn't suggest that you change the default software restriction policy settings, you can do so through the Local Security Settings console. Because there are only two levels of security, Disallowed and Unrestricted, Unrestricted is the default setting. You can configure Disallowed to be the default setting, but this might interfere with basic operational tasks. Changing the default level affects all files configured with software restriction policies.

To change the default settings:

1. Log on as an administrator.

2. Open the Local Security Settings console, and expand the Software Restriction Policies folder.

3. In the left pane, highlight Security Levels.

4. In the right pane, right-click on either Disallowed or Unrestricted, and choose Set As Default. The current default has a black circle with a checkmark in it and will not have this option. If Disallowed is chosen as the default, no software that is configured to use software restriction policies will run, no matter what access rights the user has.

Wrapping Up

In this chapter, you learned quite a bit about the security features of Windows XP, both for users and for administrators. For users, you can secure files and folders on your local computer or workgroup, set security features in Internet Explorer 6, use the built-in Internet Connection Firewall, use EFS for encryption, use local group policies, use anti-virus programs, and install and configure a UPS.

For administrators, security offerings include security hosts, smart card support, IPSec policies, the RSoP console, and software restriction policies. In a network, everyone has a role to play in keeping the computers secure.

Chapter 14

Backup, Restore, and Recovery

Backing up data is one of the most important things an administrator can do, and in large networks some type of backup is performed every day. In a small workgroup or on a standalone computer, backups might not be made as often. If you're not sure how often to back up your data, ask yourself how important the work you've done since your last backup is, and imagine having to re-create the data. Although I do full backups only once a month or so on my workgroup computers, I do back up each night the work I've completed each day.

The Backup utility included with Windows XP Professional helps you do backups easily. Backups are important to have in case the computer's hard drive fails; a virus attack occurs; or the computer is destroyed by lightning, a flood, or some other natural disaster. If data has been properly backed up, it can be restored to its original state. The Backup utility works on both FAT and NTFS drives.

Although most data backups are performed at night or after the workday is over, Windows XP Professional offers a backup type that can be used at any time. In the past, most backup utilities could not back up open files (this is why backups were performed after everyone had gone home). Now Windows XP offers the volume shadow copy, which allows you to do a backup at any time, creating an accurate point-in-time copy of the contents of the drive.

The Backup utility allows you to do all of the following:

♦ Perform a selective backup, choosing specific files and folders but not everything on the hard drive.

♦ Back up system files and configuration settings in case of a complete system failure.

♦ Back up data on remote storage drives and mounted drives.

♦ Back up the system state, including the Registry, the Active Directory database, and the Certificate Services database.

♦ Schedule regular backups.

♦ Restore backed-up files and folders.

♦ Restore system files and the system state.

♦ Back up the computer's partitions and startup files in case of a computer failure.

The Backup utility is used for fairly simple backups, not for backups that require mounting or dismounting tapes and disks. These more complicated (usually domain-related) tasks are performed through the Removable Storage component of Windows.

In this chapter, I'll discuss many aspects of backups and restorations, as well as their applications. First, I'll discuss the types of backups, types of data, and types of backup media. Then I'll discuss how to configure and use the Backup utility and how to restore data. You can also restore data by using the Automated System Recovery utility, and you can transfer files and settings to a new computer by using the Files And Settings Transfer Wizard. Finally, you'll learn tips and tricks for restoring a computer after a virus attack, and you'll learn what is needed to make that restore successful.

Types of Backups

Several types of backups are available: copy, daily, differential, incremental, normal, and volume shadow copy. Most administrators who back up data each day use a combination of these methods to obtain the best set of backups while using the least amount of time and media space. Some methods back up all data, some back up only the data that has changed since the last backup, and some back up only the files that have changed during the day. In addition, these backups have attribute bits so that the operating system can tell whether a certain file has recently been backed up and whether the file has changed. This attribute is sometimes called the *archive bit* or *archive attribute*. When a file changes, the archive attribute changes; when the file is backed up, the attribute is either cleared or reset.

Copy

The copy backup is used when selected files and folders need to be backed up. The copy backup doesn't look at archive attributes or reset them. The copy backup is good for intermediate backups of files or folders in between more complete backups, such as normal or incremental backups. Because it doesn't change the archive bit, the copy backup doesn't affect any future backup.

Daily

In a daily backup, all selected files and folders that have changed that day are backed up. This type of backup doesn't look at or clear archive bits. It simply looks for the files or folders that have been changed on a particular date and backs up those files.

Differential

In the differential backup, only files or folders that have the archive attribute are backed up. Having this attribute means that the file has changed since it was last backed up with a normal or incremental backup. The differential backup does not clear the archive attribute and is one of the faster ways to perform a backup. If you use a combination of normal and differential backups, you can restore a system with the last normal backup followed by the last differential backup.

Incremental

In the incremental backup, files and folders that have the archive attribute are backed up, just as in the differential backup. The difference between the two methods is that the incremental backup clears the archive bit. This backup type is also very fast, but restoring from an incremental backup takes longer than other types. To restore data by using incremental backups, you must use the last normal backup and then use all incremental backups made since that time.

Normal

A normal backup is sometimes called a *full backup*; all selected files and folders are backed up. When a normal (or full) backup is performed, the archive bit is not a factor. Because everything is being backed up, it doesn't matter if the file has been changed since the last backup. However, during a full backup, the archive bit is reset, and it will remain in this state until data in the file is changed. Because this is a full backup, it can be used to restore a system much faster than any other type can. On the other hand, it takes longer to complete and uses more physical media than any other backup type. This is a disadvantage, of course, especially if you have to wait for the backup to be completed every Friday afternoon before you can go home or if the price of the backup media is high.

Volume Shadow Copy

A volume shadow copy is technically a type of backup, although it's in a different category from the first five mentioned here. The volume shadow copy was not available in previous versions of Microsoft operating systems. You use a volume shadow copy when you want to make a full copy of a volume, including any open application files and any system files that are open due to system activity. During a volume shadow copy, applications can continue to write to the hard drive, and files that are open are backed up as well. These backups can thus be performed at any time during the day, although some system slowdown could occur due to the traffic.

Combining Backup Types

Many organizations do not rely on one type of backup, but instead use a combination of two or more. Normal and differential backups can be combined by performing a normal backup once a week, followed by differential backups on the other days. This takes a little more time while backing up but takes less time for restoring. Normal and incremental backups can be used the same way. If you do a normal backup once a week and incremental backups on the other days, the data takes less time to back up and more time to restore.

Finally, a combination of normal, differential, and copy backups works well for some organizations. It's done the same way as the previous two setups, but during the week a copy is performed instead of another differential or incremental backup. The copy backup is added when an organization needs a snapshot of the data but doesn't want to change any attributes when doing so.

Types of Data

Many types of data can be backed up using the Backup utility; the data most often backed up are files and folders. You can also back up system state data and data on remote computers.

Complete Volumes and Files and Folders

By using the Backup utility, you can select the volumes, files, and folders you want to back up. Figure 14.1 shows the Backup utility's window, with an entire volume selected for backup, along with specific folders. Notice that when an entire drive is chosen, the checkmark is blue and the checkbox is white; only a few files or folders are selected on a drive, both the checkmark and the checkbox are gray. In Figure 14.1, the entire C: volume and specific folders on volume D: will be backed up.

System State Data

System state data is data that is used by the system; this data includes the Registry and system boot files. If the system is a domain controller or a server, additional system state data includes the Active Directory database and Certificate Services. To back up system state data, you must be an administrator or a backup operator, and you can then back up and restore the system state data on only the local computer. You cannot back up system state data on a remote computer.

Data on Remote Computers

You can back up some of the data on remote computers, but you'll need to have permissions to access them and be logged on as an administrator or backup operator. Look at Figure 14.2,

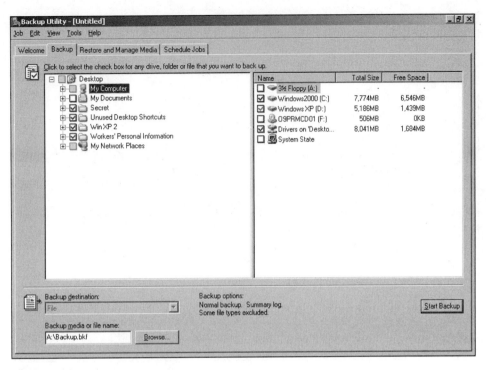

Figure 14.1
Selecting volumes, files, and folders.

and notice that Entire Network is grayed out and cannot be chosen for backup. In My Network Places, however, two files can be backed up: XP On Desktoppc and Documents On Laptop. The files that are available in My Network Places can be backed up if the user has the appropriate permissions.

Types of Backup Media

The backup media most commonly used in medium-sized and large organizations consist of tape devices because those devices are convenient and have a high capacity for holding data. These devices aren't too expensive, either, and the tapes can be reused. Data can also be stored on Zip drives, although the disks are fairly expensive and don't hold a lot of data. Similarly, rewritable CDs have become quite popular, as have optical drives. Backups can also be directed to another computer—a file server, member server, or the like—and data can be stored relatively safely there. Backing up data to a file server that is in the same room as the original data doesn't provide much security in a disaster like a flood or fire, but backing up data to another server in another building (or even another town) does.

For smaller organizations consisting of only a few users and computers, backing up the data to a Zip disk might be appropriate. You can also purchase an inexpensive tape or an Orb

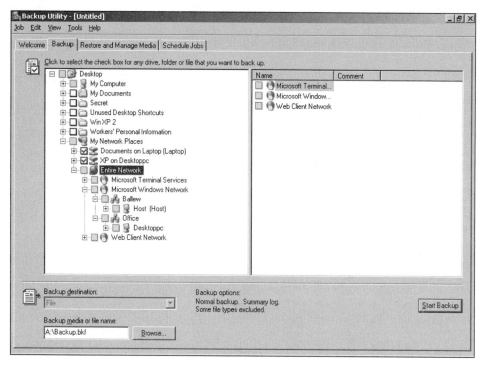

Figure 14.2
Backing up My Network Places.

drive for this purpose. Make sure that you store the backups in a safe place, though, and that the backups are tested daily to make sure they are operating correctly and restorations can be performed if necessary. There'll be more information on backup types for home users— Simple Backups and Backup Media, later in this chapter.

Precautionary Measures

For backup and restore operations to function at their highest level, several precautions need to be taken before actually assigning backup and restore operators and configuring the Backup utility. These precautions include choosing the operators and choosing an off-site location for storing the backups.

Backup Operators

Although users and groups have been discussed already (in Chapters 3 and 10), now is probably a good time to review the backup groups and the backup and restore operator. By default, a backup operator can back up *and* restore files and folders regardless of any permissions that protect those files. Backup operators can shut down the computer as well, but they cannot change any security settings on the files. The downfall of the Backup Operators group's default permissions is that a potential security flaw emerges. If a backup operator backs up files, changes the data on some of those files before restoring, and then restores the outdated files, a security lapse has occurred. A backup and restore operator can also unwittingly unleash viruses on the computer. Because of this, you should consider giving backup operators only the ability to back up and not the ability to restore. This can be done using group policies, discussed in previous chapters.

Storing Physical Media

You can make the backups more secure by moving them off site after full backups have been completed. This is necessary if the data is highly confidential or extremely important to the company's well being. You can even hire people to pick up and store the data for you. Microsoft recommends that you keep these items off site:

♦ A full backup of the entire system, performed weekly

♦ Original software installed on computers (you can store copies on site)

♦ Documents for processing an insurance claim, including purchase orders, receipts, and software-related proofs of purchase

♦ Information about hardware and software and how to reinstall it

♦ Information for reconfiguring your storage subsystem

Microsoft recommends that you keep copies of these items available on site:

♦ Daily backups

♦ Copies of operating systems

I recommend that you also keep copies of the following on site:

♦ Drivers for sound cards, video cards, USB controllers, tape drives, printers, and other hardware

♦ Copies of accounting, database, graphics, or other software

♦ Spare computer parts, such as network interface cards, monitors, or even whole computers so repairs can be done quickly

Testing the Backup

After you've configured the Backup utility and backed up some data, test the backup by restoring it. A backup will not do you any good if it doesn't work, and there are lots of things that can go wrong with a backup, ranging from a power outage to an overused tape. Make sure that your backup administrators also know how to restore data, that they have been trained, and that a plan is in place for handling the worst possible scenario.

Configuring the Backup Utility

The Backup utility has several options available for configuration. By default, the first time the Backup utility is opened, it opens in wizard mode. The Backup Wizard walks you through the process of backing up and restoring data, and it allows you to choose what you want to back up or restore; however, no advanced options are available in this mode. You can use the Backup Wizard to perform basic backups of data, as detailed later. In this section, I'll introduce the options available for configuration in the advanced mode of the Backup utility. Figure 14.3 shows the opening window for the advanced mode of the Backup utility. By understanding and setting these options before performing any backups, you can personalize how the Backup utility will work for you.

In Figure 14.3, notice that the utility window has four tabs. Selecting the Backup Wizard (Advanced) button starts the Backup Wizard. The other tabs are used to perform a manual backup, to restore and manage backup media, and to schedule jobs. You can set options for your backups by choosing Tools | Options. The Options dialog box is shown in Figure 14.4.

As you can see in the figure, several general options can be configured. The only options not enabled by default are the options to verify the data after it is backed up and to allow the use of recognizable media without prompting. You can also set options from the other tabs.

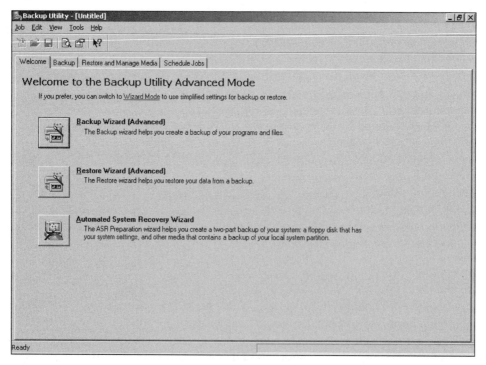

Figure 14.3
The Backup utility in advanced mode.

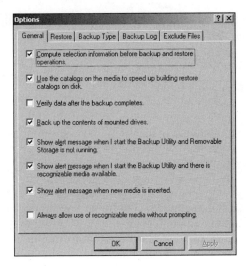

Figure 14.4
The Options dialog box for the Backup utility.

On the Backup Type tab of the Options dialog box, you can select Normal, Copy, Differential, Incremental, or Daily. On the Backup Log tab, you can select how you want to collect information related to your backups. You can choose any one of the following options:

♦ *Detailed*—Logs all information, including the names of all of the files and folders.

♦ *Summary*—Logs only key operations, such as loading a tape, starting the backup, or failing to open a file. This is the default.

♦ *None*—Does not log any activity.

On the Exclude Files tab, you can specify files that should not ever be backed up by the Backup utility. The files that are not backed up by default include power management files, memory page files, temporary Internet files, and Task Scheduler files. You can add files as well, such as animated cursor files, audio CD or video files, briefcase files, security certificate files, Microsoft Word templates, and DVD files. (Restore options will be detailed in "Using the Restore Utility," later in this chapter.)

You can also change the view of the Backup utility from the Tools menu. If you are in advanced mode, you can switch to wizard mode from this menu. You can also access the wizard by clicking the Backup Wizard button on the Welcome tab.

To set options for the Backup utility:

1. Log on as an administrator.

2. Open the Backup utility by choosing Start | Programs | Accessories | System Tools | Backup.

3. If this is the first time you've opened the Backup utility, click the Advanced Mode link on the first page of the Backup Or Restore Wizard.

4. After the Backup utility opens, choose Tools | Options.

5. Select the tabs on which you want to change the options, and make the changes you want. Choose OK when finished.

6. To switch to wizard mode, choose Tools | Switch To Wizard Mode.

Performing a Backup

You can perform a backup in a number of ways; the easiest is to use the Backup Wizard. You can back up data to tape or other removable media, you can perform manual backups, and you can schedule a backup for a later time.

Using the Backup Wizard

As I mentioned earlier, the first time you open the Backup utility from the Start menu, the utility starts in wizard mode. This means that the Backup Or Restore Wizard opens automatically. You can check the checkbox Always Start In Wizard Mode if you like, or you can switch between modes from inside the Backup program. Figure 14.5 shows the first page of the wizard.

To perform a backup by using the Backup Wizard:

1. Log on as an administrator.

2. Open the Backup utility by choosing Start | Programs | Accessories | System Tools | Backup.

Figure 14.5
Wizard mode.

3. If the Backup Wizard opens, choose Next. If the Backup utility opens, choose the Backup Wizard (Advanced) button.

4. On the Backup Or Restore page, select Back Up Files And Settings. Choose Next.

5. On the What To Back Up page, select one of the following:

   ♦ My Documents And Settings

   ♦ Everyone's Documents And Settings

   ♦ All Information On This Computer

   ♦ Let Me Choose What To Back Up

   (The last option is a manual backup and will be explained later.)

6. On the Backup Type, Destination, And Name page, choose the Browse button to choose a place for backing up the data, and then type a name for the backup. Choose Next.

7. Verify the information, and choose Finish. This will create a shadow copy of the files selected. If you want to set advanced options, choose the Advanced button instead of Finish.

8. On the Type Of Backup page, select the type of backup to create: Normal, Copy, Incremental, Differential, or Daily. Choose Next.

9. On the How To Back Up page, select the option you want to use:

   ♦ *Verify Data After Backup*—Verification reads the backed-up data to verify its integrity. This step takes extra time, but verification helps ensure that your backup is successful.

   ♦ *Use Hardware Compression If Available*—Hardware compression increases the available storage space on the backup media, and saving space reduces storage costs.

   ♦ *Disable Volume Shadow Copy*—A volume shadow copy allows files to be backed up even though they are in the process of being written to.

10. On the Backup Options page, specify whether to overwrite existing data on backups or to append the data to an existing backup. You can also choose to give only the administrator and owner access to the backed-up data and to any backups that have been appended. Choose Next.

11. On the When To Back Up page, select Now or Later. If you choose Later, you'll need to type a job name and a start date. Choose Finish. Figure 14.6 shows the backup in progress.

Performing a Manual Backup to a File, Folder, Drive, or Tape

You can perform a backup without using the Backup Wizard. Remember, you must be logged on as an administrator or backup operator to back up data.

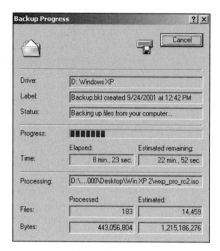

Figure 14.6
Backup in progress.

To perform a manual backup:

1. Open the Backup utility.

2. If the Backup utility starts in wizard mode, choose Advanced Mode.

3. In the Backup utility, select the Backup tab.

4. Choose Job | New.

5. Select the files and folders you want to back up, as shown in Figure 14.7.

6. If you have a local tape device, you can select it from the Backup Destination drop-down list.

7. Next to the Backup Media Or File Name text box, choose the Browse button to specify where the files should be saved. You can also browse to a tape drive in another location.

8. Choose Start Backup. This button is shown in Figure 14.7.

9. In the Backup Job Information dialog box that appears after you start the backup, choose to append this backup or to replace an existing backup with this one. To set advanced options, choose the Advanced button.

10. If you chose to set advanced options, then, in the Advanced Backup Options dialog box, check the following checkboxes as necessary:

    ◆ Back Up Data That Is In Remote Storage

    ◆ Verify Data After Backup

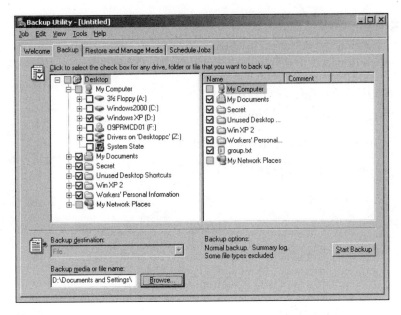

Figure 14.7
Manually selecting files and folders for backup.

- ♦ If Possible, Compress The Backup Data To Save Space

- ♦ Automatically Back Up System Protected Files With The System State

- ♦ Disable Volume Shadow Copy

11. From the Backup Type drop-down list, select Normal, Copy, Incremental, Differential, or Daily. Choose OK.

12. Choose Start Backup.

Backing Up System State Data

You can back up system state data very easily by using the Backup utility. To back up the system state:

1. Log on as an administrator, and open the Backup utility.

2. If the Backup utility starts in wizard mode, choose Advanced Mode.

3. Select the Backup tab, and choose Job | New.

4. Check the System State checkbox.

5. Choose Start Backup, verify the backup information, and set advanced options if needed. If you've set advanced options, then choose Start Backup again.

Scheduling a Backup

You can schedule a backup when manually creating a backup job through advanced options, or you can schedule a job through the Schedule Jobs tab of the Backup utility window.

Using the Schedule Jobs Tab to Schedule a Backup

To schedule a job by using the Schedule Jobs tab:

1. Log on as an administrator, and open the Backup utility.

2. If the Backup utility starts in wizard mode, choose Advanced Mode.

3. Select the Schedule Jobs tab.

4. Select a date from the calendar displayed. Choose the Add Job button.

5. When the Welcome To The Backup Wizard page opens, choose Next.

6. On the What To Back Up page, select what you want to back up:

   ♦ Back Up Everything On This Computer

   ♦ Back Up Selected Files, Drives, Or Network Data

   ♦ Only Back Up The System State Data

7. If you choose Back Up Select Files, Drives, Or Network Data, you'll need to select the files you want to back up.

8. Continue working through the wizard as detailed earlier. When you get to the When To Back Up Data page, type in a job name and a start date, and choose Set Schedule.

9. In the Schedule Job dialog box, shown in Figure 14.8, select an option in the Schedule Task drop-down list to specify how often to run the job. The choices are Daily, Weekly, Monthly, Once, At System Startup, At Logon, or When Idle.

10. In the Start Time text box, specify the start time. Choose the Advanced button.

11. In the Advanced Schedule Options dialog box, you can choose to repeat the task if necessary. The task can be configured to repeat every so many minutes or hours and to run for a specific amount of time. You can also configure the task to stop running at a specific time or after a certain duration.

12. In the Advanced Schedule Options dialog box, choose OK. In the Backup Wizard, choose Next.

13. In the Set Account Information dialog box, type a password for the administrator, and choose OK. Choose Finish.

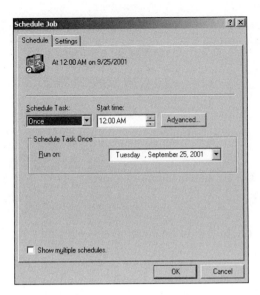

Figure 14.8
Scheduling a job.

Using Advanced Options to Schedule a Backup

To schedule a job by using advanced options:

1. Open the Backup utility.

2. Create the job manually as described in the section "Performing a Manual Backup to a File, Folder, Drive, or Tape." Then choose the Start Backup button.

3. In the Backup Job Information dialog box, choose the Schedule button.

4. In the Set Account Information dialog box, type a password for the administrator account. Choose OK.

5. In the Scheduled Job Options dialog box, on the Schedule Data tab, type a job name, and then choose the Properties button.

6. In the Schedule Job dialog box, select an option in the Schedule Task drop-down list to specify how often to run the job. The choices are Daily, Weekly, Monthly, Once, At System Startup, At Logon, or When Idle.

7. In the Start Time text box, type the start time. Choose the Advanced button.

8. In the Advanced Schedule Options dialog box, you can choose to repeat the task if necessary. The task can be configured to repeat every so many minutes or hours and to run for a specific amount of time. You can also configure the task to stop running at a specific time or after a certain duration.

9. In the Advanced Schedule Options dialog box, choose OK. In the Scheduled Job Options dialog box, select the Backup Details tab.

10. Read the job summary, and choose OK.

The Backup Report

Each time a backup is run, a backup report is created. You can view or print these reports in the Backup utility. To do so:

1. Log on as an administrator, and open the Backup utility.

2. Choose Tools | Report.

3. In the Backup Reports dialog box, highlight the report you'd like to view. Choose the View button.

   The backup report will open in Notepad.

Listing 14.1 shows a sample backup report. Notice the highlighted areas.

Listing 14.1   A sample backup report.

```
Backup Status
Operation: Backup
Active backup destination: File
Media name: "Backup.bkf created 9/24/2001 at 12:42 PM"

Backup (via shadow copy) of "D: Windows XP"
Backup set #1 on media #1
Backup description: "Set created 9/24/2001 at 12:42 PM"
Media name: "Backup.bkf created 9/24/2001 at 12:42 PM"

Backup Type: Normal

Backup started on 9/24/2001 at 12:43 PM.
Backup completed on 9/24/2001 at 1:12 PM.
Directories: 315
Files: 14459
Bytes: 1,217,944,118
Time:  29 minutes and  2 seconds


- - - - - - - - - - - - - - - - - - - -


Verify Status
Operation: Verify After Backup
Active backup destination: File
Active backup destination: D:\Documents and
Settings\Administrator.WORKSTATION01.000\Desktop\Secret\Backup.bkf
```

```
Verify of "D:"
Backup set #1 on media #1
Backup description: "Set created 9/24/2001 at 12:42 PM"
Verify started on 9/24/2001 at 1:12 PM.
Verify completed on 9/24/2001 at 1:17 PM.
Directories: 315
Files: 14459
Different: 0
Bytes: 1,217,944,118
Time:  4 minutes and  54 seconds


--------------------
```

As you can see from what's highlighted, the backup report states the name and location of the backup file, the backup type, the number of files backed up, how long the process took, and, if the files were verified after the backup, how many differences were found. This is the default log file that is created. If you configure the log file settings to write detailed logs instead of summary logs, you'll see much more information.

You can also print the report by choosing the Print button in the Backup Reports dialog box.

Simple Backups and Backup Media

If you don't want to use the Backup utility, you can perform your own simple backups daily or weekly by simply copying important data or data that's changed to Zip disks, CDs, or DVDs. You can do this by simply dragging the files to the icon for the hardware. For the average home or small-office user, a weekly backup of current files to a Zip disk might be sufficient. For other users with more data, a CD or DVD might be needed. Some users simply back up their important files when finished with them, perhaps at the end of each day. If you choose to simply drag and drop files to one of these devices, it is important that you understand what backup media options are available.

Besides backing up daily work to the media described in this section, you might also want to archive data that you don't use anymore, might not need access to often, or simply want in case of a hard drive failure. You can move the information from your computer to a Zip disk, CD, or DVD to free up hard drive space. You can also back up to the media described in this section to restore files and settings to another computer. If you're not using the Backup utility, consider backing up, moving, or copying the following sorts of items to removable media:

◆ Old email messages

◆ Graphics or photos that you don't use often

◆ Address books

◆ Large data files for completed projects

- Large files that you need to exchange with a person or another computer when a network isn't present or available

- Copies of software in case the original disk fails

- Settings for the desktop, screen colors, and personal settings

Zip Drives

A Zip drive is a small, portable device that uses a Zip disk for storing data. The computer sees the Zip drive as a type of removable media if the drive is external, or as a type of hard drive if the disk is internal. If your computer doesn't have a Zip drive, you can purchase one for about $100 and connect it via a USB port, a parallel port, or an SCSI interface.

Zip disks come in two capacities: 100MB and 250MB. The 100MB Zip disk stores the equivalent of about 70 floppy disks, and the 250MB disk can store as much data as approximately 170 floppy disks. The trademarked Zip drive was developed and sold by Iomega Corporation, but other manufacturers sell similar products.

You can drag and drop files and folders to the Zip disk, making the backup of data quite simple. Of the three media types listed here, the Zip disk holds the least amount of data but is the easiest to configure and use. The Iomega Zip drive is automatically configured by Windows XP Professional, and its installation is transparent to the user.

CDs

You can use several types of CDs for backing up and archiving data, but the regular CD-ROM isn't one of them. A CD-ROM (compact disc–read-only memory) can be written to only once. This is the type of CD that is used to distribute software, such as operating systems, applications, or computer games. A CD-ROM drive is what plays the CD on your computer. To archive and back up data on your computer or network, you'll need either a CD-R (CD–recordable) or a CD-RW (CD–rewritable) drive and discs. Although these are the most commonly used reusable CDs, there are others. CD-MO (compact disc–magneto optical) and multisession CDs are available, although soon there will be other CDs on the market that surpass even this technology.

CD–Recordable

The CD-R format is very popular, and CD-R drives can be purchased at almost any computer store. With newer computers, this drive is often included and is built in. Both internal and external drives are available, and they come in a variety of write and read speeds, such as 4X, 16X, and 24X. You can purchase a CD-R drive for about $120.

Each CD-R can be written to only once. A CD-R holds 650 to 700MB of data, about as much as 450 to 500 floppy disks or 6 or 7 Zip disks.

Using the CD-R drive is a little more complicated than using a Zip disk. Although you can drag and drop files, you often need a software program to assist you. Windows XP comes with CD-burning software, but not all CD-R drives are compatible with Windows XP, and the CD-R software must be used. To burn a CD (record a CD), you need to launch the software program and understand how it's used; if the CD is Windows XP compatible, however, you can use XP's CD-burning utility.

CD–Rewritable

Similar to a CD-R drive, a CD-RW drive can be used to write data to the CD and then to write to it again later. The CD-RW drive is also very popular and can be purchased at almost any computer store. With newer computers, this drive is often included and is built in. Both internal and external drives are available, and they come in a variety of write and read speeds, such as 4X, 16X, and 24X. You can purchase a CD-RW drive for about $150.

Each CD-RW can be written to multiple times . A CD-RW holds 650 to 700MB of data, about as much as 450 to 500 floppy disks or 6 or 7 Zip disks.

Using the CD-RW drive is a little more complicated than using a Zip disk. Although you can drag and drop files, you often need a software program to assist you. Windows XP comes with CD-burning software, but not all CD-RW drives are compatible with Windows XP, and the CD-RW software must be used. To burn a CD, you need to launch the software program and understand how it's used; if the CD is Windows XP compatible, however, you can use XP's CD-burning utilities.

Multisession CD

Multisession CDs are CD-Rs that allow data to be recorded once and then allow more data to be recorded to the end of the disc at a later date. This isn't possible with regular CD-Rs, and it can be quite useful if there isn't much data to record or if space is left on the CD. However, each session requires some lead-in space on the CD; this space is wasted and cannot be used for recording data, making this format less efficient than a regular CD-R.

Magneto-Optical CD

CD-MO discs can theoretically be written to an unlimited number of times, surpassing the technology of the CD-RW discs and drives. CD-MOs and drives are generally used by larger networks and are quite expensive. Each disc can hold up to 9.1GB, and each disc costs $500 or more. It is worth mentioning, though, because the price of these discs and drives will eventually come down, making this format a viable small-office option.

DVDs

DVD stands for *digital versatile disc*, which is a medium that can hold video, audio, and computer data. DVDs used to be called "digital video discs" before the technology was widened to include other types of data. Most DVDs hold about 4.7GB of data, about four times the amount stored on a single CD. This 4.7GB of data can be written fast (about 30 minutes). A DVD player can be external or internal, and prices generally hover around the $800 mark for a good DVD drive. Most DVD drives can write to DVDs as well as to CDs, and their read/write performance generally ranges from 4X to 24X. Most of these drives configure the DVDs that are recorded so they can be played in CD-R or CD-RW drives, too. Because of the sheer amount of data that can be saved to one of these drives, these are usually employed by small to medium-sized businesses.

There are many kinds of DVDs you can use to back up and archive data on your network. DVDs and drives are more expensive than CDs and drives, although DVDs store quite a bit more data. The most common types of DVDs and drives are DVD-ROM, DVD-RAM, DVD-Audio, DVD-R, and DVD-RW.

DVD-R

DVD-R (recordable) discs and drives are similar to CD-Rs in that they can be written to once. DVD-Rs can be read in many other types of DVD drives, including DVD-ROM drives and DVD video players. DVD-Rs are recorded in a single session, and, generally, data cannot be added to the disc after a session has ended. Each DVD-R can hold up to an average of 9.4GB of data.

DVD-RW

DVD-RW (rewritable) discs and drives are similar to CD-RWs in that they can be written to multiple times. DVD-RWs can be read in many other types of DVD drives, including DVD-ROM drives and DVD video players. DVD-RWs can contain video, text, and audio. Data can be added, and the data on the disc can be rewritten as needed. Each DVD-RW can hold up to an average of 9.4GB of data.

DVD-ROM

DVD-ROM (read-only memory) drives are read-only drives, with seven times the capacity of the CD-ROM drives that are available. This is a comparatively older technology, used in personal computers for playing DVDs. Most DVDs were originally created to hold movies and videos, and these discs can hold up to 17GB of data. DVD-ROM drives can also play CD-ROM discs.

DVD-RAM

DVD-RAM (random access memory) drives are similar to DVD-ROM drives in that they can hold any type of information, but they hold only about 2.6GB of data. DVD-RAMs can be single-sided or double-sided. Only the single-sided discs can be read by DVD-ROM drives.

DVD-Audio

DVD-audio discs and drives are fairly new and are used for recording audio data. This technology is expected to sound twice as good as what is currently available using CDs. DVD-audio drives and disks are being created at this time and are not yet currently available for purchase at the writing of this book.

Using the Restore Utility

The Restore utility is part of the Backup utility and is accessed using the same means. Restoring allows you to replace files on your computer with files from backups. Before using the Restore utility, you should look at the three configuration options. Once these options have been set, you can either use the Restore Wizard or restore data manually.

Restore Options

When you need to restore data, there will probably be some original files that are still on the computer and some that aren't. For those files that are still on the computer and healthy, you'll probably want to leave them as they are. You wouldn't want to restore them with older files. Thus, you can restore data in one of three ways: You can leave the original files on the computer intact; you can replace these files only if they're older than the backup files being restored; or you can replace all the files when you restore them. Select the appropriate option in the Options dialog box of the Restore utility.

Advanced restore options are available after you've chosen the Start Restore button. The Advanced Restore Options dialog box has five options:

♦ *Restore Security*—Enabled by default, this option restores the permissions, audit entries, and ownership for files and folders. This option is available only if you've backed up data from an NTFS folder and are restoring to an NTFS volume.

♦ *Restore Junction Points, And Restore File And Folder Data Under Junction Points To The Original Location*—Enabled by default, this option allows you to restore links to data. This option is required if you want to restore a mounted drive.

♦ *When Restoring Replicated Data Sets, Mark The Restored Data As The Primary Data For All Replicas*—This option is for servers only and does not apply to workstations.

♦ *Restore The Cluster Registry To The Quorum Disk And All Other Nodes*—This option is used only for servers that are configured as clustered servers. This option does not apply to workstations.

♦ *Preserve Existing Volume Mount Points*—This option prevents the restore operation from writing over any volume mount points you have created on the drive, partition, or volume to which you are restoring data. By default, this option is enabled, but you might deselect it if you are restoring data to a partition or drive that has been recently formatted.

Note
Remember, you will have had to back up some data by using the Backup utility before you can use the utility to restore the data.

Restoring Data by Using the Restore Wizard

To restore data by using the Restore Wizard:

1. Log on as an administrator, and open the Backup utility.

2. On the Welcome page, choose the Restore Wizard (Advanced) button. (If the Backup Wizard starts, choose Advanced Mode first.)

3. Choose Next to start the Restore Wizard.

4. On the What To Restore page, shown in Figure 14.9, select the files, folders, or drives you want to restore. Choose Next.

5. On the Completing The Restore Wizard page, choose the Advanced button.

6. On the Where To Restore page, select the location where you want to restore the files to:

    ◆ Original Location

    ◆ Alternate Location

    ◆ Single Folder

   If you choose Alternate or Single Folder, you'll have to browse to the new location before continuing. Choose Next.

7. On the How To Restore page, select one of the following:

    ◆ Do Not Replace The File On My Computer (Recommended)

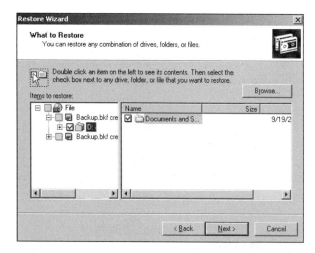

Figure 14.9

The Restore Wizard: choosing what to restore.

♦ Replace The File On Disk Only If The File On Disk Is Older

♦ Always Replace The File On My Computer

8. On the Advanced Restore Options page, select one of the options, described earlier.

9. Choose Finish.

Restoring Data Manually

Restoring data manually is slightly different from using the wizard. To restore data manually:

1. Log on as an administrator, and open the Backup utility.

2. Select the Restore And Manage Media tab.

3. Expand the File tree, and select the backup that you want to restore.

4. In the Restore Files To drop-down list, select the location where the files will be restored.

5. Choose the Start Restore button, then Advanced. Set any advanced options, and choose OK.

6. Choose OK again to begin restoring the files.

Note

Any data can be restored this way, including data that has been backed up to tape or other media.

Restoring the System State

The system state can be restored on the local computer only, and you'll need to be an administrator or backup operator to do it. To restore the system state:

1. Open the Backup utility.

2. Select the Restore And Manage Media tab.

3. Check the System State box, and choose the Start Restore button. After reading the warning box concerning writing over current system state data; then choose OK to start the restore. (To set Advanced options, choose the Advanced button.)

The Restore Report

After a restore is complete, you'll have the option of looking at the restore report. If you choose not to view the report at that time, you can always view it later by using the Tools menu in the Backup utility.

How System Restore Fits In

As you learned in Chapter 6, System Restore creates a restore point each time a backup or a restore is performed. If a backup or a restore fails or the computer becomes unstable, you can use System Restore to restore your computer to a previous state. When this is done, almost all of a user's personal files are left untouched, even if the restore point used is a week or more old.

System Restore should not be used in place of regular backups. If the hard drive crashes or lightning causes a computer failure, System Restore won't be available. In addition, if a file type is not supported by System Restore, files of that type will not be restored.

If using the Backup utility for restoring data causes the computer to become unstable, use System Restore to repair it:

1. Log on as an administrator.

2. Start the System Restore Wizard by choosing Start | Programs | Accessories | System Tools | System Restore.

3. The Welcome To System Restore page appears. Make sure that Restore My Computer To An Earlier Time is selected, and choose Next.

4. On the Select A Restore Point page, select the restore point just before the one for the recent restore or backup that failed.

5. On the Confirm Restore Point Selection page, confirm the information by choosing Next.

> **Note**
>
> *The computer must reboot for the restore process to be completed. Make sure you save your work and close any open programs before choosing Next.*

As the computer automatically reboots, you'll see the System Restore progress box. When the restoration is completed, the computer will be ready to use.

6. On the Restoration Complete page of the System Restore Wizard, you'll see confirmation that the computer was restored successfully. (If it was not restored successfully, you can choose from the available options.) Choose OK.

Using Automated System Recovery

Using Automated System Recovery (ASR) is another way to recover from a disaster. This feature should be used as a last resort, though, after Last Known Good Configuration, booting into safe mode, using System Restore, and other options, because restoring in this manner is more complex and less efficient than these other methods. ASR actually reinstalls Windows XP and re-creates the system by using the information in the ASR floppy disk that you'll make. Even though this is a last-resort recovery method, you should still create and store ASR sets at least once a month, just in case.

The ASR Wizard is used to back up the system state, system services, information about applications, and all disks that hold operating system files and components. ASR also saves the disk configurations and disk signatures, volumes, and partitions so the computer can be started. ASR also backs up portions of the Registry so that this information can be restored after a disaster.

Warning
If you use the ASR method, the hard drive will be formatted! Make sure you have current backups before using this method.

Creating an ASR Set

To create an ASR set:

1. Log on as an administrator.

2. Open the Backup utility in advanced mode.

3. Select the Welcome tab, and choose the Automated System Recovery Wizard button.

4. Choose Next to start the Automated System Recovery Preparation Wizard.

5. Select the medium to which you want to back up the data, such as a CD-R Drive or a type of removable media. You'll have a large amount of data, which will take 10 or more Zip disks. Do not place the backup data on a remote computer because networking will not be enabled when this information is needed. Choose the appropriate media. Choose Next, then Finish.

6. When the system information has been saved, you will be prompted to insert a 1.44MB floppy disk in the disk drive.

Restoring Data by Using the ASR Set

Restoring data by using ASR requires that you have the ASR floppy disk created earlier, the backup media created earlier, and the original Windows XP Professional CD. Make sure that you can access the medium on which the backup was created earlier when creating the ASR set.

With these items in hand, follow these steps to restore the computer using ASR:

1. Log on as an administrator.

2. Insert the original Windows XP Professional operating system CD into the CD-ROM drive.

3. Restart your computer. When/if prompted, select the appropriate key to boot from the CD.

4. When prompted, press the F2 key to start setup in ASR mode. This prompt appears at the bottom of the screen about three seconds after the computer has booted from the CD-ROM. (The only prompt before this one is the one to press F6 if the hard drive is an SCSI drive or needs a specific driver. If this is necessary, press F6, then F2.)

5. Insert the ASR floppy disk when prompted, and then press any key.

6. Windows XP Professional then loads necessary operating system files, formats the drive, and reinstalls Windows XP Professional. After the text portion of setup is complete, remove the ASR disk from the floppy drive so the computer can reboot successfully.

7. When the Automated System Recovery Wizard appears, choose Next or wait for the wizard to start automatically. Browse to the location of the backup file you created earlier, and continue to work through the wizard to reconstruct the system.

8. After selecting the backup files, choose Open in the Open dialog box. Choose Finish from the Automated System Recovery Wizard. The Restore Process dialog box indicates the progress of the restore process, including the number of files copied and the time elapsed. When the process is completed, Windows XP Professional will start.

9. You will now need to restore your personal files from backup.

The Files And Settings Transfer Wizard

Although the process of transferring files and settings isn't technically a backup, it certainly can be considered a type of restore. The Files And Settings Transfer Wizard helps you move data from an older computer to a new one. This wizard also lets you transfer your personal display properties, folder and taskbar options, colors, desktop settings, and browser and email settings so that you don't have to reconfigure them. You can transfer folders, too, including the My Documents, My Pictures, and Favorites folders.

Before using the wizard, you'll need to log on as an administrator and make sure the following conditions are true:

♦ Your old computer is set up the way you want it.

♦ The old computer and the new computer are connected by either a direct cable or a network.

♦ The old computer (the computer you will transfer files and settings from) is running any of the following operating systems: Windows 95, Windows 98, Windows 98 SE, Windows ME, Windows NT 4, Windows 2000, or Windows XP (32-bit version).

Using the Files And Settings Transfer Wizard

When you use the Files And Settings Transfer Wizard, you can do two types of transfers. You can either log onto the computer you want to transfer files *from*, or you can log onto the computer you want to transfer files *to*. The easiest way to transfer files is to log onto a computer that is running Windows XP Professional, and transfer files *from* this computer *to* another computer on the network. More complex is logging onto a computer that is not running Windows XP Professional and transferring files to it from a Windows XP computer. Of course, you can log onto a Windows XP Professional computer and transfer files and settings from another Windows XP Professional computer, too.

Transferring Files and Settings from One Windows XP Professional Computer to Another

In this example and the examples following, I'll work through the process of connecting to a second computer and transferring files and settings over a LAN. Later, I'll give examples of how to use other types of hardware—such as direct cables or removable media—for transferring settings.

To transfer files and settings *from* one Windows XP Professional computer to another:

1. As an administrator, log onto the Windows XP Professional computer that you want to transfer files *from*.

2. Open the Files And Settings Transfer Wizard by choosing Start I Programs I Accessories I System Tools I Files And Settings Transfer Wizard.

3. On the Welcome page, choose Next to start the wizard. On the Which Computer Is This page, select Old Computer–This Is The Computer I Want To Transfer Files And Settings From. Choose Next.

4. On the Select A Transfer Method page, select the method for transferring your data to the other computer. There are four options:

   ♦ Direct Cable (A Cable That Connects Your Computers' Serial Ports)

   ♦ Home Or Small Office Network–A Network Is The Best Way To Transfer Large Amounts Of Data

   ♦ Floppy Drive Or Other Removable Media

   ♦ Other (For Example, A Removable Drive Or Network Drive). You Can Save Files And Settings To Any Disk Drive Or Folder On Your Computer

   Depending on the choice made here, the wizard will continue in one of four ways. Select Other for this example, and browse to the location of the computer you want to transfer files to. See Figure 14.10; notice that the folder selected is the SharedDocs folder on the new computer, in this case, Laptop. Choose OK, then Next.

Note

If you select Home Or Small Office Network, you'll be prompted for a password later in the process. Choosing Home Or Small Office Network is detailed in the next example.

c:\solfire\userdata*.asp -

Figure 14.10
Browsing for a computer and folder.

5. On the What Do You Want To Transfer page, you can choose to transfer settings only, files only, or both files and settings. You can also select a custom list of files and settings if you are comfortable choosing these files manually. If you choose to select files manually, you'll be prompted with another page to select the files. Most users should choose Both Files And Settings. See Figure 14.11. Choose Next. (The transfer process can take several minutes.)

6. On the Completing The Collection Phase screen, choose Finish. Go to your new computer.

7. At the new computer, check to see if the Files And Settings Transfer Wizard is running. If so, continue with Step 8; if not, open the wizard through the Start | Programs | Accessories | System Tools menu. Choose Next to start the wizard.

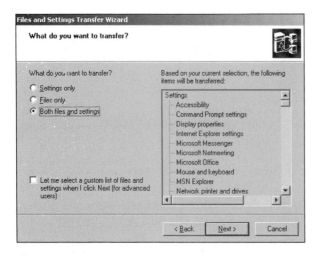

Figure 14.11
Selecting what you want to transfer.

8. On the Which Computer Is This page, select New Computer–This Is The Computer I Want To Transfer Files And Settings To, and choose Next.

9. On the Do You Have A Windows XP CD page, select I Don't Need The Wizard Disk. I Have Already Collected My Files And Settings From My Old Computer. Choose Next.

10. On the Where Are The Files And Settings page, select Other, and browse to the location of the saved files. Choose OK, then Next.

11. When the transfer is finished, log off and log back on to apply the changes.

Transferring Files and Settings to a Window XP Professional Computer from Another

The first example in this section details how to transfer a computer's files and settings to a new Windows XP computer. In this example, you'll be sitting at the receiving computer. The process is different, although the outcome is the same.

To transfer files and settings by working on the *receiving* computer:

1. As an administrator, log onto the Windows XP Professional computer that you want to transfer files *to*.

2. Open the Files And Settings Transfer Wizard by choosing Start | Programs | Accessories | System Tools | Files And Settings Transfer Wizard.

3. On the Welcome page, choose Next to start the wizard. On the Which Computer Is This page, select New Computer–This Is The Computer I Want To Transfer Files And Settings To. Choose Next.

4. On the Do You Have A Windows XP CD page, select I Want To Create A Wizard Disk In The Following Drive, and create a Wizard Disk on a floppy disk. Place a disk in the drive, and choose Next. (Of course, you won't need to do this if you've already created a disk, or if you want to put the Windows XP CD in and use the wizard there. Using a floppy disk is usually easiest, and you can use it again later. I'd suggest doing it this way.) The name of the file placed on the floppy disk is fastwiz.

   Do *not* choose Next on this page until you've completed Steps 5 and 6.

5. Go to the old computer, and insert the Wizard Disk into the disk drive.

6. At the old computer, choose Start | Run. Type "a:\fastwiz" and choose OK.

7. At the old computer, choose Next to start the Files And Transfer Wizard. Select Old Computer–This Is The Computer I Want To Transfer Files From, and choose Next.

8. On the Select A Transfer Method page, either select Home Or Small Office Network, or select Other and browse to the location. In this example, I'll choose Home Or Small Office Network; the choice Other was detailed in the previous example.

9. On the What Do You Want To Transfer page, you can choose to transfer settings only, files only, or both files and settings. You can also select a custom list of files and settings. If you choose to select files manually, you'll be prompted with another page to select the files. Most users should choose Both Files And Settings. Choose Next.

10. In the Password message box that appears, type the password. The password will be shown on the original computer, as seen in Figure 14.12.

11. Both computers will now work automatically on the transfer of files and settings. When each computer is finished, choose the Finish button on the computer with the new settings. On the computer with the new settings, log off and log back on to apply them.

Transferring Files and Settings from a Windows XP Professional Computer to a Computer Not Running Windows XP Professional

If you are sitting at a computer running Windows XP Professional, and you want to transfer the files and settings to another computer on the network that is not running Windows XP Professional, follow the directions here:

1. As an administrator, log onto the Windows XP Professional computer that you want to transfer files *from*.

2. Open the Files And Settings Transfer Wizard.

3. On the Welcome page, choose Next to start the wizard. On the Which Computer Is This page, select Old Computer–This Is The Computer I Want To Transfer Files And Settings From. Choose Next.

Note
Depending on the type of network you are running (domain or workgroup), you might be asked here to create a Wizard Disk. If prompted, create the disk on a floppy drive.

4. On the Select A Transfer Method page, select a method for transferring your data to the non–Windows XP computer. I'll choose Other and browse to the computer. If you choose Home Or Small Office Network, the directions will vary slightly, as detailed in

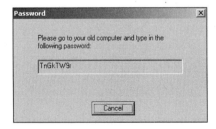

Figure 14.12
The prompt for entering a password.

the previous example. After locating the place to save the information on either a local disk or the remote machine, choose OK, then Next.

5. On the What Do You Want To Transfer page, you can choose to transfer settings only, files only, or both files and settings. You can also select a custom list of files and settings. If you choose to select files manually, you'll be prompted with another page to select the files. Most users should choose Both Files And Settings.

6. On the Completing The Collection Phase screen, choose Finish. Go to your new computer.

7. At the new computer, do one of two things:

   ♦ If you have a Wizard Disk (on a floppy), put that disk in, choose Start | Run, type "a:\fastwiz.exe", and choose OK.

   ♦ If you do not have a Wizard Disk but instead have the original Windows XP Professional CD, put that disc in, and choose Perform Additional Tasks | Transfer Files And Settings.

8. Choose Next to start the wizard.

9. On the Select A Transfer Method page, browse to the folder where the data is stored.

10. On the Where Are The Files And Settings page, select Other and browse to the location of the saved files. Choose OK, then Next.

11. On the What Do You Want To Transfer page, select Both Files And Settings. When the transfer is finished, log off and log back on to apply the changes.

Transferring Files and Settings from a non-XP Professional Computer to a Windows XP Professional Computer

If you are sitting at a computer running something *other than* Windows XP Professional, and you want to transfer the files and settings from it to another computer on the network that *is* running Windows XP Professional, follow the directions here:

1. As an administrator, log onto the computer that you want to transfer files *from*. In this example, the computer will not be running Windows XP Professional.

2. Put the Windows XP Professional CD into the CD-ROM drive, and choose Perform Additional Tasks | Transfer Files And Settings.

3. Choose Next to start the Files And Settings Transfer Wizard.

4. On the Select A Transfer Method page, either select Home Or Small Office Network, or select Other and browse to the folder where you want to save the information. (I'll select Other in this example. The results of any other choice will differ only slightly from these instructions.)

5. On the What Do You Want To Transfer page, select the information you want to transfer.

6. When the collection of data has been completed, choose Finish.

7. Log onto the Windows XP Professional computer you want to transfer the data *to*.

8. Run the Files And Settings Transfer Wizard. Choose Next to start the wizard.

9. On the Which Computer Is This page, select New Computer.

10. On the Do You Have A Windows XP CD page, select I Don't Need The Wizard Disk, I Have Already Collected My Files And Settings From My Old Computer.

11. On the Where Are The Files And Settings page, select Other and browse to the location of the data. Choose OK, then Next.

12. When the transfer is complete, log off and log back on to apply the new settings.

How Transfers Differ When You're Not Transferring over a LAN

Besides transferring files and settings over a LAN either by browsing to the new location or by using your home or office network, you can also transfer files by using removable hardware, such as Zip disks, floppy disks, and tape drives. The only difference between the steps listed previously and the steps for using removable hardware occurs on the Select A Transfer Method page, where you select one of these four options:

♦ Direct Cable (A Cable That Connects Your Computers' Serial Ports)

♦ Home Or Small Office Network–A Network Is The Best Way To Transfer Large Amounts Of Data

♦ Floppy Drive Or Other Removable Media

♦ Other (For Example, A Removable Drive Or Network Drive). You Can Save Files And Settings To Any Disk Drive Or Folder On Your Computer

If you save the information to a floppy drive or other removable media, then you only need to identify that hardware when prompted.

You can also connect to another computer via direct cable. You can directly connect two computers by using a null-modem cable (a cable that connects to the serial ports on each computer). With this method, simply choose Direct Cable when prompted.

Windows Media Services

Backing up with Windows Media Services, specifically Windows Media Player, is different from other types of backups. With Windows Media Services, you can back up the media to an audio CD. You should also back up the licenses for your digital media files in case your licenses are lost or in case you want to transfer them from an old computer to a new one.

These files are not transferred by the Files And Settings Transfer Wizard. Because the Media Player has already been covered in depth in Chapter 2, in this section I'll cover only backing up and restoring the licenses for audio files. You should back up licenses prior to upgrades or reinstallation.

Backing Up Audio Licenses

To back up the licenses for the music stored on your hard drive:

1. Log on as an administrator or backup operator. Open Windows Media Player by choosing Start | Programs | Windows Media Player.

2. Choose Tools | License Management.

3. In the License Management dialog box, choose the Browse button. Locate the floppy drive or a folder in which you want to back up the licenses. Choose OK.

4. In the License Management dialog box, choose the Backup Now button.

5. Choose OK to verify that the process has been completed.

Restoring Audio Licenses

To restore the licenses for the music stored on your hard drive:

1. Log on as an administrator or backup operator. Open Windows Media Player by choosing Start | Programs | Windows Media Player. Connect to the Internet.

2. Choose Tools | License Management.

3. In the License Management dialog box, choose the Browse button. Locate the floppy drive or other folder where the backup licenses are stored. Choose OK.

4. In the License Management dialog box, choose the Restore Now button.

5. You will then be prompted to choose OK from the dialog box shown in Figure 14.13. (See the next section for details on this privacy issue.)

6. When the transfer is complete, choose OK in the Transfer Complete dialog box.

What Information Is Collected by Microsoft When I Restore Licenses?

When you click OK to begin restoring audio licenses, Microsoft collects several pieces of information. The information collected is sent to Microsoft over your Internet connection. Sometimes, unique machine-identifying information is also sent. No "personally identifiable information" (name, address, phone number) is sent. A list of what is sent to Microsoft is provided next.

When you click the Restore Now button, you are sending information to Microsoft that uniquely identifies your computer for internal tracking purposes. Microsoft stores your unique

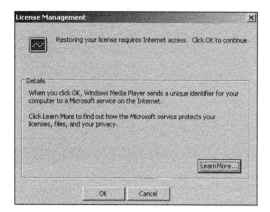

Figure 14.13
License Management details.

identifier in a database and keeps track of how often you restore your licenses. Microsoft claims not to share this information with anyone, but it also states that "Microsoft has worked with partners (such as record labels, hand-held computer manufacturers, video labels, and many others) to develop a service that enables you to move and restore digital media licenses (for legitimate purposes only) between your computers, not your computer and your friend's computer. This service allows for a limited number of license transactions." Either way, there is no way around it—if you want to restore licenses, you'll need to choose OK when prompted.

Information Sent When Using Windows Media Player

When you use Windows Media Player, the following information is sent to Microsoft:

- Microsoft collects logging items, such as connection time, IP addresses, client version, client identification, date, protocol, and so forth, most of which will not personally identify your computer.

- When you play a CD, Windows Media Player attempts to locate information about the artist over the Internet and return that information to you. Windows Media Player sends only a unique CD ID and does not send personally identifiable information.

- When you download a CD from the Internet, you often also download a license, or you might even purchase one. This license must be on your computer to play the media files. The file's ID is non-traceable and does not include any personal information.

- The information in your media library can be accessed by other software on your computer *and* on the Internet. This is necessary if you want Internet sites or other software to automatically update your media library. If you don't, you can set this at No Access (described later).

- Cookies will be downloaded to your computer.

You can protect yourself from this information collection in several ways. In Windows Media Player, choose Tools|Options, select the Player tab, and disable the relevant settings. You can also listen to music while offline, and set Internet security options to High in Internet Explorer.

Other Restore Options

A couple of other restore options are available in Windows XP. You can restore deleted files and folders from the Recycle Bin, and you can restore default security log settings. After declining a Windows Update, you can restore that also.

Restoring from the Recycle Bin

The Recycle Bin holds information that you have deleted, including files and folders. If you have accidentally deleted a file or folder, you can restore that folder to its original location through the Recycle Bin icon on the desktop or from Windows Explorer.

To restore items from the Recycle Bin:

1. Open the Recycle Bin from the desktop.

2. Right-click the file or folder you want to restore, and choose Restore.

You cannot restore the following items:

♦ Items that have been deleted from the Recycle Bin

♦ Items that were deleted from network locations

♦ Items deleted from floppy disks, Zip disks, tapes, or other removable media

♦ Items deleted that were too large to fit in the Recycle Bin (if this is the case, you'll receive a warning when deleting)

Restoring Default Security Log Settings

If you've changed the default security log settings, you can restore them to their original settings as well. If you are a member of a larger network or domain, however, network policies might prevent you from performing these steps.

To restore the default security log settings:

1. Log on as an administrator.

2. Open Network Connections by choosing Start | Settings | Control Panel | Network Connections.

3. Highlight the connection and choose Change Settings Of This Connection from Network Tasks in the left pane of the Network Connections window.

4. On the Advanced tab of the Local Area Connection Properties page, choose the Settings button.

5. On the Security Logging tab, choose the Restore Defaults button, and choose OK twice.

Restoring Declined Windows Updates

If you are using Windows Update to retrieve and download files offered by Microsoft to keep your system running smoothly, you might occasionally choose to decline an update. This might happen because the computer is too busy to handle the request or because perhaps you don't feel the need to install the downloaded files. If you decide to restore the declined updates:

1. Log on as an administrator.

2. Open the System Properties dialog box. (If Control Panel is in Category view, choose Start | Settings | Control Panel | Performance And Maintenance, and open the System icon. If Control Panel is in Classic view, choose Start | Settings | Control Panel, and open the System icon.)

3. On the Automatic Updates tab, choose the Restore Declined Updates button. Choose OK.

Note

Remember that these instructions are written for a desktop configured using the Windows Classic Theme. Classic Theme configured for the entire computer is different from Classic View applied only to Control Panel.

Preparing for and Recovering from a Virus Attack

As you already know, the best offense (against viruses on the Internet) is a good defense. The best way to recover from a virus is to have up-to-date anti-virus software on the computer and to have solid and reliable backups. I hope that after reading this chapter, you'll get in the habit of making regular backups because restoring a computer after a virus attack depends on it. If you don't have the items listed in the section "What to Keep on Hand," recovering from a backup could include reinstalling the entire system.

In this section, I'll go over what you should have in your home or office in case of a virus attack and what to do if you get one. Viruses all differ, so it's difficult to explain how to recover and restore a computer attacked by a virus that hasn't been created yet.

What to Keep on Hand

There are several things you can do to prepare yourself and your computer for a virus attack, and many of these things will actually prevent one. Make sure you have the following items on hand:

♦ Up-to-date anti-virus software, which you can purchase for about $50

♦ Copies of all original software in case reinstallation is necessary

♦ Your Windows XP Professional disk and the product ID number, plus any other ID numbers necessary to activate other software

- An Automated System Recovery disk

- A copy of your system state

- A password-reset disk

- An MS-DOS startup disk

- A complete set of backups of your data

- If you dual-boot, a copy of your boot.ini file

Make sure you also take the following precautions:

- Make sure your anti-virus software is updated daily or weekly from the manufacturer's Web site so that you are protected against the latest virus strains. Configure the software to scan for viruses at bootup.

- Use the Internet Connection Firewall.

- Do not run your computer as an administrator.

- Inform users not to open email attachments from people they don't know or if the files end in .exe or .vbs or are zipped.

- Do not install programs, drivers, or other applications from the Internet or bulletin boards. If you must use them, install them on a test computer first.

- Do not install programs from floppy disks.

- Run virus scans on any attachment or suspicious programs.

- Use strong passwords to protect against password hackers.

How Do You Know It's a Virus?

You can generally tell when you've gotten a virus because the computer doesn't perform as it should. Sometimes, the computer starts sending multiple email messages or shows weird messages on the screen. Occasionally, a virus simply slows the computer down and makes it impossible to work. You can run your anti-virus program if you suspect that a virus has gotten through. Listed here are some common signs:

- File-name extensions have changed.

- File sizes are larger.

- Files are missing or have been renamed.

- Opening files with .exe extensions produces Write Protect errors.

- The computer reboots by itself.

- You get "Invalid Drive Specification" error messages.

- You get "Sector Not Found" error messages.

- The printer, keyboard, and mouse stop functioning.

- The system hangs or freezes up.

- The computer takes a long time to boot.

- You detect any other abnormal behavior.

Detecting the Virus

You'll probably know when you've gotten a virus. It's like having the cold or the flu—you'll have the symptoms. However, you can have a virus and not have very many obvious signs. You might attribute the slow performance of your computer to a full hard drive or insufficient RAM. If you think you have a computer virus, the best option is to run anti-virus software and scan the computer's entire hard drive. You can also type "fdisk" at a command prompt to see if all partitions are intact or if any strange characters appear. You can also run virus scans from the Web sites of companies that produce anti-virus software, such as Norton AntiVirus by Symantec (**www.symantec.com**).

Restoring the Computer After a Virus Attack

Once you know you've gotten a virus, the next step is to get rid of it quickly. You should first disconnect from the Internet and the network and run an anti-virus program to see if you can catch and quarantine the virus. Occasionally, this step is successful. If this doesn't work, log back on and visit the Web site of the anti-virus software manufacturer to locate information on how to get rid of the virus. Next, visit Microsoft's Web site for specific patches and fixes.

At the time of the writing of this book, the big viruses are the Red Code Worm and Nimda. For an example of some of the steps that must be taken to get rid of a virus like these, see the sidebar.

Other Repair Options

If you're looking at Web sites for instructions about the virus (and there might not be any information if you're one of the first ones to get it), and running your anti-virus program doesn't work, you'll be forced to either wait for Web support or try these other options (in no particular order):

- Scan the hard drive, and replace all infected files with files from your backups.

- If you can't boot the computer at all, try booting from an emergency boot disk or another type of recovery disk, and boot into safe mode. Try to run the anti-virus software from there, or replace infected files.

Getting Rid of a Virus

Here is how to free a computer of the Nimda virus:

1. Run your virus program to make sure that you have the most recent virus definitions.
2. Restart the computer.

Note

When your computer restarts, it is likely that infected files will be found. Attempt to repair the infected files. Quarantine any files that are not repairable.

3. Start your anti-virus program and scan all files.
4. For each file detected as infected by W32.Nimda.A@mm or W32.Nimda.A@mm (html), choose Repair. Quarantine any file that is not repairable.
5. For each file detected as infected by W32.Nimda.A@mm (dr), W32.Nimda.enc, W32.Nimda.A@mm (dll), choose Delete.
6. Restore Admin.dll and Riched20.dll from backup, or from the Microsoft Windows or Office .cab files if necessary.
7. Remove unnecessary shares.
8. Delete the guest account from the Administrators group (if applicable).

As you can see, ridding the computer of a virus is quite a job.

♦ Try using the Disk Cleanup utility.

♦ Reformat the hard drive, and reinstall all programs and data from backups.

♦ Hire a data recovery company to come in and fix the problem.

Using the Recovery Console

There is one last option for restoring a computer. If you have backups of all of your data, the computer crashes, and you can't boot to Windows, you can use the Recovery Console to get the system up and running so you can then restore from your backups.

The Recovery Console is designed for advanced administrators of computers, and it is available for Windows XP Professional machines. You should use this option only if the computer will not boot up and all other attempts at recovery have failed, including safe mode, ASR, System Restore, and restoring from backups. With the Recovery Console, you can enable and disable system services, format disk drives, read and write to local drives, repair system files by copying missing files from floppies or CDs, and even access and format NTFS drives.

You can install and configure the Recovery Console so that it is an option at bootup, or you can simply access it from the Windows XP CD when you need it. However, if the computer can't or won't boot to the CD when the computer crashes, you've got a more difficult problem. It's best to add the Recovery Console as a boot option.

Making the Recovery Console a Bootup Option

To make the Recovery Console a bootup option:

1. Log on as an administrator.

2. Place the Windows XP Professional CD into the CD-ROM drive.

3. If the Welcome To Microsoft Windows XP screen appears, choose Exit.

4. Choose Start | Run, and type "d:\i386\winnt32.exe /cmdcons" where "d:\" is the letter of your CD-ROM drive. Choose OK.

5. In the Windows Setup dialog box that appears, choose Yes to verify that you want to install the Recovery Console in the startup options.

6. If you are connected to the Internet, dynamic updates will be downloaded automatically now. If you are not connected, or if you want to skip this option, press the Esc key, and installation will continue with the existing Setup software.

7. In the information box that is shown after installation is complete, choose OK to verify the end of the installation.

Starting the Recovery Console from the Windows XP Professional CD

If you can't boot the computer at all, you can try booting from the Windows XP Professional CD. You might need to change the computer's BIOS first, especially if your computer boots to the hard drive before the CD-ROM.

To boot the computer by using the Windows XP Professional CD and the Recovery Console:

1. Place the Windows XP Professional CD into the CD-ROM drive, and restart the computer.

2. Let the installation begin normally. At the Welcome To Setup screen, there are three options:

   ◆ To Set Up Windows XP Now, Press Enter.

   ◆ To Repair A Windows XP Installation Using Recovery Console, Press R.

   ◆ To Quit Setup Without Installing Windows XP, Press F3.

   Press R.

Recovery Console Commands

You can use the Recovery Console to perform multiple tasks. Because the console is used at a command prompt, though, using the console is more difficult than any other recovery option. You can use many of these commands at a regular command prompt without using the Recovery Console (the parameters might differ), and this can be quite useful for administrators. Commands such as **attrib, copy, dir, fixmbr, more,** and **net use** are necessities at a command prompt. Following are descriptions of these commands, what they do, and how to use them. (For those of you who have experience with using DOS commands, this material will look familiar.)

Warning

The Recovery Console should be used only by advanced administrators because making an error with one of these commands at a command prompt can cause system instability or even require reinstallation.

Attrib

The **attrib** command is used to change the attributes of a file or directory. Files and directories can be granted several attributes, including read-only, system, hidden, and compressed. For instance, if a file is read-only, you can remove the read-only attribute while in the Recovery Console so you can write to the file or alter it. You can add or remove these attributes by using these parameters:

Note

The + sets the attribute, and the – removes it.

- **+r |–r**—Sets or clears the read-only attribute.

- **+s | –s**—Sets or clears the system attribute.

- **+h | –h**—Sets or clears the hidden file attribute.

- **+c | –c**—Sets or clears the compressed file attribute.

- **[drive:][path]filename**—Specifies the file or directory for which you want to change the attributes. Only one file or directory can be changed at a time.

The syntax is:

```
attrib [+r|-r] [+s|-s] [+h|-h] [+c|c] [[drive:][path]filename]
```

Batch

The **batch** command runs a series of commands that are stored in a text file. There are two parameters:

- *input_file*—Specifies the text file that contains the batch commands to be run. This name can be a drive letter and a colon, a directory name, a file name, or any combination.

- *output_file*—Specifies the file where the output of the batch file is to be stored. If nothing is listed, the information is shown on the computer screen. This is an optional parameter.

The syntax is:

```
batch input_file [output_file]
```

Bootcfg

You can use this command for boot configuration and recovery. The boot configuration contains all of the startup options and is usually stored in the boot.ini file. A boot.ini file is what allows you to choose from multiple operating systems when a computer dual-boots, and it allows you to choose the Recovery Console as an option.

Before using the **bootcfg** command, you should make a backup copy of your boot.ini file. To do this, type "bootcfg /copy" at the command prompt before starting. See the information on the **copy** command for more details.

There are several ways to use the **bootcfg** command. It has the following switches:

♦ **/default**—Sets the default boot entry.

♦ **/add**—Adds a Windows installation to the boot list.

♦ **/list**—Lists the entries in the boot list.

♦ **/rebuild**—Looks at all of the Windows installations and prompts you to choose what to add to the boot.ini file.

♦ **/redirect**—Allows the administrator to redirect the boot loader with the specified configuration.

♦ **/scan**—Scans all files for Windows installations.

To use this command, type "bootcfg" followed by the appropriate switch.

Chdir

Use this command to see the name of the current directory or switch to the new directory.. If you use the **chdir** command without any parameters, you'll see the name of the directory; with parameters, you'll see the changes in the current folder. There are only two parameters:

♦ **[*drive:*] [*path*]**—Specifies the drive and directory you want to change if they are different from the current drive and directory.

♦ **[..]**—Specifies that you want to change the current folder.

The syntax is:

```
chdir [drive:] [path] [..]
```

Chkdsk

This command is used to check the local disks, display a status report, and correct errors on the hard disk. You can use the **chkdsk** command with or without parameters. Using the command without parameters displays the status of the disk and nothing else. The three parameters are:

- ◆ *[drive]*—Specifies the drive to check.

- ◆ /p—Performs an extensive search of the disk. This is an advanced disk-checking parameter.

- ◆ /r—Locates problems on the disk and recovers as much information as possible.

The syntax is:

```
chkdsk [drive] [/p] [/r]
```

Cls

The **cls** command simply clears the screen of all information. There are no parameters; simply type "cls" at the Recovery Console prompt.

Copy

Use this command to copy a file to another location. There are two parameters:

- ◆ *source*—Names the file to be copied. This can be a drive letter and colon, a directory name, a file name, or a combination of these.

- ◆ *destination*—Specifies the location where the file will be copied. This can be a drive letter and colon, a directory name, a file name, or a combination of these.

The syntax is:

```
copy source [destination]
```

Delete

Use this command to delete a file. There are two parameters:

- ◆ *[drive:]* *[path]*—Specifies the drive and directory you want to delete if they are different from the current drive and directory.

- ◆ *filename*—Specifies the file you want to delete.

The syntax is:

```
delete [drive:] [path] filename
```

Dir

Use this command to list the files and subdirectories on the hard drive. There are two parameters:

♦ **[drive:] [path]**—Specifies the drive and directory for which you want to see a listing.

♦ *filename*—Specifies the file name or file group for which you want to see a listing.

The syntax is:

```
dir [drive:] [path] filename
```

Disable

Use this command to disable a system service or device driver. These services are usually at the hardware level and are accessed by their system service or driver name. There are two parameters:

♦ *service_name*—Specifies the name of the system service.

♦ *device_driver_name*—Specifies the name of the device driver.

The syntax is:

```
disable {[service_name] | [device_driver_name]}
```

Diskpart

Use this command to create and delete partitions on the hard drive. There are several switches and parameters:

♦ **/add**—Used to add a partition to the hard drive.

♦ **/delete**—Used to delete a partition from the hard drive.

♦ *device_name*—Specifies the physical device you want to create the partition on, such as \Device\HardDisk1.

♦ *drive_name*—Specifies the partition you want to delete, denoted by its drive letter.

♦ *partition name*—Specifies the partition you want to delete, denoted by its partition name.

♦ *size*—Specifies the size of the partition you want to create in MB. Used with the **/add** switch.

The syntax is:

```
diskpart [/add | /delete] [device_name | drive_name | partition name] [size]
```

Enable

This command is used to enable a system service or device driver. (Compare to the **disable** command described earlier.) There are three parameters:

- *service_name*—Specifies the name of the service to enable.

- *device_driver_name*—Specifies the name of the device driver to enable.

- *startup_type*—Specifies the type of startup the service or device driver should use. There are four:

  - SERVICE_BOOT_START

  - SERVICE_SYSTEM_START

  - SERVICE_AUTO_START

  - SERVICE_DEMAND_START

The syntax is:

```
enable {service_name | device_driver_name} [startup_type]
```

Exit

The **exit** command is used to exit the Recovery Console. There are no parameters.

Expand

This command is used to extract a file from a compressed file and is commonly used with driver files. There are several parameters:

- *source*—Specifies the file that needs to be expanded.

- */F:filespec*—If the source contains more than one file, you can specify the name of the file you want to extract here, or you can use wildcards.

- *destination*—Names the destination directory for the extracted file(s).

- */d*—Lists the files without extracting them.

- */y*—Does not show the overwrite options when expanding or extracting files.

The syntax is:

```
expand source [/F:{filespec}] [destination] [/d] [/y]
```

Fixboot

This command allows you to write a new partition boot sector to the system partition. The partition boot sector is the portion of the hard disk that contains the files that load Windows XP Professional. You can use the **fixboot** command if you think the computer has been infected by a virus that has attacked the boot sector. If you use this command without any parameters, it will write a new partition boot sector to the system partition for the installation you are logged onto. There is only one parameter for the **fixboot** command, and that is the drive letter.

The syntax is:

```
fixboot [drive]
```

Fixmbr

The master boot record (MBR) gets the boot process going and is the first sector on the hard drive. If there are problems with the MBR due to a virus or other problem, you can repair it using this command. The only parameter is *device_name*, which is used to specify the hard disk containing the MBR.

The syntax is:

```
fixmbr device_name
```

Format

This command formats the drive specified. Formatting erases all data on the drive. There are three parameters:

♦ *drive*—Specifies the drive to format.

♦ */q*—Performs a quick format of the drive and does not check for bad areas on the disk.

♦ */fs:file-system*—Names the file system to be used: FAT, FAT32, or NTFS. If this parameter isn't used, the disk is formatted in the file system previously used by the disk.

The syntax is:

```
format [drive:] [/q] [/fs:file-system]
```

Help

The **help** command displays help at the Recovery Console command line. You can enter "help [commandname]" or "commandname /?".

Listsvc

The **listsvc** command simply lists the services and drivers that are used on the local computer; there are no parameters.

Logon

The **logon** command allows you to log onto your machine. There are no parameters. After using the **logon** command, you will be prompted for a password. After three unsuccessful logon attempts have occurred, the Recovery Console will exit.

Map

Use this command to see all drive letters and physical device names. This is helpful when you need to use the *device_name* parameter in other commands. The **map** command has only one parameter, **arc**. The **arc** parameter displays the ARC (Advanced RISC Computing) name; without the **arc** parameter, the device names are used.

The syntax for the arc display name is multi(0)disk(0)rdisk(0)partition(2).

The syntax for the device display name is \Device\HardDisk0\Partition2.

Multi, disk, rdisk, partition, and hard disk represent various disks and partitions that are configured on your hard drive. To see the arc path for your computer, locate the boot.ini file (it is a hidden file) and open it using Notepad.

The syntax is:

```
Map [arc]
```

Mkdir

This command is used to create a new directory or subdirectory. There are two parameters:

♦ *drive*—Specifies the drive in which to make the directory.

♦ *path*—Specifies the path and the name of the new directory.

The syntax is:

```
mkdir [drive:] path
```

More

This command is used to display the contents of a text file without modifying it. The **more** command can be used with the *drive:, path,* and *filename* parameters.

The syntax is:

```
more [drive:] [path] filename
```

Net Use

Use this command to connect to a network share or network drive. There are several parameters:

♦ *\\computername\sharename*—Specifies the computer name and the name of the share to connect to.

♦ */user:*—Specifies the user who will be making the connection.

♦ *domainname*—Specifies the domain that the user connecting to the resource belongs to.

- ◆ ***username***—Specifies the username that should be used for logging onto the resource.

- ◆ ***password***—Specifies the password for the shared resource. If the parameter isn't used, the user will be prompted.

- ◆ **/d**—Disconnects the user from the resource.

The syntax is:

```
net use [\\computername\sharename
[/user:[domainname\]username]password]|[driveletter:] [/d]
```

Rename

This command is used to rename a single file. You use the same parameters described earlier: ***drive:***, ***path***, and ***filename***.

The syntax is:

```
rename [drive:] [path] filename1 filename2
```

Rmdir

The **rmdir** command removes a directory. This command is used with the parameters ***drive:*** and ***path***, as detailed in other commands.

The syntax is:

```
rmdir [drive:] [path]
```

Set

The **set** command is used with security templates and must be enabled. To enable your computer to use the set command, access this option through Local Computer Policy\Computer Configuration\Windows Settings\Security Settings\Local Policies\Security Options from Enables The Set Command For The Recovery Console. After the **set** command is enabled, you can use it in the Recovery Console to display and set Recovery Console variables, such as allowing wildcards or removable media. The only parameter is ***variable***, which takes any of the following values:

- ◆ **AllowWildCards**—Allows you to use wildcards with Recovery Console commands.

- ◆ **AllowAllPaths**—Allows all files and directories on the hard drive to be accessed.

- ◆ **AllowRemovableMedia**—Allows files to be copied to removable media.

- ◆ **NoCopyPrompt**—Does not display a prompt when files are overwritten.

The syntax is:

```
set [variable = [string]]
```

For instance:

```
set allowallpaths = true
```

Systemroot

The **systemroot** command sets the current directory to the systemroot folder you are logged onto. There are no parameters.

Type

The same as the **more** command, the **type** command allows you to display the contents of a text file without modifying it. The **type** command can be used with the *drive:*, *path*, and *filename* parameters.

The syntax is:

```
type [drive:] [path] filename
```

Wrapping Up

In this chapter, you learned about backing up and restoring data. There are five types of backups: copy, daily, differential, incremental, and normal. You can back up many types of data. You can use the Backup utility to back up the system state, files and folders, and even data located in the My Network Places folders.

This topic extends far beyond simply using the Backup utility offered by Windows XP Professional, though. You can also back up data by using CDs, DVDs, and Zip disks. There are also several ways to restore data, such as using the restore options in the Backup utility, using Automated System Recovery, and using the Recovery Console. This chapter also discussed restoring your computer after a virus attack.

Also covered as a type of restore option was the Files And Settings Transfer Wizard. This wizard allows you to copy information from one computer to another, saving time when configuring a new computer.

Chapter 15
Mobile Computing

I f you use a mobile computer (a laptop or notebook computer), you have different requirements and options than desktop users of Windows XP Professional have. For instance, power management becomes an issue with mobile computers, and Windows XP Professional offers several power management schemes. Another issue with a laptop is obtaining the best performance for your system. You can do this by setting System options, setting hardware profiles, using encryption, and using DualView when at the office.

If you need to work on network files while your laptop is not connected to the network, you can use the Offline Files tool. Of course, this technology can create problems if you change a file at the same time a network user does, but you'll learn how to handle this conflict. Besides network files, Web pages can be made available offline, too.

The Briefcase tool can be used similarly to offline files; Briefcase allows you to take office work home or on the road. Mobile-computer users can also use NetMeeting and other conferencing options to communicate with other users. Although a couple of these topics (NetMeeting and Remote Desktop) have been covered in previous chapters, they are reviewed briefly here with the mobile-computer user in mind. Finally, this chapter discusses dialing options that are of particular interest to laptop users; these options include operator-assisted calls, redial options, call-backs, and manual calls.

Power Management

Mobile computers can plug into electrical outlets or run on batteries. Because these computers can run on batteries, there must be an effective way to manage how much power is consumed. Several power schemes are available for this purpose, and hibernation and standby options are also available. When using Scheduled Tasks, you can also specify what the computer is to do when running on batteries, in hibernation, or on standby.

Advanced Configuration and Power Interface

The Advanced Configuration and Power Interface (ACPI) is an industry standard that is used for managing power on all types of computers. For you to use all of the options available in Windows XP Professional, your laptop will need to support ACPI. If you are not sure if your computer supports ACPI, check the computer's documentation.

During Windows setup, ACPI is installed only if all components in the computer support it. If your laptop has an out-of-date BIOS or if the NIC (network interface card) or sound card isn't ACPI-supported, ACPI will not be installed. Some peripherals can cause the computer to function erratically if power management is used. Figure 15.1 shows a laptop computer's Power Options Properties dialog box on a computer that does not have ACPI installed or is not ACPI-compliant; Figure 15.2 shows the same dialog box on a computer that supports ACPI and has ACPI installed.

By using power management options (accessible through the Power Management icon in the Control Panel), you can do the following:

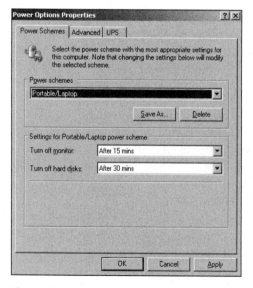

Figure 15.1
Power options for a non-ACPI-compliant computer.

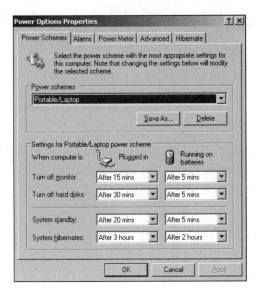

Figure 15.2
Power options for an ACPI-compliant computer.

♦ Turn off monitors and/or hard disks after a certain period of time. You can set different amounts of time for when the computer is running on batteries and when it's plugged in.

♦ Have the system go on standby or into hibernation after a certain period of idle time.

♦ Set alarms for when battery power is running low, and configure alarm actions such as immediate hibernation or shutdown of the computer.

♦ Show the power meter in the notification area of the desktop.

♦ Set advanced options such as prompting for a password after the computer has been on standby.

♦ Enable hibernation.

Choosing a Power Scheme

Although only a couple of power schemes will be effective for mobile computers that usually run on batteries, all of the schemes can be used for laptops while they're plugged in. For a laptop, users generally configure two hardware profiles: one for when the computer is being used away from the office, and one for when the laptop is plugged in at the office. This setup allows the computer to work optimally in both situations.

♦ Home/Office Desk

♦ Portable/Laptop

- ◆ Presentation

- ◆ Always On

- ◆ Minimal Power Management

- ◆ Max Battery

You should choose schemes for your laptop to use when it is plugged in as a standalone computer, when it is plugged in and connected to the network at the office, and when it is being used while out of the office. If the laptop is also used for presentations, you should consider this power scheme as well.

Note

Any of these power schemes can be changed to suit your particular needs; however, it is best to create your own power scheme instead.

As you can see from Figures 15.1 and 15.2, options are different for computers that are ACPI-compliant and those that aren't. Mainly, the differences lie in the ability of the computer to go into system standby or hibernation mode. Table 15.1 lists the default settings for the Home/Office Desk scheme.

Table 15.2 lists the default settings for the Portable/Laptop scheme.

Table 15.3 lists the default settings for the Presentation scheme.

Table 15.4 lists the default settings for the Always On scheme.

Table 15.5 lists the default settings for the Minimal Power Management scheme.

Table 15.6 lists the default settings for the Max Battery scheme.

Table 15.1   Default settings for the Home/Office Desk scheme.

Device Setting	When Plugged In	When Running on Batteries
Turn Off Monitor	After 20 Minutes	After 5 Minutes
Turn Off Hard Disks	Never	After 10 Minutes
System Standby	Never	After 5 Minutes
System Hibernates	Never	After 20 Minutes

Table 15.2   Default settings for the Portable/Laptop scheme.

Device Setting	When Plugged In	When Running on Batteries
Turn Off Monitor	After 15 Minutes	After 5 Minutes
Turn Off Hard Disks	After 30 Minutes	After 5 Minutes
System Standby	After 20 Minutes	After 5 Minutes
System Hibernates	After 3 Hours	After 2 Hours

Table 15.3   Default settings for the Presentation scheme.

Device Setting	When Plugged In	When Running on Batteries
Turn Off Monitor	Never	Never
Turn Off Hard Disks	Never	After 5 Minutes
System Standby	Never	After 15 Minutes
System Hibernates	Never	After 2 Hours

Table 15.4   Default settings for the Always On scheme.

Device Setting	When Plugged In	When Running on Batteries
Turn Off Monitor	After 20 Minutes	After 15 Minutes
Turn Off Hard Disks	Never	After 30 Minutes
System Standby	Never	Never
System Hibernates	Never	Never

Table 15.5   Default settings for the Minimal Power Management scheme.

Device Setting	When Plugged In	When Running on Batteries
Turn Off Monitor	After 15 Minutes	After 5 Minutes
Turn Off Hard Disks	Never	After 15 Minutes
System Standby	Never	After 5 Minutes
System Hibernates	Never	After 3 Hours

Table 15.6   Default settings for the Max Battery scheme.

Device Setting	When Plugged In	When Running on Batteries
Turn Off Monitor	After 15 Minutes	After 1 Minute
Turn Off Hard Disks	Never	After 3 Minutes
System Standby	After 20 Minutes	After 2 Minutes
System Hibernates	After 45 Minutes	After 1 Hour

Creating Your Own Power Scheme

If none of the default power schemes suit your needs, you can either change the default settings for the schemes already stored on your computer or create your own. It is always better to create a new power scheme than to save over the defaults. There is no "restore defaults" button in Power Options.

To create your own power scheme:

1. Open the Control Panel and then Power Options.

2. On the Power Schemes tab, select any power scheme.

3. In the drop-down lists for Turn Off Monitor, Turn Off Hard Disks, System Standby, and System Hibernates, configure the settings for when the computer is plugged in and when it is running on batteries.

4. Choose the Save As button.

5. In the Save Scheme dialog box, type a new name for the power scheme. Choose OK twice.

You can now use this power scheme whenever you want, and you can apply this power scheme when configuring hardware profiles later.

Understanding Hibernation, Standby, and Other Options

Hibernation, Standby, and other options can be used automatically or manually to conserve power on your portable computer. I have included "other options" here because some computers will use different terms to define the same state. For instance, some computers are configured to go to "sleep" instead of hibernate. You'll have to look at your computer to determine what terms are used. Here, I'll stick with the most common terms, hibernation and standby.

Note

Although your computer might be ACPI-compliant, it still might not be able to go into hibernation or on standby. Use of these modes can be prevented by devices and drivers that aren't Microsoft certified or by a lack of resources on the computer.

Hibernation

When a computer hibernates, it saves everything that is currently stored in RAM to the hard disk, turns off both the monitor and the hard disk, and then shuts down. When the computer is turned on again, the desktop is returned to the state it was in when it went into hibernation. You can configure hibernation properties in Power Options, or you can put your computer into hibernation manually. When a system is restored from hibernation, the process takes longer than restoring from standby. Hibernation is generally used at night or when you're away from your computer for similarly long periods.

To manually put your computer in hibernation:

1. Open the Control Panel and then Power Options.

2. On the Hibernate tab, make sure the Enable Hibernation checkbox is checked. Choose OK.

3. Choose Start | Turn Off Computer or Start | Shut Down.

4. In the resulting dialog box (which will differ depending on the scheme used and the options available), choose Hibernate.

Standby

You can configure the computer to go on standby automatically after it has been idle for a specific amount of time. When the computer is on standby, it conserves power by turning off hard disks and the monitor. Standby differs from hibernation in that the data stored in

RAM is not saved to the hard disk before the computer goes on standby. Computer operations can be resumed faster from standby than from hibernation, but a power loss will cause RAM to lose the data stored in it. Use standby mode when you will be away from your computer for a short period. When the computer operations are resumed, the desktop is exactly as you left it.

To put your computer on standby manually:

1. Choose Start | Turn Off Computer or Start | Shut Down.

2. In the resulting dialog box (which will differ depending on the scheme used and the options available), choose Standby.

Using a Password with Hibernation and Standby

You can require that a password be entered when the computer is awakened from hibernation or standby mode. This is a good idea if the computer is accessible to other users when you are away from it.

To require a password for awakening the computer:

1. Open the Control Panel and then Power Options.

2. On the Advanced tab, check the checkboxes Prompt For Password When Computer Resumes From Standby and Prompt For Password When Computer Resumes From Hibernation. Choose OK.

Configuring Power Buttons

When configuring power options, you should also specify what should happen when your computer's power button is pressed, when the laptop's lid is closed, and when the sleep button is pressed (if one exists). You can configure these options on the Advanced tab of the Power Options Properties dialog box, shown in Figure 15.3.

The options for each of these are as follows (these options can differ depending on the hardware installed on your system):

♦ *When I Close The Lid Of My Portable Computer*—Stand By, Hibernate, Do Nothing.

♦ *When I Press The Power Button On My Computer*—Do Nothing, Ask Me What To Do, Stand By, Hibernate, Shut Down.

♦ *When I Press The Sleep Button On My Computer*—Do Nothing, Ask Me What To Do, Stand By, Hibernate, Shut Down.

Setting Alarms

You can set two types of alarms from Power Options: Low Battery Alarms and Critical Battery Alarms. Although there are defaults, you can set these any way you see fit. You can

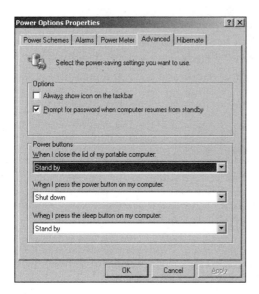

Figure 15.3
Setting options for power buttons.

specify when to activate each alarm by choosing a battery power level, such as 10 percent of power remaining, and you can set alarm actions when these levels are reached.

By default, a low battery alarm will occur when the battery power level reaches 11 percent. The notification is a text message. A critical battery alarm will occur when the battery power level reaches 5 percent, and the notification is a text message followed by the computer going into automatic hibernation. Hibernation assures that all data that is currently not saved to the hard drive will be saved before the battery runs down completely. You can change the battery levels by moving a slider bar to the level you want.

The available alarm actions for both low and critical battery alarms are:

♦ Sound Alarm

♦ Display Message

♦ When The Alarm Goes Off, The Computer Will: Stand By, Hibernate, Shut Down (you get to choose)

♦ Force Stand By Or Shutdown Even If A Program Stops Responding

♦ When The Alarm Occurs, Run This Program

When choosing to run a program when the alarm occurs, you'll really be configuring a Scheduled Task. While configuring the task, you can set a password if you need to and choose the task to run.

To configure alarms:

1. Open the Control Panel and then Power Options.

2. On the Alarms tab, move the sliders for both Low Battery Alarm and Critical Battery Alarm, or accept the defaults.

3. Choose the Alarm Action button for each alarm, and set options as needed. Figure 15.4 shows the Critical Battery Alarm Actions dialog box.

4. Choose OK in the Alarm Actions dialog box, and then in the Power Options Properties dialog box.

Power Management and Scheduled Tasks

If you have scheduled tasks configured for your laptop, you'll need to specify what you want the laptop to do if a scheduled task is supposed to run and the computer is running on batteries. You might want to run scheduled tasks only when the computer is plugged in, or you might have important tasks that must wake the computer even if it's on standby.

Note

To learn more about Scheduled Tasks, refer to Chapter 5.

The Settings tab of a scheduled task's dialog box has several options. Those that are related to power options and idle time are:

♦ Only Start The Task If The Computer Has Been Idle For At Least ___Minute(s)

♦ Stop The Task If The Computer Ceases To Be Idle

♦ Don't Start The Task If The Computer Is Running On Batteries (the default)

Figure 15.4
Alarm actions.

♦ Stop The Task If Battery Mode Begins (the default)

♦ Wake The Computer To Run This Task

To configure these options for a scheduled task:

1. Open the Control Panel and Scheduled Tasks.

2. Right-click a previously scheduled task, and choose Properties. If no tasks are scheduled, either create a task or refer to Chapter 5.

3. In the Properties dialog box for the scheduled task, select the Settings tab.

4. Configure the appropriate settings by checking the appropriate checkboxes. Choose OK.

Power Options and Airplanes

When you fly on an airplane, you'll be asked to turn off all portable electronic devices while the plane is taking off and landing and possibly even during the flight. Portable devices include not only portable video games and headsets but also your laptop.

To comply completely with this request, you'll need to physically shut down your computer. If a computer is on standby, it can still reactivate to run a scheduled task or respond to a pressed key. You must also turn off all cellular devices; therefore, if your modem is a cellular modem, you'll need to turn that off completely as well.

To turn off the computer, you'll need to choose Start | Shut Down and select Shut Down from the drop-down list.

Best Performance

To get the best performance possible out of your mobile computer, you'll want to use two new technologies provided in Windows XP Professional: ClearType and DualView. These features are used specifically on laptops to make it easier to see the screens and to incorporate laptops at the office, respectively.

There are other ways to enhance performance as well, including using System Properties, incorporating hardware profiles, copying files from your desktop, and using encryption to secure the laptop if it's ever stolen.

Choosing ClearType

ClearType can be used on laptops to make the screen fonts more readable and make them look more like what you see on a desktop computer. ClearType was created for flat screens like those on laptops and the newer versions of flat screens for desktops. ClearType won't work well on larger, more common computer monitors.

To configure your laptop computer to use ClearType:

1. Open the Control Panel and the Display icon.

2. On the Appearance tab, choose the Effects button.

3. In the Effects dialog box, check the checkbox Use The Following Method To Smooth Edges Of Screen Fonts.

4. In the drop-down list, select ClearType. Choose OK twice.

Using the System Properties Dialog Box

You can also enhance performance for your laptop from the System Properties dialog box (accessible from the System icon in the Control Panel). This dialog box has been introduced previously, but for laptop users a few options are worth noting.

The Computer Name Tab

Although you'll need to be logged on as an administrator to change settings on the Computer Name tab, you might need to do this when moving from office to office or from your office network to your home network. By choosing the Change button on this tab, you can change which network your computer is a member of. You can switch from a domain to a workgroup and vice versa, or you can simply change workgroups. For instance, at one office, you might be a member of the Office-Dallas workgroup; and at another office, you might need to log on as a member of the Office-Chicago workgroup. Additionally, you can choose the Network ID button to start the Network Identification Wizard, which can be used to connect you to a domain and create a user account. These types of manipulations are an integral part of laptop use for many administrators who visit multiple offices and domains.

The Hardware Tab and Hardware Profiles

You can do several things on the Hardware tab of System Properties, but for laptop users creating hardware profiles is the option I'll discuss here. As Chapter 12 explained, a *hardware profile* is a set of instructions that tells your computer what to do when the computer boots up. Hardware profiles are especially important for laptops because they will probably be used in different environments. For instance, you might configure one hardware profile for the office, a second one for use on the road, and a third one for working at home. The office profile could include a printer, a scanner, and a network connection. The mobile profile could include a portable printer and a telephone network connection. The home profile could include the family's printers, Zip drives, and a Remote Desktop connection.

Hardware profiles are created in the Hardware Profiles dialog box, accessible from the Hardware tab of System Properties. When you're creating a hardware profile, make sure that it includes the correct power options. For more information on hardware profiles, refer to Chapter 12.

The Advanced Tab

On the Advanced tab of System Properties, you can configure settings for performance (among other things). Configuring the performance for your laptop can improve battery life, increase the speed at which your laptop performs, and improve the appearance of the display.

There are four options:

♦ Let Windows Choose What's Best For My Computer

♦ Adjust For Best Appearance

♦ Adjust For Best Performance

♦ Custom

If you choose one of the first two in this list, the computer will be set for Windows XP mode; if you choose the third, it will be set in Windows Classic mode. If you choose Custom, you can configure almost any performance options you like. Listed next are some of the performance options available.

Note

In the Adjust For Best Performance setting, none of the following options are enabled. From this, you can deduce that enabling any of these settings uses system resources and that these settings are not necessary for the computer to function properly.

♦ Animate Windows When Minimizing And Maximizing

♦ Fade Or Slide Menus Into View

♦ Fade Or Slide ToolTips Into View

♦ Fade Out Menus After Clicking

♦ Show Shadows Under Menus

♦ Show Shadows Under Mouse Pointers

♦ Show Translucent Selection Rectangle

♦ Show Windows Contents While Dragging

♦ Slide Open Combo Boxes

♦ Slide Taskbar Buttons

♦ Smooth Edges Of Screen Fonts

♦ Smooth Scroll List Boxes

♦ Use A Background Image For Each Folder Type

- Use Common Tasks In Folders

- Use Drop Shadows For Icon Labels On The Desktop

- Use Visual Styles On Windows And Buttons

The Remote Tab

If you plan to use your computer to use Remote Assistance or Remote Desktop, you'll need to configure that on the Remote tab of System Properties. To allow Remote Assistance invitations to be sent from your laptop, you'll need to check the appropriate box. The same is true if you want to allow users to connect remotely to your laptop or if you want to connect remotely from your laptop from work. Figure 15.5 shows the Remote tab of the System Properties dialog box.

For more information on setting advanced options for and using Remote Assistance and Remote Desktop, refer to Chapter 11.

Using DualView

DualView is a new technology allowing you to attach a separate monitor to your laptop and view different items on each screen. Using DualView is similar to installing multiple monitors, as detailed in Chapter 8. DualView has several uses; on the laptop screen, for instance, you could be working on an Excel document, while the additional monitor could be showing the Internet or email. As with using multiple monitors on a desktop computer, you can use DualView on your laptop only if your display adapter and laptop support it. You can tell

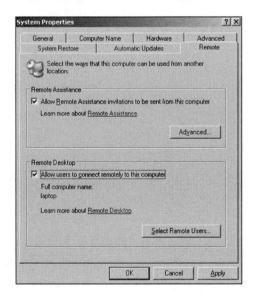

Figure 15.5
The Remote tab of the System Properties dialog box.

if you can plug in an additional monitor by looking at the back of your laptop computer. If there is a video port, you can plug in another monitor; however, this doesn't necessarily mean that DualView will work properly.

Installing a Second Monitor

If you have a video output port on your laptop, follow these steps to install the additional monitor:

1. Turn off the laptop computer.

2. Connect the monitor to the back of the laptop through the video port.

3. Plug in the monitor.

4. Turn on the laptop and the second monitor. (If the monitor is PnP-compatible, it will automatically start working.)

When you use multiple monitors with a desktop PC, you can choose a primary monitor. When you use DualView, the laptop monitor is always the primary monitor. The Display Properties dialog box should show two monitors. However, if only one monitor is shown, even though Multiple Monitors is listed and there is a second monitor attached and working, you'll need to install the monitor's driver or upgrade the BIOS on your laptop.

Note

You can install a second monitor and use it if there is a video port on the back of the laptop. However, if the laptop doesn't support DualView, you can use that extra monitor only as a duplicate monitor. The extra monitor won't be able to run separate programs, and you won't be able to drag open programs to it.

Configuring the Monitors

You can configure the new monitor (as well as the current one) through the Display Properties dialog box. When the new monitor is up and running, do the following:

1. Open the Control Panel and Display.

2. In the Display Properties dialog box, select the Settings tab.

3. Choose the Advanced button.

4. Select the Monitor tab, shown in Figure 15.6. Notice that two monitors are listed.

5. Highlight the monitor you want to configure, and choose the Properties button. In the Monitor Properties dialog box, you can add device drivers, enable or disable the monitor, and troubleshoot the monitor. Choose OK when finished.

6. On the Color Management tab of the Monitor Properties dialog box, you can set color profiles if necessary. Choose OK twice when finished.

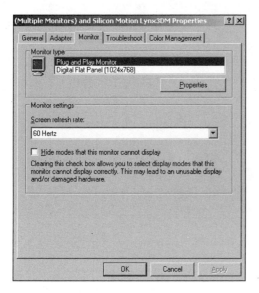

Figure 15.6
The Monitor tab.

Using the Monitors Independently or Together

With two monitors installed, you can use them to display the same desktop on both monitors, or you can use them side-by-side and drag items from one monitor to the other. Because these configurations are independent, to do either perform these steps:

1. Open the Control Panel and Display.

2. In the Display Properties dialog box, select the Settings tab.

3. Check the Extend My Windows Desktop Onto This Monitor checkbox to enable dragging from one monitor to the next, or clear this checkbox to use both monitors to display the same desktop.

Copying Files from Your Desktop Computer to the Laptop

The Files And Settings Transfer Wizard, introduced in Chapter 14, is an excellent way to transfer files from your desktop computer to your laptop. You probably won't want to transfer settings, though, because you've probably already configured the laptop to work just the way you'd like through hardware profiles and such. However, if you have a new laptop, the fastest way to get all of those desktop files over to it is to use the wizard.

The Custom setting of the Files And Settings Transfer Wizard is the only setting not covered in Chapter 14, and this is the setting you'll want to choose when copying files and folders from your desktop computer to your laptop. Although you can transfer files in other ways (using the Briefcase and Offline Files), this is a good place to start if the laptop hasn't been synchronized with the desktop and if files and folders have never been transferred by any other means.

To use the Files And Settings Transfer Wizard to transfer specific files and folders to your laptop:

1. Log onto the laptop as an administrator.

2. Open the Files And Settings Transfer Wizard by choosing Start | Programs | Accessories | System Tools | Files And Settings Transfer Wizard.

3. Choose Next to start the wizard. On the Which Computer Is This page, select New Computer.

Note

The computer you will obtain files from can be running Windows 9x, Windows ME, Windows NT 4, Windows 2000, or Windows XP (32-bit).

4. Place a new, formatted floppy disk into the laptop's floppy drive. On the Do You Have A Windows XP CD page, choose Next.

5. Once the Wizard Disk is created, go to the desktop computer from which you want to transfer the files, and place the Wizard Disk in that computer's floppy disk drive.

6. At the desktop computer, choose Start | Run, type "a:\fastwiz" in the Open box, and choose OK. Choose Next to start the Files And Settings Transfer Wizard.

7. On the Which Computer Is This page, select Old Computer.

8. On the Select A Transfer Method page, select either Direct Cable, Home Or Small Office Network, Floppy Drive Or Other Removable Media, or Other to indicate how you want to transfer the files. Because laptops and desktops are often used in an office network, in this example I'll choose Other and browse to a shared folder on the laptop. (The wizard doesn't change much with the other settings; for detailed information on all types of transfer methods, see Chapter 14.)

9. On the What Do You Want To Transfer page, select Files Only. Check the checkbox Let Me Select A Custom List Of Files And Settings When I Click Next (For Advanced Users), and choose Next.

10. On the Select Custom Files And Settings page, shown in Figure 15.7, highlight each folder you want to transfer from the Specific Folders tree, and choose either Add File or Add Folder.

11. On the same page, select the file types you want to transfer from the File Types tree, and choose Add File Type. In the Add A File Type dialog box, select a registered file type, or create a new type in the Other window. Choose Next when finished.

12. When the transfer is complete, choose Finish and return to the laptop. If the Files And Settings Transfer Wizard is still running, choose Next. If not, start the wizard again. (If you're starting the wizard again, choose I Don't Need The Wizard Disk. I Have Already

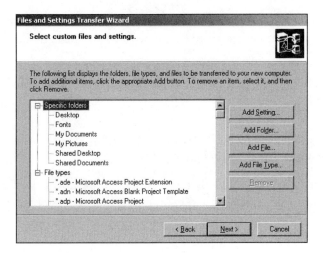

Figure 15.7
Selecting custom files and settings.

Collected My Files And Settings From My Old Computer on the Do You Have A Windows XP CD page.)

13. Browse to the location of the saved files, and choose Next. The files will begin transferring. When this process is completed, choose Finish. Then log off and log back on to apply the changes.

Using Encryption

Encryption can be used to protect files and folders stored on your laptop. Encryption is transparent to the user, meaning that you do not have to decrypt files manually before working with them; they are decrypted automatically. Encryption protects the laptop in case of unauthorized access or theft because only the person who encrypted the data can open the files. Encryption should be used on all mobile devices when possible.

Before using encryption on your laptop, make sure you understand the following:

♦ The file system must be NTFS.

♦ Encrypted files cannot be compressed, and compressed files cannot be encrypted.

♦ Encryption does not prevent files and folders from being deleted; it only prevents them from being read.

To fully protect your laptop by using encryption, you should encrypt the My Documents folder if that's where you save most of your files. This ensures that all of the files in this folder are always encrypted. If you encrypt the My Documents folder before working on a document in it, the data is always encrypted and is never written to the disk as plain text at any time.

You should also encrypt sensitive data on any laptop that is a member of a domain. This protects the network if the laptop is stolen or if the laptop is used for offline attacks of the network.

Finally, you should disable System Restore before encrypting the data, and then enable it again after encryption is done. This ensures that the encrypted files can never be restored to an unencrypted state.

To safeguard your laptop by using encryption:

1. Log on as an administrator. Open the Control Panel and System.

2. In the System Properties dialog box, select the System Restore tab, and check the Turn Off System Restore checkbox. Choose OK. Choose Yes in the System Restore dialog box to verify that you want to turn off System Restore.

3. Right-click the My Documents folder on the desktop or in Windows Explorer, and choose Properties.

4. On the General tab, choose the Advanced button.

5. Check the Encrypt Contents To Secure Data checkbox.

6. Repeat Steps 3 through 5 for all folders that contain personal or sensitive data.

7. Open the System Properties dialog box, and select the System Restore tab. Enable System Restore by clearing the Turn Off System Restore checkbox. Choose OK. (Steps 8 through 10 are optional.)

8. Open Windows Explorer, and choose Tools | Options.

9. In the Folder Options dialog box, select the View tab.

10. Check the checkbox Show Encrypted Or Compressed NTFS Files In Color, and choose OK.

Offline Files

If you use a laptop frequently, you probably do a lot of work while on the road or while away from the office. This usually means that your laptop isn't connected to the office network and you can't access the files on the network. This problem is solved by configuring your laptop to use files and folders offline, meaning that you save network files to your laptop so they're accessible when the laptop isn't physically connected to the network. When you reconnect to the network, any changes you've made are synchronized with the files on the network. During this process, you can either write over the network files, save your files to the network with different names, or both.

For you to use files and folders offline, they must first be shared. Sharing files and folders has been previously discussed and is usually done by the network administrator.

Note

Although the feature is called Offline Files, you can also use programs and folders offline. You cannot, however, access network resources such as printers or other hardware when not connected to the network.

Configuring Your Laptop to Use Offline Files

Before you can connect to a network and use offline files, you must enable your computer to do so. To enable your computer to use offline files:

1. Verify that you are not using Fast User Switching; if you are, turn it off. To turn off Fast User Switching, do the following:

   a. Open the Control Panel and User Accounts.

   b. Choose Change The Way Users Log On Or Off, and uncheck the Use Fast User Switching checkbox. Choose Apply Options.

2. Open My Computer, and choose Tools | Folder Options.

3. Select the Offline Files tab, and check the Enable Offline Files checkbox. Choose OK. See Figure 15.8.

Offline Files Configuration Options

Several configuration options are available when you're enabling or using offline files. These options and their defaults are shown in Figure 15.8 and explained in this section.

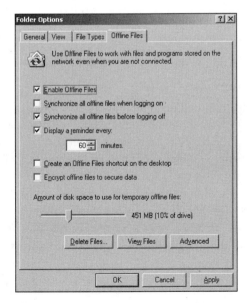

Figure 15.8
Enabling offline files.

> **Note**
>
> *Synchronization occurs when the files on the laptop and the files on the network are compared for differences. Both sets of files are then updated to reflect the changes.*

Synchronize All Offline Files When Logging On

If you want to have the most up-to-date network files available to you offline, you'll need to select this option. This ensures that you get a full synchronization each time you log onto the network. If this option isn't checked, you'll get complete files but perhaps not the most recent version.

Synchronize All Offline Files Before Logging Off

This option is checked by default and specifies that files should be synchronized each time you log off the network. This ensures that the network has the latest files and that other users can access the latest versions of files if the files are shared.

Display a Reminder Every ___ Minutes

You can set this option to send a reminder balloon every so often to notify you when computers go offline. If you do not want to receive notifications, uncheck the checkbox. By default, it is checked.

Create An Offline Files Shortcut On The Desktop

You can check this box to place a shortcut to the offline files on your desktop. From this shortcut, you can access files, view files, and work with files.

Encrypt Offline Files To Secure Data

By checking this checkbox, you can encrypt your offline files. This is a good idea because using offline files requires them to be copied to your computer; by default, these files are not encrypted.

Amount Of Disk Space To Use For Temporary Offline Files

By default, 10 percent of the laptop's hard drive is used for temporary offline files. If your files are large, contain many graphics, or contain database information, you might need to increase this number. You can do so by sliding the bar to the necessary number.

Delete Files

By choosing the Delete Files button, you can see what offline files are available and delete them if necessary. This enables you to delete these files from your computer while leaving them on the network server. You can also choose to delete only temporary offline files or to delete both the temporary offline version and the version that is configured to always be available offline.

View Files

When you choose the View Files button, the Offline Files Folder window opens. This shows all files that are being used and stored offline.

Advanced

By choosing the Advanced button, you can specify what your computer should do when it loses the connection to the network server or other computer that stores offline files. There are two choices:

♦ *Notify Me And Begin Working Offline*—Allows you to continue working on the files even if the connection is lost. This is the default.

♦ *Never Allow My Computer To Go Offline*—Specifies that network files be unavailable if you lose your connection to the network.

You can also configure exceptions to this rule by choosing Add and adding a computer on the network. This computer can have different settings for advanced options apart from the other computers on the network.

Making Files Available Offline

The first time you make a file available offline, you must not only enable the Offline Files tool but also perform other tasks. To use offline files, you must have a network drive mapped in My Computer. Network drives are letters from a to z that represent folders and network locations. If you do not have a mapped network drive, you'll need to create one.

Mapping a Network Drive

To map a network drive:

1. Log onto the laptop as an administrator.

2. Open My Computer.

3. Choose Tools | Map Network Drive.

4. In the Map Network Drive dialog box, select a drive letter from the Drive drop-down list, and browse to the folder in the Folder window.

5. To connect to this network drive each time you log onto the network, leave the check in the Reconnect At Logon checkbox. If you don't want to connect to this drive at each logon, remove the check. Choose Finish.

Using the Offline Files Wizard

After you have mapped a network drive, you can begin using offline files by running the Offline Files Wizard:

1. Open the Control Panel.

2. Right-click the network drive, and choose Make Available Offline.

3. Choose Next to start the Offline Files Wizard.

4. On the first page of the wizard, you can check the checkbox Automatically Synchronize The Offline Files When I Log On And Off My Computer (this is optional). Choose Next.

5. Check the checkboxes Enable Reminders and Create A Shortcut To The Offline Files Folder On My Desktop if you want to enable these features. Choose Finish.

6. In the Confirm Offline Subfolders dialog box, specify how you want to handle the folder's subfolders. Either choose Yes, Make This Folder And All Its Subfolders Available Offline, or choose No, Make Only This Folder Available Offline. Choose OK.

As shown in Figure 15.9, synchronization begins. When this process is completed, you can begin using the files from the network drive offline.

Using Offline Files

Now that the offline files have been configured, you can begin using the files and folders from your laptop. If you created a shortcut on your desktop, you can access them there, or you can access them from the network drive icon in My Computer. As you can see in Figure 15.10, the icons for the shared folders that are being used offline have new icons beside them that are squares with blue arrows in them. These icons indicate that these files have been synchronized with the network computer and that they are available.

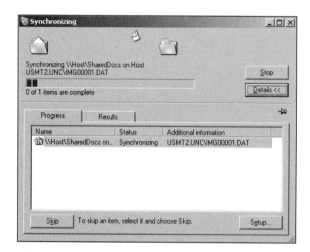

Figure 15.9
Synchronization begins.

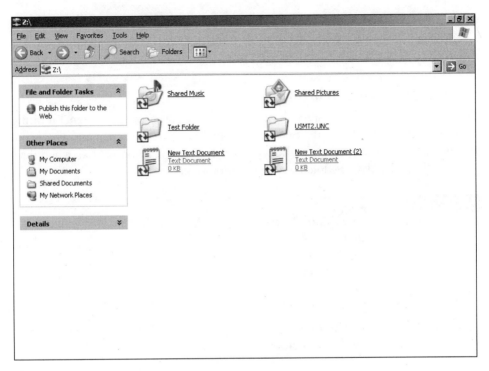

Figure 15.10
Offline files.

You can view all available offline files through My Computer. To see all of the available files on the network:

1. Open My Computer.

2. Choose Tool | Options, and select the Offline Files tab.

3. Choose the View Files button.

File Conflicts

If you are using a network file offline and you change that file, when the files are synchronized between the network and the laptop, the changes you made are saved to the network file. This happens only if you are the only person modifying the file. However, in many instances, when you are using a shared file offline, others are doing the same. Still other users might be changing the network copy of the file. As you can imagine, this can cause problems when multiple copies of the same file exist and they are all being modified at the same time. To solve this problem, you are given choices when you reconnect to the network and synchronize your files.

These choices include keeping your version, keeping the current network version, or keeping both. If you've changed an offline file, and someone deletes the file from the network, you can keep your version and save it to the network or delete it from your computer. Finally, if multiple users are logged onto your computer with files open from the same shared folder, you will not be able to synchronize your files until their files have been closed.

Synchronization Manager

The Synchronization Manager can be used to take the guesswork out of synchronizing and modifying offline files. Using the Synchronization Manager, you can manually synchronize specific files and folders, configure how you want synchronization to work when the computer is idle, and add a scheduled synchronization task.

Note

You can use the Synchronization Manager for synchronizing offline Web pages as well; see the next section.

To use the Synchronization Manager for manually synchronizing files:

1. Choose Start | Run, and type "mobsync" in the Open box. Choose OK.

2. In the Items To Synchronize dialog box, highlight the file or folder you want to synchronize, and choose the Synchronize button.

To use the Synchronization Manager for configuring logon and logoff behavior:

1. Choose Start | Run, and type "mobsync" in the Open box. Choose OK.

2. In the Items To Synchronize dialog box, choose the Setup button.

3. On the Logon/Logoff tab, open the When I Am Using This Network Connection drop-down list, and select the connection you are using to obtain your offline files.

4. In the Automatically Synchronize The Selected Items area, check any of the following checkboxes to configure how synchronization should take place:

   ♦ When I Log On To My Computer

   ♦ When I Log Off My Computer

   ♦ Ask Me Before Synchronizing The Items

   Choose OK.

To use the Synchronization Manager for configuring idle computer behavior:

1. Choose Start | Run, and type "mobsync" in the Open box. Choose OK.

2. In the Items To Synchronize dialog box, choose the Setup button.

3. On the On Idle tab, open the When I Am Using This Network Connection drop-down list, and select the connection you are using to obtain your offline files.

4. In the Synchronize The Following Checked Items area, check the boxes for the offline files you want to have synchronized when your computer is idle.

5. Check the Synchronize The Selected Items While My Computer Is Idle checkbox. Choose the Advanced button.

6. In the Idle Settings dialog box, set the number of minutes the computer must be idle before synchronization takes place. You can also specify how often you want the computer to resynchronize when the computer remains idle.

7. To conserve power when the laptop is running on batteries, check the Prevent Synchronization When My Computer Is Running On Batteries checkbox. Choose OK twice.

To use the Synchronization Manager for scheduling a synchronization task:

1. Choose Start | Run, and type "mobsync" in the Open box. Choose OK.

2. In the Items To Synchronize dialog box, choose the Setup button.

3. On the Scheduled tab, choose the Add button.

4. Choose Next to start the Scheduled Synchronization Wizard.

5. On the first page of the wizard, open the When I Am Using This Network Connection drop-down list, and select the connection you are using to obtain your offline files.

6. Check the checkboxes for the offline files for which you want to schedule synchronization. To allow your computer to connect to the network if it isn't connected, check the checkbox If My Computer Is Not Connected When This Scheduled Synchronization Begins, Automatically Connect For Me. Choose Next.

7. Select a start time (when the task is to be performed) and a start date. Choose Next.

8. Type a name for the scheduled task, and choose Next.

9. Verify the schedule and the task. Choose Finish, OK, and then Close.

Using Web Pages Offline

Besides files, folders, and applications, you can also use Web pages offline. You view the pages in Internet Explorer, and you configure this feature through the Synchronization Manager or through the Tools menu in Internet Explorer. Using Web pages offline is great for laptop users because the computer isn't always connected to the Internet or to the network. There are three options for using Web pages offline:

♦ Make The Current Web Page Available Offline

♦ Make An Existing Favorite Item Available Offline

♦ Save A Web Page On Your Computer

Making Web Pages Available

To make Web pages available offline:

1. Log onto the laptop and then onto the Internet.

2. Locate the page you want to make available offline.

3. Choose Favorites | Add To Favorites.

4. In the Add Favorite dialog box, check the Make Available Offline checkbox, and choose the Customize button.

5. Choose Next to start the Offline Favorite Wizard.

6. On the first page of the wizard, specify whether you want to make available the pages linked to the current Web page. See Figure 15.11. Select No or Yes. If you select Yes, you'll also need to specify how many levels of linked pages you want to store offline. Because downloading linked files takes up quite a bit of hard drive space, you should make sure you really need the information offline before obtaining it. Choose Next.

7. Specify how you would like to synchronize this Web page. Select one of the following:

    ♦ Only When I Choose Synchronize From The Tools Menu

    ♦ I Would Like To Create A New Schedule

    Choose Next.

8. If you choose to create a schedule, you'll need to set a day and time for the task by specifying how often to synchronize the page, what the name of the task is, and whether the computer should connect to the Internet to synchronize if it's not connected when the task is scheduled to run. Choose Next.

Figure 15.11
Setting up offline Web pages.

9. In the Does This Site Require A Password area, type your username and password if the site requires them; otherwise, select No. Choose Finish, then OK.

Using the Tools Menu

To use the Tools menu in Internet Explorer to synchronize your offline Web pages:

1. Open Internet Explorer, and choose Tool | Synchronize.

2. In the Items To Synchronize dialog box, select the Web page you want to synchronize, and choose the Synchronize Now button.

In the Items To Synchronize dialog box, you can choose the Setup button to open the Synchronization Settings dialog box. Here, you can make configuration changes, as described previously, having to do with the connection, logon and logoff properties, synchronization behavior when the computer is idle, and synchronization schedules. Both the Items To Synchronize dialog box and the Synchronization Settings dialog box are shown in Figure 15.12.

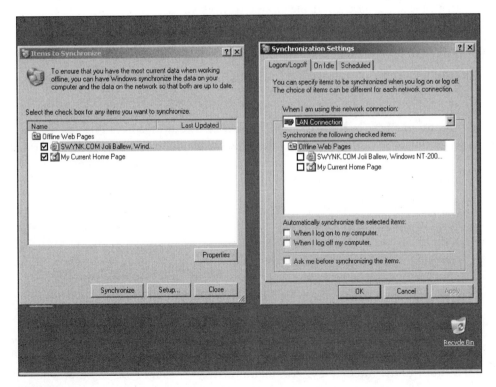

Figure 15.12
Setting up synchronization for offline Web pages.

Synchronization Manager

You can also use the Synchronization Manager to manage Web pages that are being accessed offline. In the Synchronization Manager, you can see the Web page's download size and when it was last synchronized. You can also schedule synchronization and limit the amount of hard disk space the Web page can use. Finally, you can require that an email message be sent to you when the Web page changes.

To configure offline Web pages by using the Synchronization Manager:

1. Make sure you've previously designated a Web page for offline use and synchronized it with your computer.

2. Choose Start | Run, type "mobsync" in the Open box, and choose OK.

3. In the Items To Synchronize dialog box, highlight the offline Web page for which you want to set properties, and choose the Properties button.

4. In the Web page's Properties dialog box, select the Web Document page, and verify that Make This Page Available Online is checked.

5. Select the Schedule tab. You can create a schedule, as described earlier, by choosing the Add button, or you can select an existing schedule and edit it.

6. On the Download tab, specify how many levels of linked pages you want to download.

7. On the same tab, check the Limit Hard Disk Usage For This Page To checkbox, and select a number (in KB). To configure advanced download options, choose the Advanced button. In the resulting dialog box, you can limit what is downloaded from the Web page, including images, sound and audio, ActiveX controls, and Java applets. Make changes as necessary, and choose OK.

8. On the Download tab, set an alert so that if the Web page changes you'll be sent an email message. Check the checkbox When This Page Changes, Send An E-Mail To, and type an email address and mail server. If the site requires a username and password, configure them by choosing the Login button. Close all dialog boxes when finished.

Offline File Access and Caching

You can specify whether and how files within one of your shared folders can be cached locally when the shared folder is accessed by other users. Caching is used when the computer stores files temporarily, and the word "caching" is used in a number of contexts. When you connect to the Internet and visit multiple sites, you can revisit these sites quickly by using the Back button in your browser because those network addresses are cached in your computer's memory. You can also check the History folder for recently cached addresses. Offline files and folders use caching to store the data temporarily. With shared folders, you can configure how users will cache your shared folder's data. There are three options:

◆ *Manual Caching Of Documents*—This option is the default, and it requires that users manually specify any files they want to have available when they are working offline. This is the ideal setting for files that several users will access and modify. The server version of the file is always opened.

◆ *Automatic Caching Of Documents*—This setting makes every open file in a shared folder available offline. It's a good setting for folders that contain users' documents. The files in the folder are automatically deleted as newer versions are created and accessed. The server version of the file is always opened.

◆ *Automatic Caching Of Programs And Documents*—This setting is recommended for folders that contain read-only data or applications that are run from the network. Opened files are automatically downloaded and made available when users are working offline. The files in the folder are automatically deleted as newer versions are created and accessed. The server version of the file is always opened.

Making Offline Files Unavailable

If you do not want to be able to access files from other computers while you are working offline and are disconnected from the network, you can make offline files unavailable.

To make offline files unavailable:

1. Open My Computer.

2. Choose Tools | Folder Options.

3. On the Offline Files tab, choose the Advanced button.

4. In the Offline Files–Advanced Settings dialog box, choose the Add button.

5. Choose the Browse button, and locate the computer that you do not want to be available when you are disconnected from the network.

6. Select the option Never Allow My Computer To Go Offline. Choose OK three times.

The Briefcase Tool

Using the Briefcase tool is another way to work on files and folders when you're not sitting at your desktop computer. You can use Briefcase to transfer files and folders from your desktop to your laptop by using a direct cable connection, removable media, or a network connection. The Briefcase tool is similar to the Offline Files tool in that synchronization plays a part in keeping the two sets of files up-to-date, but there are several differences, too. In this section, you'll learn how to use Briefcase, how it differs from Offline Files, how to use Briefcase with removable media, and how synchronization works.

Briefcase or Offline Files?

From reading the previous section on offline files, you can tell that offline files are generally used to work with shared files on a network (in either a workgroup or a domain). Offline files are used in networks because users can work on the files while away from their desks or from their laptops and have those files automatically synchronized when the users log off or log back onto the network.

The Briefcase tool is not so efficient in that scenario. Briefcase is most effectively used if you have a single desktop computer and a single laptop, or if you have only two or three computers in your office or workgroup. The typical scenario involves a desktop computer and a laptop; files are transferred to the laptop, modified, and then returned to the desktop computer. Those two sets of files are then synchronized so that both sets contain up-to-date information. Briefcase allows you to transfer files between computers by using a direct cable connection, a network connection, or removable media. You can create multiple briefcases to organize the data you work with.

Creating a New Briefcase

Older versions of Windows have a Briefcase icon on the desktop; Windows XP Professional does not. You can create a briefcase on your desktop very easily, though.

To create a new briefcase on the desktop:

1. Right-click an empty space on the desktop, and choose New | Briefcase.

2. Double-click the new briefcase to open it. The Welcome To The Windows Briefcase dialog box appears.

3. Read the instructions, and choose Finish.

To place files in the new briefcase:

1. Using Windows Explorer or other means, select the file or folder you want to place in the briefcase.

2. Right-click the file or folder, and drag it to the new briefcase on the desktop.

3. Choose Make Sync Copy.

Fundamentals

After you've created the new briefcase and placed files in it, you can use removable media to transfer files to other computers. There are better ways to transfer data, of course, but this serves as a good introduction to the Briefcase tool.

To transfer information from the briefcase to another computer:

1. Place a disk in the floppy drive. Right-click the new briefcase, and choose Send To | 3 _ Floppy (A:).

2. Once the files have been transferred, remove the floppy disk, and take it to the computer you want to copy the files to.

3. On the remote computer, place the floppy disk in the drive, and double-click the floppy-disk icon to see the disk's contents.

4. Work on the files as necessary, and save the changes to the disk.

5. Take the modified disk back to the original computer, and open Briefcase.

6. Choose Briefcase | Update All.

7. In the Update New Briefcase dialog box, either choose the Update button to update all files, or highlight the files you want to update and then choose the Update button.

Note

You cannot save a briefcase to another briefcase.

After you've changed files on the remote computer, you can drag those files back to the floppy disk and take the disk back to the original computer. Although this is technically the same as just saving files to a floppy disk and walking them over to the new computer, it is the only way to use Briefcase if the computers aren't networked, even though Briefcase offers much more functionality than this. For you to use Briefcase fully, the computers must be connected through either a direct cable connection or a network.

Using Briefcase When the Computers Are Networked or Physically Connected

If the two computers are connected by a direct cable or a network, Briefcase can be used much more effectively. (To explain how Briefcase works in the most common scenario, I'll use the terms "desktop computer" and "laptop computer" to indicate the two computers being used. Keep in mind, though, that the laptop computer described in this section can also be another desktop computer.)

Briefcase separates the files you work with into two categories: files that were created on the desktop computer, transferred to the laptop, and then modified; and files that were created on the laptop and have no counterpart on the desktop computer. The files that do not have counterparts are called *orphan files*. You can check the status of any file in a briefcase by opening the briefcase and choosing View | Details, or by right-clicking the file, choosing Properties, and selecting the Update Status tab. Figure 15.13 shows a briefcase with two files in it; one is up-to-date, and the other is an orphan file.

To use Briefcase between two computers such as a desktop computer and a laptop computer:

1. Make sure both computers are physically connected by either a direct cable or a network.

2. On the laptop computer, open your briefcase.

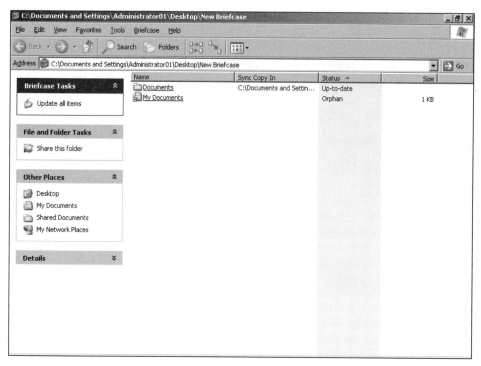

Figure 15.13
A briefcase.

3. Open My Network Places, and drag the files you want to work on to the briefcase. This will not remove the files from the desktop computer.

4. Close My Network Places. You can now disconnect from the network if necessary and continue to work on these files normally.

After you've modified the files and reconnected to the network, you'll need to synchronize the files. To synchronize the files:

1. Make sure the network or direct connection is established, and open the briefcase on the laptop computer.

2. To synchronize all files, choose Briefcase | Update All. To synchronize specific files, choose Briefcase | Update Selection.

3. In the Update New Briefcase dialog box, either choose the Update button to update all files, or highlight the files you want to update and then choose the Update button.

This updating ensures that the files on both computers are the same and are up-to-date. You can also prevent any future updates between these files by choosing Briefcase | Split From Original.

Remote Desktop for the Laptop User

Remote Desktop was detailed at length in Chapter 11, but I will briefly review it here with an emphasis on applications for the laptop user. Remote Desktop is the perfect solution for mobile users who have access to a domain or workgroup via phone lines, satellite, or cable modems. Using Remote Desktop, you can dial into a domain server, your own desktop computer, or a workgroup host computer, and access your desktop as if you were sitting right in front of the computer.

To use Remote Desktop in a domain requires the assistance of your network administrator, and in this setting your laptop will probably come already configured to use Remote Desktop. To use Remote Desktop to dial into your home computer or a workgroup computer requires that you set this up yourself, as described in Chapter 11. However, connecting using Remote Desktop is about the same for all scenarios, making this section a good read for any mobile user who will be using Remote Desktop.

Setting Up the Desktop at Work or at Home

Before you can use your laptop to connect to your desktop at work or at home, you'll need to configure the desktop computer. Before starting, make sure the following conditions have been met:

♦ The desktop computer runs Windows XP Professional.

♦ The desktop computer is connected to the Internet through an ISP or a LAN.

♦ The desktop computer has Remote Desktop enabled.

♦ You are the administrator of your computer or a member of the Administrators or Remote Desktop group.

♦ Remote users have been selected.

If you need help with any of these tasks, refer to Chapter 11.

Setting Up the Laptop

Before you can use your laptop to connect to your desktop at work or at home, you'll need to configure the laptop computer. Before starting, make sure the following conditions have been met:

♦ The laptop computer has Remote Desktop Connection client software installed.

♦ The laptop computer is connected to the Internet through an ISP or a LAN.

♦ Appropriate permissions to connect to the desktop computer have been established.

If you need help with any of these tasks, refer to Chapter 11.

Using Remote Desktop from the Laptop

Once Remote Desktop has been configured, you can connect to your desktop computer from your laptop through the Internet. The Internet connection can be a phone connection to an ISP or can be provided by your LAN.

Connecting through a LAN

To start a remote desktop session through a LAN:

1. Make sure the desktop computer is turned on and connected to a LAN.

2. Log off the host computer, and leave the Log On To Windows screen up. This will protect the computer from any unauthorized access while you are away from it.

3. On the laptop computer, open the Remote Desktop Connection by choosing Start | Programs | Accessories | Communications.

4. Expand Options to show the full dialog box.

5. On the General tab, type the computer name, or select it from the Computer drop-down list. Next, type a username and a password that give you permission to log onto the remote computer. Type the domain name (although on a LAN, this isn't always necessary).

6. On the Display tab, choose a remote desktop size and the number of colors you want to use.

7. On the Local Resources tab, choose sound and keyboard settings.

8. On the Experience tab, choose LAN (10Mbps Or Higher).

9. Return to the General tab, and choose Save As.

10. Type a name for this connection, such as "Office Connection – LAN". Choose Save.

11. Choose Connect.

12. Log onto the remote desktop the same way you would log onto it if you were sitting at the host computer. Use your name and password.

You can now work on your computer as if you were actually sitting in front of it. The computer at the office will not be accessible by any other user without a proper name and password. If someone logs onto your office computer, the session with the connecting computer will be terminated automatically.

Connecting through the Internet

To start a remote desktop session through the Internet:

1. Make sure the desktop computer is turned on and connected to the Internet.

2. If possible, log off of the host computer, and leave the Log On To Windows screen up. This will protect the computer from any unauthorized access while you are away

from it. (You might not be able to log off a standalone computer or a computer in a workgroup and still maintain an Internet connection.)

3. On the connecting computer, open the Remote Desktop Connection as described earlier.

4. Expand Options to show the full dialog box.

5. On the General tab, type the public IP address or the URL address of the computer. Next, type a username and a password that give you permission to log onto the remote computer. Type the domain name.

6. On the Display tab, choose a remote desktop size and the number of colors you want to use.

7. On the Local Resources tab, choose sound and keyboard settings.

8. On the Experience tab, choose the type of connection you have. Do *not* choose LAN (10 Mbps Or Higher).

9. Return to the General tab, and choose Save As.

10. Type a name for this connection, such as "Office Connection–Internet". Choose Save.

11. Choose Connect. If you're prompted with multiple Internet connections, choose one.

12. Log onto the remote desktop the same way you would log onto it if you were sitting at the host computer. Use your name and password.

You can now work on your remote computer as if you were actually sitting in front of it. The computer at the office will not be accessible by any other user without a proper name and password. If someone logs onto your office computer, the session with the connecting computer will be terminated automatically.

After you've established a connection, using the remote desktop is easy. The remote computer's desktop is shown in its own window, and you can perform tasks on the remote computer through this interface. You can cut and paste items from the remote computer to the local one with almost any recent version of Windows. The computers must be able to use clipboard sharing for this to work properly, and cutting and pasting work the same way between computers as they do between documents. Just locate the data on the remote computer, right-click, and choose Copy. Locate a local file on the local computer, right-click, and choose Paste.

Ending a Session

You can end a session in two ways. Either you can disconnect from the session without ending it, or you can simply log off and end the session entirely.

To end a session without disconnecting from it:

1. In the Remote Desktop window, choose Start | Shut Down.

2. In the Shut Down Windows dialog box, choose Disconnect.

To end a session and completely disconnect:

1. In the Remote Desktop window, choose Start | Shut Down.

2. In the Shut Down Windows dialog box, choose Log Off <username>.

Message Queuing

Microsoft Message Queuing (MSMQ) is a utility similar to email except that email transmits messages between *people*, and Message Queuing transfers messages between *applications*. When an email message is sent to a recipient, the message is held in a queue (perhaps at your ISP or on your domain's email server) until the recipient logs on and can retrieve it. The same is true of Message Queuing applications. While MSMQ is mainly used by system administrators and software developers in a domain, as an end user you might be asked to install MSMQ or understand MSMQ concepts.

Although Message Queuing can be used by any user on any computer, it is especially useful for laptop users because they are not always available on the corporate network and because they change locations frequently. MSMQ can also be used over HTTP transports, bringing the Internet into the equation. If messages are sent to computers while they are not on the network, a Message Queuing server saves the messages for later delivery.

For domain users, an administrator will set up the Message Queuing server, but he or she might ask you to install the Message Queuing service on your computer. If you are not a member of a domain, but you would like to use MSMQ in your workgroup, you can do that as well.

Installing Message Queuing

Message Queuing isn't installed by default with Windows XP Professional. To install Message Queuing does not require that you have the Windows XP Professional CD.

To install Message Queuing:

1. Log on as an administrator.

2. Open the Control Panel and then Add Or Remove Programs.

3. Choose the Add/Remove Windows Components button.

4. On the Windows Components Wizard page, check the Message Queuing checkbox, and choose the Details button.

5. In the Message Queuing dialog box, do the following:

   ♦ If your computer belongs to a domain, leave the Active Directory Integration checkbox checked. However, if you want to operate Message Queuing in a workgroup mode, uncheck the Active Directory Integration checkbox.

♦ If you do not want to install Message Queuing Triggers, clear the checkbox for that option. Triggers allow messages to interact with a COM (Component Object Model) component or an application.

♦ If you will send messages using HTTP, check the MSMQ HTTP Support checkbox.

♦ Leave the Common checkbox checked.

6. Choose OK, Next, Finish, and Close.

7. Right-click My Computer, and choose Manage.

8. Expand the Services And Applications tree, and expand Message Queuing. See Figure 15.14.

Using Message Queuing for Domain Users

If you are a member of a Windows 2000 or XP domain, Message Queuing is transparent. Windows XP Professional computers automatically detect the domain controllers when moved to new sites and update the directory service appropriately. Messages are then automatically sent to the computer.

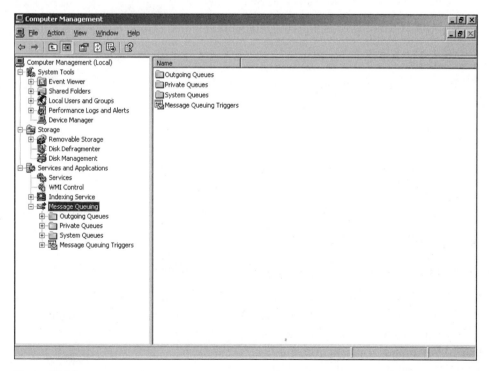

Figure 15.14
Message Queuing.

For laptop users who visit Windows NT 4 domains, the sites are not detected automatically and must be configured manually. To manually configure a new site and locate a domain controller in a Windows NT 4 environment:

1. Log on as an administrator.

2. Right-click My Computer, and choose Manage.

3. Right-click Message Queuing, and choose Properties.

4. In the Message Queuing Properties dialog box, select the Mobile tab.

5. In the New Site window's drop-down list, select the site you want to move to.

6. When prompted to restart the computer, do so.

For laptop users who need to change the domain controllers and thus change their supporting server:

1. Log on as an administrator.

2. Right-click My Computer, and choose Manage.

3. Right-click Message Queuing, and choose Properties.

4. In the Message Queuing Properties dialog box, select the Message Queuing tab.

5. Type the name of the new server. Choose OK.

To stop the Message Queuing service:

1. Log on as an administrator.

2. Open Components Services by choosing Start | Programs | Administrative Tools | Component Services.

3. Expand the Component Services tree, right-click My Computer, and choose Properties.

4. Select the MSDTC tab.

5. In the Service Control Status For MSDTC Version area, choose the Stop button.

In a domain setting, the system administrator will configure your computer for message queue length, message size, DNS (Domain Name System) properties, routing details, and other pertinent information. For more information on Message Queuing, open the Computer Management Console, expand the Services And Applications tree, highlight the Message Queuing tree, and choose Help.

Using Message Queuing for Workgroup Users

If you want to use Message Queuing in a workgroup, Message Queuing must be installed on any workgroup computer that will participate. When installing this feature, you must make sure that the Active Directory Integration checkbox is *not* checked. (See the previous installation directions.) If you are a system administrator or software developer and want to use MSMQ, you'll need to read the Help files supplied with Windows XP Professional, or perhaps purchase a book on the subject. Message Queuing is a complex utility requiring planning, configuration, and security management, and system administrator support for it is beyond the scope of this book.

Online Conferencing

Although Remote Assistance can technically be considered online conferencing, only NetMeeting is an application designed for sharing information and applications between users. Laptop users can benefit from NetMeeting conferencing in a number of ways; although NetMeeting was introduced in Chapter 9, only basic conferencing was detailed. Other options include asking other people to join the conversation, finding people by using the Find Someone utility, placing secure calls, and sharing applications with those in the meeting. This section discusses these items with an emphasis on use by the mobile-computer user.

Using NetMeeting to Share Applications

As a mobile-computer user, you will probably need to confer with others often. You might need to share ideas, collaborate on a project, or troubleshoot another computer. You might need to confer online with your boss or coworker while you're away from the office, or you can confer with others on your LAN. As you work with different people using NetMeeting, you might find that your laptop does not have the applications that those users work with, or those users don't have your applications installed on their desktop computers. To solve this problem, NetMeeting allows users to share applications in addition to files, folders, the chat area, and the whiteboard.

Note
If you do not have NetMeeting installed or you do not know how to use NetMeeting for basic conferencing, you'll need to refer to Chapter 9 to install it, and review the basic conferencing techniques.

Overview of Shared Applications
While using NetMeeting, you can allow multiple users to collaborate on a single document. If the document is an Excel file, for instance, only one user needs to have Microsoft Excel installed. NetMeeting allows the person who has the program installed to share that program with other users participating in the call. In this manner, all online participants can contribute to the document while one person is in charge of the application. Only one person can be in control of the application, and the word "Controllable" appears in the title bar of his or her program window. For other users accessing the program, a mouse pointer appears, indicating that someone else is in control of the program.

Sharing an Application

Figure 15.15 shows a NetMeeting session between two users. Once connected, the users can share an application and collaborate on a document.

Once connected to a user in NetMeeting, as shown in Figure 15.15, you can share an application by doing the following:

1. In the bottom-left corner of the NetMeeting window, select the icon of an executable file with a hand underneath it. (You will see the words "Share Program" if you hover the mouse pointer over it.)

2. In the Sharing dialog box, select the program you want to share. The file must be open to be available from the Sharing dialog box.

3. Do not check the Share In True Color checkbox unless you have a very fast connection or unless this is totally necessary; it will slow down communications. Choose Share.

4. In the Control area of the Sharing dialog box, choose the Allow Control button. This allows others to access the program and take control. Select either Automatically Accept Requests For Control or Do Not Disturb With Requests For Control. Choose Close.

5. Position the application window and the NetMeeting window so you can see both and so they don't overlap. This setup makes the program accessible to the online conferencing participants.

Figure 15.15
NetMeeting.

With the application shared, you can now work on your file with other people who are using NetMeeting. When others want to work on the file, they'll choose Control | Request Control in their NetMeeting session. When they are finished working on the file, they'll choose Control | Release Control. Figure 15.16 shows a user with control of Microsoft Photo Editor and a shared file, as well as the Control | Release Control menu option.

To stop sharing a program, choose the Share A Program button again, highlight the application, and choose the Unshare button. You can share multiple programs in most instances.

Sharing Your Computer's Desktop

You can also share your computer's desktop. However, if you are sharing your desktop, you are sharing everything on your computer, including all applications. You are also sharing My Computer, the Control Panel, and all of your open folders. This is not a safe practice because this leaves the entire computer open to whoever is connected via NetMeeting. However, it is possible.

To share your desktop, My Computer, or Control Panel:

1. Connect to another person using NetMeeting.

Figure 15.16
Sharing an application.

2. Choose the Share A Program button.

3. In the Sharing dialog box, highlight Desktop, and choose the Share button. Choose the Allow button to allow others to take control.

Joining a NetMeeting Already in Progress

To join a NetMeeting session already taking place, simply open NetMeeting and place a call to a member of the NetMeeting conference. All members will receive a call and will need to accept for you to be included in the call. If four people are in the call, and only three accept, you will not be accepted to the conference.

Getting Information and Removing Participants from the Meeting

If you are the host of a meeting, you can remove people from the meeting, and you can see information about them, including their names, their email addresses, and the hardware their computers have for audio and video conferencing. If you are a member of a meeting but are not the host, you can see other users' information but cannot remove them from the conference.

To see properties or remove a member from the meeting:

1. In the NetMeeting window, right-click a name in the Name list box.

2. Choose either Properties or Remove From Meeting.

Note
You cannot remove yourself from a meeting. Instead, you must choose Call|Hang Up.

Finding People by Using the Find Utility

By using MSN Messenger Service and by logging onto the Microsoft Internet Directory, you can locate people and invite them to join your conference. This will allow you and an MSN contact to chat using the NetMeeting interface introduced in Chapter 9.

If you want to invite someone who has an MSN passport to participate in a NetMeeting call:

1. Open NetMeeting.

2. Choose Call I Directory.

3. Using the Microsoft Internet Directory, select a name from the Find Someone window.

4. After the recipient accepts your call, choose Chat, Whiteboard, or any other means of communication.

Placing Secure Calls

You can configure your computer to accept and/or place only secure calls. Open NetMeeting, select the Security tab, and select the options shown in Figure 15.17.

Remote Desktop Sharing

The last section of this NetMeeting discussion has to do with a technology very similar to Remote Desktop; it is called Remote Desktop Sharing and is used with NetMeeting. Using Remote Desktop Sharing and NetMeeting technologies, you can access your work computer from home. Before you can connect, however, you have to configure a few options.

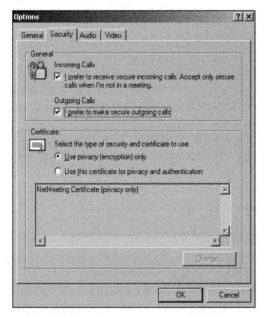

Figure 15.17
Allowing only secure calls.

Using the Remote Desktop Sharing Wizard

Before you can use Remote Desktop Sharing through NetMeeting, it must be configured using the Remote Desktop Sharing Wizard. To configure Remote Desktop Sharing:

1. Open NetMeeting.

2. Choose Tools | Remote Desktop Sharing.

3. Choose Next to start the Remote Desktop Sharing Wizard. After reading the information, choose Next again.

4. Select Yes to enable a password-protected screensaver. This is optional but recommended. Choose Next, and select a screensaver in the Display Properties dialog box that appears. Choose OK, then Finish.

5. Close NetMeeting. (Remote Desktop Sharing does not work if NetMeeting is running on the computer.)

6. Right-click the NetMeeting icon in the notification area of the toolbar, and choose Activate Remote Desktop Sharing.

Connecting by Using Remote Desktop Sharing

Once Remote Desktop Sharing has been configured as described in the previous section, you can connect to your desktop from anywhere, as long as your hardware supports it.

To use NetMeeting and Remote Desktop Sharing to connect from a laptop computer to a desktop computer:

1. On the laptop computer, open NetMeeting.

2. Choose the Place Call button, or choose Call | New Call.

3. In the Place A Call dialog box, type the name of the desktop computer.

4. Check the Require Security For This Call (Data Only) checkbox. Choose the Call button.

5. In the Remote Desktop Sharing Password box, type the username, password, and domain (if applicable).

You can end Remote Desktop Sharing by right-clicking the icon in the notification area and choosing Turn Off Remote Desktop Sharing.

Mobile Dialing Options

When a mobile user needs to connect to a network, there are several ways to do that. Most connections are made using a dial-up connection configured in Network Connections as described in Chapter 9. However, when a laptop user connects to a new network or is calling from another country, that user might need to configure a new connection and/or connect through an operator-assisted call.

Besides these optional dialing tasks, the user can also employ some of Windows XP's dialing options, such as Redial, Autodial, and even Callback if the network server and the laptop support it.

Manual and Operator-Assisted Calling

To connect to a network through a phone line when you must first speak to an operator or a switchboard operator, you can use Operator-Assisted Dialing. To make a call manually:

1. Open the Control Panel and Network Connections.

2. Choose Advanced | Operator-Assisted Calling to enable it.

3. Double-click the connection you want to dial.

4. Pick up the telephone handset, and dial the number manually, or ask the operator to dial it for you. The number is displayed in the dialog box, as shown in Figure 15.18.

5. Choose Dial immediately after you or the operator have dialed the number. When the modem takes control of the line, hang up the phone. (Be sure to disable Operator-Assisted Dialing before you dial automatically again.)

Note
Of course, you'll need to have the laptop connected to the phone line as well. An easy way is to use a telephone splitter that allows two phone lines to plug into one phone jack. A splitter costs about $3.00.

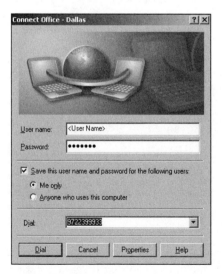

Figure 15.18
A dial-up connection.

Redial and Connection Options

Besides dialing manually, you can configure the network connection to redial if the connection isn't made. To configure Redial and other connection options:

1. Open the Control Panel and Network Connections.

2. Open the dial-up connection for which you want to configure the redial options.

3. Choose the Properties button, shown in Figure 15.18.

4. On the Options tab, set the number of redialing attempts in the Redial Attempts list.

5. In the Time Between Redial Attempts drop-down list, select an amount of time between 1 second and 10 minutes.

6. In the Idle Time Before Hanging Up drop-down list, select Never or a specific number of idle minutes.

7. If you want the connection to be redialed if the line is dropped, check the Redial If Line Is Dropped checkbox. Choose OK.

Using Autodial

Autodial is a feature of Windows XP Professional that allows a network connection to be dialed automatically when a Web address is referenced. This can occur if you select a hyperlink from a file, such as an Excel or Word document. This connection does not require any user interaction unless two or more connections exist and it is not clear which one should be chosen.

To configure Autodial:

1. Open the Control Panel and Network Connections.

2. Highlight the dial-up connection for which Autodial will be configured.

3. In the Network Connections window, choose Advanced | Dial-Up Preferences.

4. On the Autodial tab, highlight the connection for which Autodial will be used, and uncheck the Always Ask Me Before Autodialing checkbox. You can also check or uncheck the Disable Autodial While I Am Logged On checkbox. Choose OK.

Using Callback

To create a more secure environment, your network administrator might want the network server to call your computer back at a specific phone number so that the server cannot be accessed by anyone other than those who should have access. For instance, consider what could happen if someone stole your laptop computer and was able to access the files and folders on it. If this happened, the thief could also have access to the network until the theft was reported and the laptop dial-in account was closed.

Administrators also configure Callback so that the phone charges to the laptop user are not unreasonably high. Generally, calling long-distance from a remote location is quite expensive. This cost can be covered by the company instead of by the laptop user.

To configure Callback on your laptop, first make sure your network administrator has properly configured the domain servers and that an account has been created. Following that:

1. Open the Control Panel and Network Connections.

2. Highlight the dial-up connection for which Callback will be configured.

3. In the Network Connections window, choose Advanced | Dial-Up Preferences.

4. On the Callback tab, select one of the following options:

   ♦ No Callback

   ♦ Ask Me During Dialing When The Server Offers

   ♦ Always Call Me Back At The Number(s) Below

5. If you choose the third option, highlight the modem that will receive the callback, and choose the Edit button.

6. In the Call Me Back At dialog box, type the number from which you are calling.

Common Error Messages

There are many error messages you can receive when using Network Connections from a laptop (or from any other computer for that matter). The most common errors are caused because a modem is not configured correctly, incorrect information is specified, the modem is connecting or disconnecting while another connection has been started, or the connection times out before connecting to the server or ISP. Occasionally, the problem is more complex, as with a problem with the telephone lines or a remote server being down. Whatever the case, if you are out of the office and you receive any of these messages when trying to log on, and there is no administrator in sight to help you out, it can be quite frustrating. In this section, I'll list the error messages you'll most likely receive under these circumstances and why the error usually occurs. Keep in mind that most problems can be solved through patience, retyping credentials, and dialing the connection again.

600-Level Errors

Listed next are the most common 600-level errors:

♦ *600 An operation is pending*—Some other operation is in progress. This can happen when the modem has been prompted to dial a connection and is then prompted again before completing the first connection.

- 602 *The specified port is already open*—Another program is using the port that is used to dial the connection. The modem will not be able to dial until the program is closed and the port is made available.

- 604 *Incorrect information was specified*—Either the phonebook entry has changed, or the hardware itself has. Configure the new hardware, or reconfigure the phone information for the remote server.

- 605 *Port information cannot be set*—Either the phonebook entry has changed, or the hardware itself has. Configure the new hardware, or reconfigure the phone information for the remote server.

- 607 *An invalid event is detected*—This is usually an internal error. Restart your computer and try to connect again.

- 608 *A device was specified that does not exist*—You most likely chose the wrong connecting device. If this is not the case, check your current Network Connection entries for typographical errors.

- 611 *A route was specified that is not available*—Most likely, a problem exists with the computer you are dialing from. Restart your computer and try again. If problems persist, take a look at Event Viewer errors and warnings.

- 615 *The specified port was not found*—Check phonebook entries, and make sure all information is typed correctly. If no errors are found, restart the computer and try again.

- 617 *The modem is already disconnecting*—You are trying to disconnect after a Disconnect command is already pending. Wait.

- 621 *The system could not open the phonebook*—You are trying to connect using a rasphone.pbk file, which should be located in the *systemroot*\System32\Ras folder. Verify that this file is there, and then retry the connection.

- 638 *The request has timed out*—When connecting to a network, the computer is given a specific amount of time to connect, and if it doesn't connect in that amount of time, the request to connect is discarded. Check all devices to make sure they are functioning correctly, and try again.

- 642 *One of your computer's NetBIOS names is already registered on the remote network*—You cannot log onto a network with the same name as another computer that is registered. You will need to disconnect the other computer before you can log on.

- 643 *A network adapter at the server failed*—You cannot connect through this NIC until a network administrator repairs the problem. If possible, dial another phonebook entry.

- 646 *The account is not permitted to log on at this time of the day*—You have restricted logon times and cannot log on at this time.

- *647 This account is disabled*—An administrator has disabled your account. You will not be permitted to log on.

- *648 The password for this account has expired*—Press Ctrl+Alt+Del and change your password.

- *649 The account does not have permission to dial in*—If you've never dialed in, you'll need to inform your network administrator of this error. If you have dialed in before, your account might be locked out, disabled, or expired. You might also be required to call from a specific phone number, or there might be a problem with security protocols.

- *650 The remote access server is not responding*—This is most likely a problem with the network server. You'll need to phone the administrator to see the status of the network. If the server is not the problem, try switching to a different phone line, and make sure all connections are secure to your modem and the phone outlet.

- *651 The modem has reported an error*—Restart the modem if it is external, or restart the computer if the modem is internal. Check your Network Connections configuration, and make sure the remote server is available.

- *664 The system is out of memory*—Close all open programs, and redial the connection.

- *665 The modem is not properly configured*—Either the device is really not properly configured, or it is being used by another program. If the modem has been working well previously, consider the latter possibility.

Several other error messages are far more obvious, including the following:

- 668 The connection was terminated.

- 676 The phone line was busy.

- 677 A person answered the phone instead of a modem.

- 678 There was no answer.

- 680 There was no dial tone.

- 692 There was a hardware failure in the modem.

700-Level Errors

Listed next are the most common 700-level errors:

- *704 The callback number is invalid*—Make sure you've typed the number correctly. If you have, you'll need to have your administrator add this callback number to your account properties.

- *710 Serial overrun errors were detected while communicating with the modem*—Change the modem's maximum port speed.

♦ *711 The Remote Access Service Manager could not start. Additional information is provided in the event log*—You must have the PnP and Remote Access Connection Manager started on your computer for Remote Access to work properly. Make sure those services are running.

♦ *712 The two-way port is initializing. Wait a few seconds and redial*—This error occurs when you are dialing out at the same time the server is calling in. This occurs only on connections that are configured to both make and receive calls. The problem will be solved by the two computers without user input.

♦ *717 No IP addresses are available in the static pool of Remote Access Service IP addresses*—This happens on network servers that do not use DHCP to assign IP addresses. You'll have to wait for an address to become available, or have the network administrator use DHCP for allocating addresses on this server.

♦ *732 Your computer and the remote computer could not agree on PPP protocols*—You'll need to contact your administrator.

Several other error messages are far more obvious, including the following:

♦ 713 No active ISDN lines are available.

♦ 715 Too many errors occurred because of poor phone quality.

♦ 718 The connection timed out waiting for a valid response from the remote computer.

♦ 719 The connection was terminated by the remote computer.

♦ 721 The remote computer is not responding.

♦ 756 This connection is already being dialed.

♦ 771 The connection attempt failed because the network is busy.

♦ 775 The call was blocked by the remote computer.

Of course, many other errors can occur, but for the most part you can repair these problems by typing in the correct credentials, restarting the computer, waiting for an operation to end, closing all running programs, and modifying the modem's properties. Although a few problems do occur because of the remote server or because of an incorrect setting made by an administrator, many problems are solved quite easily, especially if the modem has been working properly prior to this incident.

Troubleshooting Modem Problems

If you've had any of the problems listed earlier, and you've tried restarting the computer and retyping credentials, you might need to change your modem properties. For instance, if you receive error 710, you'll need to change the speed at which your modem transfers information. You can change your modem's properties from the modem's Properties dialog box (accessible from the Control Panel), from Network Connections, and from inside Internet Explorer.

Using the Modem's Properties Dialog Box

To change your modem's properties, you can open its Properties dialog box: In the Control Panel, open Phone And Modem Options. Select the Modems tab, and select the modem you want to configure. Figure 15.19 shows a modem configured for a laptop computer.

If you cannot determine the cause of the problems occurring with your modem, you can choose the Troubleshoot button on the General tab of the modem's property sheet to have Windows XP Professional walk you through the process of finding and (one hopes) repairing the problem. You can also disable the device from here, and enable another modem if one is available.

On the Modem tab, you can change the maximum port speed. This solves problems associated with unexpected disconnects from networks or errors related to port communication problems. You should also make sure the Wait For Dial Tone Before Dialing checkbox is checked if you are using a dial-up modem.

On the Diagnostics tab, you can query the modem to see if the problem you are having is caused by your modem or the phone line or network. A successful query rules out the possibility that your modem is the problem. From this tab, you can also view the log that contains information about the query to determine what the problem is if the modem is not working.

Figure 15.19
A laptop modem's Properties dialog box.

On the Advanced tab, you can configure advanced port settings and change default preferences. You can use advanced port settings to configure a larger or smaller transmit and receive buffer (if you have errors related to buffers), and you can change the COM port to which the modem is connected. You shouldn't change the COM port if the modem has been working properly before the latest incident, though. You can change the default settings for call preferences and data connection preferences, such as how long to wait before hanging up if a call is not connected and how fast the communications should be. You can also change the default data protocol, although I'd suggest you do that only at the request of an administrator.

On the Power Management tab, you can choose to allow the computer to come out of standby mode when the modem initializes, or you can allow the computer to turn off the device to save power.

The Driver and Resources tabs are used to view and change the driver and to see the resources the modem uses, respectively. These tabs probably won't be of much use once the modem is functioning properly, and their options should not be changed in most cases.

Using Network Connections

You can also change settings from Network Connections, especially if you are having problems with Callback features or Autodial. To see what connections you have configured and to see if they are the cause of your error messages:

1. Open Network Connections.

2. Choose Advanced | Dial-Up Preferences.

3. On the Callback tab of the Dial-Up Preferences dialog box, make sure that the settings are correct if you are expecting the remote computer to call you back. One of these two checkboxes should be checked: Ask Me During Dialing When The Server Offers, or Always Call Me Back At The Numbers Below. If you select the latter, check the number to make sure it is correct.

4. On the Autodial tab, make sure Disable Autodial While I Am Logged On isn't checked if this is the problem.

Using Internet Explorer

Sometimes, changing the settings in Phone And Modem Options won't solve the problem. If this is the case, you can use Internet Explorer to change the additional properties for the modem and the dialing rules:

1. Open Internet Explorer (you do not need to be connected to the Internet).

2. Choose Tools | Internet Options, and select the Connections tab.

3. In the Dial-Up And Virtual Private Network Settings area, highlight the connection, and choose the Settings Button.

In the Settings dialog box shown in Figure 15.20, check the following items, and try these solutions:

♦ Check the Automatically Detect Settings checkbox, and choose OK twice. Try to connect again to see if these changes work.

♦ Make sure the username, password, and domain are typed correctly.

♦ Choose the Properties button, select the General tab, and make sure the phone number is correct. Configure alternatives if available.

♦ Choose the Properties button, select the Security tab, and make sure the security options are correct.

♦ Choose the Advanced button, and make sure that the Disconnect If Idle For ___ Minutes checkbox isn't checked (if the problem involves unexpected disconnects).

Wrapping Up

This chapter was written specifically for the mobile-computer user. In this chapter, I covered using power management features, enhancing laptop performance by using ClearType and DualView, configuring offline files and folders, using the Briefcase, using NetMeeting, using Message Queuing, and troubleshooting connection problems. Although most of these items can be used by desktop computer users, some features—such as hardware profiles, Briefcase, and offline files—aren't as useful.

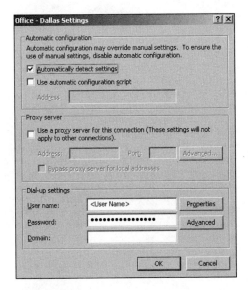

Figure 15.20
The Settings dialog box.

Appendix
Troubleshooting

This appendix is separated into many sections, and I've tried to put the sections in the order in which you should look for the answers to your troubleshooting questions and problems. In the first section, I'll discuss how to get information about your computer, such as how much RAM is installed, what type of CPU is installed, how large the hard drive is, and what resources are being used by what hardware.

When you have this information, the first step when you're troubleshooting any problem is to check the Microsoft help files. Chances are slim that the problem you are experiencing has never been experienced by a lab employee at Microsoft, and the troubleshooting guides can be quite useful. If checking Help doesn't get you anywhere, the next step is to look at Microsoft's Personal Support Center on the Internet. There, you can find late-breaking information, patches, fixes, and suggestions for getting your computer running smoothly.

The first place to look for a hardware problem is Device Manager, which uses icons to indicate problematic devices. Other problems can involve the inability to share resources or set NTFS permissions. This can be related to simple file sharing or occur because the drive isn't formatted as NTFS. In the sections "Device Manager," "File Sharing and Security," and "Problems with FAT Drives," I'll cover these types of problems.

Other problems can be categorized; printer problems and other hardware problems, software problems, and networking problems are the most common. If you are having a problem that can be categorized, consider skipping directly to that section to look for answers.

Following these "easy" troubleshooting techniques that can be used by virtually any user with any level of experience, I'll move on to more advanced troubleshooting techniques that power users can use for more stubborn problems. These techniques include using Dr. Watson, using safe mode, what to do if the computer won't boot into safe mode, using Microsoft's Support Tools, and finally, reinstalling Windows XP Professional.

Note

Before using these troubleshooting techniques, make sure you cannot use System Restore or Device Driver Rollback as detailed in Chapters 6 and 7.

Getting Information about Your Computer

There are several options for obtaining information about your computer. Even if you don't have any problems at this time, it would be a good idea to jot down notes about your computer's memory capacity, CPU, hard drive, and so on, just in case you ever need to take the computer to a repair shop or in case you can't boot the computer and you need this information for troubleshooting. You can also use the Backup utility to back up the system state, and you can create an MS-DOS boot disk for emergencies.

Using the System Properties Dialog Box

To obtain basic information about your computer, right-click My Computer and choose Properties. In the System Properties dialog box, you can find the following information:

- On the General tab:

  - The operating system name and version number

  - The person to whom the system is registered

  - The product ID number (which you need to reinstall the operating system)

  - The CPU type

  - The amount of RAM in the system

- On the Computer Name tab:

  - A description of the computer

  - The full computer name

  - The workgroup or domain name

- On the Hardware tab:

  - Device Manager

- ◆ Hardware profiles
- ◆ On the Advanced tab:
  - ◆ Performance settings
  - ◆ User profiles
  - ◆ Startup and recovery settings
  - ◆ Environment variables
  - ◆ Error-reporting settings
- ◆ On the System Restore tab:
  - ◆ Whether or not System Restore is being used
  - ◆ How much disk space System Restore is using
  - ◆ Which disks System Restore is monitoring
- ◆ On the Automatic Updates tab:
  - ◆ The notification settings for Automatic Updates (if any)
- ◆ On the Remote tab:
  - ◆ Remote Assistance settings
  - ◆ Remote Desktop settings

Getting Advanced System Information

You can obtain advanced system information through the Help and Support Center. To obtain this information:

1. Choose Start | Help And Support.

2. Under the heading Pick A Task, choose Use Tools To View Your Computer Information And Diagnose Problems.

3. Under Tools, choose Advanced System Information.

4. The right pane of the Help And Support Center window provides five options:
   - ◆ View Detailed Information (Msinfo32.exe)
   - ◆ View Running Services
   - ◆ View Group Policy Settings Applied

♦ View The Error Log

♦ View Information For Another Computer

Make your selection, and see the next few sections for more information.

Viewing Detailed Information

You can view detailed information by using the Microsoft System Information tool (Msinfo32.exe). You can run this tool from the Help and Support Center or by choosing Start I Run and entering "msinfo32". Figure A.1 shows the System Information console.

This console has five trees: Hardware Resources, Components, Software Environment, Internet Settings, and Applications. By expanding each tree, you can view just about any information that's available about your computer. For example, from the Components tree, you can view information about all of the hardware on your system. For each device, you can see a description, a manufacturer name, the status, transfer rates, driver, and more. You can print the entire description of your system by choosing File I Print.

Another tool you can use in this window is the Find What text box. Type in the name of a hardware device, software, or a resource to view information about it. Figure A.2 shows the results of a search for "adapter."

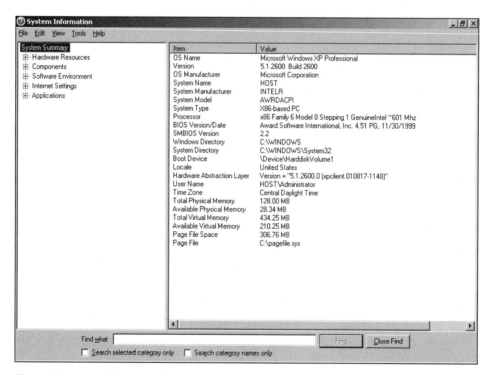

Figure A.1
The System Information console.

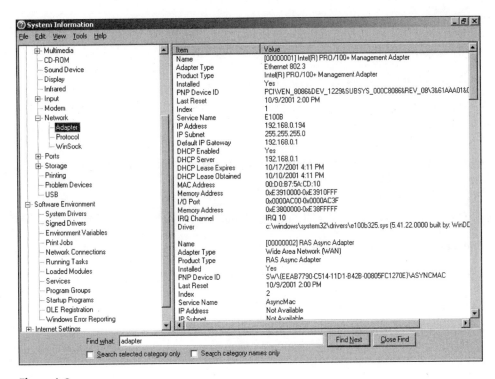

Figure A.2
System information search.

As you can see, the network adapter uses IRQ 10 and is named "Intel(R) Pro/100+ Management Adapter." Other information includes the IP address of the adapter, the default gateway, the product type, and the service name. You can then click the Find Next button to see the next entry for "adapter" in the System Information console. In this example, the next entry is the I/O address. In this example, when you continue using the Find Next button, the utility finds the display adapter, the network adapter's property sheet, the adapter driver, and more.

Viewing Running Services

When you choose to view running services, the right pane of the Help and Support Center lists the services that are currently running. The information also includes the way each service is configured to start (auto, manual, or disabled) as well as the executable file name. You can also see which services are stopped; this information can be quite useful if you're troubleshooting problems with a service. You cannot start or stop services from here, though; you do that through Start | Programs | Administrative Tools | Services.

Viewing Group Policy Settings Applied

When you choose to view which group policy settings are applied, the information is shown in the right pane of the Help and Support Center. You can see the settings for the computer and for the users of the computer.

The settings for the computer include:

♦ Computer name, domain, and site

♦ The last time the group policy was applied

♦ Startup scripts

♦ Shutdown scripts

♦ Security settings for restricted groups, the file system, and the Registry

♦ A list of the programs installed

♦ The Registry settings for the default .adm files

The settings for the user include:

♦ Username, domain, and the last time the policy was applied

♦ The user's security group memberships

♦ Internet Explorer automatic browser configuration

♦ Internet Explorer automatic proxy server settings

♦ Logon and logoff scripts

♦ Redirected folders

♦ Programs installed

From this report, you can save the information to an .htm file, or you can run the Resultant Set of Policy tool.

Viewing the Error Log

When the system encounters an error—such as failure to obtain an IP address from a DHCP server, an attempt to read from an illegal memory address, an inability to find a domain controller, a hanging application, or similar problems—an event is recorded automatically in the error log. You can view the system error log to see what types of problems have been occurring. Many errors go unnoticed or are repaired automatically or on subsequent attempts, but some errors are obvious, such as an application failing to respond.

Viewing Information for Another Computer

When choosing to view information for another computer, you are prompted to type in the path to the computer. After you select the computer, a new window opens in the Help and Support Center and displays the following options:

♦ *View General System Information About This Computer*—Displays information about the remote computer, as shown in Figure A.3. The information includes the system model

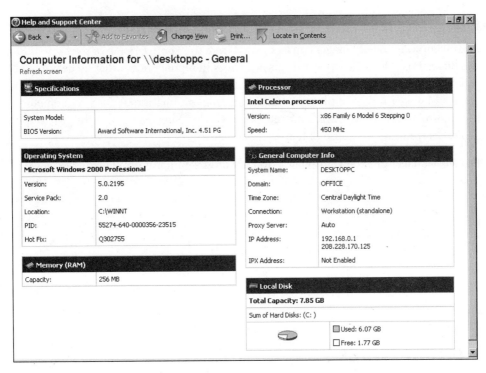

Figure A.3
System information for a remote computer.

and BIOS version, the operating system, the amount of memory, the processor, the system name, the domain, the time zone, the connection, the proxy server, the IP address, and the total capacity of the hard drive.

◆ *View The Status Of My System Hardware And Software*—Opens a new window with information on any obsolete application and device drivers, system software, and hardware (video, network, and sound card, plus USB controllers and other peripherals), plus information about the hard disk and memory.

◆ *Find Information About The Hardware On This Computer*—Opens another window describing the hardware on the remote computer, including drivers, manufacturers, and versions.

◆ *View A List Of Microsoft Software Installed On This Computer*—Opens a window listing all of the remote computer's Microsoft software, plus software in the Startup program group. This information can be extremely helpful if you are having problems starting the computer.

◆ *View Advanced System Information*—Displays the four options described earlier: viewing detailed system information, viewing running services, viewing group policy settings, and viewing the error log.

Using Device Manager to Get Information

As you know, Device Manager can be opened from the Hardware tab of the System Properties dialog box. Device Manager displays devices in alphabetical order by default and uses yellow question marks, exclamation points, and red X's to denote problems with devices. Device Manager is a good place to start collecting information about your computer, and the information can be printed for reference. Device Manager is also the first stop when you're determining the cause of hardware problems.

Device Manager offers several views. You are most familiar with viewing devices by type. You can also view:

♦ Devices by connection

♦ Resources by type

♦ Resources by connection

You can use Device Manager to view conflicts for IRQ or memory addresses, to disable or uninstall devices, and to view problems with hardware devices.

Important Notes

A few things will help you greatly when you need to troubleshoot a problem. In Chapter 14, I included a long list of items you should have. If you are reading this appendix because you already have a problem, I hope that you have these notes and disks on hand. What's most important for recovering from disaster is that you have a current backup of your computer's system state, an MS-DOS startup disk, and current backups of your data. For getting out of a tight spot when the computer won't boot, make sure you have these three things and the following information close by and current:

♦ Copies of all original software in case a reinstallation is needed

♦ Your Windows XP Professional CD and the product ID number, plus any other ID numbers necessary to activate other software

♦ An Automated System Recovery disk

♦ A copy of your computer's system state

♦ A password-reset disk

♦ An MS-DOS startup disk

♦ If you dual-boot, a copy of your boot.ini file

You can create an MS-DOS startup disk that will allow you to boot into MS-DOS in case the computer itself won't boot. To create this disk:

1. Insert a floppy disk into the floppy disk drive.

2. Open My Computer, and select the floppy drive.

3. In the My Computer window, choose File | Format.

4. In the Format 3 _" Floppy (A:) dialog box, check the checkbox Create An MS-DOS Startup Disk. Choose Start and OK.

After you have this disk, you can start your Windows XP Professional computer with it and at least locate the A:\ drive. From there, you can troubleshoot other drives on the system.

Using Windows XP Professional Help

The previous section introduced Windows XP Professional Help. There are other ways to use the help files, though, and knowing what is available in the Help and Support Center is crucial to using it properly to solve problems. You can solve many problems by using the hardware troubleshooters and by selecting specific tasks from the Pick A Help Topic section. From the home page of the Help and Support Center, you can also ask for assistance, choose a specific task, and view tips in the Did You Know section.

If you are connected to the Internet, these help files are updated daily. Figure A.4 shows the home page for the Help and Support Center. In the Did You Know section, notice that the date of the last update is shown and that you can choose to View More Headlines.

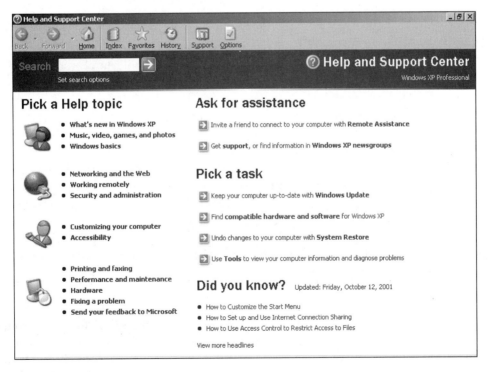

Figure A.4
The Help and Support Center.

Using the Navigation Bar

At the top of the Help and Support Center is a navigation bar with several buttons: Back, Forward, Home, Index, Favorites, History, Support, and Options. These buttons can be used to traverse the help files and change the way you work with the Help and Support Center. Several buttons are similar to those in the Internet Explorer toolbar.

Directly underneath the navigation bar is the Search box. You can type in a word or concept and then search for it by selecting the green arrow beside the text box. It is best to search for short, specific items such as "create a folder" or "use Windows Media Player."

Back and Forward Buttons

The Back and Forward buttons allow you to move to the page previously viewed or the page you were viewing before you last used the Back button. When the Help and Support Center is first opened, these two buttons are grayed out. After you move to another page by clicking a link, the Back button becomes available. These buttons do have one downfall; they cannot be used to go back to previous searches. Search results are not saved.

Home

Use the Home button to return to the Help and Support Center's home page. From there, you can use the Back button to return to the previous page viewed.

Index

The Index is a totally different way to obtain information in Help. The Index is an alphabetical list of the items in Help. You can type in a keyword and have the Index find the subject. This search tool doesn't look inside the help files, however; it only moves you to the letter of the alphabet where the word would be located in the Index. For instance, if you type in "Create a folder" and press Enter, you are taken to the entry for "CreatePool Command, Removable Storage" because the Index does not have a topic entitled "Create a folder."

Favorites

Choosing the Favorites button opens the Favorites page, which lists any items you've configured as Favorites. From this list, you can rename, remove, or display previously saved topics.

History

The History button lists the links to the previously viewed topics in Help. Using this button is a quick way to find a previously viewed topic. The History page does not show previous searches, only previously viewed topics.

Support

You can use the Support button when you want to get help from a friend, from Microsoft, or from a Windows Web site. From the Support page, you can access Remote Assistance, get information about your computer, see advanced system information, and use the System Configuration utility (Msconfig.exe, detailed later).

Options

Use the Options button when you want to change the Help and Support Center options, set Search options, or install and share Windows help files. You can configure the following:

- Whether or not to show the Favorites and History buttons on the navigation bar

- What font size to use: Small, Medium, or Large

- Whether to have the navigation bar display only text labels, only default text labels, or no text labels

You can set the following Search options:

- How many results should be shown for each search (the default is 15)

- Whether or not to highlight search words in the topic

- Whether or not to show the Suggested Topics section

- Whether or not to show Full-Text Search Matches, and whether the search should include only the title or should match similar words

- Whether or not the Microsoft Knowledge Base searches should be included in the search. The Microsoft Knowledge Base is on the Internet, so connectivity is necessary. You can choose any operating system from the Knowledge Base, and choose how the Knowledge Base is to be searched (all of the search words, any of the words, or the exact phrase)

You can choose Install And Share Windows Help, which allows you to do the following:

- Switch from one operating system's help files to another

- Install help files from another computer

- Install help files from a CD or a disk image

- Share your help files with others on the network

- Uninstall help files that you've installed from another operating system

Using the Home Page

The Home page is separated into four parts: Pick A Help Topic, Ask For Assistance, Pick A Task, and Did You Know?. These areas allow you to quickly obtain help on any subject, locate troubleshooting guides, and use support tools to diagnose computer problems. This should be the first place you look when you're trying to locate and/or solve a problem.

Pick A Help Topic

In this section, the topics are separated into four distinct sections. The first includes Windows basics such as customizing the desktop, working with files, protecting your computer, using media files, and finding out what's new in Windows XP. The second section offers assistance on networking, traversing the Web, working remotely, and securing the computer. The third section is for customizing the computer and configuring accessibility options. The fourth section includes hardware issues such as printing, faxing, maintaining performance, fixing problems, and configuring and installing hardware.

By traversing these sections, you can locate the type of information you need, and access the troubleshooting wizards. The troubleshooting wizards have their own section in this Appendix and will be detailed later.

Ask For Assistance

Asking for assistance is as simple as opening the Help and Support Center and clicking Remote Assistance. Remote Assistance was covered in depth in Chapter 11. You can also access Windows XP newsgroups and get support from Microsoft if you're connected to the Internet.

Pick A Task

Four tasks are listed under Pick A Task:

♦ Keep Your Computer Up To Date With Windows Update

♦ Find Compatible Hardware And Software For Windows XP

♦ Undo Changes To Your Computer With System Restore

♦ Use Tools To View Your Computer Information And Diagnose Problems

In many cases, these four items can solve a lot of problems. For instance, if you are having problems with a device driver, Windows Update might have a more recent one than you do. If you want to know if a piece of hardware is compatible, you can check Microsoft's Web site for the latest information. System Restore is a good first step to take when problems occur with installations of software or hardware, and you can diagnose problems by using any of the support tools in Windows XP.

Did You Know?

If your computer is always connected to the Internet, each day the information in the Did You Know? section will be different. If you aren't connected to the Internet, then each time you connect, the files will be updated. In this section, you can select a headline from the list or choose View More Headlines. When you make a choice, you'll be connected to Microsoft's Web site.

Using Help from inside Application Windows

You can obtain help from inside just about any application. In my opinion, this is the best way to get help in Windows XP Professional. Not only can you use the Index, but you can use the Contents and Search tabs as well. Figure A.5 shows the Help page for Scheduled Tasks. You can display this page by opening Scheduled Tasks and choosing Help | Help

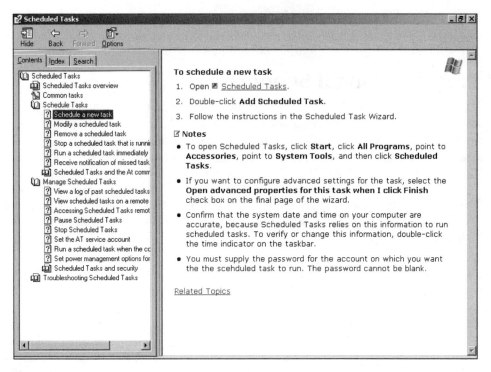

Figure A.5
Help displayed from inside the Scheduled Tasks tool.

And Support Center. The tabs shown here are available only when Help is chosen from inside an application. As you can see, the help trees have been expanded. Notice the depth of topic coverage.

The Contents Tab

Using the Contents tab, you can expand the trees as shown in Figure A.5 to view all help files on the subject requested. These files usually include information on performing common tasks, troubleshooting the Windows tool, installing and configuring the tool, understanding concepts, and performing advanced tasks. Each file contains links to additional, related topics.

The Index Tab

The Index tab is just like the Index button in the Help and Support Center. The only difference is that the Index tab lists only those topics that are related to the tool being addressed. This makes searching the Index much faster and easier.

The Search Tab

On the Search tab, you can type a keyword, and the search results will refer only to the topic at hand. For instance, typing the word "modify" in the Help and Support Center's Search box, described previously, will produce all types of topics containing the word "modify."

However, typing "modify" while using Help from inside a Windows tool displays only those topics related to that particular tool.

Microsoft Personal Support

If you've tried using the Help and Support files from the Start menu, and you've read the information in the help files from inside the Windows tool itself, you might consider accessing the Microsoft Web sites before anything else. Microsoft offers a Web site that contains articles, troubleshooting wizards, items to download, and hundreds of in-depth papers and tutorials to help you understand your computer.

You can access the online support center from inside the Help and Support Center; choose Ask For Assistance | Get Support Or Find Information In Windows XP Newsgroups | Get Help From Microsoft. Once connected to the site, you'll be prompted to input your passport name and password for verification, and then you'll be asked for your first and last name, phone number, and country. After accepting the license agreement (and terms related to privacy issues), you can enter the site. You can then choose from these options:

- Ask A Microsoft Support Professional For Help

- View My Support Requests, Which Include The Support Questions I Have Sent And Any Replies From Microsoft

- Update My Contact Information

- Go To The Passport Member Services Web Site

- View Other Support Options

Microsoft Online Assisted Support

If you choose to ask a Microsoft professional for help, you'll be prompted for the operating system. Then you'll be asked to describe the problem and include information about your computer. You can then ask to be updated by email when the problem has been addressed by Microsoft.

Other Support Options

If you choose View Other Support Options, you'll be given three options:

- Save Information About This Computer To Submit To Microsoft Online Assisted Support

- View A List Of Support Telephone Numbers

- View Operating System Upgrade Details And Known Issues

From here, you can save information about your computer, and you can find out if your computer has any known compatibility problems. These compatibility problems can cause the computer to have hard-to-find errors, startup and shutdown problems, and more. When compatibility problems are shown, you can locate the updated drivers for the hardware, disable devices, or uninstall programs to solve these problems.

Here's an example: A fairly new computer (HP Pavilion 6835), which was upgraded to Windows XP Professional in my office, had the following hardware and software incompatibilities and/or applications that would have to be reinstalled to work with Windows XP:

- Scanner: Epson Perfection 1200

- Keyboard Manager

- Software: McAfee ActiveShield

- Printer: Alps MD-5000/T-03

- SCSI Controller RDS-5000 USB Drive

- Universal Serial Bus Controller RDC-5000

- Ricoh Digital Camera RDC-5000

- Intel Graphics Technology

- Direct CD3

- Easy CD Creator 4

The incompatibilities cause the computer to be unable to scan occasionally, to hang, to freeze up, and to have to be restarted after certain applications are opened. Although these problems seem quite difficult, they can all be repaired by upgrading the software applications, upgrading the drivers for the hardware, and uninstalling outdated programs.

http://search.support.microsoft.com

Microsoft also offers a site (**http://search.support.microsoft.com**) where you don't have to use your passport to obtain information. Although this site won't take a snapshot of your system and tell you what's incompatible, you can still find lots of information.

After connecting to the site, you can search for help by product, keyword, article ID number, driver or download, or specific troubleshooting tool, or you can search by typing in a question. You can also search the Microsoft Knowledge Base, use a Search Wizard, see frequently asked questions, find software, or visit newsgroups.

If you need to request support from Microsoft, you can do that as well. Of course, getting information from a real person at Microsoft isn't free, so you'll have to decide if you want to pay on a per-incident basis or sign up for a professional support contract. Whatever the case, you can almost always find the information you need from this Web site.

Troubleshooting Wizards

From either the Help and Support Center or the online support page just mentioned (**http://search.support.microsoft.com**), you can use troubleshooters, which provide a good way to get help with solving certain problems. You can access the troubleshooters through the Fixing A Problem link in the Pick A Help Topic section of the Help and Support Center.

Windows XP Professional Troubleshooters

You can use troubleshooters to assist you in finding and repairing problems related to specific hardware (such as a printer or a DVD-RAM drive), specific problems (such as system setup), or specific applications (such as Internet Explorer). Because the problem that you are having is most likely a typical problem, troubleshooters are good places to look for answers. For instance, a common system startup problem is that an anti-virus program is running and is preventing Setup from running. Windows XP Professional provides the following troubleshooters:

- System Setup
- Startup/Shutdown
- Display
- Home Networking
- Hardware
- Multimedia And Games
- Digital Video Disks
- Input Devices
- Drives And Network Adapters
- USB
- Modem
- Internet Connection Sharing
- Internet Explorer
- Outlook Express
- File And Print Sharing
- Printing

If you decide to use a troubleshooter to solve a problem, the first step will usually be to restart your computer. Then you'll need to open the troubleshooter again, and you might need to print or copy its information before continuing.

To see the list of troubleshooters and to access a specific troubleshooter:

1. Choose Start | Help And Support Center.

2. In the Pick A Help Topic section, choose Fixing A Problem.

3. In the Fixing A Problem pane, choose Troubleshooting Problems.

4. In the right pane, choose List Of Troubleshooters.

5. Select the appropriate troubleshooter from the list. The troubleshooter will automatically start.

6. Work your way through the troubleshooter, carefully reading each screen and making the appropriate choices. Perform any tasks recommended. Figure A.6 shows a troubleshooting screen that is representative of most screens that will be shown.

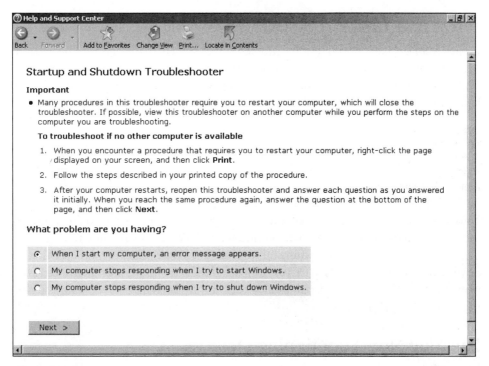

Figure A.6
A troubleshooting screen.

> **Note**
>
> *If working through the appropriate troubleshooter doesn't work, continue through this appendix, applying other troubleshooting techniques.*

Troubleshooters from Microsoft's Web Site

You can also check out the troubleshooters available from Microsoft's Personal Support Center mentioned, earlier. To see these troubleshooters:

1. Browse to **http://search.support.microsoft.com**.

2. In the My Search Is About drop-down list, select Windows XP.

3. From the I Want To Search By options, select Specific Troubleshooting Tool.

4. In the My Question Is text box, type the name of a hardware device or a software application. Click the Go icon.

5. Work through the troubleshooter when it is presented.

Device Manager

Device Manager can be used to solve problems, too. If there is anything wrong with a hardware device, the device name will be accompanied by a yellow question mark, a yellow exclamation point, or a red X. Information about Device Manager was given in Chapter 7, but a brief compendium follows here.

> **Note**
>
> *You access Device Manager by right-clicking My Computer, choosing Properties, selecting the Hardware tab of the System Properties dialog box, and choosing the Device Manager button.*

You can use Device Manager to make configuration changes, but when you're troubleshooting, you'll be most concerned with determining which devices are not functioning correctly, configuring the device settings, uninstalling and reinstalling devices, and updating device drivers. You can also use Device Driver Rollback if the latest driver installed doesn't work as planned, or you can use the Troubleshoot button to have Windows XP walk you through the troubleshooting process.

Locating Non-Functioning Devices

Locating devices that aren't functioning properly is as easy as opening Device Manager. Figure A.7 shows several problem devices listed.

Although most problems are easily located because they have a representative icon next to them, other problems can be detected when a device that should be in Device Manager

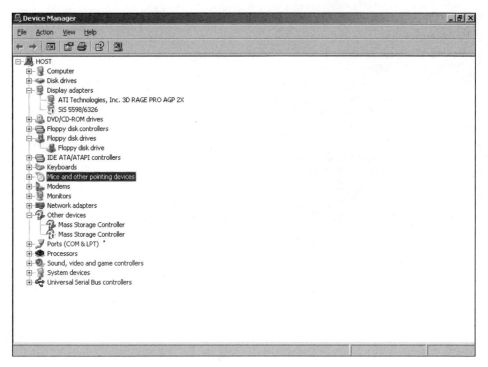

Figure A.7
Hardware problems indicated in Device Manager.

isn't listed. Missing CD-RW drives and missing modems are common problems. If you know a device is supposed to be listed but isn't, you'll most likely have to troubleshoot the problem in another way. However, you can choose Action | Scan For Hardware Changes if a new device has recently been added.

Using the Troubleshoot Button

As you can see from Figure A.8, you can choose the Troubleshoot button to have Windows XP walk you through the troubleshooting process. Right-click the device you want to troubleshoot, and choose Properties. The Troubleshoot button is on the General tab of the device's Properties dialog box.

When you click this button, Windows XP's Help and Support Center opens to guide you through the troubleshooting process.

Uninstalling and Reinstalling Device Drivers

Another thing you can try when troubleshooting through Device Manager is to uninstall and reinstall the device and the driver. Before you try this, though, make sure you have access to the existing driver. If you have obtained a newer driver, skip to the next section, "Updating Device Drivers."

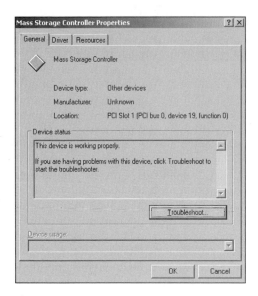

Figure A.8
The Troubleshoot button.

To uninstall and reinstall a device driver:

1. Log on as an administrator.

2. Double-click the name of the device that needs troubleshooting. This step opens the device's Properties dialog box.

3. *To reinstall the driver:* Select the General tab, and choose Reinstall Driver. *To uninstall the driver:* Select the Driver tab, and choose Uninstall. Most of the time, you'll want to reinstall the driver.

Updating Device Drivers

When new operating systems are developed, so are new device drivers. Hardware that worked fine with Windows 9x, ME, or 2000 can fail to work properly with Windows XP. When this happens, you need an updated device driver. You'll have to obtain this driver from the device manufacturer or from the Internet. Then you can update the driver in Device Manager.

To update a device driver:

1. Log on as an administrator, and open Device Manager.

2. Double-click the name of the device that needs troubleshooting.

3. In the device's Properties dialog box, select the Driver tab, and choose the Update Driver button.

Using Device Driver Rollback

If you've installed or updated a new driver and that driver doesn't function properly, you can roll back the newly installed driver. However, the device rollback goes back only to the last driver, so make sure you roll back to the first driver before trying another one.

To roll back a device driver:

1. Log on as an administrator, and open Device Manager.

2. Double-click the name of the device that needs troubleshooting.

3. In the device's Properties dialog box, select the Driver tab, and choose the Roll Back Driver button.

Configuring Device Settings

If you've located a non-functioning device through Device Manager, and you've tried reinstalling and updating the device drivers, you can try to solve the problem here as a last resort. Changing the device settings can be risky because a change in a resource for one device can affect other devices that use this resource.

If the device is working well enough that device drivers are installed, and the device functions (even somewhat), resources will have been allocated for it. These resources have to do with IRQs and memory allocation settings. Because almost all devices are PnP (plug and play) these days, I strongly discourage the changing of these settings.

However, if you must, you can use Device Manager to view resources by type or by connection, and note which resources are free. If you have a resource with a conflict, you can then manually swap the resources it uses with free resources available on the machine. (For more on how to change views in Device Manager, see Chapter 7.)

To reconfigure these settings manually:

1. Log on as an administrator, and open Device Manager.

2. Double-click the name of the device that needs troubleshooting.

3. In the device's Properties dialog box, select the Resources tab, and select the resource setting you want to change.

4. Uncheck the Use Automatic Settings checkbox, and choose the Change Settings button.

5. Make the appropriate changes, and choose OK twice.

6. Restart the computer.

Network Sharing, Security, and Connectivity

Problems sharing folders and securing them occur for several reasons, but a few are quite common. One reason is that simple file sharing is being used; another is that the computer is not connected correctly to the network; and another is that the network hasn't been set up correctly. Additionally, the hard drive must be formatted as NTFS and not as FAT for you to configure all of the file and folder security options available. Most of these problems are quite simple to repair in a workgroup, but in a domain, this is mostly the responsibility of your network administrator. If you are having a problem sharing folders or setting security in a domain, check with the administrator first to make sure that you have the correct information and that you have the required permissions to configure this sharing and security.

Simple File Sharing

Windows XP Professional has a default configuration for sharing folders and printers, and that is to use simple file sharing. If you are using simple file sharing, Figure A.9 shows what you'll see when you right-click a folder and try to share it.

If this is the page you see when you try to share or secure a folder, you need to disable simple file sharing. Notice that you cannot set permissions, set caching, or even access the Security tab from this page. In contrast, look at the Sharing tab for the same folder's properties when simple file sharing is disabled. See Figure A.10.

If you cannot see the Security tab, set permissions, or configure caching, you'll need to disable simple file sharing:

1. Right-click the Start button, and choose Explore.

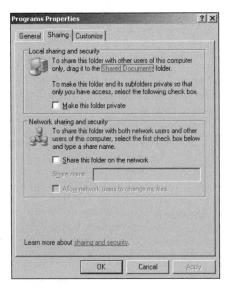

Figure A.9
A folder's properties with simple file sharing enabled.

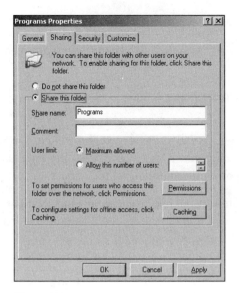

Figure A.10
A folder's properties with simple file sharing disabled.

2. In the Windows Explorer window, choose Tools | Folder Options.

3. On the View tab, scroll down to the last entry, and uncheck the Use Simple File Sharing (Recommended) checkbox. Choose OK.

Network Connectivity

You will have problems sharing on a network if you aren't correctly logged on. This is a surprisingly common problem. Other problems stem from user errors (such as the failure to look in My Network Places), failing hardware, and incorrect network protocols. If you think you have one of these problems, continue through this section; if not, skip to "Incorrect Network Setup."

Are You Logged On Correctly?

Before you panic, make sure that you've not only logged onto the network but that you've also logged onto the correct domain or workgroup. You can view network status through Network Connections and My Network Places. If in doubt, log off and log back on again. If you find that you can't log onto your network, then the problem has been solved.

Checking Network Hardware

If you're logged onto the network, but you still can't access network files, the network might be having a physical problem. You should first make sure that you have connectivity with others on the network; you do this by using the **ping** command. If you can successfully ping all of the other computers on your network, then the problem is not caused by network hardware but is instead a software or configuration problem.

To use the **ping** command to test connectivity:

1. Obtain each computer's IP address by entering "ipconfig" at a command prompt at each computer.

2. From the problem computer, open a command prompt, and enter "ping" followed by the IP address of one of the computers.

3. If the ping is not successful, you'll see a Message Timed Out error. This means that you are not making contact with the other computer. If you can successfully ping each computer on your network, proceed with other troubleshooting techniques.

4. If there are problems pinging other computers, you'll need to find out which computers can communicate and which can't. If none of the computers can communicate, consider running the Network Setup Wizard on each computer. If only a few aren't working, check their NICs, cables, and other hardware, and then use the Network Setup Wizard on them also.

Checking Network Protocols

If you still cannot locate the source of the problem, check the protocols that are installed on each computer on the network and specifically on the problem computer. Your Windows XP Professional computer should have TCP/IP installed. Depending on the type of network you use, either you'll need a static TCP/IP address, or you'll be given an address automatically. If you're a member of a domain, you'll need to ask a network administrator about the IP address; if you've set up your network using the Network Setup Wizard, you obtain an IP address automatically.

To see what protocols are installed on your computer, and to install TCP/IP if necessary:

1. Log on as an administrator.

2. Open My Network Places.

3. Right-click the local area connection, and choose Properties.

4. On the General tab, make sure that Internet Protocol (TCP/IP) is listed and is checked. If not, choose the Install button, and install it.

Incorrect Network Setup

Most connectivity problems that are not caused by failed hardware or by having simple file sharing enabled stem from incorrect network setup. If in doubt, you can always run the Network Setup Wizard on each computer just to make sure. Chapter 10 explained how to use the Network Setup Wizard. However, you cannot hurt a workgroup by running the wizard again, and if you're in a domain, network policies will prevent you from running it anyway.

To rerun the Network Setup Wizard to repair problems with network connectivity and with sharing folders and hardware:

1. Choose Start | Programs | Accessories | Communications | Network Setup Wizard.

2. Choose Next to start the wizard, and choose Next again to continue.

3. On the Select A Connection Method page, select Other. Select the appropriate option for your network, and choose Next.

4. On the Select Your Internet Connection page (if applicable), highlight the connection that you use to connect to the Internet. Choose Next.

5. On the Give This Computer A Description And Name page, verify that the computer name is spelled correctly, and choose Next.

6. On the Name Your Network page, type the name of your workgroup in the Workgroup Name text box. Choose Next twice.

7. On the You're Almost Done page, select Just Finish The Wizard, I Don't Need To Run The Wizard On Other Computers. Choose Next and Finish.

8. If sharing is now available, your problem is solved. If not, run this wizard on the other computers in your network to verify that all are connected properly.

If You Use FAT instead of NTFS

Problems can occur because you are using the FAT file system instead of NTFS. To see which file system you are using, open Computer Management and select Disk Management from the Storage tree. If you are using FAT, you cannot set NTFS permissions, and you cannot secure files and folders on your computer from other users who open files while using your computer. FAT cannot be used in domains; it can be used only in workgroups. If FAT is used, you will be unable to view the Security tab on your computer even if you disable simple file sharing.

If you want to see the Security tab and set NTFS permissions, you'll need to convert your hard drive to NTFS. This is easily done, and it does not cause any data loss or harm your computer. However, the conversion cannot be undone without data loss.

To convert your FAT drive to NTFS:

1. Log on as an administrator.

2. Choose Start | Programs | Accessories | Command Prompt.

3. At the command prompt, type convert "c: /fs:ntfs" where c: is the letter of your hard drive.

4. Acknowledge that you must reboot the computer, and then do so. The conversion will take place while the computer is rebooting.

For more information on problems with FAT drives, read the next section.

Problems with FAT Drives

You can have multiple problems if your computer isn't formatted as NTFS and is instead formatted as FAT. Several things can be done only if the drive uses NTFS. For instance, if you can't set permissions on a file, it's because setting permissions on files isn't supported with FAT; only setting permissions for folders is supported.

An NTFS drive supports the following tasks or capabilities (which FAT does not support):

♦ File encryption can be used

♦ Permissions can be set on files and folders

♦ NTFS permissions can be set

♦ Because each user must log on using NTFS security, the computer's local hard drive is protected when someone accesses the local computer

♦ You can use *sparse files* (a way that data is written to the hard disk more efficiently)

♦ Remote storage is easily accessible and more secure

♦ Recovery logging of NTFS metadata, which can be used to restore the computer quickly in case of a system problem such as a power loss or other disaster

♦ Disk quotas can be used

♦ NTFS supports larger hard drives than FAT does

♦ You have access to other NTFS files on other NTFS computers

♦ NTFS supports domains and domain configurations

If you are having a problem configuring or using any of these features, you might need to verify through the Computer Management console that the drive is formatted with NTFS

Note
Converting to NTFS was detailed in the previous section.

Internet and Email Problems

Several things can cause problems with using the Internet or with sending or receiving email. In this section, I'll assume that the connection to the Internet has previously been established as detailed in Chapter 9 and that the modem and other hardware are installed (even if they are not functioning correctly). If this isn't the case, work through Chapter 9 to set up the modem and Internet connection, and return here for troubleshooting techniques.

There are four general types of Internet and email problems: the modem isn't functioning correctly or some other hardware problem exists; the network isn't configured correctly when ICS (Internet connection sharing) is being used; the Web browser displays error messages, and Web sites can't be accessed; or email cannot be sent or retrieved. This section discusses each of these four problems.

Tip
If you think your Internet problems are due to a networking problem, you might try the techniques in the section "Network Sharing, Security, and Connectivity" before continuing here.

Modem Problems

If you connect to the Internet through a modem, and the modem isn't working correctly, isn't dialing, or displays errors messages (such as "Cannot open port"), you won't be able to connect to the Internet or send and receive email until this problem is resolved. The first step in trying to resolve any problem with a modem is to restart the computer. The second step is to verify that the phone number, logon name, and password are typed correctly. If these steps don't work, continue with the suggestions listed next (in this order):

1. In Device Manager, verify that the modem is working. If Device Manager indicates a problem with the modem (signified with a symbol next to the modem name), return to the "Device Manager" section in this appendix, and troubleshoot in Device Manager.

2. If you do not hear sounds when you're using the modem to try to connect with the Internet, make sure that the modem is turned on, that it's connected properly if it's an external modem, and (if you are comfortable with this), that it's seated correctly in the appropriate slot if it's an internal modem. Restart the computer.

3. If no obvious problem is indicated in Device Manager, double-click the modem, select the Diagnostics tab, and choose the Query Modem button. If the query is successful, continue with Step 4. If the query is unsuccessful, select the General tab, and choose the Troubleshoot button. While here, verify that the Wait For Dial Tone Before Dialing checkbox is checked, and increase the amount of time the modem will wait to be connected before giving up. Check the maximum port speed, and lower it if necessary.

4. If you do hear sounds when trying to connect with the modem, read the error message displayed. The error message is your best bet at this time.

5. If the error message concerns a protocol, verify that the correct protocols are configured for the Internet connection. If this computer has connected to the Internet previously, this is probably not an issue. Make sure TCP/IP is installed. (In Network Connections,

right-click the Internet connection, choose Properties, and select the Networking tab.) Install TCP/IP if necessary. You should also uninstall any unnecessary protocols.

6. If an error occurs and Windows states that a connection could not be established, the problem could be due to network settings or even your ISP (Internet service provider). Call your ISP to check on network status.

7. If none of these steps solves your problem, uninstall and reinstall the modem from Device Manager.

8. If the problem still isn't solved, it might not be caused by the modem.

Internet Connection Sharing Problems

The Help and Support Center provides an Internet Connection Sharing troubleshooter, and if you are having problems with ICS, this is the best place to start. If you are having any of the following problems, open the troubleshooter, choose the problem, and follow the instructions provided:

♦ You cannot receive email on an ICS client computer

♦ The ICS client dials out without notifying the user

♦ The ICS host computer won't automatically dial when a client computer requests it

♦ The DSL or cable modem is too slow

♦ You cannot browse the Internet from the host computer

♦ You cannot browse the Internet from a client computer

If you have added a domain controller to the network and set up a domain, or if any of the clients or the host is connected to a domain, ICS won't function correctly. If you have changed the client computer's configuration from automatically receiving an IP address to having a static IP address, that computer will not be able to use ICS. If the problems in the bulleted list do not pertain to you, think about changes such as these that have recently been made on your network. Undo any recent changes manually or by using System Restore. Again, the first step to solving any ICS problem is to reboot each computer in the network, let the network offer error messages, and regroup.

Internet Browser Problems

Internet browser problems can be classified as such only if you have connected to the Internet successfully. Otherwise, the problem is lies with connectivity, not with the browser or the Internet. The most common problems occur because a page cannot be displayed, there is something wrong with the toolbars and their choices, and occasionally, settings prevent you from viewing certain Web pages. Rarely, you'll see errors that are internal or errors that may cause Internet Explorer to need to be reinstalled or updated.

When You Can't View a Web Page

If you've tried to access several Web pages while surfing the Net, and you've been unable to view any of them, the problem could lie with your ISP or network server and/or with an inability to locate your DNS server. DNS (Domain Name System) servers are computers that are responsible for taking a name like **www.microsoft.com** and locating its Internet site by using its IP address (which is a series of numbers in a specific format). If you are having problems accessing only a single site, the problem probably lies with that site itself; either its Web server isn't functioning properly, or other problems exist. If you are having problems accessing only specific sites, then the problem could be a multitude of things, including restrictions set on your computer or by domain policies.

Note

Before continuing, make sure you are connected to the Internet through a network server or ISP.

The first thing you should try when you can't access any sites at all is to make sure you can ping your DNS server. If the ping fails, then either you are not connected to the Internet, or there is something wrong with your network hardware.

To identify the IP address of your DNS server and ping it:

1. Choose Start | Programs | Accessories | Command Prompt.

2. At the command prompt, type "ipconfig /all" and press Enter.

3. Locate the DNS server's IP address in the resulting output. (See the highlighted "DNS Servers" line in Listing A.1.)

4. At the command prompt, type "ping" followed by the IP address of the DNS server. Press Enter. Sample output is shown in Listing A.2.

Listing A.1   Determining the DNS server's IP address.

```
C:\>ipconfig /all
Windows IP Configuration
Host Name . . . . . . . . . . . . : host
Primary Dns Suffix  . . . . . . . :
Node Type . . . . . . . . . . . . : Mixed
IP Routing Enabled. . . . . . . . : No
WINS Proxy Enabled. . . . . . . . : No

Ethernet adapter Local Area Connection:
Connection-specific DNS Suffix  . : Ballew.com
Description . . . . . . . . . . . : Intel(R) PRO/100+ Management Adapter

Physical Address. . . . . . . . . : 00-D0-B7-5A-CD-10
Dhcp Enabled. . . . . . . . . . . : Yes
```

```
Autoconfiguration Enabled . . . . : Yes
IP Address. . . . . . . . . . . . : 192.168.0.194
Subnet Mask . . . . . . . . . . . : 255.255.255.0
Default Gateway . . . . . . . . . : 192.168.0.1
DHCP Server . . . . . . . . . . . : 192.168.0.1
DNS Servers . . . . . . . . . . . : 192.168.0.1
Lease Obtained. . . . . . . . . . : Wednesday, October 17, 2001 10:26:58 AM
Lease Expires . . . . . . . . . . : Wednesday, October 24, 2001 10:26:58 AM
```

Listing A.2   Sample output from pinging the DNS server.
```
C:\ >ping 192.168.0.1

Pinging 192.168.0.1 with 32 bytes of data:

Reply from 192.168.0.1: bytes=32 time<1ms TTL=128
Reply from 192.168.0.1: bytes=32 time<1ms TTL=128
Reply from 192.168.0.1: bytes=32 time<1ms TTL=128
Reply from 192.168.0.1: bytes=32 time<1ms TTL=128

Ping statistics for 192.168.0.1:
Packets: Sent = 4, Received = 4, Lost = 0 (0% loss),
Approximate round trip times in milli-seconds:
Minimum = 0ms, Maximum = 0ms, Average = 0ms
```

If you are still having problems viewing Web pages, open Internet Properties (in the Control Panel, choose the Internet Options icon), and make the following changes (these apply to Internet Explorer, but similar options are available in other browsers):

♦ On the General tab, choose the Delete Files button

♦ On the Connections tab, check the settings for your Internet connection, and verify that they are correct

♦ On the Programs tab, choose the Reset Web Settings button to restore default settings for your home and search pages

♦ On the Advanced tab, choose the Restore Defaults button to reset Internet Explorer default settings

If you can access only some sites, try the following in Internet Properties:

♦ On the Security tab, check the security levels and Restricted Sites. The sites you want to access might not meet current security requirements

♦ On the Privacy tab, check the settings here. These could be preventing you from accessing specific sites

♦ On the Content tab, disable Content Advisor if necessary

Try these other options:

♦ Lower the number of colors in Display Properties

♦ Verify that all video cards are on Microsoft's HCL (hardware compatibility list), and reinstall or replace them if necessary

If these solutions don't solve the problem, try the Internet Explorer Troubleshooter in the Help and Support Center.

Restoring Default Toolbars and Menus

If you are having problems with Internet Explorer's toolbars and menus, you can look at the Advanced tab in the Internet Properties dialog box to restore the defaults. (Internet Properties can be accessed through Internet Options in Control Panel.) Restoring the defaults usually solves problems related to menus and toolbars. If you want to customize the toolbars of Internet Explorer, just right-click an empty area of a toolbar, and choose the toolbars you want to see.

Downloading the Latest Version of the Browser

If you are using Internet Explorer or MSN, you can download the latest version of Internet Explorer by using Windows Update. In some cases, Windows Update also offers patches and security fixes for Internet Explorer. If you are experiencing problems that you think are related to a problem with the application, use Windows Update to obtain any fixes.

Email Problems

If your email program was working properly and now it isn't, and you can't recall changing your email settings, the problem most likely lies with your ISP or corporate network. Before getting too worked up about being unable to send or receive email, contact your ISP or your network administrator. If your ISP is running properly, or if everyone else on your network is receiving email without any problem, then you'll need to do some troubleshooting.

First, if you've changed your email account in any way—such as changing IP addresses, changing the name of the mail server, or any other such configuration—undo those changes immediately. If you haven't made any changes, verify that the settings are correct.

Verifying Mail Account Settings

You can verify mail account settings through the Tools | Accounts menu of your email program. In this example, I'll use Outlook Express.

1. Open Outlook Express, and choose Tools | Accounts.

2. On the Mail tab of the Internet Accounts dialog box, highlight the mail account you want to check. (See Figure A.11.)

3. Choose the Properties button.

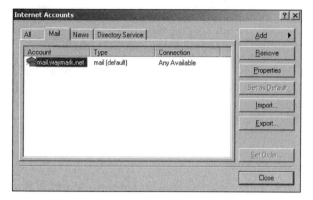

Figure A.11
Internet accounts.

4. In the Properties dialog box, verify that all information is correct. On the General tab, verify that the checkbox Include This Account When Receiving Mail Or Synchronizing is checked.

5. On the Connection tab, make sure the configuration is correct for connecting to the Internet, either through a LAN or through a specific account if required. Choose OK and Close.

If mail account settings are correct, try disabling any anti-virus programs recently installed, and make sure you have enough hard disk space to save messages.

Software Settings

You can also cause your own problems through message rules, security settings, and the way your email program is configured to read and send messages. To see if these settings are causing the problem, check the following items in your email program (I'll again use Outlook Express because it ships with Windows XP Professional):

♦ If multiple identities exist, choose File | Identities to verify that you are logged on correctly

♦ Make sure you are working online

♦ Choose View | Current View. Make sure that the Show All Messages option is selected and that Hide Read Messages and Hide Read Or Ignored Messages are not selected

♦ Choose Tools | Message Rules, and verify that configured rules are not preventing email from being received

♦ Choose Tools | Options to open the Options dialog box. Check the following

♦ On the General tab, verify that the program should check for new messages. The Check For New Messages Every _____ Minutes checkbox should be checked

- On the Maintenance tab, check the Mail checkbox so that a log will be kept for troubleshooting future problems

- On the Connection tab, in the Dial-Up section, make sure that the Hang Up After Sending And Receiving checkbox isn't checked

- On the Security tab, make sure that the checkbox Do Not Allow Attachments To Be Saved Or Opened That Could Potentially Be A Virus is not checked

Finally, if problems still exist, use Windows Update to see if there are any updates for Outlook Express, and download them if needed.

Printer Problems

If you have installed a printer and it has stopped working properly, the Printing Troubleshooter in the Help and Support Center is the best place to begin solving the problem. Most problems with printers can be solved by replacing cartridges or toner, reinstalling the printer driver through Device Manager, and even turning on and off the printer. If the Printing Troubleshooter and Device Manager can't help you solve your problem, there might be something physically wrong with the printer itself.

If the printer is a network printer that you can't access, verify that you can access other resources on the network. Error messages that are displayed when this happens are usually obscure at best. In my experience, the error messages state that the device is not working properly or is not compatible with the operating system when they should inform you that you are not connected to the network.

To sum up, solve printer problems by troubleshooting in this order:

1. Turn off the printer and then turn it back on again. Verify that it has power and that other users on the network can print to it.

2. Replace cartridges, toner, or paper if necessary.

3. Verify that you can access other resources on the same network or subnet.

4. Work through the Printing Troubleshooter in the Help and Support Center.

5. Reinstall the printer's device driver in Device Manager.

6. Uninstall the printer and reinstall it.

Hardware Problems

Hardware problems have to do with peripherals such as CD-ROM drives, CD-R and CD-RW drives, network adapters, scanners, cameras, display adapters, modems, sound cards, and more. Writing an all-encompassing troubleshooting guide for all of these would be nearly impossible. For problems that obviously are the fault of a specific piece of hardware, the best place to start is with the manufacturer's instructions and the booklet that came with the device. You can also search the manufacturer's Web site for updated device drivers and for a list of frequently asked questions. Almost any problem you could have with a device has probably already been addressed by the manufacturer, and the manuals and Web sites often provide quick answers.

The Help and Support Center also provides several troubleshooters for specific devices, and these troubleshooters can be helpful as well. Most of the troubleshooters begin with making sure the device is connected and is powered on.

Physical Connections

You might be surprised at how many technical support calls are solved simply by having the user check to see if the device is getting power and is connected properly to the computer. Although it seems unlikely that your device came unplugged, consider how many people are in and out of your office emptying trash or vacuuming the carpet after you've gone home for the night. My personal experience also tells me that electrical outlets can and do go bad. (Once you troubleshoot a device for a couple of hours and then determine that the outlet is bad, you never fail to notice that problem again.)

If you know that the external connections are good, but your problem is with an internal card or adapter, you can open the computer case and make sure the cards are seated in their slots correctly. After years of service, the inside of a computer becomes dusty, and if it has been moved numerous times, components can be knocked loose. Sometimes simply using compressed air and reseating the cards solves the problem.

Drivers

Once you know that the device is connected and plugged in, check Device Manager (if the device is listed there) to see if there are any obvious problems. If there are, return to the section on Device Manager, and try to solve the problem. If the device isn't listed or is shown to be working correctly, locate the device in either My Computer or the Control Panel to check the configuration options.

Figure A.12 shows the Properties dialog box for a CD-ROM drive. Notice the Trouble-shoot button. Work through the troubleshooter, and reinstall the device driver if this option is offered.

Hardware Compatibility

If you haven't done so already, you should make sure that the device that isn't working is on Microsoft's hardware compatibility list. You can see this list at **www.microsoft.com/hcl**. If the device isn't on this list, you can expect the device to function erratically, and you'll have to wait for an updated driver. If the device is on the list, consider the possibility that it has a physical problem.

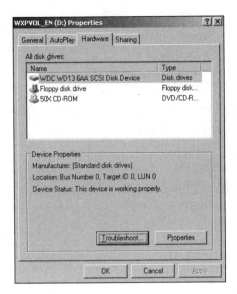

Figure A.12
The Properties dialog box for a CD-ROM drive.

Software Problems

Problems with software can be hard to figure out. If the software isn't listed on Microsoft's HCL, the problem is that the software isn't fully compatible or hasn't been tested. If this is the case, using a program that is on the list is the best solution. In other cases, application problems are hard to detect because the problems have more to do with hardware than with the program itself.

Because most application problems can't be solved by choosing a newer or compatible program, you'll need to solve the problems well enough so that you can use the application. Your first option is to try using the Program Compatibility Wizard, which was discussed in Chapter 12.

If you've tried all of the program compatibility modes and none of them work, but the program is on the HCL or works on another computer, the problem lies either with the installation of the program or in the hardware of the computer itself. As a first step, you should reinstall the software on the computer. Doing so won't erase your personal files; it will only reinstall the application.

If the program still isn't working properly, look in Device Manager for any non-working devices such as sound or video cards, or game ports, and the like. If there are no obvious problems there, you can try Windows Update for getting updated system files. If the problem still isn't solved, you'll need to contact the manufacturer of the software and compare what hardware the program needs to run and what is installed on your computer.

Figure A.13 shows a sample problem. Although Arts & Letters Express works well on three other computers in the office, when the program is run on a fourth computer, the error message shown here appears every five minutes. Although this is annoying, the program still functions and does not need to be restarted as the error message indicates. This problem seems to be caused by Intel Graphics Technology, which is included on this computer and no others on the network, and/or by the fact that the computer manufacturer has offered a BIOS update for this particular machine. The results aren't in yet.

Determining Compatibility Problems

To see if any installed hardware or software isn't compatible with your computer, and to print a list of this hardware and software:

1. Open the Help and Support Center.

2. Under the heading Ask For Assistance, choose Get Support, Or Find Information In Windows XP Newsgroups.

3. Under Support, choose Get Help From Microsoft. (You must be connected to the Internet.)

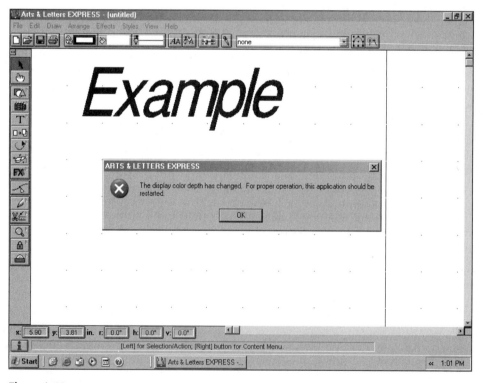

Figure A.13
Software errors.

4. Choose View Other Support Options.

5. Choose View Operating System Upgrade Details And Known Issues.

6. View the known issues in the resulting window. Repair these issues if possible by obtaining updated drivers from manufacturers' Web sites, disabling devices, or upgrading or removing problematic software.

Dr. Watson

Dr. Watson is a software-debugging program that acquires information about system and application failures and records these failures and resulting information in a log file called Drwtsn32.log. If a program error occurs, Dr. Watson starts automatically. Dr. Watson is not an anti-virus program, nor can it prevent problems from occurring or warn you when problems might occur; however, it can help technical support representatives solve problems that cause a program error. To open Dr. Watson manually, choose Start | Run and type "drwtsn32" in the Open text box.

You should check out how Dr. Watson is configured in case you ever need it. To do so, simply open Dr. Watson. The dialog box is shown in Figure A.14.

Note where the log file is located, where the crash dump information is located, and other information. You can also select options for Dr. Watson and view the currently stored application errors. To view the application errors log, highlight the log, as shown in Figure A.14, and then choose the View button. Although these logs won't help you much unless you are

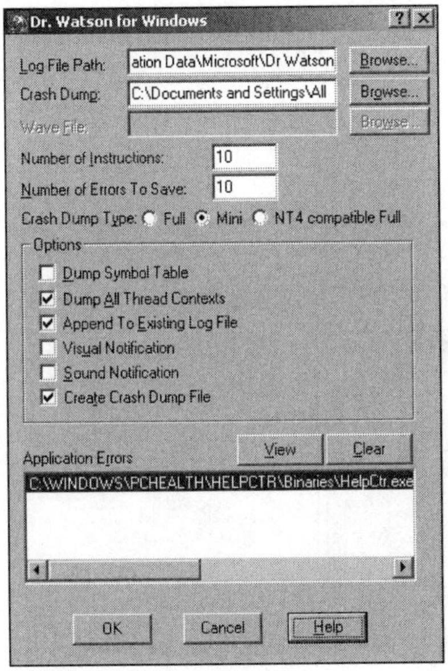

Figure A.14
Dr. Watson.

an application technician, they might give you a clue as to what problems are occurring on your system.

The System Configuration Utility

When you have problems with startup and shutdown processes, applications, devices, or the system state, you can use the System Configuration utility to troubleshoot. This utility lets you select startup options, and it can be used to identify problem files. Only advanced system administrators should use the System Configuration utility, and you must be logged on as an administrator to use it. Even then, network policies could prevent you from making changes.

If you have the correct permissions, open the System Configuration utility by choosing Start | Run and entering "msconfig.exe" in the Open text box. Figure A.15 shows the System Configuration Utility dialog box. Notice that you can choose Launch System Restore (on the General tab) to restore the computer to a previous state. This is the easiest solution if it works.

Determining the Problem

Using the System Configuration utility is just a guess-and-check troubleshooting technique. First, you load only basic devices and services, and restart the computer. If the computer boots and functions correctly, you begin adding files until you find out which ones are causing the problems. The following steps outline the process:

1. Log on as an administrator.

2. Choose Start | Run, "type msconfig.exe", and choose OK.

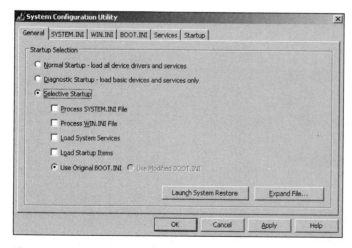

Figure A.15
The System Configuration utility.

3. On the General tab, select Diagnostic Startup–Load Basic Devices And Services Only. Choose OK, and restart the computer.

4. When the computer restarts, perform Step 2 again.

5. In the dialog box that appears, choose OK. The System Configuration utility will open automatically.

6. On the General tab, select Selective Startup, and check the Process System.ini File checkbox. Choose OK, and restart the computer.

7. Repeat Steps 4 through 6 until a file has been loaded that causes the problem that you are trying to solve. With the file in question identified, you can then replace the file or remove the driver causing the problem.

After the Problem Has Been Identified

After you've identified the file that is causing the problem, open the corresponding tab as shown in Figure A.16. For instance, if the problem was found to occur when the win.ini file was checked, use the Win.ini tab to further troubleshoot the problem.

As you can see, the computer will boot without the win.ini file (or the other files). That means that you can disable (uncheck) any driver or extension that matches the problem you are seeing. In this manner, you can locate and disable any problem file, including .dll files.

Booting Problems

If you can't boot the computer, you can try several options. The most common are Safe Mode, Safe Mode With Networking, and Last Known Good Configuration. If you are hav-

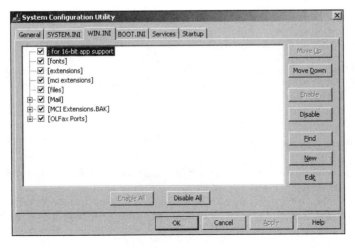

Figure A.16
The Win.ini tab of the System Configuration utility.

ing trouble booting, restart the computer, and press F8 when prompted for startup options. Choose Last Known Good Configuration (LKGC). If LKGC doesn't start the computer, you'll need to try the Safe Mode and Safe Mode With Networking options.

Safe mode can be used to help diagnose problems with device drivers, applications, video and sound cards, and more. In safe mode, only basic hardware and device drivers are loaded. You can use the mouse, the keyboard, the monitor, and basic system services, but you can't connect to another computer (unless you choose Safe Mode With Networking) or use a scanner or printer.

If you can't boot the computer normally, and LKGC won't start it either, restart the computer, press F8 when prompted, and choose Safe Mode. Once the computer has been booted into safe mode, use System Restore to restore your computer to a previous state.

If the computer won't boot to safe mode, you'll need to consider using Backup and Restore or the Automated System Recovery utility, discussed in Chapter 14.

Network Diagnostics

You can use the Network Diagnostics tool to gather information about your computer, the hardware you use, the operating system you use, how you are connected to the Internet and internal network, and how your modem and NIC are configured. You can also use this tool to locate problems on the network regarding your specific connectivity needs and applications. Network Diagnostics is generally used when you are on the phone with a technical support representative, and the information obtained allows the technician to figure out what network problems are occurring.

Configuring Network Diagnostics

To configure Network Diagnostics:

1. Open the Help and Support Center.

2. In the Pick A Task section, choose Use Tools To View Your Computer Information And Diagnose Problems.

3. In the Tools section, choose Network Diagnostics.

4. In Network Diagnostics, choose Set Scanning Options.

5. In the Actions list of checkboxes, check all of the checkboxes (unless instructed otherwise by a support technician).

6. Choose the Save Options button.

Running Network Diagnostics

To run Network Diagnostics:

1. Open the Help and Support Center.

2. In the Pick A Task section, choose Use Tools To View Your Computer Information And Diagnose Problems.

3. In the Tools section, choose Network Diagnostics.

4. In Network Diagnostics, choose Scan Your System.

5. When the scan is finished, choose the Save To File button. The file will automatically be saved to the desktop.

Understanding Network Diagnostics Output

Once the Network Diagnostics scan has been completed and saved, locate the file on the desktop, and open it. Figure A.17 shows output from a successful Network Diagnostics scan.

As you can see from Figure A.17, it is obvious if there is something wrong with connectivity between the computer and its DNS server, DHCP server, or WINS server, and it is easy to

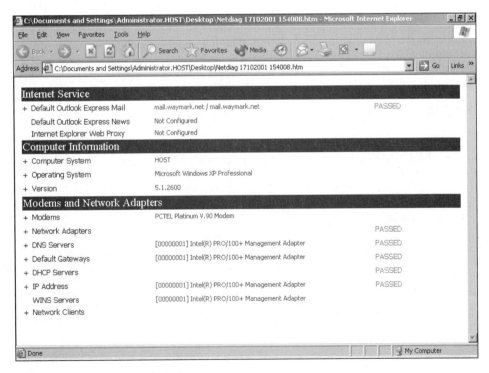

Figure A.17
Network Diagnostics output.

tell if the NIC isn't functioning correctly. When a network administrator knows that your computer has failed the Network Diagnostics test for connecting to the DNS server, he or she has also found the solution to the problem.

Command-Line Tools

If you are a command-line guru and prefer to do things at a command prompt rather than using the tools available within Windows XP, then this section is for you. Many of the command-line tools coincide with the older tools of yore and look quite familiar. Command-line tools are much different from the support tools introduced in the next section; those tools are for advanced system administrators who know how to use the output from those utilities to solve system-wide problems. The command-line tools discussed here are also different from the command-line tools introduced in Chapter 14; those are used when the Recovery Console is used for troubleshooting. These command-line tools are much easier to use and can be helpful when other troubleshooting techniques have not been successful.

Note

The commands listed in this section apply only to Windows XP Professional. The commands for other editions of Windows XP will differ.

Preparation

Before using the command-line tools the first time, you need to configure the command prompt accordingly. To configure the command prompt for using command-line tools effectively:

1. Choose Start | Programs | Accessories | Command Prompt.

2. In the upper-left corner of the Command Prompt window, click the icon next to C:\ (the root directory). Choose Properties.

3. On the Options tab, select a cursor size (Small, Medium, or Large), and set display options (Window or Full Screen).

4. Change the Buffer Size to 999 so that you can scroll through the information in the Command Prompt window.

5. Change the Number Of Buffers to 5 so that the number of lines in the Command Prompt window is increased to 5,000.

6. Change the Edit Options to Quick Edit Mode so you can copy and paste inside the Command Prompt window.

7. Select the Font tab if you want to change the font size.

8. On the Layout tab, change the Screen Buffer Size, the Window Size, and the Window Position to your specifications. The changes will be reflected in the Window Preview area.

9. On the Colors tab, change colors if you want to. Choose OK.

10. In the Apply Properties dialog box that appears, select Save Properties For Future Windows With Same Title. Choose OK.

Common Command-Line Tools

Approximately 150 command-line tools are available, and each tool has a myriad of switches and parameters that can be used with it. Instead of detailing all of these commands, I'll introduce the commands you will most likely need in a workgroup or office scenario, and I'll list only the most common switches and parameters you'll probably need for each command. At the end of this section, I'll list the additional commands (the ones that weren't introduced) and tell you how to get more information on these tools through Help and the command prompt.

> **Note**
> *Many of these tools, when used without any parameters, display the command syntax and provide help on how to use the switches. If you are not familiar with command-line tools, consider reading the syntax requirements for the switches and parameters before using the command. You can also see all of a command's switches and parameters by entering the command followed by the /? switch.*

Attrib

You can use the **attrib** command to add, remove, set, or display the attributes of a file or directory. The attributes are read-only, archive, system, and hidden. For example, to view hidden files or directories, you must first remove the hidden attribute.

The switches and parameters are:

> **Note**
> *The + sets the attribute, and the – removes it.*

- **+r** |**–r**—Sets or clears the read-only attribute.

- **+s** |**–s**—Sets or clears the system attribute.

- **+h** |**–h**—Sets or clears the hidden file attribute.

- **+c** |**–c**—Sets or clears the compressed file attribute

- [[*drive:*][*path*]*filename*]—Specifies the file or directory for which you want to change attributes. Only one file or directory can be changed at a time.

- **/s**—Applies the option to all matching files in the current directory and its subdirectories.

Chdir

Use this command to see the name of the current directory. If you use the **chdir** command without any parameters, you'll see the name of the current directory; with parameters, you'll see the changes. Use these parameters:

- **[drive:] [path]**—Specifies the drive and directory you want to change if they are different from the current drive and directory

- **[..]**—Specifies that you want to make a change to the current folder

- **/d**—Changes the current drive or the current directory for another drive

Chkdsk

Use the **chkdsk** command to check the local disks, display a status report, and correct errors on the hard disk. You can use this command with or without parameters. Using the command without parameters displays only the status of the disk. You must be an administrator to use this command. The **chkdsk** command has several parameters:

- **[path] filename**—Specifies the drive to check

- **/f**—Fixes errors on the disk

- **/v**—Displays the name of each file in the directory that is checked

- **/r**—Locates problems on the disk and recovers as much information as possible

- **/x**—Used with NTFS drives only, forces the drive to dismount first if necessary

- **/I**—Makes **chkdsk** run faster because it performs a less comprehensive check on index entries

- **/c**—Used with NTFS only, makes **chkdsk** run faster by skipping the check of cycles within the folder directories

- **/L**—Used with NTFS only, allows you to set a log file size

Cls

The **cls** command clears the screen of all information. There are no parameters; simply type "cls" at the command prompt.

Convert

Use the **convert** command to convert from a FAT drive to an NTFS drive. Use these parameters and switches:

- **volume**—Specifies the drive letter (followed by a colon) of the drive you want to convert to NTFS

- **/fs:ntfs**—Is a required switch

- **/v**—Specifies verbose mode, which displays all messages while the conversion is taking place

- **/nosecurity**—Specifies that the converted files and directory security settings are accessible by everyone

- **/x**—Dismounts the volume if necessary

Copy

Use this command to copy a file to another location. Use these parameters and switches:

- *source*—Specifies the file to be copied. This can be a drive letter and colon, a directory name, a file name, or a combination of these

- *destination*—Specifies the location and name of the file where this file will be copied. This can be a drive letter and colon, a directory name, a file name, or a combination of these

- **/d**—Allows any encrypted files that are copied to be saved as decrypted files at their final destinations

- **/v**—Verifies that the new files were written correctly

- **/y**—Prompts you when files will be overwritten

Date

The **date** command displays the current date settings and allows you to type in a new date.

Defrag

Use the **defrag** command to defragment files, including boot files, data files, and files on local disks. Use these parameters and switches:

- *volume*—Specifies the drive to be defragmented

- **/a**—Shows a summary analysis report

- **/v**—Shows a complete analysis report

- **/f**—Defragments the drive whether or not defragmentation is needed

Del

Use the **del** command to delete a file. Use these parameters and switches:

- **[*drive:*] [*path*] *filename*—Specifies the file you want to delete and the file's drive and directory if they are different from the current drive and directory.

- **/p**—Prompts for confirmation before a file is deleted

- **/f**—Forces the deletion of read-only files

- **/s**—Deletes only specified files from the current directory and subdirectories

- **/a**—Deletes files based on certain attributes

Dir

Use the **dir** command to list the files and subdirectories on the hard drive. Use these parameters and switches:

- **[drive:] [path]**—Specifies the drive and directory for which you want to see a listing

- **filename**—Specifies the file or file group for which you want to see a listing

- **/p**—Shows information one screen at a time; you must press a key to continue to the next screen

- **/q**—Shows who owns the file

- **/w**—Displays the information in wide format

- **/a**—Displays the attributes of the files

Diskcopy

Use the **diskcopy** command to copy the contents of one floppy disk to another floppy disk. Use these parameters:

- **drive1**—Specifies the drive of the source floppy disk

- **drive2**—Specifies the drive of the destination floppy disk

- **/v**—Verifies that the information is copied correctly

Doskey

Doskey is used to "remember" previous Windows XP commands and to edit command lines. Use these parameters:

- **/reinstall**—Installs the Doskey utility and erases any information in the history buffer

- **/listsize = size**—Specifies the number of commands to keep in the history buffer

- **/history**—Displays all the command in the history buffer

Note

Doskey has many other functions that pertain to creating macros and remembering previous commands. For a full explanation, type "doskey" in the Help and Support Center in Windows XP Professional.

Driverquery

The **driverquery** command displays information about the device drivers installed. Use these parameters and switches:

- **/s** *computer*—Specifies a computer other than the default local computer; use the computer's IP address with this switch

- **/u** *domain\user*—Runs the command using a specific user account; the default is the current user

- **/p** *password*—Specifies the password if one is required or the **/u** switch is used

- **/fo**—Specifies how data should be displayed. You can choose Table, List, or CSV (comma-separated values)

- **/v**—Displays detailed driver information

- **/si**—Displays digital signature information for the driver

Expand

This command is used to extract a file from a compressed file and is commonly used with driver files. Use these parameters:

- *source*—Specifies the file that needs to be expanded

- **-F:***files*—If the source contains more than one file, you can specify the name of the file you want to extract, or you can use wildcards

- *destination*—Specifies the destination directory for the extracted file(s)

- **-d**—Lists the files without extracting them

- **-r**—Renames the expanded files

Find

Use this command to search for a specific string of text in a text file or files. Any lines of text with the required string of data are displayed. The **find** command has three parameters:

- **/v**—Displays any lines that do not contain the required data

- **/c**—Counts the number of lines that contain the data requested

- **/l**—Specifies that the search not be case-sensitive

Format

This command formats the drive specified. Formatting erases all data on the drive. Use these parameters:

- *volume*—Specifies the drive to format

- */v*—Specifies the volume label

- */fs:file-system*—Specifies the file system to be used: FAT, FAT32, or NTFS. If this parameter isn't used, the disk is formatted in the file system previously used by the disk

- */a:unitSize*—Specifies the number of bytes per cluster. If this switch isn't used, the cluster size will be based on the local volume size

Gpresult

Use this command to display group policy settings and the Resultant Set of Policy (RSoP) for a user or a computer when multiple group policies exist. The **gpresult** command has several switches and parameters:

- **/s** *computer*—Specifies the computer by name or IP address; the default is the local computer

- **/u** *domain\user*—Runs the command using a specific user account; the default is the current user

- **/p** *password*—Specifies the password if one is required or the **/u** switch is used

- **/user** *targetname*—Specifies the user whose RSoP data is to be displayed

- **/scope**—Displays the results for either the user or the computer; by default, **gpresult** displays both

- **/v**—Specifies verbose output of the results

Gpupdate

Use this command when you need to update the local and Active Directory policies immediately. The **gpupdate** command has several parameters and switches:

- **/target: (computer | user)**—Specifies whether to display results for a computers or for a user. By default, both result sets are displayed

- **/force**—Ignores any optimization settings and reapplies all settings

- **/boot**—Reboots the computer after the refresh is completed

Help

This command displays help for a specified command. You can type in

```
help [commandname]
```

or

```
commandname /?
```

Ipconfig

This command displays the current TCP/IP settings and refreshes DNS and DHCP settings. The **ipconfig** command has several switches and parameters:

♦ **all**—Displays all of the information about TCP/IP settings, subnet masks, gateways, and adapters

♦ **/renew**—Renews the DHCP configuration for all the NICs on the computer

♦ **/release**—Releases the current DHCP address

♦ **/flushdns**—Resets the DNS cache

♦ **/displaydns**—Displays the contents of the current DNS cache

♦ **/registerdns**—Registers DNS names and IP addresses that are not currently configured on the local computer

Label

The **label** command allows you to create, rename, or delete the name of a hard disk (its label). The parameters are:

♦ *drive*—Specifies the drive you want to name

♦ *label*—Specifies the new name for the disk

Mkdir

Use the **mkdir** command to create a new directory or subdirectory. There are two parameters:

♦ *drive*—Specifies the drive on which to make the directory

♦ *path*—Specifies the path and the name of the new directory

MMC

The **mmc** command opens a Microsoft Management Console. In Windows XP Professional, you'll need only these two switches:

♦ *path\filename.msc*—Opens a saved console named *filename.msc*

♦ */a*—Opens the console in author mode

More

Use the **more** command to see the contents of a text file without modifying it. The **more** command has several parameters.

♦ [*drive:*] [*path*] *filename*—Specifies the file to display

♦ *command*—Specifies a command to display the output

- ◆ **/c**—Clears the screen before displaying the data

- ◆ **/s**—Changes multiple blank lines in the output to only a single blank line

- ◆ **files**—Is used to list multiple files to display

Msinfo32

Use the **msinfo32** command to display information about your hardware, system, and software. There are three switches and parameters:

- ◆ **/nfo**—Saves the exported file as an .nfo file

- ◆ **/report**—Saves the exported files as a text file

- ◆ **/computer** *computername*—Obtains information from a remote computer

Nbtstat

Use this command to display NetBIOS-over-TCP/IP protocol statistics. Use these switches and parameters:

- ◆ **-a** *RemoteName*—Specifies the name of a remote computer for which you want to display these statistics

- ◆ **-A** *Ipaddress*—Specifies the IP address of a remote computer for which you want to display these statistics

- ◆ **-c**—Displays the NetBIOS name cache, the table, and the resolved IP addresses

Netstat

This command shows all active TCP connections, the ports the computer listens on, Ethernet stats, IP routing table information, IP statistics, and more. Use these switches and parameters:

- ◆ **-a**—Displays the active TCP connections and the TCP and UDP ports that the computer listens to

- ◆ **-e**—Displays Ethernet statistics

- ◆ **-n**—Displays active TCP connections using addresses and port numbers

- ◆ **-o**—Displays active TCP connections and includes the process ID numbers for each connection

- ◆ **-p** *protocol*—Shows connections based on a specific protocol, such as TCP, UDP, etc.

- ◆ **-s**—Shows statistics by protocol

- ◆ **-r**—Displays the IP routing table

Nslookup

The **nslookup** command is used to get information about the current DNS name server. Entering "nslookup" followed by the computer name or server name produces a message about the state of the DNS server. These messages include "No response from server," "Non-existent domain," "Connection refused," "Server failure," and others. This command can be used to troubleshoot DNS problems on the network.

Ntbackup

The **ntbackup** command can be used to perform backups at the command line instead of through Windows XP's Backup utility. Use these switches and parameters:

♦ **systemstate**—Backs up the system state

♦ **@bks *filename***—Specifies the backup file that is to be used for this backup operation

♦ **/J *"jobname"***—Specifies the job name

♦ **/P *"poolname"***—Specifies the media pool from which you want to select the media. This switch cannot be used with **/A**, **/G**, **/F**, or **/T**

♦ **/G *"guid name"***—Overwrites or appends to the current tape. This switch cannot be used with **/P**

♦ **/T *"tape name"***—Overwrites or appends to the tape. This switch cannot be used with **/P**

♦ **/N *"media name"***—Specifies a new tape name. This switch cannot be used with **/A**

♦ **/F *"file name"***—Specifies the path to the disk and the file name. This switch cannot be used with **/P**, **/G**, or **/T**

♦ **/D *"set descriptor"***—Specifies a name for each backup set

♦ **/A**—Appends the data to the end of the tape. This switch must be used with either **/G** or **/T**, but not with **/P**

♦ **/V: Yes | No**—Verifies the data after the backup is completed

♦ **/R:Yes | No**—Restricts access to the tape to owners or administrators

♦ **/L : f | s | n**—Specifies the type of log file to use: full, summary, or none

♦ **/M *backup type***—Allows you to choose a backup type: normal, copy, differential, incremental, or daily

♦ **/HC:on | off**—Uses hardware compression

Pathping

Use the **pathping** command when you aren't sure where on the network your data packets are being dropped or lost. **Pathping** sends requests to all routers on the network and compiles data about those routers. If data is being lost at a specific router or in a certain subnet, troubleshooting network problems is now narrowed down to a specific area or router. Use these switches and parameters:

♦ **-n**—Does not try to resolve IP addresses to their names, and therefore speeds up the **pathping** process

♦ **-h** *maximum hops*—Sets the maximum number of hops that the **pathping** command will take to reach its destination. The default is 30

♦ **- p** *period*—Specifies how long to wait between pings; time is measured in milliseconds. The default is 250 milliseconds

♦ **- w** *timeout*—Specifies the number of milliseconds to wait for each reply. The default is 3,000 milliseconds

♦ **targetname**—Specifies the name or IP address of the destination

Ping

This command allows you to verify that your computer can communicate with another on the network. Although there are multiple parameters and switches (similar to those in **pathping**), **ping** is generally used like this:

```
PING ipnumber of destination address
```

Print

Use the **print** command to send a text file to a printer. Use these parameters:

♦ **/d:***printer*—Specifies the printer. By default, the print job is sent to LTP1, the local printer port

♦ **[***drive:***] [***path***]** *filename*—Specifies a remote printer

Rename

Use this command to rename a single file or a set of files. Use these parameters:

♦ **[***drive:***] [***path***]** *filename1*—Specifies the location of the file or sets of files you want to rename

♦ *filename2*—Specifies the new name for the file

Rmdir

Use this command to remove a directory. This command is used with the parameters *drive* and *path*, as detailed in other commands.

Runas

This command allows you to run programs with different permissions than the ones provided by the account you logged on with. This command allows an administrator to log on as a power user and still use the Administrators account with **runas** when necessary. Use these switches and parameters:

- **/profile**—Loads the user's profile

- **/no profile**—Does not load a user profile

- **/env**—Uses the current network environment instead of the local user's profile

- **/netonly**—Specifies user information for remote access users only

- **/smartcard**—Is used when credentials from a smart card are needed

- **/user:***user account name*—Specifies the user account under which the application is to be run

Secedit

This command compares your current security settings to those in a template provided by Windows XP Professional, and reports on the differences and possible weaknesses in your setup. There are four **secedit** switches, each having their own switches and parameters:

- **secedit /analyze**—Analyzes current settings

- **secedit /configure**—Applies a specific stored template

- **secedit /export**—Exports a stored template to a security template file

- **secedit /validate**—Validates the syntax of the template to be imported for analysis

SystemInfo

The **systeminfo** command displays information about the computer and its operating system, security, hardware, and product ID. Use these parameters and switches:

- **/s** *computer*—Specifies the computer by name or IP address when you want to connect to a remote computer

- **/u** *domain\user*—Runs the command using a specific user account; the default is the current user

- **/p** *password*—Specifies the password if one is required or the **/u** switch is used

- **/fo**—Specifies how data should be displayed. You can choose Table, List, or CSV (comma-separated values)

Tracert

Use this command when you need to trace a packet's progress from its source address to its destination. The information shown includes the path of the data and the routers that were used, as well as the amount of time taken at each stop. Use these parameters:

- **-d**—Does not try to resolve IP addresses to their names, and therefore speeds up the **tracert** process

- **-h** *maximum hops*—Sets the maximum number of hops that the **tracert** command will take to reach its destination. The default is 30

- **- w** *timeout* —Specifies the number of milliseconds to wait for the reply message. The default is 4,000

- *targetname*—Specifies the name or IP address of the destination

Ver

Use this command to display the version of Windows XP you are using.

Additional Command-Line Tools

As mentioned earlier, several tools that weren't introduced are far less common and more difficult to use than those just described. To get help on these tools, simply open a command prompt, and enter the name of the command-line tool, followed by the /? switch . In addition, you can type the command in the Search box of the Help and Support Center for more information. Here are the additional tools:

- **Arp**

- **Assoc**

- **At**

- **Atmadm**

- **Bootcfg**

- **Cacls**

- **Call**

- **Change**

- **Chcp**

- **Chkntfs**

- **Cipher**

- **Cmd**

- Cmstp

- Color

- Comp

- Compact

- Cprofile

- Diskpart

- Echo

- Endlocal

- EventCreate

- Eventtriggers

- Evntcmd

- Exit

- Fc

- Findstr

- Finger

- Flattemp

- For

- Fsutil

- Ftp

- Ftype

- Getmac

- GoTo

- Graftabl

- Helpctr

- Hostname

- If

- Ipseccnd

- Ipxroute
- Irftp
- Lodctr
- Logman
- Lpq
- Lpr
- Macfile
- Mode
- Mountvol
- Move
- Msiexec
- Netsh
- Ntcmdprompt
- Ntsd
- Openfiles
- Pagefileconfig
- Path
- Pause
- Pbadmin
- Pentnt
- Perfmon
- Popd
- Prncnfg
- Prndrvr
- Prnjobs
- Prnmngr
- Prnport

- Prnqctl
- Prompt
- Pushd
- Query
- Rasdial
- Rcp
- Recover
- Reg
- Regsvr32
- Relob
- Rem
- Replace
- Reset Session
- Rexec
- Route
- Rsh
- Rsm
- Sc
- Schtasks
- Set
- Setlocal
- Shift
- Shutdown
- Sort
- Start
- Subst
- Sfc

- ◆ Taskkill

- ◆ Tasklist

- ◆ Tcmsetup

- ◆ Tftp

- ◆ Time

- ◆ Tree

- ◆ Type

- ◆ Typeperf

- ◆ Unlodctr

- ◆ Verify

- ◆ Vol

- ◆ Vssadmin

- ◆ W32tm

- ◆ Winnt

- ◆ Winnt32

- ◆ Xcopy

Using Support Tools

Advanced users—such as members of the Power Users group, the Administrators group, or the Server Operators group—might want to use the support tools that come with Windows XP Professional. These tools are not installed by default because using them incorrectly could cause the system to become unstable. However, they are available from the Windows XP Professional CD and are useful when diagnosing computer problems. It is recommended that only experienced, advanced users install and use these tools.

Installing the Support Tools

To install the support tools:

1. Log on as an administrator.

2. Insert the CD. On the Welcome screen, select Perform Additional Tasks.

3. Choose Browse This CD.

4. Locate the Support | Tools folder.

5. Double-click Setup.exe.

6. Choose Next to start the Windows Support Tools Setup Wizard.

7. Read and accept the license agreement, and choose Next.

8. On the User Information page, fill in your name and organization, and choose Next.

9. On the Select An Installation Type page, select Custom, and choose Next.

10. On the Destination Directory page, verify that the volume and directory are correct, and choose Install Now.

11. Choose Finish.

Using the Support Tools

Support tools, which should be used only by experienced support personnel, are used to troubleshoot network problems. Approximately 50 support tools are available, and describing them is beyond the scope of this book. To see a list of support tools, open the Help and Support Center, and type "alphabetical list of tools" in the Search box. Select Alphabetical List Of Tools from the options for full-text searches. From here, you can choose the tools you are interested in and read information about them.

Note
One last troubleshooting tool is the Recovery Console, discussed in Chapter 14.

Reinstalling Windows XP Professional

If worse comes to worst, you might have to boot up using the Windows XP Professional CD, and reinstall the operating system. Although this situation is rare, occasionally it does happen. In addition, you might simply want to start over with a clean slate. In either case, reinstalling Windows XP Professional is quite easy.

Setting the BIOS to Boot from the CD-ROM

If you can't boot your computer at all, you can enter the computer's BIOS and set it to boot from the CD-ROM drive. This way, you can at least get to the Welcome screen of the CD to perform the reinstallation. (If you can boot to the operating system and you simply *want* to reinstall, this is not a required step.)

To set up the BIOS to boot from the CD-ROM drive:

1. Boot the computer, and watch the screen carefully. At the start of the boot process, you'll see information on how to enter "Setup" or "Computer setup." Press the appropriate key (usually the Del key or a function key).

2. In the Setup utility, you'll need to move to the section entitled BIOS Features or Advanced BIOS Features. Because different BIOS versions have different interfaces, you might have to look around a bit.

3. On the BIOS settings page, locate information that details in what order the boot process takes place. Sometimes this information is all on one line; sometimes it is on a different line for each boot device. Change the setting so that the first boot device is the CD-ROM drive.

4. Exit the utility, and save the changes.

Warning
Be extremely careful not to make any other changes to the BIOS or CMOS when exiting. Changing settings here could cause serious problems.

Gathering Required Drivers

If you can boot your system, but you want to reinstall Windows, you should list all of the hardware on your system (perhaps by printing a report as detailed in the beginning of this chapter), and gather all of the necessary drivers before continuing. Even if you can't boot the system, gathering drivers is important, especially if you have a SCSI hard drive that isn't recognized by Windows XP Professional.

You'll probably need drivers for these devices:

♦ Hard disk drive

♦ NIC

♦ Sound card

♦ Video card

♦ Modem

You might also need the name of the workgroup or domain, information about protocols and IP addressing, and/or permission from your network administrator. Make sure you know the Windows product key.

Checking Compatibility

With driver and network information in hand, let Windows XP Professional perform a compatibility report before installing. This is especially important if you've previously installed Windows XP Professional and it isn't performing exactly as you'd hoped. From the compatibility report, you can obtain additional drivers as needed, and you might even find the source of previous problems.

To have Windows XP Professional check the compatibility of your computer:

1. Either boot using the Windows XP Professional CD, or place the CD in the CD-ROM drive if the computer is started.

2. On the Welcome screen shown in Figure A.18, choose Check System Compatibility.

3. On the What Do You Want To Do page, choose Check My System Automatically.

4. On the Get Updated Setup Files page, select Yes, Download The Updated Setup Files (Recommended), and choose Next.

5. On the Report System Compatibility page, choose Details. In the Microsoft XP Upgrade Advisor dialog box, read about the compatibility problems (if any).

6. Choose OK and Finish.

If necessary, obtain any necessary drivers before continuing with the installation.

Upgrade or New Installation?

The next decision you have to make is whether you want to upgrade Windows XP Professional or perform a new installation. If you want to keep your personal files and folders,

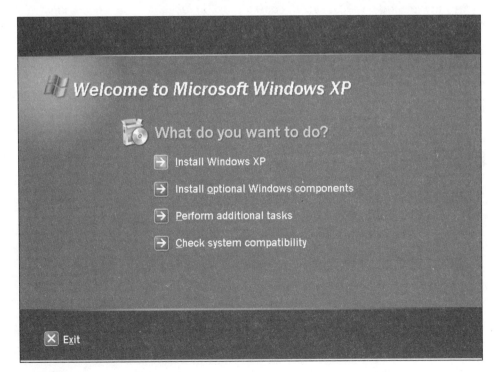

Figure A.18
Preparing to check system compatibility.

Internet settings, printer settings, hardware installations, personal settings on the desktop, items in the Favorites folder, and so on, you'll want to upgrade. Upgrading reinstalls the operating system while keeping personal files and settings.

If you want your system to look and act the way it did when you first purchased the computer (or installed Windows XP the first time), you'll want to perform a new installation. Keep in mind that with a new installation, the hard drive will be formatted, and all personal data, personal settings, and hardware settings will be lost. A new installation is just that—the operating system and the computer are just like new.

This section explains how to do a new installation and an upgrade. The only difference between the installation and upgrade processes is the number of screens you have to respond to. For instance, in an upgrade, the computer knows what time zone you are in and whether you belong to a specific workgroup or domain. In a new installation, you must input this data, reinstall all drivers, input the network information, set the date and time, and more.

Note

For a new installation, you should pencil in approximately one hour for the installation and another three or four hours for configuration. This includes installing printers and other hardware, installing their drivers, setting up a network, connecting to the Internet, and personalizing the desktop. For an upgrade, you'll need only about one hour because all personal settings and hardware are still configured.

Performing a New Installation

To reinstall Windows XP Professional, simply boot using the Windows XP Professional CD, or place the CD in the CD-ROM drive if the computer is already booted up. On the Welcome screen shown in Figure A.18, choose Install Windows XP, and follow the steps listed next:

Warning

With a new installation, the hard drive will be formatted, and all personal data, personal settings, and hardware settings will be lost.

1. On the Welcome To Windows Setup page, select New Installation. Choose Next.

2. On the License Agreement page, accept the agreement and choose Next.

3. On the Your Product Key page, type the product key. If the key doesn't work the first time, review the numbers and letters, and carefully make corrections. Choose Next.

4. On the Select Options page, choose the Accessibility Options button to open the dialog box where you set accessibility options. Set your options, and choose OK.

5. Choose the Advanced Options button if you want to change the installation folder, copy all installation files from the setup CD, or choose the installation drive and partition

during setup. In Advanced Options, check the checkbox I Want To Choose The Install Drive Letter And Partition During Setup. Choose OK.

6. In the Select The Primary Language And Regions You Want To Use drop-down list, select your primary language. Choose Next.

7. On the Get Updated Setup Files page, select Yes, Download The Updated Setup Files (Recommended), and choose Next.

8. After the computer reboots, press F6 if you need to install a third-party driver for a SCSI hard drive. You have to be quick to catch this! If you press F6, you'll be prompted by an additional screen to place the floppy disk with the driver in the floppy disk drive and press the S key.

9. At the Welcome To Setup installation screen, press Enter to continue with the installation.

10. On the Windows XP Professional Setup screen, highlight the partition where you want to install Windows XP, and press the Esc key to continue installing a fresh copy of Windows XP.

11. On the next Windows XP Professional screen, select the partition where you want to install Windows XP, and press Enter. If multiple partitions exist and you want to delete those partitions, highlight the partition you want to delete, and press D. From the resulting screen, press L to verify the deletion. Deleting a partition erases everything on the partition. If you want to create a partition in any unpartitioned space, press C, and in the resulting page, specify the partition size.

12. If prompted with a "Caution" message, press C to continue.

13. At the next Caution page, press L to continue with the installation. This will format the current hard drive and install a fresh copy of Windows XP Professional.

14. Setup then deletes existing files, copies new files, and begins the installation. This could take 15 minutes or so, depending on the speed of your computer. When this phase is completed, the computer reboots. If you have a floppy disk in the floppy disk drive, remove it.

15. The graphical phase of the installation begins and works through Preparing Installation, Installing Windows, and Finalizing Installation. You will not need to do anything until prompted. Do not worry if the screen flickers. When prompted at the Regional And Language Options page, make any changes necessary, and choose Next.

16. On the Personalize Your Software page, type your name and organization, and choose Next.

17. On the Computer Name And Administrator Password page, type a computer name and an administrator password. Choose Next.

18. On the Modem Dialing Information page, select your country, type your area code, and type a number for dialing an outside line (if applicable). Select the Tone Dialing or Pulse Dialing option, and choose Next.

19. On the Date And Time Settings page, verify the date and time, and select a time zone. Choose Next.

20. If you have a NIC installed in your computer, you'll be prompted with the Networking Settings page. Select the Custom Settings option, and choose Next.

21. On the Networking Components page, add any protocols necessary that aren't already added by default. For instance, if you need IPX/SPX, do the following: Choose the Install button; on the Select Network Component Type page, select Protocol and choose the Add button; then select NWLink IPX/SPX/NetBIOS Compatible Transport Protocol. You can also install similar features for clients and services. These steps are necessary only if you need to connect to a Novell NetWare network. Choose Next.

22. On the Workgroup Or Computer Domain page, type the name of the workgroup or the domain you want to connect to. Choose Next.

23. When the installation is completed, the computer will reboot.

24. On the Welcome To Microsoft Windows page, choose Next to begin the licensing and registration process.

25. Windows XP will attempt to connect to the Internet so that you can register your software with Microsoft. You can also begin setting up your home network or your connection to the Internet. Work through the choices in these few screens, and press F1 if you need help. (Remember, you have to get a license from Microsoft, but you do not have to register with Microsoft.)

26. On the Who Will Use This Computer page, type the names of all users who will access this computer. Choose Next.

27. On the Thank You screen, choose Finish.

In the best scenario, Windows XP starts with sound, and the display can be set for more than 16 colors. In addition, the modem and the NIC work. This isn't usually the case, though. In my experience, there are always one or two stubborn drivers or pieces of hardware that won't work correctly. After determining what those problems are, return to the appropriate chapter in this book to reinstall or configure the device.

Performing an Upgrade

Performing an upgrade takes much less time than does installing a new copy of the operating system. As with a new installation, boot to the Windows XP Professional CD, or place the CD in the CD-ROM drive if the computer is already booted up. On the Welcome screen shown in Figure A.18, choose Install Windows XP, and follow these steps:

1. On the Welcome To Windows Setup page, select Upgrade (Recommended). Choose Next.

2. On the License Agreement page, accept the agreement and choose Next.

3. On the Your Product Key page, type the product key. If the key doesn't work the first time, review the numbers and letters, and carefully make corrections. Choose Next.

4. On the Get Updated Setup Files page, select Yes, Download The Updated Setup Files (Recommended), and choose Next.

5. After the computer reboots, press F6 if you need to install a third-party driver for a SCSI hard drive. You have to be quick to catch this! If you press F6, you'll be prompted by an additional screen to place the floppy disk with the driver in the floppy disk drive and press the S key.

6. Because the upgrade is performed automatically, you won't need to do anything until the upgrade is completed. Then you'll be asked again to register and such. Complete the screens, and choose Finish.

When a Good Installation Goes Bad

Occasionally, an installation of Windows XP Professional will need to be repaired. This doesn't apply only to installations that went awry; this also applies to a Windows XP Professional installation that has been in service a while. If you find that your Windows XP Professional computer is missing files, failing to boot, or otherwise acting strangely, you can work through the upgrade steps to try to repair the installation. This doesn't always work for an existing system, but it is worth a try if installing a fresh copy of the operating system isn't an option. If an installation was stopped due to a power outage or hardware failure, installation should continue automatically. If not, simply restart the installation manually.

Wrapping Up

In this appendix, you learned how to troubleshoot various types of hardware and software problems, how to use administrative tools, and how to reinstall Windows. If you did not find what you need in this appendix, consider returning to the chapter that addresses your hardware or software, or consider contacting Microsoft for help.

Glossary

Accessibility Wizard—A wizard you can use to configure all of the Windows accessibility options at once. Accessibility options include Magnifier, Narrator, StickyKeys, and SoundSentry.

account lockout duration—The number of minutes an account will be locked out (unavailable) after the account lockout threshold has been met. The range is from 1 to 99,999 minutes. You can also set the account lockout duration to zero. This setting must be greater than or equal to the reset account counter. An account lockout value must be set for an account lockout duration to be needed.

account lockout threshold—The number of bad password attempts that can be made before the account is locked out. This can be a number from 1 to 999, or it can be set to 0 to ensure that the account will never be locked out. Failed logons from password-protected screensavers or from intentionally locking the computer using Ctrl+Alt+Del do not count against this threshold number. By default, the setting is not configured.

account policies—Policies configured for users and user accounts. There are two types of account policies: password policies and account lockout policies. Account policies always affect users no matter what computer they log onto. In a domain, an administrator configures account policies for users in the domain, but on a Windows XP Professional workstation, the policy affects only the users who log onto the computer for which the policy is configured. Account lockout policies restrict how many times a user can try unsuccessfully to log in before that user's account is locked out.

Activation—Anti-piracy technology designed by Microsoft to verify that its software products have been legitimately licensed. During the installation of Windows, the Setup Wizard asks for a product key. This is a 25-character alphanumeric code that is located on the software package, and Windows cannot be installed until this code is typed in correctly. After Windows is installed, you are prompted to register this number with Microsoft through the Internet. A snapshot is taken of the computer and its hardware, including machine-specific identifiers.

This information is referred to as a *hardware identifier*; it's used with the product ID number to create a unique picture of the computer and software. Microsoft claims that this process is totally anonymous and that no personal information is sent to Microsoft.

Active Directory—A component of Windows 2000 Server and Windows XP Server that manages user access to the network, including logging on, getting authenticated, accessing the shared resources, and accessing the directory itself. The directory stores information about all of the resources on the network and makes this information available to all users on the network. Active Directory also allows each user to use one logon to gain access to all resources.

active partition—The partition the computer boots from, typically C:. The active partition can be changed as the computer boots up, and the active partition can be a hard disk, a CD-ROM drive, or a Zip drive. You can change the active partition by pressing keys such as Del or Ctrl+Tab during startup, entering the BIOS, and making the appropriate changes.

Administrator account—An account that is set up automatically when Windows XP Professional is installed; it's the first account an administrator uses to access the new operating system. This account cannot be deleted or disabled, although administrators usually create accounts for themselves for security reasons and do not log on with the default Administrator account.

Administrators group—The least restrictive group available. Administrators have full control of the computer, the network, and user accounts. Only a few users should be in this group, and they should be chosen carefully. Even when users are in the Administrators group, they should log on as an administrator only when necessary. Otherwise, they should log on as a power user or a user. This guideline is important because certain viruses, when attacking through an administrator's account, can cause many more problems than they can when attacking through a more restricted account.

Advanced Configuration and Power Interface (ACPI)—An industry-standard technology for managing power used by the computer. For you to use all of the power management options available in Windows XP Professional, your computer will need to support ACPI. If you are not sure if your computer supports ACPI, check the documentation that came with the computer.

AT service account—An account configured to run tasks from a command line. This service account is similar to a user account and can be configured from inside Scheduled Tasks. The AT service account can be the system account or a specific account chosen by the administrator.

audit policies—Policies that allow an administrator to track such things as account logon events, directory service access, object access, and policy changes.

auditing—A way to keep track of events that take place on the local computer. Several items can be audited, and it is useful to audit at least a few of these so that when problems occur, you have a place to start when looking for a solution.

Authenticode—An industry standard for verifying the security of downloaded files from the Internet. Downloading programs, even something as simple as a screensaver, can be disastrous if the programs are not verified by a reliable source. Microsoft offers this standard to all users of Internet Explorer. As files are downloaded, it checks that the downloaded program has a valid certificate and that the publisher matches the name on the certificate. Microsoft Authenticode is not responsible for how well the program works; Authenticode establishes only that the program is safe for download and is made available by a known and reliable source.

author mode—Access mode that grants the user of a custom console full access to all MMC functionality. When a Microsoft Management Console is saved in author mode, users can add or remove snap-ins, view all portions of the console tree, and save consoles.

Auto Arrange—A menu command that arranges desktop icons by aligning them with an underlying grid. When you choose Auto Arrange, icons that you move later are still arranged in the grid and remain neatly organized. You can use the Display Properties dialog box to adjust the horizontal and vertical icon spacing.

AutoComplete—An Internet Explorer feature that automatically completes typed information for Web addresses, forms, usernames, and passwords.

Automated System Recovery (ASR)—A feature that reinstalls Windows XP and re-creates the system by using the information on the ASR floppy disk previously made. The ASR Wizard is used to back up the system state, system services, information about applications, and all disks that hold operating system files and components. ASR also saves the disk configurations and disk signatures, volumes, and partitions so the computer can be started. ASR also backs up portions of the Registry that PnP devices use and that can be restored after a disaster.

automatic updates—Service packs, hot fixes, and bug fixes that can be downloaded from Microsoft's Web site for free. You can configure how you want to be notified of these updates.

Backup Operators group—A group whose members can back up and restore users' files and folders, as well as system state files and other critical operating system files. As a precautionary measure, a common practice is to give these users permission to either back up or restore, but not both. A user could do a great deal of harm by backing up, changing, and restoring harmful data to the network. Backup operators in corporate networks have permissions that allow them to access user files and to read and write to those files. Administrators should put group policies in place to prevent these users from having this type of access.

basic disk—A hard disk that contains a primary partition and possibly extended partitions and logical drives. The basic disk's primary partition holds the operating system that came installed on the computer. Basic disks can also be used to create other types of configurations, such as spanned, mirrored, striped, and RAID 5 volumes. Basic disks can be accessed by MS-DOS and are backward-compatible with Windows NT volume sets, striped sets, mirrored volumes, and disk striping with parity. All versions of Windows, including 9x and NT, can use basic disks because this technology is an industry standard. Basic disks can be converted to dynamic disks without data loss, but the reverse is not true.

BIOS (Basic Input/Output System)—A set of software routines used to configure how the computer boots. The computer can boot from a floppy drive, hard drive, CD-ROM drive, or removable media.

Blue Screen of Death (BSOD)—The blue screen that appears when the computer encounters a STOP error. When this happens, the computer must be rebooted, sometimes by turning it off and back on, as opposed to just restarting it.

boot partition—The partition on the hard drive that holds the Windows XP operating system files. The boot partition can also be the system partition but doesn't have to be. Note that the boot partition holds the system files, and the system partition holds the boot files.

Briefcase—A Windows utility used to transfer files and folders from your desktop computer to your laptop by using a direct cable connection, removable media, or a network connection. Briefcase is similar to the Offline Files feature in that synchronization plays a part in keeping the two sets of files up-to-date.

bus topology—A network configuration in which each computer connects to a central communications cable. Each computer or resource has a unique address on the network and passes data to others using the appropriate addresses. At each end of the bus, a terminator is used to stop the signals that did not find their way from bouncing back and forth indefinitely.

caching—A process used when the computer stores files temporarily, but the word "caching" is used in a number of contexts. When you connect to the Internet and visit multiple sites, you can revisit sites quickly by using the Back button on your browser because those network addresses are cached in your computer's memory. You can also check the History folder for recently cached addresses. Offline files and folders use caching to store data temporarily.

certificate—A statement that verifies that an entity is who it says it is. Certificates identify people and Web sites on the Internet so that a visitor can verify the security of a business or individual. There are several types of certificates, including Web server, server, wireless server, and personal.

ClearType—A Windows XP feature used on laptops to make the screen fonts more readable. ClearType was created for flat screens like those on laptops and for the newer versions of flat screens for desktop PCs. ClearType won't work well on larger, more common computer monitors.

coaxial cable—A type of cable used to transport data between computers. Coaxial cable consists of a center wire surrounded by insulation and then a grounded shield of braided wire; coaxial cable is used for cable TV and some cable Internet access.

Component Services—A Windows component used by administrators, software developers, and programmers to deploy and administrator COM+ applications and to automate administrative tasks through scripts and programs. COM+ is an extension of the Component Object Model and is used to simplify the creation of these types of applications.

compression—A technology that decreases the amount of space that data takes up on the hard drive, leaving more room for additional data. Windows XP Professional offers two types of compression: NTFS compression and zipped folders.

Computer Management console—A tool used by administrators to manage a local or remote computer; the console provides a graphical interface. The Computer Management console combines several of the most-used administrative tools, such as Event Viewer, Local Users And Groups, and Disk Defragmenter.

console—A place to group programs, tools, or folders so that you or other users can access them more easily and from one location. Consoles are sometimes divided into two panes.

console tree—Located in the left pane of a Microsoft Management Console, this tree can be hidden if necessary. The tree lists the contents of the console. Clicking an area of the tree displays the corresponding console item in the right pane.

container object—An item used to group similar objects, such as printers, computers, or data. For example, a folder is a container object because it holds files.

Content Advisor—A feature used to filter out unwanted content from Internet sites that contain graphic language, nudity, sex, or violence. The Content Advisor is a great tool for administrators (and parents) who want to prevent users from accessing such sites.

cookies—Files that enable you to visit a Web site and automatically obtain information such as news or weather for your specific part of the country, or have a Web site remember your name or personal preferences. Cookies also help companies serve you better by remembering what banner ads have already been displayed and what types of books or music you generally prefer.

copy backup—A backup method used when selected files and folders need to be backed up. The copy backup does not look at archive attributes or reset them. The copy backup is good for intermediate backups of files or folders in between more complete backups, such as normal (full) or incremental backups. Because a copy backup doesn't change the archive bit, it doesn't affect any other future backup.

Daily backup—A backup method that backs up all selected files and folders that changed that day. This type of backup doesn't look at or clear archive bits. It simply looks for the files or folders that have been changed on a particular date and backs up those files.

Desktop Cleanup—A utility that moves unused shortcuts to a desktop folder called Unused Desktop Shortcuts. This utility does not move, change, or delete any files or programs; it moves only the shortcuts.

Details pane—This Microsoft Management Console pane displays the details for the item that is selected in the console tree. These details might be a list, properties of the item, or services or events that work with the item chosen.

Device Driver Rollback—An option in all of the driver Properties dialogs on the system. Driver Rollback allows you to recover from the installation of a driver that doesn't work or that causes the computer to hang or not start.

device drivers—Software that allows the operating system and the hardware to communicate with each other. Without this communication, the device would not be able to act on your command, which is forwarded from you to the operating system and then to the device and back again. Because the computer and the hardware communicate in different languages, a translator is needed. The device driver serves as this translator.

Device Manager—A tool that lists all of the hardware devices installed on the computer and that can be used to change the properties or the drivers of any device.

differential backup—A backup method that backs up only files or folders that have the archive attribute. Having this attribute means that the file has changed since it was last backed up with a normal or incremental backup. The differential backup does not clear the archive attribute and is one of the faster ways to perform a backup. If you use a combination of normal and differential backups, you can restore a system with the last normal backup followed by the last differential backup.

digital signatures—Technology that ensures that a device driver has passed a specific level of testing and that the file has not been tampered with or modified since being tested. The knowledge that the driver to be installed is safe, or that its level of safety isn't known, can help you determine if the file should be installed or not.

disk quotas—Settings that allow administrators to limit how much disk space users have access to for saving their files and other data. Disk quotas are available only on NTFS volumes.

disk striping with parity—A disk array that is like regular disk striping except that an extra disk is configured to hold parity information about the data. This parity information can be used to reconstruct the data should one of the disks crash. (Parity is a value that is calculated based on the number of ones and zeros that make up the data being saved.) Disk striping with parity works like this: Data is written to the disks in chunks simultaneously. If the RAID 5 set has five disks, then four of them get data written to them, while the fifth gets the parity information. If one of the disks fails, the data can be re-created using the parity information. These volumes have better read performance than mirrored volumes do, but when a disk is missing or has failed, the read performance suffers tremendously until the volume is repaired. RAID 5 is not available on Windows XP Professional machines but can be used in Server editions.

DLL (dynamic link library) files—Executable routines used by specific applications. These routines are stored in the library and are used only when called upon by the application.

domain—A group of network computers and devices that are administered as a unit. Domains are usually used in medium to large networks, and an administrator in the organization manages all of the users' computers and their respective user and group accounts. Large networks can have several domains, and each domain has a computer serving as a domain controller.

domain accounts—Accounts that limit or allow access to domain servers, databases, company printers, sensitive information, and more.

domain policy—A group policy created for the entire domain.

DualView—A new technology allowing you to attach a separate monitor to your laptop and view different items on each screen. DualView is similar to installing multiple monitors. DualView has several uses; on the laptop screen, for instance, you can work on an Excel document, while the additional monitor can display your Web browser or email application. Of course, this gives you extra room when you're using the laptop at the office.

dynamic disks—Disks that offer features that basic disks do not, such as the ability to extend the volume to span multiple disks instead of extending it to include extra space at the end of only the one physical disk. With a dynamic disk, you can also create fault-tolerant volumes that will protect your data if one of the physical disks fails.

electrostatic discharge (ESD)—Static that is passed from a person to a computer component, usually during installation and almost always unknowingly. ESD can cause numerous problems for computers and their components.

email community—A group of subscribers who exchange email about a certain subject. When one member of the group sends an email message, all members of the group receive it. Then all members can respond to find a solution to the posted problem or expand on ideas that are introduced. Email communities are a good way to meet people of different abilities and interests or talk with other people in your field.

Encrypting File System (EFS)—A security technique that can be used by the general user on a network. When a file is encrypted, its contents are converted into a form that only the file owner and the network administrator can decrypt. Decryption is the process of converting the file back to its original form. Users can encrypt data as they store it on an NTFS disk as long as that data is not also compressed or composed of system files.

Ethernet cables—Network cables that look like telephone cables but are larger. Ethernet cables are referred to as UTP (unshielded twisted-pair) and STP (shielded twisted-pair) cables; they also use RJ-45 connectors.

Event Viewer—A utility that stores logs that are created either automatically or manually to record the performance and integrity of programs, security, and system events on the local computer. Event Viewer can be used to troubleshoot problems related to these items.

explicit permissions—Those permissions that are created automatically when an object is created; for example, a shared folder gives the Everyone group Full Control of the objects in that folder. Explicit permissions are also those permissions that are assigned by an administrator or by the owner of the resource. When special permissions are set, those permissions are explicit.

extended partition—A part of a basic disk that can contain logical drives. You configure logical drives when you want to use more than four partitions on the basic disk. The extended partition can be configured to hold logical drives within the extended partition. Only one of the partitions can be extended.

extensions—Additional snap-in components that provide added functionality to the snap-ins. You can add extensions for only those snap-ins already installed in the custom MMC console. You cannot add snap-ins or extensions to preconfigured consoles.

Fast User Switching—A Windows XP feature that lets users switch from one identity to another easily without having to close programs or save work before doing so. For instance, if one user is logged onto the computer and working on an Excel spreadsheet, and another user needs to log on to retrieve some information from his or her address book, the first user can log off and leave Excel running. When this user logs back on, the Excel program is still running and does not have to be reopened.

Favorites—A folder that lists Web sites designated as favorites by the user. Some sites are included by default, such as MSN.com and the Radio Station Guide. You can also add your own favorites to this list and create folders for organizing them.

fiber optic cable—A type of cable used to transmit data between computers. Fiber optic cable consists of a bundle of glass threads, each of which carries data as light impulses.

File Signature Verification utility—A tool you can use to see which files on your computer are unsigned and to set file-signature verification options. You also see which warnings are shown when you install an unsigned driver. If a driver is signed, it will not be shown on this list.

FilterKeys—An accessibility option in Windows XP. You can have the computer ignore repeated keystrokes, or you can slow down the repeat rate. Settings made for the repeat rate here override the settings made in the Keyboard Properties dialog box.

firewall—A security measure that acts like a proxy server between your network and the Internet. You can use firewalls to configure what can and can't move from the Internet to the local network and vice versa. Firewalls can require both hardware and software to provide security, or they might simply be software. Firewalls are configured either by network domain administers or administrators of workgroups.

fragmentation—The storing of related data in different places on a hard drive. Because the pieces of data are not stored together in a single place and are not stored sequentially, the hard drive has to work harder to retrieve the data. You can defragment a drive by using Disk Defragmenter.

GPResult—A command-line tool that can be used to display group policy settings and RSoP (Resultant Set of Policy) settings for a user or a computer. GPResult provides information about the operating system, the user, and the computer. GPResult also provides information such as the last time the policy was applied, folders that have been redirected, disk quota information, and IP Security settings.

group policies—Policies configured by an administrator and used to specify how users' desktops will look and what they will and will not contain. See group policy object.

group policy object (GPO)—An object created by the administrator through the Group Policy snap-in. The GPO is the instrument for configuring users' desktop settings such as what users see on the Start menu, what desktop wallpaper is used, and what icons are available on the desktop.

Guest account—An account intended for users who have no configured account on the local computer but who need to access the computer briefly to check email or type a quick memo. The Guest account does not have a password, so these users can log on by typing "guest" as the username and leaving the Password box blank. When users log on using the Guest account, they receive the default profile of the local computer. Guests can run programs on the workstation and shut it down, but they have very few permissions and rights beyond that. The Guests group is the most restrictive.

handwriting recognition—Technology that allows you to input data by handwriting it instead of typing it. There are several types of handwriting hardware you can buy; the most popular at this time are graphics tablets and digital pens. These devices are installed like any other piece of hardware and come with accompanying software. The handwritten data can then be included in a document as either typed data or handwritten data.

hardware profile—A set of instructions that tells your computer what to do when the computer boots up. Hardware profiles are especially important for laptops because they will probably be used in multiple hardware settings. For instance, you might configure one hardware profile for the office, a second hardware profile for use on the road, and a third hardware profile for working at home. The office profile could include a printer, a scanner, and a network connection; the mobile profile could include a portable printer and a telephone network connection; and the home profile could include the family's printers and Zip drives and a Remote Desktop connection.

hash rule—A rule created by a hash algorithm, which is composed of data such as a session key or a piece of code that uniquely identifies a program or a file. You can configure the hash rule so that users cannot run a specific file or application.

hibernation—A power-saving mode. When the computer hibernates, it stores any unsaved information to the hard disk and then shuts down. When the computer comes out of hibernation, the information is restored.

High Contrast—An accessibility option for vision-impaired users. This option allows you to use colors and fonts that make reading the screen easier. Several high-contrast schemes are available, including ones that use large letters or white letters on a black background.

home-phone-line network adapter (HPNA)—A hardware device that provides an ideal way to configure a home network. Each computer on the network needs an HPNA, which must be plugged into the phone jacks in the home or office. Data is then sent from computer to computer via the phone lines in the home office.

hub—A piece of hardware used to connect all of the computers in the network. Using a hub is currently the most common way to create a small network, but there are other options. Cables connect the computers, converters, and hubs.

HyperTerminal—A utility that is used to connect to other computers that belong to Telnet sites, bulletin board systems, online services, and the like. This connection can be made through a modem, a null modem cable, or an Ethernet connection. This method is less common than it used to be, and HyperTerminal isn't used very much these days. However, in certain circumstances, it can prove useful.

ICS Discovery and Control—A utility that allows a client to monitor and manage the shared Internet connection from any computer on the network. All clients can use this tool to get information about the shared connection as well as to control it when necessary.

incremental backup—A type of backup in which files and folders with the archive attribute are backed up, just as with the differential backup. The difference between the two methods is that the incremental backup clears the archive bit. This backup method is also very fast, but restoring data from an incremental backup takes longer than restoring from other backup methods. To restore using incremental backups, you must use the last normal backup and then all incremental backups made since that time.

inherited permissions—Permissions that are received from their parent folder (the folder in which they are stored).

instant messaging—A communications service that enables you to chat online with another person. Windows XP Professional includes the Windows Messenger Service. All parties involved in a conversation using Windows Messenger must have a "passport" from Microsoft, which is obtained at no cost over the Internet.

Internet connection sharing (ICS)—A Windows XP feature that enables multiple computers to access the Internet through a single Internet connection, which is set up on the host computer.

Internet Connection Wizard—A wizard you can use to configure your Internet connection for the first time. This wizard is accessed through an icon on the desktop or through the Help and Support Center.

Internet service providers (ISPs)—Companies that provide access to the Internet through their own network servers. These servers are connected to other servers around the world, and information is passed between them. It is these servers and the phone and cable lines that connect them that make the Internet work. To connect to the Internet, you must have an ISP to provide you with access to these servers. The largest ISPs (at the time this book was written) are AT&T, AOL, Earthlink, and MSN.

Internet zone—A zone in Internet Explorer that contains all of the zones that haven't already been manually configured as Trusted Sites, Restricted Sites, or Local Intranet Sites. The Internet zone's default setting is Medium, meaning that safe browsing is enabled, a prompt is issued before you download unsafe content, and unsigned ActiveX controls cannot be downloaded. This setting is suitable for most Internet sites.

IP Security (IPSec) policies—Policies that can be used in both domains and workgroups to provide security when users communicate over Internet Protocol (IP) networks. IPSec protects networks from Internet and other attacks by using open encryption standards. Open standards allow different manufacturers and telecommunication companies to use IPSec without having to develop standards of their own. IPSec provides secure communications between workgroups, LANs, domain clients and servers, and physically remote offices.

Kerberos—An authentication mechanism that is used to verify users and other entities. Kerberos authentication requires a domain controller. If you are a member of a domain, your domain administrator has configured a Kerberos policy for all users.

limited accounts—User accounts that prevent users from installing software or hardware and from changing their account names or types. Users can, however, access the programs that are already installed on the computer, change their passwords and backgrounds, and somewhat personalize their computers.

local area network (LAN)—A network that is configured for the office (workgroup). This network includes only the workgroup itself; it is not part of the Internet. A local area network can also be connected to the Internet.

Local Intranet zone—A zone in Internet Explorer whose security setting is set to Medium-Low by default. Less restrictive than the Medium setting, the Medium-Low setting does not prompt you when dangerous downloads are occurring. It is appropriate for most intranets.

local policies—Policies that are configured for specific computers. Any local policy that is configured affects every person who logs onto the computer. There are three choices for setting local policies: Audit Policy, User Rights Assignment, and Security Options.

local printer—A printer that is usually installed by plugging it into the back of a computer through the LPT1 or USB port. This printer is local to the computer, and if it is a standalone computer, the printer is used only by users of this computer.

local security policy—A policy that affects the security of a local computer. Used by administrators, the Local Security Policy icon opens the Local Security Settings console. In this console, an administrator can configure account policies, local policies, public key policies, software restriction policies, and IP Security policies for the local machine. Setting these policies keeps the computer free from both accidental and malicious tampering or harm. When a local computer is a member of a domain, the local computer's security policy is the least important and the first one overridden, but you can set security policies in case other policies are not in use.

logical drives—Drives that are used to separate data on the hard disk and to further partition the extended drive. Logical drives can be configured only on basic disks because logical drives are derived from an extended partition. These logical drives can be formatted and assigned drive letters, such as E:, F:, or G:. Logical drives are listed in the Computer Management console. When logical drives are listed, not only are the extended partitions shown but so are any floppy drives, CD-ROM drives, and removable disks.

logon rights—Rights that allow or prevent user logons. These rights, which can be allowed or denied, are: Access This Computer From A Network; Log On Locally; Log On As A Batch Job; and Log On As A Service.

Magnifier utility—An accessibility option used to magnify what's on the screen so that it can be seen more easily. This provides a minimum level of functionality for users and, for the most part, is only a temporary application. You'll probably need a much better magnification utility for full-time employees who are sight impaired.

mapping a network drive—A process that allows you to assign a drive letter to a network computer or to a folder on the computer. This drive letter appears in My Computer along with the local drives on the computer. Drive mapping makes drives on other computers easy to access.

mesh topology—A network configuration in which all computers are connected to all others in some manner. This topology is applied effectively in only two networks: the Internet and the public telephone system.

metropolitan area networks (MANs)—Networks that are much smaller than WANs and that do not maintain any satellites or antennae hardware. MANs are typically created to connect multiple offices within the same city or to connect different buildings in a university campus.

Microsoft Management Console (MMC)—A shell used to group administrative tools, folders, Web pages, and other administrative items so that working with these objects is more efficient. An MMC console is made up of panes. The left pane holds the console tree (which is sort of like Windows Explorer trees), and other panes provide different views of the available consoles.

Microsoft Message Queuing (MSMQ)—A utility similar to email, except that email transmits messages between people, whereas Message Queuing transfers messages between applications. When an email message is sent to a recipient, the message is held in a queue (perhaps at your ISP or on your domain's email server) until the recipient logs on and retrieves it. The same is true of message queuing applications. MSMQ is mainly used by system administrators and software developers in a domain.

Microsoft Profile Assistant—Software that is used to store your personal information. This information can then be shared when a Web site requests it from you to make purchases or apply for services.

mirrored disks—A set of two disks, configured such that every time data is written to one disk, it is also written to the other. Mirrored disks are used when data is crucial and always needs to be available no matter what. This setup provides fault tolerance because if one disk crashes, the other is right there to provide data and information to users. Reconstructing the mirror is as simple as replacing the disk and re-creating the mirror configuration.

mounted drive—A hard disk, a floppy disk, a CD, or any other type of disk that is assigned a name instead of a letter. Members of the Administrators group can create mounted drives. A mounted drive is configured using an empty folder on an NTFS volume. The mounted drive is used the same way any other drive is used, except that the mounted drive's name is a path instead of a drive letter as with other drives. When a volume is made into a mounted drive, you can create more than 26 drives on your computer (you won't be limited by the 26 letters of the alphabet). Mounted drives make data more manageable by allowing you to assign each folder a disk quota to limit disk usage by the users who access the drive.

MouseKeys—An accessibility option that enables you to use the keyboard's arrow and keypad keys to perform functions that are normally performed with a mouse. You can also drag items by using the Insert and Delete keys.

Narrator—A text-to-speech utility for users who are unable to read what is on the computer screen due to blindness or impaired vision. Narrator reads what is on the screen, including the menu options, the contents of the active window, and even the text that has been typed. As with the Magnifier, this utility provides only minimal functionality; for everyday use, you'd want a more functional program provided by a third party.

NetMeeting—A Windows application that provides a way to communicate with other people via telephone lines and the Internet to exchange not only voice data but video data as well. With NetMeeting, users can participate in company meetings, see and speak with grandchildren across the country, and share information over a company intranet.

network printer—A printer that network users can use (with the correct permissions) for printing documents. A network printer is a member of a domain, much like a computer is. In a network, a printer is sometimes installed locally, but typically, it is connected to a print server or is part of a pool of printers. A large network can have many printers. These printers can be configured so that some users can print to certain printers, while others cannot. In very large organizations, a print operator is hired to maintain these printers.

newsgroup—An online discussion group. Participating in newsgroups can be an excellent way to obtain information on just about any subject you can imagine. For you to subscribe to a newsgroup, your ISP must have a newsgroup server. The server name is usually in the form *news.servername.xxx*. You also need news-reader software; Outlook Express works for this. After the newsgroup settings have been set up in Outlook Express, you can choose which newsgroups to subscribe to.

normal backup—A type of backup that is sometimes called a *full backup*; all selected files and folders are backed up. When a normal (or full) backup is performed, the archive bit is not a factor because it doesn't matter if the file has been changed since the last backup. However, during a full backup, the archive bit is reset, and it will remain in this state until data in the file is changed. A full backup can be used to restore a system much faster than any other type of backup can. On the other hand, it takes longer to complete and uses more physical media than any other backup type.

NTFS permissions—Permissions used with the NTFS file system. These permissions include Full Control, Modify, Read And Execute, List Folder Contents, Read, Write, and several special permissions. NTFS permissions work both over the network and when a user is sitting at the computer that offers the resource. NTFS permissions can be applied to any folders or files.

Offline Files—A Windows XP feature used to work with files and programs that are stored on network servers. When this option is enabled, you can work on the files even when your computer is not connected to the network server. Other options include synchronizing files when logging off and creating a desktop shortcut to offline files.

On-Screen Keyboard—A utility that provides a virtual keyboard shown on the screen. You can type words by using a joystick or other pointing device. Three modes are available: clicking mode, scanning mode, and hovering mode. There are lots of other options, including displaying the keyboard in different views, using an enhanced keyboard with a numeric keypad, and using a click sound to verify that you've typed a key.

organizational unit policy—The policy created for the organizational unit inside a domain. Organizational units can be departments, types of hardware, or groups of people.

parity—A value that is calculated based on the number of ones and zeros that make up the data being saved. Parity is calculated when RAID 5, disk striping with parity, is used for fault tolerance.

partitions—Portions of the disk that act like separate physical disks.

password policies—Policies governing the use of passwords. You can enforce password history, set a minimum and a maximum password age, set a minimum password length, and set a password complexity requirement. You can also store the passwords using reversible encryption. These policies can be set for domain and local user accounts.

Performance console—A tool that administrators can use to monitor the performance of the system. This console includes both System Monitor and Performance Logs And Alerts. System Monitor logs information about the system's performance and health, and it can be configured to log information about all kinds of events, such as %Processor Time and Memory Pages Per Second. Performance Logs And Alerts can be used to configure three types of data: counter logs, trace logs, and alerts. You can access the Performance console through Administrative Tools in the Control Panel.

Performance Logs And Alerts—A tool that allows an administrator to view or configure counter logs, trace logs, and alerts. Alerts can be set to go off when certain thresholds are met, such as a full hard drive or 100 percent CPU usage for a period of time.

permission—A rule that is associated with an object to regulate who or what can gain access to it. Permissions are used when referring to objects such as files and folders. The permissions Read, Read And Execute, and Write all refer to what a user can do with the file or folder. A permission is given for an object, whereas a right is given to a user.

personal area network—A small network configured for a single user and defined by a personal area of 10 meters or fewer. Individuals can configure these networks to allow their PDAs (personal digital assistants) to communicate with their laptops, or WANs (wide area networks) can be used to allow a user to connect to another user with a cell phone or pager.

personal security certificate—A certificate obtained from a third party. This certificate is like an electronic identity card. You can use this card to encrypt and decrypt data safely on the Internet. Most users won't need such security, but if you do a lot of business over the Web, getting a certificate is recommended.

personalized menus—A Windows feature that offers only those menu choices that you use most often. For instance, after you've been using the computer for a while, choose Start | Programs, and notice that not all of the programs that are available are shown. The information bubble states that these programs are not shown because they haven't been used recently. You can turn this feature off by using the taskbar and Start menu settings.

Phone Dialer—A utility that lets you make a voice call using the recipient's phone number, IP (Internet Protocol) address, or DNS (Domain Name System) name. You can use Phone Dialer with a modem, over a network, or while connected to a LAN. All you need are a microphone and speakers. To receive a call, Phone Dialer must be running.

plug and play (PnP)—A capability that allows you to plug a device into a port and have the device automatically recognized by the operating system. PnP devices are also called "plug-ins," and many devices, including Zip drives and digital cameras, can be plugged in and used without your shutting down and restarting the system.

Power Users group—A group that sits between the Administrators group and the Users group in terms of permissions and rights. Power users can do what any user can do, plus the following: modify computer-wide settings; run non-certified Microsoft applications (programs not accepted by Microsoft as fully compatible with Windows XP); run legacy applications; install applications that do not modify operating system files or add system services; customize Control Panel options, such as date, time, and power options; customize network printers; create local user accounts and local groups; manage local user accounts and local groups; and stop and start system services that do not start by default.

primary partition—The disk from which the computer boots. A primary partition is used when a basic disk is configured. You can have one, two, three, or four primary partitions, or three primary partitions and one extended partition. Primary partitions cannot be subpartitioned.

print processor—A setting used to determine what type of data is being sent from the spooler to the graphics engine. For instance, you might have a print processor that allows Macintosh clients to send PostScript files to raster printers, or one that filters ASCII files for use on a PostScript printer. Generally, the default is fine.

print quality—Print resolution, based on how many dots per inch (dpi) are used when printing a document or photo. The print quality will differ depending on the printer, but 300-dpi and 600-dpi resolutions are fairly common. The higher the print quality is set, the more ink or toner is used. To conserve on ink or toner, you can print at 300 dpi for rough drafts (some applications refer to the lower resolution as "draft output"), and save the higher resolution for final printouts.

print servers—Computers that are used to manage multiple printers from a single location.

print spooler—Software that intercepts print jobs and holds them on the hard drive of a computer until the printer is ready for them.

printer driver—A piece of software that comes with the printer. The driver is located on an accompanying floppy disk or CD. This driver must be installed so that the operating system can work with the printer.

printer pools—Groups of printers that all use the same driver and are configured so network clients can access them.

printing defaults—Print settings that are configured for all users of the computer and that apply unless printing preferences are set within an application.

printing preferences—Print settings configured through applications such as Adobe PhotoDeluxe or Microsoft Word. These preferences apply when those specific applications are used.

privileges—Access levels associated with specific objects, such as printers or files and folders. Privileges are used like permissions to ensure the security of an object. There are two types of user rights: privileges and logon rights. As with similar management tasks, administrators assign privileges and logon rights to groups rather than to individual user accounts. Multiple privileges and rights are available for administrators to grant to users.

Profile Assistant—A Windows tool used to enter personal information and store it on your hard drive for use when needed. No one else can obtain this information from your computer without your permission, and this information cannot be shared with others unless you specifically state that it is to be used.

Program compatibility mode—A mode that enables older programs to be run on a Windows XP Professional machine. All you have to do is install the program and run the Program Compatibility Wizard once to configure the program.

p1rotocol—A set of rules and conventions for sending data over a network. When data is sent from one computer to another, those computers have to agree on a number of things, including content, format, timing, sequencing, and error control. The most commonly used protocol is TCP/IP (Transmission Control Protocol/Internet Protocol). TCP/IP is the protocol (actually, a suite of protocols) that the Internet is based on, and all computers that access the Internet must have this protocol installed and configured.

Recent Documents—A list that provides quick access to the documents you have used most recently. You can show the most recently used documents and/or clear the current document list, which is accessed from the Start menu. Clearing the list does not delete the documents from the hard drive.

Recovery Console—A command-line console (separate from the Windows command prompt) designed to help you recover when your computer does not start. For advanced administrators of computers, this console is available in Windows XP Professional. You should use this tool only if the computer will not boot up and all other attempts at recovery have failed, including safe mode, ASR, System Restore, and restoring from backups. With the Recovery Console, you can enable and disable system services, format disk drives, read and write to local drives, repair system files by copying missing files from floppies or CDs, and even access and format NTFS drives. You can install and configure the Recovery Console so that it is an option at bootup, or you can simply access it from the Windows XP CD when you need it.

refresh—A command that redisplays the content on the current page. This is useful on pages where content changes often, such as news or stock pages.

Regional Options—A Control Panel tool used to set standards and formats for decimal symbols, currency, time, and date configured by country or by component. For instance, English (United States) could be chosen from Standards and Formats, but the currency and dates could be changed to something else (say, Spanish) to match the needs of a particular organization.

registration—The process of sending certain information to the manufacturer of a product you have purchased. Microsoft prompts you to register when installing Windows XP or the first time you turn on the computer. If you register with Microsoft, you'll be prompted for your name, address, ZIP code, and other personal information. You can choose to allow Microsoft to contact you with promotions and information if you'd like to. Registration is different from activation because registration is not required. Do not register if you want to remain totally anonymous with Microsoft.

Registry—A Windows file that contains information about a computer's configuration, such as the programs installed, the hardware on the system, the ports being used, and settings for folders and program icons.

remote access server—A computer that is running the Routing and Remote Access service and that allows other computers to dial into it and access information.

Remote Assistance—A feature that allows you to ask someone else who is running Windows XP to help you solve a problem on your Windows XP computer. For example, using Remote Assistance, you can allow Help Desk personnel to access your computer from the Internet to provide assistance. They will be able to view and control your computer. Remote Assistance can be used to chat with others, let others view your computer screen, and even let others work on your computer from their desktops if you allow it.

Remote Control—A feature of Remote Assistance that allows an Expert user to assist a Non-Expert user by taking control of the computer. When this happens, the Expert can use his or her own mouse and keyboard to use the Non-Expert's computer remotely. In a corporate environment, Remote Control can save time and money by saving an administrator a trip to the user's computer.

Remote Desktop—A Windows feature that allows you to use your computer from another location, such as at home. Using Remote Desktop, you can access all programs, files, and applications from your home computer just as if you were physically sitting at your computer at work.

removable storage—Storage media that are not permanently installed, such as CD changers, hardware libraries containing jukeboxes, and smaller media such as tape drives and Zip drives. The Removable Storage service is used with Microsoft Backup or other backup programs and allows you to manage the hardware from a single location. Remote Storage is a data management service used to move data that is not used often from local storage to remote storage. When the data is needed again, it is retrieved. This service allows the computer to perform better in various ways.

Replicator group—A group used for directory replication functions. This group has only one member: the domain user account used to log onto the Replicator services on the domain controller. Do not add any users to this group.

residential gateway—A hardware device that is set up between the DSL or cable modem and the local area network. These types of connections are more expensive than others and require more time to configure. However, with a residential gateway, the host computer does not have to be on for others to access the Internet, as it does with a shared Internet connection.

restore points—Records that can be used to revert the computer to a previous, stable state. By choosing a restore point in the System Restore utility, you can undo an action that was later found to have caused a problem.

Restricted Sites zone—A zone in Internet Explorer where the default security level is High; it is the safest way to browse the network but is the least functional. Cookies are disabled, and many sites will not run under this setting.

Resultant Set of Policy (RsoP)—A tool used when group policies are used in a domain to allow an administrator to check security policies at different levels of domains to see if any policies conflict. RSoP is a query engine that polls all policies and can then be used to troubleshoot hard-to-diagnose problems.

rights—Actions that can be performed by the user, such as backing up files or shutting down the computer. A right refers to a specific action that a user can take, such as logging on locally or remotely, adding workstations to a domain, or changing the system time.

ring topology—A network configuration in which each computer is connected in a circular fashion. Data can be passed by a computer only when it is that computer's turn to do so. This topology is often referred to as "token ring."

Scheduled Tasks—A tool (accessible from the Control Panel) in which you can add tasks (such as Disk Cleanup and the Files And Settings Transfer Wizard) and programs (such as Microsoft Excel or Outlook) to be run on your computer at a certain date and time. When you click Add Scheduled Task, the Scheduled Task Wizard opens to assist you with the process. You might find out that your computer came preconfigured to run specific tasks that you didn't even know about.

screen resolution—The number of pixels that are used to display the desktop and all your applications. Increasing the screen resolution makes the desktop feel larger because the items on it are smaller. There are several resolution settings; the smallest and largest both depend on the type of video card that is installed in your computer and on the type of monitor you have. Generally, you'll have choices such as 640×480, 800×600, 1,028×768, 1,152×864, and 1,280×1,024.

secure sites—Internet sites that have **https://** instead of **http://** in front of their Web addresses. Banks, Internet stores, and any other sites that receive sensitive information from you should have a secure site for doing so. Sending private information over non-secure sites is risky because others could obtain that information fairly easily.

security hosts—Authentication devices that verify whether a computer and user are authorized to connect to a remote access server in the domain. One popular security host is the RADIUS (Remote Authentication Dial-In User Service) server, which uses the RADIUS security protocol to authenticate users for dial-up and tunneled network access for ISPs, corporate networks, and small domains. RADIUS is the most widely used protocol and dial-up server at this time.

separator pages—Pages that print between various users' print jobs. When multiple users print to the same printer, documents can become hard to find and keep separate. If this is the case, you can specify that separator pages be printed between documents. The separator page can contain the user's name and document name. Separator pages use up paper and ink (or toner), so they should be used only when necessary.

SerialKey Devices—An accessibility option that allows you to install other hardware, besides the mouse and keyboard, for inputting data.

Services—A console that administrators can use to view all of the services installed on the computer. In this console, you can also stop, start, pause, or resume a service, see a description of a service, and configure what will happen if the service fails.

share permissions—Permissions applied to shared folders to restrict a shared resource's availability over the network to only certain users. Share permissions are used primarily with the FAT file system. There are three share permissions: Full Control, Read, and Change. Share permissions work only when users access the resource over the network. They do not apply if the user is sitting at the computer providing the resource. Share permissions are applied to entire folders, not to individual files.

shared printer—An extension of the local printer. When several computers are connected via a hub, as in a small home network or small business office, one or more computers in the workgroup can have locally connected printers. Those printers can be used by people who are not at the local computer (if they have the appropriate permissions to do so).

simple dynamic disk—A type of volume on a dynamic disk. You cannot configure partitions or logical drives, and simple dynamic disks can be accessed only by Windows 2000 or XP operating systems. When using a simple dynamic volume, you can increase the size of the disk by allocating space from an empty area of the same disk or a different one. However, the disks must be formatted with NTFS. When a simple volume is extended to include space on a different dynamic disk, it becomes a *spanned volume*. Simple volumes can be mirrored, but spanned volumes cannot. Simple dynamic disks are not fault tolerant; if the disk fails, all of the data on it is lost.

simple file sharing—A way to share files and folders in a workgroup. This feature might work for small home networks, but for an office, you should consider turning it off. Simple file sharing is available on both FAT and NTFS file systems.

site policy—The policy created for the local network or subnet.

skin—A file that is used to change the appearance of Windows Media Player. A skin has a distinct appearance that usually incorporates basic Windows Media Player functions, including play, previous, next, stop, and volume adjustment. In many instances, you can also play certain audio files, view visualizations, or perform other activities based on the type of skin you apply to Windows Media Player. Skins can be chosen from Windows Media Player or downloaded from the Internet. Not all skins offer the same amount of functionality.

smart cards—Credit-card-size devices that are used the same way a bankcard is used at an ATM. The smart card stores your sign-in credentials, such as a password, your public and private keys, and other information, including what floors, offices, or buildings you are allowed access to. To use the card, you must have a PIN for it. The card is used mostly in domains for the purpose of logging onto computers and obtaining access to domain resources or email.

snap-ins—Tools that can be added to MMC consoles. There are two types: standalone snap-ins and extensions. Standalone snap-ins can be added independently; extension snap-ins can be added only to extend the functionality of another installed snap-in. Examples of snap-ins include Event Viewer, Folder, Group Policy, Performance Logs And Alerts, Remote Desktops, and Security Templates.

software restriction policies—Policies that allow administrators to control which software can run on the local computer, thus protecting the computer from unintentional harm done by inappropriate programs, programs that aren't certified, or programs that aren't compatible. Some applications can damage a computer's dynamic link library (.dll) files as well, causing problems that are difficult to track. You can also protect your computer or others from email attachments that can carry viruses or untrusted code downloaded from Internet sites.

Sound Recorder—An application used to record, mix, play, and edit sounds. The Sound Recorder can also be used to link sounds to a document or insert them into a document.

SoundSentry—An accessibility option that generates a visual warning when the computer makes a sound. Designed for hearing-impaired users, this option can be configured as a flash of the active caption bar, the active window, or the desktop.

spanned volume—A logical disk composed of free space from multiple physical disks. The amount of free space on each of these disks does not have to be the same. Spanned volumes cannot be mirrored. They are written to until each disk is full, and then the next disk is written to. Spanned volumes are a good way to use multiple physical disks that have little space on each. If any one of the disks on a spanned volume fails, all of the data on the spanned volume is lost.

speech recognition—A type of software that allows you to enter information into a program such as Word 2002 without typing the words. All you have to do is speak the words into a microphone, and they appear on the screen. You can also speak words such as "bold" and "underline" to perform those tasks. The speech recognition utility isn't meant to be completely hands-free, though; it is best used along with the mouse or keyboard or both.

standard account—A user account that lets users make basic changes such as changing their account name and password and installing software and hardware that don't change the restricted operating system files. Users with a standard account can personalize their computers with screensavers and backgrounds and generally can take control of their computers when logged on under their accounts. These users can also use the programs installed on the computer and save and delete files and folders they've created.

standby mode—A power-saving mode. The computer can be configured to go on standby after it has been idle for a specific amount of time. When the computer is on standby, it conserves power by turning off hard disks and the monitor. Standby differs from hibernation because with standby mode, the data stored in RAM is not saved to the hard disk. This allows the computer to resume activity faster than from hibernation, but a power loss will also cause RAM to lose data. Standby is generally used when you will be away from your computer for a short period. When computer operations are resumed, the desktop is exactly as you left it.

StickyKeys—An accessibility option that lets you use the Shift, Ctrl, Alt, or Windows logo keys by pressing only one key at a time instead of two.

striped disks (RAID 0)—A disk configuration that does not offer fault tolerance. In a striped volume, data is written to multiple disks at the same time, making disk reads and writes faster than with other disk configurations. The data that is written to the disks is written in blocks, and the data is distributed to the disks evenly. These volumes cannot be mirrored, and they should be configured on hard disks that are the same size and model. Striped disks are used when fast performance is crucial, such as when you're collecting data from databases, when information is needed (such as stock market quotes) that must be updated frequently, or when streaming media applications are being used.

System Monitor—A tool that allows you to collect real-time information about any component in your computer, including RAM, the CPU, hard disk performance, network activity, paging files, and processes. This information can be vital when you're troubleshooting system problems such as slow access to information on the hard drive or excessive paging.

system partition—The partition on the hard drive that contains the files needed to load Windows XP. This partition can also be the boot partition, but it doesn't have to be.

System Restore—A utility that monitors changes to your system and creates restore points, or records that can be used to revert the computer to a previous, stable state. System Restore allows you to undo something that was later found to have caused a problem.

system state data—Data that is used by the system; this data includes the Registry and system boot files. If the system is a domain controller or server, additional system state data includes the Active Directory database and Certificate Services. To back up system state data, you must be an administrator or backup operator, and you can then back up and restore the system state data on only the local computer. You cannot back up system state data on a remote computer.

System Tools—A set of tools used for viewing application, security, and system logs (Event Viewer); viewing and managing shares, sessions, and open files (Shared Folders); viewing and managing users and groups (Local Users And Groups); viewing and managing counter logs, trace logs, and alerts (Performance Logs And Alerts); and viewing, configuring, and troubleshooting hardware (Device Manager).

taskbar—The blue or gray bar at the bottom of the Windows screen. The taskbar contains the Start menu, icons for Internet Explorer, MSN, and Outlook Express (you can change these), and the time.

taskbar grouping—A feature used to help you manage open programs and documents more efficiently and make them easier to find. When multiple documents are open, Windows XP groups them by type; for instance, all Word documents are grouped together, or all Excel documents are grouped together. They are then labeled as a group with the name of the program and a triangle on the right side of the button. The triangle signifies multiple documents in the group.

taskpad views—Views that appear in the details pane of a console and display shortcuts to different commands that are chosen when the taskpad view is created. These shortcuts are referred to as "tasks" and are shown as large icons in the details pane. Creating taskpad views makes the console more efficient for users by displaying the tools they'll need as large and familiar icons.

ToggleKeys—An accessibility option that has the computer sound a tone when the Caps Lock, Num Lock, or Scroll Lock key is pressed.

Trusted Sites zone—A zone in Internet Explorer that has a default setting of Low. Sites can be added through the Sites button, and all sites listed here are treated differently than in any other zone. With a setting of Low, there are minimal safeguards, no warning prompts are sent, and all ActiveX content can be run. This level is safe for only those sites that are absolutely trusted by the company or the user.

user mode—Mode that restricts what a user can do in a custom console. When a console is saved in user mode, the users who access it cannot add or remove snap-ins or save it. This is the best setting if a console has been created for users in a department or company.

User Rights Assignment—A security option that allows an administrator to view and change default settings for users' own policies such as adding workstations, changing the system time, and shutting down the system.

Users group—A group to which many network users belong in larger organizations. The Users group is very secure because its users don't have many permissions or rights and therefore have a smaller chance of causing a problem. A user's account, if hacked into, also offers very little access to sensitive network resources and data. Members of the Users group can do the following: shut down their workstations; create local groups; manage the local groups they create; run programs installed by administrators, but only if the programs are certified by Microsoft as compatible; and retain full control over anything they create.

Utility Manager—A tool that is used by administrators to configure how and when users will utilize accessibility settings. The Utility Manager allows a user to check an accessibility program's status and start or stop the program as needed. An administrator can configure accessibility options to start when a user logs on or when Utility Manager is started. Options can also be set to start after a computer's desktop has been locked and then unlocked.

visualization—A video that is shown while a piece of music is playing in Windows Media Player. You can select different videos and play them full screen, if you like.

volume shadow copy—A type of backup not available in previous versions of Microsoft operating systems. A volume shadow copy is used when you want to make a full copy of a volume, including any open application files or system files. While a volume shadow copy is being done, applications can continue to write to the hard drive, and files that are open are backed up as well. These backups can thus be performed at any time during the day, although there could be some system slowdown due to the traffic.

Windows Explorer—A utility that displays your computer's folder and file structure and allows you to move or copy the folders or files to other areas. You can also see who's on your LAN (local area network), view any mapped network drives, and rename, copy, and search for files or folders that you need.

Windows Media Player—A utility that is installed by default with Windows XP. Windows Media Player is the default audio player, which is why it opens when you're choosing to play a CD. Windows Media Player is a fully functional media utility that can do a lot more than just play your audio CDs. With Media Player, you can also listen to Internet radio stations from all over the world, copy your CDs, download videos from the Internet, and create organized lists and groups of your music and video files.

Windows Update—An extension of Windows XP Professional that is available from Microsoft's Web site. When Windows Update is used, it automatically connects to the Web site and checks for any updates or fixes that your Windows operating system needs. Windows Update then asks you if you'd like to download those updates to your computer. It is a great way for users to maintain the latest versions of drivers, applications, help files, and system files.

wireless networks—Networks that work without cables. These network configurations range from data networks to telephone communications over long distances, to walkie-talkies, infrared light devices, and radio frequencies for short distances. The onslaught of cell phones, pagers, personal digital assistants (PDAs), handheld computers, and the call for wireless Internet usage has made wireless networking almost commonplace. Wireless networks are often better in the long run in these situations because buying and maintaining personal wireless equipment is cheaper and easier than laying fiber optic lines or copper cables. Creating a wireless network can also be more cost-efficient than leasing lines in a long-term situation.

workgroup—A network configuration that usually consists of 32 or fewer computers, and in which users share files and folders by using passwords and accounts. Windows XP Professional can be used on a standalone computer, such as a single computer in a small business or a family computer that everyone shares. Using workgroups is the simplest way to share resources such as computers, printers, scanners, files, and folders. Workgroups are also referred to as "peer-to-peer networks" because computers communicate with each other directly and do not require a server.

Zip drive—A small, portable device that uses a Zip disk for storing data. The computer sees the Zip drive as a type of removable media if the drive is external, or a type of hard drive if the disk is internal. If your computer doesn't have a Zip drive, you can purchase one for about $100 and connect it via a USB port, parallel port, or SCSI interface.

Index

A

Accessibility Options, 20-22, 101-110
    Accessibility Wizard, 108-109
    handwriting recognition, 103-104
    Magnifier, 105-106
    MouseKeys, 108
    multiple monitors, 104-105
    Narrator, 106-107
    On-Screen Keyboard, 107-108
    speech recognition, 102-103
    Utility Manager, 110
Accessibility Wizard, 108-109
Accessories And Utilities, 275
Account lockout policies, 146-147
Account policies, 145-148
ACPI, 646-647
Activation, 457-458
Active Directory, 414-416, 429
Active partition, 475
ActiveX controls, 542
Add Or Remove Programs, 22, 278-279
Add Standalone Snap-in dialog box, 55
Address Book, 298-300
Administrator account, 113-114, 405
Administrators group, 406
Advanced Configuration and Power Interface (ACPI), 646-647
Advanced privacy settings, 537
Airplanes, 654
Alerts. *See* Performance Logs and Alerts.
All-in-one fax/scanner/printer/copier, 262
All programs, 4
Analysis icons, 570
Anti-virus software, 321, 559, 631
Application log, 498
AT Service account, 117, 193
AT switches, 194
attrib, 635, 741
Audio. *See* Sounds and audio.
Audit policies, 142-143

Authentication, 451
Authenticode, 541-542
Automated System Recovery (ASR), 618-620
Automatic Reset, 21
Automatic updates, 196-200
AutoPlay installations, 268-271

B

Backup, 595-614
    audio licenses, 627
    CDs, to, 612-613
    configuring the utility, 602-604
    DVDs, to, 613-614
    manual, 605-607
    operators, 600-601
    precautionary measures, 600-601
    report, 610-611
    scheduling, 608-610
    simple (without Backup utility), 611-614
    storing physical media, 601
    system state data, 607
    testing, 601
    types of, 596-598
    types of data, 598-599
    Windows Media Services, 626-628
    wizard mode, 604-605
    zip drive, to, 612
Backup Operators group, 126, 406-407, 600-601
Backup Or Restore Wizard, 604-605
Backup report, 610-611
batch, 635
BIOS, 476
Block Sender, 306
Blue screen of death, 229
Boot partition, 476
bootcfg, 636
Booting problems, 706-707, 737-738
Bottleneck, 509-510
Briefcase tool, 673-676

Built-in groups, 126-132, 405-408
Built-in user accounts, 113-116, 405
Burning CDs, 47-48
Bus topology, 338

C

Cameras, 248-250
Category view, 18-20
CD-MO, 613
CD Player, 90-91
CD-R, 612-613
CD-ROM, 612
CD-RW, 47-48, 613
CD Writing Wizard, 47
CDs, 612-613
Certificate rule, 589-590
Certificates, 540-541
Change permission, 381
Change Permissions permission, 385
chdir, 636, 742
chkdsk, 637, 742
Classic look, 4-5
ClearType, 71-72, 654-655
Clipboard, 46
cls, 637, 742
Color quality, 72
Command-line tools, 740-756
Compatible template, 565
Compressing files/folders, 468-469
Computer emergency kit, 221
Computer Management, 49-50
  console messages, 370-371
  Device Manager, 517-520
  Event Viewer, 498-507. *See also* Event Viewer.
  Indexing Service, 525
  Performance Logs and Alerts, 507-515. *See also*
    Performance Logs and Alerts.
  Services, 520-524
  System Monitor, 515-517
  users/groups, 369-370
  view connections, 371-372, 420
  WMI Control, 524
Computer Management console, 49-50
Conferencing, 324-326, 683-688
Console, 48. *See also* Custom consoles.
Console messages, 370-371
Console mode options, 57
Console tree, 48
Contacts Properties dialog box, 298

Container object, 48
Content Advisor, 26
Control Panel, 18-34
  Accessibility Options, 20-22
  Add Hardware, 22
  Add Or Remove Programs, 22
  Administrative Tools, 23
  category view, 18-20
  change appearance of, 77-79
  classic view, 19-20
  customizing toolbar, 79
  Date and Time, 24
  Display, 24
  Explorer bar, 77-78
  Folder Options, 25
  Fonts, 25
  Gaming Options, 25
  Internet options, 26-27
  Keyboard, 27
  Mail, 27
  Mouse, 28
  Network and Internet Connections, 28
  Phone and Modem Options, 29
  Power Options, 29-30
  Printers and Faxes, 30
  Regional and Language Options, 30-31
  Scanners and Cameras, 31
  Scheduled Tasks, 31
  Sounds and Audio Devices, 31-32
  Speech, 32
  System, 32-33
  Taskbar and Start Menu, 33
  User Accounts, 33-34
convert, 742
Cookies, 315-316, 534, 536
Copy, 45-46
copy, 637, 743
Copy backup, 596
Corporate networks, 403-462
  authentication, 451
  built-in groups, 405-408
  group policies, 411
  ICS, 422
  local security policy, 410
  logon procedures, 413-414
  logon rights, 409-410
  password-reset disks, 421-422
  privileges, 408-409
  Remote Access, 448-452
  Remote Assistance, 430-438. *See also* Remote Assistance.

Remote Desktop, 438-448. *See also* Remote Desktop.
removable storage, 420-421
sharing resources, 422-430. *See also* Sharing resources (corporate networks).
switching from workgroup to domain, 412
temporary/seasonal workers, 459-461
tours/tutorials, 459-461
troubleshooting, 720-723
user accounts, 404-405
viewing network resources, 414-420
wireless networking, 452-457
Counters. *See* Performance Logs and Alerts.
Cover Page Editor, 184
Create Files/Write Data permission, 384
Create Folders/Append Data permission, 385
Critical updates, 197
Custom consoles, 52-61
adding snap-ins, 54-55
changing icon/mode/name of console, 56-57
columns, 57-59
console mode options, 57
create blank console, 53
customize view, 59
extension snap-ins, 55-56
removing snap-ins, 56
snap-ins, 53-54
taskpad views, 59-61
Cut, 45-46

D

Daily backup, 597
Data Incomplete, 492
Data Not Redundant, 493
date, 743
Date and Time, 24
Decryption, 550
Default Security template, 564
defrag, 743
del, 743
delete, 637
Delete permission, 385
Delete Subfolders And Files permission, 385
Denying permissions, 387-388
Desktop, 64-71
advanced Start Menu options, 68-71
background, 64
change look of, 16
cleanup, 65-66
colors, 72-75

fonts, 71-75
icons, 15-16, 64-65
keyboard, 75-76
mouse, 76-77
multiple monitors, 259
personalized menus, 67
screen resolution, 75
screensaver, 64
shortcuts, 14-15
themes/appearance, 66-67
what is it, 14
Windows Classic theme, 68-69
Windows XP theme, 69-71
Desktop Cleanup, 65-66
Desktop folders, 15
Details, 18
Details pane, 49
Device conflict, 518
Device Driver Rollback, 238-240
Device drivers, 223-245
device types, 227-228
disable driver, 242
Driver Rollback, 238-240
driver signing, 228-231
driver warnings, 230, 234-235
how drivers work, 225
installation, 231-235
Internet, obtain drivers from, 242-244
most common drivers, 224-225
plug-and-play devices, 226-227
problems, 225-226, 237-238
remove driver completely, 240-242
safe mode, 245
third-party drivers, 244
unsigned drivers, 229-230, 234-235
upgrading, 235-237
Device Manager, 517-520
disable driver, 242
hardware profiles, 519-520
installing non-PnP devices, 518-519
reinstall hardware, 266-267
remove hardware, 283
system information, 706
troubleshooting, 716-719
views, 518
Device types, 227-228
DHCP, 400
Differential backup, 597
Digital camera, 248-250
Digital IDs, 540

dir, 638, 744
disable, 638
Disabled persons. *See* Accessibility Options.
Disk Cleanup, 209-210, 464-465
Disk Defragmenter, 465-467
Disk management
  add new disk, 486-490
  basic disk, 477, 482-484, 488
  compressing files/folders, 468-469
  convert basic disk to dynamic disk, 478-479
  convert dynamic disk to basic disk, 480-481
  Disk Cleanup, 464-465
  Disk Defragmenter, 465-467
  disk stripping with parity (RAID 5), 480, 489
  dynamic disk, 478, 484-486, 488
  formatting new disk, 490
  freeing up disk space, 467-473
  GPT, 482
  logical drives, 477
  MBR, 481-482
  mirrored disks (RAID 1), 480, 489
  mounted drive, 481
  partitions, 475-477
  performing tasks, 482-486
  quotas, 493-498
  remote disk, 473-474
  simple dynamic disks, 479, 488
  spanned disks, 479, 489
  status, 490-493
  striped disks (RAID 0), 479-480, 489
  zip compression, 469-471
Disk quotas, 493-498
Disk space, free up, 207-210, 467-473
Disk status, 490-493
diskcopy, 744
diskpart, 638
Domain controllers, 335
Domain group policy, 411
Domain Users group, 404
Domains, 334-335. *See also* Corporate networks.
doskey, 744
Download settings, 542
Dr. Watson, 735
Drive mapping, 393, 395, 430
Driver Rollback, 238-240
driverquery, 745
Drivers. *See* Device drivers.
DualView, 105, 657-659
DVD-audio, 614

DVD-R, 614
DVD-RAM, 614
DVD-ROM, 614
DVD-RW, 614
DVDs, 613-614
Dynamic Host Configuration Protocol (DHCP), 400

E

Echo effect, 89
Effective permissions, 386-389
EFS, 550-554
Email. *See* Outlook Express.
Emergency repair disk (ERD), 221
Emoticons, 311
enable, 639
Encrypting File System (EFS), 550-554
Encryption, 550-554
Enhancing performance, 526-529. *See also* Computer
  Management, Disk Management.
ERD, 221
Event Viewer, 498-507
  archiving log files, 500-501
  clearing/opening event log, 503
  creating new log view, 501
  enabling security log, 504
  finding specific event, 501-502
  interpreting events, 499-500
  options, 503-504
  remote computer, 507
  sorting/filtering event logs, 502
  types of logs, 498
  viewing events, 499
  what to audit, 505-506
exit, 639
expand, 639, 745
Explicit permissions, 397
Extended partition, 476
Extension snap-ins, 55-56

F

Failed, 491-492
Failed Redundancy, 493
Fast User Switching, 366-367
FAT, 375-377, 464, 723-724
Fax console, 183
Fax Cover Page Editor, 184
Fax Wizard, 180

Faxing, 178-186
    all-in-one fax/scanner/printer/copier, 262
    configuration, 180-182
    console, 183
    Cover Page Editor, 184
    installation, 179
    sharing/setting permissions, 186
    using the service, 185
File formats, Sound Recorder, 85-86
File Signature Verification, 228-231
Files
    compressing, 468-469
    create, 41
    delete, 43
    find/open, 42-43
    open, 42-43
    ownership, 396-397
    save, 42
    search, 43-44
    securing, 532-533
    sharing, 377-380, 422-430, 720
    Windows Explorer, 34-35
Files And Settings Transfer Wizard, 620-626
Filter Keys, 21
find, 745
fixboot, 639-640
fixmbr, 640
Folder Options, 25
Folders
    add, to desktop, 15
    compressing, 468-469
    create, 41-42
    delete, 43
    move, to another area of Start menu, 6
    ownership, 396-397
    search, 43-44
    securing, 532-533
    sharing, 377-380, 422-430
    Windows Explorer, 35-37
Font substitution, 177
Fonts
    ClearType, 71-72
    Internet Explorer, 74-75
    printers, and, 176-177
    size, 72-73
Fonts folder, 73
Foreign status, 490
Forgotten passwords, 367-369
format, 640, 745-746
Formatting new disk, 490

Freeing up disk space, 207-210, 467-473
Full backup, 597
Full Control permission, 381

G

Games, 327-329
GPResult, 584-588
gpresult, 746
GPT, 482
gpupdate, 746
Group membership change, 136-139
Group policies, 139-142, 554-556
Group Policy console, 141, 557
Group Policy snap-in, 139-140
Groups, 125-139
    add/delete users from built-in groups, 128-132
    built-in, 126-132, 405-408
    create, 132-133
    delete, 133
    membership changes, 136-139
    names, 133
    personalized, 134-139
Guest account, 114-116, 405
Guests group, 408
GUID partition table (GPT), 482

H

Handwriting recognition, 103-104
Hardware
    install. *See* Installing hardware.
    remove, 283
    small-office networks, 336-340
Hardware compatibility list (HCL), 225, 340
Hardware identifier, 457
Hardware profiles, 519-520, 655
Hash rule, 588-589
HCL, 225, 340
Healthy, 492
Healthy (At Risk), 492
Help. *See* Troubleshooting.
help, 746
Help and Support Center, 361, 707-712
Hibernation, 650
High Contrast, 21
Highly Secure template, 565
History folder, 26
Home networks. *See* Small-office networks.
Home page, 26

Home-phone-line network adapter (HPNA), 338
Hotmail account, 292-293
HPNA, 338
Hub, 337
HyperTerminal, 327

I

ICF, 545-550
Icons
  adding, 65
  arranging, 64-65
  change look of, 16
  deleting, 65
  desktop, 15-16, 64-65
  My Computer, 16
  shortcuts, 65
ICS, 333, 362, 422, 726
ICS Discovery and Control, 362-365
IIS, 276
Incremental backup, 597
Indexing Service, 525
Inherited permissions, 397-399
Initializing, 491
Install/uninstall software, 267-282
  AutoPlay installations, 268-271
  download from Internet, 274
  install from Microsoft's web site, 273
  miscellaneous Windows components, 275-278
  Program Compatibility Wizard, 271-272
  removing software, 278-282
  software that ships with hardware devices, 274-275
  troubleshooting, 733-736
  uninstalling parts of applications, 279-282
Installation
  device drivers, 231-235
  downloadable printer driver, 162
  fax services, 179
  hardware. *See* Installing hardware.
  network adapters, 341
  non-PnP devices, 518-519
  printers, 149-156
  reinstalling the operating system, 757-763
  Remote Desktop, 440-441
  software. *See* Install/uninstall software.
Installing hardware, 247-267
  all-in-one fax/scanner/printer/copier, 262
  automatic installation doesn't work, 214
  connect to Internet for driver, 242-244, 265-266
  Device Manager (reinstall hardware), 266-267

device not recognized, 263
digital cameras, 248-250
driver missing an entry, 267
modem, 253-254
multiple monitors, 256-262
remove hardware, 284
scanners, 251-253
troubleshooting, 262-267, 731-732
wireless keyboard/mouse, 255-256
Instant messaging, 307-313
Internet
  browser. *See* Internet Explorer.
  browser problems, 726-729
  connecting to, 285-291
  device drivers, 242-244, 265-266
  dial-up connection, 288, 290
  email. *See* Outlook Express.
  games, 327-329
  instant messaging, 307-313
  LAN connection, 288-291
  MSN Explorer, 321-324
  NetMeeting, 324-326
  phone calling, 312
  privacy settings, 534-538
  security, 533-545. *See also* Security.
  software, 274
  viruses, 321
  visualizations (Media Player), 95
  Windows Update, 199
Internet Connection Firewall (ICF), 545-550
Internet Connection Sharing (ICS), 333, 362, 422, 726
Internet Connection Wizard, 286-289
Internet Explorer, 313-320
  address bar, 315
  cookies, 315-316
  features, 313
  interface, 314
  Internet Options, 26-27, 317-320
  mobile computing, 696
  privacy, 316
  security, 316-317
  surfing the Web, 313-317
Internet Information Services (IIS), 276
Internet Options, 26-27, 317-320
Internet service provider (ISP), 286
Internet zone, 543
Internet-zone rules, 591
IP Security (IPSec) policies, 575-580
IP Security monitor, 579
ipconfig, 747

IPSec, 575-580
IPX/SPX, 399
ISP, 286

J

Java applets, 542

K

Kerberos policies, 147
Keyboard, 75-76

L

label, 747
LAN, 333-334, 453
Laptop computers. *See* Mobile computing.
Last Known Good Configuration (LKGC), 216-217, 738
Licensing, 459
Limited account, 117
List Folder/Read Data permission, 384
listsvc, 640
LKGC, 216-217, 738
Local accounts. *See* User accounts.
Local area network (LAN), 333-334, 453
Local Intranet, 543
Local policies, 142-145, 147-148, 554-556
Local printer, 149
Local security policy, 410
Local Security Settings console, 50-52
Log dialog box, 510
Log files. *See* Event Viewer, Performance Logs and Alerts.
logon, 640
Logon procedures, 413-414
Logon rights, 123, 409-410
Low-memory errors, 447

M

Magneto-optical CD, 613
Magnifier, 105-106
MAN, 453
Manual backup, 605-607
map, 641
Mapping a network drive, 393, 395, 430
Master boot record (MBR), 481-482
Maximizing Windows, 44
MBR, 481-482

Media Player. *See* Windows Media Player.
Mesh topology, 338
Message Queuing, 277, 680-683
Messaging, 307-313
Metropolitan area networks (MAN), 453
Microsoft Assisted Support, 39-40
Microsoft Authenticode, 541-542
Microsoft Management Console (MMC), 48-91
    columns, 57-59
    Computer Management, 49-50. *See also* Computer Management.
    console mode options, 57
    custom consoles. *See* Custom consoles.
    customize view, 59
    Local Security Policy, 50-52
    Performance, 52
    preconfigured consoles, 49-52
    taskpad views, 59-61
    terminology, 48-49
Microsoft Message Queuing (MSMQ), 680-683
Microsoft personal support, 712-713, 716
Mirrored disk problems, 492-493
Miscellaneous Windows components, 275-278
Missing status, 491
mkdir, 641, 747
MMC. *See* Microsoft Management Console (MMC).
mmc, 747
Mobile computing, 645-697
    ACPI, 646-647
    airplanes, 654
    alarms, 651-653
    autodial, 691
    Briefcase tool, 673-676
    callback, 691-692
    ClearType, 654-655
    configuring power buttons, 651
    copying files from desktop to laptop, 659-661
    dialing options, 688-692
    DualView, 657-659
    encryption, 661-662
    error messages, 691-694
    hardware profiles, 655
    hibernation, 650
    Message Queuing, 680-683
    NetMeeting, 683-688
    offline file access/caching, 672-673
    offline files, 662-668
    online conferencing, 683-688
    operator-assisted dialing, 689
    password for awakening computer, 651

performance enhancement, 654-659
power management, 646-654
power scheme, 647-650
Properties dialog box, 695-696
redial, 690
Remote Desktop, 677-680
Remote Desktop Sharing, 687-688
Scheduled Tasks, 653-654
standby, 650-651
Synchronization Manager, 668-669, 672
System Properties, 655-657
troubleshooting, 691-697
Web pages offline, 669-672
Modem, 253-254
Modem problems, 725-726
Monitors, multiple, 256-262
more, 641, 747
Mouse, 28, 76-77, 255-257
MouseKeys, 21, 108
msinfo32, 748
MSMQ, 680-683
MSN Explorer, 321-324
Multimedia utilities, 90. *See also* CD Player, Windows
    Media Player.
Multiple monitors, 104-105, 256-262
Multiple programs, switching between, 44-45
Music files, 472
My Computer
    Details, 18
    icons, 16
    Other Places, 18
    System Tasks, 17
My Network Places
    connecting to shared folder, 427
    sharing folder, 424-426
    small-office network, 373-375, 392
    view network resources, 414-417

N

Narrator, 106-107
nbtstat, 748
net use, 641-642
Net2Phone, 312
NetBEUI, 399-400
NetMeeting, 324-326, 683-688
netstat, 748
Network Diagnostics, 738-740
Network interface card (NIC), 336

Network printer, 150
Network Setup Wizard, 343-349, 722-723
Network Troubleshooter, 360
Networks. *See* Corporate networks, Small-office networks.
NIC, 336
Non-PnP devices, 518-519
Normal backup, 597
Not Initialized, 491
Notebook computers. *See* Mobile computing.
nslookup, 749
ntbackup, 749
NTFS file system, 375-377
NTFS permissions, 383-386

O

Offline status, 491
On-Screen Keyboard, 107-108
Online, 491
Online (Errors), 491
Online conferencing, 683-688
Orphan files, 675
Other Places, 18
Outlook Express, 291-307
    accessibility options, 307
    Address Book, 298-300
    attachments, 296-297
    Block Sender, 306
    creating/switching identities, 305
    folders, 294-296
    Hotmail account, 292-293
    message rule, 295
    newsgroups, 306-307
    options, 301-303
    personal identity, 299
    personalizing, 303-304
    photos, 297
    setting up an account, 291-293
    troubleshooting, 729-731
    using, 293-294

P

P3P, 535, 538
Paging file, 508
Paging options, 313
PAN, 453
Password policies, 146
Password-reset disk, 367-368, 421-422

Passwords
  forgotten, 367-369
  Guest account, 116
  local account, 120-122
  mobile computing, 651
  remembering, 452
  Remote Assistance, 437
Paste, 45-46
Path rules, 590-591
pathping, 750
Performance console, 52-53
Performance enhancement, 526-529. *See also* Computer Management, Disk Management.
Performance Logs and Alerts, 507-515
  analyzing data, 514-515
  configuring alerts, 513-514
  counter log options, 512
  creating counter logs for local computer, 510-511
  objects/counters, 507
  sample counter log, 508
  saving the log, 513
  selecting objects/counters, 508-510
  trace logs, 513
Performance objects, 507
Permissions, 124-125
  denying, 387-388
  effective, 386-389
  explicit, 397
  fax, 186
  inherited, 397-399
  NTFS, 383-386
  printer, 178
  share, 381-383
  shared printer, 152-153
Personal area networks (PAN), 453
Personal certificates, 540
Personal identity, 299
Personalize Your PC tutorial, 460
Personalized consoles. *See* Custom consoles.
Personalized groups, 134-139
Personalized menus, 67
Phone And Modem Options, 29, 695
Phone calls. *See* Telephone calls.
Phone Dialer, 326-327
Picture
  browsing for, 120-121
  sending, 297
  user accounts, 120
Picture files, 472
ping, 750

Platform for Privacy Preferences (P3P), 535, 538
Plug-and-play (PnP), 224, 226-227
Policies
  account, 145-147
  account lockout, 146-147
  audit, 142-143
  changing account/local, 147-148
  group, 139-142, 556-558
  Kerberos, 147
  local, 142-145, 554-556
  password, 146
Power Options, 29-30, 197
Power Users group, 127, 177, 407
Prefigured MMC consoles, 49-52
Primary partition, 476
print, 750
Print servers, 155
Printer permissions, 389-391
Printer pools, 155
Printer problems, 156-164, 731
  access to printer denied, 177-178
  documents do not print, 173-174
  download driver from manufacturer's web site, 160-161
  download driver from third-party site, 161-162
  fonts, 176-177
  installing downloaded driver, 162-163
  print quality poor, 174-175
  printer not detected, 157-159
  printing is slow, 175
  prompts for driver from floppy disk/CD-ROM, 159
  unable to install printer, 175-176
  updating current driver, 163
Printers, 149-173
  advanced settings, 172-173
  canceling printing, 171
  installing local printer, 150-152
  installing network printer, 155-156
  installing shared printer, 152-155
  pausing, 169-170
  print cartridge, 164-165
  printing preferences/defaults, 165-168
  problems. *See* Printer problems.
  restarting printing, 171
  resuming printing, 170-171
  troubleshooting installations, 156-164
  types, 149-150
Privacy alerts, 538
Privacy reports, 538-539
Privacy settings, 534-538
Privacy summary report, 539

Privileges, 123-124, 408-409
Problems. *See* Troubleshooting.
Profile Assistant, 539-540
Program compatibility mode, 527-529
Program Compatibility Wizard, 271-272
Properties dialog box, 695-696
Protocol, 399-401

Q

Quick Launch Toolbar, 8
Quota report, 497-498
Quotas, disk, 493-498

R

Radio, 100-101
Radio presets, 101
RADIUS, 574
RAID 0, 479-480, 489
RAID 1, 480, 489, 492-493
RAID 5, 480, 489
RAID 5 problems, 493
Read Attributes permission, 384
Read Extended Attributes permission, 384
Read permission, 381
Read Permissions permission, 385
Recovery agents, 553
Recovery Console, 633-643
Recycle Bin, 629
Registration, 458
Registration worm, 457
Reinstalling the operating system, 757-763
Remote Access, 448-452
Remote-access server, 574
Remote Assistance, 430-438
  asking for help, 431-433
  disconnect, 436
  giving help, 433-434
  password, 437
  remote control, 437-438
  Remote Desktop, contrasted, 438
  requirements, 431
  send a file, 436
  send/receive messages, 435
  settings, 436
  start talking, 436
Remote Control, 437-438

Remote Desktop, 438-448
  configuring, 441-445
  configuring host computer, 439-440
  connecting through Internet, 445
  connecting through LAN, 444
  disabling, 446
  Display tab, 442
  Experience tab, 443
  General tab, 442
  installing connection on other computers, 440-441
  laptop computers, 677-680
  Local Resources tab, 443
  Programs tab, 443
  Remote Assistance, contrasted, 438
  requirements, 438-439
  troubleshooting, 446-448
  using, 445-446
Remote Desktop Connection dialog box, 442
Remote Desktop Sharing, 687-688
Remote disk, 473-474
Removable storage, 420-421
rename, 642, 750
Replicator group, 128, 408
Residential gateway, 333
Resize
  taskbar, 10
  windows, 44
Restore, 615-633
  ASR, 618-620
  audio licenses, 627
  declined updates, 630
  default security log settings, 629
  manual, 616
  options, 615
  Recycle Bin, 629
  report, 617
  System, 618. *See also* System Restore.
  system state, 616
  transferring files/settings, 620-626
  virus attacks, 632
  Windows Media Services, 626-628
  wizard mode, 616
Restore points, 202-204, 210. *See also* System Restore.
Restore report, 617
Restore Wizard, 616
Restricted Sites, 543
Resultant Set of Policy (RSoP), 580-584
Rights, 122-123

Ring topology, 338
rmdir, 642, 750
RSoP, 580-584
runas, 751

S

Safe mode
    booting problems, 738
    drivers, 245
    System Restore, 216, 218-219
Scanners, 251-253
Scheduled Tasks, 187-196
    AT service account, 193
    create a task, 188-190
    log of past tasks, 194-195
    mobile computing, 653-654
    modify task, 190-191
    notification that task didn't run, 193
    pausing/continuing the service, 193
    power management, 195-196
    remove task, 191
    stop task, 191
    stopping/starting the service, 192
    Windows Update, and, 198
Screen resolution, 75
Search Companion, 43-44, 417-420, 427-429
search.support.microsoft.com, 713
secedit, 751
Secedit utility, 573-574
Secure Internet sites, 545
Secure template, 565
Security, 531-593
    analyzing, 569-572
    Authenticode, 541-542
    certificates, 540-541
    cookies, 534, 536
    download settings, 542
    encryption, 550-554
    files/folders, 532-533
    firewall, 545-550
    GPResult, 584-588
    group policies, 554-556
    hosts, 574-575
    IPSec, 575-580
    local policies, 554-556
    privacy alerts, 538
    privacy reports, 538-539
    privacy settings, 534-538
    Profile Assistant, 539-540

RSoP, 580-584
Secedit, 573-574
secure Internet sites, 545
Security Configuration and Analysis, 563-572. *See also*
    Security Configuration and Analysis.
security settings extension of group policy console, 572-573
smart cards, 575
software restriction policies, 588-593
templates, 563-573
UPS, 561-563
viruses, 321, 558-561
zones, 542-545
Security Configuration and Analysis, 563-572
    analyzing security, 569-572
    apply template to local computer policy, 568-569
    configuring console/importing template, 566-567
    correcting discrepancies, 571-572
    create your own template, 567-568
    creating the console, 565-566
    planning, 564
    reapplying default settings, 572
    security templates, 564-565
Security hosts, 574-575
Security log, 498
Security options for local policies, 144-145
Security templates, 563-573
Security zones, 542-545
Send Fax Wizard, 182
SerialKey Devices, 21
Services, 520-524
set, 642
700-level errors, 693-694
Share permissions, 381-383
Shared Documents folder, 393-395
Shared printer, 150
Sharing resources (corporate networks), 422-430
    administrator (My Network Places), 425-426
    connecting to other shared resources, 430
    connecting to shared folder, 426-430
    mapping network drive, 430
    My Network Places, 424-426
    Web Publishing Wizard, 423-424
Sharing resources (small-office networks), 375
    administrator connecting to shared folder, 391-393
    denying permissions, 387-388
    drive mapping, 393, 395
    effective permissions, 386-389
    file systems (FAT/NTFS), 375-377
    files/folders, 377-380
    NTFS permissions, 383-386

printer permissions, 389-391
share permissions, 381-383
Shared Documents folder, 393-395
Sharing Your PC tutorial, 460
Shortcuts, 14-15, 65
Show Sounds, 21
Signature verification, 228-231
600-level errors, 691-693
Skins, 94-95
Small network problems, 354-362, 720-723
    cannot browse Internet from client computer, 357-358
    cannot browse Internet from host computer, 356-357
    cannot locate shared folder, 358
    cannot log onto network, 358
    cannot receive email on client computer, 356
    computer's name, 354-355
    dial-up connections, 359-360
    do's/don'ts, 356
    modem, 359-360
    Network Troubleshooter, 360
Small-office networks, 331-401
    access control, 396-399
    adding a computer, 372-373
    advanced connections, 351-354
    Computer Management, 369-372
    connecting hubs/cables, 342
    connecting to workplace, 351
    console messages, 370-371
    drive mapping, 393, 395
    explicit vs. inherited permissions, 397-399
    Fast User Switching, 366-367
    forgotten passwords, 367-369
    hardware, 336-340
    ICS, 333, 362
    ICS Discovery and Control, 362-365
    ICS host, 339
    LAN, 333-334
    locating a computer, 373
    managing users, 366-372
    My Network Places, 373-375
    network adapters, 341
    Network Setup Wizard, 343-349
    other Internet connection settings, 349-350
    ownership of files/folders, 396-397
    physically connecting computers, 340-349
    planning, 335-336
    setting up client computer, 345-347
    setting up host computer, 343-345
    sharing resources. See Sharing resources (small-office networks).
    troubleshooting, 354-362. See also Small network problems.

    verifying communications, 348-349
    viewing connections, 371-372
    Windows 2000 Professional computer, 347-348
    workgroups, 331-335
Smart menus, 67
Snap-ins, 49, 53-54. See also Custom consoles.
Software. See Install/uninstall software.
Software problems, 733-736
Software restriction policies, 588-593
Sound Recorder, 82-90
    delete parts of recording, 88
    echo effect, 89
    file formats, 85-86
    insert file into existing file, 87-88
    insert/link sound file to document, 89-90
    mixing, 87
    open, 83
    playing, 85
    recording, 84
    reversing the recording, 88
    sound quality, 86-87
    voice test, 84
Sound Sentry, 21
Sounds and audio, 79-90. See also Multimedia utilities.
    give events their own sounds, 81-82
    sound effects, 82
    Sound Recorder, 82-90. See also Sound Recorder.
    sound scheme, 81
    volume controls, 80-81
Special needs persons. See Accessibility Options.
Speech recognition, 102-103
Stale Data, 493
Stand-by mode, 197
Standard account, 117
Standby, 650-651
Star configuration, 337
Start menu
    adding/removing programs, 2-3
    advanced options, 68-71
    changing menu style, 4-5
    moving folder to another area, 6
    other configuration changes, 7-8
    submenus, 5-6
Status, disk, 490-493
Sticky Keys, 21
Stored User Names and Passwords, 452
Support. See Troubleshooting.
Support tools, 756-757
Switching between applications, 44-45
Synchronization Manager, 668-669, 672

Synchronize permission, 385
System Configuration utility, 736-737
System information, 701-706
System Information console, 702
System log, 498
System Monitor, 515-517
System overview log, 514
System partition, 476
System Properties, 526-527, 655-657
System Properties dialog box, 700-701
System Restore, 201-222
    allocating more disk space, 213-214
    automatically created restore points, 202-203
    available restore points, 205-206
    changing settings, 211-213
    creating restore points, 202-204, 210
    disabling startup files, 219-220
    emergency repair, 221-222
    how it works, 204
    LKGC, compared, 216-217
    making disk space available, 207-210
    manually created restore points, 203-204
    restoring the system, 213-214
    reversible restorations, 205
    safe work, 216, 218-219
    troubleshooting, 217-221
    turning, on/off, 207
    undoing a restoration, 214-215
    what is restored, 204-205
    when used, 618
System Root Security template, 565
System summary report, 222
System Tasks, 17
systeminfo, 751
systemroot, 643

T

Take Ownership permission, 385
Task scheduler. *See* Scheduled Tasks.
Taskbar, 8-14
    grouping, 10
    hiding, 9-10
    locking, 9
    minimizing open programs/documents, 13
    moving, 8-9
    resizing, 10
    starting programs, 11-12
    toolbars, 12-13
Taskbar grouping, 10
Taskpad views, 59-61

TaskpadTest taskpad view, 61
TCP/IP, 399
Telephone calls
    free Internet calling, 312
    Phone Dialer, 326-327
Themes, 66-67
Third-party drivers, 244
Time, 24
Time-out errors, 447
Toggle Keys, 21
Token Ring, 400
Tours, 459-461
Trace logs, 513
tracert, 752
Traverse Folder/Execute File permission, 384
Trojan horse, 561
Troubleshooting, 37-40, 699-763
    available troubleshooters, 360-361, 714-716
    booting problems, 706-707, 737-738
    command-line tools, 740-756
    Device Manager, 706, 716-719
    drivers, 225-226, 237-238
    email problems, 729-731
    FAT, 723-724
    file sharing, 720-721
    hardware problems, 262-267, 731-732
    Help and Support Center, 707-712
    help from inside application windows, 710-712
    ICS problems, 726
    Internet browser problems, 726-729
    Microsoft personal support, 712-713, 716
    mobile computing, 691-697
    modem problems, 725-726
    multiple monitors, 259-261
    network connectivity, 721-723
    Network Diagnostics, 738-740
    printer installations, 156-164. *See also* Printer problems.
    reinstalling the operating system, 757-763
    Remote Desktop, 446-448
    small network, 354-362
    software problems, 733-736
    support tools, 756-757
    System Configuration utility, 736-737
    system information, 701-706
    System Properties dialog box, 700-701
    System Restore, 217-221
    upgrade, 762-763
Trusted Sites, 543
Tutorials, 459-461
type, 643

U

Uninterruptible power supply (UPS), 561-563
Unknown, 492
Unreadable, 491-492
Updates, 196-200
Upgrade, 762-763
UPS, 561-563
User accounts, 112-125, 404, 405
    add an account, 118
    built-in accounts, 113-116, 405
    delete an account, 118
    disable/enable local account, 119
    limited accounts, 117
    names, 133
    password, 120-122
    picture, 120
    privileges, 123-125
    rename local account, 119
    rights, 122-123
    standard accounts, 117
User errors, 447
User privileges, 123-124
User rights, 122-123, 408
User rights assignments for local policies, 143-144
Users group, 127-128, 407
Utility Manager, 110

V

.vbs file, 560
ver, 752
View Network Connections, 416
Virus attacks, 630-633
Virus hoaxes, 560
Viruses, 321, 558-561
Volume controls, 80-81
Volume shadow copy, 597

W

WAN, 452
Web Publishing Wizard, 423
Web-server certificates, 541
Web-site certificates, 540
Whiteboard, 326
Wide area network (WAN), 452
Windows Classic look, 4-5
Windows Classic theme, 68-69
Windows components, miscellaneous, 275-278

Windows Explorer, 34-37
Windows Installer, 591
Windows Media Player, 91-101
    copying music from CD, 96
    customizing the player, 94-95
    digital playback, 97-98
    error control, 97
    general controls, 92-93
    information sent to Microsoft, 628
    options, 98-99
    organizing the files, 100
    playing a song, 94
    radio, 100-101
    radio presets, 101
    skins, 94-95
    tour, 461
    visualizations, 95-96
    WindowsMedia.com, 100
Windows Media Player Tour, 461
Windows Messenger, 307-313
Windows Product Activation, 457
Windows Update, 196-200
Windows XP Professional Help, 707-712
Windows XP theme, 69-71
Windows XP Tour, 459
WindowsMedia.com, 100
Wireless keyboard/mouse, 255-256
Wireless networking, 452-457
WMI Control, 524
Workgroups, 331-335. *See also* Small-office networks.
Writable CDs, 47-48
Write Attributes permission, 385
Write Extended Attributes permission, 385
.wsh file, 560

Z

Zip compression, 469-471
Zip disk, 470
Zip drive, 612
Zones, 542-545

Go to Internet Explorer
" "   Tools.
" "   Delete Browsing History

Then "   files
          cookies
          history